Java from
the Beginning

INTERNATIONAL COMPUTER SCIENCE SERIES
Consulting Editor   **A D McGettrick**   University of Strathclyde

Java from the Beginning

2nd edition

Jan Skansholm

 **ADDISON-WESLEY**

An imprint of **Pearson Education**

Harlow, England • London • New York • Boston • San Francisco • Toronto
Sydney • Tokyo • Singapore • Hong Kong • Seoul • Taipei • New Delhi
Cape Town • Madrid • Mexico City • Amsterdam • Munich • Paris • Milan

Pearson Education Limited
Edinburgh Gate
Harlow
Essex CM20 2JE

and Associated Companies throughout the world

Visit us on the World Wide Web at:
www.pearsoned.co.uk

First published 2000
Second edition 2004

ISBN 0 321 15416 9

British Library Cataloguing-in-Publication Data
A catalogue record for this book is available from the British Library

Library of Congress Cataloging-in-Publication Data
A catalog record for this book is available from the Library of Congress

10 9 8 7 6 5 4 3 2 1
08 07 06 05 04

Translated by SpråkGruppen
Typeset by 35
Printed and bound in Malaysia

Contents

Contents

Contents

Preface

This book is dedicated to the new generation of computer users, for whom concepts such as windows, menus, web pages and the Internet are well known and natural. If you are used to programs with a graphical user interface and to programs that are able to communicate with remote computers via the network, then of course you expect that a book about programming should show how to construct such programs. But programs with a graphical user interface and communication programs can easily get very complicated. For this reason, they have not normally been dealt with in basic programming literature. But times have changed. Java gives us access to a new technology, which permits us to construct programs using entirely new principles. For this reason, graphical user interfaces are discussed in this book right from the start and communication is covered in detail. The most advanced examples do things that it would have been impossible to do with a more traditional programming textbook for beginners.

The new technology is based on object-oriented thinking, where programs are subdivided into autonomous modules, so-called objects. Let us use an analogy with the way that houses are built. In the old days, houses were built using relatively simple components – bricks, planks, nails etc. If you go back far enough, not even these simple components were ready-made. A person who wanted to build had to start by cutting down trees and sawing the planks needed. These days, we use ready-made modules to an increasing extent. For example, entire walls are now available ready-made, and only need to be joined together on site. This, of course, makes it quicker to build houses. Programming has been subjected to the same changes. In the old days, programmers had to write the greater part of their programs themselves. Really far back in time, you even had to construct your own programming tools (such as compilers and editors). Now we use ready-made program components which are joined together to make functioning programs. This means that programming work takes place at a higher level of abstraction than previously. It then becomes possible to construct highly advanced programs in a short time, programs which would have demanded an unreasonable amount of time and labour if you had to do everything yourself.

Java is not just a programming language. Java also has a comprehensive library of standard classes. These standard classes are described in the book, and we use them to create the program components, i.e. the objects from which the programs are constructed. (The version of Java on which the book is based is *Java 2 Platform, Standard Edition, v 1.4.*)

In this edition of the book, a collection of standard classes referred to as *Swing* are used throughout the book to implement programs with a graphical user interface. These classes offer more facilities than the classes used in the previous versions of Java, and make it possible to give the interfaces a more attractive appearance.

The book does not just cover ready-made classes, of course. It also describes "ordinary" traditional programming and shows the different building blocks – expressions, statements etc. – used in the craft of programming. If we return to the house-building analogy for an instant, we know that it is the details that are decisive for the overall finish. It is here that the skill of the building tradesmen shows. In the same way, it is important that programmers have mastered their craft, so that they can join up and utilize the program components in the best way, and adapt them to the specific needs of each task.

In the book, the objects, classes and interfaces are presented graphically by means of *UML* (Unified Modeling Language), which has now become a *de facto* standard in the presentation of object-oriented concepts.

This book was written so that it could be used by beginners. It does not assume any previous programming experience. (But previous experience is not a disadvantage.) On the other hand, it is a good idea to have a certain amount of computer literacy and to be able to use a web browser, for example.

The previous edition of this book has been used as course literature for a number of programming courses. Based on experience gained from these courses, several changes have been introduced to make the book more educational. The use of so-called dialog boxes in Swing has made it easier, right from the first chapter, to construct programs that both read input data and present results graphically.

Book arrangement

Chapter 1 gives a background to Java and discusses how compilation and program execution is done. It shows how to present data and read input data by using dialog boxes. It also discusses how to achieve choices and repetition by using `if` statements and `while` statements.

Chapter 2 discusses classes, objects and methods, but also more basic concepts such as variables, standard types and expressions.

Chapter 3 covers packages and encapsulation. It also discusses class variables and class methods, especially the way in which collections of mathematical and other functions can be constructed with the aid of class methods.

Chapter 4 gives a general background to object-orientation and shows how object-oriented relationships are described in Java.

Chapter 5 discusses how to input and decode data and how to edit the output data to be presented. Reading and writing can be done by means of dialog boxes, but text files and command windows can also be used.

Chapter 6 describes most of the standard classes used in Swing to implement graphical user interfaces. Examples of many different types of graphical components are shown.

Chapter 7 demonstrates how to construct your own graphical components, based on the standard classes in Swing. It also discusses the "drawing tools" included in Java.

Chapter 8 is an extension of Chapter 6. It shows how to position graphical components in a window using so-called Layout Managers. It also discusses how to achieve various effects by using borders and how to change the so-called Look & Feel.

Chapter 9 is mainly about arrays, vectors and lists, which are used to construct collections of data. This chapter also discusses classic concepts such as searching and sorting, and also includes object-oriented concepts such as multiple relationships.

Chapter 10 contains a full discussion of inheritance mechanisms. It discusses dynamic binding, polymorphism, abstract classes, interfaces etc.

Chapter 11 is about so-called exceptions. This is a mechanism used throughout Java to signal various kinds of errors.

Chapter 12 is about active objects and describes how to implement programs where several activities execute in parallel, so-called multiple threading. It also gives examples of programs that display moving figures.

Chapter 13 discusses event-driven programs. It includes various types of events such as mouse clicks and key presses.

Chapter 14 is a complement to Chapter 6. It covers menus, windows and dialog boxes.

Chapter 15 covers images and sound. There is a special discussion on constructing your own icons, which can be displayed in various graphical components. It also demonstrates how to display moving images.

Chapter 16 discusses streams and files. Streams are a general mechanism which Java uses to read and write data. There are a number of standard classes for streams. The chapter contains both an overview and reference sections. The chapter also discusses direct-access files and aids for working with files and folders.

Chapter 17 is about communication. It discusses the concepts of port and socket, and various forms of communication: datagram, multicast, virtual connections and client–server technology. There is also a section which describes how to send e-mail.

Chapter 18 offers an assortment. It covers how to document your Java programs. A number of language constructs are covered, which were not needed in previous chapters. There is also a section about recursion.

Chapter 19 describes the classes introduced in the Java 2 Platform to form various kinds of data structures (lists, sets and maps).

The book contains a large number of examples. Each chapter is also concluded with a number of exercises, which readers can work on themselves.

The text contains a large number of "fact boxes" which contain summaries of the classes, language constructs or concepts which have just been covered. The purpose of these boxes is to give the reader some repetition, but they should also be able to serve as quick references. The fact boxes are specially marked in the index.

Addresses

There is a website for the book, which contains more information, including solutions to all exercises. The web address is `www.cs.chalmers.se/~skanshol/Java_eng`. If you want to comment on the book, please e-mail `skansholm@cs.chalmers.se`.

Getting started

In this first chapter, we will be discussing how Java programs can be written and run. This will be demonstrated with a few simple examples. We will be looking at both programs that write in a text window and ones that make use of a graphical user interface (GUI). GUI programs can be shaped either as ordinary, independent applications, or as *applets*.

We shall be looking at examples of both techniques. This chapter begins with a short description of the properties of Java and continues with a discussion of the concepts of compilation, execution and interpretation.

1.1   What is Java?

Java is a programming language, developed by Sun Microsystems. Java became generally available in 1995. At first, Java was probably best known as a programming language used on the Internet to create dazzling effects on websites. A website can contain applets, which are small programs written in Java. When a browser such as Internet Explorer or Netscape downloads and displays a website containing a program in Java, the program will be run. Java can then generate sounds and moving pictures, or permit the user to communicate with the program by using the mouse and keyboard. But Java really is a fully fledged programming language. By using Java, just as with C++, complete application programs can be created which by no means need to be run through a browser.

Java has several characteristics that make it especially interesting:

*   Java is platform-independent. By *platform* we mean a kind of operating system that runs on a certain type of computer. For example, Windows XP on a PC is a platform, and Solaris, the Unix variant, on a workstation from Sun, is another. That Java is platform-independent means that Java programs can be run on different types of computer systems without having to be changed.
*   Java is object-oriented. In its construction Java is based entirely on object-oriented principles. A Java program therefore consists of a number of *objects* which work in conjunction with each other and which are described with the help of *classes*.

1. Getting started

- Java contains classes to generate graphical user interfaces (GUIs). *GUI programs* can be written with the help of Java, that is, programs communicating with the user through windows, menus, buttons, etc. Different platforms normally have different functions to generate GUIs. A program written, for example, in C++ and intended to be run under Windows, cannot be directly moved to another platform, let us say, X under Unix. This is because all the calls for the graphic functions have to be rewritten. The graphic functions for different platforms are also very difficult to learn to use. Meanwhile, the best part of using Java's classes to create graphics is that they, like the Java language itself, are platform-independent. We don't have to be familiar with a platform's graphic functions. It suffices to learn how Java's graphic classes work, and then we can write GUI programs for all types of computer systems! It pays for a programmer, even for a beginner, to learn to use Java's classes for graphics, since the odds are that there will be plenty of opportunities to use this knowledge.
- Java makes it possible to write parallel programs, since it supports multi-threading. This means that a Java program can describe several activities going on at the same time. For example, a moving picture can be shown at the same time as a user is allowed to enter data into the program.
- Java can be used on the Internet. As mentioned in our introduction, this is done by allowing websites to contain applets. With applets, we can create graphics on a website, download a new website, or read a file over the net. It is even possible to create programs that make use of client–server techniques.

Are there no disadvantages to using Java? Is it not extremely difficult to learn? Of course there are negative aspects, the greatest of these being the performance aspect. When a Java program is run, or *executed*, as we say, it will proceed more slowly than if the program had been written in a "normal" programming language such as C++ or Ada. This has to do with the fact that Java programs are interpreted. (We will be looking at the concept of interpreting later in this chapter.)

The question as to whether Java is difficult to learn can be answered with a yes and a no. The core of the language is relatively small. The syntax (rules of the language) is actually based on C++. A Java program looks very much like a C++ program, and anyone knowing some C++ will feel at home. In fact, the most difficult part of C++, the question of *pointers*, has been removed from Java, making it much easier to understand a Java program than one in C++. All this means that it is relatively easy to learn the language of Java itself. However, it is not enough to master the language and its syntax in order to be able to write Java programs. This is because we are not usually satisfied merely with writing simple programs that write and read text in a text window. We would like to construct GUI programs, if possible, with moving pictures and capable of communicating via the Internet. This is much more difficult! There are all the different standard classes for dealing with graphics, events, multi-threading and different ways of communicating that have to be learnt. In this respect, Java is not a small language, and a good deal of work will be necessary to learn it.

Java was released in 1995 and quickly became very popular, one reason being that it was possible to run Java applets in a web browser. Java was rapidly accepted in the computer world, and is available for all common platforms, including Windows, Mac and Unix. Sun's official description of Java is now designated *Java 2 Platform, Standard Edition* (*J2SE*). This description includes the definition of the *Java API* (Application Programming Interfaces), which is a collection of standard classes which can be used in all Java programs. In version 1.2 of J2SE, the Java API was enhanced by a collection of new classes, the so-called *Java Foundation Classes* (*JFC*). In particular, these include *Swing*, which are the classes used to generate graphical user interfaces. The latest version of J2SE comprises a *de facto* standard for Java. Sun has developed a program package which contains all the programs and class libraries you need to develop and run Java programs under J2SE. This program package is called *Java 2 SDK, Standard Edition* (*J2SDK*). (SDK is an abbreviation of "Software Development Kit".) It can be said that J2SDK is Sun's implementation of J2SE.[1] J2SDK can be downloaded free of charge from the Internet. There is also something called *Java 2 Runtime Environment, Standard Edition* (*J2RE*). J2RE contains the aids you need to run complete Java programs in your computer. J2RE is really a sub-set of J2SDK, but can be downloaded instead of J2SDK if you do not intend to develop your own Java programs.

A *package* in Java is a collection of classes that belong together. A package can also contain other packages, which, in their turn, can contain classes and packages etc. The Java API is organized in the form of packages. Most of the contents of Java API have been put in a large package called `java`. In version 1.2, the `javax` package was also added. These two packages, in their turn, contain a number of other packages designated `java.awt`, `javax.swing`, `java.lang` etc. One package of special interest is `java.lang`, which contains all the aids of a general nature which are needed in all Java programs. (This means that the contents of `java.lang` are available to all Java programs, with no special need to specify this.)

1.2   Where can we find information about Java?

Everything we need can be found on the Internet. The most important starting point is Sun's own website for Java: `www.javasoft.com`. The latest version of J2SDK can be found here, together with a mass of documentation. Sun also has a website of a more general character: `www.sun.com`.

---

[1] J2SDK used to be designated JDK (Java Development Kit). As from version number 1.2, the name J2SDK is used. It is still possible to find designations such as JDK 1.4, however, which is the same as J2SDK, version 1.4.

Another excellent website containing news about Java is the website for the magazine *JavaWorld*: www.javaworld.com with links to other interesting websites.

The site www.apple.com/java is of special interest to Mac users.

Apart from compilers, interpreters and other programs, Sun's J2SDK also contains a great deal of documentation. Of special interest is the fact that *documentation for all the classes in the Java API is there, too*. With the Java API all the information needed for practical programming work can be accessed. In addition, this documentation exists in a form facilitating the use of a browser (Netscape or Microsoft Internet Explorer) to search and read documentation on a PC. Detailed information about all classes can be retrieved easily and quickly.

The full documentation for the Java API is considerable and it would require several hundred pages to print out on paper. Since all Java programmers have access to documentation in J2SDK, this book dispenses with a thick appendix. If further details are required, more information can be retrieved from the computer. Another reason not to include the Java API documentation in the book is that Java is still being developed. Additions and adjustments are taking place all the time, and the most up-to-date information is always found in the latest version of Sun's J2SDK, while a printed book cannot be changed as often.

1.3 Traditional compiling, linking and execution

We shall now describe how programs are written and loaded into the computer so that they can be executed (run). In this section, we will begin by giving a general description of the procedure for traditional programming languages such as C++, Ada and Pascal; in the following section we shall look at the procedure for Java.

A program that is executed exists in the computer's main memory and consists of a number of connected memory cells. A memory cell, or a group of memory cells, contains an *instruction*. By combining parts of the memory cells in different ways, different instructions can be represented. A program consists of a series of *instructions* which tell the computer exactly what to do. An instruction in the program is made up of a particular combination of ones and zeros but these combinations may look different, depending on the type of computer. For the program to be run on the computer, it must be stored in the computer's main memory. We usually say that the program exists in the form of *machine code*. The machine code is a code which is very "user unfriendly", i.e. it is difficult to read *and* write. In the infancy of computers, they had to be programmed directly in machine code. Luckily, things have progressed and programmers today do not normally have to worry about the computer's machine code. Programs are now written in a *programming language* (such as C++), a more "user-friendly" form than the computer's machine code. Special translation programs can be

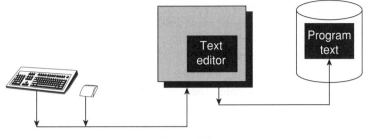

Figure 1.1

used to translate from programming language to machine code, so enabling the written program to be run on the computer.

When a program is written, it takes the form of normal text. In order to input the original *program text*, or *source code*, as it is called, the programmer can use a simple text-editing program, a so-called *text editor*. (Examples of these are Notepad in Windows and Edit in MS-DOS.) Figure 1.1 illustrates how the text editor program is run. Written text is normally put into a file on the hard disk. Exactly how the text editor functions and which commands it understands will vary from system to system. A simple text editor will do nothing more than contain the text, but more advanced text editors also "understand" the kinds of text they are processing. A text editor that knows it is editing a C++ program can help the programmer by marking different program constructions with different styles or colours.

In the next step, the program texts are translated from normal text to machine code. This is done, as shown in Figure 1.2, with the help of a special translating program, a *compiler*. Every compiler is designed to take care of a particular programming language. To be able to translate a C++ program, access to a C++ compiler must be available. Similarly, to translate an Ada program, an Ada compiler must be used. A compiler can be either a separate program, or a part of an integrated program development system. Such a system contains all the tools needed, such as text editor, compiler and debugger.

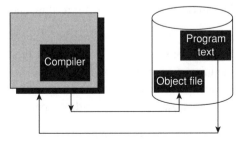

Figure 1.2

For every programming language there are special rules for how different structures may appear (compare this with the rules for sentence construction in normal languages). We say that a language has a certain *syntax*. The compiler reads the program from the text file created earlier and checks first that the program is following the rules of the language, that is, is following the given syntax. If the compiler finds errors, error messages will appear on the screen. There may also be warnings for what may not be clear errors but may look doubtful to the compiler. Sometimes, the compiler will try to correct errors if they are not too serious, but compiling will usually stop when errors have been discovered. We then have to go back to the previous step and, with help of the text editor, edit the program text and correct the errors. Once this has been done, a fresh attempt can be made to compile the program. This process often has to be repeated several times.

If the compiler does not discover errors, it goes on to translate the program from text to machine code. The compiler creates a file in which it saves the machine code generated. This file is then called an *object file*.

Since different types of computers have different machine codes, object files intended for one computer platform will not be suitable for another. Platforms must have different compilers. If we want to move a program developed on one kind of computer to another, we have to move the program text itself to the new computer and compile the program again there. This is easier if there are not too many details in the program dependent on one particular system. A program that can be moved easily from one computer platform to another is called a *portable* program. Even if programming languages are often standardized, the functions used by modern GUI programs to generate windows, menus, buttons, etc. are different on different types of computer. This means, in practice, that GUI programs are far from portable. A great deal of work is necessary to move a program to another type of computer. (As mentioned earlier, these problems do not exist with Java. We shall soon come back to this point.)

Normally, a program consists of several program parts which have been compiled *separately* so we end up with several object files. Some object files (standard object files) may have been created previously, and these will also be a part of our program. Such standard object files may include functions for reading and writing data.

In order to put object files together into a program that can be executed, we run a special linking program, a *linker*; see Figure 1.3. The linker produces a complete unit, an *executable file*. Sometimes, a special suffix, for example `exe`, may be used in the file name to indicate that the file contains an executable program. The linker can be an independent program, or can be part of a program development system.

Linking can take place either *statically* or *dynamically*. In static linking, all the parts of the program are put into the executable file, while in the case of dynamic linking,

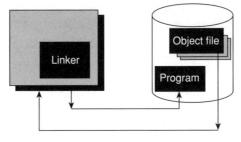

Figure 1.3

references to the required object files are placed in the executable file. The object files themselves are not found in the executable file. When a dynamically linked program is run, the different object files will be automatically retrieved and stored in the main memory, if necessary. The advantage with dynamic linking is, of course, that it saves a lot of file space since different programs often contain common parts, input and output for instance. These parts do not then need to be copied to all the executable files but can exist in only one edition, to which all the executable files will refer.

This leaves only the last step, which is to get the executable program into the main memory so that it can be run. But how does the computer know which program to run? For the answer, let us look at Figure 1.4.

In earlier diagrams, we have shown only one program at a time in the main memory, the program being executed. In fact, there are always parts of yet another program permanently stored. This is termed the *operating system*, shortened to OS. (Examples of common operating systems are Windows, MS-DOS and Linux.) The user can give commands to the operating system through the keyboard, or can point and click with the mouse. A common command is to request that a particular program is loaded and executed. The operating system will search for the required executable file and copy it into the main memory, as suggested by the diagram above. Control is then transferred to the program that has been loaded, which may run until it finishes, or until it is interrupted.

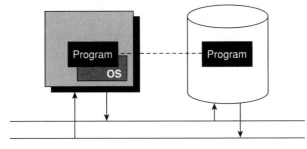

Figure 1.4

The different steps in traditional compiling

Program text (source code) is created with the help of a text editor.

The compiler translates this program text to an object file.

The linker connects several object files to an executable file.

The operating system places the executable file in the main memory, and the program runs.

1.4   Compiling and executing Java programs

Imagine what it would be like if all the different types of computer understood the same machine code! Life would be much simpler. The same compiler could be used for all platforms, and the object code produced by this compiler would also be portable, so that it could be run on any computer, without the program needing to be compiled again. Now, as we know, reality is not like this. But we could pretend that a computer existed for all kinds of object code and this is precisely how Java works. Someone has come up with a *Java virtual machine*, an imaginary computer that understands the object code produced by a Java compiler. When Java programs are compiled, however, the code generated is not called object code but *Java byte code*.[1]

Since this virtual Java machine does not really exist, it must be simulated. This is done by a special program, an *interpreter*, which reads Java byte code and ensures that the instructions in it are carried out; see Figure 1.5. On the face of it, it looks as though the Java program is "executed" in the virtual Java machine. The Java program reads input and produces output, just as in any "ordinary" program. Note, however, that it is really

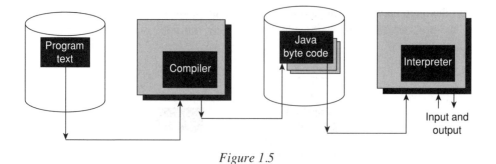

Figure 1.5

---

[1] The word *byte* is a generally accepted designation of a group consisting of eight binary digits (zeros or ones).

the interpreter that is being executed and that the Java byte code is input to the interpreter. The Java program is never actually compiled into machine code. It is in the form of Java byte code. We also see from Figure 1.5 that input to the interpreter can consist of several independent files, all of which contain Java byte code. It can be said, then, that the interpreter also carries out dynamic linking and links all files with Java byte code that are necessary for the program to run.

Have we actually gained very much by using this technique? Since the Java compiler and the Java interpreter are ordinary programs compiled into machine code, they have to be in different versions for different platforms. Different platforms, of course, have different machine code, but the work of adapting the Java compiler and the Java interpreter for different platforms needs to be done *only once* per platform. It is not the Java programmer who needs to do this; it has already been done by the development teams that produce Java. Programs written by the Java programmer are always immediately movable between different platforms, without the programs having to be changed. This is not the case when we are programming in traditional programming languages and want to move programs from one platform to another. Then, every program being moved has to be adapted to the new platform; this is work that can be very taxing for the ordinary programmer.

The technique of interpreting is not something new that applies only to Java. Programming languages that make use of interpreting have been around for a long time. The most well-known languages previously using this technique are LISP and Smalltalk. The disadvantage with interpreting is that it takes a lot longer to interpret a program than it does to execute a program that is already in the form of machine code. This difference does not matter as much as it might have done in the past, however, given the speeds of modern computers. It should also be remembered that Java programs are often interactive and have a graphical user interface. Most of the time, a program will be paused, waiting for the user to generate input data. Where the speed of a program is of paramount importance, it will be better for the programmer to use C++, for example, or Ada, where compiling takes place in the traditional way.

In order to increase the execution speed of Java programs, a technique called *just-in-time compiling* is often used. This means that the interpreter really compiles the instructions in the Java byte code into proper machine code during execution. Where these instructions are repeated later in the program, execution will proceed more quickly, since they can be executed "properly", without being interpreted.

If speed is important, another possible technique is that of writing central, complex parts of the program in a traditional language, most often C or C++, and letting the Java program call up these parts of the program. However, if this technique is used the program will no longer be platform-independent.

1.5 The first program

By using a simple example, we shall now demonstrate how compiling and execution in Java are carried out in practice. In order to do this, we need to have a Java compiler and a Java interpreter. Both of these programs are included in Sun's J2SDK, and we will assume that the latest version has been installed. This is not particularly difficult to do. (For an appropriate web address, see Section 1.2.)

A modern integrated program development system, an IDE (Integrated Development Environment), normally offers the programmer an environment with all the resources necessary to develop programs. Such systems also exist for Java. Some examples are Sun's Java Workshop, Borland's JBuilder, Symantec's Visual Café and Microsoft's Visual J++. There are also a number of shareware systems on the Internet. Not only are the obvious resources of text editor, compiler and interpreter available in an IDE but there is support to keep account of the different parts of a programming project. There is also a *debugger* (a program that makes it possible to test-run programs step by step and search for errors), and there are help texts, documentation and examples. The professional programmer will certainly make use of an IDE but here we are dealing with student programmers. We merely assume that J2SDK has been installed.

Our first Java program is comprised of only a few lines:

```
public class Welcome {
    public static void main (String[] arg) {
        System.out.println("Welcome to Java");
    }
}
```

When this program is run, it will print out the text Welcome to Java. Before we discuss how compiling and execution are handled, we should note the appearance of the program. (More detailed descriptions of the different program constructs will naturally come later in the book.)

A Java program normally consists of several *objects* which work in conjunction with one another. The different objects are created dynamically during execution. In order to describe how these objects look and behave, we use a construct called *class*. Our simple program consists of a definition of a single class with the name Welcome. This class definition is introduced with the word **class**, followed by the name of the class. Any name will do. On the first line, there is a left-hand curly bracket and on the last line, a right-hand curly bracket. These brackets indicate where the class description begins and ends. (The characters { and } correspond to the words "begin" and "end", used in many other programming languages.) The word **public** indicates that the class Welcome should be accessible to the whole program.

When the program starts, there are no objects, so there must be a starting point in the program where we have the opportunity of creating the first object (or objects). When the Java interpreter begins to execute the program, therefore, it requires the presence of a *method* in the class we began with, one with the special name of main. It is simple in this example, since the only content of the class Welcome is its method main. The definition of main begins on the second line. Let us see what there is on this line.

The word **public** indicates that the method main should be accessible from outside. It must be if the interpreter is to be able to call it. (If the word **public** had not been included, the method would only have been recognized inside class Welcome.)

The word **static** means that the method main is a *class method* (or *static method*, as we also say in Java). A class method is one that is not particular to one object but relates to the class itself. (A better description of this will be given later in the book.) Since there are no objects when the program starts, main must be a class method.

The word **void** means that the method main will not leave a result value.

The word main on the second line is, of course, the name of the method. We can normally give our methods any name we wish but in this case this method must have precisely the name of main. Note that Java differentiates between upper- and lower-case letters: we are not allowed to write MAIN or Main.

After the method's name, its *parameters* are found in brackets. In the case of main, we are able to pass arguments from the command line. We will not go further into this now but will merely state that this is the form it must have.

In a method the different steps to be performed are expressed by *statements*. A semicolon is written after each statement. In this example, there is only one statement, indicating that the text Welcome to Java is to be printed. This statement is found on the third line. The statement begins with the word System. System is a standard class found in the package java.lang in the Java API. System contains resources of a general nature. One of the items defined here is an *output stream* with the name System.out. This output stream is normally called *standard output*. Whatever is output in standard output will be automatically written in a command window on the screen. Output is generated by calling the method println for the output stream System.out. In the parentheses, we indicate the text to be written out: Welcome to Java. Note that this text must be included in double quotes.

Certain words in the program have been written in bold. These are *reserved words*, words with a special meaning in the language of Java. When we write our own programs, we do not have to mark these words in this way but we do it here simply to make the programs clearer. Note, however, that all reserved words must be written in lower case. All reserved words are listed in Appendix A.

We now type in the above program text with the help of a text editor and store it in a text file with the name `Welcome.java`. As we can see, the file name has the *suffix* `.java`. All text files containing Java programs must have this suffix. In addition, the first part of the file's name must be identical to the name of the class. It is also important here to have the same upper- and lower-case letters in the file name as in the class name.

This is what we do if we are running Windows or Unix: Open a command window (called MS-DOS Prompt in Windows). Move with the help of the command `cd` to the folder with the file `Welcome.java`. Then write the command:

```
javac Welcome.java
```

This command will start the program `javac` (Java Compiler) which compiles the Java program and generates a file containing the Java byte code for the class `Welcome`. This file will automatically be given the name `Welcome.class`. The suffix `.class` is used to mark that a file contains Java byte code.

Then run the program by giving the following command:

```
java Welcome
```

Note that we must *not* write the suffix `.class`. This command starts the Java interpreter, which reads the file `Welcome.class` as input and executes the program given there. The result is that the text

```
Welcome to Java
```

is written out in the command window.

Compiling and executing Java programs

Using a text editor, a file is created with the program text.
This file should be called `classname.java`.

The compiler translates the program text to Java byte code.
This is done with the command

```
javac classname.java
```

The interpreter executes the program by reading the Java byte code and ensuring that the instructions in it are carried out.

The interpreter is started by the command

```
java classname
```

When you debug a program it is better to use the command

```
java -Djava.compiler=NONE classname
```

When a Java program is executed the just-in-time compilation technique will normally be used to increase execution speed. This might cause problems when you debug a program. You will not be told exactly where in the program (in which lines) the errors occur. Therefore, when you debug a program it is a good thing to disable the just-in-time compilation so that a pure interpretation is performed. To accomplish this, run the program by giving the following command:

```
java -Djava.compiler=NONE classname
```

1.6   Using dialog boxes to read input data

The program in the previous section printed a text. Each time the program was executed, it printed the text Welcome to Java. We will now write a new program that prints the text Hello xxx instead, where xxx could be any name. We will call the new program Hello and for this reason, we put the program code in a file called Hello.java. (We will soon show you what the program looks like.) The program is compiled, as we have learned, with the command javac:

```
javac Hello.java
```

The next stage is to run the program, which is done with the command java. We type

```
java Hello
```

When you run the program, a so-called *dialog box* pops up, where the user is asked to write his or her name. You can see what the box looks like in Figure 1.6. In this example, the user has written the text David. When the user clicks the OK button or presses the Enter key, the dialog box disappears and the program prints the following text in the command window (MS-DOS Prompt in Windows):

```
Hello David
```

Figure 1.6 An input dialog

13

Let us now see what the program looks like.

```
import javax.swing.*;

public class Hello {
    public static void main (String[] arg) {
        String name;
        String message;
        name = JOptionPane.showInputDialog("What is your name?");
        message = "Hello " + name;
        System.out.println(message);
        System.exit(0);
    }
}
```

We will start by discussing the first line of the program. In Java, there are a number of *packages* of standard classes. One such package is javax.swing. One of the classes in this package is JOptionPane, which will be used in this program. In order for the program to use the contents of a package, you must *import* the package at the beginning of the program. This is done with a special **import** command. To specify that the javax.swing package is to be imported, type the following:

```
import javax.swing.*;
```

The * character at the end of the line can be read as "everything in the package". (Compare this with the techniques used in MS-DOS and Unix to specify file names.) It is also possible to import single classes individually. Since we are going to use the JOptionPane class in the program, we could have written the following lines instead:

```
import javax.swing.JOptionPane;
```

In normal cases, you need to use several classes in a package. This means that it would be clumsy to type an **import** command for each class. It is much easier to write *package_name.**. We will use this technique in the rest of the book. Please note that this does not make the program any faster or slower, since the Java interpreter is so smart that it includes only the classes you actually use.

You have to import every package you use in a program. The only exception is the package java.lang. The contents of this package are directly available in all Java programs, without your having to specify anything.

In computer programs, one uses so-called *variables* to store various types of data. This data can be of different types. The most common types of data are texts and numerical values. Each variable can contain data of a particular type. In this program, two variables are used. Both variables should contain text. Before you use a variable in a program, you have to *declare* it. This specifies the type of variable and what it should be called. In Java, the standard class String is used to specify that a variable contains text. In the lines

```
String name;
String message;
```

we have declared the variables `name` and `message` which are both of type `String` and thus contain texts.

The standard class `JOptionPane` contains a so-called *method* named `showInputDialog`. When you call it, it displays a dialog box on screen. In the sixth line of the program, we make such a call and type

```
name = JOptionPane.showInputDialog("What is your name?");
```

You have to write the class name, `JOptionPane`, followed by a full stop before the method name, `showInputDialog`, since the method `showInputDialog` is in the class `JOptionPane`. Inside the brackets, you write the so-called *parameters* of the message (a kind of input data to the method). The parameter that `showInputDialog` wants to have is the text typed in the dialog box. When the user has typed a text in the dialog box and clicked the OK button or pressed the Enter key, the dialog box is closed. The method `showInputDialog` then provides the text that the user typed in as its output. (We will discuss what would happen if the user clicked the `Cancel` button in Section 1.12.) We will put the text that the user typed in the variable `name`. An *assignment* is used to do this. In an assignment, there is a variable on the left of the equals sign. On the right of the equals sign, you type the expression whose value will be put in the variable.

In the next line of the program, we will type the text to be put in the variable `greeting`:

```
message = "Hello " + name;
```

An assignment is done here as well. We have specified here that the variable `message` should contain the text `"Hello"` followed by the text in the variable `name`. (The plus sign used in conjunction with texts does not mean addition; it means that the texts should be joined together.) If the user had written the name `David` in the dialog box, the variable `message` would contain the text `"Hello David"`.

The next step is to print out the contents of the variable `message` by calling the method `println`:

```
System.out.println(message);
```

The last thing that happens in the program is to write the phrase

```
System.exit(0);
```

This is a call to a standard method called `exit` which is included in the class `System`. This method ensures that the program is terminated in the correct way. It is necessary to include this line when you use dialog boxes in the way that we have done in this program. If we were to fail to call `exit`, the program would hang up and would not be terminated.

The text in the buttons of a dialog box is automatically written in the relevant language for the installation. (This is discussed at further length in Section 5.2.) You can also choose the text to be shown in the frame of a dialog box yourself. The call to showInputDialog then becomes more complicated, however. If you want to have the text Question instead of Input in the frame in the dialog box in Figure 1.6, you should make the call

```
name = JOptionPane.showInputDialog(null, "What is your name?",
                    "Question", JOptionPane.QUESTION_MESSAGE);
```

1.7   Using dialog boxes for messages

In the program Hello, it might seem to be illogical to write in a command window when you read the name in a dialog box. So we will make a new version of the program, where the greeting is written out in a new dialog box. We call the new program Hello2.

```
import javax.swing.*;

public class Hello2 {
    public static void main (String[] arg) {
        String name;
        String message;
        name = JOptionPane.showInputDialog("What is your name?");
        message = "Hello " + name;
        JOptionPane.showMessageDialog(null, message);
        System.exit(0);
    }
}
```

If you run the new variant of the program with the same input data as previously, the dialog box shown in Figure 1.7 is generated. As you can see, we have made only one change. We have changed the line where println was called to the following:

```
JOptionPane.showMessageDialog(null, message);
```

showMessageDialog is another method included in standard class JOptionPane. It is used to display dialog boxes with messages. As parameter two, in front of the brackets, we specify the message to be displayed. The first parameter must be included and we give it the value null. (This parameter is really used to specify the window on the screen over which the dialog box should be displayed, but if you give it the value null, the dialog box will be displayed in the centre of the screen.) When the user clicks the OK button, the dialog box and message disappear and the program continues to the next line. (The method showMessageDialog does not provide a result value that needs to be processed.)

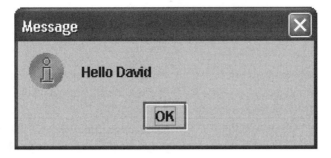

Figure 1.7 A message dialog

It is possible to make a number of simplifications in the program. For example, we can form an expression at the same time as `showMessageDialog` is called, to specify the text to be displayed.

```
JOptionPane.showMessageDialog(null, "Hello " + name);
```

The variable `message` is then not needed. We can even put the call of `showInputDialog` directly into the expression and write

```
JOptionPane.showMessageDialog(null,
    "Hello " + JOptionPane.showInputDialog("What is your name?"));
```

We will not need the variable `name` either. However, it is never wrong to use variables if they make a program clearer or easier to understand.

We can also mention here that you can create dialog boxes where the text is displayed on several lines. To achieve this, you put the combination `\n` in the text, at all places where you want a new line to start. For example, we can write the phrase

```
JOptionPane.showMessageDialog(null, "Hello\n" + name);
```

This will put the text `Hello` on one line, with the name on the line below.

It is possible to control the text displayed in the frame in a dialog box that displays a message. For example, if we want the text Information to be displayed instead of Message in the box in Figure 1.7, we change the way `showMessageDialog` is called:

```
JOptionPane.showMessageDialog(null, message, "Information",
                      JOptionPane.INFORMATION_MESSAGE);
```

1.8   An alternative way to start Java programs

When you have a program such as `Hello2`, it can appear to be clumsy to start the program by entering `java` in a command window (MS-DOS window). The command window is not used by the program, after all. You might want to be able to start the program by clicking an icon, just as you do with most other programs in a system that uses a graphical user interface. This can be achieved relatively simply. For example, to start the program Hello2 in this way, all you have to do is create a text file with a single line

```
java Hello2
```

This text file can be created with any text editor. In Unix or Linux, you save the file under any name and then change the file properties to make it executable. In Windows, you make this file into a so-called BAT file and call it Hello2.bat, for example. You then open the folder where the file is resident, select the file with the right mouse button and select the Create shortcut option. A new file is then created with the name Shortcut to Hello2.bat. Change the name of this file to something simpler, such as Hello2. Then select the new file with the right mouse button and select the Properties shortcut option. In the window that pops up, you select the Program tab. Under the Run: heading, you select the Minimized alternative and then select Close when terminated. Finish by selecting OK or Run. It is then very easy to start the program Hello2 by clicking the new shortcut.

1.9   Using numerical variables

So far, we have worked with texts. We will now start to study programs where you can calculate things. As a first example we will construct a program that calculates what it costs to rent a car. Assume that you know how many days you want to rent the car, and what it costs per day. You can then get the program to ask for this information in two dialog boxes, and then calculate the total cost and display it in a third dialog box. For example, the program can produce the three dialog boxes displayed in Figure 1.8. (These boxes are not all displayed at the same time; they appear one at a time.)

This is what the program looks like:

```java
import javax.swing.*;

public class CarRent {
  public static void main (String[] arg) {
    int noOfDays;
    double costPerDay;
    double totalCost;
    String input;
    input = JOptionPane.showInputDialog("Number of days?");
    noOfDays = Integer.parseInt(input);
    input = JOptionPane.showInputDialog("Cost per day?");
    costPerDay = Double.parseDouble(input);
    totalCost = costPerDay * noOfDays;
    JOptionPane.showMessageDialog(null,
                            "Total cost: " + totalCost);
    System.exit(0);
  }
}
```

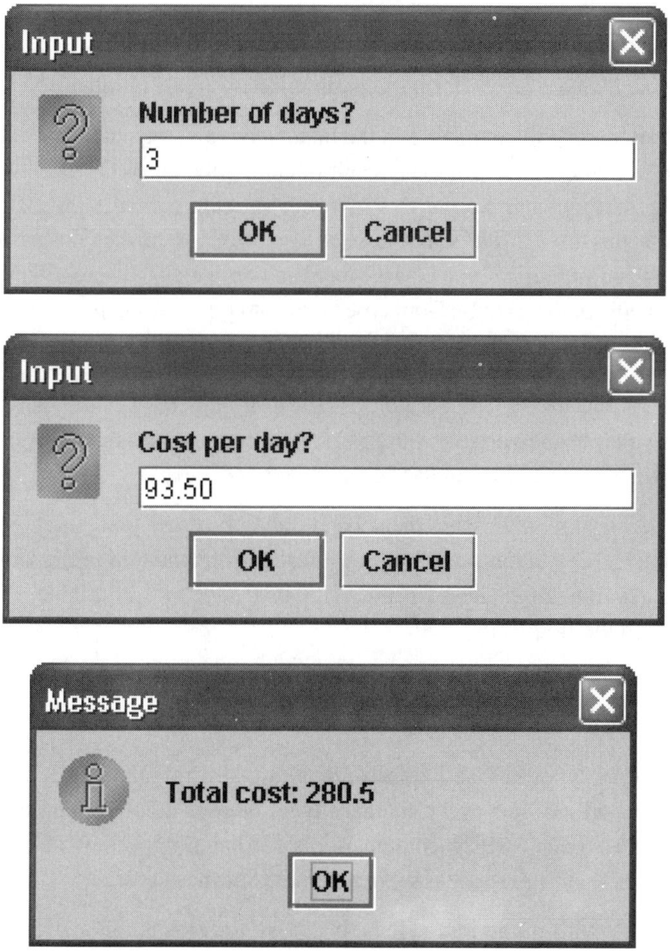

Figure 1.8

As mentioned previously, variables are a kind of container in which you can put data. In this program four variables, noOfDays, costPerDay, totalCost and input, are used. You have to declare a variable before you can start to use it in a program. In other words, you have to say what the variable should be called and what type of data it should contain. In our program, the declaration of the variable noOfDays is done on the line that starts with int. This line says that the variable should be called noOfDays and that it should contain values of the type int. (One generally says that the variable *is of* type int or that it *has* type int.) Type int is a so-called standard type in Java and "int" is an abbreviation of the word "integer", which means numbers with no fractions or decimal places. The variable noOfDays will thus contain integers, i.e. numbers with no decimal point. The variables costPerDay and totalCost are declared on the lines that start with the word `double`. The type `double` is another standard type in Java and is used to declare variables that can contain numerical values with a decimal portion. `costPerDay` and `totalCost` will thus contain ordinary (real) numbers.

If the user were to type the number 3 in the first dialog box, the numerical value 3 would be put in the variable `noOfDays`. The result of calling the method `showInputDialog` would be the text `"3"` and we put this text in a variable named `input`. However, we cannot assign this text to the variable `noOfDays` without further discussion. This is because texts and numerical values are stored in completely different ways. We have to do a so-called *type conversion* from type `String` to type `int`. This is done on this line:

```
noOfDays = Integer.parseInt(input);
```

which converts the text in the variable `input` to a numerical value of type `int` and assigns this value to the variable `noOfDays`. The conversion is done by a tool called `parseInt`, which is part of a standard class called `Integer`.

When the user has typed 93.50 in the second dialog box, the text `"93.50"` is assigned to the variable `input`. In the same way, we must convert the text in the variable `input` to a numerical value of type `double` and assign this value to the variable `costPerDay`. This is done on the line

```
costPerDay = Double.parseDouble(input);
```

where we have used the tool `parseDouble` in standard class `Double`.

In addition to the types `int` and `double`, there are several standard types, which we will see in Section 2.3. For every standard type, there is a corresponding class, such as `Integer` and `Double`, which contains tools for handling values of that type. The methods `parseInt` and `parseDouble` are examples of these tools.

When you work with numerical values, it is easy to form mathematical expressions by using the mathematical operations + - * and /, which refer to the four rules of arithmetic. The first three function in the way you would expect. The division operator / gives a normal result if one of its operands is a real number, but if *both* its operands are integers, the result will be an integer, not a normal quotient. (We will discuss this in greater detail in Section 2.4.1.) On the next line of the program, we form a numerical expression:

```
totalCost = costPerDay * noOfDays;
```

In this line, the total price is calculated and assigned to the variable `totalCost`. The result is then displayed in a dialog box by using the call

```
JOptionPane.showMessageDialog(null,"Total cost: " + totalCost);
```

This contains the expression `"Total cost: "` + `totalCost`. It looks as if we are adding a text to a real number, which seems strange. But this is not an addition, it is a text concatenation. This is because if one of the two operands for the operator + is of type String, the other operand will *automatically* be converted to type String as well. (In other words, we do not explicitly have to do a type conversion from type **double** to type String.) After this, a concatenation of the two texts is done. In this example, the numerical value in the variable totalCost will automatically be converted to text form before concatenation.

One question that pops up naturally when we have got this far is whether you really have to use dialog boxes. Can't you read input data directly from the command window from which the program is started, and also write output data to this window? Yes, it is quite possible to do this. The way this is done will be described in detail in Chapter 3. The reason that we do not go into detail now is that it is, unfortunately, rather complicated to read from command windows in Java.

1.10 **if statements**

In all the examples we have seen so far, the statements have been executed in sequence, from beginning to end. But two more basic things are needed to make it possible to write more interesting programs: a program should be able to choose alternative statements to execute (selection) and to execute the same statement several times (repetition). We can use an **if** statement to achieve choices, which we will discuss in this section. Repetition is covered in the next section.

As an example, we will study the program below, which calculates the total price when you have purchased a number of items of the same type. The program reads input data from two dialog boxes. In the first, you specify the number of units you have purchased, and in the second you give the price per unit. The program calculates the total price and shows the result in a third dialog box. To make the program a bit more interesting, we assume that you get a discount of 10% if you spend more than $1,000. The program is as follows.

```java
import javax.swing.*;

public class Price {
    public static void main (String[] arg) {
        String input;
        input = JOptionPane.showInputDialog("Number of items?");
        int numberOfItems = Integer.parseInt(input);
        input = JOptionPane.showInputDialog("Cost per item?");
        double itemPrice = Double.parseDouble(input);
        double totalPrice = itemPrice * numberOfItems;
        double discount;
        if (totalPrice > 100) {
            discount    = totalPrice * 0.10;
            totalPrice = totalPrice - discount;
```

```
        }
        JOptionPane.showMessageDialog(null,
                                "Total cost: " + totalPrice);
        System.exit(0);
    }
}
```

Reading of input data from the dialog boxes is done in the same way as for the `CarRent` program on page 18. The only difference is that we have used the facility of initializing variables at the same time as declaring them. For example, we have written

```
int numberOfItems = Integer.parseInt(input);
```

This is exactly the same as making first a declaration and then an assignment:

```
int numberOfItems;
numberOfItems = Integer.parseInt(input);
```

When you declare a variable, you can thus choose if you want to initialize it or not. If you do not initialize a variable in a method (a so-called local variable), it will contain an undefined rubbish value from the start. In this case, you will have to make sure that you assign a sensible value to the variable before you read it.

The part of the program we particularly want to study is the four lines starting at the reserved word `if`. After this word, there must be an expression *in brackets*. This must be a so-called *logical expression*, which must have one of the values `true` or `false`. Here, we see `totalPrice > 1000`. (The `>` means "greater than", of course.) If the expression is true, the statements inside the following brackets `{}` will be executed. If the expression is false, these statements will not be executed. To make it easier to see the statements that will be executed conditionally, we have moved the text a little to the right. This is called *indenting*. It is very important that you indent your programs, to make them easier to read and understand.

Indenting

A program is made legible by moving the text on the lines over to the right, so that they reflect the structure of the program.
A well-structured program is always indented.
Use indents whenever you write programs.

You can have any number of statements inside the brackets in an `if` statement. Frequently, there is only one statement. In this case, you do not have to put any brackets round the statement if you do not want to. For example, we could write

```
if (totalPrice > 1000)
    totalPrice = totalPrice - totalPrice * 0.10;
```

An **if** statement can have an **else** section, a series of statements which are executed if the condition is false.

```
if (totalPrice > 1000) {
   discount   = totalPrice * 0.10;
   totalPrice = totalPrice - discount;
}
else
   JOptionPane.showMessageDialog(null, "No discount, sorry");
```

Here, *either* the two statements inside the brackets will be executed, *or* the statement after the **else** will be executed.

You can also put several statements in the **else** section, but you must then use brackets:

```
if (totalPrice > 1000)
   totalPrice = totalPrice - totalPrice * 0.10;
else {
   JOptionPane.showMessageDialog(null, "No discount, sorry");
   JOptionPane.showMessageDialog(null, "Buy more next time");
}
```

When there are brackets round the statements after **if** there must *not* be a semicolon in front of **else**, but if there are no brackets, there *must* be a semicolon.

if statement, different forms	

if (*expression*)
    statement;
───────────
if (*expression*)
    statement;
else
    statement;
───────────
if (*expression*) {
    one or more statements
}
else {
    one or more statements
}
	if (*expression*) {
	    one or more statements
	}
	───────────
	if (*expression*)
	    statement;
	else {
	    one or more statements
	}
	───────────
	if (*expression*) {
	    one or more statements
	}
	else
	    statement;

Even if the **if** has only two alternatives, it can be used in multiple choice situations. Let us assume that there are two discount levels in our example. If you spend more than

$5000 you get 15% discount and if you spend less than $5000 but more than $1000, you get 10% discount. If you spend less than that, you do not get a discount. We can then write the `if` statement as follows:

```
if (totalPrice > 5000)
   totalPrice = totalPrice - totalPrice * 0.15;
else if (totalPrice > 1000)
   totalPrice = totalPrice - totalPrice * 0.10;
else
   JOptionPane.showMessageDialog(null, "No discount, sorry");
```

Two `if` statements have been combined here, so that the `else` section of the first `if` statement contains a new `if` statement.

The statement(s) in the `if` statement or `else` may be any kind of statement, including new `if` statements. When you have one `if` statement inside another one, we say that they are *nested*. The structure becomes clearer if they are indented in a different way:

```
if (totalPrice > 5000)
   totalPrice = totalPrice - totalPrice * 0.15;
else
   if (totalPrice > 1000)
      totalPrice = totalPrice - totalPrice * 0.10;
   else
      JOptionPane.showMessageDialog(null,"No discount, sorry");
```

When you have pure multiple choice situations, normal practice is to indent in the first way, so that the program text will better reflect the logic of the program.

1.11 Using dialog boxes to choose alternatives

Sometimes, you may want to allow the program user to choose from several alternatives. To demonstrate this, we change the conditions for the `Price` program slightly. Assume that you no longer get a discount if you spend more than $1000, but you get a 10% discount if you are a member of the shop's customer club instead. To find out if the customer is a club member or not, we get the program to display the dialog box in Figure 1.9. In this box, the user can click one of the buttons.

Dialog boxes of this type are generated in the program by calling method `showCon-firmDialog`, which is part of class `JOptionPane`. You specify the text to be displayed in the box as the parameter. When the user has clicked one of the buttons, the dialog box is closed and the method `showConfirmDialog` gives an integer as the result. This integer is the number of the button that the user clicked. Please note that numbering starts at 0, which means that the method returns the value 0 if the user clicks the `Yes` button, value 1 if the user clicks the `No` button and value 2 if the user clicks the `Cancel`

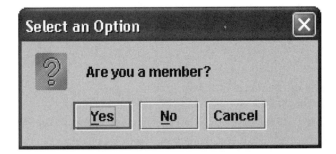

Figure 1.9 A dialog box used to ask a question

button. We can thus generate the dialog box in Figure 1.9 and read the user's answer with the aid of the program line

```
int answer = JOptionPane.showConfirmDialog(null,
                            "Are you a member?");
```

After this, we can investigate the value in the variable answer to find out whether the customer is a member of the customer club. We change the condition in the if statement as follows:

```
if (answer == 0) {
   discount = totalPrice * 0.10;
   totalPrice  = totalPrice - discount;
}
```

Please note that we have written *two* equals signs. The character == means "equal to". You cannot use a single equals sign, because this is used for assignments. In addition to the two comparison operators > and == which we have seen examples of here, Java also contains comparison operators <, <=, >= and != ("not equal to").

In all the dialog boxes we have shown so far, the text on the buttons and the text in the window frames have had a standardized appearance. This can be changed so you can have any text you want. To avoid confusing things early on, we will wait until later before we start showing how to do this.

1.12 while **statements**

The simplest method of achieving repetition in a Java program is to use a while statement. We will start with a simple example. The program lines

```
int j = 0;
while (j < 6) {
   System.out.println(j);
   j = j + 2;
}
```

give the printout

```
0
2
4
```

Execution of the `while` statement takes place as follows. The expression in brackets after the `while` is executed first. (You can use the same comparison operators as in the `if` statement here.) If the expression is false, nothing more is done here; the `while` statement is fully executed. If the expression is true, on the other hand, the statements inside the brackets are executed once. When these statements have been executed, the expression inside the brackets is processed again. If it is false, the `while` statement is terminated and if it is true, the statements inside the brackets will be executed again, etc. In the example above, we will do three loops of the `while` statement. The variable `j` starts off with the value `0` and is then incremented by `2` at the end of each loop. This means that at the end of the third loop, `j` has assumed the value of `6`. The expression `j<6` then becomes false and the `while` statement is terminated.

In a `while` statement, you can leave the brackets out if there is only one statement to be executed every loop, in the same way as for an `if` statement.

while statement, different forms	

while (*expression*)
 statement;
	while (*expression*) {
	     one or more statements
	 }

The next example shows a somewhat unrealistic job situation. You have been offered a very dangerous, risky job. The wages are also quite unusual. You are offered 1 cent for the first day's work, 2 cents for the second day, 4 cents for the third day, 8 cents for the fourth day, etc. In other words, the wages double each day. Since you are careful with your health, but can still accept a certain level of risk to become rich, you want to find out what the offer really means. You ask the question: how many days do I need to become rich? We write the following program to answer that question:

```java
import javax.swing.*;

public class Rich {
   public static void main (String[] arg) {
      String input = JOptionPane.showInputDialog("Amount?");
      double desired = Double.parseDouble(input);
      int noOfDays = 1;
      double dailyWage = 0.01;
      double totalSum  = 0.01;
      while (totalSum < desired) {
```

```
        noOfDays = noOfDays + 1;
        dailyWage = dailyWage * 2;
        totalSum = totalSum + dailyWage;
    }
    JOptionPane.showMessageDialog(null,
                "You will be rich after " + noOfDays + " days");
    System.exit(0);
  }
}
```

When you run the program, it might look like Figure 1.10.

The three variables noOfDays, dailyWage and totalSum are used in the program. They are initialized to default values which reflect the situation after you have worked one day. The variable desired should contain the result you want. We input the value for this variable by using a dialog box.

The three statements inside the while will be repeated once per working day as from day two. We see that each day, the day counter is incremented by 1, the new day's wages (which are twice the old wage) are calculated and the new day's wages are added to the total sum. After two days noOfDays will have value 2, dailyWage will have value 0.02 and totalSum will have value 0.03. Since the value in the variable

Figure 1.10

27

`totalSum` increases all the time, the condition after `while` must become false sooner or later, and the `while` statement is terminated.

The variable `noOfDays` is incremented every day, and each loop corresponds to a worked day. This means that the variable `noOfDays` contains the number of days worked when the `while` statement has stopped executing.

Sometimes, you may have to break off a `while` statement in the middle of a repetition. You can then use a `break` statement. A `break` statement can be placed among the statements which are executed each time, and has the form:

```
break;
```

A `break` statement should, of course, be included in an `if` statement so that it can only be executed conditionally.

When a `break` statement is executed, the `while` statement is terminated at once and a jump is made to the first statement immediately after the `while` statement. It should be pointed out that `break` statements can also be used with the other two repetition statements in Java, namely `for` statements and `do` statements, which are described later on in the book.

---

break statement

May be placed among the statements performed at every round of a repetition statement. Immediately aborts the repetition statement.
There is a jump to the first statement after the repetition statement.
Is often placed in an `if` statement:

```
if (conditions_to_end)
    break;
```

As an example, we will do a minor modification to the `Rich` program. In the new version, you will be able to do repeated calculations. Each time the program has calculated and displayed the number of days you need to work, it starts from the beginning again and allows the user to input a new desired amount in the top dialog box in Figure 1.10. The program then does repeated calculations until the user clicks the `Cancel` button in the dialog box, instead of filling in the desired sum. How can the program know if the user has clicked the `Cancel` button? As you know, the `showInputDialog` method usually returns the text that the user has typed in, but if the user clicks the `Cancel` button, a special value called `null` is returned instead. This value means "no text". (We do not get this value if the user leaves the input field blank and clicks the `OK` button. In this case, the `showInputDialog` returns a text of zero length.) The new version of the program is as follows:

```
import javax.swing.*;

public class Rich2 {
  public static void main (String[] arg) {
    while (true) {
      String input = JOptionPane.showInputDialog("Amount?");
      if (input == null)
        break;
      double desired = Double.parseDouble(input);
      int noOfDays = 1;
      double dailyWage   = 0.01;
      double totalSum = 0.01;
      while (totalSum < desired) {
        noOfDays = noOfDays + 1;
        dailyWage = dailyWage * 2;
        totalSum = totalSum + dailyWage;
      }
      JOptionPane.showMessageDialog(null,
                    "You will be rich after " + noOfDays + " days");
    }
    System.exit(0);
  }
}
```

We have encapsulated the previous statements in a new `while` statement. The condition for this statement might appear a bit strange. The fact that the word `true` appears inside the brackets would normally mean that this `while` statement would be repeated an infinite number of times. However, there is a `break` statement which makes it possible to terminate the repetitions. Each time we display the dialog box, we test whether the variable `input` has value `null`. If this is the case, the user has clicked the `Cancel` button. We then terminate the `while` statement by using a `break` statement. When the `break` statement has been executed, the program jumps to the first statement immediately after the `while` statement, i.e. to the statement where we call `exit`.

One thing to be noted in this example is that you can have `while` statements and `if` statements inside a `while` statement. Of course, you can also have `while` statements and `if` statements inside an `if` statement.

1.13 A GUI program

Modern programs use a graphical user interface (GUI) to communicate with the user. This means that the programs display windows on the screen. These screens can contain various GUI components, such as buttons, menus and texts. The programs we have studied in previous sections have, admittedly, used dialog boxes to communicate with the user, but you can hardly claim that these programs are "real" GUI programs.

Figure 1.11

The thing that is needed is a window which is permanently displayed on the screen. We will give a brief introduction to the way a GUI program is constructed. (This will be discussed in greater detail later in the book, when we have learned the basics of Java and the principles of object-oriented programming.)

We will start by studying a simple GUI program, which will display the same welcome phrase as the `Welcome` program on page 10, but this time the program will create a new window and the text will be displayed in it. When you run the program, it will look like Figure 1.11. (The text should really be blue and the background yellow, but this does not show up in black and white print.) Please note that this is not a dialog window, it is a "proper" window, which is displayed on screen until we terminate the program by clicking the close box on the window.

We will call our program `Greeting` and thus will put it in a file called `Greeting.java`. The program is compiled with the command

```
javac Greeting.java
```

You then run the program as usual, by typing

```
java Greeting
```

(It is also possible to start the program by clicking an icon, if you use the procedure described on page 17.)

We let the program consist of two classes, `Greeting` and `Welcome2`. It is permissible to put several classes in the same text file, but in this case, you must state **public** for one of the classes, which should be the class that contains the method **main**. It is this class that determines what the text file should be called. In this example, we put `main` in the class `Greeting`, so the file should be called `Greeting.java`. The program looks like this:

```java
import java.awt.*;
import javax.swing.*;

public class Greeting {
  public static void main (String[] arg) { // start of program
    Welcome2 w2 = new Welcome2();  // create a Welcome2 object
  }
}

class Welcome2 extends JFrame {
  public Welcome2() {  // Constructor, called automatically
    JLabel l = new JLabel("Welcome to Java", JLabel.CENTER);
    getContentPane().add(l);  // put l in the window
    l.setOpaque(true);           // opaque background
    l.setBackground(Color.yellow);
    l.setForeground(Color.blue);
    l.setFont(new Font("SansSerif", Font.BOLD, 24));
    setSize(400,150);                // the size of the window
    setVisible(true);                // make the window visible
    setDefaultCloseOperation(EXIT_ON_CLOSE);
  }
}
```

The program contains a new feature, which is *comments*. A comment starts with // and applies to the rest of the line. There are two other ways to write comments in Java. We will come back to this later.

In the first two lines of the program, we import the two packages java.awt and javax.swing. These two packages contain a number of classes which can be used to write GUI programs. There are tools for graphics (fonts, colours, drawing tools etc.), tools for creating various components (menus, buttons, lists etc.) and tools for organizing and positioning components in a suitable manner in the window. The java.awt package has been included in Java since the earliest versions of the language, whereas javax.swing is newer and has only been added in the latest versions of the language. The javax.swing package contains a large number of classes which replace or supplement the classes found in java.awt. You can get by with just java.awt when you write GUI programs in Java, but in this book we will use the newer classes in javax.swing. However, we cannot manage with just the javax.swing package, since several classes we need are in java.awt. This program contains the Font and Color classes from the java.awt package, for example, whereas the JFrame and JLabel classes are in the javax.swing package.

Execution of the program starts as usual with the method main. The only thing that happens in main is that a new object is created, of class Welcome2. This is done in the expression new Welcome2(). The result of this expression is a *reference* (a kind of pointer) to the new object. This reference is saved as a variable, which we call w2. The line

```java
Welcome2 w2 = new Welcome2();
```

31

is really a *declaration* of a new variable called w2. The word Welcome2, which is placed first, specifies that the new variable should be a reference and that it should be able to refer to objects that belong to the Welcome2 class. The word w2 is the name we give the variable. The equals sign means that the variable should be *initialized* and on the right of the variable is the value it should take.

The Welcome2 class describes what the window should look like. In the declaration of the Welcome2 class, we use a technique which is central to object-oriented programming, namely *inheritance*. There is a standard class called JFrame which describes windows. When you create an object of class JFrame, a window is created automatically which can be displayed on the screen, on which you can then place various objects (such as buttons and menus). We want our class Welcome2 to have the same properties as JFrame. So we let it inherit properties from class JFrame. This can be done by writing the first line in Welcome2 as follows:

```
class Welcome2 extends JFrame {
```

A class can contain a so-called *constructor*. This is a kind of initiation method which is automatically called each time you create a new object of the class. A constructor always has the same name as the class in which it is found. The class Welcome2 has a constructor. It starts on the second line of the class Welcome2. When the statement **new** Welcome2() is executed in the method main, this constructor will be *automatically* called. The program lines found in the constructor in the class Welcome2 will thus be executed when you start the program.

In the constructor, an object of the standard class JLabel is created first. An object of this class, in its simplest form, describes a text to be displayed in a window. When you create an object of class JLabel, you can specify the text to be displayed and how the text should be positioned. In our program, we write

```
JLabel l = new JLabel("Welcome to Java", JLabel.CENTER);
```

This is a declaration where we declare a variable of name l and type JLabel. The expression on the right of the equals sign is the value to which l should be initialized. Variable l should be initialized, so that it contains a reference to the JLabel object which contains the text "Welcome to Java" and where the text is centred.

On the next line in the program, we write

```
getContentPane().add(l); // put l in the window
```

This is where we say that a JLabel object should be placed in this window. Every window of type JFrame has a "work surface", which is called contentPane. The call getContentPane() gives a reference to this work surface. You can position one or more GUI components on this work surface. This is done with a method called add. It is, of course, of interest to be able to control where each component is placed on the work surface. We will describe how this is done in Chapter 6. This is easy in the `Welcome2` program, however. Since we place only one component, it ends up in the centre and fills the entire window.

On the following lines in the program, we will specify further properties of the `JLabel` object `1`. The methods `setBackground` and `setForeground` are used to specify background and foreground colours. They must have an object of the class `Color` as their parameter. Colours are described in Java with so-called RGB numbers. These are three integers in the range 0–255 which specify the amount of red, green and blue in the object. For example, yellow is described with the numbers (255,255,0), white with (255,255,255) and black with (0,0,0). The class `Color` contains a number of ready-made objects which describe the most common colours. For example, it contains the objects `Color.black`, `Color.white` and `Color.red`. You can also define your own colours by combining the RGB numbers as you like. A light blue object could be created with the declaration

```
Color lightBlue = new Color(175,175,255);
```

Pre-defined colours in the class java.awt.Color			
`Color.black`	0, 0, 0	`Color.magenta`	255, 0, 255
`Color.blue`	0, 0, 255	`Color.orange`	255, 200, 0
`Color.cyan`	0, 255, 255	`Color.pink`	255, 175, 175
`Color.gray`	128, 128, 128	`Color.red`	255, 0, 0
`Color.darkGray`	64, 64, 64	`Color.white`	255, 255, 255
`Color.lightGray`	192, 192, 192	`Color.yellow`	255, 255, 0
`Color.green`	0, 255, 0		

In the program, the call

```
l.setOpaque(true);       // opaque background
```

is important. This specifies that the `JLabel` object should be opaque. If we had not included this line, `1` would have become transparent. The text would, admittedly, have been printed in blue, but the background would not have been visible. The window background colour (probably grey) would have been visible instead.

The method `setFont` specifies the font to be used. As its parameter, it must have a reference to an object of the class `Font`. The program contains the statement

```
l.setFont(new Font("SansSerif", Font.BOLD, 24));
```

1. Getting started

As the parameter, we give a new object of the type `Font`. When you create an object of type `Font`, you have to specify the name of the typeface. We have chosen `SansSerif` here. After this, you have to specify whether you want plain, bold face or italic style by writing `Font.PLAIN`, `Font.BOLD` or `Font.ITALIC`. It is also permissible to combine the last two. You can have bold face italic, for example, and you specify the style as `Font.BOLD|Font.ITALIC`. Finally, you have to specify the size of the typeface. The typefaces with direct support[1] are `Serif`, `SansSerif`, `Monospaced`, `Dialog`, `DialogInput` and `Symbol`. The first three correspond to the typefaces `TimesRoman`, `Helvetica` and `Courier`.

If you have a `Font` object and want to read its properties, you can specify the methods `getFontName`, `getStyle` and `getSize`. For example, the following line gives `SansSerif` printout:

```
System.out.println(f.getFontName());
```

When you create a new object of class `JFrame`, or of a class which has inherited properties from class `JFrame`, a window is created. The window is not displayed on screen automatically, however. To make the window visible, you have to demand this explicitly, and we do this by including the following statement in the constructor:

```
setVisible(true);
```

When you have a window on screen similar to the one shown in Figure 1.11, it is normal practice to close the window by clicking the closing box in the window frame or selecting the alternative `Cancel` (or equivalent) on the window menu. When the window is closed, the program that displays the window is generally closed as well. To make a window of type `JFrame` function in this way, we have to add the following statement to the constructor:

```
setDefaultCloseOperation(EXIT_ON_CLOSE);
```

If we had not included it, it would not have been possible to close the window and terminate the program in the normal way. (It would have been possible to type CTRL-C in the command window from which the program was started, however.)

Of course, we can use dialog boxes in programs that display windows. If we replace the first line in the constructor in class `Welcome2` with the following two lines:

---

[1] You can, of course, choose any installed typeface. The following statements are required to get a printout of the names of all available typefaces:

```
String[] tab = GraphicsEnvironment.
    getLocalGraphicsEnvironment().getAvailableFontFamilyNames();
for (int i=0; i < tab.length; i++)
    System.out.println(tab[i]);
```

34

```
String name =JOptionPane.showInputDialog("What is your name?");
JLabel l = new JLabel("Welcome " + name, JLabel.CENTER);
```

the program will input the user's name in a dialog box and then display a window with the text `Welcome xxx`, where xxx is the name. (Compare this with the program `Hello2` on page 16.)

1.14 An applet

All the programs we have seen so far are examples of *standalone programs*, or *standalone applications* as they are also called. In this section, we will provide an introduction to *applets*. The word applet is an invented word which means a "tiny application", a mini-program). An applet cannot be executed independently but is a routine which is called from another program. In the first instance, it was intended that applets should be called from a web browser. To demonstrate how this functions, we will start by writing a further version of the program that displays the text `Welcome to Java`. We will call the class `Welcome3` and put it in a file called `Welcome3.java`.

```
import java.awt.*;
import javax.swing.*;

public class Welcome3 extends JApplet {
    public void init() {
        JLabel l = new JLabel("Welcome to Java", JLabel.CENTER);
        getContentPane().add(l);     // put l in the window
        l.setOpaque(true);           // opaque background
        l.setBackground(Color.yellow);
        l.setForeground(Color.blue);
        l.setFont(new Font("SansSerif", Font.BOLD, 24));
    }
}
```

As you can see, the class `Welcome3` is very similar to the class `Welcome2` on page 31. There are only three real differences.

We can see the first difference on the third line. The class `Welcome3` *inherits its properties from the standard class* `JApplet`, not from the class `JFrame`. An object of class `JApplet` has more or less the same properties as a `JFrame`; there is a window associated with the object and you can write and draw in this window, and put various components in it. (But the window does not have its own frame and cannot be displayed by itself on the screen. It must be displayed as a component in another window.) In addition, an object of class `JApplet` has certain unique properties, which means that it can be called from a web browser.

The other difference between classes `Welcome2` and `Welcome3` is that an object of class `Welcome3` *is not created in a method with the name* `main`. This is because the web browser takes care of creating an object from the applet. One can imagine that the following line is executed by the web browser:

```
Welcome3 w3 = new Welcome3();   // is done in the web browser
```

The third and last difference is that in the class `Welcome3`, we have not defined a constructor. *A method of name* `init` *is defined* instead. Please note that in this method, almost the same things are done as in the constructor in class `Welcome2`. The difference is that we have omitted the calls to the methods `setSize`, `setVisible` and `setDefaultCloseOperation`. The size of the applet will be defined by the web browser and the visibility of the applet will also be handled by the web browser. The method `init` is called automatically by the web browser as soon as an applet has been created. One can imagine that the following line is executed by the web browser:

```
w3.init();   // is done in the web browser
```

This means that the method `init` is called once when the applet object is created.

The class `Welcome3` is compiled in the same way as other classes. We enter the command

```
javac Welcome3.java
```

Just as before, a file is then created containing Java byte code. The file will be given the name `Welcome3.class`.

Please note that you *cannot* execute the file `Welcome3.class` by giving the command `java`. To make this possible, there must be a method of name `main`, which we do not have. The file `Welcome3.class` should be read and executed by the web browser instead. A web browser normally reads text files which contain instructions for how the text and images should be displayed on the screen. These instructions are written in a special language called HTML (HyperText Markup Language). To tell a web browser to start up a certain applet, you have to create a text file containing suitable HTML instructions. We cannot describe the entire HTML language, so we will show only what is absolutely necessary to be able to execute applets. (The HTML specification can be found on the www.w3.org website. A "Beginners Guide" is available from the web address www.ncsa.uiuc.edu/General/Internet/WWW.)

Using a text editor, we create the following file and give it the name `Welcome3.html`.

```
<html>
  <head>
    <title>Welcome3</title>
  </head>
  <body>
    My first applet.
    <br>
```

```
    <applet code=Welcome3.class width=400 height=150></applet>
    <br>
    The applet is only visible if Java Plug-in is installed.
    <br>
    <a href="http://java.sun.com/getjava/">Get Java Plug-in.</a>
  </body>
</html>
```

An HTML file consists of various components. Each component starts with a *tag* of the form `<name>` and is terminated by `</name>`. The first part of an HTML document must be a header, followed by a title. This title is displayed in the web browser title frame. Then follows the body copy containing the text to be displayed in the website. You can put in any text here. For example, we have written the text `My first applet`. You can also put in headings, lists and various editing commands. (The command `<br>` means that you have to start a new line.)

The specially interesting feature is the line containing an `applet` tag:

```
<applet code=Welcome3.class width=400 height=150></applet>
```

This specifies that the web browser should start the applet contained in `Welcome3.class`. The parameters `width` and `height` specify the size of the space to be associated with the applet. The files `Welcome3.html` and `Welcome3.class` must be in the same folder in the file system for the call to the applet to work. If this is not the case, you must also have a `codebase` parameter. This is used to specify the folder where the `class` file is resident. For example, if the file `Welcome3.class` is in the folder `c:\own\jan\java\examples\Chap1` you can write

```
<applet code="Welcome3.class" width="400" height="150"
        codebase="c:\own\jan\java\examples\Chap1">
</applet>
```

If an applet uses several classes, these can be put in so-called archive files (please refer to Section 3.1). An `applet` tag can then have a parameter called `archive`, which contains a list of the archive files to be used. (This is not needed for the `Welcome3` applet, however.)

```
<applet code="Welcome3.class" width="400" height="150"
        archive="extraClasses.jar,specialClasses.jar">
</applet>
```

To execute `Welcome3`, we can now start the web browser and specify the search path to file `Welcome3.html`. We can also double-click the file `Welcome3.html`. If we use Internet Explorer we see a screen as in Figure 1.12.

Please note that to be able to execute an applet, you also need to write an HTML file in addition to the program text. In the rest of this book, we will work with both

Figure 1.12 Execution of the applet in a web browser

free-standing programs and applets. Whenever we construct applets, we are going to assume that there is an HTML file, unless otherwise mentioned.

It is necessary to install a so-called *plug-in* module to allow a web browser to execute applets that use Swing classes. So at the end of our HTML file, we have put in a link to the Sun website, `http://java.sun.com/getjava/`, from which this module can be downloaded. Please note that this installation must be done locally by *every* user. If you set up a central server which posts a web page containing an applet that contains Swing classes, you take the risk that many users will fail to install the plug-in module and are thus unable to run the applet. For this reason, it could be wise to use the older and simpler classes in `java.awt`. This is because these can be executed by all web browsers without needing to install a special plug-in module. Later on in the book, we will also include examples of applets that use `awt` classes.

Sometimes you may wish to test applets locally on your own computer, without having to use a web browser. You can then use a program called `appletviewer`, which is included in J2SDK. The `appletviewer` program must have an HTML file as input data, as with a web browser. To test our applet, `Welcome3`, we can give the following command:

```
appletviewer Welcome3.html
```

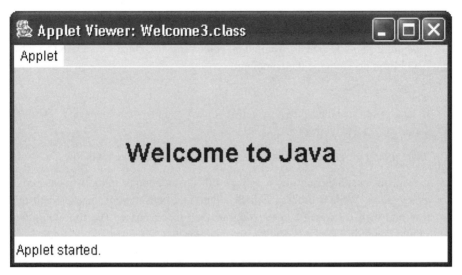

Figure 1.13 Executing an applet with the Applet Viewer

The screen in Figure 1.13 is then displayed. The `appletviewer` program admittedly reads the entire HTML file, but it only bothers about the text in the applet tags.

Compilation and execution of applets

Use a text editor to create a file with the program text.
The file should be called `class_name.java`.

The compiler translates the program text to Java binary code.
This is done with the command

```
javac class_name.java
```

Create the corresponding HTML file with the text editor
(preferably with the name `class_name`.html).
The file must contain an applet tag:

```
<applet code=class_name.class width=n height=n> </applet>
```

Add `codebase` if the class file is not in the same folder.

The program can be executed by a web browser.
In this case, double-click the HTML file or input the search path to the web browser.

The program can also be executed by means of the `appletviewer`.
This is done with the command

```
appletviewer classname.html
```

1.15 Exercises

1. Find out if Sun's J2SDK is installed on your computer. Open a command window (DOS Prompt) and type the command

```
java -version
```

If Java is not installed please install it (or ask your system manager). The web address (URL) is on page 3.

2. Write a Java program which outputs your name in a command window.

3. In English-speaking countries, a car's petrol consumption is normally measured in *miles/gallon*. Write a program which inputs fuel consumption measured in this way and then convert it to *litre/100 km*. Use dialog boxes. The following data should be used: *1 mile = 1.609 km* and *1 gallon = 3.785 litres.*

4. Write a program which calculates the volume and area of a sphere. Use the radius of the sphere as the input data. The following formulae are given

$$V = \frac{4\pi r^3}{3} \qquad A = 4\pi r^2$$

5. When you are going to insure a car, you usually sign up for full coverage if you have a newish car (younger than five years old). If the car is older, you might think that you can get by with third party, fire and theft.
   a) Write a program that advises you on the type of insurance to obtain. The program input data should be the year (this year) and the model year. One of the following messages: *Choose full coverage* or *Choose third party, fire and theft* should be displayed, depending on whether the car is older or younger than five years.
   b) Some insurance companies have special policies for veteran and classic cars which are at least 25 years old. Supplement the program so that it gives the message: *Choose a veteran/classic car policy* if the car is at least 25 years old.

6. When you input data into a program, it is frequently necessary to check that the data that the user types in are reasonable. Modify the program in Exercise 4 so that it checks that the radius is greater than 0 before it does the calculation. If this is not the case, a new dialog box should be displayed, which asks the user to type in a correct value. This procedure should be repeated until a correct value has been input.

7. In diving competitions, each jump is assessed by seven judges who give points on a scale from 0 to 10. The points for each jump are calculated as follows: Ignore the highest and lowest scores given by the judges. Then calculate the average of the remaining five scores. The points for the jump are then calculated by multiplying the average obtained by 3 and then by a figure corresponding to the level of difficulty of the jump. Write a program that first inputs the level of difficulty of the jump, and then the scores given by the seven judges. The program should calculate and display the points for the jump.

8. Modify the program in the previous exercise so that it can be used to calculate the final points for an arbitrary number of jumps. Each new calculation starts by asking the level of difficulty. The user can then specify that the program should be terminated by pressing `Cancel`.

9. Write and test-run a standalone Java program that outputs your name. Try using different typefaces, background colours and print colours. Also compose your own colour by specifying RGB numbers.

10. Do the same thing as in the previous exercise, but design the program as an applet instead. Also write the associated HTML file. Test-run the program with the aid of both a web browser and the `appletviewer` program.

Classes and objects

In object-oriented programming, programs are constructed from a number of well-defined units called *objects*. In this chapter we shall discuss basic concepts and the associated terminology, with particular attention to *classes* and *objects*, and shall demonstrate how these are constructed in Java. In order to do this, we shall also describe how *variables* and *methods* can be declared.

2.1 Object-orientation

The classical picture of a computer program is of a "box" into which we put input data and from which we take output data. The task the program has is to transform a flow of data. This traditional way of looking at computer programs is usually called the *function-oriented* view. The *object-oriented* view is quite different. There, a computer program is conceived as a kind of *model* of the reality the program has to work with. The separate units in a program, the *objects*, are then models of real, or devised, things in the program's environment. It is then the task of the computer program to manipulate these objects. We use classes, as illustrated in Figure 2.1, to represent and describe characteristics of objects.

Let us begin by discussing the concept of an object in detail. Each object has a unique identity. We deal with objects by their names or by references (as used in Java). For instance, we could construct the object `theFlower`, representing a real flower, or the object `theWindow`, which describes a window on the screen. Every object has certain properties, which can be described by *attributes* and *operations*. Attributes are used to keep track of the object's status, since each object has a definite status which can be changed during execution. Each object has its own unique set of attributes. Normally, they are hidden within the object so that they are not accessible from outside and can only be changed by the object itself. This is called *information hiding*. As an example, we can study an object `theLift`, whose status can be described using two attributes, `direction` and `floor`. The attribute `direction` can have one of the values `stationary`, `up`, or `down`, while the attribute `floor` can contain an integer stating which

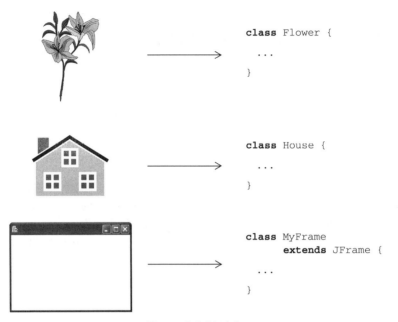

```
class Flower {
    . . .
}
```

```
class House {
    . . .
}
```

```
class MyFrame
        extends JFrame {
    . . .
}
```

Figure 2.1 Models

floor the lift is currently at. Different object-oriented languages use different terms for "attribute". In Java, the term "instance variable" is used, in C++ it is called a "data member", and in Ada, a "component". From now on we will be using the term *instance variable*. We may sometimes use the simpler term *variable* when it is clear that an instance variable is intended and not some other kind of variable.

The second category of properties of an object is the *operations* that can be performed on it. For the object `theLift`, for instance, there might be the operations `goTo`, `stop` and `whichFloor`. The method `goTo` is used to get the lift to a particular floor, `stop` is used to stop the lift, and `whichFloor` is used to find out which floor the lift is currently at. In Java, an operation like this is called a "method", in C++ it is a "member function", while in Ada the term "primitive operation" is used. From now on, we will be using the term *instance method* to emphasize that a particular method is employed for a particular instance of a class.

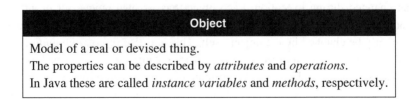

Object
Model of a real or devised thing.   The properties can be described by *attributes* and *operations*.   In Java these are called *instance variables* and *methods*, respectively.

Lift
direction : int floor : int
goTo(v : int) stop() whichFloor() : int

Figure 2.2 A class diagram

As stated, an object is a model of a real or devised thing. How then is an object described in a program? This is where the concept of *class* comes in. A class is a kind of template or pattern which describes the appearance of a collection of objects with a common construction and set of properties. A class is therefore a *description*, and different classes can describe different sets of objects. A diagram of class Lift is given in Figure 2.2. In our diagrams we will use UML[1] (Unified Modeling Language). UML contains rules for visual presentation of classes, objects, and other concepts related to object-orientation. UML has been adopted as standard by the OMG (Object Management Group) and has been generally accepted.

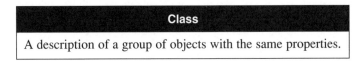

Class

A description of a group of objects with the same properties.

In UML, a class is drawn as a rectangle with three compartments. The class name is placed in the top compartment, the attributes are placed in the middle compartment and the operations in the bottom compartment. In Figure 2.2, the types of the attributes and the types of the operations' parameters and return values are given. This is not necessary. It is permissible just to state the names of attributes and operations. (In the figure the direction of an elevator is described by an integer number. We can let −1 mean down, 0 stationary, and 1 up.)

An object that belongs to a particular class is said to be an *instance* of the class. Several objects may belong to any one class. Figure 2.3 contains a UML diagram showing two

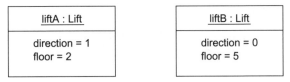

Figure 2.3 Object diagrams

---

[1] *UML Notation Guide* (available from the website www.omg.org).

instances of the class Lift. An object diagram contains two compartments. In the top compartment, the name of the object and the class to which the object belongs are shown underlined. The second compartment shows the attributes and their current values.

In the figure there is one lift on the way up and currently at floor no. 2 and another one has stopped at floor no. 5. In UML, if the name of an object is of no interest, it may be omitted. In this case the colon should be retained. If we omit the name of a Lift object, for instance, the top compartment should show the text : Lift.

2.2 Class definitions

As we have already seen, there is a special language construct in Java to define classes. The definition of class Lift will have the following form, for example:

```java
public class Lift {
    // instance variables
    private int direction;  // -1 down, 0 stationary, 1 up
    private int floor;

    // instance methods
    public void goTo(int v) {
        ...
    }

    public void stop() {
        ...
    }

    public int whichFloor() {
        ...
    }
}
```

A class definition starts off with the reserved word class. Before this word, you might have the so-called modifier public, which specifies whether the class should be generally available or not. (Please refer to Section 3.2.) After the word class you specify the class name, which is Lift in this case. Inside the class definition, we have placed the instance variables first and the methods last. (It is not necessary to use this order. You can put each definition in any order, but we will comply with the model in this book.)

Class Definition

modifier class *name* {
    declarations of instance variables
    definitions of methods
}

The definitions of the methods have only been shown in outline. In the following sections, we will describe how to declare instance variables and methods in greater detail.

When we declare a class, we ourselves may decide what it is to be called. The name of something in a program usually goes under the name of *identifier*. An identifier can have an arbitrary length and consist of letters, digits, dollar signs or underscores but it must not begin with a digit. By "letter", we do not mean merely the letters "a" to "z", as in the English alphabet, but also foreign characters. It is therefore eminently possible to use letters such as ê, ã and ö in identifiers. Note that lower-case and upper-case letters are treated as being different. The names n1 and N1 would indicate two different things. We are not allowed to use reserved words as names. For example, we may not declare variables called while and if, since these are reserved words.

We previously wrote the class name Lift, starting with a capital L. From now on, we will let all class names begin with a capital letter. We will be giving instance variables and methods names beginning with lower-case letters, such as sec, for instance, or width. (This is a convention that is generally accepted in Java.) We do this to make it easy to distinguish class names from the names of variables and methods. If a name includes several words, such as MyFrame, numberOfCars, highestValue and timeForLunch, we normally let each word begin with a capital (excepting the first word, in the case of variables and methods).

2.3 Variables

Variables can be used in several ways in a program:

- They can be used as *local variables*. These are variables which are used as containers for temporary calculation results *inside* a method. All variables used in the example in Chapter 1 were of this type.
- They can be used as *instance variables*, such as the variables direction and floor in the class Lift in the previous section.
- They can be used as *class variables*. This is described in Section 3.3.
- In addition, one can say that the *parameters* for methods, which are described in Section 2.7, are also a kind of variable.

There are two classes of variable types, *reference variables* and *simple variables*. Reference variables are used to refer to various objects. Simple variables are a type of container which can hold data. A particular simple variable can only contain data of a particular *type*. In the corresponding way, a particular reference variable can only refer to objects that belong to a particular class (or subclass below it).

Before you can start to use a variable in a program, you have to say what the variable should be called and what type it should have. Specifying this is referred to as *declaring* the variable. A variable declaration has the following form:

```
modifier type variable_name = initial_value;
```

Modifiers are reserved words such as `final` and `private`, which specify that the variable should have certain properties. You use the initial value if you want to specify that the variable should contain a particular value from the start. The initial value can be a simple constant value or an expression. Modifiers and initial values may be omitted, which means that the simplest form of variable declaration is:

```
type variable_name;
```

If the default value is omitted for an *instance* variable or a *class* variable, it will automatically be initialized to a so-called *default value* (standard value). The default value depends on the type in question. The default value of simple numerical variables is 0, for example, and the default value for reference variables is `null`, an empty reference. This means that a reference variable without an initial value does not refer to an object.

Please note that this does not apply to so-called *local* variables, the ones defined inside methods. These must always be initialized before you read their values for the first time.

If several variables are to have the same type, you can define them on the same line:

```
modifier type name1, name2, name3;
```

You can specify initial values here, as well. For example, you can have the form:

```
modifier type name1 = init1, name2, name3 = init3;
```

An initial value is only valid for the variable immediately before it, which means that the variable `name1` in this example is given the initial value `init1` and `name3` is given the initial value `init3`.

The word `final` is a special modifier. You use this when you want to define *constant* variables. For example, you can write

```
final type v = init;
```

This means that the variable `v` is initially given the value `init` and cannot then be changed. It is actually permissible to omit initialization when you declare a variable which is marked `final`. In this case, the variable must be given a value before it is used for the first time. This value must not be changed later on.

2.4   Simple variables and built-in types

There are eight built-in types. These are the types `boolean` and `char`, together with six types used to describe *numerical* data, i.e. ordinary numbers. The type `boolean` is used to describe truth values. The type `char` is used to describe single graphical characters, i.e. numbers and letters. We start by describing the numerical types.

2.4.1 Numerical types and expressions

The types `byte`, `short`, `int` and `long` are used to describe whole numbers or integers (numbers without decimals), while types `float` and `double` are used for real numbers (numbers with decimal parts). What distinguishes the different numerical types, apart from their ability to store decimals, is the number of bits in the computer's memory taken up by variables of these types. A variable of type `byte` is always 8 bits long, for example, while a variable of type `int` is always 32 bits long; see details in the table below. The type we choose will depend on the size of the numbers we wish to store in a program. We will generally be making use of types `int` and `double` ("double" stands for "double precision", a relic from the programming language C).

Built-in numerical types			
type	size	least value	greatest value
`byte`	8 bits	−128	128
`short`	16 bits	−32 768	32 767
`int`	32 bits	−2 147 483 648	2 147 483 647
`long`	64 bits	−9 223 372 036 854 775 808	9 223 372 036 854 775 807
`float`	32 bits	Roughly -3.4×10^{38} to an accuracy of 7 digits	Roughly 3.4×10^{38} to an accuracy of 7 digits
`double`	64 bits	Roughly -1.7×10^{308} to an accuracy of 15 digits	Roughly 1.7×10^{308} to an accuracy of 15 digits

An instance variable that is one of the numerical built-in types is automatically initialized to the value 0 unless a special initialization value is indicated in the declaration. Here are some examples of declarations of simple numerical variables:

```
int i, j, lowestPoint=10, highestPoint=50;
final int maxSize=500;
double x, y;
```

Expressions for the calculation of numerical values often occur in programs. Such expressions are called *numerical expressions*. With these, we can use the ordinary mathematical operations of addition, subtraction, multiplication and division, indicated by the signs +, -, * and / respectively. The most common form of numerical expression has two operands, which can be variables or constant values. Some examples are:

```
i + j        x + 12.6       1 - i         x - y
x * y        i * maxSize    i / 10        x / y
```

The two operands may be of different numerical types. The type of the result of a numerical expression is determined by the type of the operands. If one of the operands has type `double`, the result will be of this type. Otherwise, a search is made to see whether one of the operands has type `float` and, if so, the result will be of type `float`. If not, a search is made to see whether one of the operands has type `long` and, if so, the result will be of type `long`. Otherwise, the result will be of type `int`, independent of the type the operands have.

Division requires further explanation. If one of the operands is a real number, ordinary division takes place and the result will be a real number. If, on the other hand, both the operands have an integer type, for example `int`, then *integer division* is performed. This means that we will see how many times the right-hand operand "goes into" the left-hand one. If, for example, the variables i and j are of type `int` and have the values 14 and 5, respectively, the result of the expression i/j will be 2, since 5 goes 2 times into 14. The result will *not* be 2.8. To obtain the remainder in a division operation, we can use the operator %. If, as previously, the variables have values of 14 and 5, respectively, the expression i%j will produce a result of 4.

More complicated expressions can be created by combining several operators. An example is i+j*maxSize. In a complicated expression, the priorities of the operators determine the order in which the expression is calculated. Operators with higher priority are calculated before those with lower priority. If two operators have the same priority, calculation will be performed from left to right. In the case of numerical operators, *, / and % have the highest priority, while the operators + and - have the lowest priority. An example is the expression -2+4/2*3, which will have the value 4. Parentheses can also be used to control the order of calculation. For instance, the expression (-2+4)/ 2*3 will have a value of 3. A list of all operators is given in Appendix A.

Numerical operators	
+ - *	addition, subtraction and multiplication
/	division (integer division if both operands are integers, ordinary division otherwise)
%	gives the remainder of an integer division
Operators * / and % have higher priority than + and -	

We often need to indicate constant values in an expression. We have already seen several examples of this. In the following example, 12.6 and 10 are constant values.

```
x + 12.6    i / 10
```

Such constant values are normally called *literals* in a programming language. In Java, we distinguish between integer literals and real literals. In the above expression, 10 is an integer literal and `12.6` is a real literal. It is normal to indicate integer literals in ordinary *decimal* form. They will then consist of the digits 0–9. If we let an integer literal begin with the digit 0, the compiler will interpret this as an *octal* number and the literal may then contain only the digits 0 to 7. The literal `025`, for example, is interpreted as 21 in the decimal system (2*8+5). Integer literals can also be given in *hexadecimal* form. The literal is then introduced by the signs `0x`, or `0X`, and then a number of hexadecimal digits are given. These hexadecimal digits are the normal digits 0 to 9, together with the letters A, B, C, D, E and F. (We can also use lower-case letters.) The literal `0x2c`, for example, is interpreted as 44 (2*16+12). Integer literals normally have type `int`. If we had to represent a number so large that it could not be contained in a variable of type `int`, we would write the letter L last. The literal would then have type `long` instead. For example, we can write the literal `150000000000L`.

Real literals can be written either in the ordinary way or in exponential form. In the ordinary form, there are a number of integer digits, a decimal point and a number of decimals. Note that it should be a decimal *point* and not the continental decimal *comma*. We are allowed to leave out integer digits or decimals but never the decimal point. Some examples of this are:

```
12.3    0.057    789.    .5    0.
```

The exponential form is handy when indicating very small or very large numbers. Some examples of numbers in exponential form are:

```
1.234E2    23.456e-32    1.E16    56e-55    832E12
```

The exponential part introduced by the letter E, or e, indicates how the number is to be raised. For example, `1.234E2` means "1.234 times 10 raised to the power of 2" and `23.456e-32` means "23.456 times 10 raised to the power of –32". A real literal will have type `double`. (We can write the letter F right at the end, for example `7.8e17F`, if we want a real literal to have type `float`.)

For each of the eight built-in types, there is a corresponding class in the `java.lang` package. This corresponding class has the same name as the type, but with an upper-case first letter. For example, there is a class called `Byte` and another called `Double`. Exceptions from this name rule are the types `int` and `char`. For these types, the corresponding classes are called `Integer` and `Character`, respectively. These corresponding classes are generally referred to as "wrapper classes". They contain various constants and methods which have to do with the relevant built-in type. In Chapter 1, we saw an example of how we could use the methods `parseInt` and `parseDouble` in the classes `Integer` and `Double` to convert texts to numerical values. All wrapper classes (except the class `Boolean`) contain the two constants `MIN_VALUE` and `MAX_VALUE`, which specify the smallest and the largest value that the type can assume. (But for the types `float` and `double`, `MIN_VALUE` specifies the smallest positive value that is greater than zero.) We can do the following initializations, for example:

```
int k = Integer.MIN_VALUE;
double z = Double.MAX_VALUE;
```

Then `k` is initialized to the least possible value of type `int` and `z` to the greatest possible value of type `double`. The classes `Float` and `Double` also contain the constants `NEGATIVE_INFINITY` and `POSITIVE_INFINITY`, which describe an infinitely large negative number and infinitely large positive number, respectively. We can use the method `isInfinite` to test whether a value is infinitely large. For example, the expression `Double.isInfinite(z)` gives the value `true` if `z` contains an infinitely large number. Certain numerical operations, division by 0, for instance, give an undefined result. There is a method called `isNaN` in the classes `Float` and `Double`, which can be called to check whether a real variable contains such an undefined value. (`NaN` stands for "not a number".)

Type `boolean` is used to describe logical values. For this type, only two values are allowed, `false` and `true`. An instance variable of type `boolean` that has not been explicitly initialized will automatically be given the value `false`. It is perhaps a little unusual to find variables of type `boolean`. Type `boolean` is mostly used in connection with comparisons which, as we shall see, may be found in `if` statements and `while` statements. A *comparison expression* has type `boolean` and is constructed using a *comparison operator*. The comparison operators are:

```
<   >   <=   >=   ==   !=
```

They mean "less than", "greater than", "less than or equal to", "greater than or equal to", "equal to" and "not equal to", respectively. Note especially that the operator "equal to" is written with two equal signs. Here are some examples:

```
i > j      lowestPoint == 10      x <= 5.75      i != 0
```

Comparison Operators					
`==`	equal to	`<`	less than	`>`	greater than
`!=`	not equal to	`<=`	less than or equal to	`>=`	greater than or equal to

We can construct more complicated *logical expressions* with the help of the operators `&&`, `||` and `!`, which carry out the operations *and*, *or* and *not*. These operators also yield a result of type `boolean`. The expression `A&&B` is true if *both* `A` and `B` are true and false otherwise. The expression `A||B` is true if *at least one* of `A` or `B` is true, and false otherwise. The expression `!A` is true if `A` is false and false if `A` is true. Some examples:

```
temp>20 && temp<30
i==1 || i==3 || i==5 || i==7 || i==9
!(temp>20 && temp<30))
```

The operators && and || have lower priority than the arithmetical operators +, -, * and / and the comparison operators <, >, etc. This means that expressions such as

```
i + j > k * 1 && m == n
```

are interpreted as

```
(i + j) > (k * 1) && (m == n)
```

The operators && and || are calculated from left to right, and the calculation is terminated as soon as possible. This means that if the left-hand operand of the operator && is false, the right-hand operand will never be calculated. Conversely, if the left-hand operand of the operator || is true, the right-hand operand will never be calculated. In the following expression the division is not carried out if k is equal to zero.

```
k != 0 && n/k > 10
```

Logical Operators		
A && B true if *both* A and B are true	A || B true if *at least one* of A or B is true	! A true if A is false
&& and || have *lower* priority than comparison operators ! has *higher* priority than arithmetical operators and comparison operators		

2.4.2 Type `char`

Single, printable characters are stored with the built-in type `char`. You can declare variables of this type, just as with other variables.

```
char c1, c2;
```

The characters are surrounded by single apostrophes. For example, we can make the assignment

```
c1 = 'A';
c2 = 'é';
```

Not all characters can be specified in this way. This applies to special characters such as tabs and characters that indicate a new line, together with characters that are not found on the keyboard you use. When you write these, you have to use so-called *escape sequences*. An escape sequence starts with the character \ and should be interpreted as one single character. In Chapter 9, we will specify how to use various escape sequences in greater detail and how the various characters are coded. Right now, we will restrict ourselves to the escape sequences \t and \n, which happen to mean tabulator and new line character, respectively. We can make the variable `c1` contain a new line character by making the assignment

```
c1 = '\n';
```

Values of type `char` can be output with `println` in the same way as other values:

```
System.out.println(c2);    // the character é will be printed out
```

You can also combine values of type `char` with texts, by using the operator `+`.

```
System.out.println("c2 contains the character: " + c2);
```

Values of type `char` can easily be compared by means of the usual comparison operators. For example, we can write

```
if (c1 == '%')
   System.out.println("per cent");
if (c1 >= '0' && c1 <= '9')
   System.out.println("digit");
```

Please note that comparing characters does not always give correct alphabetical comparisons. Upper- and lower-case letters are different, for example, and most characters with accents, dots and other decorations do not come in alphabetical order.

There is a wrapper class called `Character`, which is associated with type `char`. This contains methods for investigating and converting values of type `char`. (Please refer to the fact box.) The last comparison above could have been done with

---

Wrapper Class Character

In this table, `c` designates a value of type `char`. The methods should be called with the name `Character` before them, e.g.: `Character.isDigit`

`isDigit(c)`	gives `true` if `c` contains a number, otherwise `false`
`isLetter(c)`	gives `true` if `c` contains a letter, otherwise `false`
`isLetterOrDigit(c)`	gives `true` if `c` contains a letter or digit, otherwise `false`
`isLowerCase(c)`	gives `true` if `c` contains a lower-case letter, otherwise `false`
`isUpperCase(c)`	gives `true` if `c` contains a capital letter, otherwise `false`
`isWhitespace(c)`	gives `true` if `c` contains a so-called white character (space, tab, end of line character), otherwise `false`
`toLowerCase(c)`	if `c` contains a capital letter, the corresponding lower-case letter is returned, otherwise the value in `c` is returned
`toUpperCase(c)`	if `c` contains a lower-case letter, the corresponding capital letter is returned, otherwise the value in `c` is returned
`getNumericValue(c)`	gives an integer, which contains the character's Unicode

```
if (Character.isDigit(c1))
    System.out.println("digit");
```

and the following statement makes the character É end up in the variable c1. (c2 contains the character é.)

```
c1 = Character.toUpperCase(c2);
```

2.5   Reference variables

In Java, we cannot access objects directly. We always have to access them through a reference. Suppose, for example, that we have defined a class called Lift which describes how lifts work. We can then declare a new variable, which we will call a.

```
Lift a;
```

This does not mean, as we might perhaps be inclined to believe, that the variable a has type Lift. It means that a is a *reference variable* which has the ability to *refer to* lifts; a has the type "reference to Lift". Since no initialization value has been indicated in the declaration, a will automatically get the default value **null**. This means that the variable a will not, for the present, be referring to an object. We can look upon a as being a container that contains an empty reference. See Figure 2.4.

Figure 2.4 An uninitialized reference variable

To make a refer to an object, we first have to *create* an object, that is, a new instance of the class Lift. This is done with the operator **new**. We can write, for example:

```
a = new Lift();
```

Then we will have the situation in Figure 2.5. Note that the object itself lacks a name. It is the reference that is called a. We can now reach the object through the reference. We can, for instance, write

```
a.goTo(5);
```

Figure 2.5 A reference variable and an object

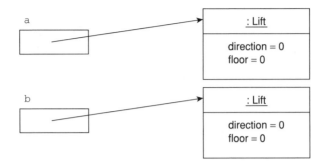

Figure 2.6 Two reference variables and two objects

Naturally, it is possible to initialize reference variables directly in the declaration.

```
Lift b = new Lift();
```

We now have two reference variables and two lifts. See Figure 2.6.

When we use the operator **new**, the Java system reserves memory space for the new object. The space for objects no longer in use must be returned so that accessible memory space will not be exhausted. In some programming languages, such as C++, a programmer had to take great care that this was done correctly but in Java this is extremely simple: we do nothing! There is no operator to return memory space. The system automatically carries out *garbage collection* and if it discovers objects without references to them, it will return their memory space. If we know that we no longer need an object, we can make it possible for the system to return memory space by ensuring that there is no longer a reference to the object. For example, we can assign the value **null** to a reference variable. If we have reference variables declared inside methods, we do not even need to do this, since these reference variables will cease to exist once execution of the method is complete. We should also point out that in Java, it is not possible to have *lingering* references to objects that no longer exist. This is because we cannot declare objects directly but always have to use **new**. The system will not release memory space as long as there is a reference to it.

Automatic garbage collection is naturally very convenient for the programmer. There is only one disadvantage: it can take time. This means that Java is not always a convenient programming language to use for constructing real-time programs.

It is often asserted that there are no pointers in Java but this is not true. In fact, it could be said that the opposite is nearer the truth; as soon as we start working with objects, we will be using pointers, for reference variables are nothing other than pointers. When people say that there are no pointers in Java, what they really mean is that there are few opportunities for the programmer to manipulate pointers. The programmer can only declare reference variables and assign values to them.

From now on, we will be mentioning references less, for practical reasons. If we make the call `a.goTo(5)`, for example, it would be correct to say that we are calling the method `goTo` for the object to which the variable `a` is referring, but this is clumsy. So we simply say that we are calling the method `goTo` for object `a`. Everything takes place through references, however, and it is important to remember that `a` in this case is not an object but a reference to an object. When it is important to emphasize the difference between references and objects, for example when making assignments, we will naturally keep the two concepts separate.

2.6 Assignment

Variables, as we have seen, may be initialized directly upon declaration but we can also make use of an *assignment statement*. One of these might have the form

```
variablename = expression;
```

What is happening here is that the expression to the right of the equals sign is being calculated first. This value is then placed in the variable. For a value to be assigned to a variable, the value must have the same type as the variable. Therefore, the expression to the right of the equals sign in an assignment statement must either have the same type as the variable to the left, or its value must be able to be converted automatically into the type of this variable. Where *numerical types* are concerned, that is, types containing mathematical numbers, it is important that "safe" type conversions can take place automatically. (A type conversion is safe when the value cannot be corrupted, that is, when the value can always be held in the new type.) Conversions from an integer type to a longer one are safe, as is the conversion from an integer type to a real type. Here are some examples of assignments:

```
int i;
double d;
d = i;     // OK! Safe type conversion
i = d;     // INCORRECT!! Attempt at a dangerous type conversion
```

If we wish to make "dangerous" type conversions, we must use an explicit type conversion, a *cast*. We will then write the type to which we wish the value of the expression to be converted in parentheses, in front of the expression in the right-hand section. We can then write, for example:

```
i = (int)d;    // OK. Explicit type conversion
```

When you convert from a real type to an integer type, as in this example, the decimals are "truncated". This is *not* the same as rounding off.

We can also make assignments to reference variables. If we suppose, as previously, that the variables `a` and `b` are references to the class `Lift`, we can write

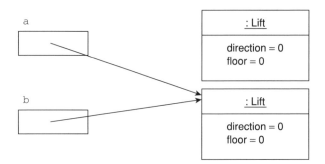

Figure 2.7 Assignment to reference variables

```
a = new Lift();    // OK! new gives a reference as result
a = b;             // Permissible but probably not what we intended
```

In the last assignment statement, we assigned b to a. This will mean that the reference in variable b will be assigned to variable a. After the assignment both references will then be pointing at the *same* object. See Figure 2.7. The object that b points to will *not* be copied to the object that a points to.

Certain classes, but not all, have a method called clone which can be called if we wish to make a copy of the whole object. For example, the standard class Calendar, which we will be using later, has such a method. Now suppose that we have two reference variables c1 and c2, which can refer to objects of class Calendar. In order to make a copy of the object to which c2 refers and to let c1 refer to the copy, we can write

```
c1 = (Calendar) c2.clone();
```

Assignment

variablename = expression;

The value of the expression to the right of the equals sign is calculated first.
This value is then placed in the variable on the left.
The variable's earlier value is destroyed.
The expression on the right must have the same type as the variable, or be able to be converted automatically to this type.
"Safe" type conversions are made automatically for numerical types.

Where assignments to reference variables are concerned, the reference itself is changed, not the object to which the variable refers.

Explicit type conversions are sometimes necessary:

variablename = (desired type) expression;

(Here we need an explicit type conversion, since the method `clone` gives a reference to an object of the base class `Object` as result.) Not only standard classes can have a method called `clone`. We could also define one for our own classes but this is more complicated so we will not go into it now.

2.7 Methods

Instance methods (which we will just call "methods" in this chapter for the sake of simplicity) describe what you can do with an object, and how the object is manipulated. We will use the following program as the point of departure for our discussions:

```java
// This class is placed in the file TimeDemo.java
public class TimeDemo {
  public static void main(String[] arg) {
    Time t1 = new Time();   // create a Time-object
    Time t2 = new Time();   // create a Time-object
    int a=17, b=8, c=20;
    t1.set(a, b, c);              // put the time 17:08:20 in t1
    t2.set(23, 59, 59);           // put the time 23:59:59 i t2
    t1.tick();                    // increment t1 by one second
    t2.tick();                    // increment t2 by one second
    t2.tick();                    // increment t2 by one second
    String s1 = t1.toString(); // s1 gets the value "17:8:21"
    String s2 = t2.toString(); // s2 gets the value "0:0:1"
    System.out.println(s1);       // print s1
    System.out.println(s2);       // print s2
  }
}
```

```java
// This class is placed in the file Time.java
public class Time {
  // instance variables
  private int h, m, s;
  private boolean showSec = true;

  // methods
  public void set (int hour, int min, int sec) {
    // check that the time is OK
    if (hour>=0 && hour<24 &&
        min>=0 && min<60 && sec>=0 && sec<60) {
      h=hour; m=min; s=sec;
    }
    else
      System.out.println("Illegal time");
  }
```

```
public void setShowSec(boolean show) {
    showSec = show;
}

public int getHour() {
    return h;
}

public int getMin () {
    return m;
}

public int getSec () {
    return s;
}

public void tick() { // moves the time forwards one second
    s = s+1;
    if (s == 60) {
        s = 0;
        m = m+1;
    }
    if (m == 60) {
        m = 0;
        h = h+1;
    }
    if (h == 24)
        h=0;
}

public String toString () {        // returns "hh:mm:ss"
    String t = h + ":" + m;        // or "hh:mm"
    if (showSec)
        t = t + ":" +  s;
    return t;
}
```

}

The program has been constructed from two classes, TimeDemo and Time. When you run the program, execution of the method main in the class TimeDemo starts. Two reference variables are first declared there, t1 and t2, which are initialized so that they each refer to a separate instance of the class Time. After this, the method set is called to get the two Time objects to contain different times. Each call to the method tick makes the indicated Time object tick forwards one second. The method toString is used to read the value of a Time object. The method main is terminated by printing out the values read. A test run of the program gives the printout

```
17:8:21
0:0:1
```

We will start by discussing the class Time. The details of the way in which calls are made to methods will be described in Section 2.7.2. The class Time has three instance variables, h, m and s, which are used to keep track of hours, minutes and seconds. In addition, there is an instance variable showSec, which specifies whether seconds should be included in printouts. There are seven methods. You call the method set when you want to set an object to describe a certain point in time. You call the method setShowSec to specify whether seconds should be displayed. The methods getHour, getMin and getSec read and return values of h, m and s respectively. The method tick moves the Time object forwards one second. (Please note that the class Time does not describe a clock that ticks forwards all by itself. You have to call the method tick from some other part of the program for the Time object to be moved forwards one second. One example of the way this is done is shown in Section 2.8.) The result of the method toString is a text of format hh:mm:ss or hh:mm, depending on whether seconds are to be displayed. We have defined this method to give automatic type conversion from the class Time to the class String. If the variable t is a Time object, it is permissible to write the expression as "The time is" + t. The method toString will then be called automatically to do the conversion.

2.7.1 Definition of methods

A method definition consists of two sections – a *head* and a *body*. In the method's head, you specify how the method should be used. For example, we can study the method set. Its head is as follows:

```
public void set (int hour, int min, int sec)
```

The first thing specified is the visibility of the method (we will come back to this later on). After this, we specify the type of the result returned by the method. In this example, there is the reserved word **void**. This means that the method does not return a value. Next, there is the name of the method. After the method's name, you specify what should be put into the method, by giving a list of the method's *parameters*. For each parameter, you specify its type and name. We specify here that the method has three parameters, hour, min and sec, which are all of the built-in type int. This is very similar to a declaration of three variables, and inside the method set, the parameters will also be regarded as variables. When the method is called, hour, min and sec will contain the values given as arguments for the method. Please note that when you declare parameters, you must write the type name in front of *each* parameter name. In other words, you must not write (**int** hour, min, sec) as you can do when you declare variables. Nor is it permissible to initialize parameters. Some methods do not have parameters. The method getHour, for example, has the head

```
public int getHour()
```

You then write empty brackets after the name of the method. Here, you can also see that the method getHour should give a value of type **int** as its result. A method can give a result of any type, both built-in types and references.

61

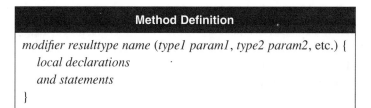

In the body of a method, which is surrounded by curly brackets, you describe what should be done when the method is called. This may contain declarations and statements. `getHour` does not contain any declarations and there is only one statement:

```
return h;
```

A `return` statement does two things. It specifies the value which should be given as the result of the method, and it terminates the method. (If there is another statement immediately after the return statement, this other statement would then not be executed.) There must be a statement after the word `return`. The type of this statement should be the same as the type specified in the method head. If this is not the case, there will be an automatic type conversion to this type (if possible). If a method returns a reference, the object to which the object refers will not be copied and given as the result; it is the actual reference that will be given as the result. If, for example, you have written the following in a method:

```
MyClass r = new MyClass();
...
return r;
```

the return value will be a reference to the object created on the first line. You will not get a copy of this object.

---

return Statement

`return` *expression*;

Terminates a method and returns the value *expression* as result.
The expression's type should be the same as the method's result type.
Must be in methods with result types other than `void`.

Methods with the result type `void` may have simple `return` statements:

`return`;

You can have several `return` statements in a method, but it is very common to have only one, which is placed last in the body of the method. All methods with a return type that is not `void` must have a `return` statement. Methods whose return type is `void`, i.e.

methods that do not leave a value, do not need to have a `return` statement. In this case, execution of the method is terminated when you get as far as the concluding curly bracket. Methods whose return types are `void` can have `return` statements, but in this case there should not be any statement after the word `return`.

The instance variables declared in a class are directly accessible inside the methods of the class (but not in methods defined with the modifier `static`). Let us study the methods in the class `Time` more closely. The three methods `getHour`, `getMin` and `getSec` are simple. They just return the value of the corresponding instance variable. The method `setShowSec` is also simple.

The method `set` is a bit more complicated. It receives three integers, `hour`, `min` and `sec`, which specify the current moment in time. The task of the method is to set the instance variables `h`, `m` and `s` to `hour`, `min` and `sec` respectively, but before it does this, it has to check that the parameters have permissible values. They must not be < 0. The parameters `min` and `sec` must not exceed 59 and `hour` must not exceed 23. An `if` statement is used to do the check.

```
if (hour>=0 && hour<24 &&
    min>=0 && min<60 && sec>=0 && sec<60) {
  h=hour; m=min; s=sec;
}
else
   System.out.println("Illegal time");
```

The method `tick` is used to increment the `Time` object by one second. This is done as follows. First, the seconds are incremented by 1. If seconds then become 60, exactly one minute has passed. So minutes are incremented by 1 and seconds are reset to zero. If minutes then become equal to 60, exactly one hour has passed. So hours are incremented by 1 and minutes are reset to zero. Finally, if it is found that exactly 24 hours have passed, a whole day has passed and hours are reset to zero.

The method `toString` looks like this:

```
public String toString () {      // returns "hh:mm:ss"
   String t = h + ":" + m;       // or "hh:mm"
   if (showSec)
      t = t + ":" +  s;
   return t;
}
```

A *local variable*, `t`, is declared on the second line. This is a reference variable which refers to an object of standard class `String`. It is initialized to a text with format hh:mm, where hh and mm are the values of the instance variables h and m in text form. (As we have seen previously, integer variables are automatically converted to type `String` when you use the operator + for texts.) If seconds are also to be displayed, a new text is then formed where the seconds are added last.

2.7.2 Calling methods

A method description is just a description of how a certain action is to be carried out. To really get anything done, you have to call the method. The method is called by means of the dot operator. You then write the name of the object[1] you want to execute the method on, followed by a full stop, and then the name of the method. The following line in class `TimeDemo` on page 59 is a call to the method `set` for object `t1`.

```
t1.set(a, b, c);
```

It is permissible to call other methods for the same object. In this case, you do *not* need to write an object name and full stop before the method name. It is then understood that the call applies to the same object as the one you are currently handling.

In a method call, you write a list of *arguments* after the method name. When the call is executed, the values of the arguments are calculated. (In the call of the method `set`, no calculations are needed since the values are already there in the variables `a`, `b` and `c`.) After this, the argument values are inserted into the method. The argument values are *copied* to the corresponding parameters. When `set` is called, the value of the first parameter is copied to the parameter `hour`, the value of the second parameter is copied to the parameter `min` and the value of the third parameter is copied to the parameter `sec`. Please note that none of the variables `a`, `b` and `c` is affected by this or what happens later on in the method `set`. This technique of transferring argument values to a method is generally called *call by value* and means that the values of the arguments are copied to local copies inside the method. Another way of expressing it is to say that `hour`, `min` and `sec` are value parameters. In Java, calls by value are *always* used. All parameters are thus value parameters. But note that *when you have parameters of reference type, the actual reference is copied, not the object you refer to.* Let us assume that the class `TimeDemo` contains both `main` and a method `tickBoth`, with format (don't worry right now about why it is called **static**):

```
static void tickBoth(Time x, Time y) {
    x.tick();
    y.tick();
}
```

Also assume that we add the following lines at the end of `main` in the class `TimeDemo`:

```
tickBoth(t1, t2);
String s3 = t1.toString();
String s4 = t2.toString();
System.out.println(s3);
System.out.println(s4);
```

---

[1] In actual fact, one writes the name of a variable which refers to the object you want to execute the method on but we will express ourselves in a simpler manner as from now.

This gives us two new printout lines:

```
17:8:22
0:0:2
```

This shows that it really is the references that are copied when `tickBoth` is called. If the actual object had been copied, the objects that `t1` and `t2` refer to would not have been changed by the call. Here, `x` comes to refer to the same object as `t1` and `y` will refer to the same object as `t2`.

Method Calls

referencename.methodname(a1, a2, . . . an)

A reference name and dot can be left out if another method in the same class is called. The call then applies to the same objects.
a1, a2, ... an are *arguments*. They are allowed to be expressions.
Their types should agree with corresponding parameters.
The following take place:

1. The values of *a1, a2, . . . an* are calculated.
2. Arguments *a1, a2, . . . an* are copied to their corresponding parameters.
    This is termed *call by value*.
    If the arguments are references, they are copied, and not the objects.
3. The statements inside the method are carried out.
4. The method is terminated in a `return` statement, or when the last statement has been executed.
5. Methods with a return type other than `void` must have a `return` statement. For methods, the method's call value will equal the value in the `return` statement.
6. Execution continues after the method has been called.

A call of a method that has the result type `void` is regarded as a statement in the program. Calls of the methods `set` and `tick` are thus statements. A call of a method that does not have the result type `void` is regarded as an expression and can thus be put at any place in the program where expressions are allowed. For example, they can be included as a component of a larger expression. In the following declaration, the text to the right of the equals sign is an expression:

```
int totalHour = t1.getHour()+t2.getHour();
```

The arguments of a method can be expressions. They do not need to be simple values. For example, you can write

```
t1.set(totalHour+2, t1.getMin(), 0);
```

We could have used this in the `TimeDemo` program. We would not have had to declare the variables `s1` and `s2` if we had written

```
System.out.println(t1.toString());
System.out.println(t2.toString());
```

In actual fact, we could have simplified things further by just writing

```
System.out.println(t1);     // t1.toString will be called
System.out.println(t2);     // t2.toString will be called
```

The standard method `println` has been designed so that it automatically checks whether the argument it receives is of type `String`. If not, it automatically calls the method `toString` for the argument in question.

2.8   Example – displaying the time

In this section, we will show some examples of how the class `Time` from Section 2.7 can be used as a "building block" in a program. We start off by constructing a program that outputs the current time in the command window (MS-DOS window). When you run the program, you might get the following output:

```
The time is 18:56:3
```

The program looks like this:

```
import java.util.*;
public class DisplayTime1 {
    public static void main (String[] arg) {
        Time t = new Time();
        Calendar c = Calendar.getInstance();
        t.set(c.get(Calendar.HOUR_OF_DAY),
              c.get(Calendar.MINUTE),
              c.get(Calendar.SECOND));
        System.out.println("The time is " + t.toString());
    }
}
```

We have used the standard class `Calendar` in the program to find out what the time is. This class is included in the package `java.util`, which has been imported on the first line. An object of class `Calendar` contains a certain moment in time (both date and time). The easiest way to create an object of class `Calendar` is by calling method `Calendar.getInstance`. This gives a reference to a `Calendar` object which contains the current moment in time. The class `Calendar` contains a method called `get`, which you can use to obtain information from a certain `Calendar` object. You specify a constant for the method `get`, which says what you want to read, as the parameter for `get`. If you want to read the year, you specify the parameter `Calendar.YEAR` and if you want to read the hour, you give the parameter `Calendar.HOUR_OF_DAY`. (There is also a parameter called `Calendar.HOUR`, but this gives the hour in the 12-hour system, where you use a.m. and p.m.) The result from the method `get` is an integer. In our program, we create a new object of class `Time`, and then we call the method `set` to initialize the moment in time. We then use the class `Calendar` to initialize the moment in time object so as to describe the current time.

It might not be very exciting to have the current time written in a command window. It becomes a bit more elegant if we display the time in a window as in Figure 2.8.

Figure 2.8

Accordingly, we will construct a program `DisplayTime2`, which generates a window like this. Each time you run the program, the current time is displayed. We use the program `Greeting` on page 31 as our model. The main difference is that we replace the text `"Welcome to Java"` by a text that contains the current time. We get this text in the same way as in the program `DisplayTime1`, by using an object of class `Time`. We also initialize the `Time` object here by using the class `Calendar` and call `toString` to get the time in text form. We have also made a few minor adjustments, compared with the program `Greeting`. The window's background colour has been changed to black and the foreground colour to white. In addition, the size of the window has been reduced. Our new program looks like this:

```
import java.awt.*;
import javax.swing.*;
import java.util.*;

public class DisplayTime2 {
  public static void main (String[] arg) {
    TimeFrame f=new TimeFrame(); //create a new TimeFrame object
    }
  }

class TimeFrame extends JFrame {
  public TimeFrame() {    // Constructor, called automatically
    Time t = new Time();
    Calendar c = Calendar.getInstance();
    t.set(c.get(Calendar.HOUR_OF_DAY),
          c.get(Calendar.MINUTE),
          c.get(Calendar.SECOND));
```

```
        JLabel l = new JLabel(t.toString(), JLabel.CENTER);
        getContentPane().add(l);      // put l in the window
        l.setOpaque(true);            // opaque background
        l.setBackground(Color.black);
        l.setForeground(Color.white);
        l.setFont(new Font("SansSerif", Font.BOLD, 24));
        setSize(200,75);              // the window's size
        setVisible(true);             // make the window visible
        setDefaultCloseOperation(EXIT_ON_CLOSE);
    }
}
```

The program `DisplayTime2` shows a constant text. It would have been even more interesting if we had displayed a proper clock, a clock which was automatically incremented once a second. We will now write a program that displays a clock like this. When you run the program, it looks just like Figure 2.8, but the clock ticks forwards.

```
import java.awt.*;
import javax.swing.*;
import java.util.*;
import java.awt.event.*;

public class DisplayClock {
    public static void main (String[] arg) {
        TimeFrame v=new TimeFrame(); //create a new TimeFrame object
    }
}

class TimeFrame extends JFrame implements ActionListener {
    private Time t = new Time();
    private JLabel l;

    public TimeFrame() { // Constructor, called automaticaly
        javax.swing.Timer tim = new javax.swing.Timer(1000, this);
        tim.start();          // start the timer
        Calendar c = Calendar.getInstance();
        t.set(c.get(Calendar.HOUR_OF_DAY),
              c.get(Calendar.MINUTE),
              c.get(Calendar.SECOND));
        l = new JLabel(t.toString(), JLabel.CENTER);
        getContentPane().add(l);      // put l in the window
        l.setOpaque(true);            // opaque background
        l.setBackground(Color.black);
        l.setForeground(Color.white);
        l.setFont(new Font("SansSerif", Font.BOLD, 24));
        setSize(200,75);              // the window's size
        setVisible(true);             // make the window visible
        setDefaultCloseOperation(EXIT_ON_CLOSE);
    }
```

```
public void actionPerformed(ActionEvent e) {
    // we get here automatically, once per second
    t.tick();
    l.setText(t.toString());
}
}
```

This program is, without doubt, the most advanced we have met in the book so far. It is actually an example of a so-called *event-driven program*. We will discuss event-driven programs in Chapter 6 when we cover graphical user interfaces. So we will just give a brief description now. (It is not necessary to understand all the details now. You can even skip this example and come back when you have read Chapter 6.) The program DisplayTime2 has been used as the model. What we have added is a so-called *timer*, which ensures that the method tick for our Time object is automatically called once a second. The package javax.swing contains a standard class called Timer. If you generate an object of this type, it can execute in the background and generate so-called *events* (a kind of interrupt signal) at regular intervals. We use one of these Timer objects in the program. We declare a variable called tim, which refers to this object. This is done on the line

```
javax.swing.Timer tim = new javax.swing.Timer(1000, this);
```

Here, we were obliged to write javax.swing.Timer instead of just Timer. This is because there is another class which is also called Timer. This is in the package java.util, which we also import into this program. If we had just written Timer, the compiler would not have been able to decide which of the classes we meant.

When we create the Timer object, we give it the two parameters 1000 and this. The first parameter, which has value 1000, specifies that the timer should generate an event every 1000 milliseconds, i.e. once a second. The other parameter informs the Timer object about who should listen to the events that are generated. Here, we have written this. We are in the constructor for the class DisplayClock. The word this thus means the object of class DisplayClock, which we are initializing, or in other words the object to which the variable v in method main refers.

Any object at all can be a listener to a timer. There are only two things needed: the first is that you write implements ActionListener in the class definition and the second is that you have defined a method in the class with the name actionPerformed. Both these requirements are met in the class TimeFrame. The following will happen. Each time the timer generates an event, i.e. once a second, the method actionPerformed will be called. In this method, we first call the method tick to increment our Time object tp by one second and then the method setText to change the text displayed in the JLabel object l.

For this to work, the variables `tp` and `l` must be available inside the method `actionPerformed`. In the program `DisplayTime2`, we declared these variables as *local* variables inside the constructor, but if they are declared in the constructor, they will only be visible inside it. In this program, we have therefore moved the variables `tp` and `l` out and declared them as *instance* variables in the class `TimeFrame`. They then become visible to all the methods in this class, including the method `actionPerformed`.

Finally, please note that the standard classes that handle events are defined in the package `java.awt.event`, which we have to import at the beginning of the program.

2.9   Standard class `String`

In Java, we use both ready-made classes and classes we have written ourselves. When you use a ready-made class, you do not normally need to know how the class methods are implemented, you just have to know how they are called. The standard class `String` is an important example of a ready-made class. As we saw in Chapter 1, we use this class to describe texts. An expression with the format `"a text"` is perceived as a constant object of the class `String`. In the declaration

```
String s1 = "Java";
```

the initialization statement is an object of class `String`, and `s1` is a reference variable which is initialized to refer to this object. A `String` object can be printed out by means of the method `System.out.println`. The following statement gives the printout `Java`.

```
System.out.println(s1);
```

Objects of class `String` are always constant; it is not possible to change the text. On the other hand, you can use the operator `+` to form new `String` objects. You can write

```
String s2 = "From the Beginning";
s1 = s1 + " " + s2;
```

The variable `s1` will now refer to a new `String` object which contains the text `"Java From the Beginning"`. The object `s1` used to refer to (the one that contained the text `"Java"`) will no longer be used and its space will automatically be returned when the system next does garbage collection. The operands for the operator `+` must be of type `String`. The following lines show how a value of type **int** is automatically reformatted to type `String`.

```
int i = 5;
s2 = "Number " + i;
System.out.println(s2);
```

The printout becomes

```
Number 5
```

Values of types other than the simple built-in types can also be automatically converted to type `String`. For this to be possible, the relevant class must have a method called `toString` and this must return a value of type `String`.

The automatic conversions to `String` are not only done in conjunction with the operator `+`, they are also done when the method `System.out.println` is called. For example, you can write

```
System.out.println(i);
```

There are many methods in the class `String`. These can be used to test text etc. A summary is given in the fact box. The most important are `length`, `charAt`, `substring`, `equals` and `compareTo`.

The method `length` returns an **int** giving the length of the current text. If the variable `s1` refers to the text `"From the Beginning"`, the following statement outputs 18.

```
System.out.println(s1.length());
```

A `String` object contains an internal sequence of characters of type **char**. You can use the method `charAt` to test individual characters in a text. This method returns values of type **char**. You must always give the number of the character you want to test as the argument. Numbering always starts from 0, so that the first character has number 0. For example, the statements

```
System.out.println(s1.charAt(2));
System.out.println(s1.charAt(s1.length()-1));
```

give the printout

```
v
g
```

The method `substring` gives a sub-text as its result. There are two variants of this method: one in which you just specify the start point for the sub-text you want to select and one where you specify both the beginning and the end. If `s1`, as previously, refers to the text `"Java From the Beginning"` we could write

```
String s3 = s1.substring(13);    // s3 refers to "Beginning"
String s4 = s1.substring(0, 4); // s4 refers to "Java"
```

Please note that indexing takes place from 0 and that in the second version of the method, you have to specify the number of the position *after* the end position.

We use the method `equals` when we want to test if two texts are equal:

```
if (s1.equals(s2))
   System.out.println("The texts are equal");
```

java.lang.String	
In the following list, s1 and s2 denote objects of class String, c a value of type char and n and m integer indices greater than, or equal to, 0.	
s1.length()	gives the number of characters in s1
s1.charAt(n)	gives the character at position n in s1
s1.substring(n)	gives the subtext of s1 that begins in position n
s1.substring(n, m)	gives the subtext of s1 that begins in n and ends in m−1
s1.compareTo(s2)	gives a value that is 0 if s1 and s2 are equal, <0 if s1 comes before s2 alphabetically and >0 if s2 comes before s1. NB: Only works for the "pure" letters a–z
s1.equals(s2)	gives true if s1 and s2 are equal, false otherwise
s1.equalsIgnoreCase(s2)	gives true if s1 and s2 are equal, false otherwise lower- and upper-case letters are regarded as being the same
s1.startsWith(s2)	gives true if s1 begins with s2, false otherwise
s1.startsWith(s2,n)	gives true if s1, with its beginning in position n, contains the subtext s2, false otherwise
s1.endsWith(s2)	gives true if s1 ends with the subtext s2, false otherwise
s1.indexOf(c)	gives the position for the first occurrence of the character c in s1, gives −1 if the character c is not in s1
s1.indexOf(c,n)	gives the position for the first occurrence, from position n and onwards, of the character c in s1
s1.lastIndexOf(c)	gives the position for the last occurrence of the character c in s1
s1.lastIndexOf(c,n)	gives the position for the last occurrence, from position n and backwards, of the character c in s1
s1.indexOf(s2)	gives the position for the first occurrence of the text s2 in s1
s1.indexOf(s2,n)	gives the position for the first occurrence, from position n and onwards, of the text s2 in s1
s1.lastIndexOf(s2)	gives the position for the last occurrence of the text s2 in s1
s1.lastIndexOf(s2,n)	gives the position for the last occurrence, from position n and backwards, of the text s2 in s1
s1.trim()	gives a copy of s1, where the beginning and ending blank characters and tab characters have been removed
s1.replace(c1,c2)	gives a copy of s1 where the character c1 has been exchanged for the character c2 everywhere
s1.toUpperCase()	gives a copy of s1 where all lower-case letters have been exchanged for capitals
s1.toLowerCase()	gives a copy of s1 where all the capitals have been exchanged for lower-case letters
String.valueOf(x)	gives a text where the value of x has been converted into text form. x must either be of a simple, built-in type, or of a class where the method toString is defined

The method `equals` gives a result of type **boolean**, which specifies whether the texts are equal or not. Please note that you should not write `s1=s2` or `s1==s2` inside the brackets in the `if` statement. The first expression is an assignment of `s2` to `s1`. The second expression is admittedly a comparison, but it compares the values of the reference values, not what they refer to. This means that the second expression can only be true if both `s1` and `s2` refer to the *same* `String` object.

The method `compareTo` is used to test if a certain text comes before or after another text in alphabetical order. The method returns an integer. This number is less than zero if the first text comes first, greater than zero if the second text comes first and equal to zero if both texts are equal. You could write

```
if (s1.compareTo(s2) < 0)
   System.out.println(s1 + " is before " + s2);
else if (s1.compareTo(s2) > 0)
   System.out.println(s2 + " is before " + s1);
else  // == 0
   System.out.println(s2 + " and " + s1 + " are equal");
```

A warning must be issued for the method `compareTo`. It compares the two texts character by character. Upper- and lower-case letters are regarded as being different. In addition, alphabetical order only works for the letters a–z. Accented letters such as é do not have correct alphabetical order. This means that the method `compareTo` is not suitable for comparing texts that contain languages other than English. In Section 9.2, we will describe what to do when you want to compare texts with correct alphabetical order in various languages.

2.10 Initialization of objects

When we declare an instance variable, as was discussed previously, it is automatically given a default value. But we can also give it an explicit initialization value. On page 46, we defined the class `Lift`. This had two instance variables, `direction` and `floor`. Both were uninitialized and were therefore given the default value 0, but we could very well initialize the variables explicitly. If we want an instance variable `floor` to be initialized to 1, we can write code as follows. Then *every* new `Lift` that is created will start off at floor 1.

```
class Lift {
   // instance variables
   private int direction;
   private int floor = 1;
   as previously
}
```

It is useful to be able to initialize instance variables directly, but if we want to do somewhat more complicated initializations or if we want the person who creates a new object to be able to influence the initialization values, this mechanism is not enough. We can then use something referred to as a *constructor*. A constructor is a special initialization method which is automatically called each time we create an object. As an example, we can make a new variant of the class Time on page 59.

```
public class Time {
   // instance variables
   private int h, m, s;
   private boolean showSec = true;

   // constructors
   public Time() {}

   public Time(int hour, int min, int sec) {
      set(hour, min, sec);
   }
   // methods
   as previously
}
```

It is lines 6–9 that are of interest here. A constructor is a kind of method. The special thing about a constructor is that it has the same name as the class in which it is included, and *it must not have a return type*. What we define here is the constructors, both with the name Time. In Java, you can have several constructors for the same class, on condition that they have a different number of parameters, or different types of parameters. The first constructor in the class Time does not have parameters, and the second has three parameters of type int. The first constructor does not do anything at all, since it does not contain any statements. This means that the instance variables are all automatically given the default value of 0. The second constructor has to use the parameter values to initialize instance variables. It does not do this directly, however, but calls the method set, which does the actual work. The reason that the initializations are not done directly in the constructor is that you have to check that the parameters contain correct values. The method set does this, and it is easier to call it than to repeat the checks in the constructor. Please note than when calling set, no object name is written before the method name. This is because you are calling a method in the *same class* and the call refers to the *same object* as the one you are initializing.

Constructors are not called in the same way as ordinary methods. They are called automatically instead, each time you create a new object. The constructor called is determined by the argument given in the expression after new. For example, assume that we have the program lines

```
Time t1 = new Time();
Time t2 = new Time(10, 20, 30);
System.out.println(t1);
System.out.println(t2);
```

On the first line, the parameterless constructor will be called, since no arguments are specified. On the second line, the constructor that has three parameters is called. The three instance variables in `t1` are all given the value 0 and `t2` is given the values 10, 20 and 30. The printout from the program lines then becomes

```
0:0:0
10:20:30
```

It might seem to be unnecessary to define the first constructor, the one with no parameters. It does not do anything. The reason that you have to define a parameterless constructor anyway is that you have to have one if you write expressions with the format **new** `classname()`, i.e. do not specify an argument. If you have a class where you have not defined any constructors at all, the Java compiler will define a parameterless constructor *itself* (which does not do anything). This is the reason that we were able to create objects of class `Time` previously, although we had not defined any constructors. But if you have declared one or more constructors for a class, the Java compiler does *not* define a parameterless constructor, and you have to do it yourself if you want to have one. In a parameterless constructor, you can of course give the instance variables any values you want, not just default values.

Constructors

Have the same name as the class.

Are not allowed to have a return type.

There may be several of them but then they must have a different number of parameters, or parameters of different types.

Unless we define our own constructors, a constructor without parameters is defined automatically (and this does nothing).

If we define our own constructors, we have to define a constructor without parameters ourselves, if we want one.

A constructor can call another constructor:

  this(*argument*);

Since there are two constructors for the class `Time`, there are two ways to create new objects with **new**. You either specify hours, minutes and seconds as arguments, or you do not specify any arguments at all. But sometimes you might want to omit the seconds and just specify hours and minutes. or just hours. We might want to write

```
Time t3 = new Time(15, 45);
Time t4 = new Time(18);
```

We have to add two constructors to make this possible.

```
public class Time {
  // instance variables
  private int h, m, s;
  private boolean showSec = true;

  // constructors
  public Time() {}

  public Time(int hour, int min, int sec) {
    set(hour, min, sec);
  }

  public Time(int hour, int min) {
    this(hour, min, 0);
    showSec = false;
  }

  public Time(int hour) {
    this(hour, 0);
  }
  // methods
  as previously
}
```

There are now four constructors. We have discussed the first two previously. The next to last one has hours and minutes as parameters, and the last one only has hours as its parameter. The interesting thing here is the two lines that contain the word `this`. We use the reserved word `this` inside a method to get a reference to the object we are working on right now. Constructors are not called in the same way as ordinary methods, but a constructor can actually call another constructor. This is done by using `this`. The statement

```
this(hour, min, 0);
```

means that the constructor that has three parameters is called. In the corresponding way, the constructor with one parameter calls the constructor with two parameters. Allowing one constructor to call another is a useful trick, since the tasks that each constructor does are often very similar, and we do not then need to repeat the common statements.

2.11 Overloaded methods

In the previous section, we saw that although constructors in a class all have the same name (class name), we could have any number of constructors, provided that they had different parameters. This also applies to ordinary methods. You can have any number of methods with the same name, on condition that the methods have either a different number of parameters, or different types of parameters. Methods that have the same name are called *overloaded* methods. When you call an overloaded method, the compiler decides which of the overloaded methods you mean by studying the arguments you have specified. The method where the numbers and types of parameters correspond is chosen. If none of the methods suits, or if more than one can be chosen, you get an error when the program is compiled.

Let us add a new method called `tick` to the class `Time`. You might not always want to increment the time by just one second. The new method thus has an integer parameter which specifies the number of seconds to be incremented.

```
public class Time {
   as previously
   public void tick(int n) {
      while (n>0) {
         tick();
         n = n - 1;
      }
   }
}
```

The two methods `tick` are then overloaded and you can now do a call with both the following formats. In the second case, the new method `tick` is called.

```
t1.tick();
t1.tick(35);
```

In the new version of the method `tick`, we do the number of laps of the **while** statement that the parameter n specifies. On each lap, the original version of method `tick` is called once. This means that the time is incremented by one second per lap. The variable n is decremented by 1 per lap. This means that after each lap, n will contain the number of remaining seconds to be ticked forwards. When n has become zero, the test statement will be false, and the **while** statement is terminated. Please note that if you tried to increment time backwards by calling `tick` with a negative argument, nothing would happen since the test statement would be false right from the start.

2.12 Standard class `Point`

One example of a class we could study is the standard class `Point` in the `java.awt` package. The class `Point` describes a point in a window. The class contains the two instance variables x and y, which specify the x and y coordinates of the point. The class `Point` has approximately the following appearance:

```
public class Point {
   // instance variables
   public int x;
   public int y;
```

```java
// constructors
public Point() {
    this(0, 0);
}

public Point(Point p) {
    this(p.x, p.y);
}

public Point(int x, int y) {
    this.x = x;
    this.y = y;
}

// methods
public void setLocation(Point p) {
    setLocation(p.x, p.y);
}

public void setLocation(int x, int y) {
    move(x, y);
}

public void move(int x, int y) {
    this.x = x;
    this.y = y;
}

public void translate(int dx, int dy) {
    x = x + dx;
    y = y + dy;
}

public boolean equals(Object obj) {
    // checks whether obj is a point and whether it has the same
    // x and y coordinates as this point
    ... // the details are left out
}
}
```

There are three constructors, one without parameters, one that receives the x and y coordinates of the new point and one that makes the point into a copy of another point p. There are methods for moving a point to a particular location, displacing it along both the x and y axes and comparing two points with each other. (There is a summary in the fact box.)

One thing worth noticing is that at a couple of places in the class, such as in the method move, we have written this.x and this.y. This has been done since we have parameters x and y, with the same names as the instance variables. If you just write x and y, this means the parameters, whereas this.x and this.y means the instance variables.

	java.awt.Point
new `Point()`	creates a new point with value `(0,0)`
new `Point(x,y)`	creates a new point with value `(x,y)`
new `Point(q)`	creates a new point which is a copy of the point `q`
`p.x`	gives the x coordinate for point `p`
`p.y`	gives the y coordinate for point `p`
`p.equals(q)`	checks whether points `p` and `q` are the same
`p.setLocation(q)`	sets `p` to a copy of `q`
`p.setLocation(x,y)`	sets `p` to the value `(x,y)`
`p.move(x,y)`	the same as `p.setLocation(x,y)`
`p.translate(dx,dy)`	translates `p` `dx` in the x direction and `dy` in the y direction

2.13 Exercises

1. Construct a class `Counter`, which calculates integers that may only take on values within a certain interval. When a counter is initialized, the counter's start value should be indicated, and we should also be able to indicate the least and greatest value the counter can assume. (If no limit values are indicated, the counter will be allowed to assume all values of type **int**.) Methods should be found to increase and decrease a counter by 1. If a counter then gets a value that is not allowed, an error text should be printed out. We should also be able to read the counter's value.

2. Construct a class `Person`. A person should have a name, an address and an age. Make use of the class `String`. Form a constructor and some appropriate methods for class `Person`.

3. Construct a class `Card` which describes a card in an ordinary pack of cards. The value and colour of a card should be indicated when the card is created. Methods should be found to read the value and colour of a card. In addition, define a method `toString` that makes it possible, in a simple way, to write out the card in the form `Queen of Hearts`, `8 of Clubs`, `Ace of Spades`, etc.

4. A company has a storeroom which contains several different types of article and there may be several different examples of each article in stock. The following information will be interesting to know for each article: the *article identification* (a code of 4 characters), the article description (a text with at most 30 characters), the *number of articles* of a particular kind in stock and the *sales price*. Write a class `Article`, which defines an article. Methods should be found so that articles of the actual kind can be bought and sold. We should also be able to get information about an article.

5. In the package `java.awt`, there is a standard class called `Dimension`. Check the documentation on this class and try to define your own variant of it. (For simplicity's sake, you may assume that the method `equals` has a parameter of type `Dimension` instead of type `Object`.)

6. In the package `java.awt`, there is a standard class called `Rectangle`, which makes use of class `Point` from Section 2.12 and class `Dimension` from Exercise 5. Check the documentation on class `Rectangle` to see if you can understand how it is used and what the different methods do.

More about classes

3

A Java program can use a large number of classes. To structure a program, it is thus necessary to assemble the classes into so-called packages. In a well-structured program, each class also has to have a clean interface to other classes. You have to decide exactly which methods and variables are to be visible. In addition to packages and visibility, this chapter also covers class methods and class variables.

3.1 Package

We have seen how classes can be used to describe what individual objects look like. In a class, we collect and encapsulate everything that describes individual objects. Since a program normally uses many different kinds of objects, a program has to have access to many different classes. To keep track of all these classes, there is a concept in Java at a "higher level" than a class, which is the concept of a *package*. Classes that belong together in some way are collected together in a package. In other words, a package contains a group of classes. In Java, there are a large number of ready-made standard packages. Several programs which we have studied have used the standard packages `java.awt` and `javax.swing` to implement graphics. However, you can also construct your own packages and put your classes into them. We will discuss how this is done in this chapter.

Package construction

The first thing that should be done when designing a package is to find a name for it. In order to distinguish between package names and names of classes, we usually let the names of packages begin with a lower-case letter. Suppose, for example, that we want to design a package with the name `myPackage`. The next step is to create a folder in the file system where the package is to go. The name of the folder must be the same as that of the package. In our example then, the package should be called `myPackage`. This folder can be put anywhere in the file system. Suppose that we put it in `c:\own\java\classes`.

The third step is to design the classes that are to go into the package. In Java, we do not collect all the classes of a particular package into a single file. Instead, each class is usually defined separately, each one in its own file. On the first line in each such file, we should give a special **package** command, in front of any **import** command, indicating which package the class is to go into. If no **package** command is included in a program file, the package defined in the file will land in an *anonymous* package in the folder in question.

As an example, we define a class C1 which will go into the package myPackage. As usual, we give the file the same name as the class and add the suffix .java. The file including class C1 will therefore be called C1.java. We put the file C1.java into the new folder c:\own\java\classes\myPackage. Class C1 has the following form.

```
// the file C1.java
package myPackage;        // C1 will be included in myPackage

public class C1 {         // a visible class
  ...
}
```

Each file is then compiled as usual. Class C1 is compiled with the command

```
javac C1.java
```

A file with the name C1.class is then generated in c:\own\java\classes\myPackage. (It is really the class files that must be placed into a folder with the same name as the package; the java files may be placed anywhere.)

We now define yet another class, which is placed in the package myPackage.

```
// the file C2.java
package myPackage;        // C2 will be included in myPackage
class C2 {                // a local class
  ...
}
```

Class C2 looks almost the same as class C1 but there is an important difference. **class** C2 is written on the third line, while **public class** C1 is on the third line in the file C1.java. If the word **public** is given first in a class definition, the class will generally be visible everywhere in a program, even in other packages, but if the word **public** is missing, the class will be a local class and visible *only* in the package it is in. For every class included in a package, we can therefore indicate whether the class should be local (only visible inside the package), or visible everywhere.

Up to now, we have assumed that each class definition has been placed in its own file. This is the normal thing to do but in fact it is permissible to place several class definitions in the same file, in which case at most one of the classes may be `public`, and the name of this class will determine the name of the file. The other classes in the file will not be accessible to classes lying outside the file in question. This is useful if a class needs to make use of one or more help classes that should not be visible from outside. The help classes are then defined in the same file as the public class.

Sub-packages

As was mentioned above, a package can contain other packages, that is, it can be said to contain *sub-packages*. We call such a package a *super-package*. A sub-package must have a name consisting of the super-package's name followed by a dot and then the sub-package's name. For example, we can create a new package `myPackage.special`, which will be placed in `myPackage`. (Compare with the way a file name is given in a file system.) The folder in the file system where a sub-package is placed must have the same name as the sub-package, and the folder must be placed in the folder where the super-package is. If, for example, the package `myPackage` is in the folder `c:\own\java\classes\myPackage`, the sub-package `myPackage.special` should be placed in the folder `c:\own\java\classes\myPackage\special`. The hierarchical construction of the packages should be directly mirrored in the folders created in the file system.

We can now define a class `C3` and place it in the new package `myPackage.special`.

```
// the file C3.java
package myPackage.special;

public class C3 {
    ...
}
```

We place the `C3.java` file in the folder `c:\own\java\classes\myPackage\special`.

Of course, a sub-package may in turn be a super-package and contain other packages. For example, we can create a package with the name `myPackage.special.more`. If, as before, we assume that the classes in the package `myPackage` are in the folder `c:\own\java\classes\myPackage`, the classes in `myPackage.special.more` must be in the folder `c:\own\java\classes\myPackage\special\more`.

We can design a hierarchical package structure using sub-packages, where the position of the packages corresponds to their logical role in the program. Class libraries, that is, collections of generally useful packages, can be designed in this way. Java's standard packages also follow this model. We start with a super-package called `java`, and then the different sub-packages, for example, `java.awt`, `java.io` and `java.util`, will be included in this folder.

Archive files

In order to compress the size of the `class` files included in a package, and to make these files faster to download, they are often compressed and put in a so-called *archive* file. This is done with a special program called `jar`, which is included in J2SDK. The program `jar` is run from the command line. Assume that we have a package called `myPackage`, as previously, that we have compiled the classes included in the package and that they are resident in a folder called `C:\own\java\classes\myPackage`. To generate an archive file containing the classes in the package `myPackage`, we start the command interpreter (MS-DOS Prompt), go to the folder `c:\own\java\classes` and then type the following command:

```
jar cf myPackage.jar myPackage\*.class
```

The flags `cf` represent "create" and "file". After the flag `f`, you give the name of the archive file to be created. This can have the same name as the package and its name must end with the suffix `.jar`. The last argument specifies the files to be included in the archive file. Here, we have specified that all the files in the folder `myPackage` whose names end in `.class` should be included. (The full documentation of `jar` is on the Sun website at `java.sun.com/j2se/1.4/docs/tooldocs/win32/jar.html`.)

All the standard packages in Java are distributed in the form of archive files.

Import command

When a program wants to use one of the classes in a package, it must import the class, as we saw earlier. The simplest thing here is to import the entire package. For example, if we wish to use classes `C1` and `C2` in a program, we can write

```
import myPackage.*;
```

since both classes lie in the package `myPackage`. If we wish to use class `C3` from package `myPackage.special`, we can write

```
import myPackage.special.*;
```

The environment variable CLASSPATH

A package can be put at any location in the file system. But we have to tell the Java interpreter where the package is, so that it can find the package. This is done by setting an environment variable called `CLASSPATH`. This should contain a list of names of folders and any archive files that should be searched. In MS-DOS, we can give the command:

```
set CLASSPATH=.;c:\own\java\classes;d:\project\div\graphics.jar
```

Packages

By using a `package` command, which must first be placed in a program file, we indicate that a class should go into a particular package.

  `package` *package_name;*

The classes in a package must be placed in a folder with the name *package_name*. The folder *package_name* must be found in a folder indicated in CLASSPATH.

A package can, in turn, contain other packages. The dot notation is then used.

  `package` *package_name.sub-package_name;*

The classes in a sub-package must be in a folder with the name
package_name\sub-package_name

We have to type a semicolon between each name in the list. Here, we have specified three names – first . which means the current folder you are in right now, then `c:\own\java\classes` and lastly `d:\project\div\graphics.jar`. We have assumed, as previously, that we will use the package `myPackage` and that the classes in this package are resident in `c:\own\java\classes\myPackage`. (Please note that in CLASSPATH we specify the names of the folders that *contain* the packages; we do not give the names of the packages themselves.) We have also assumed that other packages will be used as well, and that the classes in these packages are in the archive file `d:\project\div\graphics.jar`. When you run Windows it is a good idea to use the Control Panel to set the environment variable CLASSPATH. This will then be set automatically each time the computer is started.

If you use Unix or Linux, the command can have the following appearance. A colon is then used between each name in the list.

  `setenv CLASSPATH .:/own/java/classes:/project/div/graphics.jar`

It is a good idea to put the command in an initialization file (`.cshrc`, `.profile` or equivalent, depending on your Unix version). You will not then have to retype the command each time you log in.

If you use an integrated application development system, and run the compilations and runs from inside it, there may be a menu with setting alternatives (options) where you can specify the CLASSPATH you want to have.

In CLASSPATH, you do not have to specify the location of the standard classes. The Java compiler and the Java interpreter know where they are anyway. If you do not use any of your own packages, you do not normally need to set CLASSPATH.

It is a good idea to have a folder where you store all your own "standard packages". This means that they will be available to every program you write. In addition, you will not have to copy any of the classes in these packages, and thus avoid the problem of maintaining several versions.

3.2   Encapsulation and visibility

In the previous section, we were able to use the word `public` to determine whether a particular class should be visible outside the package in which it is included. This applied to whether we wanted the *entire* class to be visible or not. In this section, we will discuss visibility for *individual* instance variables, class variables and methods *inside* a class. Note that what we discuss in this section does *not* apply to local variables, i.e. variables declared inside methods. These variables are always only visible inside the method in which they are declared, and also have a limited life. They cease to exist at the moment that the method has terminated its execution.

As an example we can study the instance variables h, m and s in class `Time` in Section 2.7. These variables were automatically initialized to 0 in each new instance of class `Time`. Because the methods `set` and `tick` are the only methods that change instance variables and since both of these methods check that these instance variables have correct values, we would like to be certain that an object of type `Time` will always describe a correct time of day. But suppose that someone succeeded in directly changing one of the variables without making use of either of the methods `set` and `tick`. Then we could not be sure that the time was correct. In order to prevent such a possibility, the instance variables have been encapsulated in the class so that they cannot be accessed directly from outside it. We achieve this by writing `private` in the declaration of the variables. On the other hand, we want all methods to be visible and able to be called from outside. For this reason, they have been declared with the word `public`. These words are modifiers and indicate the nature of the *visibility* to be applied.

When instance variables and methods are declared, we can indicate the nature of their visibility for each of them and write one of the reserved words `public`, `private` or `protected`. The word `public` means that what is being declared is accessible from anywhere in the program, even from other classes. The word `private` means that what is being declared is only accessible inside the actual class. The word `protected` means that what is being declared is only accessible within the actual class, in other classes within the actual package and in any subclasses of other packages.

If we do not write one of the words `public`, `private` or `protected` when we declare an instance variable or a method, whatever we declare will have *package visibility*. This means that the instance variable or method will be visible in all other classes in the package in which the actual class is included but never from classes that are part of

Visibility				
visible in	private	*package*	protected	public
another class in the same package	no	yes	yes	yes
a subclass in another package	no	no	yes	yes
a class in another package	no	no	no	yes

other packages. The idea here is that all the classes included in a particular package should be able to "rely on" each other, so that it would be safe to allow them free access to instance variables. However, the problem is that if we do not indicate that the class we are defining is to go into a special package, it will go into a default package that includes all of the classes in the actual folder of the file system and we cannot be sure that these classes will belong together to the degree that they can have access to each other's instance variables.

Visibility can be marked in UML diagrams. An example of this will be shown in Figure 3.1 on page 93.

3.3   Class variables

Sometimes we deal with attributes common to all the objects belonging to a certain class. Such components are usually called *class variables* in the context of object-orientation. In Java they are also called *static variables*. This name is an unfortunate relic of C and C++ resulting from the fact that we make use of the reserved word `static` when we declare class variables. The word "static", which indicates that something does not change, is misleading. Class variables are not necessarily static in this sense. They can be changed. In order to avoid misunderstandings, therefore, we will be using the term "class variables" from now on, but the word `static` must of course be used in the program code itself. What is special about a class variable is that it only exists in a single instance, and this instance is shared by all the objects belonging to the actual class. A good example of a class variable is a variable that keeps a check on how many instances of a particular class there are at any one time. Another, rather different example is a bank account. For every bank account, there is a particular balance and a particular account holder. These data must, of course, be available in one instance for each account, and so they are ordinary instance variables. The interest rate, on the other hand, is a class variable. Since all accounts (at least accounts of the same kind) will have the same interest rate, it will be wholly unnecessary to store the interest rate in every single account. It suffices that it can be found in one place, being common for all accounts. We shall then use a bank account as an example and write its definition:

```java
public class Account {
  // class variables
  private static double interestRate;

  // class methods
  public static double getInterest() {
    return interestRate;
  }

  public static void setInterest(double newInterest) {
    interestRate = newInterest;
  }

  // instance variables
  private int customerNo;
  private double balance, interestEarned;

  // constructor
  public Account(int customer) {
    customerNo = customer;
  }

  // instance methods
  public double getBalance() {
    return balance;
  }

  public void transaction (double amount) {
    //negative amount => withdrawal
    if (amount<0 && balance+amount<0)
      System.out.println("Withdrawal cannot be done!");
    else
      balance = balance+amount;
  }

  public void getDailyInterest() {
    interestEarned=interestEarned+balance*interestRate/100/365;
  }

  public void addInterest() {
    balance = balance+interestEarned;
    interestEarned = 0;
  }
}
```

For every account there are three class variables which keep a check on customer numbers, the current balance and the interest earned during the year. Interest earned is calculated on a daily basis but is not added to the balance until the end of the year.

First, we shall briefly describe the operations that have nothing to do with class variables. The constructor initializes a new account. A unique customer number is provided as argument to the constructor. The instance variables balance and interestEarned will automatically get a value of 0. We call the method getBalance if we wish to check the balance in a particular account. The method transaction is called each time a deposit or withdrawal is made on the account. A deposit is indicated as a positive amount and a withdrawal as a negative amount. If we try to take out more money than is available in an account, we get an error text. The method getDailyInterest is called once a day and it calculates the interest earned during that day. The interest earned is added to the instance variable interestEarned. (The interest rate is expressed as a percentage and must therefore be divided by 100. Division by 365 is carried out because we want to calculate the interest earned for one day and not a whole year.) The method addInterest is called at the end of every year (or when the account is closed). This method adds the total interest earned during the year to the balance, and the class variable interestEarned is then set at zero.

There is a class variable, interestRate. This is declared with the reserved word static. There are also two methods getInterest and setInterest, which are used to read and change the interest rate. These are so-called class methods. We will discuss them in the next section. Both class variables and class methods can have modifiers, such as **private**, which determine their visibility. The same rules apply to instance variables and instance methods.

Ordinary instance methods have access to the class variables and can read and change them. For example, the interest rate is necessary in the method getDailyInterest in order to calculate the daily interest. If a class variable is changed in an instance method, the change will affect all the objects of the actual class, since they all share this class variable.

A class variable is found in only one place. A class variable is initialized when the class is loaded into the Java interpreter, that is, when the class is used for the first time in a program. As with other variables, we can indicate a special initialization value if we wish. If we had wanted the interest rate automatically to be 5% every time we started the program, we would have been able to write

```
private static double interestRate = 5;
```

If no initialization value has been indicated, then the class variables, like instance variables, will get a default value. In class Account, the class variable interestRate will get a value of 0. Constructors are *not* used to initialize class variables. The job of constructors is, of course, to initialize the variables dealing with a particular *instance* of the class. If we want to create more complicated initializations of class variables, we can use special *class initializers* (also called *static initializers*). They look like this:

```
static {
    declarations and statements
}
```

and could be placed anywhere inside the class definition. What is happening is that the declarations and statements inside the class initializer are executed just once, when the class is loaded in the Java interpreter. The class variables can then be initialized.

Class variables are often used to define constants that should be generally available. As an example, let us return to the class Lift on page 46. This uses an integer internally to keep track of the current direction of the lift. Downwards is represented by the number −1, stationary by 0 and upwards by the number 1. Now assume that we want to be able to read this direction from outside. So we define a new method called getDirection, which returns this integer. To prevent whatever calls this method from having to keep track of which number represents what in each direction, we also define three constant class variables called DOWN, STATIONARY and UP. Note that the class variables are defined as **public** to make them accessible from outside and as **final** so that they cannot be changed. Also note that we use upper-case letters in their names. This is not necessary, but it is a convention in Java to do it this way, to make it easy to see that they are constant variables.

```
class Lift {
   private int direction;   // -1 down, 0 stationary, 1 up
   ... // as previously
   public static final int DOWN = -1, STATIONARY = 0, UP = 1;
   public int getDirection() {
     return direction;
   }
}
```

Now assume that we have a variable 1 in another part of the program, which refers to a lift, and we want to know if this lift is on its way upwards. We can then write the code

```
if (l.getDirection() == Lift.UP)
   ...
```

Apart from not having to keep track of the fact that upwards is represented by the number 1, the program becomes much clearer. Since the variable UP is declared in the class Lift we must include the class name, of course, and write Lift.UP. If we had just written UP, there would have been a compilation error.

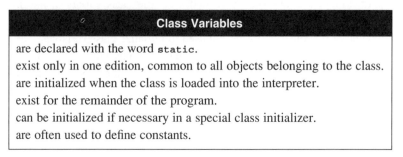

Class Variables

are declared with the word **static**.
exist only in one edition, common to all objects belonging to the class.
are initialized when the class is loaded into the interpreter.
exist for the remainder of the program.
can be initialized if necessary in a special class initializer.
are often used to define constants.

It is common practice to define constants with this technique. It is used frequently in Java's standard classes. Many of the methods in the standard classes have constants (frequently integers) as parameters, or give constants as a result. We have an example of this in the following statement, where we create a JLABEL object and specify that it should contain the text "Hello".

```
JLabel l = new JLabel("Hello", JLabel.CENTER);
```

The second parameter for the constructor should be an integer which specifies how the text should be placed. We do not need to know the integers that mean left, centred, right or other locations. We can use the constant variables which are declared in the class JLabel. In this, we have used the variable CENTER. There is another, similar example in the following call (please refer to page 68):

```
c.get(Calendar.HOUR_OF_DAY)
```

Here, the method get has an integer parameter which specifies the value to be returned (year, month, hours, minutes etc.) and we use the constant variable HOUR_OF_DAY, which is declared in the class Calendar.

3.4   Class methods

Methods marked with the word **static** are called *class methods* (or *static methods*) in Java. The methods getInterest and setInterest in the class Account (please refer to page 88) are examples of these methods. These two methods are special, since they do not handle individual accounts. They use only class variables, and no instance variables. If you try to use an instance variable in a class method, you will get a compile fault.

A class method is not called for one special object, and so it can be called even if there are no objects of the relevant class. The calls

```
Account.setInterest(4.5);
double ir = Account.getInterest();
```

change and read interest. When a class method is called, the class name is written in front of the dot. It is also possible to call class methods in the same way as instance methods, by writing the name of an object instead of the class name. We can write

```
Account acc = new Account(12345);
acc.setInterest(5.1);
```

However, this is pointless and even misleading, since the function setInterest does not in any way read or change the object acc. What it does do is change something that affects all the objects of the class.

91

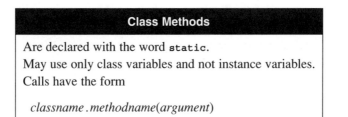

It is not unusual to have classes that contain only class methods. These methods can carry out various mathematical calculations, for example. A class of this kind is then used to encapsulate the methods. We do not intend to create any objects from the class. Study the following class, for example:

```
public class Functions {

   public static double meanValue (double x, double y) {
      return (x + y) / 2;
   }

   public static double quadraticSum (double x, double y) {
      return x * x + y * y;
   }

   public static boolean commonFactors (int i, int j) {
      int k=2;
      while (k <= i && k <= j) {
         if (i % k == 0 && j % k == 0)
            return true;
         k = k + 1;
      }
      return false;
   }
}
```

We have included three mathematical functions in this class. The first calculates the average of two numbers and the second calculates the sum of the squares of two numbers. The third decides whether two given integers i and j have any common factors, or in other words, if there is any integer, apart from the number 1, that both of them can be divided by exactly. To do this test, the method runs through all numbers k, which are equal to or greater than 2, and less than or equal to the smaller of i and j. If there is a number k which both i and j can be divided by, with no remainder, then the two numbers have a common factor, but not otherwise.

Using the class, we could calculate and print the average of the two variables a and b by writing

```
System.out.println(Functions.meanValue(a,b));
```

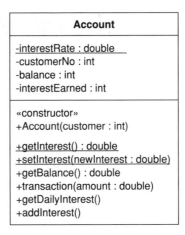

Figure 3.1 A class diagram with class variables and methods

As another example, we can show the following lines where we test whether the two variables m and n have any common factors. (We assume that m and n have previously been assigned values in the program, and that they have the type int.)

```
if (Functions.commonFactors(m, n))
    System.out.println("The numbers have commom factors");
else
    System.out.println("The numbers have no commom factors");
```

We finish this section by showing, in Figure 3.1, a UML diagram for the class Account. In UML, class variables and class methods are underlined, as shown in the figure. The visibility of the variables and methods of a class can be shown in a UML diagram. In that case the name is preceded by a visibility marker, which is one of the characters "+", "−" or "#", denoting public, private and protected visibility, respectively. If the visibility marker is omitted, the visibility is not defined. Also note that a UML diagram can contain keywords enclosed in « ». This is called a *stereotype*. In the figure the constructor is marked in this way.

3.5 The standard class Math

Let us now discuss the class Math in the package java.lang, which is an example of a serviceable class containing class methods. There are a number of methods in this class used to calculate ordinary mathematical functions, for example trigonometric functions, square roots, exponents and logarithms. There are also methods, min and max, which can be used to calculate the lesser or greater of two numbers. We can also find the mathematical constants π and e in class Math. A synopsis is given in the fact box. Note that angles are measured in *radians*. A complete revolution (360 degrees) corresponds to 2π radians.

java.lang.Math	
`PI`	the number π
`E`	the number e
`abs(a)`	gives the absolute value of `a`
`max(a,b)`	gives the greater of `a` and `b`
`min(a,b)`	gives the smaller of `a` and `b`

The following methods return a value of type **double**.
The arguments `x` and `y` should also be real numbers.

`exp(x)`	gives e^x
`log(x)`	gives the natural logarithm (ln) of `x`
`sqrt(x)`	gives $\sqrt{x}$
`ceil(x)`	gives the least integer that is `>= x`
`floor(x)`	gives the greatest integer that is `<= x`
`pow(x, y)`	gives x^y (If `x<=0`, `y` must be an integer)
`round(x)`	rounds off `x` to an integer of type **long**
`random()`	gives a random number in the interval 0 to 1
`sin(x), cos(x), tan(x)`	`x` is indicated in radians
`asin(x), acos(x), atan(x)`	gives arcsin etc.
`sinh(x), cosh(x), tanh(x)`	hyperbolic functions

Calls of the methods in `Math` can be a part of numerical expressions such as

```
3.6*Math.sqrt(z)    Math.log(z)/Math.PI    Math.abs(Math.sin(y))
```

Note that the class name must be written first, since the methods in class `Math` are all class methods.

As a final example, we show a statement which uses the well-known Pythagoras theorem $c^2 = a^2 + b^2$ to calculate the length of the hypotenuse in a right-angled triangle. In this formula, `c` designates the length of the hypotenuse and `a` and `b` are the lengths of the other two sides. Now assume that we have input the values `a` and `b` in the program, and have assigned them to variables called `a` and `b`. We can then declare a third variable called `c` and initialize it so that it contains the length of the hypotenuse. We use the formula $c = \sqrt{a^2 + b^2}$, of course.

```
double c = Math.sqrt(Functions.quadraticSum(a,b));
```

Here, we have used both the standard class `Math` and our own class `Functions` (please refer to page 92).

3.6   Exercises

1. Write a class `c` which contains a class variable `totNumber`, which automatically holds the total number of objects of class `c` that have been created. The class `c` should also contain a class method which returns the value of the class variable.

2. Develop the previous exercise so that every object of class `c` has an instance variable that is automatically assigned a unique identification number. (*Hint.* Devise a constructor without parameters and read off the class variable `totNumber` in it.) There should be a method that makes it possible to read the identification number but it should not be possible to change it.

3. There is a package called `extra`, as a supplement to the book. You can find this package on the book's website. Set up the package as a "standard package" on your own computer. You can put the package folder anywhere in your file system.

4. A palindrome is a text that is the same whether you read it forwards or backwards (e.g. "*Madam, I'm Adam*" and "*Able was I ere I saw Elba*"). Write a program that inputs a word from a dialog box and then shows a message that says whether the word is a palindrome or not. The actual test of the input word should be done in a class method which receives the text as a parameter and returns a value of type `boolean`.

5. A "perfect number" is a number where the sum of the factors of the number, including 1 but excluding the number itself, is equal to the number. A couple of examples are the numbers 6 and 28. Write a class method which determines whether a given positive number is perfect or not. Put the method in a class called `c`.

6. *Euclid's algorithm* to determine the largest common denominator of two positive integers m and n can be written as follows:

    –   Divide *m* by *n* and call the remainder from the division *r*.
    –   If *r*=0 the calculation is finished and the result is contained in *n*.
    –   If not, make *m* equal to *n* and *n* to *r* and return to step 1.

    Use this algorithm to write a class method called `sgd`, which calculates the largest common denominator of two positive integers. Put the method into a class called `Euclid`. Then supplement the class with a method called `main`, which uses dialog boxes to input an arbitrary number of pairs of positive integers, and output the largest common denominator of each pair.

7. If you did not have access to the standard package `Math`, you could have used so-called Maclaurin polynomials to calculate the value of certain common functions. For example, the function *sin* can be calculated with the following infinite polynomial:

$$\sin(x) = x - \frac{x^3}{3!} + \frac{x^5}{5!} - \frac{x^7}{7!} + \frac{x^9}{9!} - \dots$$

Write a class c which contains the class method `sin`. The method should have a parameter of type `double` and should calculate and return the value *sin(x)*. The calculation should be done with the aid of the polynomial above. Start by calculating the first term and then calculate the next term on the basis of the previous term. Repeat this until the last term calculated is less than 10^{-5}.

8. The standard package `Math` contains a class method `sqrt` which calculates the square root of a number. Assume for a moment that the class `Math` does not exist. Your task is now to write a class c which contains its own class method which functions in the same way as `sqrt` in `Math`. You can use "Newton's method" to calculate the square root of a number, which functions as follows:

Start off by guessing a number $g \geq 0$. When you have guessed g, you know that there is another number such that $g \cdot h = x$. (The number h can thus be written as $h = x/g$.) If you have been lucky and have guessed well, g and h will be more or less equal and you have found the solution. In most cases, you will not have made such a good guess. You can make a new, better guess g_{new} by taking the average of g and h:

$$g_{new} = \frac{g + \frac{x}{g}}{2}$$

You can now replace g by g_{new} and calculate a new number h. By taking the average of the new values g and h, you can make a new, even better guess, etc. Use this method to implement a method that calculates $\sqrt{x}$. Use the value of $x/2$ as the first guess and let the guessing continue until the difference between the two guesses is less than 10^{-6}.

Object-oriented program development

When we develop big programs with object-oriented design we say that we carry out *object-oriented program development*. Object-oriented program development is normally divided into the different phases of object-oriented analysis, object-oriented design and object-oriented programming, and we will be discussing these phases.

A feature of object-oriented program development is the relationship between different objects. We will demonstrate how the UML (Unified Modeling Language) can be used to give a visual presentation of such relationships, and we will also discuss how relations between objects are described in Java.

4.1   Object-oriented analysis

In Chapter 2, we stated that object-oriented program development was a kind of model building. The first question we might now ask ourselves is "What shall I build a model of?" To be able to answer this question, we have to try to understand and establish what the program is supposed to do. In object-oriented program development, this phase is termed *object-oriented analysis*. In this phase, we try to get a feel for the problem, to understand the conditions involved and make a first, fairly rough model of our program. To put this in more concrete terms, we must

- find the objects that will be part of the model
- describe the different attributes of objects
- establish the relations between the different objects
- put the objects into groups.

It may be necessary to go through these steps repeatedly, since we have to make sure that all the required operations are carried out by an object. The result of an object-oriented analysis is documented in various forms by diagrams that illustrate the model, while these diagrams can be complemented with tables and other written information. In the following discussion we talk about objects, but we must keep in mind that the discussion is also about classes, since we use classes to describe objects.

The first step, to find the objects, may seem complicated. How do we find the "right" objects? If the program is considered as a model of reality, there is a natural way to let every real "thing" in the environment be represented as an object. At this stage, we should also be doing our utmost to reuse previously constructed classes. Examples of these are different types of container classes, such as tables or queues, or classes that describe visuals on the screen.

Another strategy that has been suggested is to write down, in words, an informal description of what the system should do. In this description, we underline all the nouns and let them be candidates for an object. All the verbs would be candidates for the operations on the objects. This may seem straightforward but the problem with this strategy is that there probably will be too many objects. Nouns need not only designate prospective objects. A noun could also indicate a property, or a condition of an object.

We could also study how the system works as a whole and select a number of *use cases*, or scenarios. If we think of an object as something that provides services, we could check that all the services in our use cases are available. If, for example, a program is to be constructed to check a bank's cashpoint, we could look at the use cases, "a customer wants to withdraw money", "a customer wants to check the balance of an account" and so on.

Of course, no one collection of objects will be the only right one. Different collections can produce results that are equally good. Clearly, the quality of a program will finally depend on the experience, knowledge and intuition of its creator.

In order to see more clearly when constructing big programs, we group objects, that is, we divide a program into its *subsystems* and select the objects to be included in the different subsystems. One way of doing this is to collect all the objects that work closely together and communicate often with one another and establish a subsystem for them. We may allow objects that interface with their surroundings to form their own subsystems. For instance, there might be a subsystem that handles communication with a database. If we can isolate a group of objects with a small and well-defined interface in respect of the rest of the system and this group can offer well-defined services to the other subsystems, then we will have found a "client–server" model.

In Java, packages can be used to create subsystems. We have seen how it was possible, for every class that was a part of a package, to indicate whether the class should be local (only visible inside the package) or visible everywhere. When packages are used to form subsystems in an object-oriented program, classes used internally in the subsystem may be allowed to be local. Visible classes are used to give the subsystem a well-defined interface for other subsystems in a program. Then these other sub-systems will see only the visible classes and need not "know" how the package is constructed internally.

To be able to carry out an object-oriented analysis in a big program development project, we must have the support of a *system development method*. This is a sort of work schedule which indicates how we will accomplish the process of constructing models, that is, of finding objects, attributes and relations. This method also stipulates the different forms of the diagrams to be produced, and it usually provides software support, that is, programs that help with the selection of diagrams and other information that might be required. Examples of some common object-oriented system development methods are OMT[1], Objectory[2] and Coad/Yordon's OOA-OOD[3].

In this section we will use UML notation in our diagrams, just as we did in Chapter 2. UML is not a system development method, but different methods can prescribe that UML should be used.

An object-oriented analysis should establish the relations between the various objects. We will discuss three different kinds of relation:

- *knows*
- *has*
- *is*.

In UML, a relationship between classes is called an *association*. An association exists between classes `c1` and `c2` if, for instance, `c1` has attributes of type `c2`, if `c1` calls methods in `c2` or if some of the methods in `c1` have parameters of type `c2`. Figure 4.1 shows an association between the classes `Person` and `Flight`. The relation is illustrated as a *path* (a line) between the class diagrams. An association can be given a *name*, which is written near the path. In Figure 4.1 the name is *books*. The name may have an optional small black triangle, which indicates the direction in which the association name should be read. (It is not always necessary to read from left to right.) At the end of an association path it is possible to write a *role_name*, which indicates the role played by the class in the association. In our example a person is a *passenger*. At the end of an association we may also attach a *multiplicity*. A multiplicity could be either a simple number or an interval. `a..b` means that the number of objects of the current class should be in the interval `a` to `b`. The character * means an unlimited number. (The

Figure 4.1 Association

---

[1] Rumbaugh *et al.*, *Object-Oriented Modeling and Design*, Prentice Hall, 1991.
[2] Jacobsson, Christensen, *Object-Oriented Software Engineering*, Addison-Wesley Publishing Company, 1992.
[3] Coad, Yourdon, *Object-Oriented Analysis*, 2nd Edition, Prentice Hall, 1991. Coad, Yourdon, *Object-Oriented Design*, Prentice Hall, 1991.

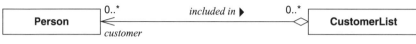

Figure 4.2 One-way association

interval 0..* may be written as a single star *.) In Figure 4.1 a person can book a seat on 0 or more flights and a flight can have at most 300 passengers.

Figure 4.1 describes a *knows* relation. A passenger must know which flights he has booked a seat on and a particular flight must have a passenger list, that is, know its passengers. In other words, Figure 4.1 describes a bi-directional relation. But relations do not always have to be bi-directional. This is demonstrated in Figure 4.2.

A customer list must contain information about all the customers, but it is not necessary for the customers to know that they are on a list. Arrows may be attached to the ends of an association path to indicate the direction of the association, its *navigability*. In Figure 4.2 the arrow at the class `Person` shows that the association is from right to left. UML does not state how an association without arrows should be interpreted. It could mean that the association is bi-directional, but it could also mean that no information about navigability is given.

The "diamond" on the path near the class `CustomerList` in Figure 4.2 indicates that the class `CustomerList` is an *aggregate*. This means that it is composed of a number of persons. When the diamond is hollow, as in Figure 4.2, it means that the aggregate "knows of" its parts.

Associations may also exist between objects of the same class. A person may be married, for example, and therefore have an association with his or her spouse. This is demonstrated in Figure 4.3.

Figures 4.1, 4.2 and 4.3 all describe the *knows* relation. The next relation we will describe is the *has* relation, which states that an object is constructed with the help of another object, that it has this object as one of its parts. This is also sometimes called *composition*. For example, a car has an engine, and a book has a number of different chapters. Figure 4.4 illustrates how we can graphically describe that a motor has a

Figure 4.3 Association to the same class

Figure 4.4 Composition

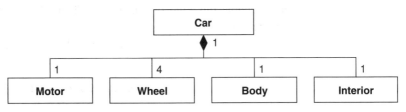

Figure 4.5 Composition with different classes

number of cylinders. Note that the "diamond" should be filled. In UML, composition is considered to be a stronger form of aggregation, a form where the parts are *encapsulated* in the aggregate. If, for instance, the aggregate is copied then all its parts would also be copied.

Of course, an object can consist of several different sub-objects. In Figure 4.5 we illustrate that a car is composed of an engine, wheels, body and interior.

It is easy to confuse the *knows* relation with the *has* relation. We should not be fooled by the word "has". That a car has an owner does not mean that an owner is a component in the construction of the car. The *knows* relation is represented in programs with the help of references. To describe, for example, that a car has an owner, we let the class Car contain an instance variable which is a reference to an object belonging to the class Person.

The third important relation in object-oriented program development is the *is* relation. This is used to state that a class has certain general properties that can be common to other classes: "a squirrel is a mammal"; "a dog is a mammal". The common properties are then described in a separate superclass (in our example, in the class Mammal). We can have *is* relations in several stages: "a mammal is an animal"; "an animal is a living thing". Figure 4.6 illustrates *is* relations for different kinds of vehicle. In UML the

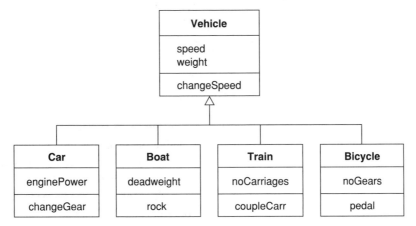

Figure 4.6 Generalization

word *generalization* is used to denote this kind of relation. In Figure 4.6 the class `Vehicle` is a generalization of the more specific classes `Car`, `Boat`, `Train` and `Bicycle`. In a UML diagram there should be a hollow arrow from the specific class to the general class.

In object-orientation, we make use of the concept of *inheritance* to describe *is* relations. When we have to describe a class, we can begin with a class that already exists and add or subtract attributes. The new class is said to *inherit* the properties of the old class, which is said to be a *superclass* of the new class. The new class is then a *subclass* of the old class. Suppose, for example, that we have a class `Person`. Some of the instance variables in this class will be `name` and `address`. Suppose further that we wish to describe students at a university. We can then create a new class `Student`, a subclass of the class `Person`. This means that the new class will automatically get all the attributes in the class `Person`. Therefore, we do not have to redefine the instance variables `name` and `address`. The only thing that we need to do is to declare the new attributes and relations we want to have in the subclass `Student`. We could conceive of relations that indicated the courses a student had taken, as well as an operation that could give a printout of the grades the student had achieved. Figure 4.7 uses both *inheritance* and *knows* relations to illustrate the classes `Person`, `Student`, `Teacher` and `Course`. Both students and teachers are persons. A student takes a number of courses. A teacher teaches a certain number of courses. A course has one teacher. A course has several students.

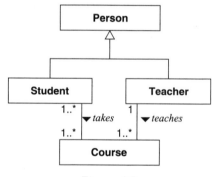

Figure 4.7

A class that is a subclass of another class can in turn be a superclass with its own subclasses. This means that a class hierarchy, with a tree-like structure, can be built. One of the ideas behind inheritance is that the programmer can make use of "ready-made" classes kept in a *class library*. In Java, there is, of course, the API. In this way, we will not have to keep writing new program code. Moreover, ready-made classes have been tested and are more likely to be free of errors than those we have constructed ourselves.

4.2   Object-oriented design

So far, we have mainly discussed object-oriented analysis – the first phase in object-oriented program development. After the analysis phase comes the design phase. *Object-oriented design* may be said to be the activity where plans are drawn up and "drawings" made for object-oriented programs.

The boundary between the analysis and design phases is rather vague. Generally, it can be said that in the analysis phase an idealized model is made, while in the design phase this model is given substance. Another way to express this is to say that during the analysis phase we think about *what* is to be done, while in the design phase we consider *how* it is to be done.

The design phase can be divided into two parts: *system design* and *object design*. System design has to do with making global decisions for the system. At this point we ask questions such as how the new system is to be split into subsystems and how it will communicate with its environment. The operating system to be used for the new system is also something that has to be decided. Part of the environment for the new system might well be a GUI (as Windows or X), database handlers and communication programs. This is easier when we program in Java, since most things are platform-independent.

During the object design phase, we start with the objects that have been selected in the analysis phase, then add all the details, object by object. For example, we determine how an object's various methods are to be performed through the application of appropriate algorithms (see Section 4.4) and describe the parameters the different methods will have. In the object design phase, we also determine how objects are to be constructed internally and whether previously constructed objects can be used again.

A decision as to which programming language will be used to write the program must be made before the design phase is over, since the program language will affect aspects of different objects as well as the system's method of communicating with its environment.

It should be pointed out again here that object-oriented analysis and design often merge, that it is not unusual for the analysis phase to encroach on the design phase. It is also an *iterative* process, where a return to the analysis phase is sometimes necessary if something in the design phase has to be changed or if new functionality is to be added. The programmer must be flexible in developing object-oriented programs.

4.3   Object-oriented programming

The object of the programming phase is to implement the system, that is, to realize it in the form of a computer program that can be run. Naturally, we try to write as "good" a program as possible. A program is "good" if it satisfies the following requirements:

- it is correct
- it is effective
- it is reusable
- it is adaptable.

The first requirement is that the program should be *correct*. It should be able to perform the operations defined in earlier phases of the program development without error. Of course, this is a very important requirement. If a program is littered with errors, it will not matter that it has good properties.

The next requirement is that a program should be *effective*, that is, it should use the resources of the computer system well. Under certain conditions, for example in connection with real-time systems, this may be a deciding factor in whether the program can be used but this requirement may not always be of great importance.

Is a correct and effective program always a good program? Naturally, it depends on what we mean by "good". To shed some light on this issue, we can look at the cost of producing software. This can be divided into two parts: development costs and maintenance costs. Program development would be simplified if we had greater freedom in using pre-existing program components in the same way as occurs with mechanical and electronic systems. In other words, we can require software to be reusable. It is advantageous if we can construct software with the help of ready-made, reusable and well-tested components, instead of writing everything ourselves. Then we can achieve

- lower program development costs
- faster program development
- improved software quality.

It is a known fact that many programmers spend much of their time programming variants of satisfactorily developed programs. Why must this be so? One of the reasons may be that programmers are not used to reusing programs. They may think that it must take at least as long to find a program component and find out how it works as to write it themselves. Another reason may be that it is not as easy for a programmer to find a suitable program component as it is, say, for an electronics design engineer to find a VLSI circuit. If software components are to be reusable, they must conform to certain conditions, whether it is a question of the operating system or the ability to handle certain kinds of data. The number of variants can be endless. What is required of a reusable program component is that it should be applicable under different conditions. In other words, it should be "general". In this context, Java can provide the programmer with many advantages, since its various components are platform-independent.

Before proceeding further with our discussion of reusable programs, a few words should be mentioned concerning the other side of program development costs:

maintenance costs. A program does not deteriorate, so software maintenance costs cannot be compared with, for example, the maintenance costs for a car. The two main aspects of maintenance costs are correcting errors in the software that should already have been discovered during its construction, and adapting software to changed circumstances and requirements. That the latter should be necessary is probably because the program specifications were incorrect from the beginning, because there was a lack of foresight, or because it was simply not possible to forecast how certain conditions would develop with the passing of time.

Maintenance costs can be low, therefore, if it has been possible to keep a program free of errors from the beginning (by the use of well-tested components, for example), and if the program is intrinsically adaptable.

The program will tend to be more adaptable if it is constructed from several independent modules, each one being employed for a special, well-defined task. Then changes in the program will simply entail a procedure where a component is exchanged or removed, as with the repair of a TV set. Therefore, we will want to avoid interfering with the structure of programs, as far as possible. If changes have to be made, they should be well thought out.

Our ability to take in a complex situation is limited. So it is extremely important that the number of contact paths between modules in a system, together with each module's interface with anything outside it, be kept to a minimum. All the information in a module that is local, that is only necessary to be known for the module itself, should be hidden. When the module is used, the user should not need to think about its internal construction. This is where the concept of *information hiding*, which was touched on earlier, comes in. Again, it is a question of packaging, and the packaging can have a favourable effect on both development and maintenance costs.

In object-oriented programming, we try to write programs that are correct, effective, reusable and adaptable, by allowing individual modules in a program to be constructed of objects – objects that facilitate information hiding. Objects are, of course, described with the help of classes, and to know which objects are required, we have to refer back to the design phase.

For the result to be satisfactory, an *object-oriented programming language*, a language with the relevant constructs, should be used. There are, above all, two constructs which are usually required of an object-oriented programming language:

- *Information hiding*. It should be possible to put everything that describes an object's properties into one place in a program. This includes both data and operations. The details belonging to a particular object should be capable of being hidden so that other objects do not need to see these details or have access to them. In Java we use classes to accomplish this.

- *Inheritance.* When describing a class, we should begin with the properties of other classes, adding the new properties as required. In other words, we should try to use previously constructed classes and, making use of the inheritance mechanism, modify and adapt them to our own actual requirements.

These constructs can be found in Java but also in other object-oriented languages such as C++ or Ada.

4.4   Algorithms

When constructing methods for various objects, we are confronted with the difficulty of finding appropriate ways of solving sub-problems. A description of how certain (parts of) problems are solved, a calculation method, is called an *algorithm*. An algorithm consists of a number of elementary operations and directions concerning the order in which operations should be performed. We can make demands of an algorithm:

- It should solve the given problem.
- It should be unambiguous (not "fuzzy" in its formulation).
- If the problem has an ultimate objective (for example, that it should calculate a certain value), the algorithm should terminate after a finite number of steps.
- Note that not all algorithms should terminate. If you have, for example, an algorithm which describes how a control program in a nuclear power station should function, you will not want this algorithm to come to an end.

As a matter of fact, we come across different kinds of algorithms every day. One example is a cookery recipe. Here the problem is to prepare a certain dish, and the algorithm gives us the solution. Another example is provided by assembly instructions (Who has not attempted to assemble a bookshelf from IKEA?) and other kinds of operational instructions. Anyone who knits will realize that a knitting pattern is an algorithm.

Algorithms can be expressed in many different ways. A common way is to indicate the algorithm in normal language. Pictures and symbols can also be used (IKEA again) or formalized language (e.g. mathematical notation). Flow charts are another well-known example. We will be dealing with programming here, so what is naturally most interesting for us is that algorithms can be expressed in a programming language.

Algorithm
Description of how a particular problem is to be solved (a calculation method).

Let us look at an example. We shall describe an algorithm that shows how the sum `1+2+3+...+n` can be evaluated, where `n` is a given integer > 0. One way of describing the algorithm in natural language is:

1. Set 'sum' to 0 and the counter k equal to 1.
2. Repeat the following steps until k is greater than n:
    2.1 Add 'sum' and k and save the result in 'sum'.
    2.2 Increase the value of k by one.
3. The result required is now the number in 'sum'.

Expressed as part of a Java program, the algorithm looks like this:

```java
int sum=0, k=1;
while (k<=n) {
    sum = sum + k;
    k = k + 1;
}
// the result is now in the variable sum
```

To enable it to construct general algorithms, the description method we use must be able to express the following three constructs:

- A *sequence* is a series of steps that are carried out sequentially in the order they have been written. Each step is performed exactly once.

    An example is the assembly instructions for bookshelves:

    1. Put the side pieces in position.
    2. Screw the back piece on to the sides.
    3. Put the shelves into the frame.

- *Selection.* Selection means that one of two or more alternatives should be chosen.

    Example. Calculate the absolute value of a number t.

    If t > 0, the result is the same as t
    otherwise the result is –t.

- *Iteration.* Part of the algorithm should be capable of repetition, either a defined number of times or until a certain condition has been met.

    We saw an example of repetition a defined number of times in the algorithm above, when the sum 1+2+3+...+n was calculated.

    An example of the other type of repetition could be:

    Whisk the eggs vigorously
    until they become fluffy.

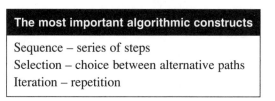

The most important algorithmic constructs

Sequence – series of steps
Selection – choice between alternative paths
Iteration – repetition

Another kind of construct that is commonly used in algorithms and can sometimes replace iteration is *recursion*. This construct seldom appears in "everyday" algorithms and may therefore seem a little strange. The principle is to break down the original problem into smaller but structurally similar problems. The smaller problems can then be solved by reapplying the same algorithm. The previous example, calculating 1+2+3+...+n, can be solved using recursion in the following way:

1. If n= 0, set the result to 0,
2. otherwise do this:
   2.1 Compute the sum 1+2+3+ ... (n-1) using the algorithm.
   2.2 The required result is obtained by adding n to the result from step 2.1.

When a complicated problem has to be solved, it is helpful to split it into smaller sub-problems and solve them separately. These sub-problems can then be split into further sub-problems and so on. This is a very important technique in algorithm and program design and is known as *top-down design*. Let us look at a real-world algorithm that describes how to wash a car. A first, rough algorithm may be simply:

1. Wash car.

This can quickly be expanded to:

1.1 If you are feeling lazy:
    1.1.1 Wash it at a car wash.
1.2 otherwise
    1.2.1 Wash it by hand.

Step 1.1.1 can be refined to:

1.1.1.1 Drive to the nearest car wash.
1.1.1.2 Buy a token.
1.1.1.3 Wait in line.
1.1.1.4 Have the car washed.

Step 1.1.1.4 can be refined further:

1.1.1.4.1 Drive into the car wash.
1.1.1.4.2 Check that all the doors and windows are closed.
1.1.1.4.3 Get out of the car.
1.1.1.4.4 Put the token into the machine.
1.1.1.4.5 Wait until the car wash is finished.
1.1.1.4.6 Get into the car.
1.1.1.4.7 Drive away.

In this way, different parts of an algorithm can be refined until a level is reached where the solution becomes trivially simple.

> **Top-down design**
>
> Divide a problem into sub-problems.
> Solve the sub-problems individually.
> Divide the sub-problems into further sub-problems.
> Continue in this way until all the sub-problems are easily solvable.

There are usually several alternative algorithms for solving a particular problem. In general, it is sensible to design an algorithm that is as simple and easily understood as possible, because there is a better chance that it will work as intended.

4.5   Relations in Java

In this section we shall illustrate the various kinds of relation, discussed in Section 4.1, in greater detail.

4.5.1   The *knows* relation

Because we always make use of references in Java, it will be a simple matter to describe the *knows* relations. We will use class `Person` as an example. A person has a name and address and, in addition, we have added another relation that says that a person can be married. Compare with Figure 4.3 on page 100. We let class `Person` have an instance variable `husbOrWife`, which is a reference variable.

```java
public class Person {
  private String name, address;
  private Person husbOrWife;  // reference to another Person

  // constructor
  public Person(String n) {
    name = n;
  }

  public String getName() {
    return name;
  }

  public void setAddress(String adr) {
    address = adr;
  }

  public String getAddress() {
    return address;
  }
```

```java
public void marry(Person p) {
   husbOrWife = p;       //provide a reference to husband or wife
   p.husbOrWife = this; //let husb. or wife refer to this person
}

public void divorce() {
   husbOrWife.husbOrWife = null;
   husbOrWife = null;
}

public Person marriedTo() {
   return husbOrWife;
}
}
```

Because the instance variable husbOrWife is not initialized in the constructor, husbOrWife will from the beginning contain the value null for every new person. To establish a relation between two persons, the method marry is called. We can write

```java
Person p1 = new Person("Robert");
Person p2 = new Person("Carol");
p1.marry(p2);
```

In the call of the method marry, we allow the object p1 refers to, that is, the object Robert, to be the actual object. As argument, we give a copy of p2, in other words, a reference to the object Carol. The method marry does two things: on the one hand, it permits the instance variable husbOrWife in the actual object to refer to the same object as the parameter p, and on the other, it changes the instance variable husbOrWife in the object p refers to, so that it refers to the actual object. As a result, a bi-directional relation arises. (We do not always need bi-directional *knows* relations, but in this example it is necessary.) After the call of the method marry, the two reference variables p1 and p2.husbOrWife will refer to the same object (to Robert). Similarly, p2 and p1.husbOrWife will refer to the same object (to Carol).

Each Person object has its own name and its own address. For example, we can make the call:

```java
p1.setAddress("2 Old Mill Road");
p2.setAddress("36 Prince Street");
System.out.println(p1.getAddress());
```

The output will be:

```
2 Old Mill Road
```

which shows that Robert's address remains unaffected by the second call. As a result of the *knows* relation, any changes that might be made in one of the two objects will indirectly affect the other. For example, we can reach Carol's new address via Robert:

```java
System.out.println(p1.marriedTo().getAddress());
```

The method `marriedTo` returns a copy of the instance variable `husbOrWife`, in this example a reference to Carol. The output will be:

```
36 Prince Street
```

If we are dealing with a *knows* relation but, for the time being, an object does not know some other object, we indicate this by giving the reference variable the value `null`. If we call the method `divorce`

```
p1.divorce();
```

the reference variable `husbOrWife` in the method `divorce` is set to `null` for both objects involved. Note that the two statements

```
husbOrWife.husbOrWife = null;
husbOrWife = null;
```

inside the method `divorce` must be performed in the right order. Once the reference variable `husbOrWife` in the actual object has been set to `null`, the connection will be broken and we will not be able to reach the other object to alter it.

4.5.2   The *has* relation

When we use classes to construct models of reality, we often find that certain objects are constructed with the help of others, which are encapsulated in the bigger object. In other words, there is a *has* relation. As an example of how we describe this in Java, let us look at the class `Flight`, which describes regular flights. Every flight is described by five instance variables: the flight number, destination, commentary, departure time and time of arrival. The first three are text strings but it is the departure and arrival times that are the interesting things here, and there is a *has* relation involved. A flight *has* a departure time and arrival time. These times are described with the help of two objects of class `Time` from Chapter 2. However, since we cannot declare objects directly in Java, we will have to use two reference variables. The class `Flight` then looks like this:

```java
public class Flight {
  private String no, destination, comment = "";
  private Time dep, arr; // departure and arrival times

  // constructor
  public Flight (String flightNo, String dest,
                 int depHour, int depMin,
                 int arrHour, int arrMin) {
    no  = flightNo;
    destination = dest;
    dep = new Time(depHour, depMin);
    arr = new Time(arrHour, arrMin);
  }
```

```
   // methods
   public void setComment(String com) {
      comment = com;
   }

   public void delay (int min) {
      dep.tick(min*60);
      arr.tick(min*60);
      setComment("Delayed");
   }

   public Time getDep() {
      return new Time(dep.getHour(), dep.getMin());
   }

   public Time getArr() {
      return new Time(arr.getHour(), arr.getMin());
   }

   public String getDestination() {
      return destination;
   }

   public String toString() {
      return no + " " + destination + " " + dep + " " + comment;
   }
}
```

The constructor has six parameters. When we create a flight, we indicate the flight number, destination and departure and arrival times, expressed in hours and minutes. For example, we can write

```
Flight f = new Flight("BA1853", "London", 8, 10, 10, 55);
```

The constructor creates two new objects of class `Time` and allows the instance variables `arr` and `dep` to refer to these. We can set the instance variable `comment` separately by calling the method `setComment`.

We use the class `Time` in class `Flight` in the normal way. The method `delay`, which we call to indicate that a flight has been delayed, will in turn call the method `tick` for class `Time` (the second version, the one with a parameter) both for the time of departure and for the arrival time. Note that class `Flight` has no more knowledge of class `Time` than any other outsider. It cannot reach the enclosed instance variables in any of the time objects directly but instead must use the methods defined for this purpose.

We find in the method `toString` the expression

```
no + " " + destination + " " + dep + " " + comment
```

Since `dep` is an object of class `Time`, the method `dep.toString` for class `Time` will be automatically called to make the conversion to type `String`.

The method `toString` for class `Flight` will be called automatically if we try to write out a flight object with the help of the method `println`. The three statements

```
System.out.println(f);   // f.toString is called automatically
f.delay(15);
System.out.println(f);   // f.toString is called automatically
```

for example, give the output:

```
BA1853 London 08:10
BA1853 London 08:25 Delayed
```

In order to read the departure and arrival times and the destination of a flight from outside, we call the methods `getDep`, `getArr` and `getDestination`, respectively. These are very interesting. Note that in `getDep` and `getArr` we do not directly return the instance variables `dep` and `arr`. Instead, we create *copies* of the objects that `dep` and `arr` point to and return references to these copies. We do this so that an outsider will not have direct access to the private instance variables. For example, we may make these statements from outside:

```
Time t = f.getDep();
t.tick(60);
```

If `t` had been a reference to the same time object as the one that `f.dep` refers to, we would naturally have changed the departure time "behind the back" of the flight object, which would not have been a good thing, but because this change is made in a copy, it is quite safe to do so.

Because we also have to use reference variables for *has* relations in Java, we must be careful to hand back references. If we allow an outsider class to have access to a reference to an enclosed object, one that we "have", then it will no longer be a question of a *has* relation but a *knows* relation, in which case various objects will be able to know an enclosed object and affect it. The difference between *has* relations and *knows* relations is sometimes very subtle, indeed.

Let us look at the method `getDestination`. We do not make a copy in this. It merely says **return** `destination`. What happens then if we make the following statements?

```
String s = f.getDestination();
s = "Paris";
System.out.println(f);
```

Won't the destination for flight `f` be changed? When the first line is executed, `s` of course refers to the same text as `f.destination`. Then should not the text also be changed for `f`? No, because there is never any danger where references to objects of the standard class `String` are concerned. As we saw in Section 2.9, we can never *change* anything in an object of this kind. The second line, above, therefore means that a *new* `String` object is created containing the text `Paris` and that `s` is set to refer to the new object. The instance variable `f.destination` will not be affected. It will still refer to the old `String` object, the one with the text `London`.

4.5.3 The *is* relation

The third relation we now look at is that of inheritance, or the *is* relation. Inheritance is dealt with thoroughly in Chapter 10, which is devoted entirely to this concept. We merely give a brief introduction here. When we define a new class, we can start with an already existing class and add or change characteristics. We then say that the new class is a *subclass* of the old one and that the old class is a *superclass* of the new one. As a demonstration of this relationship, we will define a new class `TimeWithAlarm`.

```
import java.awt.*;

public class TimeWithAlarm extends Time {
   private int ah, am, as;
   private boolean alarmOn = false;

   public void setAlarm (int hour, int min, int sec) {
   if ( hour>=0 && hour<24 &&
         min>=0 && min<60 && sec>=0 && sec<60) {
      ah = hour; am = min; as = sec;
      alarmOn = true;
   }
   else
      System.out.println("Incorrect time");
   }

   public void alarmOff() {
      alarmOn = false;
   }

   public void tick() {
      super.tick();
      if (alarmOn && getHour() == ah &&
          getMin() == am && getSec() == as) {
        Toolkit.getDefaultToolkit().beep();
      }
   }
}
```

This class is used to trigger the functioning of an alarm clock. The instance variables ah, am and as indicate when it is time for the alarm to ring. On the third line, we see that the reserved word **extends** has been used to indicate that a class will be a subclass of another class. The new class inherits both instance variables and methods from the superclass. This means, for example, that an object of class `TimeWithAlarm`, in addition to the instance variables ah, am and as, also has the instance variables h, m and s, inherited from class `Time`. An object of class `TimeWithAlarm` also has all the methods in class `Time`, for example `set` and `getHour`, in addition to the new methods `setAlarm` and `stopAlarm`. The method `tick` requires a comment. It exists in class `Time` but has been redefined in class `TimeWithAlarm`. If we call the method `tick` for an object of class `TimeWithAlarm`, the new version will then be called.

The new version of `tick` begins by calling the version of `tick` in the superclass. This is done by the statement **super**`.tick()`. A check is then made to see whether the time is equal to the alarm time. If so, the method `beep` (in the standard class `Toolkit`) is called to get the computer to emit a "beep". For example, we may have the following program lines:

```
TimeWithAlarm ta = new TimeWithAlarm();
ta.set(11, 59, 58);
ta.setAlarm(12,0,0);
ta.tick();
ta.tick();
```

The computer will then "beep" when the last statement has been executed.

Inheritance is a crucial, central mechanism in object-oriented programming. It is the best way of making use of such ready-made program parts as the standard GUI classes.

4.6 Exercises

1. Construct a class `Car` that describes a car. A car should have a registration number and a text containing the make and model of the car. A car should also know its owner, a member of the class `CarOwner`, which will be a subclass of the class `Person` (cf. Exercise 2 on page 79). In addition, define the class `CarOwner`. For simplicity's sake, you should specify that a car owner may own only one car. Write methods that can be called when a car is bought or sold.

2. Construct the classes `Vehicle` and `Train` in Figure 4.6.

3. Construct the classes `Person` and `Teacher` in Figure 4.7.

4. A table contains n different numbers. Describe, in natural language, an algorithm that searches a table and finds the least number. The algorithm should give as result the position number in the table (an index between 1 and n) of this least number.

5. A table contains n different numbers. Describe an algorithm that changes the contents of the table so that the numbers appear in order of size (the smallest number first and the largest last). Use a method that first places the least number in the table's first position, then the next least number in the table's second position, and so on. (*Hint*: Make use of the algorithm in the previous exercise.)

Reading and writing

5

In this chapter, we are going to study how to read and decode input data and how to edit printouts. We will also discuss how we can read and write text files.

5.1 Editing numerical values

When you display a result on screen or write it to a file, you frequently want to edit the printout to make it look neat. In Section 1.9, we designed a program which calculated what it cost to rent a car. The dialog boxes which the program created are shown in Figure 1.8 on page 19. The last of these boxes contains the message: `"Total cost: 280.5"`. If you run the program in a country that uses a decimal comma instead of a decimal point, you might have preferred to have the result presented as `280,50`. The text `280.5` shown in Figure 1.8 is produced by the expression

```
"Total cost: " + totalCost
```

in the program. The value in the variable `totalCost`, which has type **double,** is converted automatically to text format and we, the programmers, are not able to influence the way in which this conversion is done.

As another example, we can take the class `Time` on page 59 in Chapter 2. The printouts of times are not very good. For example, we could get the printout

```
17:8:21
```

What we want is to have hours, minutes and seconds always printed with two figures, irrespective of the value they have. In Figure 2.8 on page 67, we might have wanted to have the time presented as `18:56:03`. The conversion from integers to text is done in the method `toString` in class `Time`. If you write an expression there with the following format:

```
h + ":" + m
```

the values of the integers `h` and `m` will be converted to text format. This text will contain exactly the number of characters needed to display the values of the variables. If `t` has value 17 and `m` has the value 8, there will be two characters for the value of `h` and one character for the value of `m`. This cannot be influenced by the programmer either.

It is necessary to use a *formatter* to format texts the way you want them. The `java.txt` package contains a standard class called `NumberFormat`, which contains everything necessary. This class contains tools for formatting numbers in different ways. The easiest way to obtain a formatter is to call the class method `getInstance` in the class `NumberFormat`. On the line below, for example, we declare a variable `nf` and let it refer to a formatter.

```
NumberFormat nf = NumberFormat.getInstance();
```

The class `NumberFormat` contains a method called `format`. You call this to format a number. The result of the call is a text. Assume, for example, that `x` is a number with value `2318604.123` and that we write the line

```
String s = nf.format(x);
```

The way formatting is done is controlled by the formatter `nf`. The variable `s` will contain the text `"2,318,604.123"`, `"2.318.604,123"` or `"2 318 604,123"`.[1] The format used is determined by the so-called *local conventions* used. The first format obtained is the English format. In the next section, we will describe how to control the local formats used.

The class `NumberFormat` contains methods for controlling the number of integer numerals and the number of decimal places. (Please refer to the fact box.) In addition, you can specify whether the numerals in a number should be grouped or not. This means that the numerals are bunched, normally three at a time, to increase legibility. These formatting facilities are enough for most needs. It is possible to change the properties of a formatter dynamically by calling different methods and you can also use several different formatters with different properties. As an example, we show what to write to specify that you want a maximum of six decimal places in the printout.

```
nf.setMaximumFractionDigits(6);
```

This rounds off to six decimal places. If you do not specify the number of decimal places you want, you get up to three decimals.

It must be pointed out that the method `format` cannot format very small or very large numbers. These numbers need the exponential form to be displayed correctly.[2]

---

[1] In the last format, an ordinary space character is not used between the groups of numerals. Instead, a "no-break space" with Unicode `00A0` is used, which looks like an ordinary space character if displayed in a graphical user interface, such as a dialog box. In an MS-DOS box, it gives the wrong appearance, however.

[2] In the class `ExtendedWriter`, which is discussed in Section 5.4.2, there is a method `useExponent` which you can use to test whether a number can be formatted with the method `format`.

Number formatting

Use class `java.text.NumberFormat`

Get an object of class `NumberFormat`:

```
NumberFormat f = NumberFormat.getInstance(); // local conventions
```

or

```
NumberFormat f = NumberFormat.getInstance(l); // l is a Locale
```

Call the method `format` to convert a number `x` into text:

```
f.format(x)
```

Formatting characteristics are given by the method calls:

```
f.setMaximumFractionDigits(n);    // maximum of n decimals, default 3
f.setMaximumIntegerDigits(n);     // maximum of n integer digits
f.setMinimumFractionDigits(n);    // minimum of n decimals
f.setMinimumIntegerDigits(n);     // minimum of n integer digits
f.setGroupingUsed(true);          // the digits should be grouped
f.setGroupingUsed(false);         // the digits should not be grouped
```

As an example, we show how you can change the program `CarRent` on page 18 so that the dialog box containing the result has the appearance of Figure 5.1.

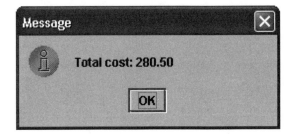

Figure 5.1

We do this by putting the following line first in the program:

```
import java.text.*;
```

then we replace the lines

```
JOptionPane.showMessageDialog(null,
                        "Total cost: " + totalCost);
```

by the following lines:

```
NumberFormat nf = NumberFormat.getInstance();
nf.setMinimumFractionDigits(2);
```

119

```
nf.setMaximumFractionDigits(2);
JOptionPane.showMessageDialog(null,
                            "Total cost: " + nf.format(totalCost));
```

Let us discuss the method `toString` in the class `Time` as an example. We write a new version in which we use a formatter. The new version is as follows:

```
public String toString () {
   NumberFormat nf = NumberFormat.getInstance();
   nf.setMinimumIntegerDigits(2);
   String t = nf.format(h) + ":" + nf.format(m);
   if (showSec)
      t = t + ":" +  nf.format(s);
   return t;
}
```

Using this modification of the method `toString`, the printout from the demonstration program `TimeDemo` on page 59 is:

```
17:08:21
00:00:01
```

and in the box in Figure 2.8 on page 67, the text will be presented as `"18:56:03"`.

5.2   Local conventions

The conventions for writing numbers vary from country to country. For example, the English-speaking countries use a full stop between the integers and the decimals, while in most of the European countries, for example, a decimal comma is used. Conventions are normally determined by the operating systems in use. If we have an English system, for example, we will use English conventions. We can also explicitly indicate the conventions we want by calling the method `setDefault` in the standard class `Locale` of the package `java.util`. We must then give as arguments the codes for the language and country.[1] For example, English has the code `en`, Chinese `cn`, Russian `ru`, Spanish `es`, French `fr`, German `de`, Italian `it` and Portuguese `pt`. Some examples of country codes are Great Britain `GB`, USA `US`, Canada `CA`, Australia `AU`, Argentina `AR` and Brazil `BR`. For example, to indicate that we want to have Spanish conventions, we can write

```
Locale.setDefault(new Locale("es","ES"));
```

The class `Locale` also contains some pre-existing `Locale` objects for a number of "common" countries and languages. Some examples are shown in the fact box.

---

[1] We can use a method `getAvailableLocales` in the class `NumberFormat` to check the languages and countries that are installed on the computer used.

---

java.util.Locale

Conventions for different languages are handled with the help of the class
`java.util.Locale`. An object of this class describes a local convention. Local
conventions determine such things as the format for dates, times and numerals.
There is always a default `Locale` object set by the system from the beginning.

In the following list, `l` indicates a variable of type `Locale`.

new `Locale("`*language*`","`*country*`")`	Creates a new `Locale` object. *language* and *country* are ISO codes
`Locale.getDefault()`	Gives a reference to the default `Locale` object
`Locale.setDefault(l);`	Gives `l` to the default `Locale` object
`Locale.UK`	A British `Locale` object
`Locale.US`	An American `Locale` object
`Locale.JAPAN`	A Japanese `Locale` object
`Locale.CHINESE`	A `Locale` object for Chinese
`Locale.FRENCH`	A `Locale` object for French
`l.getLanguage()`	Returns the language code for `l` (a `String`)
`l.getCountry()`	Returns the country code for `l` (a `String`)

If we now make the declaration

```
NumberFormat sp = NumberFormat.getInstance();
```

we will get a `NumberFormat` object which makes use of the conventions currently set as
default. In this example, the conventions are Spanish. A `NumberFormat` object can be
obtained for any convention, without changing the default conventions. We would get
a `NumberFormat` object following the American conventions if we wrote, for example:

```
NumberFormat us = NumberFormat.getInstance(Locale.US);
```

In class `NumberFormat` there is a method called `format`. It is called to format a number,
and the result of a call is a text. Suppose, for example, that x is a number with the value
`2318604.123` and that we write the statement

```
System.out.println(sp.format(x));
```

The object `sp` will direct the formatting here. We will get Spanish conventions, and the
printout will be

```
2.318.604,123
```

If we had instead given the statement

```
System.out.println(us.format(x));
```

the printout would have been

```
2,318,604.123
```

Since the class `Locale` contains a method `toString`, it is easy to print out information about a `Locale` object. The statement

```
System.out.println(Locale.getDefault());
```

would give the following printout if you were using a Spanish installation:

```
es_ES
```

5.3   Parsing input data

When you input data from a dialog box, this data comes in the form of text, i.e. a value of type `String`. If you have numerical input data, this must be converted from type `String` to a numerical type, i.e. to types `int` or `double`. We call this *parsing* (or *decoding*) the data. We have previously seen that you can use the methods `Integer.parseInt` and `Double.parseDouble` to do this, but we will now look at an alternative way. We will use the fact that the class `NumberFormat` can not only be used to get printouts in the desired format. It also contains a method called `parse`, which does the conversion from text format to numerical value. This gives us the facility of inputting data with a decimal comma instead of a decimal point if we should want to do so. To make it as simple as possible for the programmer, we will not use the method `parse` in the class `NumberFormat` directly, however. We will introduce our own auxiliary class called `Parse`, which uses an object of class `NumberFormat` internally to do the decoding.

The class `Parse` is easy to use, and you do not need to know or understand how it works internally to be able to use it. We will show what the class looks like here, but will not bother to discuss how it is constructed. (Readers who are interested in details should refer to the documentation of the class `NumberFormat`, especially the description of the method `parse`.)

```java
import java.text.*;
public class Parse {

  private static NumberFormat form=NumberFormat.getInstance();

  public static void setFormat(NumberFormat f) {
    form = f;
  }

  // parse an integer number
  public static int toInt(String s) {
    return Integer.parseInt(s.trim());
  }
```

```
// parse a real number
public static double toDouble(String s) {
   ParsePosition p = new ParsePosition(0);
   form.setGroupingUsed(false);
   Number n = form.parse(s.trim(), p);  // try to parse
   if (n == null || p.getIndex() != s.trim().length()) //error?
      throw new NumberFormatException(); // yes, throw exception
   return n.doubleValue();  // no, parsing OK
   }
}
```

5.3.1   Simple parsing of texts with single numerical values

Our new class Parse contains the two class methods toInt and toDouble. Both should give values of type String as a parameter, and as results they give values of types int and **double** respectively. Assume, for example, that we have a variable s which is of type String and which contains the text "123,45". (Here, we assume that the program uses Spanish conventions. If it had used English conventions, we can assume that s would contain the text "123.45".) Also assume that x is a variable of type **double**. The following call then means that the text in s is parsed and that the variable x is assigned the value 123.45:

```
x = Parse.toDouble(s);
```

The method Parse.toInt works in the same way, but when it is used the text must not contain a decimal point (or decimal comma).

As an example of how these auxiliary methods can be used, we will study a new version of the program CarRent on page 18. The new program is as follows:

```
import javax.swing.*;
import java.text.*;
public class CarRent2 {
   public static void main (String[] arg) {
      String s = JOptionPane.showInputDialog("Number of days?");
      int noOfDays = Parse.toInt(s);
      s = JOptionPane.showInputDialog("Cost per day?");
      double costPerDay = Parse.toDouble(s);
      double totalCost = costPerDay * noOfDays;
      NumberFormat nf = NumberFormat.getInstance();
      nf.setMinimumFractionDigits(2);
      nf.setMaximumFractionDigits(2);
      JOptionPane.showMessageDialog(null,
                       "Total cost: " + nf.format(totalCost));
      System.exit(0);
   }
}
```

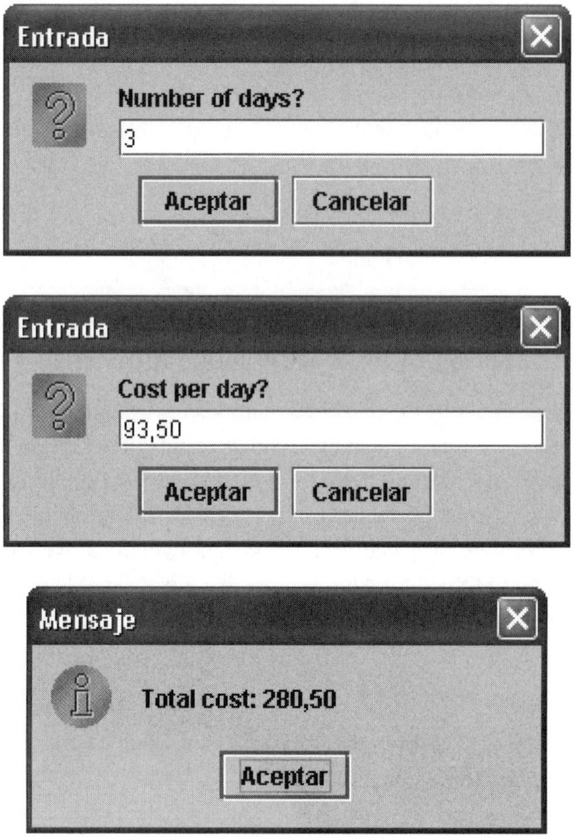

Figure 5.2

Now assume for a moment that we are using a computer with a Spanish installation of Windows. Figure 5.2 shows an example of dialog boxes which can then be generated by the program.

We see that the user can write a decimal comma instead of a decimal point when inputting the price per day. This can be done since the method `Parse.toDouble` automatically adapts itself to the local conventions used in the current installation. This can easily be changed, however. In the class `Parse`, a formatter of type `NumberFormat` is used internally. We can specify that the class `Parse` should use a different formatter. Assume, for example, that we have previously declared the formatter `usa`:

```
NumberFormat usa = NumberFormat.getInstance(Locale.US);
```

If we put in the following statement before the call for `Parse.toDouble`, this will demand that a decimal point is used in the input data.

```
Parse.setFormat(usa);
```

To make it easy to run the program CarRent2, the class Parse must be available. An easy way to achieve this is to put the file containing the class Parse in the same folder (sub-directory) in the file system as the file that contains the class CarRent2. The class Parse is usable in more programs than the program CarRent2, however. For this reason, the class Parse has been put in a package of auxiliary classes which are a complement to the book and can be downloaded from the book's website. The package is called extra, and the classes in the package are thus put in an archive file called extra.jar. You should download this file to your own computer. When you have downloaded the file, you can put it anywhere in the file system, for example in the folder c:\javautil. For the Java interpreter to be able to find the extra package, you have to set the CLASSPATH variable as we discussed in Section 3.1. If you are running Windows and the file extra.jar is in the folder c:\javautil, the command for setting CLASSPATH should have the following appearance:

```
set CLASSPATH=.;c:\javautil\extra.jar
```

You must, of course, put an **import** command into the programs that want to use the class extra:

```
import extra.*;
```

The version of the class Parse in the package extra is more comprehensive than the one we have shown here. This is because it contains methods for decoding numerical data for all the standard types in Java. The methods are all listed in the fact box.

The class extra.Parse

The following calls assume that s is a text of type String.
If s is **null**, an error signal of type NullPointerException is given. If s contains incorrect data, an error signal of type NumberFormatException is given.

Parse.toByte(s)	Decodes s, gives a number of type **byte**
Parse.toShort(s)	Decodes s, gives a number of type **short**
Parse.toInt(s)	Decodes s, gives a number of type **int**
Parse.toLong(s)	Decodes s, gives a number of type **long**
Parse.toFloat(s)	Decodes s, gives a number of type **float**
Parse.toDouble(s)	Decodes s, gives a number of type **double**

Uses a formatter internally, of type NumberFormat with local conventions. The formatter can be changed by the following call, where r is another formatter:

```
Parse.setFormat(r)
```

5.3.2 Error checking

When you read the input data in a program, it is a good idea to check that the input data is correct. The methods `Parse.toDouble` and `Parse.toInt` generate special error signals, so-called exceptions, if the input data is incorrect, as do methods `Integer.parseInt` and `Double.parseDouble`. Faulty input data means characters that cannot be included in a number, such as letters. Integers must not contain a decimal point or decimal comma. The methods `Parse.toDouble` and `Parse.toInt` permit you to have space characters first or last in the text to be decoded, but this is regarded as an error by methods `Integer.parseInt` and `Double.parseDouble`. This means that it might be an advantage to use the methods `Parse.toDouble` and `Parse.toInt` even if you are not interested in getting a decimal point in the input data.

If the input data for one of the four methods above is faulty, the method generates an error signal of type `NumberFormatException`. We have not discussed error signals yet (this will not be done until Chapter 11), but it might be useful to know what to do to handle any error signals right now. If an error signal is not handled, the program will crash if the user happens to enter incorrect data and you might not want the program to behave that way. For this reason, we will now see what to do, without getting involved in a deep discussion about how error signals work.

As an example, we will see what to do to discover if the parameter for method `Double.parseDouble` contains incorrect data. (You can use the same technique for methods `Parse.toInt`, `Integer.parseInt` and `Double.parseDouble` as well.) Assume that the `String` variable s contains input data and we want to decode the value in s and assign it to variable x of type **double**. Instead of just writing

```
x = Parse.toDouble(s);
```

we insert the statement into a so-called **try** statement as follows:

```
try {
   x = Parse.toDouble(s)
}
catch (NumberFormatException e) {
   // you get here if s contains an incorrect number
   ...
}
```

If s contains incorrect data, nothing strange will happen, but the program will continue as usual by executing the first line after the lines above. If s contains incorrect data, the program jumps to the place we have marked with three dots. This is where you put in the statement(s) you want to have executed if incorrect input data is given.

One frequently wants to give the user another chance to input data if it was incorrect. To make this possible, we can encapsulate the **try** statement in a **while** statement. To demonstrate this, we replace the lines

```
s = JOptionPane.showInputDialog("Cost per day?");
double costPerDay = Parse.toDouble(s);
```

in the program CarRent2 on page 123 by the following lines:

```
s = JOptionPane.showInputDialog("Cost per day?");
double costPerDay = 0;
boolean ok = false;
while (!ok) { // continue util the parsing succeeds
  if (s == null)
    System.exit(0);   // The user clicked "Cancel"
  try {
    costPerDay = Parse.toDouble(s); // try to parse
    ok = true;     // the parsing was successful
  }
  catch (NumberFormatException e) {
    // the parsing failed
    s = JOptionPane.showInputDialog
                ("Incorrect number!\nEnter cost per day?");
  }
}
```

We start off by showing the dialog box and assigning the input text to variable s. Each lap of the **while** statement represents an attempt to decode input data. The **while** statement is repeated until decoding succeeds (or until the user clicks the "Cancel" button). The variable ok, which contained the value **false** from the beginning, is changed to contain the value **true** after a successful decoding event has taken place. Each time decoding fails, a new dialog box is displayed containing an error message.

5.3.3   Decoding text with several items of data

Sometimes, the same text can contain several items of data which have to be decoded. Assume, for example, that we replace the two top dialog boxes in Figure 5.2 by a single box, as shown in Figure 5.3. We can display this dialog box and input the typed text in the same way as previously, by typing the declaration

```
String s = JOptionPane.showInputDialog
        ("Enter number of days, cost per day, and type of car");
```

If the user has input the data correctly, the variables will now contain three sections (so-called *tokens*), delimited by one or more space characters. If the data had been input as in Figure 5.3, variable s would contain the text "3 93.50 Fiat". There is a standard class in java.util called StringTokenizer which you can use to pick the individual sections out of a text. This is quite easy. You start off by creating an object of class StringTokenizer and in the constructor you specify the text to be divided up.

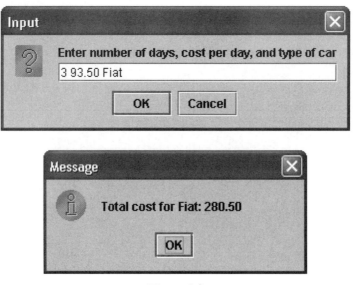

Figure 5.3

In our example, we are going to divide up the text in the variable input data, so we write the declaration

```
StringTokenizer stok = new StringTokenizer(s);
```

We now use the variable `stok` to divide the text up. You pick the pieces out, one at a time, by calling the method `nextToken`. We write the following lines:

```
String noTxt    = stok.nextToken();
String priceTxt = stok.nextToken();
String car      = stok.nextToken();
```

The variable `noTxt` will then contain the text `"3"`, `priceTxt` will contain the text `"93.50"` and the variable `car` will contain the text `"Fiat"`. The variables `noTxt` and `priceTxt` can then be decoded in the usual way with the methods `Parse.toInt` and `Parse.toDouble`. We show the full program here. (We have simplified it somewhat by calling the methods `Parse.toInt` and `Parse.toDouble` directly, without intermediate storage of the results in the variables `noTxt` and `priceTxt`.)

```
import javax.swing.*;
import java.text.*;
import java.util.*; // continues the class StringTokenizer

public class CarRent3 {
    public static void main (String[] arg) {
        String s = JOptionPane.showInputDialog
            ("Enter number of days, cost per day, and type of car");
```

```
StringTokenizer stok = new StringTokenizer(s);
int noOfDays    = Parse.toInt    (stok.nextToken());
double costPerDay = Parse.toDouble(stok.nextToken());
String car = stok.nextToken();

double totalCost = costPerDay * noOfDays;
NumberFormat nf = NumberFormat.getInstance();
nf.setMinimumFractionDigits(2);
nf.setMaximumFractionDigits(2);
JOptionPane.showMessageDialog(null,
    "Total cost for " + car + ": " + nf.format(totalCost));
System.exit(0);
  }
}
```

The class `StringTokenizer` contains more methods. If you are going to divide up a text which contains an unknown number of components, you could use the method `hasMoreTokens` to test whether the text contains more components.

java.util.StringTokenizer

Divides up a given text s into components, so-called *tokens*.

new `StringTokenizer(s)`	creates an object to divide s up into tokens. Characters `"\t\n\r\f"` are regarded as dividers.
new `StringTokenizer(s,d)`	creates an object to divide s up into tokens. The characters in d (a `String`) are regarded as dividers.
new `StringTokenizer(s,d,`**true**`)`	creates an object to divide s up into tokens. The characters in d (a `String`) are regarded as dividers. The dividers are also regarded as tokens.

In the following methods, t is a `StringTokenizer` object which is created as above.

`t.countTokens()`	gives the number of remaining tokens in s
`t.hasMoreTokens()`	specifies if there are any more tokens in s
`t.nextToken()`	gives the next token in s
`t.nextToken(d)`	gives the next token in s. Characters in d (a `String`) are counted as dividers instead of the ones in the constructor

The following program displays a dialog box in which the user can write a number of real numbers, with space characters in between. The program then calculates the total of the numbers entered, and shows the result in another dialog box.

```
import javax.swing.*;
import java.text.*;
import java.util.*;

public class CalculateSum {
  public static void main (String[] arg) {
    String s = JOptionPane.showInputDialog("Enter the numbers");
    StringTokenizer stok = new StringTokenizer(s);
    double sum = 0;
    while (stok.hasMoreTokens())
      sum = sum + Parse.toDouble(stok.nextToken());
    NumberFormat nf = NumberFormat.getInstance();
    JOptionPane.showMessageDialog(null,
        "The sum of the numbers is " + nf.format(sum));
    System.exit(0);
  }
}
```

5.4 Data input and printout in command windows

A program can communicate with its surroundings in several different ways. So far, we have mainly used dialog boxes, but we have also seen examples of how we can write in a command window (MS-DOS Prompt) by using the method `System.out.println`. In this section, we will also see what to do to read data from the keyboard, via the command window Unfortunately, it is not necessarily easy to carry out input and output in Java, especially if we have to enter numerical data or want to format output. There are several reasons for this. One is that Java was primarily intended for the construction of GUI programs. Another reason is that Java is so general. When we input or output data, we use *streams*. Much can be done with streams but big demands are made of the programmer if he or she is to use them correctly. A third reason is that, because Java offers so much, we tend to raise our expectations of our programs, as compared with other programming languages. We do not have to produce input and output in a standard form dictated by the programming language. We can opt for the format used by the country in which we happen to be. The text input and output can also be coded in different forms in the various countries, and completely different alphabets can be used. We no longer have to put up with a situation where incomprehensible gobbledegook appears on the screen as soon as we use letters other than the "basic" a to z, that is, accented letters of the type ñ, ë and à.

If we try to write data making use of the standard classes in Java, we soon find out that it is a difficult business. When we program, however, it is essential to be able to input and output text easily. Even if the programs we write are GUI programs we may have to produce test output while developing the program. We may also need to read or write data from files. Unfortunately, there are no standard classes in Java for input and output that are easy to use. To make it easier for the programmer, therefore, we have constructed our own help classes, and these are described in Section 5.4.2. However, we shall begin by describing how we can read and write text with the help of Java's standard classes.

5.4.1 Reading and writing by using standard classes

The language of Java does not itself contain constructs for data input and output. To read and write data, therefore, we have to make use of streams. The stream classes are defined in the standard package `java.io`. A *stream* is a flow of data streaming in or out of a program; we differentiate between *input streams* and *output streams*. A stream may be originally from a file, from the keyboard, from a communication line such as a modem, or from some other input unit in the computer. Similarly, an output stream may be stored in a file, shown on the screen, or be sent out on a communication line. The class `System` (in the package `java.lang`) contains three different streams we can use in our Java programs. They are defined as class variables, with the names `System.in`, `System.out` and `System.err`, and correspond to *standard input*, *standard output* and *standard error*. Normally, *standard input* is connected to the keyboard, which means that everything we write there lands in the stream `System.in`. Both *standard output* and *standard error* are usually connected to a text window.

Printout

The stream `System.out`, which we have used in the book until now, is an object of class `PrintStream`. Two of the methods for this class are `print` and `println`. The difference between these two is that `println` places the printout cursor in a new line after printout has taken place. When there are repeated printouts, `println` sees to it that every printout lands in a new line. When we use `print`, on the other hand, printouts will follow each other on the same line. If, for example, we want to print out

```
What is your name?
```

we will use `print`:

```
System.out.print("What is your name? ");
```

We should not need to use `println` here, since it is natural for the user to print out the answer on the same line as the question.

We should know, in connection with the stream `System.out`, that it uses a *buffer*. This means that the printout will not necessarily be directly visible in the text window when it has been printed out by the program. This is particularly misleading in *interactive programs*, which write out questions for the user to answer. The program can wait for an answer to its question, although the question has not yet been presented to the user of the program. To be sure text shows up immediately, we sometimes have to empty the buffer, which is done by calling the method `flush`.

```
System.out.flush();
```

This should be done after method `print` has been called. If, on the other hand, we call `println`, this will not be necessary, as the buffer will be emptied automatically.

One problem with the stream `System.out` is that we do not always get correct printout, that is, when `LATIN_1` code (see Section 9.1) is not used in the text window. This is especially common when we use MS-DOS Prompt in Windows. It can also happen when the user is working in a language not based on the Latin alphabet. For instance, we may give the statement

```
System.out.println("Would you like some pâté?");
```

This printout looks fine if we are running a Unix system, for instance, which uses `LATIN_1` to code characters. But if we are running a PC (even if we are using Windows), then `LATIN_1` is not used in MS-DOS windows,[1] for historical reasons. Printout can then assume the sinister appearance

```
Would you like some pótú?
```

The coding used in MS-DOS works well with `LATIN_1` when we only need the first 128 characters, but for the remaining 128 (amongst them, all the accented letters) another coding system is used. This is not only a problem for MS-DOS. In all the countries that do not use the Latin alphabet, text is coded in some way other than with `LATIN_1`.

Let us now look at how we can print out numerical data for the stream `System.out`. The easiest way is simply to call the method `print` or `println` directly, with a numerical variable as argument, or to use the operator `+` together with a text. The numeral will then be converted automatically to text. We can write, for example:

```
int n = 8150;
double d = 0.058;
System.out.println(d);
System.out.println("n = " + n);
```

The printout will then be

```
0.058
n = 8150
```

---

[1] In Windows windows, on the other hand, `LATIN_1` is used. This is why this problem does not arise in GUI programs.

We will always get a standard format, where the number of decimals is determined automatically. Note, too, that we will always get a decimal point in the printout, even if we have a non-English installation. The standard format generally works well with integers, but in the case of real numbers it can look awful. Let us insert the statement:

```
System.out.println("Result: " + (n*d));
```

We will then get the printout:

```
Result: 472.70000000000005
```

For technical reasons, the last decimal place of the result may not always be exact when using real numbers.

If we want to be able to format printout, or use local conventions, we have to use a `NumberFormat` object, as described in Section 5.1. For example, if we run a Spanish system and give the statements

```
NumberFormat nf = NumberFormat.getInstance();
nf.setMaximumFractionDigits(1);
System.out.println("Result: " + nf.format(n*d));
```

the printout will be

```
Result: 472,7
```

Note that we now get the decimal comma automatically, instead of a decimal point.

Input

Data written at the keyboard will land in the stream `System.in`, which is an object of the class `java.io.InputStream`. We cannot read directly from this stream, however. Instead, we have to connect another stream to it. We do this using the model in Figure 5.4. In the program it is convenient to use a stream of class `BufferedReader`. This cannot be connected immediately to the stream `System.in`. We have to use an intermediary stream of class `InputStreamReader`, as shown in the figure. When we create a new stream in a program, we indicate, as parameter to the constructor, the other stream the new stream should read from. In order to create a new stream `myIn`, in accordance with the figure, we write the declaration:

```
BufferedReader myIn = new BufferedReader
                    (new InputStreamReader(System.in));
```

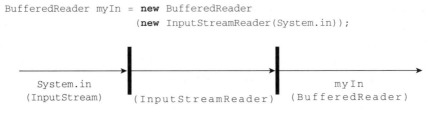

Figure 5.4

5. Reading and writing

In class `BufferedReader`, there is a serviceable method called `readLine`, which reads in a whole line at a time. In order to use `readLine`, we must declare a variable of type `String` which will refer to the input line.

```
String s;
```

We then write out a question to the user:

```
System.out.print("What is your name? "); System.out.flush();
```

Note that we have to call `flush`, since we are using `print` and not `println`. The input itself is now done with the method `readLine`. It returns a reference to a `String` object containing the input line.

```
s = myIn.readLine();
```

We finish by writing out the greeting

```
System.out.println("Hello " + s + "!");
```

Note that the method `readLine` waits until the user has entered a whole line and finished it by pressing the Enter key. The end-of-line character (or end-of-line characters, if the Enter key produces more than one) is read by `readLine` but will *not* be included in the text that is returned.

Input errors may sometimes arise when entering data. The input methods, for example `readLine`, will then generate an error signal of class `IOException`. The method in which such an error signal arises must either itself deal with it, or send it on. How we deal with error signals is described later in the book. We choose the simpler alternative here, sending the error signal further on. This will happen automatically but at the beginning of the method, where the reading is done, we must indicate that an error signal might arise. We do this by writing **throws** *event name* after the parameter list at the beginning of the method. If, for example, the call of `readLine` lies in the method `main`, the introduction to `main` must have the following appearance:

```
public static void main (String arg[]) throws IOException {
```

When entering data, the user often has to indicate that he or she does not intend to write any more. A technique using *end of file* is used where, at the keyboard, the user writes a special combination of characters indicating an end to the input. In MS-DOS this combination of characters is usually Ctrl-Z and in Unix Ctrl-D. If *end of file* is indicated when the program has called the method `readLine`, `readLine` will return the value `null`, that is, an empty reference. Note that this is not the same thing as a blank line. If we simply press Enter when the program has called `readLine`, it will return not `null` but a reference to a `String` object containing a text of length 0.

There is also a method in class `BufferedReader` called `read`, which reads a single character at a time. For example, we can give the following statements:

134

```
System.out.print("Type a character "); System.out.flush();
char c = (char) myIn.read(); // type conversion needed
System.out.println("You typed " + c);
```

The method read will give, not as we might think, a char as result but a value of type int. This is why an explicit type conversion to type char must be made before the result can be assigned to the variable c. The method read does not return a char because read gives the value −1 when the user has indicated *end of file*. A value of type char cannot be negative, so type int is used instead.

The method read waits, just like method readLine, until the user has pressed the Enter key. The difference is that read only reads *a single character*. Suppose, for example, that the execution of the program lines given above produces the following output:

```
Type a character Z (the user presses the Enter key having typed Z)
You typed Z
```

When the user presses the Enter key, one or two characters are put in the input stream. If we are running a Unix system, the character '\n' will be produced, and in MS-DOS the two characters '\r' and '\n' are produced. (These characters are described in Chapter 9.) This, or these, character(s) remain in the input buffer after the character 'Z' has been read into the program and will be the first character, or characters, to be read the *next* time read or readLine is called. The method readLine is recommended rather than read, since readLine functions in the same way in both Unix and MS-DOS.

Unfortunately, the standard class BufferedReader contains no methods for the input of numerical data. Therefore, if we want to read an integer or a real number, we first have to read the input line in the form of text and then make a type conversion to the numerical type we want. The following lines demonstrate how we can read an integer for the variable i and a real number for the variable x:

```
System.out.print("Enter an integer number: ");
System.out.flush();
String s = myIn.readLine();
int i = Integer.parseInt(s);
System.out.print("Enter a real number: ");
System.out.flush();
s = myIn.readLine();
double x = Double.parseDouble();
```

The type conversion methods parseInt and parseDouble assume, as we know, that the user of the program has input the numerical values in "English" format, with a decimal point. Another alternative is to use the methods Parse.toInt and Parse.toDouble, as we did in Section 5.3.1. It is then possible to use a format which complies with local conventions, such as using a decimal comma instead of a decimal point. Putting space characters in front of the input number will not cause an error either. To input an integer to variable i and a real number to x, we can write the statements:

```
System.out.print("Enter an integer number: ");
System.out.flush();
String s = myIn.readLine();
int i = Parse.toInt(s);
System.out.print("Enter a real number: ");
System.out.flush();
s = myIn.readLine();
double x = Parse.toDouble(s);
```

If we want to do an error check on input data, we can use exactly the same technique as described in Section 5.3.2. It is also possible to input lines with several items of input data on the same line. We can then use the class `StringTokenizer`, as described in Section 5.3.3, to divide up the input text into several sections.

5.4.2   Reading and writing with the use of help classes

As we can see from the last section, it could be complicated to read and write using Java's standard classes. In this section we shall be describing the three classes `ExtendedReader`, `ExtendedWriter` and `Std`, which will make things much easier for the programmer. We will put these three classes into our own "standard package"

Methods in the class extra.ExtendedReader	
`readLine()`	reads a line, returns a `String`, always begins reading on a new line, gives **null** upon *end of file*
`readWord()`	reads a word (a sequence of non-blank characters), returns a `String`, gives **null** upon *end of file*
`readInt()`	reads and returns an **int**, makes error checks
`readLong()`	reads and returns a **long**, makes error checks
`readDouble()`	reads and returns a **double**, makes error checks
`readChar()`	reads a character, returns an **int** with the character code, gives -1 upon *end of file*
`lookAhead()`	looks ahead at the next character in the input stream without taking it up yet, gives the same return value as `readChar`
`skip(n)`	skips n characters, returns a number of skipped characters
`skipLine()`	skips the rest of the line read in
`more()`	gives **true** if there are more non-blank characters to be read
`setFormat(r)`	indicates that the `NumberFormat` object r will be used
`getFormat()`	returns the `NumberFormat` object that is used
`getFileReader(`*name*`)`	a class method that returns a new `ExtendedReader` object which reads from the file *name* (*name* is a `String`)
`close()`	closes the file connected to the stream

extra. For this package, see page 125. These program texts are available from the book's website. In order to take advantage of help classes, users will have to take home the program texts and compile them. Users must then make sure that the compiled files are in the package extra. They must also set the environment variable CLASSPATH so that the Java interpreter can find the package extra. How this is done is dealt with on page 125.

The class ExtendedReader is a subclass of the standard class BufferedReader, and it contains several methods for various kinds of data input. We can input text, either in the form of entire lines, or in words and numerals.

The class ExtendedWriter is a subclass of the standard class PrintWriter. With the help of class ExtendedWriter we can print out and format various kinds of data. Real numbers can be written either in standard form or exponentially. If a real number is so small or so large that it cannot be written in the normal way, printout in the exponential form will take place automatically.

Instance methods in the class extra.ExtendedWriter	
println()	begins a new line in the printout
print(x)	writes out x with exactly the number of positions needed. x can be a value of one of the simple built-in types, a String, a **char** array, or of a class having the method toString
println(x)	the same as print(x) followed by println()
print(x,n)	the same as print(x) but using *at least* n positions in the printout; filling up takes place to the left of x for numerical types and for the types **bool** and **char**, filling up takes place to the right of x for other types, and blank characters are used if setFillChar has not been called
println(x,n)	the same as print(x,n) followed by println()
print(x,n,d)	writes out a real number x, with a total of at least n positions, of which d are used for decimals
println(x,n,d)	the same as print(x,n,d) followed by println()
printExp and printlnExp	write out a real number exponentially; they exist in the same variants as print and println, respectively
setFillChar(c)	indicates that c will be a fill-in character
setFormat(r)	indicates that the NumberFormat object r will be used
getFormat()	returns the NumberFormat object used by the stream
close()	closes the stream
flush()	empties the stream's buffer

5. Reading and writing

The class `Std` contains declarations of three ready-made streams, `in`, `out` and `err`. The stream `in` is an object of the class `ExtendedReader`, and the streams `out` and `err` are objects of class `ExtendedWriter`. These three streams correspond to *standard input*, *standard output* and *standard error*, respectively. *Standard input* is normally related to the keyboard, and the two others to a text window on the screen. From now on, we shall be using the streams `Std.in` and `Std.out` to read and write.

To demonstrate how reading and writing proceeds using the new help classes, let us look at a program that calculates the cost of hiring a car. We will assume that we know the number of days for which we wish to hire the car, together with the hire charges per day. It would then be easy to calculate the total cost. However, we shall make the program a little more realistic by supposing that we are in Spain on holiday and that the hire cost is given in euros. Shunning mental arithmetic, we want the program to write out the total cost in both euros and US dollars. To this end, we will have to give the current exchange rate as input data. We also would like to be able to make several calculations, consecutively, to compare the costs for different numbers of days and different cars with varying daily hire charges. The exchange rate does not change between calculations, so we shall enter this only once at the beginning. We now show what such a program looks like. Whatever is written in italics has been written by the user. Everything else will have been written by the program.

```
Exchange rate? 0.93
Type of car? Opel Corsa
Number of days? 3
Cost per day? 96.50
Total cost for Opel Corsa: 289.50 euro ($269.24)

Type of car? Ford Focus
Number of days? 3
Cost per day? 113.25
Total cost for Ford Focus: 339.75 euro ($315.97)
Type of car?  (here the user indicates end of file)
```

The program is terminated when the user indicates that he or she does not intend to enter more input data, by writing a special combination of characters at the keyboard. In an MS-DOS window this is usually Ctrl-Z and in Unix Ctrl-D.

The program will look like this:

```
import extra.*;
public class Travel {
   public static void main (String[] arg) {
      String car;
      int noOfDays;
      double costPerDay, totalCost;
      final double exch;
```

```
Std.out.print("Exchange rate? ");
exch = Std.in.readDouble();

while (true) {
    Std.in.skipLine(); // read type of car from a new line
    Std.out.print("Type of car? ");
    car = Std.in.readLine();
    if (car == null)  // end of file ?
        break; // break the while statement
    Std.out.print("Number of days? ");
    noOfDays = Std.in.readInt();
    Std.out.print("Cost per day? ");
    costPerDay = Std.in.readDouble();
    totalCost = noOfDays * costPerDay;
    Std.out.print("Total cost for " + car + ": ");
    Std.out.print(totalCost, 1, 2);
    Std.out.print(" euro ($");
    Std.out.print(totalCost*exch, 1, 2);
    Std.out.println(")");
    }
  }
}
```

First, we declare the variables that will be used. The variable `exch` has been declared as **final** because it will not be changed once it has got its value.

The class `Std` is constructed so that printout will take place in accordance with local conventions. If we use `println` for some output, the output marker will automatically be moved forward to a new line *after* the data is printed out, while the output marker remains at the end of the same line if we use `print`. When real numbers are written out, for example in the statement `Std.out.print(totalCost,1,2);`, format arguments can be given. The second argument means that output should take place with *at least* one output position. The last argument means that we want two decimals in the output.

When we used the stream `System.out`, we had problems with output in windows not using `LATIN_1` code. This applied, for example, to MS-DOS windows in Windows. We do not have this problem with `Std.out`. If, for example, we give the statement

```
Std.out.println("Would you like some pâté?");
```

the printout will be correct:

```
Would you like some pâté?
```

The class `Std` is constructed such that at the start of the program it checks to see whether Windows is running. This done, it will check the language that is used in the installation, and the streams will be initialized so that translation takes place automatically to and from the MS-DOS coding used in the actual country. (If an English system is being run, MS-DOS code 437 will be used.)

When the stream `System.out` was used in interactive programs, the method `flush` had to be called following output to ensure that text would show up immediately. If instead we use `Std.out`, we do not have to worry about this, as the output buffer will be emptied automatically before input operation. Interactive questions and answers will then always take place in the correct order.

Let us now read from the stream `Std.in`. We use either method `readInt` or method `readDouble` to read in numerals. These methods give as result an **int** and a **double**, respectively, and if we do not indicate anything else, they will assume that input data follows local convention. Both these methods will check to see that input data has been indicated correctly. Were we to make a mistake, for example by writing a letter instead of a digit, we would get an error message asking us to enter the number again.

```
Exchange rate? 0.p3
Illegal number. Try again
0.93
Type of car? Opel Corsa
```

The car model is a text, and to read texts we use the method `readLine`. This method reads in a whole line and gives as result a reference to a `String` object containing the text read in. If the user writes Ctrl-Z (or Ctrl-D) to indicate *end of file*, `readLine` will return an empty reference, that is, the value **null**.

When we want to write out numerical values together with texts, we can also use the operator + for texts. The printout of the result for our car hiring program could then take place with the statement:

```
Std.out.println("Total cost for " + car + ": " + totalCost +
                "euro ($" + totalCost*exch + ")");
```

But then the conversion from numerals to text will not be carried out by class `Std`, but in standard fashion. We will neither get local conventions in the printout nor be able to format the number of positions and the number of decimals in the printout. If we had used this statement in the car hire program, the final output in our example on page 138 would have been:

```
Total cost for Ford Focus: 339.75 euro ($315.96750000000003)
```

The stream `Std.out` uses a `NumberFormat` object internally to format output; in the same way, `Std.in` uses a `NumberFormat` object to interpret input numbers. If we do not want local conventions for reading and writing, we can tell these streams to use another `NumberFormat` object. We do this with the help of the method `setFormat`. If we want French conventions in our program, we can write, for instance:

Class methods in the class extra.ExtendedWriter	
`formatNum(x)`	formats x with exactly as many positions as are required; x can be a value of a simple numerical type, gives as result a value of type `String`
`formatNum(x,n)`	the same as `formatNum(x)` but uses *at least* n positions, filling up takes place with blank spaces to the left of x
`formatNum(x,n,t)`	the same as `formatNum(x,n)` but filling up takes place with the character t to the left of x
`formatNum(x,n,d)`	the same as `formatNum(x,n)` but with d decimals
`formatNum(x,n,d,t)`	the same as `formatNum(x,n,d)` but filling up takes place with the character t to the left of x
`formatExp`	formats a real number in exponential form; exists in the same variants as `formatNum`
`useExponent(x)`	gives **true** if the number x is so small or large that it must be written out or formatted in exponential form
`adjustLeft(s,n,t)`	returns a copy of the text s adjusted to the left in at least n positions; filling up takes place with the character t
`adjustRight(s,n,t)`	returns a copy of the text s adjusted to the right in at least n positions; filling up takes place with the character t
`toFixedLength(s,n)`	returns a copy of the text s adjusted to the left in precisely n positions; truncation or filling up takes place with spaces
`setStaticFormat(r)`	sets the `NumberFormat` object r to be used by the class methods
`getStaticFormat()`	returns the `NumberFormat` object used by the class methods
`getFileWriter(`*name*`)`	gives a new `ExtendedWriter` object, which writes to a new file *name* (*name* is a `String`)
`getFileWriter(`*name*`,`**true**`)`	gives a new `ExtendedWriter` object, which adds text to the end of the file *name*

```
NumberFormat r = NumberFormat.getInstance(Locale.FRENCH);
Std.in.setFormat(r);
Std.out.setFormat(r);
```

A decimal comma is then used instead of the decimal point for input and output. We can also change the characteristics of a `NumberFormat` object. For example, if we want the digits to be grouped in threes when numerals are printed out, we can enter:

```
Std.out.getFormat().setGroupingUsed(true);
```

There are also some serviceable class methods in class `ExtendedWriter`, the method `formatNum`, for example, which formats a numeral in the same way as with output, but instead of writing out the number, the formatted number is returned as a `String`.

5.5 Text files

The variables used in a program exist in a computer's primary memory but only for as long as the program is running. However, many programs need to store data permanently. To do this, we have to use a secondary memory (often a disk memory). Data in the secondary memory is stored in the form of *files*. A file is an arbitrarily long sequence of bytes (8 bits). These bytes most often contain characters coded in accordance with the LATIN_1 code (see Chapter 9) or some other code. A file containing such characters is called a *text file*. But there are many files that do not contain text. Such files are usually called *binary files*. In this section we shall only be discussing text files. To read or write a file in Java, we have to connect a stream to the file. The simplest way of doing this is to use our own help classes ExtendedReader and ExtendedWriter. After describing how this is done, we describe the procedure, in Section 5.5.2, should we only want to use Java's standard classes.

5.5.1   Using help classes

To connect a new stream to an existing text file, we can use the class method getFileReader in the class ExtendedReader. This method should have an argument of type String which contains the file's name (the name the file has in the file system). We can give either a simple name or a search path. For example, we can write:

```
ExtendedReader f1=ExtendedReader.getFileReader("report.txt");
ExtendedReader f2=ExtendedReader.getFileReader(" c:\\x\\y.dat");
```

Note that we must write a double \\ character. This is because the character \ has special significance. Two streams are created here, f1 and f2. (If the file indicated as argument does not exist, the method getFileReader will return the value **null**.) We can then use the methods in class ExtendedReader and read from the files exactly as we do from Std.in. For example, if we wish to read in the first line in file f1, we write:

```
String line = f1.readLine();
```

We shall now write a program that illustrates how input is read from text files. Suppose we have a situation involving an automatic pump at a self-service petrol station. Every time a customer buys petrol, the pump will register the number of litres bought, the date, the time of day and the number of the customer's account card, on magnetic tape. From time to time, the service staff come to retrieve the magnetic tape. Information on it is read into a computer and stored in the form of a text file, in which there is a line for every purchase. Each line has the form:

```
nnn.nn dd/mm/yy hh:mm:ss xxxxxxxxxxxxx
```

As can be seen, the number of litres of petrol sold comes first in the line. Let us suppose that the file has the name log.txt. Our program will then read in all the data recorded

and write out the total amount of petrol sold within a certain period. Output might look
like this:

```
First time: 14/10/03 09:14:25
Last time:  17/10/03 11:02:37
Total number of litres: 5679.18
```

The program will look as follows:

```
import extra.*;
public class Petrol {
  public static void main (String[] arg) {
    ExtendedReader f = ExtendedReader.getFileReader("log.txt");
    // read the first line
    double litre = f.readDouble();
    String date  = f.readWord();
    String time  = f.readWord();
    String cardNo = f.readWord();
    Std.out.println("First time: " + date + " " + time);
    double tot = litre;

    // read other lines
    while (f.more()) {
      litre = f.readDouble();
      tot += litre;
      date = f.readWord();
      time = f.readWord();
      cardNo = f.readWord();
    }

    Std.out.println("Last time: " + date + " " + time);
    Std.out.print  ("Total number of litres: ");
    Std.out.println(tot, 1, 2); // left-adjusted, 2 decimals
  }
}
```

Note that we have to use the method more to see when the file will end. This is because
numerals come first in every line. If we try to call the method readDouble or readInt
when the file has ended, we will get an error message.

It is just as easy to store output in a text file. We then use the method getFileWriter
in class ExtendedWriter to connect a stream to a file. For example, we can write:

```
ExtendedWriter w = ExtendedWriter.getFileWriter("newfile.txt");
```

If the file newfile.txt does not already exist, it will be created. But if there is a file
with this name already, it will be overwritten with new information. To avoid this, we
can use an alternative form:

```
ExtendedWriter w = ExtendedWriter.getFileWriter
                    ("newfile.txt", true);
```

The existing file will not be overwritten. Instead, the new information will be added at the end of the file. If, for some reason, a new file cannot be created, the method `getFileWriter` will return the value `null`.

We can now use all of the methods in class `ExtendedWriter` to write to the file, in exactly the same way as we write to `Std.out`. For example, we can write:

```
w.print("Result: ");
w.println(x, 1, 3);
```

The next program we will look at copies one text file to another. When the program starts, it asks for the names of the two files. When copying is finished, the program tells us the number of lines copied. This could look like this:

```
Input file? myfile.txt
Output file? copy.txt
518 lines copied
```

If the input file does not exist, or if an output file cannot be created, the program produces an error message and will be interrupted. The program reads one line at a time from the input file. It is an easy matter to see when the file has ended, since the method `readLine` returns the value `null` when it can read no further.

```
import extra.*;
class FileCopy {
  public static void main (String[] arg) {
     // open the input file
     Std.out.print("Input file? ");
     String name = Std.in.readWord();
     ExtendedReader inFile = ExtendedReader.getFileReader(name);
     if (inFile == null) {
        Std.out.println("Cannot find " + name);
        System.exit(1);
     }

     // open the output file
     Std.out.print("Output file? ");
     name = Std.in.readWord();
     ExtendedWriter outFile =ExtendedWriter.getFileWriter(name);

     if (outFile == null) {
        Std.out.println("Cannot create" + name);
        System.exit(2);
     }

     // copy
     int n=0;
```

```
    while (true) {
       String line = inFile.readLine();
       if (line == null)
          break;
       outFile.println(line);
       n = n + 1;
    }
    outFile.close();  // NB Important!
    Std.out.println(n + " lines copied");
  }
}
```

Note that we should always close an output file when we have finished writing. If this is not done, characters remaining in the buffer will never be printed out.

5.5.2   Using standard classes

If we want to make use of standard classes only, it is simplest to use the classes `FileReader` and `FileWriter`. Using these classes, we can connect a stream to the file we want to read from or write to. When creating the stream, we simply give the file's name as parameter to the constructor. Let us begin by discussing how files are read. In a program, we should not read directly from a stream of class `FileReader`. Instead, we should use a stream of class `BufferedReader` and connect it to the `FileReader` stream. (Compare this with our procedure for reading from standard input, in Section 5.4.1.) For example, we can create a stream `inFile` and connect it to the file `indata.txt`.

```
BufferedReader inFile = new BufferedReader
                        (new FileReader("indata.txt "));
```

If there is no file with this name, the constructor would give an error signal of type `FileNotFoundException`. If we did not trap this error, we would have to write the words **throws** `FileNotFoundException` at the beginning of the actual method. The method `readLine` can now be used to read one line at a time from the file. If we want to read in numerical data, then we ourselves must make the conversion from text to the numerical type we want, exactly as we did when reading from the keyboard.

When writing output in a program, we may want to make use of a stream of class `PrintWriter`. The methods `print` and `println` are in this class, and they can be used in exactly the same way as when we write to the stream `System.out`. A `PrintWriter` stream should be connected to a file using a `FileWriter` stream but we do not do this directly. Instead, we make use of an intermediary stream of class `BufferedWriter`. For example, we can make the following declaration to create `outFile`, a `PrintWriter` stream which can be used for output to a file called `outdata.txt`.

```
PrintWriter outFile = new PrintWriter(new BufferedWriter(
                      new FileWriter("outdata.txt ")));
```

There will be an error signal here too, of type `FileNotFoundException`, if the file cannot be opened.

We conclude by giving an alternative version of the program `FileCopy` on page 144.

```
import java.io.*;
class FileCopy2 {
  public static void main (String[] arg)
                    throws IOException, FileNotFoundException {
    // create a stream from standard input
    BufferedReader myIn = new BufferedReader
                          (new InputStreamReader(System.in));
    // open the input file
    System.out.print("Input file? "); System.out.flush();
    String name = myIn.readLine();
    BufferedReader inFile = new BufferedReader
                            (new FileReader(name));

    // open the output file
    System.out.print("Output file? ");
    name = myIn.readLine();
    PrintWriter outFile = new PrintWriter(new BufferedWriter
                                    (new FileWriter(name)));
    // copy
    int n=0;
    while (true) {
      String line = inFile.readLine();
      if (line == null)
        break;
      outFile.println(line);
      n++;
    }
    outFile.close();
    System.out.println(n + " lines copied");
  }
}
```

5.6   Dates and times

It is not unusual to have to read the time and the passing of time, and display them in edited format. (We saw an example of this in Section 2.8.) For this reason, we will round off this chapter by describing Java's standard classes for date and time.

5.6.1   The class `Date`

The most basic class in Java for describing times is the class `Date` in the package `java.util`. An object of class `Date` will describe a specific time that includes both the stroke of the clock (in Greenwich Mean Time, GMT) and the date. Times are stored with an accuracy of one millisecond. Internally in the class, they are stored as the number of milliseconds that have elapsed since 1 January 1970. We could indicate these milliseconds when creating an object of class `Date` but for the constructor an argument is not normally indicated. The computer's clock is then read automatically, and the new object will contain the time when it was created:

```
Date nu = new Date();  // describes the actual time
```

What we get is a snapshot. The object `now` is not changed when the time continues but it will contain the time when it was created. In earlier versions of Java, class `Date` was used to convert to years, months, days, hours, etc., but class `Date` cannot manage to present dates and times in an international format. Instead we have to make use of the standard classes `Calendar` and `DateFormat`. We shall describe both of them but must first deal with another standard class, the class `TimeZone`. Like the classes `Calendar` and `DateFormat`, it lies in the package `java.util`.

5.6.2   The class `TimeZone`

It is well known that different places in the world use different time zones. In Central Europe, for example, they are one hour ahead of GMT, and on the American East Coast, they are five hours behind GMT. To read and present the time correctly, we have to know what time zone is being used. In Java we use the class `java.util.TimeZone` to keep track of time zones. There is always an actual time zone (default time zone). We can get the actual time zone by calling the class method `getDefault`:

```
TimeZone tz = TimeZone.getDefault();
```

Another class method in the class `TimeZone` is `getTimeZone`, which gives an arbitrary time zone as result. A text with the zone's designation is given as parameter. (The class method `getAvailableIDs` gives a list of designations that can be used.) Some examples are "GMT", "ECT" (European Central Time) and "JST" (Japanese Standard Time). For example, we can write:

```
tz = TimeZone.getTimeZone("JST");
```

The default time zone can be changed by a call of the class method `setDefault`, which should have a `TimeZone` as parameter:

```
TimeZone.setDefault(TimeZone.getTimeZone("ECT"));
```

The idea here is that an actual time zone (default time zone) will be set automatically by the Java interpreter and information retrieved from the operating system. Unfortunately, this does not always work as we would like it to, so we can insert a call of the method `setDefault` at the beginning of our program, as described above. Another solution is to use an extra parameter for the `java` command when starting the program. For instance, if the program is called `Pr`, we can give the command:

```
java -Duser.timezone=EST Pr
```

With the D parameter, we can indicate several properties for the Java interpreter. For example, we could indicate the correct language and country if the system does not do so automatically. We could write:[1]

```
java -Duser.timezone=ECT -Duser.language=fr -Duser.region=FR Pr
```

5.6.3 The class `Calendar`

The best way of describing time in Java is to make use of the class `java.util.Calendar`. An object of class `Calendar` contains a `Date` object internally, so that we do not need the class `Date` ourselves when using `Calendar`. Then to create a new `Calendar` object, we can call the class method `getInstance`:

```
Calendar cal = Calendar.getInstance();
```

The object created is initialized automatically to describe the actual time. The `Calendar` object will also keep track of the time zone concerned, an important factor when the time is to be read. The default time zone will apply if a time zone is not indicated in the call above. If we want to, we can create a `Calendar` object for another time zone. If `tz` is a `TimeZone`, as before, we can write:

```
Calendar cal = Calendar.getInstance(tz);
```

The most interesting of the methods in class `Calendar` is the method `get`, used to read the time. It gives a whole number as result. The method `get` will have an argument indicating whatever aspects of the time we wish to read. We might wish to read the year, the hour, or the number of the week, for instance. A number of constants we use as arguments are defined in class `Calendar`. We could write:

```
int v = cal.get(Calendar.WEEK_OF_YEAR);  // reads the week number
int m = cal.get(Calendar.MINUTE);        // reads minutes
int s = cal.get(Calendar.SECOND);        // reads seconds
int i = cal.get(Calendar.MILLISECOND);   // reads milliseconds
int h = cal.get(Calendar.HOUR_OF_DAY);   // reads hours
```

Examples of other constants are YEAR, MONTH, DAY_OF_MONTH and HOUR. The latter reads the time in the 12-hour system, with AM and PM. Please note that the months are

---

[1] If this is thought to be inelegant, it might be a good idea to create the command in advance. In MS-DOS, for example, we can create a BAT file, or make use of the command `doskey`. In Unix, a script file can be created, or an alias defined.

numbered from 0, strangely enough, which means that `cal.get(Calendar.MONTH)` returns the number 0 if the month is January and value 11 if `cal` contains the month December.

If you want a `Calendar` object to describe some point in time other than the present, you can call the method `set`, which functions along the same lines as the method `get`. For example, we can zero the hours by doing the call:

```
cal.set(Calendar.HOUR_OF_DAY, 0);
```

You can also change a `Calendar` object by calling the method `add`. Using it, you can add (or subtract) the number of time units. The call

```
cal.add(Calendar.DAY_OF_MONTH, 10); // move 10 days ahead
```

changes the object `cal` so that it describes a point in time ten days forwards, and the call

```
cal.add(Calendar.MONTH, -3);        // move 3 months back
```

changes `cal` so that it describes a point in time three months previously.

You can also change the time zone for a `Calendar` object:

```
cal.setTimeZone(tz);
```

5.6.4 The class `DateFormat`

The last class to discuss is the class `DateFormat`, which can be found in the package `java.text` (as against the other classes in this section, which lie in the package `java.util`). We use the class `DateFormat` when we want to convert a time into text form. We first have to get a suitable instance of the class `DateFormat`. We can call one of the class methods `getTimeInstance`, `getDateInstance`, `getDateTimeInstance` and `getInstance`. The first one gives an object that formats a point in time as the stroke of the clock. The second one gives an object that formats the time as a date, and the last two give objects that format both the date and the stroke of the clock. This is best illustrated in an example; we will begin by creating four different objects for formatting:

```
DateFormat f1 = DateFormat.getInstance();
DateFormat f2 = DateFormat.getTimeInstance();
DateFormat f3 = DateFormat.getDateInstance(DateFormat.SHORT);
DateFormat f4 = DateFormat.getDateTimeInstance
                    (DateFormat.SHORT, DateFormat.MEDIUM);
```

The class methods `getTimeInstance` and `getDateInstance` can have an extra argument that indicates formatting style. We can choose between FULL, LONG, MEDIUM, SHORT and DEFAULT. The class method `getDateTimeInstance` must always have two arguments, one for date and one for time.

5. *Reading and writing*

As an alternative, we can create a formatter of class SimpleDateFormat (which is a subclass of DateFormat). In the constructor, we specify how we want the text to be formatted by using a special text. The exact rules for the appearance of this text are fairly comprehensive. So we will just refer the reader to the documentation of the class SimpleDateFormat. One example is shown here: We declare a further formatter:

```
DateFormat f5 = new SimpleDateFormat("EEE d MMM yyyy");
```

(Here, EEE represents the name of the day of the week, d is the number of the day, MMM is the name of the month and yyyy is the year.)

We will now write out a time in five different ways. The conversion to text is done by the method format. It will have an object of class Date as argument and give a text as result. We will begin by creating a Date object:

```
Date now = new Date();
```

If we had already had a Calendar object cal and had wanted to write this out instead, we could have written:

```
Date now = cal.getTime();
```

We now call the method format for the five different objects, f1, f2, f3, f4 and f5:

```
System.out.println(f1.format(now));
System.out.println(f2.format(now));
System.out.println(f3.format(now));
System.out.println(f4.format(now));
System.out.println(f5.format(now));
```

The formatting of the time and date will depend on the local conventions applied; see Section 5.2. If English conventions apply, the printout could be:

```
01/06/02 17:51
17:51:38
01/06/02
01/06/02 17:51:38
Sat 1 Jun 2002
```

If we had instead indicated American conventions, for instance by giving the statement:

```
Locale.setDefault(Locale.US);
```

the printout of the first four lines would have had the form:

```
6/1/02 5:51 PM
5:51:38 PM
6/1/02
6/1/02 5:51:38 PM
```

150

It is an easy matter to change the time zone without changing the default time zone. We could make the statements:

```
f2.setTimeZone(TimeZone.getTimeZone("JST"));
System.out.println("In Japan the time is now " +f2.format(now));
```

and we would get the printout:

```
In Japan the time is now 00:51:38
```

We finish off by writing a new version of the program DisplayTime1 on page 66. Our own class Time is not actually needed. We can simplify the program by using a formatter.

```
import java.util.*;
import java.text.*;
public class DisplayTime3 {
  public static void main (String[] arg) {
    DateFormat f = DateFormat.getTimeInstance();
    System.out.println("The time is" + f.format(new Date()));
  }
}
```

5.7   Exercises

1. Write a program that calculates and prints out the number of kilometres a car has travelled during the last year and, in addition, calculates the car's average petrol consumption per kilometre. Input data for your program should be the daily meter reading and the meter reading for a year, together with the number of litres of petrol consumed during the year (indicated as a real number). The output should look like this:

```
Number of kilometres travelled:  1487
Number of litres of petrol:       1235.4
Consumption per kilometre:        0.83
```

2. Put in tests to check the input data in the program CarRent3 on page 128.

3. Write a program that calculates the amount of change you should receive when you have gone shopping, together with the type of bills. Input data for the program should be the price to be paid for goods and the amount actually tendered. For the sake of simplicity, let us suppose that all amounts are a whole number of US dollars. For example, if your shopping cost $51 and you paid with a $100 bill, your program should write out that you get change consisting of two $20 bills, one $5 bill and four $1 bills (or coins).

4. Suppose that a bank gives *p%* interest on deposited capital. Suppose further that you can deposit *d* dollars. Write a program that shows how the capital accrues interest, calculated as compound interest, during the first 10 years. The output of your program should indicate the size of your capital, including interest, after each of the 10 years. The interest rate and the capital deposited should be the input data for your program. Use dialog boxes.

5. A text file called `temp.txt` contains temperatures that are recorded at one o'clock in the afternoon at a certain place, for one month. Write a program that reads the file, calculates and prints out the highest recorded temperature, together with the average of all temperatures.

6. A text file contains information about a number of persons, and there are two lines in the file for every person. The person's name and address are on the first line, while on the second line are the person's age, height and weight. The height is given in centimetres (cm). In order to carry out a medical enquiry on very tall persons, you want to try to find all persons at least 200 cm tall. Your task is to write a program that reads files containing personal data. Your program should create a new text file that only contains data on very tall persons. The name of this file should be read in by the program.

7. Write a program that reads a text file and writes out the number of letters, digits and other characters the file contains. *Hint*: Make use of some of the class methods in the standard class `Character`.

8. In the Romany language, all the consonants are doubled and an 'o' is placed between the doubled consonants. Vowels and other characters remain unchanged. A text file contains a secret message written in the Romany language. Write a program that reads in the file and writes out the secret message in plain English on the screen. If, for example, the file contains the text `"hoheyoy alololol yoyou roromomanoniesos"`, the function should write out `"hey all you romanies"`.

9. Write a program that works as a very simple calculator. The user should be able to input simple expressions in a dialog box. The expressions should have the format `a ? b`, where `a` and `b` are real numbers and `?` is one of the characters `+ - *` or `/`. The program should then calculate the expression and show the result in a another dialog box. Design the program so that this procedure can be repeated an arbitrary number of times. The program should not terminate until the user clicks `Exit` in the input dialog box. Put in error traps. For simplicity, you can demand that the user should type a space character between each section of the expression. *Tip*: Use the class `StringTokenizer`.

10. Assume that you have a text file which contains a number of words. Each word is on a separate line in the file. The task is to construct a class `Randomword`, which selects a word from the file at random. The class Randomword should contain a parameterless method called oneWord, which gives a String as its result containing one of the words in the file. Each time you call oneWord, one of the words in the file should be chosen at random, with the same probability. The class Randomword should also contain a constructor with a parameter that contains the name of the file.

Tip: In the constructor, you input the entire file, line by line, and count the number of words in the file. Say that the file contains n words. In the method oneWord, you then randomly choose a number k, which is in the interval from 1 to n. You then read k words from the file and give the last word as the result. You have to open the file again every time you are going to read it from the beginning.

GUI components

6

In Chapter 1, we had a small foretaste of how to write programs with graphical user interfaces (GUIs). Most GUI programs have similar interfaces. For example, they use buttons and pull-down menus. Java contains a number of standard classes, which are easy to use, when you want to create GUI components in a program. In this chapter, we will discuss these standard GUI classes. The most important components which can be included as components in a window will be covered here. In Chapter 7 we will show how you can construct your own GUI components and in Chapter 8 we discuss various techniques for assembling components and influencing their appearance. Further GUI components, such as menus and dialog boxes, are discussed in Chapter 14. The goal of this chapter is also to illustrate how useful and powerful the concept of classes is, and how you can use ready-made classes to implement a quite sophisticated program relatively easily.

6.1 A summary

Java contains two sets of standard GUI classes: *awt* (Abstract Window Toolkit) and *Swing*, which are defined in packages `java.awt` and `javax.swing` respectively. The older of them is awt, whereas Swing has been introduced in later versions of Java. Swing contains newer, "hotted-up" versions of most classes in awt, plus a set of new classes. The classes in Swing that have direct equivalents in awt have the same name, but with a `J` in front. The class `JButton`, for example, is a class in Swing which replaces the class `Button` in awt.

We will use the Swing package in this book. However, you cannot just replace awt by Swing, since the basic classes in Swing are subclasses of the corresponding classes in awt. This means that all Swing classes are subclasses of awt classes, directly or indirectly. As we discussed in Section 1.14, it can also be suitable to use the older awt classes when you implement applets.

Swing offers the programmer more facilities than awt. Swing is also more flexibly constructed, which means that it is easier to construct new classes, which describe new

GUI components, for example, and to modify the screen display to suit different platforms.

The basic difference between awt and Swing is that most classes in Swing generate so-called *lightweight* components, whereas the classes in awt give *heavyweight* components. When a heavyweight component is to be displayed on screen, the tools in the computer's operating system or window manager are used. These components are specific to each platform. For this reason, a menu in Windows looks different from a menu for a Macintosh. On the other hand, a lightweight component is "drawn" directly by the Java program, and its appearance is thus independent of the system on which it is run. In Swing, it is only the components of classes JApplet, JFrame, JDialog and JWindow that are heavyweight components. These components are referred to as top-level components. All other components are lightweight components.

Another property of Swing is that it uses a technique called MVC, *Model View Controller*. In this technique, each class makes an internal separation between a component's state (*Model*), its graphic appearance on the screen (*View*) and its behaviour when various events occur (*Controller*). A component that describes a button could have states of pressed or released, which can be displayed graphically in different ways on screen, and the component can react when you click it with the mouse. In Swing, this has been solved so that each class uses a special auxiliary component internally, a so-called *UI delegate*, which is responsible for drawing the component and managing events that have to do with the component. (A *UI delegate* thus both handles the appearance of a component, *View*, and serves as a *Controller*.)

Because Swing uses lightweight components and the MVC technique, it is easy to change the appearance of components dynamically. For example, you can give components a "Windows look" or a "Macintosh look". In Java, this is called changing the *Look & Feel*. If you do not specify anything specially in your program, the components have a special "Java look", which is usually called *Metal Look & Feel*. It is also possible to create your own *Look & Feel* if you should want to. That is outside the scope of this book, however.

Swing is a highly complex package, but as luck would have it, you do not need to know all its classes and how they are constructed to be able to use Swing.

In Figure 6.1 the standard classes in awt are shown. (The superclasses are on the left and the subclasses on the right. The class Panel, for example, is a subclass of Container, which in its turn is a subclass of Component.) The Swing classes that are direct subclasses of awt classes are also shown in the diagram, in the shaded area. Note particularly that the class JComponent is a subclass of the class Container.

- Component is a superclass for all GUI components, both in awt and in Swing. It contains general properties for all components, such as size and colour.

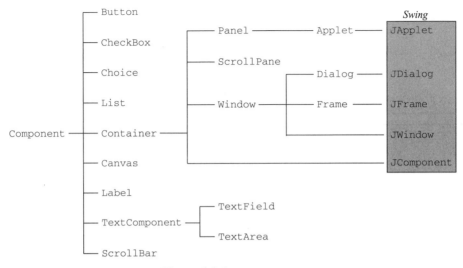

Figure 6.1 Awt components

- `Container` Most GUI components cannot be displayed separately on screen. They have to be put in a container. These containers are described by class `Container`. In class `Container` a method is described, `add`, which is used to place components in the container.
- `Applet` and `JApplet` are subclasses of `Container` and are thus able to contain components. An `Applet` does not have its own window and cannot be displayed separately on screen. An applet is normally called from a web browser or from the program `appletviewer`, which creates a window into which the applet is placed.
- `JWindow` describes an independent window on screen. A `JWindow` component does not have a frame or a title bar.
- `JFrame` describes an independent window with a frame and a title bar.
- `JDialog` describes a dialog box which can be displayed and removed during program execution. Temporary messages etc. can be displayed in this box.

Figure 6.2 shows the components in Swing. (Some classes have been omitted.) We see that all these classes have a common superclass `JComponent`. Since this is a subclass of class `Container`, which is a subclass of class `Component`, all Swing components inherit properties from the awt classes `Component` and `Container`.

We will give a brief summary here of what each Swing class does. More detailed descriptions can be found in separate sections later on in the book. We will restrict ourselves to discussing Swing classes at this point. The classes in awt with correspond-ing names can do more or less the same things, but they lack some of the properties that Swing classes have. One of these properties is that you can put borders round Swing components, but not round awt components. You should avoid mixing Swing

157

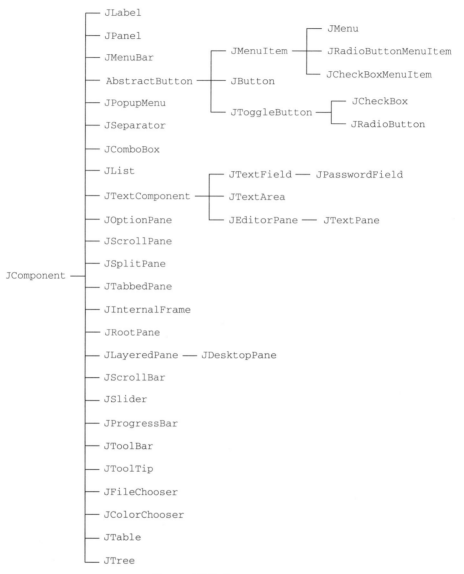

Figure 6.2 Swing components

components and awt components in the same program. The only exception to this rule is that when you use Swing, you must also use the awt classes Component and Container.[1]

---

[1] If you have installed Java on your computer, and want to see examples of what Swing components look like on screen, you can try running the SwingSet demonstration program, which is found on the website http://java.sun.com/products/javawebstart/demos.html.

- JComponent is the superclass for all the lightweight components in Swing. It contains more general properties, in addition to the ones inherited from classes Component and Container. A couple of examples are the way that borders are handled round components and tips.
- JLabel describes a simple text or an image which can be displayed in a window. The text can be changed by the program, but not by the user.
- JPanel describes a sub-window. A JPanel object cannot be displayed by itself on screen, but must be encapsulated in a Container, such as in a JFrame. You can use the class JPanel to construct quite complicated GUIs in a hierarchical manner. You can allow a window to contain several sub-windows. Each of the sub-windows can be constructed separately, independently of the others. These sub-windows can then be subdivided into further sub-windows and so on.
- AbstractButton contains common properties for all buttons and menu choices.
- JButton describes buttons which can contain text and images.
- JCheckBox describes a box with associated text or images which the user can select or not, depending on whether he or she wants a certain property to be enabled or not.
- JRadioButton is more or less the same as JCheckBox but you link several JRadioButton components to give a group where only one alternative can be selected.
- JMenuBar, JMenu, JPopupMenu, JSeparator, JMenuItem, JRadioButtonMenuItem and JCheckBoxMenuItem all have some connection with menus. The class JMenuBar describes a menu bar that can be located at the top of a window. Classes JMenu and JPopupMenu describe complete menus, which can contain several different menu choices. Menus generated by JMenu must be put on a menu line. JSeparator describes the lines that can be inserted into a menu to make it easier to find the right menu choice. Classes JMenuItem, JRadioButtonMenuItem and JCheckBoxMenuItem represent the choices that can be made in a menu, and their function corresponds with components JButton, JCheckBox and JRadioButton.
- JComboBox describes a menu with several choices, one of which can be selected by the programmer. When the user is not using the menu, a box containing the selected menu choice is displayed. (The class JComboBox corresponds to class Choice in awt.).
- JList describes a list which is displayed in a box. The user can select one or more choices from the list.
- JTextComponent is a superclass of the three classes JTextField, JTextArea and JEditorPane. The class JTextField is used when you want a single line for the user to enter text, which will be used as input data for the program. If more than one line has to be displayed and edited by the user, use another class, JTextArea. The class JEditorPane describes components in which more advanced text can be displayed in different formats, such as HTML files. The class JTextPane is a complicated class which can be used to create components that function as a word processor.

- `JOptionPane` describes a dialog box. We have seen several examples of dialog boxes earlier on in the book.
- `JScrollPane` is a sub-window which can contain a single component. A `JScroll-Pane` can be smaller than the component it contains. In this case, you can have a scroll bar at the edges, so you can see part of the component at a time.
- `JSplitPane` is a sub-window which can contain two windows with a split between the two components. The two components can be placed either side by side or one on top of the other.
- `JTabbedPane` is a sub-window which can contain an arbitrary number of components. The components are arranged as a set of "file cards". Only one component is visible at a time, and each component has a tab which can be used to choose the component which is displayed. (This is the same idea as at many places in Windows. If, for example, you select the icon called *My Computer* and click it with the right mouse button, then select the "Properties" menu choice, a window pops up which contains a number of file cards. You can choose the card you want to see by clicking one of the tabs at the top.)
- `JInternalFrame` is used to create internal windows and frames. A component such as `JInternalFrame` works in the same way as a `JFrame` but with the major difference that it can only exist inside a larger window. (Compare this with the way that you can open several windows inside the surrounding window in many word processors, such as Microsoft Word, to edit several files at the same time.)
- `JRootPane` and `JLayeredPane` are special containers which are found inside window components (`JApplet`, `JFrame`, `JDialog`, `JWindow` and `JInternalFrame`.) A window contains a single `JRootPane` which keeps track of three different components of the window: the menu bar, work surface (`contentPane`) and a "glass pane" which can overlay the window. To help it, the window's `JRootPane` has a `JLayeredPane`, which arranges the window components in different layers on the screen. Generally, programmers seldom need to use classes `JRootPane` and `JLayeredPane`.
- `JDesktopPane` is a subclass of the class `JLayeredPane`. You can use a `JLayered-Pane` when you want to create windows which will contain internal windows in their turn, i.e. components of type `JInternalFrame`. A `JDesktopPane` contains a `DesktopManager` which handles the internal windows, i.e. moves them and converts them into icons.
- `JScrollBar` describes a scroll bar where the user can specify a value which lies between two set value.
- `JSlider` describes a more advanced scroll bar than `JScrollBar`. You can add a ruler and text.
- `JProgressBar` is used to show how far a time-consuming process has come. This could show how much of a file has been downloaded, for example.
- `JToolBar` is a panel containing buttons and other components which can be inserted under the menu bar in a window. (Compare this with the panel containing forwards

and reverse buttons etc. in Microsoft Internet Explorer.) It is not entirely necessary to insert a JToolBar under the menu bar. A JToolBar can also be made floating, so that it can be dragged to another location on the screen.

- JToolTip describes a text containing explanations which pops up if you hold the cursor over a certain component for a short while.
- JFileChooser describes a dialog box in which the user can select a file name, such as when a file is being opened or saved. (The corresponding class in awt is FileDialog.)
- JColorChooser describes a dialog box in which the user can choose a colour.
- JTable is an advanced class which is used to present data in the form of tables.
- JTree is an advanced class which is used to present data in the form of a tree. Compare this with the way in which the file system with its files and folders is often displayed in many common programs, such as the *Explorer* in Windows.

6.2 JComponent **and** Container

In this section, we will discuss the most common properties of components in the basic classes JComponent and Container. The fact box contains a summary of the methods that a programmer generally needs to use. Since all lightweight components in Swing are subclasses of JComponent, which in its turn is a subclass of Container, the methods for all lightweight components are found in Container and JComponent.

JComponent **and** Container
In the table below, j *describes a component of class* JComponent, c *describes a component of class* Container *and* w *is a* Container *which describes a window (i.e. of the class* JFrame, JWindow, JDialog *or* JInternalFrame*)*

c.setBackground(q)	sets c's background colour to q (of class Color)
c.getBackground()	gives c's background colour
c.setForeground(q)	sets c's foreground colour to q (of class Color)
c.getForeground()	gives c's foreground colour
c.setFont(f)	sets the typeface to be used in c
c.getFont()	gives the typeface which is used in c
j.setBorder(b)	sets the border b (of class Border) which will be drawn in j
j.getBorder()	gives j's border
c.getInsets()	returns a value i of class Insets. i.top, i.bottom, i.left and i.right give the space that c's border requires.
j.setOpaque(*bool*)	specifies whether j should be opaque (default: false)
c.setEnabled(*bool*)	specifies whether c should be activated
c.isEnabled()	shows whether c is activated
c.setVisible(*bool*)	specifies whether c should be visible

JComponent **and** Container **(continued)**	
`w.setSize(x,y)`	sets window w's size
`w.setSize(d)`	sets window w's size (d's type is Dimension)
`c.getSize()`	gives c's size, returns Dimension
`c.getWidth()`	gives c's width
`c.getHeight()`	gives c's height
`j.setMinimumSize(d)`	sets j's minimum size (d's type is Dimension)
`c.getMinimumSize()`	gives c's minimum size, returns Dimension
`j.setMaximumSize(d)`	sets j's maximum size (d's type is Dimension)
`c.getMaximumSize()`	gives c's maximum size, returns Dimension
`j.setPreferredSize(d)`	sets j's desired size (d's type is Dimension)
`c.getPreferredSize()`	gives c's desired size, returns Dimension
`w.pack()`	calculates w's size (also for JPopupMenu)
`c.getX(), c.getY()`	gives the x and y coordinates for c's origin (in c's parent's coordinate system)
`c.getLocationOnScreen()`	gives c's location on screen, returns a Point
`c.setCursor(r)`	sets the cursor in c to r (of class Cursor)
`c.getCursor()`	gives the cursor in c
`j.setToolTipText(s)`	sets s (of type String) as help text to j
`j.getToolTipText()`	gives a String with the help text that belongs to j
`c.requestFocus()`	moves the focus to the component c
`c.hasFocus()`	tests whether c is in focus (returns a **boolean**)
`j.setNextFocusableComponent(x)`	places x after j in the focus chain
`j.getNextFocusableComponent()`	gives the focus to the next component
`j.requestDefaultFocus()`	moves the focus to the first component in the chain
`c.repaint()`	demands that c and all its children should be drawn
`j.revalidate()`	demands that the positioning of the children should be redone
`j.setDoubleBuffered(`*bool*`)`	specifies whether double buffering should be used
`paintComponent(g)`	is automatically called when j is drawn. g is of type Graphics. Can be redefined in subclasses to JComponent
`paint(g)`	is automatically called when Container is drawn. g is of class Graphics. Can be redefined in subclasses to Container, e.g. Applet and JApplet. Is *not* used in subclasses of JComponent
`c.getParent()`	gives the Container c is placed in
`j.getTopLevelAncestor()`	gives the Window component j is placed in
`j.getRootPane()`	gives the RootPane of the window j is placed in
`w.getContentPane()`	gives the "working area" of the window w

	JComponent and Container (continued)
`c.add(x)`	places the component x in c
`c.add(x, n)`	places the component x in place no. n in c
`c.getComponent(n)`	gives component no. n in c
`c.remove(x)`	removes the component x from c
`c.remove(n)`	removes component no. n from c
`c.removeAll()`	removes all components from c
`c.setLayout(1)`	specifies that 1 should be used as `LayoutManager` in c
`c.getLayout()`	gives the `LayoutManager` which is used by c
`c.getComponents()`	gives a list (an array) containing the components in c

In addition to the methods in the fact box, there are also a number of methods which are connected with events and listeners. We will describe these methods at various points in the book, and a summary is given in Chapter 13. Each method in the fact box is defined in class `Component`, `Container` or `JComponent`. In order to make the summary more or less comprehensive, we have included a large number of methods in the fact box, including ones we do not need yet. In this chapter, we will discuss only the most basic methods. The others will be discussed later when we use them. We see that there are many different properties that can be influenced. The most commonly used ones are probably the ones related to the colour, font and size of components. Assume, for example, that b is an object of class `JButton`, and we want its foreground colour to be blue. We then write

```
b.setForeground(Color.blue);
```

Positioning of child components

The last group of methods in the fact box is used when you want to use a `JComponent` as container and put other, so-called child components into it. Since class `JComponent` is a subclass of class `Container` you could, theoretically, place GUI components in all lightweight components in Swing. It is not good practice to do this, however. You should only place GUI components in components intended to be used as containers, for example components of class `JPanel`.

The most important method is `add`, which is used to place components in the container. For example, if we have an object p which is of class `JPanel` and an object b which is of class `JButton` we can place b in panel p:

```
p.add(b);
```

Note that this does not mean that the `JButton` object b is displayed directly on screen. Each `Container` has a list containing references to the graphic components which are to be placed in the container. The method add just inserts the object b into this list. The actual drawing of the components in the container takes place on occasions when the container is drawn. This can be either the first time it is drawn or when it is redrawn because it has been fully or partly concealed by other components.

Classes JFrame, JWindow, JApplet, JDialog and JInternalFrame are somewhat special. They all describe a window (in some cases the outermost window) we are working with. When we have windows of this type, we should *never place the child components straight away in the window*. This should be done in the window's "working area", its so-called ContentPane. For example, if we have a window w of type JFrame and want to position a JButton object b we can write

```
w.getContentPane().add(b);
```

We have to do it this way because classes JFrame, JWindow, JApplet, JDialog and JInternalFrame are constructed internally from special components which are used to handle different layers of the window, and to handle the menu bar. If we attempt to place a component directly in a window, we destroy this set-up.

If we want to place several components in a window, it becomes clumsy to write w.getContentPane() in each location. We can do this declaration first:

```
Container c = w.getContentPane();
```

and then use the variable c:

```
c.add(b);
```

Layout managers

One of the goals of Java is that programs should be portable between different platforms. For this reason, it is not intended that the programmer make a detailed specification of the size and location of the GUI components. Instead, the programmer should specify a *strategy* for the way positioning should be done. There are several strategies that can be used. These are the classes FlowLayout, BorderLayout, GridLayout, GridBagLayout, CardLayout and BoxLayout. These classes are all subclasses of class LayoutManager. Each time a window is redrawn, the window calls a LayoutManager which looks after the actual positioning of the components in the window. You can tell the window about the LayoutManager to be used by calling the method setLayout. This has a LayoutManager as a parameter. The simplest strategy is FlowLayout. If we want this to be used to position components in container c we write

```
c.setLayout(new FlowLayout());
```

The FlowLayout strategy briefly means that the components are each lined up in turn, going from left to right. If a component does not fit on one line, a new line is started below the current one.

In the first examples, we will also use the `GridLayout` strategy to position components. When you use this strategy, the space is divided up into a number of equal-sized boxes and you specify the number of lines and columns you want the window to be divided into. For example, if you want to have `r` lines and `k` columns in a `Container` `c` you write

```
c.setLayout(new GridLayout(r,k));
```

The components are then lined up from right to left. Each component will then automatically be so large that it fills its box.

If you do not call the `setLayout` method, each container will still have a pre-defined `LayoutManager`. A component of class `JPanel`, for example, has a `LayoutManager` of class `FlowLayout` and a window's "working surface", its `ContentPane`, has a `LayoutManager` of class `BorderLayout`. (We will explain how `BorderLayout` works in Section 8.1.3.)

Size of components

We can distinguish three cases: applets, windows and internal components. The size of an applet is specified in the HTML file from which the applet is started. For this reason, you should never specify the size of an applet in the program. The size of a *window* (for example, a `JFrame`) can be specified in two ways. You can either call the method `setSize` and specify the size directly, or you can call the method `pack`. When you call `pack`, the size of the window is calculated automatically, so that it just fits the components it has been placed in. The size of an *internal component* (which is inside a window) is determined by the `LayoutManager` you use. Thus, for internal components, calling the method `setSize` seldom has any effect. If you specially want an internal component to be a certain size you can, instead, call the methods `setMinimumSize`, `setMaximumSize` and `setPreferredSize`. The `LayoutManager` can then consider these requests when it calculates the size that the component will have. For example, you could write

```
c.setMinimumSize(new Dimension(100, 50));
```

to say that you want the component `c` to be at least 100 pixels wide and 50 high. The class `Dimension`, which is used here, is a simple standard class with two public instance variables: `width` and `height`. If you have a `Dimension` object `d` you can easily access these values by writing `d.width` and `d.height`.

One thing that should also be noted is that the `LayoutManager` does not calculate the size of internal components directly. This is not done until the `LayoutManager` needs to decide how the components are to be placed in the container, which is not normally done until the surrounding window is made visible or you call `pack`. If you call `getSize` for a component before this has been done, the response is that the width and length of the object are 0.

Drawing of the components

All components that belong to class JComponent or one of its subclasses have a pre-defined method called paintComponent, which is called automatically each time the component needs to be redrawn. In classes that are not subclasses of JComponent, e.g. JApplet, the corresponding method is called paint. In method paintComponent the actual drawing is done. To help it, paintComponent is automatically given a kind of toolbox containing drawing tools as a parameter. This toolbox is of type Graphics.

Please note that your program should never call method paintComponent. This is done automatically. If you want a component to be redrawn, you should call method repaint. This makes sure that the following things happen: the component background is redrawn (if it is opaque); the component is redrawn; if the component has a border it is redrawn; and last, but not least, all the component's child components are redrawn.

If you change the size of a component when running a program, the LayoutManager has to redo the position of the components in the container involved. You can demand that this should be done by calling the method revalidate.

In most cases, you do not need to worry about method paintComponent since it is already available for all standard classes. However, it can happen that you want to create your own subclass from one of the standard classes. You will then have to redefine the method paintComponent. We will see examples of this later on in the book.

Demonstration example

Before you read on, it might be a good idea to reread Section 1.13 and pay special attention to the program Greeting on page 31, where we have used some of the methods in the classes JComponent and Container. We will now construct another program which shows how to use some of the methods available for these classes. When you run the program, it will look like Figure 6.3. We have placed three JLabel

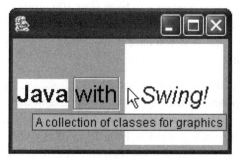

Figure 6.3 JCompDemo

objects in the window. For the right-hand `JLabel`, we have also added a help text, which is displayed shortly after you hold the cursor over the text *Swing!*.

```java
import java.awt.*;
import javax.swing.*;
import javax.swing.border.*;   // contains classes for frames

public class JCompDemo extends JFrame {
  public JCompDemo() { // Constructor for the class JCompDemo
    Container c = getContentPane();
    c.setLayout(new FlowLayout());
    c.setBackground(Color.lightGray);

    JLabel l1 = new JLabel("Java", JLabel.CENTER);
    l1.setOpaque(true);            // opaque background
    l1.setBackground(Color.white);
    l1.setForeground(Color.blue);
    l1.setFont(new Font("SansSerif", Font.BOLD, 24));

    JLabel l2 = new JLabel("with", JLabel.CENTER);
    l2.setForeground(Color.black);
    l2.setFont(new Font("SansSerif", Font.PLAIN, 24));
    l2.setBorder(new EtchedBorder());

    JLabel l3 = new JLabel("Swing!", JLabel.CENTER);
    l3.setOpaque(true);            // opaque background
    l3.setBackground(l1.getBackground());
    l3.setForeground(l1.getForeground());
    l3.setFont(new Font("SansSerif", Font.ITALIC, 24));
    l3.setPreferredSize(new Dimension(100,100));
    l3.setToolTipText("A collection of classes for graphics");

    c.add(l1); c.add(l2); c.add(l3);
    pack();        // compute the size of the window
    setVisible(true);            // make the window visible
    setDefaultCloseOperation(EXIT_ON_CLOSE);
  }

  public static void main (String[] arg) {
    JCompDemo j = new JCompDemo();
  }
}
```

The program has the same structure as the program `Greeting` on page 31. One important difference, however, is that we have put method `main` in the same class as the rest of the code. We can then avoid having an extra class just for `main`. A GUI program of this type can be designed in several ways, but we will use this layout in future. This program is encapsulated in a class of its own, which is a subclass of another class, `JFrame`. In this example, we call our own class `JCompDemo`. Our new class will then inherit all its properties from class `JFrame`, which means that an object of this class can be displayed as a window on screen. The method `main`, in which execution starts, contains only a single declaration, where we create an object of our new class, i.e. an object which describes a window. In this example, the object is called `j`. When a new object is created, the class constructor is called, as we know, to initialize the new object. In our GUI program, we will put most of the code that has to do with the appearance of the window in the constructor.

In the constructor for our program, we first specify that `FlowLayout` should be used, and that the window background colour should be light grey. Note that we specify these properties for the "work surface" of the window, its `ContentPane`. We then create three objects, `l1`, `l2` and `l3` of class `JLabel`. Among other things, this class can be used to display ordinary texts. (We will discuss the class `JLabel` in greater detail later on.) For each `JLabel` object, we specify the text to be displayed and the font to be used. For `l1`, we say that we want its background colour to be white and its foreground colour to be blue. In addition, we specify that `l1` should be transparent. For `l2` we specify that the foreground colour should be black, but we do not specify a background colour. The reason for this is that `l2` is transparent, which means that the window's background colour will be visible behind the text. Around `l2` we have also put a simple border to emphasize its size, in the window. (We have used the simple type of frame, `EtchedBorder`, but we will discuss different types of borders later on in this chapter.)

In the last `JLabel` component `l3` we want to have the same background colour and foreground colour as in `l1`. So we read off these properties for `l1` and use them as input data when we set the corresponding properties for `l3`. (Of course, we could have written `setBackground(Color.white)` and `setForeground(Color.blue)` for `l3` as well, but we will do it the other way for the sake of exercise.) We want `l3` to have size 100 by 100. It would have been tempting to write

```
l3.setSize(100,100);
```

but this would not have worked, since the `LayoutManager` calculates the size itself, and would have changed the size we specified. What we should do instead is to ask the `LayoutManager`, if possible, to give `l3` size 100 by 100. We do this by calling the method `setPreferredSize`. In this case, the `LayoutManager` considers our request and lets `l3` have the size we wanted.

For `l3` we also demonstrate how to add a help text to a lightweight component in Swing. This is very easy. We just call the method `setToolTipText` and specify the text to be displayed as the parameter.

The method `add` is called to add the three components `l1`, `l2` and `l3` to the work surface of the window. After this, it calls the method `pack`. When this is called, the `LayoutManager` calculates the size of each component, calculates how they should be placed in the window, and then calculates a suitable size for the entire window. Since

Figure 6.4

we have specified that FlowLayout should be used, the components will be laid out in a line from left to right. We could have specified a size for the window ourselves, instead of calling pack. For example, we could have written

```
setSize(150,180);
```

Then the window would have looked like Figure 6.4. Here, the components do not all fit on one line in the window. Since we use FlowLayout a new row will be started.

Please note that when we call methods pack, setVisible and setDefault-CloseOperation in the constructor we do not write any object name in front of the method name. The methods for "the current object" are then called, which is the object that describes the window, or in this case the object j of class JCompDemo. (It would have been possible to write **this**.pack() etc. in the constructor, but this would not have been so elegant.)

6.3 JLabel

The class JLabel is one of the most useful Swing classes. We have already seen several examples of how it can be used to display texts in a window. Components of class JLabel can show more than just simple texts, however, which we will discuss in this chapter. As the point of departure for discussion, we will study a program which displays the window in Figure 6.5. As you can see, the window has been subdivided into eight equal-sized windows, consisting of two lines of four windows. To do this arrangement of the windows, the program uses a LayoutManager of class GridLayout. In each box, the program places a JLabel object. In the program, these objects are called 11, 12, . . . 18. To make the boxes clearer, the program surrounds each box with a border of type EtchedBorder. We will start by listing the entire program, and will then discuss the details.

169

Figure 6.5 JLabelDemo

```java
import java.awt.*;
import javax.swing.*;
import javax.swing.border.*;  // contains classes for frames
import java.net.*;            // contains the class URL

public class JLabelDemo extends JFrame {
  public JLabelDemo() {
    Container c = getContentPane();
    c.setLayout(new GridLayout(2,4));  // 2 rows, 4 columns

    JLabel l1 = new JLabel("Plain text");
    JLabel l2 = new JLabel(new ImageIcon("work.gif"));

    URL u = null;
    try { u = new URL("http://www.xyz.se/pub/info.gif"); }
    catch (MalformedURLException e) {}
    JLabel l3 = new JLabel(new ImageIcon(u));

    JLabel l4 = new JLabel(new ImageIcon("hammer.gif"),
                                       JLabel.RIGHT);
    l4.setVerticalAlignment(JLabel.BOTTOM);

    JLabel l5 = new JLabel("Under construction",
                  new ImageIcon("work.gif"), JLabel.RIGHT);
    l5.setHorizontalTextPosition(JLabel.CENTER);
    l5.setVerticalTextPosition(JLabel.BOTTOM);

    JLabel l6 = new JLabel("Strike!",
                  new ImageIcon("hammer.gif"), JLabel.LEFT);
    l6.setVerticalAlignment(JLabel.BOTTOM);
    l6.setHorizontalTextPosition(JLabel.RIGHT);

    JLabel l7 = new JLabel(new ImageIcon
        ("C:\\jdk1.4\\demo\\jfc\\Java2D\\images\\clouds.jpg"));
    l7.setLayout(new GridLayout(1,1));
    l7.add(new JLabel("Background"));

    JLabel l8 = new JLabel(
      "<html><body><b>HTML-text</b>" +
```

```
        "<p>with <i>varying</i> <u>font</u> <small>and</small> " +
        "<big>size</big></body></html>");

    EtchedBorder e = new EtchedBorder();
    l1.setBorder(e); l2.setBorder(e);
    l3.setBorder(e); l4.setBorder(e);
    l5.setBorder(e); l6.setBorder(e);
    l7.setBorder(e); l8.setBorder(e);
    c.add(l1); c.add(l2); c.add(l3); c.add(l4);
    c.add(l5); c.add(l6); c.add(l7); c.add(l8);
    setSize(450,175);
    setVisible(true);
    setDefaultCloseOperation(EXIT_ON_CLOSE);
  }

  public static void main (String[] arg) {
    JLabelDemo j = new JLabelDemo();
  }
}
```

A JLabel can contain either text, an icon (an image) or both text and an icon. You can use the methods setText and setImage to specify what a JLabel should contain, but the simplest way is to specify the contents by giving the constructor a suitable parameter. On lines

```
JLabel l1 = new JLabel("Plain text");
JLabel l2 = new JLabel(new ImageIcon("work.gif"));
```

in the program, it creates the first two JLabel objects. When a JLabel is to contain an icon, the parameter can be an object of class ImageIcon. The expression

```
new ImageIcon("work.gif")
```

creates such an object. As the parameter, we can give the name of a file which contains an image in one of the formats gif or jpg.[1] It is also possible to have moving gif images. When you give a simple file name, as in this example, it is assumed that the file is in the same directory as the program. It is also possible to specify a full search path. For example, you could write

```
new ImageIcon("C:\\own\\pictures\\work.gif")
```

Please note that if you are running Windows and use the character \ when you specify a file name, you have to use double \\ in the program. This is because the character \ is regarded as a special character by the Java compiler.

It is also possible to download an image from another computer via the Internet. The parameter you give the constructor should then be the web address. This is done by

---

[1] There are a large number of images available on the Internet. One way to find the right websites is to search for "free clip art".

means of an object of class URL (Uniform Resource Locator). Our program contains an example of how this is done. The icon in the third JLabel component is downloaded from web address www.xyz.se/pub/info.gif. You first create a URL object with the expression

```
u = new URL("http://www.xyz.se/pub/info.gif");
```

This expression could generate an error signal, however, a so-called exception, so it must be encapsulated in a **try** statement. We will not go into depth about this right now. (Exception handling is discussed in Chapter 11.) After this, you use the URL object as a parameter when you create the icon.

```
JLabel 13 = new JLabel(new ImageIcon(u));
```

The contents of a JLabel (i.e. text, icon or text plus icon) can be placed at various places in the space that the component occupies in the window. You can specify both horizontal and vertical positions. We can do this by calling the methods setHorizontalAlignment and setVerticalAlignment. As the parameter for the horizontal position, we can give one of the values JLabel.LEFT, JLabel.CENTER or JLabel.RIGHT and for the vertical position, we give one of the values JLabel.TOP, JLabel.CENTER or JLabel.BOTTOM. The horizontal position can also be given as a parameter for the constructor when we create a JLabel object. For the fourth JLabel component in our program, we write

```
JLabel 14 = new JLabel(new ImageIcon("hammer.gif"),
                                      JLabel.RIGHT);
14.setVerticalAlignment(JLabel.BOTTOM);
```

The vertical position always becomes JLabel.CENTER unless you specify something else. The horizontal position becomes JLabel.CENTER for icons and JLabel.LEFT for images unless otherwise specified.

The fifth JLabel object in the program is an example of a JLabel which contains both a text and an icon. This is created on line

```
JLabel 15 = new JLabel("Under construction",
                  new ImageIcon("work.gif"), JLabel.RIGHT);
```

In other words, both text and image are given as parameters for the constructor. You must also specify the horizontal position of the contents.

When you have a JLabel that contains both a text and an icon, you can give both the position of the contents as a whole and the text's *relative* position in relation to the icon. This is done by means of the two methods setHorizontalTextPosition and setVerticalTextPosition. Here as well, the parameters we give are one of the values JLabel.LEFT, JLabel.CENTER or JLabel.RIGHT and JLabel.TOP, JLabel.CENTER or JLabel.BOTTOM. In the program, we put the text Under construction in the centre, underneath the icon, by making the statements

```
15.setHorizontalTextPosition(JLabel.CENTER);
15.setVerticalTextPosition(JLabel.BOTTOM);
```

Please note that in 15 the contents are right justified in general (icon plus text), whereas the text is centred in relation to the icon.

If you do not specify a *relative* text position, the horizontal and vertical default values are JLabel.CENTER, which means that the text ends up on the centre of the icon. Study the sixth JLabel component:

```
JLabel 16 = new JLabel("Strike!",
                   new ImageIcon("hammer.gif"), JLabel.LEFT);
16.setVerticalAlignment(JLabel.BOTTOM);
16.setHorizontalTextPosition(JLabel.RIGHT);
```

Here, the contents are located down on the left, whereas the text ends up on the right of the icon, centred vertically in relation to it.

In the seventh box in the window, we use a JLabel with an icon as the background. We start by creating a JLabel object which contains the desired background:

```
JLabel 17 = new JLabel(new ImageIcon
      ("C:\\jdk1.4\\demo\\jfc\\Java2D\\images\\clouds.jpg"));
```

Since the class JLabel is a subclass of another class, JComponent, we can use 17 as a container and put the child components on it. However, to do this, we must make sure that we have a LayoutManager. In our program, we have chosen to use GridLayout with only one box (one line and one column):

```
17.setLayout(new GridLayout(1,1));
```

We can then put components in 17, e.g.

```
17.add(new JLabel("Background"));
```

Since components are normally transparent unless we say otherwise, the icon is visible in the background.

In the last box in the program, we demonstrate that the text in a JLabel can actually be in HTML format. In other words, you can put in simple so-called HTML tags in the text to insert carriage returns and to control the font and size to be used for individual words. The following declaration is made in the program code:

```
JLabel 18 = new JLabel(
  "<html><body><b>HTML-text</b>" +
  "<p>with <i>varying</i> <u>font</u> <small>and</small> " +
  "<big>size</big></body></html>");
```

We will not teach HTML coding in this book, but we can include a brief list of some of the symbols used: <b> means bold face, <i> means italic, <u> underlined text,

173

`<small>` small text, `<big>` large text and `<p>` that you should start a new paragraph. The symbols frequently occur in pairs, where the first specifies that something should start, and the other one specifies that something should end. `<b>` means that bold face starts, for example, and `</b>` means that bold face is concluded.

The properties associated with class `JLabel` are summarized in the fact box.

JLabel
Shows a text and/or an icon. Icons should be of type `Icon` (actually implements the interface `Icon`). They are commonly of class `ImageIcon`.

hor specifies horizontal alignment: `JLabel.LEFT`, `JLabel.CENTER` or `JLabel.RIGHT`
ver specifies vertical alignment: `JLabel.TOP`, `JLabel.CENTER` or `JLabel.BOTTOM`

new `JLabel(txt)`	creates a left-justified `JLabel` with text `txt`
new `JLabel(txt, hor)`	creates a `JLabel` with text `txt` and alignment *hor*
new `JLabel(ic)`	creates a centred `JLabel` with icon `ic`
new `JLabel(ic, hor)`	creates a `JLabel` with icon `ic` and alignment *hor*
new `JLabel(txt, ic, hor)`	creates a `JLabel` with text `txt` and icon `ic` in c and with alignment *hor*
`l.setText(txt)`	sets the text in `l` to `txt`
`l.getText()`	returns the text in `l`
`l.setIcon(ic)`	sets the icon in `l` to `ic`
`l.getIcon()`	returns the icon in `l`
`l.setDisabledIcon(ic)`	sets the icon displayed when `l` is deactivated
`l.getDisabledIcon()`	returns the icon displayed when `l` is deactivated
`l.setHorizontalAlignment(hor)`	specifies horizontal placement for the contents in `l`
`l.setVerticalAlignment(ver)`	specifies vertical placement for the contents in `l`
`l.setHorizontalTextPosition(hor)`	specifies horizontal alignment: for text in relation to the icon in `l`
`l.setVerticalTextPosition(ver)`	specifies vertical alignment: for text in relation to the icon in `l`
`l.setIconTextGap(n)`	sets the distance between the icon and the text to n pixels
`l.setLabelFor(c)`	specifies that `l` should be a label for the component c
`l.getLabelFor()`	gives the component `l` is a label for
`l.setDisplayedMnemonic(x)`	sets the keyboard shortcut for `l` to `Alt-x` (x is of type `char`)

6.4   `JButton`

The next standard class we will study is `JButton`. We use this when we want to place buttons in a window, buttons that the user can click. We can create buttons with text, with an icon or with both text and an icon:

```
JButton okKnapp    = new JButton("OK");
JButton exKnapp    = new JButton(new ImageIcon("exit.gif"));
JButton ringKnapp  = new JButton("Phone",
                                 new ImageIcon("phone.gif"));
```

You can control how the text and icon can be positioned on a button, in the same way as for the class `JLabel`, by calling the methods `setHorizontalAlignment`, `setVerticalAlignment`, `setHorizontalTextPosition` and `setVerticalTextPosition`. The only difference is that it is a good idea to give the parameter the value `JButton.LEFT`, `JButton.CENTER` etc. For example, you could write

```
okButtonsetHorizontalAlignment(JButton.RIGHT);
ringButtonsetHorizontalTextPosition(JButton.LEFT);
```

If you do not specify anything special, the contents of the button will be centred, both horizontally and vertically, and if you have both a text and an icon, the text ends up on the right of the icon. A button is also given a border and becomes transparent.

As an example, we will study a program which displays the window in Figure 6.6. When the program starts, it looks like the upper window in the figure. By clicking one of the two buttons at the bottom of the window, the user can switch between English and Swedish text. When English text is displayed, the button for displaying English

Figure 6.6 JButtonDemo

text has been made inactive, and in the corresponding manner when Swedish text is displayed, the button for displaying Swedish text is inactive. To terminate the program, the user can click either the button at the top right or, as usual, the closing box in the window frame.

The program is as follows:

```java
import java.awt.*;
import java.awt.event.*;   // contains listener classes
import javax.swing.*;

public class JButtonDemo extends JFrame
                         implements ActionListener {
  private JLabel  lab = new JLabel("Welcome!", JLabel.CENTER);
  private JButton exi = new JButton("Cancel");
  private JButton eng = new JButton("In English, please!",
                            new ImageIcon("flag_eng.gif"));
  private JButton swe = new JButton("På svenska, tack!",
                            new ImageIcon("flag_swe.gif"));

  public JButtonDemo() { // constructor for class JButtonDemo
    Container c = getContentPane();
    c.setLayout(new GridLayout(2,2)); // 2 rows, 2 columns
    c.add(lab); c.add(exi); c.add(eng); c.add(swe);
    c.setBackground(Color.white);      // white content pane
    lab.setFont(new Font("SansSerif", Font.ITALIC, 20));
    exi.setFont(new Font("SansSerif", Font.BOLD, 14));
    // connect listeners
    exi.addActionListener(this);
    eng.addActionListener(this);
    swe.addActionListener(this);
    eng.setEnabled(false);    // English is shown
    setSize(350,100);
    setVisible(true);
    setDefaultCloseOperation(EXIT_ON_CLOSE);
  }

  // listener method
  public void actionPerformed(ActionEvent e) {
    if (e.getSource() == exi)
      // The user clicked the button Cancel (Avsluta)
      System.exit(0);
    else if (e.getSource() == eng) {
      // The user clicked the button In English, please!
      lab.setText("Welcome!");
      exi.setText("Cancel");
      eng.setEnabled(false);
      swe.setEnabled(true);
    }
```

```
    else if (e.getSource() == swe) {
        // The user clicked the button På svenska, tack!
        lab.setText("Välkommen!");
        exi.setText("Avsluta");
        swe.setEnabled(false);
        eng.setEnabled(true);
    }
}

public static void main (String[] arg) {
    JButtonDemo j = new JButtonDemo();
}
}
```

As usual, execution starts in the method `main`, whose only task is to create a new object of class `JButtonDemo`. When this happens, we end up in the constructor for the class `JButtonDemo`. Here, the work surface is initialized first, to make it white, and we use a `LayoutManager` of type `GridLayout`. The window is divided into two lines with four boxes on each line. In the window, four components are to be placed: a `JLabel`, `lab`, and three buttons called `exi`, `eng` and `swe`. These variables have been declared and initialized outside the constructor. They then become instance variables of class `JButtonDemo`. The reason that we have declared them as instance variables is that we want them to be available to other sections of the class, even outside the constructor.

This is an example of a so-called *event-driven program*. In this kind of program, the program sits and waits for various types of event that might occur – such as if the user types something or clicks a mouse button – and for each type of event the program could do something. In this example, the program should only bother about events that occur when the user clicks one of the three buttons.

In an event-driven program, we tell it what should happen when each event occurs. In Java, this is done by defining special *listeners* (*event listeners*). There are a number of different event listeners for different types of event. When you click a button, this creates an event of type `ActionEvent`. An event of this type should be trapped by an event listener of type `ActionListener`. In the general case, an event listener can be an object of a special listener class, but in many cases this can be done more easily, as you can specify that the graphic component you construct should also function as a listener. We will use this technique in this chapter. (A more general description of event listeners and listener classes is given in Chapter 13.)

Definitions of the classes that have to do with events are found in the standard package `java.awt.event`. For this reason, this package is imported on the second line. Please note that we wrote **implements** `ActionListener` at the beginning of the definition of class `JButtonDemo`. This says that an object of class `JButtonDemo` (apart from everything else) should be a listener to events of type `ActionEvent`. The word

implements has to do with a so-called *interface*, which is a special type of inheritance. (This is described more fully in Section 10.9.)

The following lines in the constructor are important:

```
exi.addActionListener(this);
eng.addActionListener(this);
swe.addActionListener(this);
```

This calls the method addActionListener for each of the three buttons. The argument specifies the object that should be the listener to events that occur in the component in question. Here, we have given the argument this. This means that the current object (in other words, this JButtonDemo object) should be an event listener. An event listener must always be registered in this way, so that it knows which component it should be connected to and listen to.

An event listener of type ActionListener must have a method called action-Performed. This method will be called automatically when the event in question occurs. In other words, this method will be called every time the user clicks one of the buttons. You, yourself, must define the method actionPerformed in your event listener. The method has a parameter e which is of class ActionEvent (defined in the package java.awt.event). The parameter e contains general information about the type of event that has occurred. Among other things, there is a method getSource which gives a reference to the object in which the event occurred. In the if statement

```
if (e.getSource() == exi)
   System.exit(0);
```

a call is made to System.exit only if the event occurred in the object exi or, in other words, if the user has clicked the button exi. In the corresponding way, we investigate in the method actionPerformed if the user has clicked the button eng or swe.

The fact box shows the constructors and the most common methods for class JButton. All methods are inherited from the superclass AbstractButton. This class, as we saw in Figure 6.2, is also a superclass of classes JMenuItem and JToggleButton. This means that the methods are also available for these classes and for their subclasses. You can define several different icons for one button. You could have different icons for when a button is depressed and when the cursor is moved across it. In the fact box, we have only included methods for handling the default icon and the icon for a deactivated button. Please refer to the online documentation for the other icons.

As an alternative to using the mouse, you can use keyboard shortcuts to select the button you want to click. We then use the method setMnemonic. For example, to give the button eng the keyboard shortcut Alt-E you write

```
eng.setMnemonic(KeyEvent.VK_E);
```

AbstractButton

In the following methods, b is an object in a subclass of `AbstractButton`.
Icons should be of type `Icon` (really implements the interface `Icon`).
They are commonly of class `ImageIcon`.

hor should be	`JButton.LEFT, JButton.CENTER` or `JButton.RIGHT`
ver should be	`JButton.TOP, JButton.CENTER` or `JButton.BOTTOM`

new `JButton()`	creates a `JButton`
new `JButton(txt)`	creates a `JButton` with text `txt`
new `JButton(ic)`	creates a `JButton` with icon `ic`
new `JButton(txt, ic)`	creates a `JButton` with text `txt` and icon `ic`
`b.setText(txt)`	places the text `txt` in b
`b.getText()`	returns the text in b
`b.setIcon(ic)`	sets the icon on b to `ic`
`b.getIcon()`	returns the icon in b
`b.setDisabledIcon(ic)`	sets the icon displayed when b is deactivated
`b.getDisabledIcon()`	returns the icon displayed when b is deactivated
`b.setHorizontalAlignment(`*hor*`)`	specifies horizontal placement for the contents
`b.setVerticalAlignment(`*ver*`)`	specifies vertical placement for the contents
`b.setHorizontalTextPosition(`*hor*`)`	specifies horizontal alignment: for text in relation to the icon in b
`b.setVerticalTextPosition(`*ver*`)`	specifies vertical alignment: for text in relation to the icon in b
`b.isSelected()`	gives a **boolean** which specifies whether b is selected or not
`b.setBorderPainted(`*bool*`)`	specifies whether a border should be painted
`b.setContentAreaFilled(`*bool*`)`	specifies whether b should be transparent
`b.setMnemonic(KeyEvent.VK_x)`	sets the keyboard shortcut to `Alt-x`
`b.doClick()`	clicks (from the program) on b
`b.setActionCommand(txt)`	links the text `txt` to b
`b.setAction(a)`	links an `Action` object a (see Chapter 14) to b
`b.getActionCommand(txt)`	reads the text connected to the button b

Connect an event listener l of class `ActionListener` to b:

```
b.addActionListener(l)
```

Define the method `actionPerformed` in the listener:

```
public void actionPerformed(ActionEvent e) {
    // you get here when the user clicks on the button b
}
```

The following method can be called in the listener:

`e.getSource()`	returns the object where the event happened

The key to be used is defined by means of a constant VK_?, which is defined in class KeyEvent. The character ? is replaced by the letter you want to use. On the button, the (first) corresponding letter will be underlined.

The user can also use the Tab and Shift-Tab keys to select the correct button and the Enter key to click the selected key. We will show you what to do to achieve this in Section 13.6 on page 423.

6.5 JToggleButton, JCheckBox and JRadioButton

When the user clicks an ordinary button on the screen, i.e. a button of class JButton, the button is drawn depressed while the user keeps the mouse button depressed. When the user releases the mouse button, the button is displayed in its non-depressed normal position on the screen again. The class JToggleButton and its two subclasses JCheckBox and JRadioButton describe buttons that work somewhat differently. When the user clicks one of these buttons, it remains in its depressed state and it has to be clicked again to get it back to its normal position.

The thing that distinguishes the three classes JToggleButton, JCheckBox and JRadioButton is how the buttons are displayed visually on the screen. A component of class JToggleButton looks like an ordinary button, i.e. it looks like a button of class JButton, but it can assume the depressed position. A component of class JCheckBox is displayed as a so-called *check box*, a square box with associated text. If the button is in the depressed position, a tick is displayed in the box, and the box is empty otherwise. A component of class JRadioButton is displayed as a small round button with associated text. If the button is depressed, a mark is displayed on the button. Components of class JRadioButton are generally linked together in groups, in which only one button at a time can be depressed. Components of class JCheckBox, on the other hand, are not generally linked to each other. Several boxes can be selected at the same time.

Classes JCheckBox and JRadioButton are used more frequently than JToggleButton. The appearance of components of class JCheckBox and JRadioButton is demonstrated in Figure 6.7. A text is displayed at the top left of the program (a JLabel). On the right of the text, there are three radio buttons which are used to choose the colour in which the text will be displayed. At the bottom of the window, there are three check boxes. These are used to choose whether the text will be displayed in italic style, if it should be centred and if there should be a black background or not. Since the text can be displayed in only one colour at a time, only one of the radio buttons can be selected. The three check boxes are independent of each other, however.

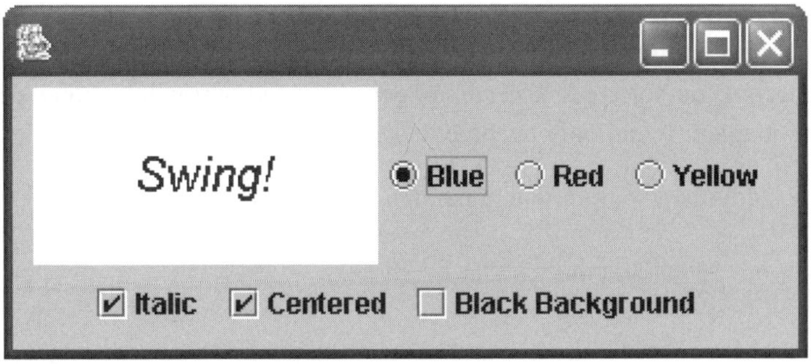

Figure 6.7 JToggleDemo

Since the class JToggleButton is a subclass of another class, JAbstractButton, the three classes JToggleButton, JCheckBox and JRadioButton have all the methods noted in the fact box on page 179. It should be specially noted that the method isSelected can be used to sense whether a button is selected, i.e. depressed or not.

There is the same set of constructors for the classes JToggleButton, JCheckBox and JRadioButton. These constructors are summarized in the fact box below.

Constructors for JToggleButton, JCheckBox, JRadioButton, JCheckBoxMenuItem and JRadioButtonMenuItem

Here, *JB* designates one of JToggleButton, JCheckBox, JRadioButton, JCheckBoxMenuItem or JRadioButtonMenuItem.
ic designates an icon of type Icon. ic could belong to class ImageIcon.

new *JB*()	un-selected without text
new *JB*(txt)	un-selected with text txt
new *JB*(txt, *selected*)	with text txt (*selected* is a **boolean**)
new *JB*(ic)	un-selected with icon ic
new *JB*(ic, *selected*)	with icon ic (*selected* is a **boolean**)
new *JB*(txt, ic)	un-selected with text txt and icon ic
new *JB*(txt, ic, *selected*)	with text txt and icon ic (*selected* is a **boolean**)

To form groups of radio buttons, we use the class ButtonGroup. It is easy to form a group by creating an object from this class. (We call the group g.)

```
ButtonGroup g = new ButtonGroup();
```

After this, we specify the radio buttons that will belong to the group by calling the method add. Assume, for example, that we have defined four radio buttons with names ra, rb, rc and rd. We can then let them belong to group g by making the call

```
g.add(ra); g.add(rb); g.add(rc); g.add(rd);
```

In the group, only one button can be selected at a time. If the user clicks one of the buttons in a group, this button will be selected. The button that was selected will automatically become de-selected. You cannot get a selected button to become de-selected by clicking it again. It can only become de-selected if another button is selected.

Let us now study the program that generates the window in Figure 6.7.

```java
import java.awt.*;
import java.awt.event.*;
import javax.swing.*;

public class JToggleDemo extends JFrame
                         implements ActionListener {
  private JLabel l   = new JLabel("Swing!", JLabel.CENTER);
  private Font plain = new Font("SansSerif", Font.PLAIN, 20),
              italic = new Font("SansSerif", Font.ITALIC, 20);
  private JRadioButton r1 = new JRadioButton("Blue", true),
                       r2 = new JRadioButton("Red", false),
                       r3 = new JRadioButton("Yellow", false);
  private JCheckBox x1 = new JCheckBox("Italic", true),
                    x2 = new JCheckBox("Centered", true),
                    x3 = new JCheckBox("Black Background",false);

  public JToggleDemo() {    // Constructor
    Container c = getContentPane();
    c.setLayout(new FlowLayout());

    // the text
    c.add(l);
    l.setForeground(Color.blue);
    l.setFont(italic);
    l.setHorizontalAlignment(JLabel.CENTER);
    l.setBackground(Color.white);
    l.setOpaque(true);
    l.setPreferredSize(new Dimension(150,75));

    // the radio buttons
    c.add(r1); c.add(r2); c.add(r3);
    ButtonGroup colors = new ButtonGroup();
    colors.add(r1); colors.add(r2); colors.add(r3);
    r1.addActionListener(this);
    r2.addActionListener(this);
    r3.addActionListener(this);

    // the check boxes
    c.add(x1); c.add(x2); c.add(x3);
    x1.addActionListener(this);
    x2.addActionListener(this);
    x3.addActionListener(this);
```

```
      setSize(350, 150);
      setVisible(true);
      setDefaultCloseOperation(EXIT_ON_CLOSE);
    }

    // listener method
    public void actionPerformed(ActionEvent e) {
      Object b = e.getSource();
      if (b == r1)                        // blue
        l.setForeground(Color.blue);
      else if (b == r2)                   // red
        l.setForeground(Color.red);
      else if (b == r3)                   // yellow
        l.setForeground(Color.yellow);
      else if (b == x1)                   // italic
        if (x1.isSelected())
          l.setFont(italic);
        else
          l.setFont(plain);
      else if (b == x2)                   // centred
        if (x2.isSelected())
          l.setHorizontalAlignment(JLabel.CENTER);
        else
          l.setHorizontalAlignment(JLabel.LEFT);
      else if (b == x3)                   // black background
        if (x3.isSelected())
          l.setBackground(Color.black);
        else
          l.setBackground(Color.white);
    }

    public static void main (String[] arg) {
      JToggleDemo j = new JToggleDemo();
    }
  }
```

We declare the components to be displayed in the window as instance variables of the class. There are a `JLabel` object `l`, three `JRadioButton` objects `r1`, `r2` and `r3`, plus three `JCheckBox` objects `x1`, `x2` and `x3`. We also declare two `Font` objects which describe plain and italic styles. Positioning of the components is done in the usual way in the constructor. We use `FlowLayout`, which means that the components are then lined up from right to left. The check boxes end up in a line of their own at the bottom of the window, since we have chosen a certain size of window to force a new line for the check boxes. (This is a simple, but not terribly good solution, since the position of the components changes if the size of the window changes. It is better to use panels, which we will see later on.)

When the user clicks a check box or a radio button this, as usual, generates an event of class ActionEvent. (It also generates events of class ItemEvent, but it is simpler to handle ActionEvent.) To trap an event like this, we have to link up an event listener of class ActionListener to the tick box or radio button. We make the class itself the listener, so we write **implements** ActionListener at the beginning of the definition of the class. The method actionPerformed is called automatically when the user clicks one of the tick boxes or radio buttons. We use the method getSource to find out which button the user clicked. The result type from this method is of type Object and we put the result in a variable which we call b to avoid having to call the method several times.

6.6 JPanel

The class JPanel is a subclass of JComponent. An object of class JPanel can thus be placed as a child component in a window, but it also has the property that, by using the method add, you can place other GUI components inside it. We use panels as tools when we want to construct a somewhat more complicated GUI. The window can then be constructed hierarchically. Each panel is made to describe one *sub-window*. This is because each panel has its own coordinate system and its own LayoutManager. You can describe each panel separately and then assemble the panels in a larger window. You could easily create a new JPanel by writing

```
JPanel p1 = new JPanel();
```

In the new panel, a LayoutManager of type FlowLayout will be used. If you want to have FlowLayout you can specify the parameter to tell the constructor which LayoutManager will be used in the panel. For example, you could write

```
JPanel p2 = new JPanel(new GridLayout(5,3));
```

A new JPanel automatically becomes transparent.

As an example, we will make a few changes to the program JButtonDemo from page 176. In the constructor, we replace the two lines

```
c.setLayout(new GridLayout(2,2)); // 2 rows, 2 columns
c.add(lab); c.add(exi); c.add(eng); c.add(swe);
```

by the following lines:

```
c.setLayout(new GridLayout(2,1)); // 2 rows, 1 column
JPanel p = new JPanel();
c.add(lab); c.add(p);
p.add(eng); p.add(swe); p.add(exi);
```

The work surface is divided into two lines. The top line contains the JLabel object lab and the lower line contains a JPanel which is called p. On panel p the three buttons are

Figure 6.8 JButtonDemo with JPanel

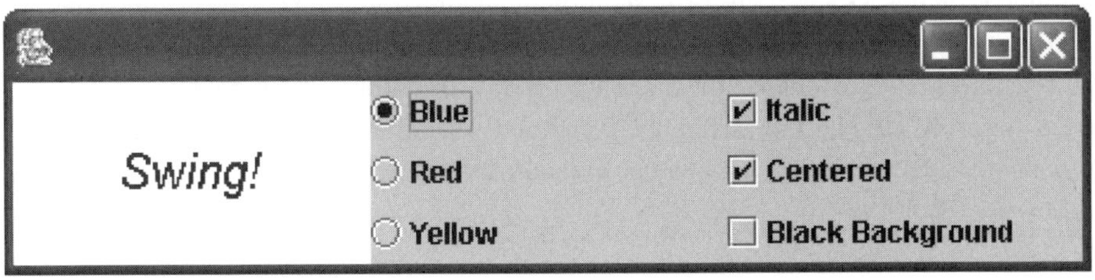

Figure 6.9 JToggleDemo with JPanel

placed: `eng`, `swe` and `exi`. Since a `JPanel` uses `FlowLayout` by default, the buttons will be placed in line after each other on the panel.

We will do another small change. We will allow the program to work out a suitable size for the window itself. So we replace the call to `setSize` by the statement

```
pack();
```

The screen display when the program starts is shown in Figure 6.8.

We will also make a few changes to the program `JToggleDemo` on page 182. We want the radio buttons and tick boxes to be placed as shown in Figure 6.9. No major changes are needed. We use `GridLayout` with one row and three columns. In the first column, we place a `JLabel` object `l`, which contains the text `Swing`. In the other columns, we place two `JPanel` objects `p1` and `p2`:

```
c.setLayout(new GridLayout(1,3));
c.add(l);
JPanel p1 = new JPanel(), p2 = new JPanel();
c.add(p1); c.add(p2);
```

The next step is to specify the appearance of the panels. We make both panels use `GridLayout` with three rows and one column. The three radio buttons are placed in `p1` and the three tick boxes are placed in `p2`:

185

```
p1.setLayout(new GridLayout(3,1));
p2.setLayout(new GridLayout(3,1));
p1.add(r1); p1.add(r2); p1.add(r3);
p2.add(x1); p2.add(x2); p2.add(x3);
```

We will make the program work out a suitable size for the window itself by replacing the call of setSize by the statement

```
pack();
```

6.7 JTextField

Earlier on, we discussed how we could read input data from dialog boxes and command windows. We will now see how we can use the text field to input data to a GUI program. Text input can be done by means of the standard class JTextField. In Section 6.3 we discussed the standard class JLabel. The class JTextField is also used for texts, but the big difference compared with class JLabel is that the user can *change* the text displayed. This is not possible for a JLabel.

We can create a new object of class JTextField in one of the following four ways:

```
JTextField t = new JTextField();
JTextField t = new JTextField(n);
JTextField t = new JTextField("a text");
JTextField t = new JTextField("a text", n);
```

The first declaration gives an empty JTextField object with indeterminate (short) length. The second declaration gives an empty JTextField object with space for n characters.[1] The third declaration gives a JTextField object which initially contains the text "a text". The last declaration gives a JTextField object which contains n characters, and which initially contains the text "a text".

An object of class JTextField, just as with other GUI components, can be placed inside a Container by using the method add. A JTextField object is displayed as a box on the screen. At any time, you can change the size of a JTextField object by calling the method setColumns:

```
t.setColumns(n); // change the size to n characters
((JComponent)t.getParent()).revalidate(); // rearrange
```

and you can get the program to specify the text to be displayed in the box by using the method setText:

```
t.setText("a text"); // show the text "a text"
```

---

[1] The width of the letter "m" (lower-case m) is used as the dimension of each character. Please note that the text field will not have space for n characters, since its border occupies a certain amount of space. It is wise to add a few extra characters.

6.7.1 Inputting simple text

The interesting thing about a JTextField object is that the user can write text in its box. Inside the program, you can see what the user has written by calling the method getText. This method gives the text in the box as its result.

```
String txt = t.getText(); // read the text
```

If you want, you can select the text in a window. Text is then displayed in inverted colours, i.e. white colour on a blue ground. This is done with the method selectAll.

```
t.selectAll(); // select the whole text
```

You can also select part of the text:

```
t.select(i, j); // mark character number i to j
```

and you can read the selected portion of the text with the method getSelectedText:

```
String txt = t.getSelectedText(); // read the selected text
```

When the user presses the Enter key in a JTextField box, this creates an event of type ActionEvent, which means that you can use an event listener to sense when the text in a JTextField box has been changed. Of course, in the usual way, you have to link an

---

JTextField

Please refer to the fact box for JTextComponent on page 209.
Used to input text in GUI programs.

new JTextField()	space for 0 characters
new JTextField(n)	space for n characters
new JTextField("*text*")	contains the text *text* from the beginning
new JTextField("*text*",n)	space for n characters, contains the text *text* from the beginning

Connect an event listener l of class ActionListener to x:

```
x.addActionListener(l)
```

Define the method actionPerformed in the listener:

```
public void actionPerformed(ActionEvent e) {
   // you get here when the user presses the Enter key
   ...
}
```

The following method can be called in the listener:

e.getSource()	returns the object where the event happened
x.getText()	returns the text in the tick box

Figure 6.10 JTextField

event listener to the `JTextField` object. As an example, we will look at a program which produces the window in Figure 6.10.

```
import java.awt.*;
import java.awt.event.*;
import javax.swing.*;

public class Hi extends JFrame implements ActionListener {
  JTextField answer   = new JTextField(20);
  JLabel      greeting = new JLabel();

  public Hi() {      // Constructor
    Container c = getContentPane();
    c.setLayout(new FlowLayout());
    c.add(new JLabel("What is your name? ", JLabel.RIGHT));
    c.add(answer);
    c.add(greeting);
    greeting.setHorizontalAlignment(JLabel.RIGHT);
    answer.addActionListener(this);
    setSize(375,90);
    setVisible(true);
    setDefaultCloseOperation(EXIT_ON_CLOSE);
  }

  public static void main (String[] arg) {
    Hi h = new Hi();
  }

  // listener method
  public void actionPerformed(ActionEvent e) {
    // this method is called when the user presses Enter
    String name = answer.getText();
    greeting.setText("Hi " + name + "!");
  }
}
```

6.7.2   Inputting numeric data

When you are going to input numerical data into a GUI program, you can use the standard class `JTextField`. We have discussed previously, in Section 5.3.1 on page 123,

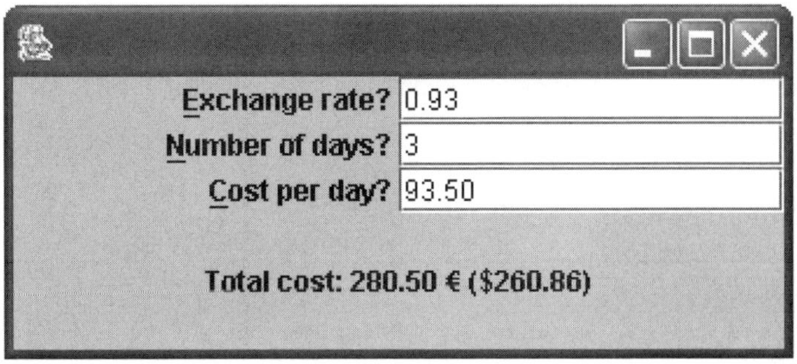

Figure 6.11 JTextField, numeric data

how we can decode numerical data which has been input from a dialog box. Decoding numerical data which has been input from a `JTextField` component can be done in exactly the same way. In other words, you can use the method `Integer.parseInt` or `Double.parseDouble`, but a more general way is to use the methods `toInt` and `toDouble` in the class `Parse`, as we did in Section 5.3.1.

We will demonstrate how inputting numerical data from `JTextField` components can be done by writing a new version of the program `Travel` on page 138, which calculated what it cost to rent a car. The version of the program shown on page 138 used a command window to communicate with the user. The new version will use a GUI. When you run the program, it might look like Figure 6.11. The window is divided into an upper section and a lower section. In the lower half of the window, we put a `JLabel` component which shows the results of the calculation. In the upper half of the window, we put a `JPanel` component which is subdivided into three lines and two columns in its turn. In the left-hand column, three `JLabel` components have been positioned and in the right-hand column there are three `JTextField` components.

The window in Figure 6.11 demonstrates how `JLabel` components and `JTextField` components can occur in pairs and comprise a so-called form. For each `JTextField` component there is an associated `JLabel` component which specifies what should be written in the text field. You can link a `JLabel` component to a `JTextField` component by calling the method `setLabelFor`. The parameter you then give is a reference to the `JTextField` component. We will use this in the program. One advantage of making this connection is that you can use the method `setDisplayedMnemonic` to specify a keyboard shortcut. This is illustrated in Figure 6.11. When you run the program, you can give the keyboard combinations Alt-E, Alt-N and Alt-C. For example, if you write Alt-C, the cursor ends up in the text field on the right of the text `"Cost per day?"`.

The program is as follows. In method `main` we create an object of class `Travel2`. The class constructor is then called and draws the components in the window. We make the current object be an event listener to events in all three `JTextField` components and must then call method `addActionListener` for each of these components. All coding and decoding of data is done in the event listener method.

```java
import java.awt.*;
import java.awt.event.*;
import javax.swing.*;
import java.text.*;
import extra.*; // contains the class Parse

public class Travel2 extends JFrame implements ActionListener {
  JTextField exchAnswer = new JTextField(15);
  JTextField dayAnswer  = new JTextField(15);
  JTextField costAnswer = new JTextField(15);
  JLabel l1 = new JLabel("Exchange rate? ", JLabel.RIGHT);
  JLabel l2 = new JLabel("Number of days? ",  JLabel.RIGHT);
  JLabel l3 = new JLabel("Cost per day? ", JLabel.RIGHT);
  JPanel p = new JPanel();            // upper half
  JLabel result = new JLabel();       // lower half

  public Travel2() { // Constructor
    Container c = getContentPane();
    c.setLayout(new GridLayout(2,1)); // 2 rows 1 column
    c.add(p);
    c.add(result);
    // put the components in the upper half of the window
    p.setLayout(new GridLayout(3,2)); // 3 rows 2 columns
    p.add(l1); p.add(exchAnswer);
    p.add(l2); p.add(dayAnswer);
    p.add(l3); p.add(costAnswer);

    // connect the forms and assign keybord shortcuts
    l1.setLabelFor(exchAnswer); l1.setDisplayedMnemonic('E');
    l2.setLabelFor(dayAnswer);  l2.setDisplayedMnemonic('N');
    l3.setLabelFor(costAnswer); l3.setDisplayedMnemonic('C');
    result.setHorizontalAlignment(JLabel.CENTER);

    // connect the listener
    dayAnswer.addActionListener(this);
    costAnswer.addActionListener(this);
    exchAnswer.addActionListener(this);
    pack();
    setVisible(true);
    setDefaultCloseOperation(EXIT_ON_CLOSE);
  }

  // listener method
  public void actionPerformed(ActionEvent e) {
    // read exchange rate
    String input = exchAnswer.getText();
    double exch = Parse.toDouble(input);
```

```
    // read number of days
    input = dayAnswer.getText();
    int noOfDays = Parse.toInt(input);

    // read cost per day
    input = costAnswer.getText();
    double costPerDay = Parse.toDouble(input);

    // calculate and display total cost
    double totalCost = noOfDays * costPerDay;
    NumberFormat nf = NumberFormat.getInstance();
    nf.setMinimumFractionDigits(2);  // 2 decimals
    nf.setMaximumFractionDigits(2);
    String s = "Total cost: " + nf.format(totalCost)+" \u20AC";
    s = s + " ($" + nf.format(totalCost*exch) + ")";
    result.setText(s);  // display new result
  }
  public static void main (String[] arg) {
    Travel2 t2 = new Travel2();
  }
}
```

The strange character string \u20AC used in the result text is a so-called Unicode sequence. These sequences can be used to designate characters you cannot type on the keyboard. The sequence \u20AC designates the euro symbol. (Special characters and Unicode will be discussed in Section 9.1.)

It is sensible to check that the input numerical values are correct in a program of this type. This can be done in the same way as in Section 5.3.2.

6.8 JComboBox

In this section, we will describe the class JComboBox. A JComboBox is a kind of menu from which you can make different choices.[1] The current choice is displayed at the top of the menu. One possible appearance is demonstrated in Figure 6.12. In the usual case, only the selected choice is displayed (as in the left-hand window). When you press the button with the mouse button, the entire menu is displayed and you can select an alternative. (Please refer to the right-hand window in the figure.)

The methods associated with class JComboBox are summarized in the fact box. You can construct a menu by first creating a JComboBox object and then adding to the alternatives with the method addItem:

---

[1] A JComboBox is really a combination of a button or text field and a JList object in a popup window. The class JList describes lists where you can select one or several alternatives. We discuss the class JList in Section 9.13.

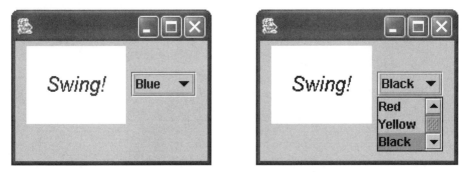

Figure 6.12 JComboBox with texts

```
JComboBox box = new JComboBox();
box.addItem("Blue"); box.addItem("Red"); box.addItem("Yellow");
box.addItem("Black"); box.addItem("Green");
```

The alternatives in a JComboBox can be of any type, but the most common is to use texts, as here. We will demonstrate how we can use icons as an alternative later on. Instead of calling the method addItem for each alternative, we can use a constructor which has a list of the various alternatives as its parameter. The list should be an array or a vector. We have not gone into arrays and vectors yet, but since they are quite simple we will show an example here. The JComboBox object above can be created more easily with the following lines, where we declare the list of alternatives on the first line.

```
String[] colors = {"Blue","Red","Yellow","Black","Green"};
JComboBox box = new JComboBox(colors);
```

The number of alternatives to be shown on the list can be specified by using the method setMaximumRowCount. For example, you could write

```
box.setMaximumRowCount(3);
```

If there are more alternatives than the number shown, you automatically get a slider on the right of the list, so that the user can scroll through it.

The program that generates the window in Figure 6.12 is as follows. When the user selects an alternative in the JComboBox object, this creates an event of type Action-Event. We can then link an event listener of class ActionListener to the JComboBox object. For a JComboBox object, you can use the method getSelectedIndex to find out the alternative that was selected. You then get the number of the alternative as a parameter. (The alternatives are numbered from 0.)

JComboBox

In the table below, x designates a component of class JComboBox.

new JComboBox()	creates an empty JComboBox
new JComboBox(v)	creates a JComboBox, the alternatives are given by v, v is of class Vector or an array containing Object
x.addItem(a)	adds the alternative a to x
x.insertItemAt(a, n)	adds the alternative a at place number n
x.removeItemAt(n)	removes alternative number n
x.removeItem(a)	removes the alternative a
x.getItemAt(n)	gives alternative number n (of type Object)
x.getItemCount()	gives the number of alternatives
x.getSelectedIndex()	gives the number of the selected alternative, or −1 if no alternative is selected
x.getSelectedItem()	gives the selected alternative (of type Object)
x.setSelectedIndex(n)	selects alternative number n
x.setSelectedItem(a)	selects alternative a
x.setEditable(*bool*)	specifies whether the user is allowed to input text
x.setMaximumRowCount(*r*)	specifies the maximum number of lines shown

Connect an event listener l of class ActionListener to x:

```
x.addActionListener(l)
```

Define the method actionPerformed in the listener:

```
public void actionPerformed(ActionEvent e) {
   // you come here when the user has selected an alternative
   // or if the user can write text in the box and press Enter
}
```

The following method can be called in the listener:

e.getSource()	returns the object where the event happened

```
import java.awt.*;
import java.awt.event.*;
import javax.swing.*;

public class JComboDemo extends JFrame implements ActionListener{
   private JLabel l = new JLabel();
   private String[] colors = {"Blue","Red","Yellow",
                              "Black","Green"};
   private JComboBox box = new JComboBox(colors);
```

```
public JComboDemo() { // Constructor
   Container c = getContentPane();
   c.setLayout(new FlowLayout());
   c.add(l); c.add(box);
   l.setForeground(Color.blue);
   l.setFont(new Font("SansSerif", Font.ITALIC, 20));
   l.setHorizontalAlignment(JLabel.CENTER);
   l.setBackground(Color.white);
   l.setOpaque(true);
   l.setText("Swing!");
   l.setPreferredSize(new Dimension(100,75));
   box.setMaximumRowCount(3);
   box.addActionListener(this);
   setSize(200, 150); setVisible(true);
   setDefaultCloseOperation(EXIT_ON_CLOSE);
}

// listener method
public void actionPerformed(ActionEvent e) {
   if (box.getSelectedIndex() == 0)
      l.setForeground(Color.blue);
   else if (box.getSelectedIndex() == 1)
      l.setForeground(Color.red);
   else if (box.getSelectedIndex() == 2)
      l.setForeground(Color.yellow);
   else if (box.getSelectedIndex() == 3)
      l.setForeground(Color.black);
   else if (box.getSelectedIndex() == 4)
      l.setForeground(Color.green);
}

public static void main (String[] arg) {
   JComboDemo j = new JComboDemo ();
}
}
```

We will also show an example of using icons as an alternative in a JComboBox. In Figure 6.13 a window is shown which contains a JComboBox, which contains three alternatives: a German, a French and a British flag. Depending on the alternative selected it displays the text *Willkommen!*, *Bienvenue!* or *Welcome!*.

We can start off with the program JComboDemo above and do a few simple changes. We start by using the following texts to replace the statements in the constructor where we define the text to be displayed and the menu alternatives available:

```
l.setText("Willkommen!");
l.setPreferredSize(new Dimension(150,75));
box.addItem(new ImageIcon("flag_ger.gif"));
box.addItem(new ImageIcon("flag_fra.gif"));
box.addItem(new ImageIcon("flag_eng.gif"));
```

Figure 6.13 JComboBox with icons

We also write a new event listener method:

```
// Listener method
public void actionPerformed(ActionEvent e) {
   if (box.getSelectedIndex() == 0)
      l.setText("Willkommen!");
   else if (box.getSelectedIndex() == 1)
      l.setText("Bienvenue!");
   else if (box.getSelectedIndex() == 2)
      l.setText("Welcome!");
}
```

When you have JComboBox components where the alternatives are texts, you might want to design them so that the user can write text in the box displayed at the top of the menu. The user then has another way to choose alternatives. In Figure 6.14 you can see what it looks like. This is a new version of the program Hi on page 188. The program is designed so that the user can either choose and select a name on the list, or write a new name. The list is empty at the beginning. Each time the user writes in a new name which was not previously on the list, the program automatically adds the new name.

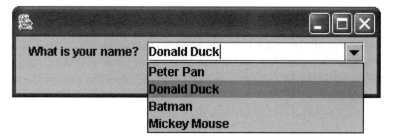

Figure 6.14 Editable JComboBox

The program is as follows. We can quite easily replace the text field by a JComboBox. Note that this has been made editable by calling setEditable.

```java
import java.awt.*;
import java.awt.event.*;
import javax.swing.*;

public class HiAgain extends JFrame implements ActionListener {
  JComboBox answer = new JComboBox();
  JLabel    greeting = new JLabel();

  public HiAgain() {      // Constructor
    Container c = getContentPane();
    c.setLayout(new FlowLayout());
    c.add(new JLabel("What is your name? ", JLabel.RIGHT));
    c.add(answer);
    c.add(greeting);
    greeting.setHorizontalAlignment(JLabel.RIGHT);
    answer.setPreferredSize(new Dimension(220,20));
    answer.setEditable(true);
    answer.addActionListener(this);
    setSize(375,90);
    setVisible(true);
    setDefaultCloseOperation(EXIT_ON_CLOSE);
  }

  // listener method
  public void actionPerformed(ActionEvent e) {
    String name = (String) answer.getSelectedItem();
    greeting.setText("Hi " + name + "!");
    if (answer.getSelectedIndex() == -1)   // a new name?
      answer.addItem(name);
  }

  public static void main (String[] arg) {
    HiAgain h = new HiAgain();
  }
}
```

6.9 JSlider

Numerical data can be input to a GUI program, as we have seen, by using dialog boxes or components of class JTextField, but in some cases another class JSlider offers a more elegant approach. A JSlider object is a slider which the user can use to set values. If you want to, you can place a "ruler" along the slider, which makes it easier to see the value being set. There is also a simpler class, JScrollBar, but when you use it, you cannot use a ruler. So we will content ourselves with describing the more advanced class JSlider.

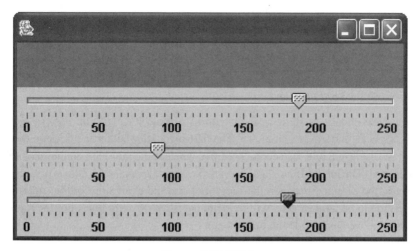

Figure 6.15 JSlider

To demonstrate how the class `JSlider` works, we will write a program which displays a box. The user can then use three sliders, one for each primary colour, to choose the colour displayed in the box. For each primary colour, the user can set an arbitrary value between 0 and 255 and the colour in the box is displayed with the colour combination set. This is shown in Figure 6.15.

When you create a `JSlider` object, you can specify various properties. To create the top slider in Figure 6.15 we could write

```
JSlider r = new JSlider(JSlider.HORIZONTAL, 0,  255, 0);
```

The first argument specifies the orientation. You can choose between `JSlider.HORI-ZONTAL` and `JSlider.VERTICAL`. Arguments number two and three specify the minimum and maximum values for the slider. The last argument specifies the default value. The following conditions must always be met:

```
minimum <= value <= value+extent <= maximum
```

(The value `extent` specifies the width of the thumb grip that the user pulls along. It is easiest not to specify any value for `extent`. It then becomes equal to zero, but the thumb grip is still drawn the way it should be.)

You can use the methods `setMinimum`, `setMaximum` and `setValue` to change the variables dynamically from the program. If you were to specify values that do not coincide with the condition above, the methods "correct" the values of the variables automatically so that the condition is still true.

The position of a slider can be read from the program. We then use the method `getValue`. A horizontal slider usually has its lowest value on the left and its highest value on the right. A vertical slider usually has its lowest value at the bottom and its highest value at the top. This can be changed to the other way round. In this case, we call the method `setInverted` with value **true** as argument.

The user can operate a slider in three ways: pull the thumb grip, click the "track" of the slider, or use the keys `PgUp` and `PgDn`.

You can also choose to show a slider with or without a ruler. You use the methods `setPaintTicks` and `setPaintLabels`. The first specifies whether the lines on the ruler should be displayed, and the second specifies whether the numbers on the ruler should be displayed. The methods `setMajorTickSpacing` and `setMinorTickSpacing` are used to specify the distance between the long lines and the short lines on the ruler. If the numbers are to be written, they will be written against the long lines. For the top slider in the figure, we have made the calls

```
r.setPaintTicks(true);      r.setPaintLabels(true);
r.setMajorTickSpacing(50);  r.setMinorTickSpacing(5);
```

These specify that a slider with both lines and figures should be drawn, and that the distance between the long lines should be 50 units and the distance between the short lines 5 units.

The program that generates the image in Figure 6.15 is as follows. The window is subdivided into four rows, with one column on each row. At the top, we have a `JLabel` object, and underneath there are three lines with a `JSlider` object on each row. For each `JSlider` object, the foreground has been set to the colour that the slider controls.

```
import java.awt.*;
import java.awt.event.*;
import javax.swing.*;
import javax.swing.event.*;  // contains ChangeListener

public class JSliderDemo extends JFrame
                              implements ChangeListener {
   JLabel  l = new JLabel();
   JSlider r = new JSlider(JSlider.HORIZONTAL, 0,  255, 0);
   JSlider g = new JSlider(JSlider.HORIZONTAL, 0,  255, 0);
   JSlider b = new JSlider(JSlider.HORIZONTAL, 0,  255, 255);

   public JSliderDemo() {
      Container c = getContentPane();
      c.setLayout(new GridLayout(4, 1, 0, 5));
      c.add(l); c.add(r); c.add(g); c.add(b);
      l.setOpaque(true);
      l.setBackground(new Color(r.getValue(), g.getValue(),
                             b.getValue()));
      r.setForeground(Color.red);
      g.setForeground(Color.green);
```

```
      b.setForeground(Color.blue);
      r.setPaintTicks(true);        r.setPaintLabels(true);
      g.setPaintTicks(true);        g.setPaintLabels(true);
      b.setPaintTicks(true);        b.setPaintLabels(true);
      r.setMajorTickSpacing(50); r.setMinorTickSpacing(5);
      g.setMajorTickSpacing(50); g.setMinorTickSpacing(5);
      b.setMajorTickSpacing(50); b.setMinorTickSpacing(5);
      r.addChangeListener(this);
      g.addChangeListener(this);
      b.addChangeListener(this);

      setSize(400, 225);
      setVisible(true);
      setDefaultCloseOperation(EXIT_ON_CLOSE);
   }

   // listener method
   public void stateChanged(ChangeEvent e) {
      l.setBackground(new Color(r.getValue(), g.getValue(),
                                b.getValue()));
      l.repaint();   // repaint the pane with the new color
   }

   public static void main (String[] arg) {
      JSliderDemo j = new JSliderDemo();
   }
}
```

When the user operates a slider, this generates an event of type ChangeEvent. To manage events like this, you have to use an event listener of class ChangeListener. Please note that we wrote **implements** ChangeListener at the beginning. The declarations of the classes that relate to ChangeEvent are in the package javax.swing.event, which must be imported. When an event occurs the method stateChanged is called and we have to write our own version of it. This is where we read the three sliders and redraw the box with the new colour.

When the user pulls a slider, this generates many events of type ChangeEvent in one sequence. Sometimes, you are only interested in reading the slider position during the last of these events. You can then use the method getValueIsAdjusting to sense whether the slider is still moving, and ignore the current value if it is. This can make the program more efficient, of course, since it does not have to process all the temporary values. In our program above, we probably want to process all the values. We want to see how the colour in the square gradually changes when we move the slider. But if we were only interested in the final value, and did not want to see the gradual change in colour, we could write the listener method as follows:

JSlider

new JSlider(*position, min value, max value, init value*)
   position is JSlider.HORIZONTAL or JSlider.VERTICAL

x.setValue(n)	sets the value
x.getValue()	reads the value
x.setMinimum(n)	sets the minimum value
x.getMinimum()	reads the minimum value
x.setMaximum(n)	sets the maximum value
x.getMaximum()	reads the maximum value
x.setInverted(*bool*)	specifies whether the scale should be inverted or not
x.setPaintLabels(*bool*)	specifies whether figures should be displayed on the "ruler"
x.setPaintTicks(*bool*)	specifies whether lines should be displayed on the "ruler"
x.setMajorTickSpacing(n)	sets the distance between the long lines
x.setMinorTickSpacing(n)	sets the distance between the short lines
x.getValueIsAdjusting()	gives **true** if the user is changing the value

Connect an event listener l of class ChangeListener to x:

```
import javax.swing.event.*;
   ...
x.addChangeListener(l)
```

Define the method stateChanged in the listener:

```
public void stateChanged(ChangeEvent e) {
   // you get here when the user changes the JSlider
   ...
}
```

```
// listener method
public void stateChanged(ChangeEvent e) {
   JSlider source = (JSlider) e.getSource(); //type conversion
   if (!source.getValueIsAdjusting()) {      // not adjusting?
     l.setBackground(new Color(r.getValue(), g.getValue(),
                               b.getValue())));
     l.repaint();    // repaint the pane with the new color
   }
}
```

In the example we have shown, we made the class lay the figures out on the ruler. In the class JSlider, you can also specify the figures to be displayed on the ruler yourself. It does not have to be numbers. We will leave this to your own reading, however.

Figure 6.16 JSpinner

6.10 `JSpinner`

Another way to input numerical data into a GUI program is to use the class `JSpinner`. A `JSpinner` is displayed on screen as a text field with associated arrows. Using these arrows, the user can make a choice. The user can also input data directly in the text field. One possible appearance is demonstrated in Figure 6.16, which has been generated by a program that is used to order theatre tickets. The figure contains three `JSpinner` components alongside each other. A `JSpinner` can display numerical values, ordinary texts or times. These three variants are demonstrated in the figure.

When you are going to create a `JSpinner`, start by creating a so-called *model*, which describes the data to be displayed in the `JSpinner`. There are three standard classes which you can use to create these models: `SpinnerNumberModel`, `SpinnerListModel` and `SpinnerDateModel`. We will start by demonstrating how to create a `JSpinner` that will display integers. We first declare a model and then a `JSpinner` that will use the model. This can have the following appearance:

```
SpinnerNumberModel mod1 = new SpinnerNumberModel();
JSpinner spin1 = new JSpinner(mod1);
```

If you do not give the model's constructor any parameters you get a `JSpinner` that contains the value 0 from the beginning. The increment, i.e. the amount that the value displayed in the `JSpinner` is changed each time you press the up or down arrows, becomes 1. There will not be any upper or lower limit for the values.

If you want to, you can influence the `JSpinner`'s properties by giving parameters to the model's constructor. You then specify the start value, the smallest and largest value and the increment. A `JSpinner` that has start value 50, permissible values between 0 and 100 and increment 5 is created by the following program lines:

```
SpinnerNumberModel mod2 = new SpinnerNumberModel(50, 0, 100, 5);
JSpinner spin2 = new JSpinner(mod2);
```

To create a `JSpinner` that displays a list of different texts, first create a model of the class `SpinnerListModel`. For example, to create a `JSpinner` that you can use to choose different colours, we write

JSpinner

First create a *model* of what is to be included in the JSpinner. You can display numerical values, a list of texts or times. This is done in one of the following ways:

```
new SpinnerNumberModel() // default value: 0, step: 1
new SpinnerNumberModel(value, min, max, step)
new SpinnerListModel(l)  // l is an array or is of type List
new SpinnerDateModel()   // default value: now, step: day
new SpinnerDateModel (value, min, max, step)
  // step is Calendar.HOUR_OF_DAY, Calendar.DAY_OF_MONTH etc.
```

Then create a JSpinner and link the model to it:

```
new JSpinner(model)
```

Method for models:

`m.setValue(obj)`	sets the value (`obj` has type `Object`)
`m.getValue()`	reads the value (return value of type `Object`)
`m.getNextValue()`	gives the value after the current value
`m.getPreviousValue()`	gives the value before the current value

For numerical models, there are also

`m.getValue()`	reads the value (return value of type `Number`)
`m.setMinimum(n)`	sets the min value, n is a subclass of `Number`
`m.setMaximum(n)`	sets the max value, n is a subclass of `Number`
`m.setStepSize(n)`	sets the increment, n is a subclass of `Number`

For models for times, there are also

`m.getDate()`	reads the value (return value of type `Date`)
`m.setStart(d)`	sets the minimum value, d is of class `Date`
`m.setEnd(d)`	sets the maximum value, d is of class `Date`
`m.setCalendarField(s)`	sets increment, s is defined in class `Calendar`

You can change the editor for a JSpinner sp which displays dates:

```
sp.setEditor(new JSpinner.DateEditor(sp,"pattern"));
```

You can link an event listener l of class ChangeListener to a JSpinner sp:

```
import javax.swing.event.*;
  ...
sp.addChangeListener(l)
```

In this case, define the method stateChanged in the listener:

```
public void stateChanged(ChangeEvent e) {
   // you get here when the user changes a JSpinner
}
```

```
String[] colors = {"Blue", "Red", "Yellow", "Black", "Green"};
SpinnerListModel mod3 = new SpinnerListModel(colors);
JSpinner spin3 = new JSpinner(mod3);
```

(Note that we use the same technique to define lists here as we did on page 192 when we specified the alternatives that should be found in a JComboBox.)

A JSpinner that displays times can be created quite simply with the following lines:

```
SpinnerDateModel mod4 = new SpinnerDateModel();
JSpinner spin4 = new JSpinner(mod4);
```

If you do not give the model's constructor any parameters, the JSpinner will be initialized so that it displays today's date and the present time. The increment will be one day and there will not be any upper or lower limit for the times that can be displayed. If you want to change the increment size, you can call method setCalendarField. For example, to change JSpinnern spin4 so that the increment becomes an hour, we write

```
mod4.setCalendarField(Calendar.HOUR_OF_DAY);
```

The parameter should be one of the constants, e.g. DAY_OF_MONTH, defined in standard class Calendar.

You can also set an upper and lower limit for a JSpinner that displays times by calling the methods setStart and setEnd. These should preferably have a parameter of the standard class Date (please refer to page 146). We show examples of this below.

Times are a bit complicated since they can be displayed in several different ways. Each JSpinner contains an internal, so-called *editor* which determines how the value should be displayed on screen. If you do not specify otherwise, times will be displayed in their full form, with both date and time of day. You may not always want things to look like this. You can then specify that another editor should be used. For example, to specify that JSpinner spin4 should only display hours (00–23), you write

```
JSpinner.DateEditor e = new JSpinner.DateEditor(spin4,"HH");
spin4.setEditor(e);
```

An editor that edits times is, as can be seen, an object of class JSpinner.DateEditor. When we create an editor, we use a text to specify how the times should be edited. The same rules apply as when we create an object of class SimpleDateFormat (please refer to page 150). Here also, please refer to the documentation of class SimpleDateFormat for further details.

For all types of JSpinner models, there are methods you can call to read or change the JSpinner's properties. These are summarized in the fact box. It is of particular interest to be able to read the text displayed in a JSpinner. It is a good idea to use the method getNumber for JSpinners that display numerical data, getValue for JSpinners that display text and getDate for JSpinners that display times. Please note that these methods should be called for the *model* that is linked to the JSpinner. To read the text displayed in spin1, spin3 and spin4 above, we could write

```
int value   = mod1.getNumber().intValue();
String col  = mod3.getValue().toString();
Date time   = mod4.getDate();
```

We will now show the program that generates the window in Figure 6.16. When this program is run, the user should set suitable values by using the three JSpinner components. Each time the user clicks the Book button, a printout is generated in the command window, containing the current order. For example, if you click the button when it looks as shown in the figure, you get the following printout:

```
4 tickets, 1st balcony, 11/23/02
```

(American conventions have been used.) The program is as follows:

```
import java.awt.*;
import java.awt.event.*;
import javax.swing.*;
import java.util.*;    // contains Calendar
import java.text.*;    // contains DateFormat

public class Ticket extends JFrame implements ActionListener {
   private JButton b = new JButton("Book");

   // create a spinner for number of tickets
   private SpinnerNumberModel modNumber =
                              new SpinnerNumberModel(1, 1, 10, 1);
   private JSpinner sp1 = new JSpinner(modNumber);

   // create a spinner for seat
   private String[] se = {"front stalls", "back stalls",
                  "1st balcony", "2nd balcony", "3rd balcony"};
   private SpinnerListModel modSeat = new SpinnerListModel(se);
   private JSpinner sp2 = new JSpinner(modSeat);

   // create a spinner for date
   private SpinnerDateModel modDay = new SpinnerDateModel();
   private JSpinner sp3 = new JSpinner(modDay);

   public Ticket() {   // constructor
      // set editor for sp3
      sp3.setEditor(new JSpinner.DateEditor(sp3,
                                        "EEE d MMM yyyy"));
      // set lower and upper limits for date
      Calendar cal = Calendar.getInstance();
      cal.add(Calendar.DAY_OF_MONTH, -1);
```

```
      modDay.setStart(cal.getTime());
      cal.add(Calendar.MONTH, 6);
      modDay.setEnd(cal.getTime());

      Container c = getContentPane();
      c.setLayout(new FlowLayout());
      c.add(sp1); c.add(sp2); c.add(sp3); c.add(b);
      b.addActionListener(this);
      pack(); setVisible(true);
      setDefaultCloseOperation(EXIT_ON_CLOSE);
   }

   // listener method
   public void actionPerformed(ActionEvent e) {
      if (e.getSource() == b) {
         // read no of tickets, seat and date
         int    noOfTickets = modNumber.getNumber().intValue();
         String seat = modSeat.getValue().toString();
         Date   day  = modDay.getDate();

         // print the information
         DateFormat f =
                   DateFormat.getDateInstance(DateFormat.SHORT);
         System.out.println(noOfTickets + " tickets, " +
                         seat + ", " + f.format(day));
      }
   }

   public static void main (String[] arg) {
      Ticket tick = new Ticket ();
   }
}
```

A couple of details can be mentioned. The first applies to the constructor. It calls the methods setStart and setEnd to set the upper and lower limits for the JSpinner that displays the date. It should be possible to order tickets as from today's date and six months ahead. To form the two limits, we use the auxiliary object cal of type Calendar (please refer to Section 5.6.3). The object cal is initialized automatically, so that it contains the current date. We then reduce this by one day to get the lower limit. (This should not really be necessary, but it does not work otherwise.) After this, cal is incremented by six months to create the upper limit.

The second detail refers to editing the date. In the JSpinner we have used an editor with format code "EEE d MMM yyyy", which means that the date in the JSpinner is displayed in the format Sat 23 Nov 2002. In the listener method, we use a different format for the printout. The formatter used there is f, which edits the date in format 11/23/02. (Of course, we could have edited the date in the same way in both places, but we did it this way to demonstrate the possibilities.)

In the program above, we have just linked an event listener to button b. No event listeners are linked to the JSpinner components. It is also possible, however, to link an event listener to a JSpinner. When the user clicks forwards to a new value in a JSpinner, this creates an event of type ChangeEvent. To process these events, we proceed in exactly the same way as we did for components of type JSlider in Section 6.9. We connect an event listener of class ChangeListener to the JSpinner component.

6.11 JScrollPane

Sometimes, one wants to be able to study something which is larger than the dimensions of the available space. You can then use the method JScrollPane. A JScrollPane object contains a component, a so-called *viewport*. This component can be any type of component, including a JPanel. If the viewport components are larger than the JScrollPane object, you can have a slider on the edges, so that the user can decide which part of the component he or she wants to see. You can create a JScrollPane object sp and place an arbitrarily chosen component comp in it by using the program line

```
JScrollPane sp = new JScrollPane(comp);
```

This can also be done in two stages:

```
JScrollPane sp1 = new JScrollPane();
sp.setViewportView(comp);
```

In the constructor in class JScrollPane you can include two extra parameters, which specify whether you always or never want to have a horizontal and vertical slider. Unless you specify otherwise, the slider will automatically be added if a JScrollPane object is larger than the component it contains.

As an example, we will study a program which displays the windows in Figure 6.17. The window contains two JScrollPane objects placed side by side. Both JScrollPane objects contain JLabel objects with icons on them. Both JScrollPane objects are smaller than the components they contain, which is why the sliders have been generated.

```
import java.awt.*;
import javax.swing.*;

public class JScrollDemo extends JFrame {
    JLabel l1       = new JLabel(new ImageIcon("Sara.jpg"));
    JLabel l2       = new JLabel(new ImageIcon("Flowers.jpg"));
    JScrollPane sp1 = new JScrollPane(l1);
    JScrollPane sp2 = new JScrollPane(l2);

    public JScrollDemo() {
        Container c = getContentPane();
```

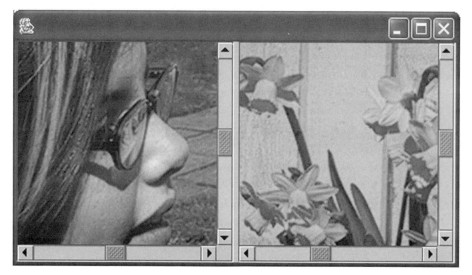

Figure 6.17 JScrollPane

```
        c.setLayout(new GridLayout(1, 2, 5, 0));
        c.add(sp1); c.add(sp2);
        setSize(450,250); setVisible(true);
        setDefaultCloseOperation(EXIT_ON_CLOSE);
    }

    public static void main (String[] arg) {
        JScrollDemo j = new JScrollDemo();
    }
}
```

Since we use `GridLayout` the `JScrollPane` object's size will be decided by the size of the surrounding window as usual, and the size will be changed automatically if you drag the window to make it larger or smaller. If you make the window so large that an entire image is visible, the slider for the image will disappear.

The properties of class `JScrollPane` are summarized in the fact box. Please note that there are methods you could use to position arbitrarily chosen objects, such as headings. A column header ends up at the top of the columns and a line header ends up at the furthest left. Both types of header are dragged along when the user drags a `JScrollPane` component's slider. There is also a method which can be used to position components in the four corners of a `JScrollPane` component.

A `JScrollPane` object can contain only one viewport component. For this reason, it is common practice to make it a `JPanel` on which you can then place other components. It is common to want sliders round the entire window. We can then replace the

---

JScrollPane

In the following constructors, `c` is an arbitrary component.

`v` should be `JScrollPane.VERTICAL_SCROLLBAR_AS_NEEDED`,
`JScrollPane.VERTICAL_SCROLLBAR_NEVER` or `JScrollPane.VERTICAL_SCROLLBAR_ALWAYS`

`h` should be `JScrollPane.HORIZONTAL_SCROLLBAR_AS_NEEDED`, `JScrollPane.HORIZONTAL_`
`SCROLLBAR_NEVER` or `JScrollPane.HORIZONTAL_SCROLLBAR_ALWAYS`

new `JScrollPane()`	new, empty `JScrollPane`. Gives sliders when necessary
new `JScrollPane(c)`	new `JScrollPane` in which the component `c` is placed. Gives sliders when necessary
new `JScrollPane(v,h)`	as above, but the sliders are determined by `v` and `h`
new `JScrollPane(c,v,h)`	as above, but the sliders are determined by `v` and `h`
`x.setViewportView(c)`	places the component `c` in `x`
`x.setColumnHeaderView(c)`	places the component `c` as a column header in `x`
`x.setRowHeaderView(c)`	places the component `c` as a line header in `x`
`x.setCorner(h, c)`	places the component `c` in the corner `h` in `x`

   `h` should be `JScrollPane.UPPER_LEFT_CORNER`, `JScrollPane.UPPER_RIGHT_CORNER`,
   `JScrollPane.LOWER_LEFT_CORNER` or `JScrollPane.LOWER_RIGHT_CORNER`

---

window's work surface, its `contentPane`, with a `JScrollPane` which contains a `JPanel`. We then place the window components on this panel instead of placing them on the window's `contentPane`. In the programs, you could replace the call

```
Container c = getContentPane();
```

by the following lines

```
JPanel c = new JPanel();
JScrollPane sp = new JScrollPane(c);
setContentPane(sp);
```

The only thing you need to remember in this case is that a `JPanel` has `FlowLayout` as default, whereas a `contentPane` has `BorderLayout` as default.

6.12 `JTextArea` and `JTextComponent`

The class `JTextField` was used to allow the user to provide input data on one line. If you want to display a longer text, or allow the user to edit more than one line, you can use the class `JTextArea`. This class has many similarities with class `JTextField` (they both have a common superclass `JTextComponent`). For example, both classes can be used to allow the program to read text written by the user, or the portion of text that the user has selected. (Please refer to the fact box.)

JTextComponent

In the table below, `t` designates an object of class `JTextComponent` or one of its subclasses, such as `JTextField`, `JTextArea` and `JEditorPane`.

`t.setEditable(`*bool*`)`	specifies whether the user is allowed to edit the text
`t.setText("`*text*`")`	changes the text in `t` to `"`*text*`"`
`t.getText()`	returns the text
`t.getSelectedText()`	returns the selected portion of the text
`t.select(i,j)`	selects the text between positions `i` and `j`
`t.selectAll()`	selects the entire text
`t.getSelectionStart()`	gives the position where selection started
`t.getSelectionEnd()`	gives the position where selection ended
`t.read(r, `**`null`**`)`	reads the text from the stream `r` (of type `Reader`) and puts the read text in `t` (previous text is erased)
`t.write(w)`	writes the text in `t` to the stream `w` (of type `Writer`)

When we create a new object of class `JTextArea` we have several opportunities. For example, if you want to create a `JTextArea` with `r` rows and `k` columns, you write

```
JTextArea a = new JTextArea(r, k);
```

If you want to have a slider round the text area, you should put the `JTextArea` object in a `JScrollPane` object:

```
JScrollPane sp = new JScrollPane(a);
```

JTextArea

Please refer to the fact box for `JTextComponent`.

`new` `JTextArea()`	creates an empty text area
`new` `JTextArea("`*text*`")`	creates a text area with text *text*
`new` `JTextArea(r,k)`	creates a text area with `r` rows and `k` columns
`new` `JTextArea("`*text*`",r,k)`	`r` rows and `k` columns with text *text*
`a.append("`*text*`")`	adds the text *text* last in the text area `a`
`a.insert("`*text*`",i)`	inserts the text *text* starting from position `i`
`a.replaceRange("`*text*`",i,j)`	replaces the text between position `i` and `j` with *text*
`a.setRows(r)`, `a.setColumns(k)`	sets the numbers of rows and columns
`a.getRows()`, `a.getColumns()`	returns the numbers of rows and columns
`a.setLineWrap(`*bool*`)`	specifies whether long lines should be wrapped or not
`a.setWrapStyleWord(`*bool*`)`	specifies whether any line wrapping may only be done at word borders

The user can write text in the area and then cut and paste as normal, but we can also get the program to add and delete text. It is also possible to specify that only the program can change the text in the text area. This could be useful if you want to display a text to the user, such as a help text. A summary of the most important methods is given in the fact boxes. Assume, for example, that we have a `String` variable `s` and that we want to insert the text in `s` last in the text area. We can then make the call

```
a.append(s + "\n"); // add s + new line character
```

You can see a demonstration here of inserting the character `\n` to force a new line in the text area, after the inserted text.

We will now show a quite advanced program, a text editor. It is surprisingly simple to construct the program, using the standard classes. When you run the program, you see a window as in Figure 6.18.

The user can edit the text in the usual way in the text area. If you want to open and import an existing text file, you write the name of the file at the top left of the text field, and then click the button `Open`. The previous contents of the text area are erased and the new file is read. If you click the button `Save` the program will save the text displayed in the text area to the specified file.

The window has been divided into two sections. At the top, there is a panel containing five components: a `JLabel`, a `JTextField` object and three buttons. The components on the panel are placed using `GridLayout` (one row and five columns.) Under the panel, there is a `JTextArea` object. The panel and the `JTextArea` object are placed on the

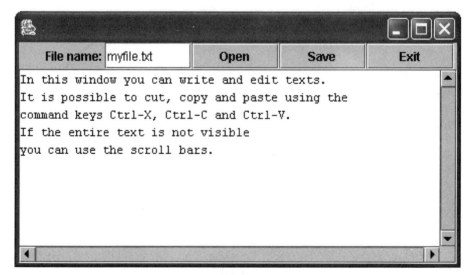

Figure 6.18 A text editor

window using `BorderLayout`. (We do not have to specify explicitly that `BorderLayout` should be used, since `BorderLayout` is the default for a window's `contentPane`.) We have not yet considered `BorderLayout`, but it can briefly be said that when you place components, you specify the direction in which they should be placed. In addition, you can specify the position CENTER. The panel containing the buttons is placed in the NORTH. The text area is placed in the CENTER, which means that it will get all the extra space if the window is enlarged. The program is as follows:

```java
import java.awt.*;
import java.awt.event.*;
import java.io.*;
import javax.swing.*;

public class TextEdit extends JFrame implements ActionListener {
    JPanel p = new JPanel();
    JTextField name = new JTextField();
    JButton    open = new JButton("Open");
    JButton    save = new JButton("Save");
    JButton    exit = new JButton("Exit");
    JTextArea  area = new JTextArea(10,60);
    JScrollPane sp  = new JScrollPane(area,
                      JScrollPane.VERTICAL_SCROLLBAR_ALWAYS,
                      JScrollPane.HORIZONTAL_SCROLLBAR_ALWAYS);

    public TextEdit() {
        Container c = getContentPane();
        p.setFont(new Font("SansSerif", Font.PLAIN, 12));
        area.setFont(new Font("Monospaced", Font.PLAIN, 12));
        c.add(p,  BorderLayout.NORTH);
        c.add(sp, BorderLayout.CENTER);

        // put the components in the panel p
        p.setLayout(new GridLayout(1,5));
        p.add(new JLabel("File name: ", JLabel.RIGHT));
        p.add(name); p.add(open); p.add(save); p.add(exit);
        name.addActionListener(this);
        open.addActionListener(this);
        save.addActionListener(this);
        exit.addActionListener(this);
        pack();
        setVisible(true);
        setDefaultCloseOperation(EXIT_ON_CLOSE);
    }

    public void actionPerformed(ActionEvent e) {
        // check which button the user has pressed
        if (e.getSource() == name || e.getSource() == open)
            readFile(name.getText());
        else if (e.getSource() == save)
```

```
         saveFile(name.getText());
      else if (e.getSource() == exit)
         System.exit(0);
   }

   private void readFile(String fileName) {
      try {
         FileReader r = new FileReader(fileName);
         area.read(r, null);
      }
      catch (IOException e) {}
   }

   private void saveFile(String fileName) {
      try {
         FileWriter w = new FileWriter(fileName);
         area.write(w);
      }
      catch (IOException e) {}
   }

   public static void main (String[] arg) {
      TextEdit t = new TextEdit();
   }
}
```

Some details can be mentioned. The method `readFile`, which is called when the user has pressed the button `Open`, calls the method `read` to read the file and display the text in the text area, so that it becomes visible in the window. To get a stream which is linked to the file, we use the same technique as in Section 5.5.2. However, we do not need a stream of class `BufferedReader`; it is enough to use the class `FileReader`.

Both method `read` and the constructor in class `FileReader` can generate error signals of type `IOException`. We have worked round this problem previously, by writing **throws** `IOException` in the method header. This cannot be done when we use listener methods, however. For this reason, we must use the other technique and trap any errors ourselves. This is done here in a so-called **try** statement. We will not go into the details here. Exceptions are covered in detail in Chapter 11.

The method `saveFile` has the same structure as the method `readFile`. Here also, we must use a **try** statement to trap error signals.

6.13 JEditorPane

The class `JTextArea` which we studied in the previous section is used to display and edit simple text. This contains the properties found in common text editors. The class `JTextPane` is an advanced class which can handle texts containing various forms of editing information, such as information about fonts and colours. Using this class (plus a number of other standard classes), we can implement word-processing programs etc. The class `JTextPane` is quite complicated to use, which means that there is no space for full description in this book. We will, however, include a brief discussion of the simpler superclass `JEditorPane`.

The class `JEditorPane` contains a number of ready-made tools for processing simple texts, and texts in HTML format and rtf format. In other words, you can use a `JEditorPane` component to display web pages. This means that it is relatively simple to write your own web browser, using this class, but since the class is not able to manage all the formats used in web pages, it is more suitable for displaying simple sites. It can be used to display local pages (in HTML format), for example, which contain various types of documentation. We will take a look one of these programs here.

When you first start the program, you see a dialog box in which you are asked to write a link to the page to be displayed. You can then write either a simple file name in your own computer, or a web address. The program then opens a window in which the requested page is displayed. One possible appearance is Figure 6.19, where we have given the file name `http://java.sun.com/j2se/1.4/docs/index.html`. The user can then click a link on the web page displayed, just as with an ordinary web browser. The program will then display the page to which the link leads.

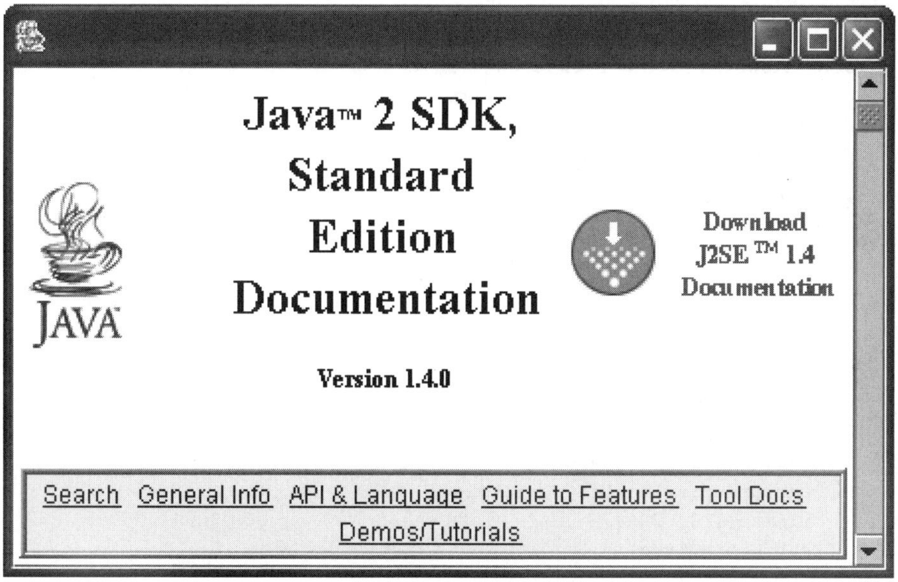

Figure 6.19 JEditorPane

The class `JEditorPane` is a subclass of `JTextComponent` and thus has all the properties displayed in the fact box on page 209. The most important new method is `setPage`, which is used to specify the page to be displayed. The method `setPage` should have a parameter which contains the link to the page you want. The parameter can be either an ordinary text (a `String`) or an object of class `URL` (Uniform Resource Locator). The latter contains a unique address. (Please refer to Chapter 17.)

When the user points to a link on the displayed page, this creates an event of type `HyperlinkEvent`. To trap an event like this, you must have an event listener of type `HyperlinkListener` and this event listener must have a method called `hyperlinkUpdate`. There are two usable methods in the class `HyperlinkEvent`, which can be called from inside the listener method. The first is `getURL`, which returns a `URL` object which contains the link that the user pointed to. The other interesting method in class `HyperlinkEvent` is `getEventType`, which says what type of event it was. The return value can be `HyperlinkEvent.EventType.ENTERED`, `HyperlinkEvent.EventType.EXITED` or `HyperlinkEvent.EventType.ACTIVATED`. The first two say that the user moved the cursor over the link or moved the cursor away from the link, respectively. The last value, which is what we are interested in here, says that the user double-clicked the link.

The program that generates the window in Figure 6.19 is as follows.

```java
import java.awt.*;
import java.io.*;
import javax.swing.*;
import javax.swing.event.*;

public class HTMLViewer extends JFrame
                              implements HyperlinkListener {
  JEditorPane page = new JEditorPane();
  JScrollPane sp   = new JScrollPane(page);

  public HTMLViewer(String adr) throws IOException {
    if (!adr.startsWith("http://") && !adr.startsWith("file:"))
      // no protocol was specified by the user, add http
      if (adr.startsWith("www"))
        adr = "http://" + adr;
      else
        adr = "file:" + adr;
    page.setPage(adr);          // show the start page
    setContentPane(sp);
    page.setEditable(false);    // important
    page.addHyperlinkListener(this);
    setSize(450, 280);
    setVisible(true);
    setDefaultCloseOperation(EXIT_ON_CLOSE);
  }
```

```
// listener method
public void hyperlinkUpdate(HyperlinkEvent e){
    if (e.getEventType() == HyperlinkEvent.EventType.ACTIVATED)
        try {
            page.setPage(e.getURL()); // show the new page
        }
        catch (IOException ie) {}
}

public static void main (String[] arg) throws IOException {
    String s = JOptionPane.showInputDialog("Start page?");
    HTMLViewer w = new HTMLViewer(s);
}
}
```

Two things can be mentioned. The first is that the method `setPage` can generate an error signal of type `IOException`. For this reason, we write **throws** `IOException` in the constructor and in `main`, but in the listener method we must trap the error and are therefore obliged to encapsulate the call in a **try** statement, just as in the program `TextEditor` in the last section.

The second thing applies to links on the network. A link must always specify the so-called protocol in its general form. If you want to specify a web address, the link must be preceded by the text `"http://"`, and if you want to specify a file on your own computer, the link must be preceded by the text `"file:"`.

In `main` the start link is read from the dialog box. The text read is then used as a parameter for the class constructor. In the constructor, a check is made to ensure that the user specified the protocol at the beginning of the link. If this is not the case, the constructor will add the text which describes the protocol itself. If the link begins with the text www, it will assume that it is an address on the network, and in other cases it will assume that it is a local file.

6.14 Applets

There are no major differences between an independent program that uses Swing components and an applet that also does so. As we saw in Section 1.14, there are three differences in principle: we must make the class we construct be a subclass of `JApplet` instead of `JFrame`, we do not need to have a method called `main` and we must have a method called `init` instead of a constructor. To demonstrate this, we will start by writing an applet version of the program `Travel2` on page 190:

```
import java.awt.*;
import java.awt.event.*;
import javax.swing.*;
```

215

```java
import java.text.*;
import extra.*; // contains the class Parse

public class Travel3 extends JApplet implements ActionListener {
   JTextField exchAnswer = new JTextField(15);
   JTextField dayAnswer  = new JTextField(15);
   JTextField costAnswer = new JTextField(15);
   JLabel l1 = new JLabel("Exchange rate? ", JLabel.RIGHT);
   JLabel l2 = new JLabel("Number of days? ",  JLabel.RIGHT);
   JLabel l3 = new JLabel("Cost per day? ", JLabel.RIGHT);
   JPanel p = new JPanel();          // upper half
   JLabel result = new JLabel();     // lower half

   public void init() {
      Container c = getContentPane();
      c.setLayout(new GridLayout(2,1)); // 2 rows 1 column
      c.add(p);
      c.add(result);

      // put the components in the upper half of the window
      p.setLayout(new GridLayout(3,2)); // 3 rows 2 columns
      p.add(l1); p.add(exchAnswer);
      p.add(l2); p.add(dayAnswer);
      p.add(l3); p.add(costAnswer);

      // connect the forms and assign keybord shortcuts
      l1.setLabelFor(exchAnswer); l1.setDisplayedMnemonic('E');
      l2.setLabelFor(dayAnswer);  l2.setDisplayedMnemonic('N');
      l3.setLabelFor(costAnswer); l3.setDisplayedMnemonic('C');
      result.setHorizontalAlignment(JLabel.CENTER);

      // connect the listener
      dayAnswer.addActionListener(this);
      costAnswer.addActionListener(this);
      exchAnswer.addActionListener(this);
   }

   // listener method
   public void actionPerformed(ActionEvent e) {
      as on page 190
   }
}
```

The listener method has exactly the same appearance as in the normal program. In method `init` we did not include anything that concerned the size of the window, (pack, setVisible etc.).

The applet can be run in a web browser, or by using the program `appletviewer`. When you run the applet, it will look just like Figure 6.11, although the components are embedded in a web browser or in a window created by the `applet viewer`. The HTML file from which the applet was started could look like this:

```
<html>
  <head>
    <title>Travel3</title>
  </head>
  <body>
    <applet code=Travel3.class width=400 height=150
      archive=extra.jar></applet>
    <br>
    The applet is only visible if the Java Plug-in is installed.
    <br>
    <a href="http://java.sun.com/getjava/">
    Get Java Plug-in.</a>
  </body>
</html>
```

The file `Travel3.class` is normally in the same folder on the server as the HTML file. For this reason, we have just written `code=Travel3.class`. But the applet needs more classes to be able to function. The web browser finds the standard classes automatically. They are either built into the web browser or in a plug-in (if you use Swing). But if you have several of your own classes, you must make sure that the web browser can find them. In this example we use our own class `Parser` in the listener method. This class is in the package `extra`, which was stored in the `jar` file `extra.jar`. For this reason, the HTML file includes `archive=extra.jar`. We have then assumed that the `jar` file is in the same folder as the HTML file, but it would have been possible to give a relative or full search path.

As we mentioned in Chapter 1, each user has to install a plug-in module to be able to run applets that use Swing. For this reason, it can be wise not to use the classes in Swing when you implement applets that have to be generally available. You will have to content yourself with using the older classes in the package awt. In most cases, it is relatively easy to use awt when you know how Swing works. In general, the number of classes in awt is less than those in Swing, and the classes in awt have fewer and simpler properties than the classes in Swing. The properties they have in common generally have the same or similar names, but there can sometimes be differences. (For example, radio buttons and check boxes are created with the same class, `CheckBox`, in awt whereas we have seen that different classes are used in Swing.)

All Swing components are subclasses of class `JComponent`, whereas the awt classes are only subclasses of `Component` and, in some cases, of `Container`. In the fact box on page 161, you can easily see which methods are found only in Swing and not in awt. These are the methods that have a 'j' in front of them, such as the method `setBorder`. In particular, one should note that awt components cannot have borders, cannot be transparent and cannot have help texts (tool tips).

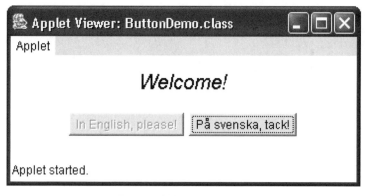

Figure 6.20 ButtonDemo

Another important difference is that awt does not have a `ContentPane`. The components are always placed directly in the applet.

To illustrate the differences, we will show an example of an applet that uses awt. We will implement a new version of the program `JButtonDemo` on page 176. If you run the applet in `appletviewer` it will look like Figure 6.20. We use the awt classes `Button`, `Label` and `Panel` instead of the corresponding Swing classes. As you can see, there are no flags on the buttons. This is because you cannot have icons on buttons and `Label` components in awt. In addition, we have deleted the button `Cancel`. This is because we are now building an applet, and an applet cannot terminate the web browser (or `appletviewer`) in which it is executed. For this reason, it would be meaningless to try to call `System.exit`. After these changes, the applet looks as follows:

```
import java.awt.*;
import java.applet.*;        // contains the class Applet
import java.awt.event.*;     // contains listener classes

public class ButtonDemo2 extends Applet
                        implements ActionListener {
  private Label  lab = new Label("Welcome!", Label.CENTER);
  private Button eng = new Button("In English, please!");
  private Button swe = new Button("På svenska, tack!");

  public void init() {
    setLayout(new GridLayout(2,1)); // 2 rows, 1 column
    Panel p = new Panel();
    add(lab); add(p);
    p.add(eng); p.add(swe);
    setBackground(Color.white);
    lab.setFont(new Font("SansSerif", Font.ITALIC, 20));
    // connect listeners
    eng.addActionListener(this);
```

```
      swe.addActionListener(this);
      eng.setEnabled(false);        // English is shown
   }

   // listener method
   public void actionPerformed(ActionEvent e) {
      if (e.getSource() == eng) {
         // The user clicked the button In English, please!
         lab.setText("Welcome!");
         eng.setEnabled(false);
         swe.setEnabled(true);
      }
      else if (e.getSource() == swe) {
         // The user clicked the button På svenska tack!
         lab.setText("Välkommen!");
         swe.setEnabled(false);
         eng.setEnabled(true);
      }
   }
}
```

Please note that we must import the package `java.applet` since the definition of the class `Applet` is included in this package. To make the text *Welcome!* stretch across the entire first row, we have used `GridLayout` with two rows and one column. On the first row we put a `Label` object and on the second row we put a panel containing the two buttons.

The HTML file which starts the applet can be very simple. We do not need any extra classes, apart from `ButtonDemo`, and since we do not use Swing, we do not include a link to a Java plug-in.

```
<html>
   <head>
      <title>ButtonDemo</title>
   </head>
   <body>
      <applet code=ButtonDemo.class width=350 height=100>
      </applet>
   </body>
</html>
```

6.15 Exercises

1. Download any two .gif files from the Internet. Put them in a folder on your own computer and rename the image files `image0.gif` and `image1.gif`. Then write a program that shows a window with components, a `JLabel` which should contain

the two downloaded images and a `JButton` with text `Switch image`. Each time the user clicks the button, the `JLabel` component should change so that the other of the two images is displayed.

2. Write a GUI program that allows the user to input his or her name, height and weight in three dialog boxes. When the user has provided the input data, the program should display a text of format *Hello NN, You weigh xx.x kg/cm*.

3. Solve Exercise 1 on page 151. Give the program a GUI.

4. Amend the program `TextEdit` on page 211 so that a `JComboBox` is used instead of a text field to input the text name. Design the program so that it automatically remembers the last five file names it has edited and displays them in a menu under the input box. The names of the files can be saved in a text file between different program runs.

5. Solve Exercise 3 on page 151. Give the program a GUI.

6. Write a program that shows two thermometers side by side. One thermometer should display the temperature expressed in degrees Celsius (°C) and the other in degrees Fahrenheit (°F). The thermometers should be displayed by means of two `JSlider` objects. When the user pulls the thumb grip on one of the thermometers, the other one should be changed as well. In addition to the thermometers, their current values should be printed in numerals. 0°C corresponds to 32°F and 100°C corresponds to 212°F. You can use the formula °C = (°F − 32) × 5/9 to convert from °F to °C.

7. Write a program that plays the game "Stone, scissors and paper". The program should randomly "think of" a stone, scissors or paper and display a window where the user can also choose. After this, the program should decide who won and show a message. Design the program so that you can run it several times in sequence. The program can then also show how many times the user has won or lost.

8. Construct a program that runs a simplified version of the "hangman" game. Assume that there is a ready-made text file called `word.txt` that contains a number of words. In each session of the game, the program chooses one of the words in the file at random, and the person who runs the program has to guess what the word is. You guess one word at a time, and may only guess wrong a certain number of times. Give the program a graphical user interface that contains three lines. At the top, there is the unknown word. Each time you have to try to guess a word, it displays the same number of question marks that there are letters in the word. Each time you guess a letter correctly, the question mark is replaced by the right letters.

In the centre, there is a text field in which the user writes the letters he or she guesses. The user inputs one letter at a time and presses Enter after each letter is input. The program then checks whether the latest input letter is included in the unknown word. If this is the case, the letter is shown in its correct place in the word.

At the bottom of the window, there is a `JSlider` whose thumb grip moves one step to the right each time the user has guessed a letter wrongly. When the slider reaches the right-hand edge, the user has failed to guess the word. This happens when the user has made as many wrong guesses as the number of letters in the word. For example, if the word consists of five letters, 20% of the total length of the bar is filled each time the user guesses wrongly. If the user fails to guess the word, the correct word can be displayed in red, in the top field of the window. After each session, you can allow the correct word to remain visible at the top of the window until the user presses Enter again. Then a new, unknown word can be retrieved, the question marks displayed at the top, the input field emptied, and the slider indicator returned to 0%.

Tip: To select random words, the program can use the class `Randomword` from Exercise 10 on page 152.

Constructing your own GUI components

As well as using standard graphic components directly, you can also create your own GUI components by letting a class inherit properties from a standard class. It is relatively easy[1] to create GUI components, and we will demonstrate how it is done in this chapter. In conjunction with this, we will also discuss the standard classes you can use to draw your own images.

7.1 Example – class `Flight`

In the first example, we will write a program that displays flight information on the screen. We will use the class `Flight` which we wrote on page 111 and implement a new version of the program. The goal is to write a program that displays the window in Figure 7.1.

BA1853	London	8:10	Delayed
AF3142	Paris	8:20	Boarding gate 15
TP0678	Lisbon	8:35	
SK5971	Gothenburg	8:40	

Figure 7.1 Flights

As you can see, the window consists of four lines, and each line contains information about a flight. One can say that the window consists of four sub-windows placed

---

[1] If you want to construct your own GUI components going by the rule book and using the MVC technique, as is done in Swing, it gets more complicated.

underneath each other. Sub-windows can be specified by using the class JPanel. For this reason, we will let Flight be a subclass of class JPanel and redefine the class Flight from page 111.

```java
import java.awt.*;
import javax.swing.*;

public class Flight extends JPanel {
  private String no, destination, comment = "";
  private Time dep, arr;
  private JLabel numL, desL, depL, comL = new JLabel(comment);

  // constructor
  public Flight (String flightNo, String dest,
                 int depHour, int depMin,
                 int arrHour, int arrMin) {
    no = flightNo;
    destination = dest;
    dep = new Time(depHour, depMin);
    arr = new Time(arrHour, arrMin);
    numL = new JLabel(no);
    desL = new JLabel(dest);
    depL = new JLabel(dep.toString());
    setLayout(new GridLayout(1,4));
    add(numL); add(desL); add(depL); add(comL);
    setBackground(Color.white); setForeground(Color.black);
    setPreferredSize(new Dimension(400, 25));
  }

  // methods
  public void setComment(String com) {
    comment = com;
    comL.setText(comment);
    repaint();
  }

  public void paintComponent(Graphics g) {
    super.paintComponent(g);  // paint the panel
    numL.setForeground(getForeground());
    desL.setForeground(getForeground());
    depL.setForeground(getForeground());
    comL.setForeground(getForeground());
    numL.setFont(getFont());
    desL.setFont(getFont());
    depL.setFont(getFont());
    comL.setFont(getFont());
  }

  Other methods as previously
}
```

Only relatively few additions have been made:

- The third line specifies that the class `Flight` should be a subclass of class `JPanel`.
- On the sixth line, four new instance variables are defined, `numL`, `desL`, `depL` and `comL`. These are references to objects of class `JLabel` and will be used to display flight number, destination, departure time, arrival time and any comments about the flight. From the start, we initialize `comL` so that it contains an empty text.
- The constructor has been extended by two statements which specify the GUI components that will be used in the flight in question. The `JLabel` objects which will contain the flight number, destination and departure time are created and initialized. The departure time is described with the instance variable `dep`, which is of class `Time`, and to get the departure in the form of a `String` we call the method `toString`. For each flight, we display the four `JLabel` components `numL`, `desL`, `depL` and `comL`. These will be placed in order on one line. For this reason, we use `GridLayout` with one row and four columns. Please note that when we write `add(numL)` etc. in the constructor, we mean that `numL` should be placed on the object in question, i.e. the `Flight` object we are in the process of initializing. In the constructor, we also specify that we want a white background (remember that a `JPanel` is normally opaque) and a black foreground.
- In method `setComment` the text is updated in `comL`. In addition, we have added a call of `repaint`, so that the flight in question is updated on the screen.
- We have added our own version of method `paintComponent`. As we discussed on page 166, this method is called automatically each time a component needs to be drawn. In our own version of `paintComponent` we have put in statements which ensure that the four `JLabel` objects `numL`, `desL`, `depL` and `comL` are displayed with the foreground colour and the typeface specified for the current `Flight` object. (The calls `getForeground()` and `getFont()` report the foreground colour and typeface for the current `Flight` object.) We have to do this so that it is possible, from outside, to change the foreground colour and typeface of a `Flight` object. (This is because if the foreground colour of a panel is changed, for example, the foreground colour of the objects placed on it is not changed automatically.) Our class `Flight` is a subclass of the class `JPanel` and in this class there is a ready-made version of `paintComponent` which makes sure that the panel background and all its child components are drawn. Since we want this method to be called, the first thing we have put in our version of `paintComponent` is the call

```
super.paintComponent(g);
```

Now, we need a class which creates the flights and places them underneath each other in a window. We create a window containing four components, placed on four lines. Since flights are a subclass of `JPanel`, they can be placed on the window directly, using the method `add`. We make the background colour black and leave one pixel between the components vertically. This means that we get horizontal lines.

```
import java.awt.*;
import javax.swing.*;

public class FlightDemo extends JFrame {
  Flight f1, f2, f3, f4;

  public FlightDemo() {
    Container c = getContentPane();
    f1 = new Flight("BA1853", "London",     8, 10, 10, 55);
    f2 = new Flight("AF3142", "Paris",      8, 20, 10, 50);
    f3 = new Flight("TP0678", "Lisbon",     8, 35, 12, 40);
    f4 = new Flight("SK5971", "Gothenburg", 8, 40,  9, 30);
    c.add(f1); c.add(f2); c.add(f3); c.add(f4);
    c.setLayout(new GridLayout(4, 1, 0, 1)); //4 rows, 1 column
    c.setBackground(Color.black);        // black lines
    pack();                         // calculates the window's size
    setVisible(true);
    setDefaultCloseOperation(EXIT_ON_CLOSE);

    f1.delay(15);
    f1.setFont(new Font(f1.getFont().getFontName(),
                  Font.ITALIC, f1.getFont().getSize())));
    f2.setComment("Boarding gate 15");
    f2.setForeground(Color.red);
  }

  public static void main(String[] arg) {
    FlightDemo demo = new FlightDemo();
  }
}
```

In the program, we have specified that the flight f1 should be displayed in italic script
(since it is delayed). We want to retain the same typeface and the same size, so we read
the information from the previous Font object in f1.

7.2 Graphics

When you define your own subclass, it is common practice in method paintComponent
(or paint if you use awt), to have to draw your own illustrations. In the class
java.awt.Graphics, several methods are defined which can be used to draw various
kinds of figures and texts. To acquaint ourselves with some of these drawing tools, we
will construct a component which draws the pretty illustration in Figure 7.2. We will
use Figure 7.3 to demonstrate how the illustration is constructed.

We call our new class CatPainter. We thought that our component might be used in
an awt applet, so we do not use Swing, but let the component be a subclass of the awt
class Panel.

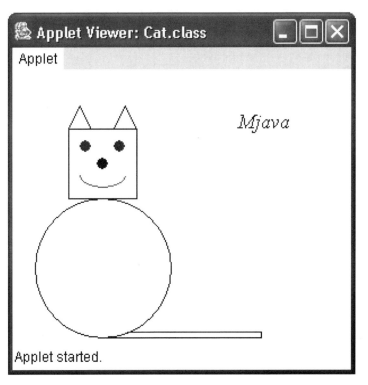

Figure 7.2

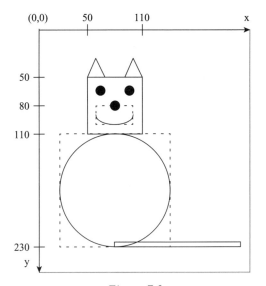

Figure 7.3

```
import java.awt.*;

public class CatPainter extends Panel {
    public CatPainter() {
        setBackground(Color.white);
    }

    public void paint(Graphics g) {
        super.paint(g);
        g.setColor(Color.black);
        g.drawRect(50, 50, 60, 60);        // head
        g.drawRect(80, 225, 140, 5);       // tail
        g.setColor(Color.white);
        g.fillOval(20, 110, 120, 120);     // white body
        g.setColor(Color.black);
        g.drawOval(20, 110, 120, 120);     // paint body
        g.fillOval(75, 75, 10, 10);        // nose
        g.setColor(Color.blue);
        g.fillOval(60, 60, 10, 10);        // eyes
        g.fillOval(90, 60, 10, 10);
        g.setColor(Color.black);
        g.drawLine(50, 50, 60, 30);        // ears
        g.drawLine(60, 30, 70, 50);
        g.drawLine(110, 50, 100, 30);
        g.drawLine(100, 30, 90, 50);
        g.setColor(Color.red);
        g.drawArc(60, 80, 40, 20, 180, 180);  // mouth
        // draw the name
        g.setColor(Color.black);
        g.setFont(new Font("Serif", Font.ITALIC, 18));
        g.drawString("Mjava", 200, 50);
    }
}
```

The applet that generates the window in Figure 7.2 is very simple:

```
import java.awt.*;
import java.applet.*;

public class Cat extends Applet {
    public void init() {
        setLayout(new BorderLayout());
        add(new CatPainter());
    }
}
```

Its only component is an object of class CatPainter.

In the constructor in class CatPainter the background colour is set to white. The most interesting method is paint, which is called automatically each time the component has to be redrawn. Please note that if CatPainter had been a Swing component instead, we would have redefined the method paintComponent. The parameter g refers, as we said previously, to an object of class java.awt.Graphics. A common characteristic of all the methods in class Graphics is that they have a coordinate system which originates from the top left corner of the drawing area. (Please refer to Figure 7.3.) The units are pixels.

7.2.1   Rectangles

When you draw rectangles, you can choose between ordinary rectangles, rectangles with rounded corners and rectangles with a three-dimensional effect. To draw the cat's head in the program, we use the method drawRect, which draws an ordinary rectangle. The first two arguments for drawRect specify the x and y coordinates of the top left-hand corner of the rectangle. The last two arguments are the width and height of the rectangle. The cat's tail is also drawn as an ordinary rectangle.

There is also a corresponding method called fillRect. This draws filled rectangles. fillRect has the same arguments as drawRect.

To draw rectangles with rounded corners, we use the methods drawRoundRect and fillRoundRect. If we had wanted to give the cat's head rounded corners, we could have written

```
g.drawRoundRect(50, 50, 60, 60, 10, 10);
```

The last two arguments specify the distance in from the corners that rounding should start. The penultimate argument specifies the width and the last one specifies the height. The arguments specify the diameter of the rounding. This means that if you have specified the value *n* as the argument, the rounding will start *n/2* pixels from the corner.

The methods draw3DRect and fill3DRect draw rectangles with a three-dimensional appearance.[1] They have an extra argument compared with drawRect. This last argument specifies whether we want the rectangle to appear to be raised from the screen or recessed. For example, you could make the call

```
g.draw3DRect(100, 200, 75, 60, true);
```

Here, **true** means that the rectangle should be raised.

7.2.2   Circles and ellipses

To draw circles and ellipses, we use the methods drawOval and fillOval. When we draw an ellipse, we should remember that it is drawn inside a rectangle, which is

---

[1] Unfortunately, the three-dimensional effect is hardly visible. This is particularly true if the printout colour used is black.

implied in Figure 7.3. The arguments of methods `drawOval` and `fillOval` define the location and dimensions of the enclosing rectangle. These arguments are thus the same as the arguments of method `drawRect`, i.e. x and y coordinates, width and height.

The reason that we draw the tail before the body is that the top left corner of the tail will be concealed by the body. To achieve this, the drawing colour is first changed from black to white, and then the body is drawn as a filled circle. The top left corner of the tail will then be overwritten with white. When this is done, we go back to black and draw the body.

The cat's nose and eyes are also drawn as circles. Note again that it is the coordinates and dimensions of the surrounding rectangles that are specified.

7.2.3 Lines

The cat's ears are drawn as lines, where each ear is two lines. To draw the lines, we use the method `drawLine`. This has four arguments. The first two specify the x and y coordinates of the line's start point and the last two specify the x and y coordinates of the line's end point. There is, unfortunately, no way to specify the thickness of the line or if you want broken lines.

7.2.4 Arcs and segments

The cat's mouth is drawn as an arc. Drawing is done with the method `drawArc`. An arc is part of an ellipse. The first four arguments for `drawArc` define, as with the method `drawOval`, the position and size of the rectangle inside which the ellipse is drawn. In our program, the call of `drawArc` is as follows:

```
g.drawArc(60, 80, 40, 20, 180, 180);   // mouth
```

The surrounding rectangle thus has its top left-hand corner at point (60,80) and is 40 pixels wide and 20 pixels high. In Figure 7.4 you can see an enlargement.

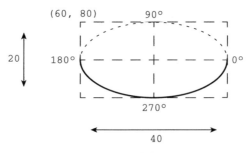

Figure 7.4

The last two parameters specify the section of the ellipse to be drawn. We use angle measurement to describe this. Imagine that there is a clock in the centre of the ellipse, as shown in the illustration. We traverse the clock anticlockwise, starting from three o'clock, which corresponds to 0°. A complete circuit comprises 360°. This means that twelve o'clock corresponds to 90°, nine o'clock to 180° and six o'clock to 270°. The fifth argument for drawArc specifies the start of the section of the arc to be drawn. In our example, we will therefore start at 180° (nine o'clock). The last argument does *not* specify the end of the section of the arc, as you might think, but the length of the arc, i.e. the number of degrees it should have. In our example, the last argument has a value of 180°, which corresponds to a half circle. When the last argument has a positive value the arc is draw anticlockwise, and if the last argument has a negative value the arc is drawn clockwise.

To draw segments of circles and ellipses, we use the method fillArc. This has exactly the same arguments as drawArc. The difference is that fillArc draws the entire "piece of cake" specified, not just the contour.

7.2.5 Texts

Printing the name in Figure 7.2 is relatively easy. This is done with program lines

```
g.setColor(Color.black);
g.setFont(new Font("Serif", Font.ITALIC, 18));
g.drawString("Mjava", 200, 50);
```

The actual text is written on the last line. It says there that the text printout should start at points (200,50). The vertical distance is to the text *baseline*, not the top left-hand edge as for rectangles. If you want to position texts more accurately and need to know the exact width and height of the text, you can use the standard class FontMetrics, but we will not go into all the details you need to know.

7.2.6 The class Graphics2D

The drawing tools we have discussed here are all found in the class Graphics. There is also a subclass of the class Graphics which is called Graphics2. Using the methods in class Graphics2 you can achieve more advanced graphics. For example, you can draw lines of differing thicknesses, fill figures with colours that change shade and have different patterns, move and rotate figures, work with overlapping figures and manipulate images. The parameter for the method paintComponent is of type Graphics, but in actual fact this parameter refers to an object of class Graphics2. If you want to use drawing tools in class Graphics2 you do an explicit type conversion:

Some graphic methods	
`drawLine(x1,y1,x2,y2)`	Draws a line from point ($x1$, $y1$) to ($x2$, $y2$).
`drawRect(x,y,w,h)` `fillRect(x,y,w,h)`	Draws an unfilled or filled rectangle with its top left-hand corner at (x, y), width w and height h.
`drawRoundRect(x,y,w,h,m,n)` `fillRoundRect(x,y,w,h,m,n)`	Draws an unfilled or filled, rounded rectangle with its top left-hand corner at (x, y), width w and height h. The rounding is $m/2$ wide and $n/2$ high.
`draw3DRect(x,y,w,h,up)` `fill3DRect(x,y,w,h,up)`	Draws an unfilled or filled 3-dimensional rectangle with its top left-hand corner at (x, y), width w and height h. up = `true` $\Rightarrow$ raised
`drawOval(x,y,w,h)` `fillOval(x,y,w,h)`	Draws an unfilled or filled ellipse drawn inside a rectangle with its top left-hand corner at (x, y), width w and height h.
`drawArc(x,y,w,h,s,l)` `fillArc(x,y,w,h,s,l)`	Draws an arc or a segment of an ellipse drawn inside a rectangle with its top left-hand corner at (x, y), width w and height h. s is the start of the arc (in degrees) and l is the arc length (in degrees). If $l>0$, drawing is done anticlockwise.
`drawPolygon(xp, yp, n)` `drawPolygon(p)` `fillPolygon(xp, yp, n)` `fillPolygon(p)` `drawPolyline(xp, yp, n)`	Draws a filled or unfilled polygon or a number of joined-up lines. xp and yp are arrays (please refer to Section 9.4) containing the x and y coordinates of the points. n is the number of points. In the alternative forms, p is a `Polygon` (see Section 9.9).
`drawString(txt,x,y)`	Draws the text, starting at point (x, y). The y coordinate specifies the baseline of the texts.

```
public void paintComponent(Graphics g) {
   Graphics2D g2 = (Graphics2D) g;
   // g2 can now be used instead of g
   ...
}
```

There is not space in this book to describe the class `Graphics2`. If you are interested, please refer to web address `java.sun.com/docs/books/tutorial/2d/`.

7.3   The class `CircleDiagram`

In the next example, we will construct a class which can be used to display pie diagrams. We call the new class `CircleDiagram`. One possible appearance is Figure 7.5, where we have positioned three components of the new class.

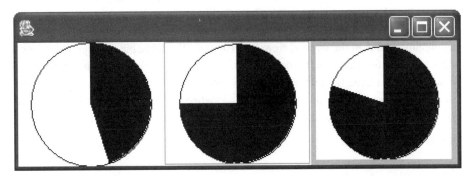

Figure 7.5 Circle diagram

We will start by studying the program that generates the window in Figure 7.5.

```
import java.awt.*;
import javax.swing.*;
import javax.swing.border.*;

public class CircleDemo extends JFrame {

  public CircleDemo() {
    Container c = getContentPane();
    CircleDiagram d1 = new CircleDiagram();
    CircleDiagram d2 = new CircleDiagram(-100, 100);
    CircleDiagram d3 = new CircleDiagram(0, 100000);
    d2.setBorder(new EtchedBorder());
    d3.setBorder(new LineBorder(Color.lightGray, 5));
    d1.setValue(45);
    d2.setValue(50);
    d3.setValue(80000);
    c.add(d1); c.add(d2); c.add(d3);
    c.setLayout(new GridLayout(1, 3));
    setSize(450,155);
    setVisible(true);
    setDefaultCloseOperation(EXIT_ON_CLOSE);
  }
```

```
    public static void main(String[] arg) {
      CircleDemo demo = new CircleDemo();
    }

}
```

The program creates three objects d1, d2 and d3 of class CircleDiagram. An object of class CircleDiagram contains a value which governs the amount of the circle that should be filled in. We can set this value by calling the method setValue. The value must be within a set interval. The highest and lowest values in this interval can be given as parameters for the constructor. If you do not specify any parameters, it is assumed that the interval is 0 to 100. Thus, in the program above, d1 contains a value in the interval from 0 to 100, d2 contains a value in the interval from −100 to 100 and d3 contains a value in the interval from 0 to 100,000. The three pie diagrams are placed in line. To demonstrate how borders function when you draw your own components, we let d2 and d3 have borders. Around d2 we put a border of type EtchedBorder and around d3 we put a border of type LineBorder, where we let the line thickness be five pixels. (A discussion about different types of borders comes below in Section 8.4.)

Our own class CircleDiagram is as follows:

```
import java.awt.*;
import javax.swing.*;
public class CircleDiagram extends JPanel {

  private int value, minimum, maximum;
  public CircleDiagram(int min, int max) {    // constructors
    if (min < max) {
      minimum = min; maximum = max; value = minimum;
    }
    else
      System.out.println("Illegal minimum and maximum values");
    setBackground(Color.white);
  }

  public CircleDiagram() {
    this(0, 100);              // set interval to 0..100
  }

  // methods
  public void setValue(int v) {
    if (v < minimum)
      value = minimum;       // value too small, set to minimum
    else if (v > maximum)
      value = maximum;       // value too large, set to maximum
    else
      value = v;             // value OK
    repaint();
  }
```

```
public int getValue() {
   return value;
}

public void paintComponent(Graphics g) {
   super.paintComponent(g);  // paint background
   Insets i = getInsets();   // thickness of surrounding border
   int w = getWidth()-i.left-i.right;   // width available
   int h = getHeight()-i.top-i.bottom; // height available
   int diam = Math.min(h,w);       // the circle's diameter
   // calculate start position for surrounding rectangle
   int x = i.left + (w-diam)/2;
   int y = i.top  + (h-diam)/2;
   g.drawOval(x, y, diam, diam); // paint the entire circle
   double part = (double) (value-minimum) / (maximum-minimum);
   int partFilled  = (int)(part * 360 + 0.5);
   g.fillArc(x, y, diam, diam, 90, -partFilled); // clockwise
}
}
```

We let the class be a subclass of standard class `JPanel`. The class `CircleDiagram` contains three instance variables, which specify the current value and the smallest and largest values in the interval. There are two constructors. The first has the interval limits as its parameter. The second constructor is parameterless. It calls the first constructor in its turn, with parameters 0 and 100. In the constructor, the background colour is set to white. Since a `JPanel` is opaque (unless you specify something else) and `CircleDiagram` is a subclass of `JPanel`, this white background will be drawn.

The two methods `setValue` and `getValue` are simple. It is worth noting that in `setValue` is a check made that the specified value is inside the permissible limits.

The most interesting method is `paintComponent`, which is called automatically each time a component of class `CircleDiagram` is to be drawn on screen. In this method, a call is first made to the corresponding method in the superclass `JPanel`. This method will draw the background colour of the components. The next step is to specify the size of the circle. The circle should be so large that it exactly fits the available drawing area. Its diameter should thus be equal to the lesser of the drawing area's width and height. When we calculate the width and height of the drawing area, we start off with the total width and height of the component, but we must deduct the area occupied by the component's border. (A border is drawn *inside* the component.) To find the thickness of the border, we use the method `getInsets`. When we are going to draw a circle, we have to specify the coordinates of the top left-hand corner of the rectangle which surrounds the circle. The circle must be centred in both height and width. For this reason, the x coordinate is calculated to give the same space on the left and right of the circle, and the y coordinate is calculated to give the same space above and below the circle. Remember that a JPanel has its own coordinate system with origin (0,0) at the top left of the component.

When the x and y coordinates have been calculated, the first method called is drawOval, which draws a circle which is not filled. Next to be called is fillArc, which has to draw the "piece of cake" to be filled in. The amount to be filled in is determined by the value of the variable value. First, a calculation is made in the variable part of the amount of space to be filled in. The variable part will then be given a real value between 0 and 1. (Please note that we must do a type conversion to **double** to avoid an integer division.) This value is then multiplied by 360 to express the value in degrees. (We add 0.5 to get correct rounding-off when the result is converted to an integer.)

7.4 Exercises

1. Write and test run an applet that draws an image you have designed yourself.

2. What changes need to be made to the program FlightDemo on page 226 and in the class Flight to convert the program to an applet instead?

3. Construct a class Bar which can be used to display horizontal or vertical bars. Objects of class Bar should be able to function as GUI components in a Java program. So let class Bar be a subclass of the standard class JPanel. In the class Bar there should be a method, setPercent, which you call to govern the amount of the bar that should be filled in. (The rest should be white.) The method setPercent should have a percentage between 0 and 100 as its parameter. The parameter should be of type **double**. If the method is called with an incorrect parameter value, it should give an error printout. When you create a new bar, 0% of the bar should be filled in from the beginning. There should be a constructor which has a parameter of type **boolean**. You then use this parameter to specify whether the bar should be horizontal or vertical (**true** means vertical).

4. Give class Car in Exercise 1 on page 115 the property that it is a JPanel, so that it can be displayed graphically on screen. The registration number and make of car should be displayed. Then write a program that displays three cars side by side.

Layout and appearance 8

In the previous chapter, we discussed the classes that describe individual components in a graphical user interface. In this chapter, we will go further and discuss how each component should be positioned in relation to others, and how you can influence their appearance. We will discuss `LayoutManagers`, borders and so-called *Look & Feel*. We will also discuss a couple of special components which can be used to create sub-windows.

8.1 Layout managers

Positioning of the components in a `Container` is controlled, as we have discussed previously, by a `LayoutManager`. There are several subclasses of the class `LayoutManager`. Programmers make greatest use of `FlowLayout`, `GridLayout`, `BorderLayout`, `CardLayout`, `BoxLayout` and `GridBagLayout`. So far, we have used only the classes `FlowLayout` and `GridLayout`, but it is now time to present the others as well.

8.1.1 `FlowLayout`

The simplest `LayoutManager` class is `FlowLayout`. When `FlowLayout` is used, the components are lined up from left to right. If a component does not fit on one line, a new line is started below the current one, and the component is placed on this line. When the components are placed on a line, they are normally centred. When you create a new `FlowLayout` manager, it is also possible to specify that the components should be placed on the left or right of the lines. You can also specify a distance between the components. If you do not specify anything particular, they will be placed next to each other. The size of each component is not changed by the `LayoutManager`. A `JButton` or `JLabel` object will assume a size so that its text just fits, for example.

We show an example. In the following program, we position five components in a window: two buttons, a `JLabel`, a `JTextField` and a `JPanel`. The size of the first four components is determined by their texts, but note that we must give the desired size of the `JPanel` explicitly, or the length and width will be zero and it will not be visible.

FlowLayout

Is used as a default for the class `JPanel`.

new `FlowLayout()`	the components are centred
new `FlowLayout(a)`	*a* is `FlowLayout.LEFT` or `FlowLayout.RIGHT`
new `FlowLayout(a, dx, dy)`	*dx* and *dy* indicate the distance between components

```
import java.awt.*;
import javax.swing.*;

public class LayoutDemo extends JFrame {
   JButton b1 = new JButton("1");
   JButton b2 = new JButton("Button 2");
   JLabel 13 = new JLabel("Label 3");
   JTextField t4 = new JTextField("Text 4");
   JPanel p5 = new JPanel();

   public LayoutDemo() {
      Container c = (Container) getContentPane();
      p5.setBackground(Color.white);
      p5.setPreferredSize(new Dimension(75,75));
      c.setLayout(new FlowLayout());
      c.add(b1); c.add(b2); c.add(13); c.add(t4); c.add(p5);
      pack();
      setVisible(true);
      setDefaultCloseOperation(EXIT_ON_CLOSE);
   }

   public static void main (String[] arg) {
      LayoutDemo y = new LayoutDemo();
   }
}
```

When this program is run, it can look as in the window on the left in Figure 8.1. What is particular to `FlowLayout` is that the arrangement of components will automatically be changed if the height or width of the window is changed. In the part on the right in Figure 8.1, for instance, we have made the window narrower and longer. As a result, two new rows have been created automatically in the window.

8.1.2 GridLayout

We have seen many examples of the use of `GridLayout`. The window is divided into a number of rows and columns, and components are arranged in a row from left to right. All the components will be equally large, regardless of anything else having been indicated. If, for example, we make the following changes in the constructor in class `LayoutDemo` from Section 8.1.1:

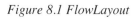

Figure 8.1 FlowLayout

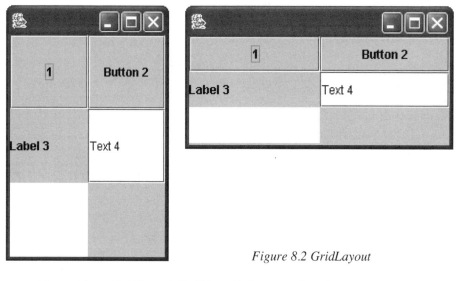

Figure 8.2 GridLayout

```
c.setLayout(new GridLayout(3,2));  // 3 rows, 2 columns
c.add(b1); c.add(b2); c.add(l3); c.add(t4); c.add(p5);
```

the window will look as in Figure 8.2. We can see that the size of the components is entirely determined by the window size and that it will be changed automatically when we drag on the window.

GridLayout	
new GridLayout(*r,c*)	puts the components into *r* rows and *c* columns
	0 indicates an arbitrary number of rows and columns
new GridLayout(*r,c,dx,dy*)	*dx* and *dy* indicate the distance between components

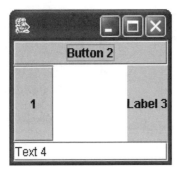

Figure 8.3 BorderLayout

8.1.3 `BorderLayout`

When we use `BorderLayout`, the window is divided into five sections. The components are arranged along the window's four sides and in the middle of the window. When we add components, we give an argument that will indicate which of the sections the component is to be put into. A point of the compass is used. In order to demonstrate this, we once more change inside the constructor in the class `LayoutDemo`:

```
c.setLayout(new BorderLayout());
c.add(b1, BorderLayout.WEST);  c.add(b2, BorderLayout.NORTH);
c.add(13, BorderLayout.EAST);  c.add(t4, BorderLayout.SOUTH);
c.add(p5, BorderLayout.CENTER);
```

The window will look as in Figure 8.3.

If a window's size is changed, for example by dragging on it, the size of its components will automatically be changed, as demonstrated by the figure. However, the components' inner placement will remain unchanged. The size of the different components is determined automatically in the following way: the components NORTH and SOUTH will

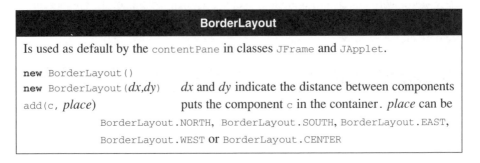

BorderLayout
Is used as default by the `contentPane` in classes `JFrame` and `JApplet`.

`new BorderLayout()`
`new BorderLayout(`*dx,dy*`)`   *dx* and *dy* indicate the distance between components
`add(c, `*place*`)`   puts the component `c` in the container. *place* can be
        `BorderLayout.NORTH`, `BorderLayout.SOUTH`, `BorderLayout.EAST`,
        `BorderLayout.WEST` or `BorderLayout.CENTER`

have exactly the height they need but will be stretched out horizontally to fill the whole window. The components EAST and WEST will have exactly the width they need. They will be stretched out vertically to fill the space between the components NORTH and SOUTH. Finally, the component CENTER will be large enough to fill the space left over when the other components have been arranged in the window.

8.1.4 BoxLayout

If you want to place several components on a line, you can use either FlowLayout or GridLayout, where you specify that you want to have a line with a certain number of columns. Both of these approaches have their disadvantages, however. If you use FlowLayout, you risk having the components end up on several lines if the available space is too narrow. In addition, you have relatively little opportunity of influencing the mutual arrangement of the components on the line. For GridLayout, the disadvantage is that all the components end up the same size, irrespective of what kind of component each one is. This seldom looks very attractive. Swing contains a new LayoutManager, BoxLayout, which is specially constructed to manage this a bit better. BoxLayout can be used to set several components out horizontally on a single line, or vertically in a single column. The components are laid out from left to right, or from the top down. If there is not enough room for the components, a new line or column is started. When the components are placed, BoxLayout considers the desired size of each component, minimum size and maximum size. In addition, you can specify the relative displacement of each component, the so-called *alignment*.

We will now demonstrate this and will start by making more changes to the constructor in the program LayoutDemo on page 238:

```
c.setLayout(new BoxLayout(c, BoxLayout.X_AXIS));
c.add(b1); c.add(b2); c.add(l3); c.add(t4); c.add(p5);
```

The only change we have made so far is that BoxLayout is used instead of FlowLayout. Please note that the constructor for class BoxLayout should have two parameters. The first is a reference to the Container to be handled, and the second specifies whether the components should be placed horizontally (X_AXIS) or vertically (Y_AXIS). If we run the program, it will look like Figure 8.4. The first three components have fixed sizes,

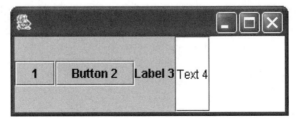

Figure 8.4 BoxLayout, floating sizes

241

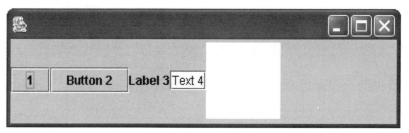

Figure 8.5 BoxLayout, fixed sizes

but the last two do not. The height of the window is determined by our setting the size of the last component, the panel p5, to 75 by 75. If you drag the window to make it higher, both the JTextField components t4 and p5 will become higher and fill the entire height. This is because these components do not have a maximum height. If you drag the window to make it wider, t4 will increase in width, whereas the other four components will be unchanged. We can prevent a component from becoming too large or too small by specifying its maximum and minimum sizes. For example, you could give components t4 and p5 fixed sizes by changing their minimum and maximum sizes so that they are equal to the sizes you want.

```
t4.setMinimumSize(t4.getPreferredSize());
t4.setMaximumSize(t4.getPreferredSize());
p5.setMinimumSize(p5.getPreferredSize());
p5.setMaximumSize(p5.getPreferredSize());
```

This is demonstrated in Figure 8.5. In the figure, we have dragged the window to make it larger than it was to start with. We see that all components retain their sizes. When you make the window wider, it is filled out with a grey background on the right and when you make it higher, all the components centred in height end up on one line.

All components are normally placed beside each other, as in Figure 8.5, but if you want, you can insert invisible components as padding. There is an auxiliary class called Box which contains a number of useful methods. The following program lines show how you can insert a fixed space between the two buttons b1 and b2 and a flexible distance between buttons b2 and JLabel object 13. When you run the program, it will look like Figure 8.6.

Figure 8.6 BoxLayout, with invisible components

```
c.add(b1);
c.add(Box.createRigidArea(new Dimension(20,1)));
c.add(b2);
c.add(Box.createHorizontalGlue());
c.add(l3); c.add(t4); c.add(p5);
```

The method `createRigidArea` creates an invisible component of fixed size which you can put where you want.[1] Since we want to have 20 pixels between the buttons `b1` and `b2`, we have given this component width 20. The height is not really important, but it should not be higher than any of the other components in the relevant container, because it would affect the height of the container otherwise.

The method `createHorizontalGlue` creates an invisible "rubber band component", a component whose width can vary when you make the window wider or narrower. In Figure 8.6 we have made the window wider. Please note that the invisible "rubber band component" fills the distance formed between the components `b2` and `13`.

Let us now demonstrate what happens when we place the components vertically instead. We make a few small changes to the statements that set out the components:

```
c.setLayout(new BoxLayout(c, BoxLayout.Y_AXIS));
c.add(b1);
c.add(Box.createRigidArea(new Dimension(1,20)));
c.add(b2);
c.add(Box.createVerticalGlue());
c.add(l3); c.add(t4); c.add(p5);
```

We now let the second parameter for the constructor for `BoxLayout` have the value `Y_AXIS`, we change the size of the fixed, invisible component so that it is 20 pixels high and we use the method `createVerticalGlue` to get a vertical, invisible "rubber band component". Its appearance is shown in the left-hand section of Figure 8.7, where we have stretched the window vertically. As can be seen, the side positioning is somewhat strange. Each component is justified in relation to an imaginary vertical line (a y axis). In the left-hand part of Figure 8.7 the two buttons and `JLabel` object are left justified in relation to the y axis, whereas the two lowest components are centred in relation to the y axis. You can specify the amount that individual components will be adjusted sideways by calling the method `setAlignmentX`. This has a parameter of type `float`, whose value should be in the range from 0 to 1. Value 0 means that the component should be placed furthest left and value 1 means that the component should be placed furthest right. All values in between are possible. The value 0.5 means that the

---

[1] It should be pointed out here that there are two, somewhat simpler methods in class `Box` which you can use instead of the method `createRigidArea`. These are `createHorizontalStrut` and `createVerticalStrut`. They can cause problems when you have more complicated windows, however, so it is recommended that you use `createRigidArea`.

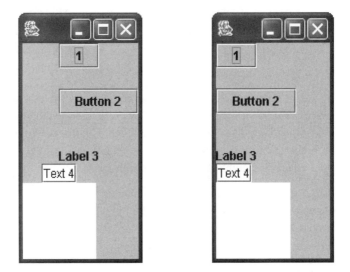

Figure 8.7 BoxLayout, vertical

component should be centred, for example. You can also use parameters such as the constants LEFT_ALIGNMENT, CENTER_ALIGNMENT and RIGHT_ALIGNMENT. To make components line up neatly when you use a vertical BoxLayout, it is frequently suitable to give them all the same sideways justification. For this reason, we modify the two lowest components in our example to make them left justified as well.

```
t4.setAlignmentX(LEFT_ALIGNMENT);
p5.setAlignmentX(LEFT_ALIGNMENT);
```

Its appearance is shown in the right-hand section of Figure 8.7.

BoxLayout

The following statement specifies that the container p (for example, a JPanel) should have BoxLayout. *alignment* should be BoxLayout.X_AXIS (horizontal) or BoxLayout.Y_AXIS (vertical).

```
p.setLayout(new BoxLayout(p, alignment));
```

Box.createRigidArea(new Dimension(b,h))	invisible component, fixed size
Box.createHorizontalGlue()	invisible component, flexible width
Box.createVerticalGlue()	invisible component, flexible height
comp.setAlignmentX(*just*)	in vertical positioning, adjusts *comp* sideways
comp.setAlignmentY(*just*)	in horizontal positioning, adjusts *comp* in height

just is a real number in the interval from 0 to 1. Value 0 means left or top, and value 1 means right or lowest. The constants TOP_ALIGNMENT, LEFT_ALIGNMENT, CENTER_ALIGNMENT, RIGHT_ALIGNMENT and BOTTOM_ALIGNMENT can be used.

When you have a horizontal `BoxLayout`, you can similarly call the method `set-Alignmenty` to specify the height justification of the components in relation to an imaginary x axis. You can then use the constants `TOP_ALIGNMENT`, `CENTER_ALIGNMENT` and `BOTTOM_ALIGNMENT`. If you do not make any of these adjustments, all components will be centred in relation to the x axis, which is visible in Figures 8.4, 8.5 and 8.6.

For `BoxLayout`, we can finally mention that you can create components of class `Box`. A component of this class is a `Container` which is automatically initialized so that it gets a `LayoutManager` of type `BoxLayout`.

8.1.5 `CardLayout`

`CardLayout` differs from other `LayoutManagers` in that not all components are visible at the same time. We define a kind of card instead, which the user can leaf through and study one at a time. In many programs and operating systems, such as in Windows, a card with tabs is used to let the user see various formulae and set various alternatives. You can use `CardLayout` to construct components which are similar to these cards, but it gets a bit complicated. However, Swing contains a class called `JTabbedPane` which has been specially implemented to construct cards with tabs, and it is a good idea to use it instead. For this reason, we will include only a brief description of `CardLayout`. We discuss the class `JTabbedPane` in Section 8.3.

We show an example here of one way to use `CardLayout`. We declare a panel `p` in which we want to lay three cards, which are panels in their turn. In other words, we declare a `LayoutManager` of class `CardLayout`:

```
JPanel p = new JPanel();
JPanel one = new JPanel();
JPanel two = new JPanel();
JPanel three = new JPanel();
CardLayout m = new CardLayout();
```

We can then specify that `m` should be `LayoutManager` for panel `p` and lay the three panels `one`, `two` and `three` as cards in `p`:

```
p.setLayout(m);
p.add("no 1", one);
p.add("no 2", two);
p.add("no 3", three);
```

When you use `CardLayout` you can give each card a name, as here. You give a text as an extra parameter to method `add`. You can then use this name when you want to specify the card to be displayed. In the class `CardLayout` there is a method `show` which can be called as follows:

```
m.show(p, "no 2");
```

In the class `CardLayout` there are also methods for displaying the first or last card, or for leafing through the cards. For example, you could write

`m.first(p);`

CardLayout	
`m = `**`new`**` CardLayout()`	one component (a card) is displayed at a time
`m = `**`new`**` CardLayout(`*dx,dy*`)`	*dx* and *dy* indicate the distance around the card
`w.add(c)`	`w` is a `Container` object
`w.add("`*name*`", c)`	adds to the component `c` the name *name*
`m.show(w, "`*name*`")`	displays the component (the card) *name*
`m.first(w)`	displays the first component (the first card)
`m.last(w)`	displays the last component (the last card)
`m.next(w)`	displays the next component (card)
`m.previous(w)`	displays the previous component (card)

You must have a reference to the `LayoutManager` used to be able to call the methods that display each card. One way to get this reference is to call the method `getLayout()` for the container in question.

8.1.6 GridBagLayout

We have saved the most powerful, but also the most complicated `LayoutManager` until last. When we use `GridBagLayout`, the window is separated into a number of boxes, exactly as with `GridLayout`, but all the windows are of unequal size. In addition, we can let certain components monopolize several boxes. To demonstrate how `GridBagLayout` works, we shall design the window in Figure 8.8. To the left in the figure is displayed the window when it is just big enough for all components to have the space they need, and to the right the window has been dragged out in respect of both its length and width.

The window is divided into four rows and three columns. The rows are numbered from the top and the columns from the left. Note that we begin numbering with 0. The uppermost row is then row no. 0 and the column furthest to the left column no. 0. There are two `JCheckBox` objects in the window; they are placed in boxes (0,0) and (1,0). The dark field is a `JPanel` object. It takes up four boxes, that is, the columns 1 and 2 and rows 0 and 1. In the third row (row no. 2), there is a `JLabel` object with the text `"File"` to the left (in column no. 0). In columns 1 and 2, there is a `JTextField` object. The last row (no. 3) contains three buttons, each in its column.

When we want to use `GridBagLayout`, we begin by declaring a `LayoutManager` of class `GridBagLayout`. This is easy, since there is only one constructor, which has no parameters. It would be a good idea to give the `LayoutManager` a name, since we will

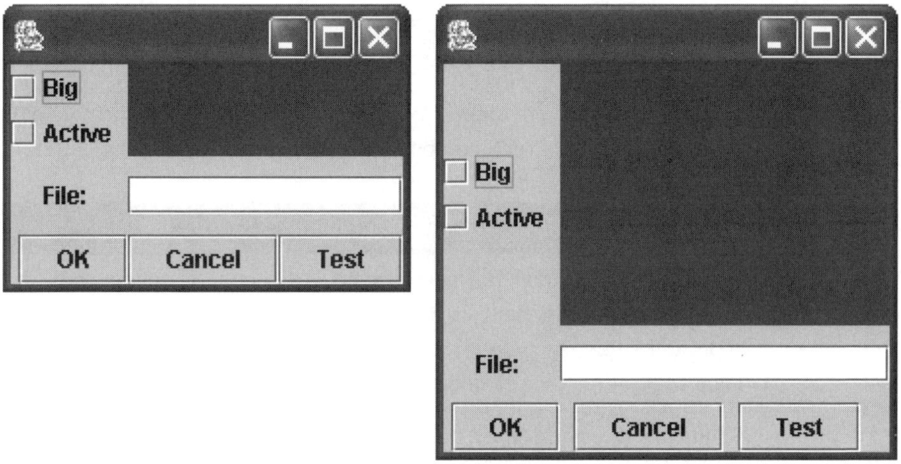

Figure 8.8 GridBagLayout

have to refer to it later. We shall call it m here. We also indicate that m will be the
LayoutManager in the actual window.

```
GridBagLayout m = new GridBagLayout();
Container c = (Container) getContentPane();
c.setLayout(m);
```

The different components will then be added, one by one. What is different with
GridBagLayout is that when we add each component, we have to indicate explicitly
the *properties* each one is to have. Such properties might indicate, for example, where
the component is to be placed. In the fact box, there is a synopsis of the properties
that can be indicated. A special class called GridBagConstraints is used to indicate
a component's properties. We begin by declaring a reference variable for an object of
this class. Note that we wait a while before creating the object itself.

```
GridBagConstraints con;
```

For every component (or group of similar components), a new object of class
GridBagConstraints is created:

```
con = new GridBagConstraints();
```

We then fill this object with the properties we want. If, for example, we want a
component to begin in box (2,3), we write:

```
con.gridy = 2; con.gridx = 3; // row and column
```

and if we want it to be two boxes high, we write:

```
con.gridheight = 2;
```

When we have indicated all the properties we want, we connect them to the component
in question. For example, if the component is called comp, we write:

```
m.setConstraints(comp, con);
```

We then add the component to the actual window in the usual way.

```
c.add(comp);
```

This procedure is repeated for all components. It is convenient to create a new `GridBagConstraints` object for every component because there are many different

Properties for GridBagLayout	
gridx gridy	Indicate the column no. and row no., respectively, for the box in which the component is to begin. (Numbering starts with 0.) Default value: Relative, which means that the component is put to the right of (gridx) or under (gridy) the component last added.
gridwidth gridheight	Indicate the number of boxes which the component will include horizontally and vertically. Default value: 1. The value REMAINDER means the remainder of the row or column.
fill	Indicates how the component will fill out the whole box (or boxes). Permitted values: NONE, BOTH, HORIZONTAL and VERTICAL. Default value: NONE.
anchor	Indicates where in the box (or boxes) the component is to be put if it is smaller than the space available. Permitted values: CENTER, WEST, NORTH, EAST, SOUTH, NORTHWEST, NORTHEAST, SOUTHWEST and SOUTH-EAST. Default value: CENTER.
ipadx ipady	Indicates the extra space (expressed in pixels) the component will be allotted in addition to its minimum size. Default value: 0.
insets	Indicates the amount of filling out that will be put *around* the component. Is assigned a value of class Insets, which has the constructor Insets(*up, left, down, right*). Default value: Insets(0,0,0,0).
weightx	Is used to determine how the extra horizontal space will be allotted between the columns. For each column the values of weightx for all its rows are examined and the maximum of these weightx values will be the column's actual weight. The horizontal extra space is then allotted between the columns in proportion to their weights. If all the columns have a weight of 0, no column will get extra space. Default value: 0.
weighty	Is used to determine how the extra vertical space is to be allotted between the rows. Works in the same way as weightx. Default value: 0.

properties that may be specified. For each property, there is a default value. Creating a new `GridBagConstraints` object means that we can be sure that all of its properties have this default value.

We will now show how the window in Figure 8.8 is built up. We begin as before by declaring a `LayoutManager` and a reference to a `GridBagConstraints` object.

```
GridBagLayout m = new GridBagLayout();
Container c = (Container) getContentPane();
c.setLayout(m);
GridBagConstraints con;
```

We first arrange the two check boxes `Big` and `Active`. We set `weighty` to 1 for both row no. 0 and row no. 1. This will mean that any extra vertical space will be allotted to these two rows (each one gets the same amount).

```
// The check boxes
JCheckBox bx1 = new JCheckBox("Big");
JCheckBox bx2 = new JCheckBox("Active");
con = new GridBagConstraints();
con.weighty = 1;
con.anchor = GridBagConstraints.SOUTHWEST;
con.gridy = 0; con.gridx = 0; // row and column
m.setConstraints(bx1, con);
c.add(bx1);
con.anchor = GridBagConstraints.NORTHWEST;
con.gridy = 1; con.gridx = 0; // row and column
m.setConstraints(bx2, con);
c.add(bx2);
```

The next component to be arranged is the `JPanel`, which takes up four boxes.

```
// The JPanel object
JPanel p = new JPanel();
p.setBackground(Color.darkGray);
con = new GridBagConstraints();
con.gridy = 0; con.gridx = 1;          // row and column
con.gridwidth = 2;                     // takes up two columns
con.gridheight = 2;                    // takes up two rows
con.fill = GridBagConstraints.BOTH;    // fill up all the space
m.setConstraints(p, con);
c.add(p);
```

We now put the two components in the third row. There will be a `JLabel` object with the text `File:` in the left-hand column, and in the other two columns a `JTextField` object.

```
// The JLabel object
JLabel dl = new JLabel("File: ", JLabel.RIGHT);
```

249

```
con = new GridBagConstraints();
con.gridy = 3; con.gridx = 0;          // row and column
con.insets = new Insets(10,0,10,0); // 10 pixels above and below
m.setConstraints(dl, con);
c.add(dl);

// JTextField-object
JTextField dt = new JTextField();
con.gridwidth = 2;                          // takes up two columns
con.fill = GridBagConstraints.HORIZONTAL; // fill up both
con.gridy = 3; con.gridx = 1;              // row and column
m.setConstraints(dt, con);
c.add(dt);
```

Finally, we put the three buttons OK, Cancel and Test in the lowest row.

```
// The last row
JButton ok = new JButton("OK");
JButton av = new JButton("Cancel");
JButton te = new JButton("Test");
con = new GridBagConstraints();
con.gridy = 4; con.gridx = 0; // row and column
con.ipadx = 5; // enlarge the buttons before and after the texts
con.anchor = GridBagConstraints.EAST; // adjust the first one
m.setConstraints(ok, con);
c.add(ok);
con.weightx = 1; // give columns no.1 and no.2 any extra space
con.gridy = 4; con.gridx = 1; // row and column
con.anchor = GridBagConstraints.CENTER;
m.setConstraints(av, con);
c.add(av);
con.gridy = 4; con.gridx = 2; // row and column
con.anchor = GridBagConstraints.WEST;
m.setConstraints(te, con);
c.add(te);
```

Here we have set weightx to 1 for columns 1 and 2, so that these will be allotted all the extra horizontal space. Because we had previously allotted all the extra vertical space to rows 0 and 1, the JPanel object will be enlarged automatically if we make the window larger (see the right-hand window in Figure 8.8).

8.2 JSplitPane

LayoutManagers are the main tool for controlling how components are placed, but there are also a couple of special components which are useful. In this section, we will study the class JSplitPane, which can be used to divide an area up into two sections. You can either divide the surface horizontally, so that the two components are placed beside each other, or vertically, so that the two components are placed on top of one

Figure 8.9 JSplitPane

another. A dividing line is automatically placed between the two components. This divider can be moved, to make one component larger than the other.

As an example, we will write a new variant of the program JScrollDemo on page 206. In the new variant, only one image is displayed at any time, and there is a list on the left of the image, where the user can choose which image is displayed. One possible appearance is Figure 8.9.

The program is as follows:

```java
import java.awt.*;
import java.awt.event.*;
import javax.swing.*;

public class Picture extends JFrame implements ActionListener {
    JLabel l1 = new JLabel(new ImageIcon("sara.jpg"));
    JLabel l2 = new JLabel(new ImageIcon("flowers.jpg"));
    JLabel l3 = new JLabel(new ImageIcon("flag_eng.gif"));
    JScrollPane scroll = new JScrollPane(l1);
    JPanel  p = new JPanel();
    JButton b1 = new JButton("Girl");
    JButton b2 = new JButton("Flowers");
    JButton b3 = new JButton("Flag");
    JSplitPane split= new JSplitPane(JSplitPane.HORIZONTAL_SPLIT,
                                     p, scroll);

    public Picture() {
        Container c = (Container) getContentPane();
        c.add(split);
```

251

```
        scroll.setMinimumSize(new Dimension(100, 100));
        p.setLayout(new BoxLayout(p, BoxLayout.Y_AXIS));
        p.add(b1); p.add(b2); p.add(b3);
        b1.setBorderPainted(false); b1.addActionListener(this);
        b2.setBorderPainted(false); b2.addActionListener(this);
        b3.setBorderPainted(false); b3.addActionListener(this);
        setSize(350,250);
        setVisible(true);
        setDefaultCloseOperation(EXIT_ON_CLOSE);
    }

    public void actionPerformed(ActionEvent e) {
        if (e.getSource() == b1)
            scroll.setViewportView(l1);
        else if (e.getSource() == b2)
            scroll.setViewportView(l2);
        else if (e.getSource() == b3)
            scroll.setViewportView(l3);
    }

    public static void main (String[] arg) {
        Picture p = new Picture();
    }
}
```

In the program we create a `JSplitPane` component with declaration

```
JSplitPane split = new JSplitPane(JSplitPane.HORIZONTAL_SPLIT,
                                  p, scroll);
```

The first parameter specifies whether the split should be horizontal or vertical. The two other parameters specify the two components which will be found in the `JSplitPane` component. The first one, `p`, is a `JPanel` which in its turn contains three buttons `b1`, `b2` and `b3`. The other component, `scroll`, is a `JScrollPane` which contains a `JLabel` containing the image to be displayed. In the program, we have declared three `JLabel` components `l1`, `l2` and `l3`, which contain different images. The component `scroll` has been initialized so that when the program starts, the `JLabel` component contains `l1`. This can be changed when the user clicks one of the buttons. The program contains a listener which senses the button that the user has clicked, and changes so that the `JLabel` component with the corresponding image is placed in `scroll`.

A `JSplitPane` component can contain only two components. These can be modified dynamically. We might have been able to do the above operations in two stages.

```
JSplitPane split = new JSplitPane(JSplitPane.HORIZONTAL_SPLIT);
...
split.setLeftComponent(p);
split.setRightComponent(scroll);
```

The user can drag the line that divides the two components. As we have done in the program, you can set the minimum size of a component, to stop it becoming too small. It is then impossible to move the divider so that the component becomes smaller than you have specified. The initial position of our divider depends on the sizes requested. For this reason, it can sometimes be necessary to set them, to give the window the desired size from the beginning.

The location of the divider can also be influenced by calling the method `set-DividerLocation`. There are two versions of it. The first version has a parameter of type `int`, which specifies the location of the divider expressed in pixels. The second version has a parameter of type `double`. The value of the parameter should be between 0 and 1, and it specifies the relative position of the divider. The following statement would put the divider midway between the two sub-components:

```
split.setDividerLocation(0.5);
```

JSplitPane	
Only contains two components. In the following lines, *orient* will be `JSplitPane.HORIZONTAL_SPLIT` or `JSplitPane.VERTICAL_SPLIT`	
new `JSplitPane(orient)`	creates `JSplitPane`
new `JSplitPane(orient,a,b)`	creates `JSplitPane` with components a & b
`sp.setLeftComponent(c)`	lays c as the left-hand component in sp
`sp.setRightComponent(c)`	lays c as the right-hand component in sp
`sp.setTopComponent(c)`	lays c as the upper component in sp
`sp.setBottomComponent(c)`	lays c as the lower component in sp
`sp.setOrientation(orient)`	specifies orientation (left–right or up–down)
`sp.setDividerSize(n)`	specifies the thickness of the divider
`sp.setDividerLocation(n)`	moves the divider to position n (pixels)
`sp.setDividerLocation(x)`	moves the divider to relative position x (x must be a real number between 0 and 1)
`sp.getDividerLocation()`	gives the position of the divider (in pixels)
`sp.resetToPreferredSizes()`	resets the divider to the default position

8.3 JTabbedPane

As we saw in Section 8.1.5, we could use `CardLayout` if we wanted to place components on top of each other, like cards in a deck of cards. One occasion when you want to position components in this way is when you want a card index with tabs. (This is the same idea as at many places in Windows. For example, if you select the icon *My Computer* and click it with the right mouse button, then select the "Properties" menu

Figure 8.10 JTabbedPane

choice, a window pops up which contains a number of cards. You can then choose the card you want to see by clicking one of the tabs at the top.) The problem with `CardLayout` is that you have to design each card separately and make sure yourself that the correct card is displayed. This is quite complicated. There is a much simpler solution, however, which is to use `JTabbedPane`. A component of this type is automatically given tags, and different cards are displayed when the user clicks the tabs.

As an example, we will study a program that creates the windows in Figure 8.10. There are three cards with associated tabs on top of each other in this window. The first card, which is not visible in the figure, contains a game (a board with four buttons). The second card contains a text area, and the third one contains an image. The program is as follows:

```java
import java.awt.*;
import javax.swing.*;

public class JTabbedDemo extends JFrame {

    JButton b1 = new JButton("1");
    JButton b2 = new JButton("2");
    JButton b3 = new JButton("3");
    JButton b4 = new JButton("4");

    JTextArea a = new JTextArea("Work area");
    JLabel fl = new JLabel(new ImageIcon("flowers.jpg"));

    public JTabbedDemo() {
        Container c = (Container) getContentPane();
        JTabbedPane tp = new JTabbedPane();
        c.add(tp);
```

```
      // card 1
      JPanel card1 = new JPanel();
      tp.addTab("Game", card1);
      card1.setLayout(new GridLayout(2,2));
      card1.add(b1); card1.add(b2); card1.add(b3); card1.add(b4);

      // card 2
      JScrollPane card2 = new JScrollPane(a);
      tp.addTab("Work", new ImageIcon("hammer.gif"), card2);

      // card 3
      JScrollPane card3 = new JScrollPane(fl);
      tp.addTab("Flowers", null, card3, "Shows daffodils");

      setSize(200,250);
      setVisible(true);
      setDefaultCloseOperation(EXIT_ON_CLOSE);
   }
   public static void main (String[] arg) {
      JTabbedDemo t = new JTabbedDemo();
   }
}
```

A single component is placed in the window's working area, a JTabbedPane component which is created with the declaration

```
JTabbedPane tp = new JTabbedPane();
```

We have not given the constructor a parameter here, but you can have a parameter which specifies where the tabs should be placed. They can be placed on any side of the cards. If you do not say anything, they are placed on top.

To add a card to a JTabbedPane component, you can use the method addTab. There are various versions of it. You specify the text to be written on the tab and the component to be found on the corresponding card as the parameters. You could also specify an icon to be placed on the tab, and a help text (tool tip). It is common practice to let each card contain a JPanel or a JScrollPane, so that you can then set out further components on the cards. In the program above, card number 1 contains a JPanel and card numbers 2 and 3 contain JScrollPane components We have put a text on the tab of card number 1, whereas the tab on card number 2 also contains an icon. On card number 3 we have also added the tool tip "Shows daffodils", which pops up if the user holds the cursor over the tab for about one second.

The most useful methods for class JTabbedPane are summarized in the fact box. Please note that you can add cards and remove them dynamically, and that you can change the appearance of tabs by changing the background and foreground colours. You can also change the text or icon on a tab. You can get the program to sense the cards which are currently on display, by calling the method getSelectedIndex.

JTabbedPane

Contains several components (cards) with associated tabs on top of each other.

new JTabbedPane()	creates a JTabbedPane with tabs on top
new JTabbedPane(1)	creates a JTabbedPane with tabs at location 1

b should be JTabbedPane.TOP, JTabbedPane.BOTTOM, JTabbedPane.LEFT or JTabbedPane.RIGHT

The method addTab adds a card which contains the component c:

tp.addTab(t,c)	the tab only contains the text t
tp.addTab(t,ic,c)	the tab contains the text t and icon ic
tp.addTab(t,ic,c,tip)	the tab contains the text t, icon ic and tool tip tip
tp.insertTab(t,ic,c,tip,j)	as addTab but the card becomes no. j
tp.removeTabAt(j)	removes card no. j
tp.removeAll()	removes all cards
tp.getTabCount()	gives the number of cards
tp.getSelectedIndex()	gives the number of the currently selected card
tp.setEnabledAt(j,*bool*)	specifies whether card j should be selectable or not
tp.setComponentAt(j,c)	sets the component on card no. j to c
tp.setTitleAt(j,t)	sets the text on tab no. j to t
tp.setBackgroundAt(j,b)	sets the background colour on tab no. j to b
tp.setForegroundAt(j,b)	sets the foreground colour on tab no. j to b
tp.setIconAt(j,ic)	sets the icon on tab no. j to ic
tp.setDisabledIconAt(j,ic)	sets the icon for "not selectable" on tab no. j

8.4   Borders

All graphic components that are subclasses of class JComponent can have borders. You can use the method setBorder to put a border round any component. Swing contains a number of classes which you can use to create borders. (It is also possible to define your own border classes, but we will refrain from discussing this.) We have already seen an example of how standard class EtchedBorder can be used. In this section, we will also describe the other border classes. In Figure 8.11 there are examples of what borders created by using each standard class can look like. In the figure, we have created twelve JLabel components and put different types of borders round them. The window has been divided up into four rows, with three components on each row. Each JLabel contains the name of the type of border used. We call the JLabel objects a11, a12, a13, a21 etc., where the first figure is the line number and the second is the column number. JLabel objects are initialized as follows (a11 is shown as an example):

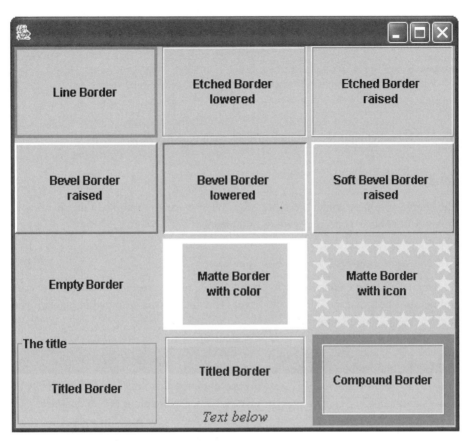

Figure 8.11 Borders

```
JLabel all = new JLabel();
all.setHorizontalAlignment(JLabel.CENTER); // centre the text
all.setForeground(Color.black); // makes the text easier to read
```

To place a particular text in a `JLabel` object, we then use our usual method `setText`. We could write:

```
all.setText("Line Border");
```

Some of the `JLabel` objects in the figure have text which is displayed on two lines. To achieve this, we have made use of the fact that the text on a `JLabel` can be in HTML format. (See Section 6.3.) To make this easy for ourselves, we write a small auxiliary method called `htmlText`. This method generates the HTML code needed to display two lines of centred text. As parameters, we specify the texts to be displayed. For example, to put a text in the second box on the top line in Figure 8.11, we make the call:

```
a12.setText(htmlText("Etched Border", "lowered"));
```

The auxiliary method `htmlText` is as follows:

```
private String htmlText(String line1, String line2) {
    return "<html><body><center><b>" + line1 +
            "<p>" + line2 + "</body></html>";
}
```

Given this background, we can now discuss each type of border.

8.4.1   `LineBorder`

The simplest form of border is `LineBorder`. We can see an example in the first box in Figure 8.11. This is generated with the statements

```
a11.setText("Line Border");
a11.setBorder(new LineBorder(Color.green, 3));
```

As parameters for the constructor in class `LineBorder` we specify the colour we want and the thickness that the line should have. (The thickness is specified in pixels.) You can also have rounded corners.

LineBorder	
new `LineBorder(col)`	gives a border with colour `col` and thickness 1
new `LineBorder(col,n)`	gives a border with colour `col` & thickness n
new `LineBorder(col,n,`*round*`)`	gives a border, colour `col`, thickness n
	round (**boolean**) specifies rounded corners

8.4.2   `EtchedBorder`

A border of type `EtchedBorder` looks as if it had been punched. You can choose whether the border should be raised or lowered. The first line in Figure 8.11 contains examples of both types of `EtchedBorder`. The following statements give the components the appearance they have in the figure:

```
a12.setText(htmlText("Etched Border", "lowered"));
a12.setBorder(new EtchedBorder());
a13.setText(htmlText("Etched Border", "raised"));
a13.setBorder(new EtchedBorder(EtchedBorder.RAISED));
```

Borders of this type look like they have been illuminated from the top left corner. This is achieved by means of two colours, one for the illuminated parts of the border and one for the parts of the border which are in shadow. If you do not specify anything particular, suitable colours are chosen for light and shadow based on the background colour of the component, but you can also specify the colours to be used yourself.

EtchedBorder	
new EtchedBorder()	gives a downwards "punched" border
new EtchedBorder(light,shadow)	gives a downwards "punched" border, is drawn with colours light and shadow
new EtchedBorder(type)	gives a "punched" border, type specifies whether it is punched downwards (EtchedBorder.LOWERED) or upwards (EtchedBorder.RAISED)
new EtchedBorder(type,light,shadow)	punching and colours are specified

8.4.3 BevelBorder and SoftBevelBorder

When we put a border of type BevelBorder or SoftBevelBorder round a component, the component will look as if it is raised or recessed. The border will appear to be illuminated from the top left, and have sloping corners. We can see examples of this on the second line in Figure 8.11. This line has been implemented with the statements

```
a21.setText(htmlText("Bevel Border", "raised"));
a21.setBorder(new BevelBorder(BevelBorder.RAISED));
a22.setText(htmlText("Bevel Border", "lowered"));
a22.setBorder(new BevelBorder(BevelBorder.LOWERED));
a23.setText(htmlText("Soft Bevel Border", "raised"));
a23.setBorder(new SoftBevelBorder(BevelBorder.RAISED));
```

There is no great difference between BevelBorder and SoftBevelBorder. If you look carefully, you will see that the latter has a somewhat thinner "shadow side".

BevelBorder and SoftBevelBorder	
new BevelBorder(type)	gives a "sloping" border. type specifies whether the component should appear to be recessed (BevelBorder.LOWERED) or raised (BevelBorder.RAISED)
new BevelBorder(type,light,shadow)	drawn with colours light and shadow
new BevelBorder(type,lightOut,lightIn,darkOut,darkIn)	light sides are drawn with colours lightOut (furthest out) and lightIn (furthest in), dark sides with darkOut and darkIn
new SoftBevelBorder(type)	
new SoftBevelBorder(type,light,shadow)	
new SoftBevelBorder(type,lightOut,lightIn,darkOut,darkIn)	

As you can see from the fact box, you can choose the colours to be used in the border to create the three-dimensional effect yourself. You can choose either two colours, one colour for the dark, shaded parts of the border and another colour for the illuminated parts, or four colours. If you choose four colours, two colours are used to draw the dark sections and two to draw the light sections of the border.

8.4.4 `EmptyBorder`

By using the class `EmptyBorder` you can create an invisible border around a component. We have put one at the furthest left on the third line of Figure 8.11. The program that creates the window contains the statements

```
a31.setText("Empty Border");
a31.setBorder(new EmptyBorder(5, 20, 5, 20));
```

When you create an empty border, you specify the thickness you want the border to be on each of the four sides. An empty border is not visible, but the effect of one is that the space for the actual content of the component is reduced by the thickness of the border. The class `EmptyBorder` is possibly not so interesting by itself, but it has a more useful subclass called `MatteBorder`, which we will discuss in the next section.

EmptyBorder

new `EmptyBorder(u,l,d,r)`	gives an empty border with thickness `u` on top, `l` on the left, `d` at the bottom and `r` on the right

---

8.4.5 `MatteBorder`

By using the class `MatteBorder` you can create a border with any thickness and colour around a component. This is similar to using a mask to frame a drawing or photograph. When you create one of these, you specify the thickness the border should have on each side, and the colour it should have. The border in the centre of the third line in Figure 8.11 is created with the statements

```
a32.setText(htmlText("Matte Border", "with color"));
a32.setBorder(new MatteBorder(5, 20, 5, 20, Color.white));
```

As an alternative to letting the border be a single colour, you can specify that an icon should be used. The icon will then be repeatedly drawn on the border. It will look as if you have used wallpaper. One example is shown on the furthest right of the third line in Figure 8.11. We have included the following statements in the program:

```
a33.setText(htmlText("Matte Border", "with icon"));
a33.setBorder(new MatteBorder(new ImageIcon("star.gif")));
```

When we do not specify the thickness of the border, as here, it will automatically be the same height and width as the icon. It is possible to specify the thickness of the border even when an icon is used, however. (Please refer to the fact box.)

MatteBorder	
new MatteBorder(u,l,d,r,col)	a border with colour col, thickness u on top, l on the left, d at the bottom and r on the right
new MatteBorder(u,l,d,r,ic)	a border with icon ic, thickness u on top, l on the left, d at the bottom and r on the right
new MatteBorder(ic)	a border with icon ic, frame thickness is determined by icon size

8.4.6 `TitledBorder`

The class `TitledBorder` makes it possible to put a text in or beside any border. The border on the left of the last line in Figure 8.11 has been achieved with the following statements:

```
a41.setText("Titled Border");
a41.setBorder(new TitledBorder("Title in border"));
```

We have only specified the text to be put on the border here. When you do not specify the type of border you want, and where the text should be put, a standard border is chosen automatically, and the text is inserted in a standard fashion. You can use greater precision, however. (Please refer to the fact box.) You can specify the type of border it should be, where the text should be positioned and the font and colour in which the text is displayed. The text can be placed left justified, right justified or centred, at the

TitledBorder	
The adjustment *adj* below should be `TitledBorder.`*x*, where *x* is LEFT, CENTER or RIGHT. Positioning *po* should be `TitledBorder.`*y*, where *y* is ABOVE_TOP, TOP, BELOW_TOP, ABOVE_BOTTOM, BOTTOM or BELOW_BOTTOM	
new TitledBorder(txt)	gives a border with text txt
new TitledBorder(bor,txt)	gives a border with text txt on the frame bor
new TitledBorder(bor,txt,*adj*,*po*)	as above, the text ends up on position *po* with adjustment *adj*
new TitledBorder(bor,txt,*adj*,*po*,f)	as above, with font f
new TitledBorder(bor,txt,*adj*,*po*,f,col)	as above, with colour col
tb.setTitle(txt)	sets (changes) the text txt in border tb

top or bottom edge of the border. It can be placed either above, on or below the edge. To generate the border around the component in the centre of the last line in Figure 8.11 we could write the following statements:

```
a42.setText("Titled Border");
a42.setBorder(new TitledBorder(
            new EtchedBorder(), "Text below",
            TitledBorder.CENTER, TitledBorder.BELOW_BOTTOM,
            new Font("Serif",Font.ITALIC,15), Color.blue));
```

It is possible to change the text in the border dynamically. For example, you could write the statement

```
((TitledBorder)a42.getBorder()).setTitle("Another text");
```

The method `getBorder` answers with a reference of type `Border`, which is a common superclass (actually an interface) for all the classes that describe borders. In the statement above, it is thus necessary to do an explicit type conversion to the particular subclass `TitledBorder`.

8.4.7 `CompoundBorder`

The class `CompoundBorder` is somewhat special. This is because it is used to join two borders together. The constructor has two parameters, which refer to the two borders to be combined. We first specify the border to be on the outside and then the one to be on the inside. The last box in Figure 8.11, for example, was created with the statements

```
a43.setText("Compound Border");
a43.setBorder(new CompoundBorder(
                new LineBorder(Color.green, 10),
                new EtchedBorder(EtchedBorder.RAISED)));
```

Here, we have put a combined border around the component `a43`. On the outside there is a 10-pixel-wide green border of type `LineBorder` and inside it there is a border of type `EtchedBorder`. There is, of course, nothing to prevent one of the parameters in the constructor for class `CompoundBorder` from referring, in its turn, to another object of class `CompoundBorder`. This makes it possible to create combined borders which consist of more than two borders.

CompoundBorder		
new CompoundBorder(outer, inner)	gives a combined border with border `outer` furthest out and border `inner` furthest in	

8.5   Look & Feel

In the introduction to Chapter 6 we said that the components in Swing are drawn by a special auxiliary component, a so-called UI delegate. When it is going to draw a Swing component, it retrieves information from its environment about the way drawing should be done. You can choose the style that Swing components should have by specifying the so-called *Look & Feel* to be used. At present, there are four ready-made Look & Feel styles to choose from: *Metal*, *Windows*, *Motif* and *Mac*. The latter three correspond to the appearance the components would have if you ran an "ordinary" program under Windows, under Unix with Motif or on a Macintosh. Metal and Motif Look & Feel are available for all platforms, whereas Windows and Mac Look & Feel are only available when you run Windows or use a Mac. Unless you specify something else, you automatically get the Metal Look & Feel. This gives a special "Java look".

To specify the Look & Feel you want, you tell your program to call the class method `UIManager.setLookAndFeel`. This method should have a text containing the name of the Look & Feel you want to use as its parameter. The names are quite long and complicated, which is shown in the table below:

Look & Feel	Name
Metal	`javax.swing.plaf.metal.MetalLookAndFeel`
Windows	`com.sun.java.swing.plaf.windows.WindowsLookAndFeel`
Motif	`com.sun.java.swing.plaf.motif.MotifLookAndFeel`
Mac	`com.sun.java.swing.plaf.mac.MacLookAndFeel`

`UIManager.setLookAndFeel` generates various types of exceptions if you give an incorrect name or if the Look & Feel you have given is not available for that platform. For this reason, you have to encapsulate the call of `setLookAndFeel` in a **try** statement. As an example, we show how you can specify that you want Motif Look & Feel.

```
try {
   UIManager.setLookAndFeel
                 ("com.sun.java.swing.plaf.motif.MotifLookAndFeel");
}
catch (Exception ex) {}
```

For a call like this to have any effect, it must be done before the first Swing component is created. If you want to change the Look & Feel dynamically, then you must call the method `SwingUtilities.updateComponentTreeUI` after calling `UIManager.setLook-AndFeel`. The method `SwingUtilities.updateComponentTreeUI` should have a reference to the outermost component as its parameter. This should normally be a reference to the outermost `JFrame` component. For this reason, you can put the call of

`SwingUtilities.updateComponentTreeUI` in the class that describes the program's outermost `JFrame` and give the reference **this** as the parameter:

```
try {
  UIManager.setLookAndFeel
                  ("com.sun.java.swing.plaf.motif.MotifLookAndFeel");
  SwingUtilities.updateComponentTreeUI(this);
}
catch (Exception ex) {}
```

As an example, we will make a few changes to the program `TextEdit` on page 211. When we run the program in its original form, it automatically uses the Metal Look & Feel and we get the appearance shown in Figure 6.18 on page 210. We will now add a `JComboBox` at the bottom of the window. Using this, the user can select a particular Look & Feel. The appearance when you have chosen Windows and Motif Look & Feel respectively is shown in Figures 8.12 and 8.13.

To achieve this, we add the following declarations to the program `TextEditor`:

```
JComboBox box = new JComboBox();
JPanel boxp = new JPanel();
```

After this, we put the `JComboBox` in panel `boxp` and put the panel at the bottom of the window. We also link an event listener to the `JComboBox`:

```
boxp.add(box);
c.add(boxp, BorderLayout.SOUTH);
box.addActionListener(this);
```

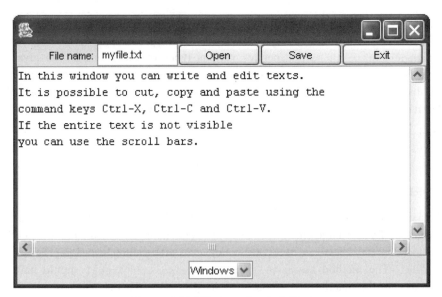

Figure 8.12 Windows Look & Feel

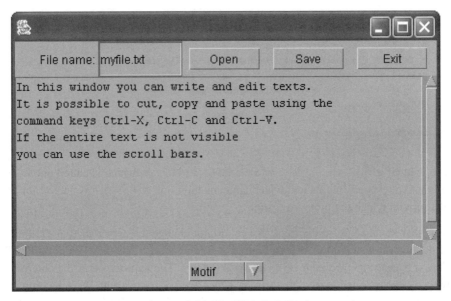

Figure 8.13 Motif Look & Feel

We then add five alternatives in the JComboBox:

```
box.addItem("Metal"); box.addItem("Windows");
box.addItem("Motif"); box.addItem("Mac");
box.addItem("System");
```

The first four alternatives correspond to the four different Look & Feel styles available. If the user specifies the last alternative, which is called System, the program should choose the Look & Feel that is "natural" for the platform that the program is run on. This means, for example, that the Windows Look & Feel should be chosen if the program is run under Windows and that the Mac Look & Feel should be chosen if the program is run on a Macintosh.

The last addition to the program is done in the listener method. So we will insert the following if statement, which controls what happens when the user chooses an alternative in the JComboBox:

```
if (e.getSource() == box) {
  String name = "";
  if (box.getSelectedIndex() == 0)
    name = "javax.swing.plaf.metal.MetalLookAndFeel";

  else if (box.getSelectedIndex() == 1)
    name ="com.sun.java.swing.plaf.windows.WindowsLookAndFeel";
  else if (box.getSelectedIndex() == 2)
    name = "com.sun.java.swing.plaf.motif.MotifLookAndFeel";
```

```
   else if (box.getSelectedIndex() == 3)
      name = "com.sun.java.swing.plaf.mac.MacLookAndFeel";
   else if (box.getSelectedIndex() == 4)
      name = UIManager.getSystemLookAndFeelClassName();
   try {
      UIManager.setLookAndFeel(name);
      SwingUtilities.updateComponentTreeUI(this);
   }
   catch (Exception ex) {}
}
```

The method UIManager.getSystemLookAndFeelClassName which is called in the last alternative responds with a text which contains the Look & Feel that is natural for the platform on which the program is run.

Note that the changes to the Look & Feel do not change the appearance of the frame of the outermost window. In both Figures 8.12 and 8.13, it has the "Windows look". This is because the program is run under Windows. The appearance of the outermost window is controlled by the platform on which the program is run. If we had run the program under Unix instead, the window would have had a "Motif look". Irrespective of the platform you run on, it is still possible to have the "Metal look" on the outermost window as well. You could get it to look like Figure 8.14.

To achieve this, you can call the class method JFrame.setDefaultLookAndFeel-Decorated. The call should be made before the window is created. In the program TextEditor you could write the method main as follows:

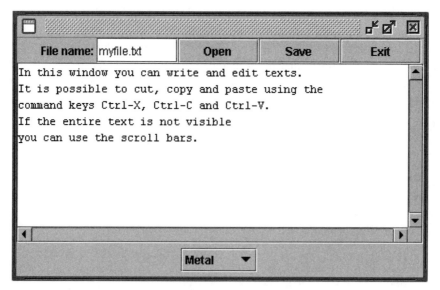

Figure 8.14 Metal Look & Feel, in the outermost window as well

```
public static void main (String[] arg) {
  JFrame.setDefaultLookAndFeelDecorated(true);
  TextEdit t = new TextEdit();
}
```

Finally, it should be mentioned that you can completely remove the border around the outermost window. We do this by calling the method setUndecorated for the JFrame in question. In the constructor, you could add the call

```
setUndecorated(true);
```

8.6 Exercises

1. Amend program Picture on page 251 so that it uses a JTabbedPane instead, from which you can choose the image to be displayed.

2. Figure 6.9 on page 185 was generated by using GridLayout. This means that all three columns were of equal width. Attempt, by using BoxLayout, to position the components so that the two right-hand columns are no wider than necessary to leave space for their components.

3. Use GridBagLayout to design a graphic form which can be used to input various information about the programmer. In addition to your name, you should be able to give your age, marital status (single, married or partnership) and your favourite programming language(s) (you should receive a list to choose from). There should also be two buttons: one labelled Cancel which terminates the program and one labelled Finished. When you click this one, the information about the programmer should be output in a command window (use the stream System.out). After this, all notes on the form should be deleted, so that new information can be input.

4. Try to solve the task in Exercise 3 without using GridBagLayout. *Tip*: BoxLayout can be useful.

5. Construct a JLabel with a border consisting of four colours.

6. Construct a JFrame without border. Add a small button at the top right, which the user can use to close the window and terminate the program.

Characters, arrays and vectors

We have previously discussed the class `String`, which is used to describe texts. We have also briefly discussed the type `char`, which is used to describe individual letters. This chapter starts with a more detailed discussion of the type `char` together with a discussion on how characters and texts are compared. After this, we discuss arrays and vectors, which are used to construct tables that contain several items of data.

9.1 Character codes and character literals

We normally use a group of eight bits to store a character in the computer. A group of this kind is called a *byte*. In the past, only seven of these eight bits were used. The eighth bit, or *parity bit*, was reserved for checking purposes. The other seven bits could be combined in 128 different ways, which meant that there were 128 different character codes. There is a generally accepted standard, called the *ASCII standard*, which determines the characters that can be coded with the seven available bits, and for each pattern of seven bits, there is one character designated in the standard. For example, "%", "9" and "A" are represented, respectively, by

```
00100101 00111001 01000001
```

These bit patterns can be interpreted as binary integers, called *character codes*. The character codes lie between 0 and 127; the characters "9" and "A" will, for example, have the character codes 57 and 65, respectively. The ASCII standard contains the letters a–z (both upper and lower case), the digits 0–9, various special characters (for example, "!" and ".") and a set of non-printing control characters.

ASCII is an American standard that was developed on the assumption that the language used would be English. The English alphabet has the 26 letters, a–z, derived from the Latin alphabet. Almost all other living languages use either the Latin alphabet, with other characters, or other non-Latin alphabets or characters. The ASCII standard is, however, spread throughout the world. The fact that ASCII contains only the letters a–z has been a problem and a constant source of irritation to everyone working in programming in the non-English-speaking countries. An obvious solution to this problem would be to allow for more characters. If we dropped the use of the first bit in each byte as a parity bit, we could have eight bits instead of seven, and 256 different characters could be represented instead of 128. We could then use the characters from 128 to 255 to represent new letters and other characters. There is an international standard (ISO 8859), also called *LATIN_1*, specifying the characters to be designated by the different codes. When we use Windows or a Unix system (but not MS-DOS) we follow this standard. LATIN_1 corresponds to the ASCII standard for the character codes 0 to 127. Character codes 128 to 255 are used partly for non-printing control characters and partly for a set of printable characters. Among the characters in LATIN_1 there are the letters with diacritics that are used in the Romance and Germanic languages, for example á, å, è, æ, ö, ü, ñ and ç. All these characters exist in both lower and upper case. The only exceptions are the German character ß, indicating a double s, and the character ÿ. Apart from the letters with diacritical marks, LATIN_1 also contains various graphic characters such as §, £ and ¶.

Of course, using LATIN_1 instead of ASCII only solves the problem for countries where the Western European languages are used. Java, however, aims to ensure that it.can be used anywhere in the world and so it has gone a step further. Letters and characters are coded in Java with 16 bits instead of 8. As a result, no fewer than 65,536 different characters can be encoded. Java uses the Unicode standard. The characters in this standard come from many different alphabets from all over the world. In addition, there are a number of special characters for graphics. The Unicode codes from 0–255 agree with the LATIN_1 standard. A complete listing of all the Unicode characters can be found at www.unicode.org.

In Java, variables of the standard type `char` are 16 bits long and contain character codes in accordance with the Unicode standard.

Character literals, or constant character values, are written between apostrophe marks. For instance, if we want to declare a variable of type `char` and insert a plus character into it, we can write:

```
char ch = '+';
```

The following assignments are also permitted:

```
ch = 'ê'; ch = '¿';
```

Character literals for characters that can be written can be easily indicated, as demonstrated above. Exceptions are the characters ′ (apostrophe), ″ (double quotes) and \ (backslash). When we wish to indicate these characters, we have to use *escape sequences*. An escape sequence is introduced by the character \ and is interpreted as a single character. For example, to assign an apostrophe to the variable `ch1` and a backslash to the variable `ch2`, we can write:

```
ch1 = '\''; ch2 = '\\';
```

Escape sequences are also used to indicate control characters that cannot be written. Some of the most common control characters have been given special escape sequences. For example, \n means new line and \t tabulator. If we want to indicate a character that we cannot write and that lacks a special escape sequence, we can use an escape sequence where the character's code is directly indicated. If we want to indicate a character included in LATIN_1, we can write an *octal number*[1] consisting of, at most, three digits after the character \. The highest octal number that can be indicated in this way is 377, which corresponds to decimal 255. Some examples are:

```
'\0'  '\33'  '\177'  '\266'  '\377'
```

It is impossible to type most of the characters in the complete Unicode standard on a normal keyboard. To indicate characters with character codes higher than 255 (decimal), we can use a Unicode sequence. This has the form '\uxxxx'. The number xxxx will consist of four digits and is written in *hexadecimal* form.[2] If we have two variables ch1 and ch2, both of type **char**, for instance, we can write:

```
ch1 = '\u2663'; ch2 = '\u03A8';
```

Then the variable ch1 will contain the character ♣, while the variable ch2 will contain the character ψ.

We do not only use Unicode in the type **char**. Java also uses Unicode internally in the compiled classes. It is therefore permissible to use Unicode letters in class names, variables, and so on, while we can also use Unicode sequences in the program code itself. If, for example, we write the declaration

```
double π = 3.1416;
```

but do not have a text editor that allows us to enter π, we can instead write

```
double \u03C0 = 3.1416;
```

We will show a program that reads a text file and prints the file out, as a demonstration of handling individual characters. Input is done with the method read in the class BufferedReader. (See page 133.) During printout, all tabulator characters are replaced by three space characters, and all upper-case letters are also translated to lower-case letters.

---

[1] Only the digits 0–7 may be used in an octal number. For instance, the decimal number 8 is written as 10 in octal form. Octal 20 corresponds to decimal 16 and octal 100 corresponds to decimal 64.

[2] The digits 0–9 are used in a hexadecimal number and the letters A–F are used to indicate the decimal numbers from 10 to 15. Thus the hexadecimal number F corresponds to decimal 15 and the hexadecimal number 10 corresponds to decimal 16. Hexadecimal 20 corresponds to decimal 32 and hexadecimal 100 corresponds to decimal 256.

Escape sequences		
\n	*new line*	moves the printout position to the beginning of the next line
\b	*backspace*	moves the printout position one step to the left
\r	*return*	moves the printout position to the beginning of the next line
\f	*form feed*	moves the printout position to the beginning of the next page
\t	*tab*	moves the printout position to the next tab stop
\'	*single quote*	apostrophe mark
\"	*double quote*	quotation marks
\\	*backslash*	gives the character \
nnn		the character with the octal character code *nnn*
\u*xxxx*		the character with the hexadecimal Unicode *xxxx*

```java
import java.io.*;
public class CharDemo {
  public static void main (String[] arg) throws IOException {
    // create a stream from standard input
    BufferedReader myIn = new BufferedReader
                        (new InputStreamReader(System.in));
    // open the input file
    System.out.print("Input file? "); System.out.flush();
    String name = myIn.readLine();
    BufferedReader inFile = new BufferedReader
                        (new FileReader(name));
    // read and write out the file
    int i;
    while ((i = inFile.read()) != -1) {
      char c = (char) i;
      if (c == '\t')
        System.out.print("    ");
      else if (Character.isUpperCase(c))
        System.out.print(Character.toLowerCase(c));
      else
        System.out.print(c);
    }
    System.out.flush(); // NB! Important!
  }
}
```

In the program, the class methods `isUpperCase` and `toLowerCase` in the wrapper class `Character` (see page 51) are called.

The expression after **while** might look somewhat strange, so we should say something about assignments in Java. An expression of the form a=b is called an *assignment expression*. In an expression of this kind, a's value is, of course, assigned to b but, in fact, the *whole* expression has a value in the same way that an expression of the form a+b has a value. The value of an assignment expression is the value that is assigned. The value of the expression

```
i = inFile.read()
```

is, therefore, the value that is assigned to the variable i. In the **while** statement

```
while ((i = inFile.read()) != -1)
```

the value of i is compared with –1. Note the importance of the parentheses around the assignment expression. The operator != has a higher priority than = and would have been carried out first had the parentheses not been included, producing a compilation error. Note, too, that we have to read in the characters to a variable of type **int** and not a variable of type **char**, since a variable of type **char** cannot contain the value –1.

We call the method flush last of all in the program to empty the printout buffer. If this were not done, a number of characters (perhaps all of them) that were to be written out could remain in the buffer and, therefore, not be seen on the screen. The printout buffer is cleared automatically every time println is called, or something is entered from the keyboard; since we have not done anything like this in the program, we have expressly to empty the buffer by calling flush.

An object of class String contains a text consisting of a series of elements of type **char**, that is, of elements coded with 16-bit Unicode. If a text contained a character that could not be written at the keyboard, we would be able to use Unicode sequences:

```
String s = "\u03B1\u03B2"; // s contains the text "αβ"
```

Escape sequences may also be used in text:

```
System.out.println("\"method\" is called \"function\" in C++");
```

The printout will then be:

```
"method" is called "function" in C++
```

9.2 Comparisons of characters and texts

An internal order is defined between the different values of type **char**, which is determined, quite simply, by the code representing the characters. A character with a small character code will come before a character with a larger code. Note especially that upper- and lower-case letters are not regarded as being the same and that the normal alphabetical order will not apply to letters with accents or other diacritics. The program lines below compare two characters and write them out in order of size. (We suppose that the variables ch1 and ch2 both have type **char**.)

```
ch1 = 'A'; ch2 = 'a';
if (ch1 < ch2)
   System.out.println(ch1 + " is smallest");
else
   System.out.println(ch2 + " is smallest");
```

The output will be:

```
A is smallest
```

Capitals are treated as being smaller than lower-case letters.

In Section 2.9 we saw that we were able to use the method `compareTo` in the standard class `String` to compare two texts. This method will compare the incoming characters one by one in the same method as above, that is, the character code determines their internal order. The method `compareTo` will therefore not function as we would like when we compare natural text, especially if the text is written in a language other than English. Let us take an example: let us suppose that the variables `s1` and `s2` have type `String`:

```
s1 = "pâté"; s2="prince";
if (s1.compareTo(s2) < 0)
   System.out.println(s1 + " is before " + s2);
else if (s1.compareTo(s2) > 0)
   System.out.println(s2 + " is before " + s1);
else
   System.out.println(s2 + " and " + s1 + " are equal");
```

The output will be:

```
prince is before pâté
```

The solution to our problem is to use a *collator* that knows the rules for sorting letters in the language in question. We can get a collator by declaring an object of the standard class `java.text.Collator`:

```
Collator co = Collator.getInstance();
```

The class method `getInstance` gives a collator that knows the rules for the language currently serving as a default `Locale` (see page 121). For example, if we use French conventions, the collator `co` will know the French rules.

To compare two texts, we can now use the method `compare` for the collator `co`:

```
s1 = "pâté"; s2="prince";
if (co.compare(s1, s2) < 0)
   System.out.println(s1 + " is before " + s2);
else if (co.compare(s1, s2) > 0)
   System.out.println(s2 + " is before " + s1);
else
   System.out.println(s1 + " and " + s2 + " are equal");
```

The method `compare` has, as parameters, the two texts to be compared. The result it gives is the same value as the method `compareTo` in class `String`, that is, a value that is 0 if the two texts are equal, less than 0 if the first text comes before the second, and greater than 0 if the second text comes before the first. The output from these program lines will now be (with English conventions):

```
pâté is before prince
```

The comparisons will not be entirely perfect yet. For example, if we let `s1` contain the text `"Prince"` and `s2` the text `"prince"`, we will get the output:

```
prince is before Prince
```

If we let `s1` contain the text `"Irene"` and `s2` the text `"Irène"`, we will get the output:

```
Irene is before Irène
```

This is because the collator `co` regards upper- and lower-case letters as being different. Moreover, it also sees letters with accents and the corresponding letters without accents as being different. Meanwhile, we can solve this problem by telling the collator `co` how exacting it is to be when comparing different letters; this is done with the method `setStrength`. This has a parameter that indicates the collator's strength. There are three levels: PRIMARY, SECONDARY and TERTIARY. If the level is set at PRIMARY, the collator will only differentiate between different letters, upper- and lower-case letters being regarded as equal. Letters with diacritics are seen as being the same as letters without them. If the collator is set to SECONDARY, upper- and lower-case letters are regarded as equal but letters with diacritics are not seen as being the same as letters without them. If the TERTIARY level is chosen, upper- and lower-case letters are treated as being unequal, as are letters with and without diacritics.

If no level has been indicated for a collator, the TERTIARY level will be chosen, which is why the collator `co`, in our example above, sorted things in such an odd way. The best thing is to set the level to PRIMARY, which will give normal alphabetical comparisons:

```
co.setStrength(Collator.PRIMARY);
```

Using the same example as before, we will now get the correct comparisons:

```
prince and Prince are equal
Irène and Irene are equal
```

When we create a collator, we can indicate the language conventions we want to have. The class `getInstance`, for example, can have as parameter a `Locale` object. If we want a collator to make a comparison in accordance with Portuguese language rules, for instance, we can write:

```
Collator co_pt = Collator.getInstance(new Locale("pt", "PT"));
```

Summing up, we can say that if ordinary alphabetical comparisons are called for, a collator should be obtained that has been adjusted to the language conventions desired. The collator's level should then be set to PRIMARY.

We can also use a method equals, in class Collator, to check whether, from an alphabetical point of view, two texts are the same. We can write

```
s1 = "Irene"; s2="Irène";
if (co.equals(s1,s2))
    System.out.println(s1 + " and " + s2 + " are equal");
```

Alphabetical comparison of texts

Obtain a collator of class java.text.Collator:

```
Collator c = Collator.getInstance();
```

or

```
Collator c = Collator.getInstance(new Locale("language","country"));
```

Set the collator's level to PRIMARY:

```
c.setStrength(Collator.PRIMARY);
```

The texts are then compared with method compare or equals:

c.compare(s1,s2)   gives a value that is 0 if s1 and s2 are alphabetically equal, < 0 if s1 comes before s2 and >0 if s2 comes before s1

c.equals(s1,s2)   gives true if s1 and s2 are alphabetically equal, false otherwise

---

9.3   The for statement

So far in the book, we have used a while statement to achieve repetition. In this section, we will take a look at a further statement that can be used, which is the for statement. The reason that we introduce the for statement now is that it is often suitable to use it when you work with the arrays we will discuss in the next section. One usually uses a for when one has a repetition where there is a counter that should be incremented or decremented each time round. The for statement in Java differs slightly from the corresponding statement in other program languages (except C and C++). After the reserved word for there is a bracket that contains three separate components, an initialization section, a conditional section and a change section. There should be a semicolon between each component. The for statement has the format:

```
for (init; condition; change)
    statement;
```

The statement on the second line can consist of several statements in curly brackets, just as for `if` statements and `while` statements. Execution proceeds in the following way: First *init* is computed and then *condition*. If *condition* is true, *statement* is performed. When this has been done, *change* is computed. Now *condition* is computed once again. If it is still true, another round is performed, which means that first *statement* and then *change* are computed again; *condition* is then computed and checked again, the whole process being reiterated until this expression is shown to be false. Note that *init* is performed only once, before the first round, while the other expressions are computed once per round, *condition* before each round and *change* after each round.

Here are a few examples of `for` statements. The following statement writes out the multiplication table for 12, that is, 1 times 12, 2 times 12 and so on, up to 12 times 12:

```
int i;
for (i=1; i<=12; i=i+1)
   System.out.println(i*12);
```

If we have a counter, as we do here, computation need not take place with 1. The counter can be changed at will at the end of each round. For instance, we could just as well write:

```
int i;
for (i=12; i<=144; i=i+12)
   System.out.println(i);
```

We could also declare the counter in the initialization expression. It will then only be known inside the `for` statement. (But the counter must not be given the same name as another variable declared outside the `for` statement in the actual method.)

```
for (int i=12; i<=144; i=i+12)
   System.out.println(i);
```

We might as well take this opportunity to introduce the operators `++` and `--`, as well as the composite forms of the assignment operator. Statements such as

```
i = i + 1;
k = k - 1;
```

are very common. In Java there are a couple of useful operators, `++` and `--`, to increase or decrease a variable's value by 1. The statements above could be written as

```
i++;
k--;
```

The increment and decrement operators come in two variants. We can set `++` or `--` either in front of the variable name (the *prefix* variant) or after it (the *postfix* variant):

```
++i;   // prefix
k--;   // postfix
```

9. Characters, arrays and vectors

In the above examples, it will not matter which of the two variants we choose but there is still an important difference. The expressions `i++` and `++i` both mean that the variable `i` is increased by 1, but the *values* of the expressions are different. The value of the expression `i++` is the value `i` had *before* the increase, and the value of the expression `++i` is the value `i` has *after* the increase. The same thing applies to the `--` operator. This difference is best illustrated by an example:

```
int i, k, m, n;
i = 4; k = 7;
m = i++ * k--; // postfix.  m gets the value 4*7, or 28
i = 4; k = 7;
n = ++i * --k; // prefix.   n gets the value 5*6, or 30
```

Apart from increasing and decreasing it by 1, we may often wish to change a variable's value in other ways, for instance by adding a particular value to the variable or multiplying a variable by a certain number. Some examples are:

```
i = i + 2;
j = j - k;
k = k * i;
```

In such situations it can be useful to use the composite forms of the assignment operator. Then the above statements could be written as

```
i += 2;     // same as i = i + 2;
j -= k;     // same as j = j - k;
k *= i;     // same as k = k * i;
```

There are several composite forms of the assignment operator (see the fact box).

The operators ++, -- and composite assignments

`++`   increases the value of the operand by 1. The value of `k++` is `k`'s old value. The value of `++k` is `k`'s new value.

`--`   decreases the value of the operand by 1. The value of `k--` is `k`'s old value. The value of `--k` is `k`'s new value.

`+=   -=   *=   /=   %=`

composite assignment operators.

The expression: `x •= y;`
is equivalent to: `x = x • (y);`

These operators work well together with the **for** statement. For example, we can write:

```
for (int i=1; i<=12; i++)
   System.out.println(i*12);
```

or

```
for (int i=12; i<=144; i+=12)
   System.out.println(i);
```

<table>
<tr><td colspan="1">for statement</td></tr>
</table>

```
for (init; condition; change)
   statement;
```

The equivalent of the statements:

```
init;
while (condition) {
   statement;
   change;
}
```

Parts *init*, *condition* and *change* could be left out but the semicolon must remain.

Each part can consist of several expressions with the comma character in between.

Each of the three different parts *init*, *condition* and *change* in parentheses in the `for` statement could easily contain several expressions. For instance, we might sometimes want to initialize several variables at the beginning of a repetition. Here is an example where we want to compute the value of x^n. Let us suppose that x has type `double` and n type `int`. The result will be computed in a variable r of type `double`. Both the variable r and a counter i must be initialized before the first round. Note especially that when one of the parts *init*, *condition* and *change* contains several expressions, the *comma character* must be inserted between them:

```
for (r=1.0, i=1; i <=n; i++)
   r *= x;
```

Sometimes the statement to be repeated in every round will be an *empty statement*, that is, nothing will be done, in which case we just write a semicolon on its own. The `for` statement, above, could then be written as follows:

```
for (r=1.0, i=1; i <=n; i++, r*=x)
   ;
```

But then, as in this example, the semicolon should be written in a separate line to show that there is an empty statement. Because a semicolon is interpreted as an empty statement and will be the statement repeated at every round, *a semicolon should never be written directly after a right-hand parenthesis character*. This applies to `while` statements as well.

One of the three parts of a `for` statement can be omitted. If, for example, there are no initializations to be done, the initialization part will not be necessary. If a part is omitted, it must be marked by a semicolon. There must always be two semicolons between parentheses in a `for` statement. We can even leave all the parts out. If the *condition* part is left out, it will be regarded as being "true":

```
for (;;)
   System.out.println("Help, I can't stop");
```

9.4   Arrays of simple variables

A simple variable, for example a variable of type `int` or `double`, can contain only one value at a time. However, we often need to be able to deal with collections containing several different values of the same type. We then make use of *arrays*. An array is a table that contains several components of the same kind, where the various components are numbered. We can use a special kind of reference variable to handle arrays. We can call this an *array variable*. We begin by declaring an array variable which we will call f.

```
double[] f;
```

Here it is clear that f is an array variable, that is, a reference variable that can refer to an array, and not an ordinary variable, since `[]` appears after the type name. The word `double` indicates that the array's components will be of this type. As is the case with all reference variables, f will automatically get the initialization value `null` unless we initialize it. There are two ways of initializing an array variable. The first is by using `new`.

```
double[] f = new double[5];
```

Initialization means that f will refer to an array with five components. We show this in Figure 9.1. Each component in an array is automatically initialized to its default value, the value a single variable of the actual type would have obtained. Because the components in the array are of type `double`, they are initialized to the value 0.

Every component in an array has a unique number, or *index*, as it is usually called. Note especially that the numbering of components *always* takes place from 0, so that the first component will have the index 0. (It is not possible in Java to indicate how we want the components to be numbered. The first component will always have the index 0.) It follows then that the index for the last component in an array will always be a number that is one less than the number of components in the array. The instance variable

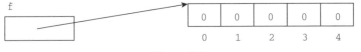

Figure 9.1

length can be used to determine the number of components in an array. Here, for example, the expression f.length will have a value of 5. When we want to access a particular component in an array, we make use of the component's index to do the *indexing*. If, for example, we wanted to put the value 2.75 into the last component (the one with the number 4) in the array f, we would write the statement:

```
f[4] = 2.75;
```

We also make use of square brackets here. The index indicated in square brackets does not need to be a constant. It could be an arbitrary integer expression. If the variables i and j are of type int, we can write:

```
f[i+j] = 2.75;
```

The important thing here is that the index expression should have a value lying inside the array's boundaries. In this example, the value of i+j will lie in the interval 0 to 4. The Java interpreter will check that the correct index has been indicated. If the value of an index expression lies outside the array's boundaries, an error signal is generated – an exception of type ArrayIndexOutOfBounds. If this error signal is not dealt with, the program will be interrupted.

The components in an array can be of arbitrary type. For instance, we can declare another array variable and let it refer to an array with six components of type int:

```
int[] a = new int[6];
```

As we have seen when creating an array, all its components will be initialized to a default value unless otherwise specified. An array can also be initialized when it is being created. If we wanted, we could write:

```
int[] b = {13, 23, 55, 4};
```

This is the other way to initialize an array variable. Note that we do not need to use new when writing in this way. A new array will still be created. The number of components in the new array will be determined by the number of components that are enumerated in the curly brackets. Here we create a new array having four components and they will get the initialization values 13, 23, 55 and 4. The initialization expressions inside the curly brackets do not need to be constants. They can be arbitrary expressions. For example, if the variables i and j had type int, we would write:

```
int[] b = {i, i-1, i+j, 18};
```

It is only during the initialization stage that it is permissible to give values to the components all at once. For example, the following statement would not be allowed:

```
b = {0, 0, 0, 0};   // not allowed!
```

If, for example, we wanted to assign the value 5 to all the components in b, we could do this for each component, one at a time, like this:

```
for (int i=0; i<b.length; i++) // b.length has the value 4
    b[i] = 5;
```

This is a little unwieldy. Better is the following construction:

```
b = new int[]{5, 5, 5, 5};
```

But note that now we create a *new* array, letting b refer to the new array. The array that b referred to earlier will be an item for automatic garbage collection.

Because array variables are reference variables, we must be careful when making assignments of arrays. In the following statement, for example, the variable a is set to refer to the *same* array as the variable b.

```
a = b;   // copies the reference
```

What this would look like is shown in Figure 9.2.

If we want to assign the whole array b to a, we must instead make a copy of the array b refers to. This we do by using the standard method clone.

```
a = (int[]) b.clone(); // copies the array
```

The method clone returns a value of class Object, and so an explicit type conversion to type int[] is required. Instead, we will now get the situation shown in Figure 9.3. Note that a is a reference and that it is the reference itself that is changed so that a will refer to a *new* array. This means that it does not matter what a referred to earlier. As

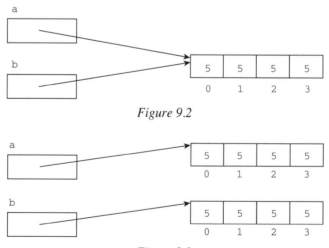

Figure 9.2

Figure 9.3

can be seen, the length of the array that a referred to earlier does not need to agree with the length of array b.

If we want to copy a number of components from one array to another, we can use the class method `arraycopy` in the standard class `System`. Suppose, for example, that we have declared yet another array

```
int[] c = {10, 20, 30, 40, 50, 60};
```

Further suppose that array b looks as in Figure 9.3. We now make the call:

```
System.arraycopy(c,2,b,1,2);
```

The first argument is the array that we will copy from and the second indicates where in this array we will begin to copy. Copying will, therefore, begin with component number 2 in array c. The third argument is the array we will be copying to, and the fourth element will indicate the starting position in this array. Here copying will, therefore, take place to component number 1 and onwards, in array b. The last argument indicates the number of components to be copied, in this example, 2. The result of the above statement will thus be that components 1 and 2 in array b will be changed. Components 0 and 3 will remain unchanged. As a result, array b will contain the values {5, 30, 40, 5}. Note that `arraycopy` will change inside the array that b refers to. The reference b itself will not be changed. (Compare this with the use of the method `clone`, above.) Of course, it is possible to write a repetition statement instead of using `arraycopy`.

Care must be exercised when making comparisons of arrays. If we wrote, for example,

```
if (a == b) // permitted but not what is intended
```

it would certainly be allowed, but the contents of the arrays would not be compared. Instead, a check is made to see whether a and b are referring to the *same* array.

Arrays, the basics	
type[] f;	declares a reference to an array
type[] f = **new** *type*[*number*];	declaration and initialization
type[] f = {*value, value ... value*};	declaration and initialization
f = **new** *type*[]{*value, value ... value*};	f is assigned a new array
f = g;	f refers to the same array as g
f = (*type*[]) g.clone();	f refers to a *copy* of g
f.length	gives the number of components in the array f
System.arraycopy(f1,*startpos1*,f2,*startpos2*,*number*);	
copies *number* of components from f1[*startpos1*] to f2[*startpos2*]	
f == g	checks whether f and g refer to the same array

283

9. Characters, arrays and vectors

The class `java.util.Arrays` contains some class methods (static methods) that are useful when dealing with arrays. A compilation of these is given in the fact box. For example, we can check whether two arrays `f` and `g` are equal by writing:

```
if (Arrays.equals(f,g))
```

java.util.Arrays	
`equals(a1,a2)`	gives `true` if the arrays `a1` and `a2` are equal (contain the same number of components and the components are equal)
`fill(a,v)`	gives all the components in array `a` the value `v`
`fill(a,i1,i2,v)`	gives components no. `i1` to `i2-1` in array `a` the value `v`
`sort(a)`	sorts the components in array `a` in ascending order
`sort(a,c)`	as above but uses `c` to compare components (`c` will implement the interface `Comparator`)
`sort(a,i1,i2)`	sorts components no. `i1` to `i2-1` in array `a`
`sort(a,i1,i2,c)`	as above but uses `c` to compare components
`binarySearch(a,k)`	searches for component `k` in the array `a`, gives `k`'s index in the array if `k` exists, otherwise -1
`binarySearch(a,k,c)`	as above but uses `c` to compare components (`c` will implement the interface `Comparator`)
`asList(a)`	converts an array `a` to a list (see Section 19.2)

Objects of standard type `String` contain an array in which the components are of type `char`. It is easy to convert an array of `char` to a `String` object and vice versa:

```
char[] v = {'J', 'a', 'v', 'a', ' ', 'c', 'l', 'a', 's', 's'};
String s = new String(v);       // s gets the value "Java class"
String t = new String(v,1,3);   // t gets the value "ava"
char[] w = t.toCharArray();     // w gets the value {'a', 'v', 'a'}
```

On the third line we choose a sub-array of `v`. The "1" means that the sub-array will begin in position 1, and the "3" means that the sub-array will be three characters long.

It is also easy to convert an array of `byte` to a `String` object and vice versa:

```
byte[] b = s.getBytes();        // b contains the text "Java class"
String p = new String(b);       // p gets the value "Java class"
String q = new String(b,1,3);   // q gets the value "ava"
```

It should be mentioned here that (unfortunately) there is another way of declaring arrays in Java. The array variable `f` that we previously declared as

```
double[] f;
```

can also be declared in the following way:

```
double f[];
```

So we can set the square brackets after the variable name instead of after the type name. This way of writing is inherited from the programming language C, where arrays were declared in this way, but it is illogical and misleading, since the square brackets really are a part of the type indication. If we look at the following example:

```
int[] g1, h1;    // recommended way of writing
```

we see that this is written in the usual way. The result will be that the variables `g1` and `h1` both get type `int[]`, which is quite natural. The indication of the type, that is, `int[]`, comes first, and then the variables that will have this type are enumerated afterwards. However, if we write,

```
int g2[], h2[];
```

we see that the square brackets must be repeated for each variable. If these are omitted for a variable, the variable will not be an array but an ordinary variable. For instance, if we write the following, `g3` will be an array variable, while `h3` will be an ordinary `int`:

```
int g3[], h3;
```

We therefore recommend the normal way of writing, where square brackets are written together with the type name (even if old C programmers might be offended!).

As an example we will now look at a simple program which reads in, from the keyboard, several real numbers constituting a series of measurements. The program will then compute the mean value of the measurements and write it out. Finally, the program will write out all the measurements that are greater than the mean value:

```
import java.io.*;
public class ForDemo {
  public static void main (String[] arg) throws IOException {
    BufferedReader myIn = new BufferedReader
                        (new InputStreamReader(System.in));
    System.out.print("How many measurements? ");
    System.out.flush();
    final int no = Integer.parseInt(myIn.readLine());

    double sum = 0;
    double[] m = new double[no];
    for (int i = 0; i<no; i++) {
      System.out.print("Measurement no. " + i + "? ");
      System.out.flush();
      m[i] = Double.parseDouble(myIn.readLine());
      sum += m[i];
    }
```

```
    double mean = sum / no;
    System.out.println("The mean is " + mean);
    System.out.println("Measurements greater than the mean:");
    for (int i = 0; i<no; i++)
      if (m[i] > mean)
        System.out.println("Measurement no. " + i +
                            " is " + m[i]);
  }
}
```

This could produce the following output when the program is run:

```
How many measurements? 5
Measurement no. 0? 4.0
Measurement no. 1? 4.5
Measurement no. 2? 3.5
Measurement no. 3? 3.8
Measurement no. 4? 4.2
The mean is 4.0
Measurements greater than the mean:
Measurement no. 1 is 4.5
Measurement no. 4 is 4.2
```

9.5 Searching and sorting

It is common to want to implement a computer program that can search for certain information in tables or lists. It is then natural to use arrays in programs and there are two operations which are frequently performed on arrays: *searching* and *sorting*. (In the fact box on page 284 we saw that the standard class java.util.Arrays contains ready-made methods for sorting arrays and searching in arrays, but for the sake of clarity, we will discuss searching and sorting in this section anyway.)

We will first demonstrate a simple way to search in an array. Assume that we have an integer array a containing n elements. We could have created and initialized the array with the program lines

```
// read the numbers
BufferedReader myIn = new BufferedReader
                      (new InputStreamReader(System.in));

System.out.print("How many numbers? "); System.out.flush();
final int n = Integer.parseInt(myIn.readLine());
int[] a = new int[n];
for (int i = 0; i<n; i++) {
  System.out.print("Number " + i + "? "); System.out.flush();
  a[i] = Integer.parseInt(myIn.readLine());
}
```

We now want to investigate whether a certain number is found in the array. We demonstrate simple, so-called *linear searching*. We search from the beginning of the array a until we find the element containing the number we are searching for, or we have searched through the entire array without finding the number we were looking for.

```
// linear search
System.out.print("What number are you looking for? ");
System.out.flush();
int searched = Integer.parseInt(myIn.readLine());
int j;
for (j = 0; j < n && a[j] != searched; j++)
   ;
if (j < n)
   System.out.println("The number is in place no. " + j);
else
   System.out.println("The number was not found");
```

The first condition in the `for` statement, j<n, tests whether the index j is still inside the array. If this is the case, it tests whether character number j is the number it was looking for. If not, it does another circuit, which means that j is incremented by one. After the end of the `for` statement, we can test j's value. If this value is inside the array limits, the `for` statement must have been terminated since the condition a[j]!=searched was false. In other words, one must have found the number searched for in position j.

One frequently wants to have sorted arrays. One reason is that they can then be searched faster. There are many common algorithms which describe how arrays should be sorted. We will now describe a few program lines which sort the array a and print the numbers out in order of size. We will use an algorithm which is generally referred to as *selection sort* to do the actual sorting. The basic idea is to search for the smallest number in the array, and put it in the first position in the array, after which you look for the next smallest element and put this in the second place in the array, etc. The algorithm can be described as follows:

1. Set k to the index for the first element in the array.
2. While k is less than or equal to the index for the last element in the array.
   2.1 Look for the smallest number in the part of the array which starts with the number k and which ends with the last number in the array.
   2.2 Let the smallest number (from stage 2.1) and the number k change places.
   2.3 Increment k by 1.

Stage 2.1 can be refined to:

2.1.1 Set m to k.
2.1.2 Let i run from k+1 to the last index in the array.
   2.1.2.1 If the number i is less than the number m, set m to i.
2.1.3 The smallest number is now in place number m.

287

Stage 2.2 can be refined to:

2.2.1 Move the number k to a temporary place.

2.2.2 Move the number m to place number k.

2.2.3 Move the number in the temporary place to place number m.

Using this, we can write the following program lines.

```
// Selection sort
for (int k = 0; k < n; k++) {
   // Search for the smallest among the numbers no. k to n-1
   int m = k;
   for (int i = k+1; i < n; i++)
     if (a[i] < a[m])
        m = i;
   // Let the numbers k and m swap places
   int temp = a[k];
   a[k] = a[m];
   a[m] = temp;
}
// Print out the sorted array
System.out.println("The numbers, sorted:");
for (int i=0; i<n; i++)
   System.out.print(a[i] + " ");
System.out.println();
```

If you want to search for a particular value in a sorted array, you can of course use linear searching as we did above. But if you utilize the fact that the array has been sorted, you can do a much more efficient search, a so-called *binary search*. We will now demonstrate how this is done. We use the following approach.

First take a look at the element in the middle of the array. Assume that this element contains the value *m*. If the number searched for is less than *m*, we know that this number, if it exists, must be in the left-hand section of the array, since the array is sorted. On the other hand, if the number searched for is bigger than *m*, the number must be in the right-hand section of the array. The case that the number searched for is equal to *m* remains. This solution is trivial, since we just happened to find the number right away. Having studied the element in the centre of the array, we have either found the number searched for, or know which half of the array to search in.

When we continue to search, we can regard the half we are going to search through as a new array, smaller than the original one. We can then reuse the same idea over again, i.e. study the element in the centre of the new, smaller array. If the searched-for number is not equal to the value of this element, we can decide whether we are going to continue searching in the right- or left-hand section of the array. We can now apply the same technique once again on the new, even smaller sub-array. This procedure is repeated, with ever smaller sub-arrays, until we have found the number we are looking for or until the sub-array is so small that it does not contain any elements. In the latter case, the number we are looking for is not in the array.

If we translate this procedure to program code, it can have the following appearance. We still assume that we will search through array a. We use the variables first and last to keep track of the first and last index in the array we will search in. These variables are initialized so that they describe the entire array from the start.

```
// binary search
System.out.print("What number are you looking for? ");
System.out.flush();
int searched = Integer.parseInt(myIn.readLine());
int first = 0, last = n-1, middle = 0;
while (first <= last) {
   middle = (first + last)/2;
   if (searched < a[middle])
      last = middle-1;
   else if(searched > a[middle])
      first = middle+1;
   else // equal
      break;  // the number was found
}
if (searched == a[middle])
   System.out.println("The number is in place no. " + middle);
else
   System.out.println("The number was not found");
```

This method of searching is much more efficient than simple linear searching. If you have an array containing 100 elements, for example, a binary search algorithm will only have to search seven elements in the worst case to determine whether a certain number is in the array or not. If you had used linear searching, you would have to have searched 100 elements in the worst case. The larger the array, the larger is the gain in efficiency. In an array containing 10,000 elements, a binary search would have needed to search thirteen elements in the worst case, whereas a linear search would have required a search of up to 10,000 elements.

9.6 Arrays containing reference variables

The components of the arrays we have studied so far have been of simple, built-in types such as int and double, but we can also have arrays where the components are reference variables. By using arrays like these, we can build tables of objects. Suppose, for example, that we have defined a class Point that describes points on the screen:

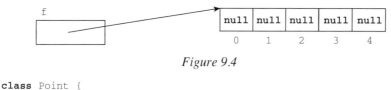

Figure 9.4

```
class Point {
  int x, y;
  Point(int xx, int yy) {// constructor
    x = xx; y = yy;
  }
}
```

There are two instance variables x and y and a constructor. We can now define an array variable that can be used to describe a pentagon:

```
Point[] f = new Point[5];
```

This will look as in Figure 9.4. Note that the individual components in the array are not points but *references* to points. Initialization will take place automatically so that all the components will get the value null. If we want a component to refer to an object, we can make an assignment, exactly as for ordinary, simple variables. For example, we can write:

```
f[2] = new Point(4,3);
```

We will then get the situation in Figure 9.5.

We can now access the object that component 2 in the array refers to, by using indexing. We could write the statement

```
System.out.println(f[2].x);
```

and this would give 4 as output.

It is also possible to initialize the components in an array when making a declaration. For example, we can write:

```
Point[] g = {new Point(1,1),   new Point(0,1),
             new Point(-1,1),  new Point(0,0)};
```

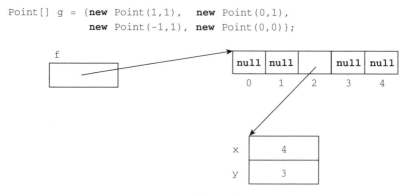

Figure 9.5

Here we have an array with four components. Each component is a reference that refers to an object of class `Point`.

Of course, we can declare array variables where the components can be references to any kind of object. An especially interesting case is one where the components can be references to objects of class `String`. This makes it possible to create tables of texts, as in the following example. Note that the texts can be of different lengths.

```
String[] message = {"Turn off the tap",
                    "Open the window",
                    "Turn off the computer",
                    "Start the fan"};
```

As usual, we use indexing to get to the different texts. The statements

```
i = 2;
System.out.println(message[i]);
```

could give the printout

```
Turn off the computer
```

We shall now demonstrate a slightly larger example of the use of arrays. Suppose that a company has a number of sales representatives working on commission. The total number of reps is at most 100. Every time a rep has sold something, a record of the sale is left with the company. A sales record consists of the rep's number and the amount the goods have been sold for. What we are now going to do is to construct a program that inputs a lot of sales records and outputs a compilation of how much the different reps have sold. In this compilation, we would also like to see how much commission the reps are to have. The commission on a sale is 10% of the total sales amount if this is less than, or equal to, $5,000. If the total sale exceeds $5,000, the commission is 15% of the amount exceeding $5,000. We show what the program could look like when it is run. Everything in italics has been written by the user. Everything else is written by the program. Sales figures can be entered in any order, and different sales figures can be entered for a particular rep (for instance, Linda Sands and Eric Anderson have each made two sales).

```
Agent? Linda Sands
Amount? 1000
Agent? Curt North
Amount? 50
Agent? Eric Anderson
Amount? 1200
Agent? Jenny Linden
Amount? 2500
Agent? Linda sands
Amount? 6000
```

```
Agent? Eric Anderson
Amount? 100
Agent? Katie Ward
Amount? 6000
Agent? The user enters Ctrl-Z here

                         Amount   Commission
                         ======   ==========
Linda Sands              7,000       800
Curt North                  50         5
Eric Anderson            1,300       130
Jenny Linden             2,500       250
Katie Ward               6,000       650
```

The following class is used in the program to describe reps:

```
class Agent {
   static final double limit=5000;
   static final double proc1=0.1;
   static final double proc2=0.15;
   String name;
   double sum;

   Agent(String n) {  // constructor
      name=n;
   }

   double commission() {  // computes the commission
      if (sum <= limit)
         return sum * proc1;
      else
         return limit * proc1 + (sum-limit) * proc2;
   }
}
```

There are two instance variables called name and sum. The latter contains the total sum of a rep's sales. There are three constant class variables (limit, proc1 and proc2) used to keep an account of the percentage rates and the limit applicable when sales commission is to be calculated. By defining these variables as constants, it is easy to make changes in the program if information has to be changed – for instance, if the limit for the higher percentage rate were to be raised. Note especially that the three constant variables are class variables (static). They will therefore only be found in a single edition that will be shared by all of the sales reps.

In class Agent, there is also a constructor and a method commission that calculates the commission for the rep concerned. The main program is in the following class:

```
import java.io.*;
import extra.*;
import java.text.*;

public class Report {
   static Collator co = Collator.getInstance();

   public static void main (String arg[]) {
      Agent[] a = new Agent[100];
      int noOfAgents = 0;
      co.setStrength(Collator.PRIMARY);
      // read in sales information
         while (true) {
            Std.out.print("Agent? ");
            String nn = Std.in.readLine();
            if (nn==null) // no more information
               break;
            Std.out.print("Amount? ");
            double amount = Std.in.readDouble(); Std.in.skipLine();

            // search for the name nn
            int i;
            for (i=0; i<noOfAgents && !co.equals(nn,a[i].name); i++)
               ;
            if (i == noOfAgents) {  // not found, create new rep
              a[i] = new Agent(nn);
              noOfAgents++;
            }
            a[i].sum += amount;
         }

         // write a compilation
         Std.out.getFormat().setGroupingUsed(true);
         Std.out.println();
         Std.out.println();
         Std.out.print(" ", 20);            // 20 spaces
         Std.out.println("   Amount  Commission");
         Std.out.print(" ", 20);            // 20 spaces
         Std.out.println("   ======  ==========");

      for (int j=0; j<noOfAgents; j++) {
         Std.out.print  (a[j].name, 20);
         Std.out.print  (a[j].sum,    10, 0);
         Std.out.println(a[j].commission(), 10, 0);
      }
   }
}
```

In this program, we have used the auxiliary package extra, which is described in Section 5.4.2. This is done to facilitate data entry and to make it easier to print out a table.

In method `main` we have declared an array variable `a` which is initialized so that it refers to an array with space for up to 100 reps. The variable `noOfAgents` is used to keep track of the number of sales reps who have handed in their sales figures. To start off with, this variable was equal to zero.

The program starts by inputting the sales figures. This is done in a `while` statement. On each lap, the program inputs the rep's name and the sales total he or she has made. The `while` statement is terminated if the user indicates *end of file* (presses Ctrl-Z or Ctrl-D) when the program asks for the rep's name. Each time a new sales figure is input, the program checks to see if the current rep is already in the array `a`. This is done by means of a linear search, using the same technique as we discussed on page 287. The only difference, compared with the example on page 287, is that we have an array with a `String` object instead of arrays containing integers. So we use a collator to test whether the two names are the same. It is worth noting that the collator treats upper- and lower-case letters as equals. (We "just happened" to write a lower-case letter in Linda Sands' name the second time in the comparison example, but it worked anyway.)

If we have searched through all the components without finding a rep with the relevant name, a new rep is created and put last in the array `a`, and `noOfAgents` is incremented by one. The total sales sum is then automatically initialized to 0 for the new rep.

The new amount is added to the previous amount for the current rep in the `while` statement at the end of each round.

There will be three columns in the printout. The first will contain the names of the reps left justified, while the two others will contain the sales amounts and the commissions right justified. We would like the numbers to be written out in groups of three, so that it would be easier to read. To indicate this, we call the method `setGroupingUsed` for the editor used by class `Std`. To get the printout adjusted, we make use of the fact that we can give an extra argument to the printout methods. This argument will indicate the total number of printout positions, so that when real numbers are printed out, the number of decimals desired can be indicated as well. Note that texts will be left justified and numerical values right justified, exactly as required in this program.

9.7 Arrays as parameters

We can, of course, have array variables as parameters. The following method gives all the components in an array the same value:

```
static void initAll(int[] f, int value) {
    for (int i=0; i<f.length; i++)
        f[i] = value;
}
```

If, for example, we have made the declaration

```
int[] a = new int[6];
```

we can make the call

```
initAll(a,1);
```

Then all components in the array a will get the value 1. Note that the array itself is not copied during the call. The variable a is a *reference* to the array, and the parameter f will then be a copy of this reference. This means that f will refer to the same array as a.

You can also have arrays containing reference variables as parameters. To demonstrate this, we will go back to the program that processed sales reps in the previous section. We then note that the reps are not written in alphabetical order. If we want alphabetical order, we have to sort the array containing reps before we print it out. In Section 9.5 we discussed the *selection sort* algorithm. We will use another relatively simple technique here, which is generally referred to as *insertion sort*. The idea is to start off with an empty array and then put the components into the array, one at a time. The first component is placed at place number 0. The next component is placed before or after the first component, depending on which component is larger. The third component is then placed in the correct order in relation to the previous two, etc. We make sure that the new array we set up is sorted correctly after each insertion. Each time we are going to insert a new component into the array, we start from the rear and search forwards until we find the correct place for the new element. At the same time as we do this search, we move the components one place to the right to make space for the new component.

We can write the following method, which inserts a new rep into the array a. The last parameter indicates the number of components that were previously inserted into the array. These components lie in positions 0 to number-1.

```
static void insert(Agent newAgent, Agent[] a, int number) {
    int i=number-1;
    for (; i>=0 && co.compare(newAgent.name, a[i].name)<0; i--)
        a[i+1] = a[i];  // move one step to the right
    a[i+1] = newAgent;  // insert the new rep
}
```

We let the index i run through the array, from the back to the front. This process stops when i has become less than 0, or when the correct place has been found for the new element. The new rep's name is compared with the name of the reps in the array with the help of the collator co. A component that has been checked is moved one step to the right. When the run of the index through the array is interrupted, there will, therefore, be a free place for the new component.

This technique involves beginning with an empty array and putting the components in one by one. But how should we deal with a full array with its components unsorted? Let us look at the following method, which sorts an already full array. The method has two parameters. The first is the array a that has to be sorted, and the other one indicates the number of elements in the full array. (If all the elements in the array were filled, this parameter would not be required, since we would then be able to find the number of components in the array by writing a.length.)

```
// insertion sort
static void sort(Agent[] a, int number) {
    for (int i=1; i<number; i++)
        insert(a[i], a, i);
}
```

The following idea has been used. There is a sorted part of the array on the left and an unsorted part on the right. From the beginning, the sorted part consists of only a single component (in position 0). We then run through the unsorted part of the array, beginning at index 1, inserting the components one by one into the sorted part. This is done with the method insert. The sorted part will then grow, until all of the components finally lie in this part and the array will be sorted.

To sort all the reps in our program from the previous section, we merely need to add the following call just before the table of reps is displayed:

```
sort(a, noOfAgents);
```

In our program of sales reps we read in information about the different reps one by one, inserting the new reps into array a. If we were able to use the method insert when inserting the reps, would the array not be sorted from the beginning, in which case we would not need to call the method sort? This is true. Let us look at how the sales rep program can be changed to accommodate this interesting idea.

When we have input a new sales figure into the program (name and sales total), we will investigate whether the current agent is already in the array a. We used linear searching to do this previously, but since array a is sorted now, we can use binary searching instead (please refer to page 288). We do this search in a separate method binarySearch. The method binarySearch has the following appearance. It has three parameters. The first is the name we are going to search for. The second is the array and the third is an integer which gives the number of elements in the array. The result of the method is the index for the place in the array where the name we are searching for is found. If the name is not found in the array, the value −1 is returned.

```
// binary search
static int binarySearch(String searched, Agent[] a, int n) {
    int first=0, last=n-1;
    while(first <= last) {
        int middle = (first + last)/2;
        if (co.compare(searched, a[middle].name) < 0)
            last = middle - 1;
        else if (co.compare(searched, a[middle].name) > 0)
            first = middle + 1;
        else // equal
            return middle;
    }
    return -1;   // not found
}
```

We can use the method binarySearch and make the section of the program where we investigate whether the latest input name is already included among the agents look as follows:

```
// search for the name nn
if ((i = binarySearch(nn, a, noOfAgents)) == -1) {
    Agent nyAgent = new Agent(nn);
    nyAgent.sum = amount;
    insert(nyAgent, a, noOfAgents);
    noOfAgents++;
}
else
    a[i].sum += amount;
```

A check is made to see whether the actual sales rep is in array a whenever a name and an amount is read in. In order to do this, the method binarySearch is called. The result of the search is assigned to the variable i, and then a check is carried out to see whether the value assigned to i was equal to –1. If it was, the rep was not found. We have to create a new rep and insert it into the array. The method insert, which we described earlier, is called to do this. If there already is a sales rep with the name nn in the array, a new rep will not be inserted into it. The variable i will then contain the index for this rep, and we instead increase the total sales amount for the sales rep concerned.

9.8 Parameters for `main`

In command operating systems such as Unix and MS-DOS, we start a program by writing a *command line*. In a command line, we first indicate the program's name, and then give arguments for the program. These arguments are normally names of files but there can be other kinds of arguments, too, such as flags of different kinds. The program name and its various arguments are usually bounded by blank characters. If, for example, we wrote the command line

```
prog -x /r fill
```

this would mean that the program called `prog` should be run and that it should have the three arguments `-x`, `/r` and `fill`. This procedure can also be followed for Java programs. Let us suppose, for example, that we want to run the Java program `MainDemo`. Because Java programs cannot be executed directly but have to be executed by the Java interpreter, we write:

```
java MainDemo -x /r fill
```

As we have seen, a standalone Java program (but not an applet) must have a method `main` in which execution begins. Up to now, we have not worried very much about the definition of `main`, so let us now look at the following simple class:

```
class MainDemo {
   public static void main (String[] arg) {
      for (int k=0; k<arg.length; k++)
         System.out.println("Argument " + k + ": " + arg[k]);
   }
}
```

On the second line, we can see that the method `main` has one parameter. It is called `arg` and has type `String[]`. This parameter is therefore an array variable that refers to an array where the components are objects of class `String`, that is, texts. We do not call the method `main` as we do other methods, from inside the program. Instead, it is called from the Java interpreter when program execution begins. Let us suppose that we have written the command line as it stands above. The Java interpreter will then create an array with three components and give this array as argument to `main`. The text `"-x"` will be found in `arg[0]`, the text `"/r"` in `arg[1]`, and the text `"fill"` in `arg[2]`. We see that `main` in class `MainDemo` contains a **for** statement that runs for the same number of rounds as the length of the array `arg`. At every round, the text of the corresponding argument is displayed. The printout in this example will be:

```
Argument 0: -x
Argument 1: /r
Argument 2: fill
```

Let us take another example. The program `MainDemo2` will display a message. This might look as in Figure 9.6. The message is given as the first argument in the command

Figure 9.6

line. A number, indicating the number of times the message is to be displayed, is given as the second argument. To get the window in Figure 9.6, we give the command

```
java MainDemo2 "Time's up!" 3
```

Note that we have to put an argument in double quotes if it contains blank characters. The program will be shaped such that the second argument can be left out. The message will then be written out once. For example, we can write:

```
java MainDemo2 "Shut down the computer"
```

The program is as follows:

```java
import java.awt.*;
import javax.swing.*;
public class MainDemo2 extends JFrame {

   public MainDemo2(String message,int noOfLines){ //Constructor
      Container c = getContentPane();
      c.setLayout(new GridLayout(noOfLines,1));
      for (int i = 1; i <= noOfLines; i++)
         c.add(new JLabel(message, JLabel.CENTER));
      pack();
      setVisible(true);
      setDefaultCloseOperation(EXIT_ON_CLOSE);
   }

   public static void main (String[] arg) {
      int n;
      if (arg.length < 2)
         n = 1;   // argument no.2 is missing, write once
      else
         n = Integer.parseInt(arg[1]); // read argument no.2
      MainDemo2 m = new MainDemo2(arg[0], n);
   }
}
```

In `main` we read the arguments from the command line. In the `if` statement, we check whether the user has given both arguments or not. If the user has omitted the second argument, it is set to 1. Once the arguments have been read, they are supplied as parameters to the constructor. Since the constructor expects that the second argument should be an `int`, it has to be translated from `String` to `int` in `main`.

9.9 Parameters for applets

It is not only standalone programs that can have parameters. Applets, too, can have parameters. But since applets do not have a `main` method, a different way is used to send parameters to applets. Applets are started not from a command line but from an

Figure 9.7

HTML file, and an applet's parameters are therefore given in the HTML file. As an example of this, we will look at an applet called `PolyDemo` that draws a polygon in a window. This applet will have two whole numbers as parameters. The first parameter indicates the number of corners the polygon is to have. If, for example, we give the parameter 7, a heptagon will be drawn. The second parameter indicates the heptagon's size. We have to imagine that the heptagon is inscribed in a circle, where the parameter indicates the circle's radius, expressed in pixels. Figure 9.7 shows the picture that the applet `PolyDemo` would generate if it were called with parameters of 7 and 100.

The HTML file that starts the applet `PolyDemo` is as follows:

```
<html>
  <head><title>PolyDemo</title></head>
  <body>
    <applet code=PolyDemo.class width=250 height=250>
      <param name=number value=7>
      <param name=radius value=100>
    </applet>
  </body>
</html>
```

In an HTML file, the parameters are indicated inside an `applet` tag, between `<applet>` and `</applet>`. For every parameter, a `param` tag of the following form is added.

```
<param name=parameter name value=parameter value>
```

As can be seen, for every parameter, the parameter's name and value are indicated. We have given the parameter that indicates the number of corners the name `number` and the parameter that indicates the circle's radius the name `radius`.

There is a method called `getParameter` in class `Applet`. We use this method to access a parameter's value inside an applet. For example, we can write the statement:

```
String s = getParameter("number");
```

We give as argument the parameter's name. We get as result a `String` object containing the parameter's value in the form of a text. If the parameter, as is the case here, is a whole number, a conversion from text to type `int` must be made:

```
n = Integer.parseInt(s);
```

The class `JApplet` is not a subclass of `JComponent`. For this reason, in class `PolyDemo` we should not redefine method `paintComponent`; we should redefine method `paint`. In method `paint` we draw the polygon by a simple call to method `fillPolygon`:

```
g.fillPolygon(x, y, n);
```

The parameters `x` and `y` are two arrays. They will contain x and y coordinates for the polygon's corners. The third parameter is a number indicating the number of corners. The array variables `x` and `y` are initialized, and the values of the components are computed in the method `init` when the applet is initialized.

We put the polygon's centre in the middle of the window. This central point is described by the variables `x0` and `y0`. A little basic mathematics will now be necessary to understand how we calculate the coordinates to be placed in arrays `x` and `y`. (It is not necessary to understand this, so this part can be skipped.) To determine the points in the arrays `x` and `y`, we begin with a circle of radius 1, placed in the mid-point `(x0,y0)`. The x coordinate of a point `(xi,yi)` in a circle is given by the expression `xi=x0+cos(v)`, where v is the angle between the x axis and a line drawn from `(x0,y0)` to `(xi,yi)`. The y coordinate is similarly given by the expression `yi=y0-sin(v)`. Mathematically speaking, there should normally be a + sign, but we have written a − sign instead because the y axis goes downwards in a Java window and not upwards, as is usually the case. We get the angle v by dividing a complete revolution (360 degrees) into n equal angles, where n is the number of corners in the polygon.

We shall now use the standard class `Math` (see Section 3.5). We shall need the methods `sin` and `cos` in our program. The coordinates in the arrays `x` and `y` can now be computed by the following statements:

```
angle = 2*Math.PI/n;      // translate from degrees to radians
for (int i=0; i<n; i++) {
   double v = i*angle;
   x[i] = x0 + (int)Math.round(r * Math.cos(v));
   y[i] = y0 - (int)Math.round(r * Math.sin(v));
}
```

The method `Math.round` rounds off a real number to an integer of type `long`. We then have to make an explicit type conversion of this value to type `int` because the components in arrays `x` and `y` are of type `int`.

We are now ready to see the entire `PolyDemo` class:

```
import java.awt.*;
import javax.swing.*;
public class PolyDemo extends JApplet {
   int n, r, x0, y0;
   double angle;
   int[] x, y;

   public void init() {
      String s = getParameter("number");
      n = Integer.parseInt(s);
      s = getParameter("radius");
      r = Integer.parseInt(s);
      x0 = getSize().width/2;
      y0 = getSize().height/2;
      x = new int[n];
      y = new int[n];
      angle = 2*Math.PI/n;
      for (int i=0; i<n; i++) {
         double v = i*angle;
         x[i] = x0 + (int)Math.round(r * Math.cos(v));
         y[i] = y0 - (int)Math.round(r * Math.sin(v));
      }
   }

   public void paint(Graphics g) {
      g.fillPolygon(x, y, n);
   }
}
```

9.10 The classes `Vector` and `ArrayList`

So far, we have used arrays to form collections of data. It is relatively easy to use arrays, but there are a number of disadvantages. For example, you have to determine the size of the array when you create it, and you cannot add elements at any location without moving the elements around in the array. In the package `java.util`, however, there are two very useful standard classes called Vector and ArrayList. Objects of these classes function more or less like arrays but do not have the limitations that arrays have. The two classes have roughly the same properies. Therefore any one of them can be used. In this section we will demonstrate the class Vector, but we might as well have used the class ArrayList in all the examples.

To demonstrate how the classes Vector and ArrayList can be used, we will set up a data collection that contains texts. We start by declaring a Vector object. (The class ArrayList could have been used instead.)

```
Vector v = new Vector();
```

We then have a vector of size 0, i.e. one that does not contain any components. There are some methods which can be used to add components to a data collection. The simplest is add, which adds a new element last in the collection. You could write

```
v.add("EEE");
v.add("VVV");
v.add("XXX");
```

The vector v will then contain the three components "EEE", "VVV" and "XXX" in locations 0, 1 and 2. You can find the size of a data collection by calling the method size. The call v.size() now gives the value 3. You can explicitly specify the size by calling the method setSize. If you reduce the size, the components that do not fit in the collection will be deleted and if the size is increased, the new components will be given the value null.

There is also a version of the method add in which you can specify the location where the new element should be inserted. The previous components are displaced one place to the right to make space for the new component. If we were to write

```
v.add(0, "JJJ");    // insert "JJJ" first
```

the component "JJJ" will be inserted at location number 0, i.e. first in the vector. The previous components in v will be displaced one place to the right, so that they end up in positions 1, 2 and 3. The size of v will be increased from 3 to 4.

You can also change a specific component. This is done with the method set. We could change component number 1 so that it contains the text "AAA":

```
v.set(1, "AAA");    // change "EEE" to "AAA"
```

A common feature of methods add and set is that the last parameter is of type Object. The class Object is a common superclass for all classes in Java. This means that you can insert any type of object at all into a data collection. It is even possible to put different kinds of objects into the same collection. We will come back to this later.

The method `remove` can be used to remove components. The argument used is the index of the component we want to delete. For example, you could write

```
v.remove(3);      // remove "XXX"
```

When you remove a component, all the components on the right of the removed component are moved one space to the left and the size of the collection is reduced by one.

To read the value of a particular component in a vector or list, without making any changes, we can use the method `get`. This has an index as its parameter, specifying the component to be read. The method `get` returns a value of type `Object`, i.e. a reference to any type of object at all. This means that we often have to do an explicit type conversion to the type we want to have. Assume, for example, that we want to print out component no. 1 in vector v. We could then give the statements

```
String s = (String) v.get(1);   // explicit type conversion
System.out.println(s);
```

On the first line, we do an explicit type conversion from type `Object` to type `String`. (In this particular case, we did not really need to do an explicit type conversion, since the method `println` also has a variant which has a parameter of type `Object`.) Another example of use of method `get` is given in the following line, where we copy element number 1 and put the copy last. (It is the reference to the text object that is copied, not the actual text.)

```
v.add(v.get(1));   // copy "AAA"
```

One frequently wants to run through all the elements in a collection of data. If we want to run through all the elements in a vector or list v we could, of course, write a `for` statement where we let an index rise from 0 to `v.size()-1` and call `v.get` each time round. There is a more general technique, however. We use a so-called *iterator*. An iterator is an auxiliary object which can be coupled to a particular collection of data. The iterator knows how a collection of data is constructed internally, and it can run through it in an effective manner. We call the method in the iterator to do a run through the data, instead of calling methods in the collection of data.

We will start by showing how we can use iterators of the standard class[1] `java.util.ListIterator`. To get an iterator which is linked to a particular vector or list, we can call method `listIterator`. The expression `v.listIterator()` results in an iterator which has the ability to search through the vector v. The two most important methods in class `ListIterator` are `hasNext`, which returns the value **true** if there are

---

[1] This is not really a class, it is an *interface*, but it does not make any difference now.

several components left in the data collection you are looking through, and the method next, which returns the next component in the data collection. The method next returns, as does method get, a value of type Object. For this reason, you need to do an explicit type conversion in most cases when you have called next. In the class ListIterator there are further methods, such as methods for searching through a vector or list backwards. (Please refer to the fact box.) It can also be mentioned that there is a somewhat simpler iterator class, Iterator, which you can also use, but which does not permit you to search through a data collection backwards.

java.util.ListIterator	
next()	gives the next element in the vector or list
previous()	gives the previous element in the vector or list
hasNext()	specifies if there are more elements (forwards)
hasPrevious()	specifies if there are more elements (backwards)
nextIndex()	gives the index for the next element (forwards)
previousIndex()	gives the index for the next element (backwards)
add(o)	inserts the object o in the current position in the vector or list
remove()	removes the element in the current position from the vector or list.
set(o)	replaces the element in the current position by the object o

To demonstrate how this works, we construct a **for** statement that searches through the vector v and prints all the components in it. The variable i is the iterator. This is an object of class ListIterator and is initialized so that it is connected to the vector v.

```
for (ListIterator i=v.listIterator(); i.hasNext(); ) {
   s = (String) i.next();
   System.out.println(s);
}
```

The printout will become

```
JJJ
AAA
VVV
AAA
```

In the classes Vector and ArrayList an array is used internally to keep track of the components. The length of this array is called the *capacity* of the vector or list. The number of components included in the collection, i.e. its size, is always less than or equal to the length of the internal array. In other words, the size of a vector or list is always less than or equal to its capacity. If you add so many components that the capacity of the vector or list is not enough, a new, larger internal array will automatically be allocated. This means that the capacity of a vector or list is automatically

java.util.Vector and java.util.ArrayList

See also the fact boxes on page 627 and page 629.

new `Vector()`	new vector of capacity 10, doubled if necessary
new `Vector(k)`	new vector of capacity k, doubled if necessary
new `Vector(k, d)`	new vector of capacity k, is incremented by d if necessary
new `Vector(w)`	new vector which becomes a copy of the vector or list w
new `ArrayList()`	new list of capacity 10, doubled if necessary
new `ArrayList(k)`	new list of capacity k, doubled if necessary
new `ArrayList(w)`	new list which becomes a copy of the vector or list w
`setSize(n)`	sets the size to n (not for class `ArrayList`)
`size()`	returns the size (number of components)
`isEmpty()`	gives **true** if the vector/list does not contain any components
`capacity()`	returns the capacity
`ensureCapacity(k)`	ensures that the vector/list has at least capacity k
`trimToSize()`	sets the capacity so that it is equal to the size
`add(x)`	inserts x last in the vector/list, the size is incremented by 1
`add(i,x)`	inserts x in place no. i, previous components as from place no. i are displaced to the right, the size is incremented by 1
`set(i,x)`	inserts the object x in place no. i, the previous component in this location is removed
`remove(i)`	removes component no. i, components as from location no. i+1 are displaced to the left, the size is decremented by 1
`remove(x)`	removes object x
`clear()`	removes all components, the size becomes equal to 0
`get(i)`	returns the component in place no. i, return type: `Object`
`firstElement()`	returns the first component (not for class `ArrayList`)
`lastElement()`	returns the last component (not for class `ArrayList`)
`contains(x)`	gives **true** if the object x is found in the vector/list
`indexOf(x)`	gives the index of (the first) x, or gives −1 if x is not found
`indexOf(x,i)`	as `indexOf(x)`, but starts to search at location no. i (not for class `ArrayList`)
`lastIndexOf(x)`	gives the index of (the last) x, or gives −1 if x is not found
`lastIndexOf(x,i)`	as `lastIndexOf(x)`, but searches backwards from i (not for class `ArrayList`)
`copyInto(a)`	copies the components to array a (not for class `ArrayList`)
`clone()`	gives a copy of the vector/list (only the references are copied)
`listIterator()`	returns a `ListIterator` which starts from position no. 0
`listIterator(k)`	returns a `ListIterator` which starts from position no. k

increased when necessary. Unless you specify something specially when you create a vector or list, it will start off with capacity 10 and each time the internal array is not large enough, an array which is twice as large will be allocated. The capacity will be doubled. If you know more or less what capacity a vector or list will need, you can specify the capacity when you create a new vector or list. You can then avoid time-consuming and unnecessary memory allocations. For example, you could write

```
Vector v = new Vector(500); // capacity 500
```

For objects of class `Vector` it is also possible to specify the amount of capacity that should be added each time the size becomes so large that the capacity is not sufficient.

```
Vector v = new Vector(500, 50); // increase by 50
```

If a vector or list has reached its final size, you can save space by calling method `trimToSize`, which reduces the vector's capacity so that it is equal to the size of the vector.

The classes `Vector` and `ArrayList` contain more methods than we have shown here. For example, there are methods for searching for a particular object. There is a summary in the fact box.

One important thing to note about classes `Vector` and `ArrayList` is that they can only be used to create collections where the element types are defined by means of classes. This means that the classes `Vector` and `ArrayList` cannot be used to create collections of simple data types such as **int** and **double**. If you want to have data collections with numerical elements, you can use a wrapper class, such as `Integer` and `Double`. For example, the following program lines create a vector `w` with two elements of type `Double`. On the last line, element number 1 is read and its value is copied to an ordinary simple variable of type **double**.

```
Vector w = new Vector();
w.add(new Double(1.5));
w.add(new Double(2.7));
double x = ((Double) w.get(1)).doubleValue(); //x becomes 2.7
```

Several new standard classes for collections of data were introduced in J2SDK version 1.2. The class `ArrayList` is one of these new classes. (We will describe these classes in Chapter 19.) To make class `Vector` fit into the new pattern, several of the methods in class `Vector` were given new names. The old names can still be used, however. The method `add` was called `addElement` or `insertElementAt` (depending on whether it has one or two parameters), `set` was called `setElementAt`, `get` was called `elementAt`, `remove` was called `removeElementAt` and `clear` was called `removeAllElements`. New iterator classes were also added. To search through objects of type `Vector`, iterators of type `Enumeration` were previously used. For example, we could have written

```
for (Enumeration e=v.elements(); e.hasMoreElements(); ) {
  s = (String) e.nextElement();
  System.out.println(s);
}
```

We see that the method `listIterator` in the class `Vector` corresponded to a method called `elements` and that methods `hasNext` and `next` in the class `ListIterator` corresponded to methods called `hasMoreElements` and `nextElement`.

9.11 Multiple relations

In Section 4.5, we discussed how we could describe the different kinds of relations that exist between objects. Arrays and vectors can be used to describe relations where an object has several sub-components of the same kind, or knows several other objects that are all of the same class. We then declare instance variables that are array variables or vectors. We will begin by describing a multiple *has* relation. As an example, we will look at the standard class `Polygon` in the package `java.awt`. The definition of the class has this structure:

```
public class Polygon {
  public int npoints = 0;   // number of corners
  public int xpoints[];     // x coordinates for the corner points
  public int ypoints[];     // y coordinates for the corner points

  public Polygon() {
    // creates a polygon without corners
  }

  public Polygon(int xpoints[], int ypoints[], int npoints) {
    // creates a polygon with the corner points xpoints, ypoints
  }

  public void addPoint(int x, int y) {
    // adds a new corner at the point (x,y)
  }

  more methods
}
```

The interesting things here are the two instance variables `xpoints` and `ypoints`, arrays containing the x and y coordinates of the corner points. This is a typical *has* relation: a polygon *has* a number of corner points. These instance variables have been declared as **public** so that the corner points can be read from outside.

There are two constructors. When we build up a polygon, we can either use the constructor that has corner points as parameters, or we can start with a polygon without corners and then call the method `addPoint` for each corner that is to be added. To

java.awt.Polygon	
new Polygon()	creates a new polygon without corners
new Polygon(xp,yp,n)	creates a new polygon with n corners. The x and y coordinates are given by the arrays xp and yp
p.addPoint(x,y)	adds the corner (x,y) to the polygon p
p.npoints	the number of corners in the polygon p
p.xpoints	array with the x coordinates of the corners in the polygon p
p.ypoints	array with the y coordinates of the corners in the polygon p
p.translate(dx,dy)	moves the polygon p
p.contains(x,y)	gives **true** if the point (x,y) lies in the polygon
p.contains(q)	gives **true** if the point q (of standard class Point) lies in the polygon p
p.getBounds()	gives the smallest rectangle (of standard class Rectangle) that encompasses the polygon p

demonstrate the latter technique we will show a new, somewhat simpler version of the applet PolyDemo on page 302. Instead of using two arrays to keep account of the corner points, we shall make use of an object of class Polygon:

```
import java.awt.*;
import javax.swing.*;

public class PolyDemo2 extends JApplet {
    int n, r, x0, y0;
    double angle;
    Polygon p = new Polygon();

    public void init() {
        String s = getParameter("number");
        n = Integer.parseInt(s);
        s = getParameter("radius");
        r = Integer.parseInt(s);
        x0 = getSize().width/2;
        y0 = getSize().height/2;
        angle = 2*Math.PI/n;

        for (int i=0; i<n; i++)
            p.addPoint(x0 + (int)Math.round(r * Math.cos(i*angle)),
                       y0 - (int)Math.round(r * Math.sin(i*angle)));
    }

    public void paint(Graphics g) {
        g.fillPolygon(p);
    }
}
```

Note that we have called the method `fillPolygon` with an object of class `Polygon` as parameter. In the class `Graphics`, both of the methods `drawPolygon` and `fillPolygon` are overloaded. They exist in two versions, one version that has arrays with coordinates as parameters, and one that has an object of class `Polygon` as parameter.

The class `Polygon` has a number of useful methods. For example, we can check whether a particular point lies within a polygon or not; see the fact box.

We shall also see how the *knows* relation can be described with the help of arrays. A particular object can know several other objects that are all of the same kind. As an example, we will extend the class `Person` on page 109, so that it will be possible to describe that a person can have one child or several children.

```
public class Person {
   private String name, address;
   private Person husbOrWife;
   private Vector children = new Vector();

   public void newChild(Person b) {
      children.add(b);
   }

   public Vector getChildren() {
      return new Vector(children);   // create and return a copy
   }

   other methods as on page 109
}
```

We have declared a private instance variable `children`, which is a vector. The components in this vector should be of type `Person`, i.e. references to the `Person` object. Every person has references to his or her children: the person *knows* his or her children. Each time the person has a new child, there is a call to method `newChild`. As a parameter, you get a reference to the new child. This reference is put last in the vector `children`.

The method `getChildren` is called when you want to find out, from outside, how many children a person has. It would have been very easy to simplify this method. It would only have needed the statement

```
return children;
```

The reason that we have chosen not to do it this way is that the variable `children` is a reference to the vector containing children. If we had made this reference available, it would have been possible to make changes to the vector. This breaches the encapsulation principle that each object is responsible for its instance variables.

Instead, we have chosen to allow the method `getChildren` to return a reference to a *copy* of the vector that the instance variable `children` refers to. It will then be impossible, from outside, to change vector `children` and add or delete children, etc. Please note that when you create a copy of a vector, you copy the *references* found as components in the vector. The objects they refer to are not copied.

Here are some program lines that demonstrate how the new methods in class `Person` can be called:

```
Person p = new Person("Carl Gustaf");
p.newChild(new Person("Victoria"));
p.newChild(new Person("Carl Philip"));
p.newChild(new Person("Madeleine"));
Vector b = p.getChildren();
System.out.println(p.getName() +" has "+b.size()+ " children:");
for (ListIterator i=b.listIterator(); i.hasNext(); ) {
    Person p2 = (Person) i.next();
    System.out.println("    " + p2.getName());
}
```

The output will be:

```
Carl Gustaf has 3 children:
    Victoria
    Carl Philip
    Madeleine
```

9.12 Multi-dimensional arrays

The arrays we have looked at up to now have provided us with an index to select individual components. This kind of array is very useful for describing collections of several data objects, where these naturally lie in a long line. Sometimes, however, we are presented with tables that cannot be described in this way. An example of this is Table 9.1, which describes daily air and water temperatures in the Algarve, in southern Portugal. In Java, we can make use of arrays with several indices, or *multi-dimensional arrays*, to describe this kind of array. For example, we can declare an array variable `m` that can refer to tables where the individual components are of type `int`.

```
int[][] m;
```

The type for `m` is `int[][]`. The square brackets indicate that `m` is an array variable with two indices. We can now let `m` refer to a table consisting of three rows and four columns.

```
m = new int[3][4];
```

We can, of course, initialize `m` directly with the declaration

```
int[][] m = new int[3][4];
```

Table 9.1 Daily air and water temperatures in the Algarve

	January	February	March	April	May	June	July	August	September	October	November	December
Minimum	11.5	12.0	12.9	13.5	17.0	20.5	22.2	22.5	21.5	16.0	13.5	9.9
Maximum	19.0	20.5	21.0	23.0	27.0	29.0	33.0	35.0	31.5	27.0	22.0	20.0
Median	15.0	15.5	17.0	19.0	20.1	24.0	27.0	27.4	26.5	22.7	17.5	14.5
Water	17.0	17.5	20.5	21.0	21.5	23.0	25.0	26.0	26.0	22.7	21.0	17.5

A two-dimensional arrangement of numbers is usually called a *matrix*. We could then say that m is a matrix of three rows and four columns. We are allowed to have as many indices as we like but, in practice, it is unusual to have more than two, so we will confine ourselves to just two.

The variable m is really a reference to a one-dimensional array of three elements, where each component is in turn a reference to an array consisting of four components of type `int`. We say that m is an *array of arrays*. Figure 9.8 shows what m will look like.

We do not have to create the dimensions of a multi-dimensional element all at once. For example, we can write:

```
int[][] f = new int[10][];
```

The variable f is initialized to refer to a one-dimensional array of 10 components. Each component is in turn a reference that is automatically initialized to the value `null`. We can then initialize the 10 components one at a time. For instance, we could write:

```
f[6] = new int[7];
```

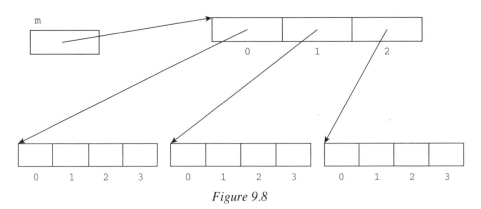

Figure 9.8

The component number 6 in the array f would refer to an integer array of seven components. Not all the components in a multi-dimensional array need refer to arrays that are of a similar length. If we made the statement

```
for (int r=0; r<10; r++)
    f[r] = new int[r+1];
```

f would describe a triangular number formation, where the first row would have one component, the second row two components, the third three, and so on. We can use length to check the lengths of rows and columns. The expression

```
f.length  // = number of rows
```

will get the value 10 and indicates the number of components in the array f refers to, or, in other words, the number of rows in the formation. The expression

```
f[r].length  // the number of columns in row no. r
```

will give the number of columns in row no. r.

Multi-dimensional arrays can be initialized in the declaration. For example, Table 9.1 could be described with the variable temp, declared in the following way:

```
double[][] temp =
    { {11.5, 12.0, 12.9, 13.5, 17.0, 20.5,
       22.2, 22.5, 21.5, 16.0, 13.5,  9.9},
      {19.0, 20.5, 21.0, 23.0, 27.0, 29.0,
       33.0, 35.0, 31.5, 27.0, 22.0, 20.0},
      {15.0, 15.5, 17.0, 19.0, 20.1, 24.0,
       27.0, 27.4, 26.5, 22.7, 17.5, 14.5},
      {17.0, 17.5, 20.5, 21.0, 21.5, 23.0,
       25.0, 26.0, 26.0, 22.7, 21.0, 17.5} };
```

We can see that every row of the table comes between curly brackets.

We can have multi-dimensional arrays where individual components are references. As an example, let us look at the following table which describes the team colours for different football teams. Each row in the table indicates the colours of a team's kit:

```
String [][]kit = { {"blue", "yellow"},
                   {"red", "white", "blue"},
                   {"red", "yellow"},
                   {"green", "black", "white"} };
```

Notice that it is permitted to have rows of different lengths even when a multi-dimensional array is declared in this way.

The easiest way of accessing an individual element in a multi-dimensional array is to use indexing. For example, we can write:

```
m[1][2] = 14;
```

We normally use nested repetition statements to run through multi-dimensional arrays. If, for instance, we want to set all the elements in m to zero, we write:

```
for (int i=0; i < 3; i++)
   for (int j=0; j < 4; j++)
      m[i][j] = 0;
```

But it is pointless to insert constant values for the number of rows and columns. It would be better to use length, in accordance with the following model:

```
for (int i=0; i < m.length; i++)
   for (int j=0; j < m[i].length; j++)
      m[i][j] = 0;
```

Using this technique, we can also run through two-dimensional arrays where the rows are of different lengths:

```
for (int i=0; i<kit.length; i++) {
    System.out.print("Team no. " + i + " :");
    for (int j=0; j<kit[i].length; j++)
      System.out.print(" " + kit[i][j]);
    System.out.println();
}
```

Multi-dimensional arrays are allowed to be parameters of methods. We now conclude by demonstrating a method that adds two matrices a and b, element by element, and puts the result into a third matrix c. (We have assumed that the matrices have the same number of rows and columns.)

```
static void add (int[][] a, int[][] b, int[][] c) {
   for (int i=0; i < c.length; i++)
      for (int j=0; j < c[i].length; j++)
         c[i][j] = a[i][j]+b[i][j];
}
```

9.13 The class JList

One way to present arrays and vectors graphically is to use the class JList. Using this class, you can display a list in which the user can select one or more choices. To give an impression of how this works, let us start with an example. On page 193 we wrote a program that used a JComboBox in which we could choose the colour in which a message should be displayed. In Figure 6.12 on page 192 you can see what it looks like. We will implement a new version of the program. In the new version, we will use a JList component instead of a JComboBox. When you run the program, you can see what the new version will look like in Figure 9.9.

Figure 9.9 JListDemo

The program is as follows:

```
import java.awt.*;
import javax.swing.*;
import javax.swing.event.*;   // contains ListSelectionListener

public class JListDemo extends JFrame
                          implements ListSelectionListener {
  private JLabel l = new JLabel();
  private String[] colors = {"Blue","Red","Yellow",
                               "Black","Geen"};
  private Color[]  col = {Color.blue, Color.red, Color.yellow,
                           Color.black, Color.green};

  // Declare a list and put it in a JScrollPane
  private JList list = new JList(colors);
  private JScrollPane sp = new JScrollPane(list);

  public JListDemo() { // Constructor
    Container c = getContentPane();
    c.setLayout(new FlowLayout());
    c.add(l); c.add(sp);
    l.setForeground(Color.blue);
    l.setFont(new Font("SansSerif", Font.ITALIC, 20));
    l.setHorizontalAlignment(JLabel.CENTER);
    l.setBackground(Color.white);
    l.setOpaque(true);
    l.setText("Swing!");
    l.setPreferredSize(new Dimension(100,75));
    list.setVisibleRowCount(3);
    list.setSelectionMode(ListSelectionModel.SINGLE_SELECTION);
    list.addListSelectionListener(this);
    pack();
    setVisible(true);
    setDefaultCloseOperation(EXIT_ON_CLOSE);
  }

  // listener method
  public void valueChanged(ListSelectionEvent e) {
    l.setForeground(col[list.getSelectedIndex()]);
  }
```

```
public static void main (String[] arg) {
    JListDemo j = new JListDemo ();
}
}
```

The list is created with the declaration

```
private JList list = new JList(colors);
```

We have given an array containing the texts to be included in the list as the parameter for the constructor. We could also have given a vector as the parameter. The elements do not need to be texts. They can be any object. If you have elements which are texts or icons, this is easy. This is because the JList knows how the elements should be displayed in the list. If you have elements of other types, it gets more complicated. You then have to write your own class, a so-called ListCellRenderer, which describes how the elements should be displayed. We will abstain from discussing this.

A list frequently contains more elements than can be displayed on the screen at any one time. For this reason, it is a good idea to give the list a slider. The class JList does not do this itself; you have to put the list in a component of type JScrollPane:

```
private JScrollPane sp = new JScrollPane(list);
```

There are several properties you can describe for a list (see the fact box). In our program, for example, we have specified that three lines at a time should be visible.

```
list.setVisibleRowCount(3);
```

Sometimes you want to allow users to be able to select several elements from a list, and sometimes you want them to be able to select only one element. In our example, we want only one colour at a time to be selected. For this reason, we make the call

```
list.setSelectionMode(ListSelectionModel.SINGLE_SELECTION);
```

Here, we have written SINGLE_SELECTION. The two other choices are SINGLE_-INTERVAL_SELECTION and MULTIPLE_INTERVAL_SELECTION. The latter applies unless you specify something else. The user will then be able to select several choices, by using the Shift and Ctrl keys in combination with mouse clicks. The choices made can be in several different intervals. If you have specified SINGLE_INTERVAL_SELECTION, the user can select several choices but these must be in a contiguous interval.

When the user selects a choice in a list, this generates an event of type ListSelection-Event. An event listener that listens for these events must be of type ListSelection-Listener and have a method called valueChanged. In our program, we have made the class itself be the listener in the usual way. In the listener, we call the method getSelectedIndex to find out the number of the selected alternative. We then use this number to index the correct colour in array col.

JList

In the table below, l designates a component of class JList.

new JList(v) creates a JList, the alternatives are given by v,
 v is of class Vector or an array containing Object

new JList(m) creates a JList, the alternatives are given by m (a ListModel)

l.setListData(v) specifies that the alternatives should be determined by v
 v is of class Vector or an array containing Object

l.setModel(m) alternatives should be determined by m (a ListModel)

l.getModel() gives the model (a ListModel) which is used

l.setVisibleRowCount(r) specifies the maximum number of lines in the list

l.setFixedCellHeight(h) specifies the height (in pixels) of the alternatives

l.setFixedCellWidth(b) specifies the width (in pixels) of the alternatives

l.setSelectionMode(s) specifies how selection may be done, s is
 z.SINGLE_SELECTION, z.SINGLE_INTERVAL_SELECTION or
 z.MULTIPLE_INTERVAL_SELECTION, and z = ListSelectionModel

l.getSelectedValue() gives the selected alternative (of type Object)

l.getSelectedValues() gives an array with the selected alternatives

l.setSelectedValue(a, *scroll*) selects alternative a, *scroll* is a **boolean**

l.getSelectedIndex() gives the number of the selected alternative, or −1 if
 no alternative is selected

l.getSelectedIndices() gives an integer array with the selected alternatives

l.setSelectedIndex(n) selects alternative number n

l.setSelectedIndices(h) selects the alternative specified in the integer array h

l.isSelectionEmpty() gives **true** if no alternatives are selected

l.clearSelection() makes sure that no alternatives are selected

To listen for the event that the user selects an alternative:
Connect an event listener y of class ListSelectionListener to l:

 l.addListSelectionListener(y)

Define the method valueChanged in the event listener:

```
public void valueChanged(ListSelectionEvent e) {
   // you get here when the user has selected an alternative
}
```

When you create a list by giving an array or vector as parameter to the constructor, you cannot add or subtract individual selections afterwards. In this case, you have to specify all the alternatives again by calling the method setListData. To get a more flexible list, you can make use of a *model*. This is a separate object which contains the list selections. This is an example of using the technique MVC (*Model View Controller*), which we discussed briefly at the beginning of Chapter 6.

The simplest way forward is to let the model be an object of class DefaultListModel. This class has more or less the same methods as class Vector. For example, you can add or delete elements. All the methods in the fact box on page 306 are found, with a few exceptions for this class as well. An important exception is the version of add which adds a new element last. This method is called addElement instead of add. Another important exception is method remove (the one that has an object as parameter). It is called removeElement. (Nor is it possible to link iterators of class ListIterator to objects of class DefaultListModel. If you want to use iterators, you will instead have to use class Enumeration. Please refer to page 308.)

We will now study an example where models are used. We will also demonstrate how it functions when you have lists in which several choices can be selected. We will write a program that a Christmas album vendor could use. When you run the program, it might look like Figure 9.10. The left-hand list displays all the items in the product range. For each customer, the vendor selects the items the customer wants to buy. When you click the button containing the right arrow, a copy of the selected choices is moved to the right-hand list. You can select one item at a time, or several at a time. It is possible to purchase several items of the same kind. This is done by selecting the same item several times. It is also possible to change your mind and remove items from the right-hand list. In this case, you select the items you do not want to purchase and click the button with the left-hand arrow. The total cost of the selected items is displayed below the lists. When the customer is satisfied with his or her order, you click the "Order" button. A dialogue is then displayed, where you fill in the customer's

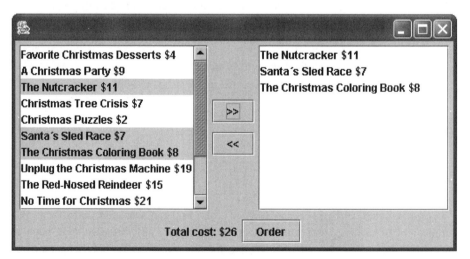

Figure 9.10

name and address. When this has been done, the program prints out a summary of the order in the command window. For the example in the figure, the printout has the following appearance:

```
Order number 1
Susan Wilson, 22 First Lane, Rumford
   The Nutcracker $11
   Santa's Sled Race $7
   The Christmas Coloring Book $8
Total cost: $26
```

When the printout is done, the right-hand list is emptied and all selections on the left-hand list are removed. The program can then be used for the next customer. The program can, of course, be adjusted so that the printout above is put into a text file to be printed out. Another alternative is to send the order by e-mail. (We will show how this is done in Chapter 17.)

The program is as follows:

```java
import java.awt.*;
import java.awt.event.*;
import javax.swing.*;
import java.io.*;
import java.util.*;

public class Order extends JFrame implements ActionListener {
   // create two Model objects
   private DefaultListModel mod1 = new DefaultListModel(),
                            mod2 = new DefaultListModel();
   // create two lists
   private JList l1 = new JList(mod1),
                 l2 = new JList(mod2);

   private JButton to = new JButton(">>"),
                   delete = new JButton("<<"),
                   ord = new JButton("Order");

   private JLabel costLabel = new JLabel("Total cost: $0");
   private int no;    // Order number

   public Order() throws IOException { // Constructor
      // put the components in the window
      JPanel arrows = new JPanel();
      arrows.setLayout(new GridLayout(2,1, 0, 10));
      arrows.add(to); arrows.add(delete);
      JPanel row1 = new JPanel(), row2 = new JPanel();
      getContentPane().add(row1, BorderLayout.CENTER);
      getContentPane().add(row2, BorderLayout.SOUTH);
      JScrollPane sp1 = new JScrollPane(l1),
                  sp2 = new JScrollPane(l2);
```

```
    row1.add(sp1); row1.add(arrows); row1.add(sp2);
    row2.add(costLabel); row2.add(ord);

    // Read the file with titles and put the titles in list 1
    BufferedReader file = new BufferedReader(
                              new FileReader("titles.txt"));
    String line;
    while ((line = file.readLine()) != null)
      mod1.addElement(line);

    // set properties for the lists
    l1.setVisibleRowCount(10);
    sp2.setPreferredSize(sp1.getPreferredSize());

    to.addActionListener(this);
    delete.addActionListener(this);
    ord.addActionListener(this);
    pack();
    setVisible(true);
    setDefaultCloseOperation(EXIT_ON_CLOSE);
  }

  public void actionPerformed(ActionEvent e) {
    if (e.getSource() == to) {        // The >> button
      // read the selected titles in list 1
      Object[] sel1 = l1.getSelectedValues();
      // copy the selected titles to list 2
      for (int i=0; i < sel1.length; i++)
        mod2.addElement(sel1[i]);
      updateCost();
    }
    else if (e.getSource() == delete) {   // The << button
      // read the selected titles in list 2
      Object[] set2 = l2.getSelectedValues();
      // delete the selected titles from list 2
      for (int i=0; i < set2.length; i++)
        mod2.removeElement(set2[i]);
      updateCost();
    }

    else if (e.getSource() == ord) {    // The Order button
      String name = JOptionPane.showInputDialog
                                   ("Name and address?");
      if (name != null) {
        // print out the order
        System.out.println("Order number " + ++no);
        System.out.println(name);
        // run through all titles in list 2
        for (int i=0; i < mod2.size(); i++)
          System.out.println("   " + mod2.get(i));
        System.out.println(costLabel.getText());
        System.out.println();   // extra empty line
```

```
        // prepare for next customer
        l1.clearSelection();  // no selections in list 1
        mod2.clear();         // clear list 2
      }
    }
  }

  // internal method
  private void updateCost() {
    int totCost = 0;
    // run through all titles in list 2
    for (int i=0; i < mod2.size(); i++) {
      // split the text of title no. i
      StringTokenizer t = new  StringTokenizer
                                      ((String)mod2.get(i));
      String s = "";
      // Search for the last word in title no. i
      while (t.hasMoreTokens())
        s = t.nextToken();
      // s now contains the price, the dollar sign included
      s = s.substring(1);  // remove the dollar sign
      totCost += Integer.parseInt(s);
    }
    costLabel.setText("Total cost: $" + totCost);
  }

  public static void main (String[] arg) throws IOException {
    Order b = new Order ();
  }
}
```

The program first creates two list models `mod1` and `mod2` of class `DefaultListModel` and then two lists `l1` and `l2`. They are initialized so that the models `mod1` and `mod2` are linked to them:

```
private JList l1 = new JList(mod1),
              l2 = new JList(mod2);
```

Since we have models linked to two of the lists, we will be able to add and remove elements from them dynamically.

In the constructor, the components are first placed in the window. The two lists are then placed in a component each, of type `JScrollPane`, so that they are given sliders.

The next stage is to fill in the left-hand list so that it contains all the books, magazines etc. in the product range. We assume that there is a text file called `titles.txt` which contains the current product range. There is a line in the file for each item. The line contains the name of the item, followed by a price. The prices are always specified in whole dollars, with a dollar sign before them. Example lines in the file might be:

```
Christmas Cooking $13
The Best Christmas Songs $5
```

In the constructor, a stream is opened to the file called `titles.txt` and one line at a time is input. Each input line is added to the left-hand list by calling the method `addElement` for the model that is linked to the list, i.e. model `mod1`.

We then specify that 10 lines at a time should be visible in the left-hand list. The statement

```
sp2.setPreferredSize(sp1.getPreferredSize());
```

might need a comment. It specifies that `sp2`, i.e. the `JScrollPane` that contains the right-hand list, should be the same size as `sp1`, the `JScrollPane` that contains the left-hand list. This is because we want the lists to be the same size in the window.

In the usual way, the event listener is linked to the three buttons. If the user has clicked the button `">>"` or `"<<"` the method `getSelectedValues` for the left-hand or right-hand list is called to find the choices that the user has selected. If the user has clicked the button `">>"` the selected choices are added to the right-hand list by calling method `addElement`. If the user has clicked the button `"<<"` the selected choices are removed from the left-hand list by calling method `removeElement`. In both cases, the right-hand list is changed. For this reason, the method `updateCost` is called.

The method `updateCost` calculates the total price of all items in the right-hand list and displays this price in the `JLabel` component `costLabel`. To do this, it uses `mod2`, the model for the right-hand list. Each line in the list is read by calling method `get`, and the line read is then subdivided into its individual "words". (By "words", we mean groups of non-space characters which are surrounded by space characters.) To do this, it uses the `StringTokenizer` in the manner described in Section 5.3.3 on page 127. We are only interested in the last "word", the one that contains the price. When we have found this, we delete the initial dollar sign before we decode the price.

9.14 Exercises

1. Reconstruct the program on page 272 so that it does not print out the file that has been read. The program should instead change the contents of the file so that all tab characters are replaced by three spaces and all capitals are replaced by lower-case letters. *Hint*: Because only one file can be read or written, you must make use of another file, a temporary one. Write out the result in the temporary file, then copy the result to the original file.

2. A *prime number* is a positive integer greater than 1 which cannot be divided exactly by any other integer excepting itself and 1. A number will be a prime number if it cannot be divided exactly by a smaller prime number. Use this fact to

construct a program that computes the first 50 prime numbers and puts them into a table. (If you want to decide whether a certain number *k* is a prime number or not, you can check to see whether *k* can be divided exactly by any of the numbers put into the table so far.) The program should terminate when the table with your 50 prime numbers has been printed out.

3. There is a very simple but not particularly effective sort algorithm called "bubble sort". With this method, we run through the array to be sorted, again and again. As soon as we find two elements in the array lying side by side that are not in the right order, we let them change places. Running through an array is terminated when the places of none of the elements have been changed. The "lighter" elements, those having small values, will successively "bubble up" to the front of the array during execution – hence the name of this sort method. Write a class method that gets an integer array as parameter and sorts the array with the help of this algorithm.

4. In Exercise 3 on page 115, you had to construct the classes `Person` and `Teacher` in Figure 4.7. Your task is now to construct both of the other classes in Figure 4.7, that is, the classes `Student` and `Course`. A student can study several courses, and a course can have several students. Use multiple *know* relations.

5. The simplest form of noughts and crosses is played on a board of 3 × 3 squares. One player marks with crosses, and the other noughts. Thus, during a game, a given square can be empty, contain a cross, or contain a nought. The first player to get three characters in a row, column or diagonal has won.

   Construct a class `Board` that represents a board for the game of noughts and crosses. The class should be a subclass of the standard class `JPanel`, so that a board can be drawn in a window. The constructor should construct an empty board, and the following methods should exist:

   `read` returns a value of type **char**, which gives the marking of a particular square. Row and column numbers are given as parameters.

   `place` places a mark (a nought or a cross) into a particular square. Marking, row and column are all given as parameters.

   `move` moves a mark from one square to another. Row and column numbers, for both the old and the new square, are given as parameters.

   `win` indicates whether a player has won. Returns a **char** that contains the winner's mark. If nobody has won, a blank character is returned.

   `paintComponent` draws the board. It will get a parameter of class `Graphics`.

6. In Exercise 4 on page 79, we defined a class `Article` that describes the kinds of article in stock. Your task now is to use this class to write a program that keeps

track of all the articles in stock. You may assume that there is a text file containing information about the different kinds of articles. Each row in the file contains information about a kind of article, that is, the article designation, article description and the sales price. The program will first read the text file and place the information into an array with components of type `Article`. (Assume that there are no more than 1000 kinds of article in the warehouse.) Input can be terminated when, for example, the user of the program indicates the article designation "0000". The program will then repeatedly read commands from the keyboard and perform the tasks required. The different commands are:

`info xxxx`	Write out all the information about article xxxx
`sell xxxx n`	Register that n items of article xxxx have been sold
`buy xxxx n`	Register that n items of article xxxx have been put into the warehouse

7. Standard class `java.utils.Arrays` contains a method called `equals` which investigates whether two arrays are equal. Write your own version of this method. Also do a version that compares two vectors.

8. If you have an array containing integers, you can define a rotation of the array one step to the right as an operation that places the first number in the array on the second location in the array, the second number in the third location etc. The last number in the array is placed in the first location. Write a class method that rotates an array an arbitrary number of steps to the right. The method should have two parameters, the array to be rotated and an integer that specifies the number of rotation stages.

9. The concept of vectors is also used in mathematics. The length of a vector does not denote the number of elements in the vector in this case, however. The length of a vector $(v_1, v_2, \ldots v_n)$ is defined instead by the formula:

$$l = \sqrt{v_1^2 + v_2^2 + \ldots + v_n^2}$$

Write a class method that calculates the mathematical length of a vector where the components are of type `Double` (i.e. a wrapper class). The vector is specified as the parameter for the method.

More about inheritance 10

What distinguishes an object-oriented language from a traditional programming language is the fact that it contains constructs enabling the use of *inheritance*. By making use of inheritance we can create new classes from already existing ones by extending them with new attributes and operations. We can, for instance, express relations such as "an athlete is a person" or "a book is a document". In Java, inheritance is introduced by creating *subclasses* of already existing classes.

By using inheritance we can create objects that are only partly equal to other objects. Such objects are defined by what are called *polymorphous classes*. In dealing with polymorphic classes, we make use of a mechanism called *dynamic binding*. Both of these important concepts are handled in this chapter.

10.1 Definition of subclasses

By way of an introduction, we shall make use of the following class, which describes houses in a very general way. The instance variables length, width, noOfFloors and lastRenovation are provided for a building, together with a method area that calculates the total surface area. Apart from this method, there should be methods to change and read the instance variables but we shall leave this for the moment.

```java
public class Building {
   double length;
   double width;
   int noOfFloors;
   int lastRenovation; // year

   public double area() {
      return length * width * noOfFloors;
   }
}
```

Now let us suppose that we want to describe a house, that is, a building made for people to live in. We can create a new class House that is a subclass of class Building.

The new class will then automatically get the attributes that are to be found in class `Building`. Therefore, we shall not have to redefine the instance variables `length`, `width`, `noOfFloors` and `lastRenovation`. The only thing we need to do is to declare the new attributes we want in the subclass `House`. Now suppose that we want to add an instance variable indicating whether the house has been given additional insulation or not, together with a method that makes it possible to insulate a house after it has been built. The definition of class `House` will be:

```
public class House extends Building {
   boolean additionallyInsulated;

   public void insulate() {
      additionallyInsulated = true;
   }
}
```

Note that when we define a subclass, we use the reserved word **extends**, writing after this the name of the superclass. An object of class `House` will now get five instance variables: `length`, `width`, `noOfFloors` and `lastRenovation`, inherited from class `Building`, and `additionallyInsulated`, declared in class `House`. The inherited method `area` will also be available for objects of class `House`. If we now make the declarations

```
Building b = new Building();
House h = new House();
```

we will get the situation in Figure 10.1. Note that the object b refers to has only a `Building` part, while the object h refers to has both a `Building` part and a `House` part.

In class `Building`, we did not indicate visibility for the instance variables (**private**, **protected**, or **public** do not appear in our definition), which means that these instance variables will be visible only for other classes in the same package. If we suppose that

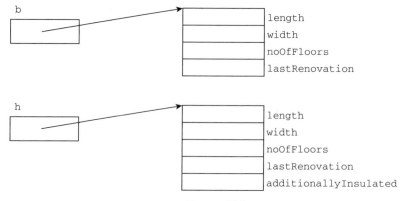

Figure 10.1

class House lies in the same package as class Building, the instance variables in class Building will be directly visible in class House. If we want to be able to put subclasses into packages other than the package the superclass is in, we will have to indicate **protected** visibility for the instance variables we want to be visible in the subclasses.

Definition of subclass

class *subclass name* **extends** *superclass name* {
    declarations of additional instance variables
    definitions of additional methods
}

A class that is a subclass of another class can in turn be a superclass of its own subclasses. For example, we can define a class that describes houses with several flats. We add to the new class an instance variable that indicates the number of flats in the building, together with an instance variable that indicates when the building's interior was last renovated. In addition, we have added a method that routinely computes the rent that the building's owner can receive every year. The new class is as follows:

```
public class BlockOfFlats extends House {
    int numberOfFlats;
    int lastRenovation; // refers to interior renovation
    static final double rentPerM2 = 100;

    public double calculatedRentalIncome() {
        return area() * rentPerM2;
    }
}
```

There are two things worth noting here. The first is that the variable rentPerM2 is a *class variable* and not an instance variable. This is because we gave the word **static**. The rent per square metre is, of course, not unique to each house. It applies to all the houses generally. This information therefore does not have to be included in all BlockOfFlats objects. As a result, an object of class BlockOfFlats will not have an instance variable called rentPerM2. Let us suppose that we now make the declaration

```
BlockOfFlats f = new BlockOfFlats();
```

We will get the situation as shown in Figure 10.2.

The second thing worth noting is that an instance variable was declared in class BlockOfFlats with the same name as an instance variable in a superclass. This was the instance variable lastRenovation. This is permitted and can sometimes be the intention of the programmer. In this example, we might let the instance variable declared in class Building refer to exterior renovation, while the one declared in class

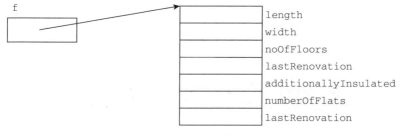

Figure 10.2

`BlockOfFlats` could refer to interior renovation. When we are dealing with two instance variables of the same name, what happens is that the instance variable in the superclass is *hidden* by the instance variable of the subclass. For example, if we write

```
f.lastRenovation = 1998;
```

the instance variable declared in class `BlockOfFlats` will be changed. (We suppose that this statement lies in a class of the same package, so that the instance variables are directly visible.) How should we then proceed if we wanted to access a hidden variable? To demonstrate this, we must broach the subject of references to subclasses. We shall then return to the subject of hidden variables in Section 10.3.

A class may have several subclasses. The class `Building`, for example, can also have the subclasses `FactoryPremises` and `Cinema` and class `House` can have the subclass `Bungalow`. In this way, we can build a class hierarchy that will have a tree-like structure. The different classes we have discussed are illustrated in Figure 10.3.

One of the ideas behind inheritance is that, during the programming process, we should be able to make use of ready-made classes belonging to a *class library*. In Java, for example, there is the API. By so doing, we would not have to write so much program code. In addition, these ready-made classes would probably be better tested and contain fewer errors than classes we ourselves construct.

In Java, all the classes have a common, highest superclass called `Object`. If we wrote a class definition having the form

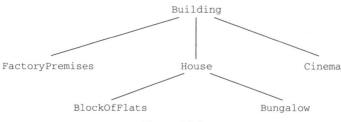

Figure 10.3

```
class C {
   ...
}
```

this would actually mean

```
class C extends Object {
   ...
}
```

In Figure 10.3, therefore, we should really put class `Object` at the top. Class `Object` is defined in the package `java.lang` and has a number of methods common to all classes.

The word `final` can be written at the beginning of a class definition:

```
final class C {
   ...
}
```

This indicates that it is forbidden to define subclasses of this class.

10.2 References to subclasses

There are a couple of important rules governing the relations between references and subclasses. The most important of these is:

Wherever there is a value of the type "reference to `C`*", an expression of the type "reference to* `Csub`*" will suffice if* `Csub` *is a subclass of* `C`*. There is then an automatic type conversion to type "reference to* `C`*".*

This is because the instance variables of a superclass will always constitute a part of the object of the subclass. A `House`, for example, will always have a `Building` part – a `House` *is* a kind of `Building`. Suppose there is another method in class `Building` that compares whether the actual building is bigger than another building:

```
public boolean bigger(Building another) {
   return area() > another.area();
}
```

Let us further suppose that the variable `b`, as before, has type "reference to `Building`" and the variable `h` type "reference to `House`". Then we are allowed to write the expression:

```
b.bigger(h)
```

The next rule follows as a consequence of the first:

A reference variable that has type "reference to `C`*" may refer to objects that are of class* `C` *or a subclass of* `C`*.*

It is therefore possible to do the following:

```
Building b = new Building(); // b now refers to a Building
House h = new House();
BlockOfFlats f = new BlockOfFlats();
b = h;    // b now refers to a House
b = f;    // b now refers to a BlockOfFlats
```

Note that a consequence of this rule is that a reference variable of type "reference to Object" is allowed to refer to any object at all, since class Object is a superclass common to all classes.

On the other hand, we cannot simply assign a reference of a superclass to a reference of a subclass. The assignment

```
h = b;    // ERROR!!
```

is not allowed, for example. We cannot be sure that the object b refers to is a House. It might well be a FactoryPremises. If we are absolutely certain that the assignment is correct, we can use an explicit type conversion:

```
h = (House) b;    // Correct, but dangerous!
```

If b referred to something that was not a House there would be an interruption when the program was executed. A more reliable procedure would be first to test whether b referred to a House. To do this, we can use the **instanceof** operator:

```
if (b instanceof House)
    h = (House) b;    // Reliable
```

10.3 Hidden instance variables

We saw in Section 10.1 that there was an instance variable lastRenovation in class BlockOfFlats with the same name as an instance variable in the superclass Building. We wondered then how we might access the hidden variable of the superclass. Now, we must differentiate between two different instances of this: when we want to access the superclass's variable from a method in the subclass and when we want to access the superclass's variable from outside. We will begin with the first case. As an example, we shall demonstrate how a method renovate in class BlockOfFlats can be added. This method has two parameters that indicate when an exterior or interior renovation was last carried out:

```
public void renovate(int exterior, int interior) {
    super.lastRenovation = exterior;
    lastRenovation = interior;
}
```

We can see here that, in a method of a subclass, we can use the reserved word `super` to gain access to things in a superclass.

If we want to access a hidden variable from outside, the word `super` cannot be used. Instead, we have to use references. If we wrote

```
Building b;
f = new BlockOfFlats();
b = f;
```

the reference variables `b` and `f` would refer to the same object, a `BlockOfFlats`, after the last statement. If we now write the statement

```
b.lastRenovation = 1999; // exterior renovation
```

the instance variable in class `Building` will be affected. If, on the other hand, we write

```
f.lastRenovation = 2002; // interior renovation
```

the instance variable declared in class `BlockOfFlats` will be affected. When we deal with hidden instance variables, it is thus the *reference variable's type* that will decide which variable is intended.

Hidden instance variables

An instance variable `v` in a subclass that has the same name as an instance variable in the superclass *hides* the instance variable in the superclass.

We can write `super.v` to access the instance variable in the superclass.

If `a` is a reference variable of type "reference to superclass" and `b` is a reference variable of type "reference to subclass", then `b.v` is the subclass's variable and `a.v` is always the superclass's variable, regardless of whether `a` happens to refer to a superclass or to a subclass.

10.4 Polymorphism and dynamic binding

We saw in Section 10.1 that we were allowed to indicate the same name of an instance variable in a subclass as in a superclass. One or more of a superclass's methods can also be redefined in a subclass. It can then be said that the new subclass's method *overrides* the method in the superclass. To demonstrate this, we extend class `BlockOfFlats` with a new method that calculates the total surface area for a block of flats. When the surface area of the flats is calculated, the area covered by the stairs has to be deducted. (We shall suppose that the stairs take up 5% of the building's total area.) The method `area` in class `Building` will not therefore give the correct result. The new method is as follows:

```
public class BlockOfFlats extends House {

   as previously

   public double area() {
      return length * width * noOfFloors * 0.95;
   }
}
```

We now declare two objects, a `House` and a `BlockOfFlats`, and we give them the same length, width and number of floors.

```
House h = new House();
BlockOfFlats f = new BlockOfFlats();
h.width = 10; h.length=20; h.noOfFloors = 3;
f.width = 10; f.length=20; f.noOfFloors = 3;
```

We now calculate their area:

```
System.out.println(h.area());
System.out.println(f.area());
```

The result will be:

```
600.0
570.0
```

In the first case, the method `area` in class `Building` is called, and in the second the method `area` in class `BlockOfFlats`. We now declare a new reference `h2` of type "reference to `House`" and let it refer to the same `BlockOfFlats` as the variable `f`:

```
House h2;
h2 = f;
```

We now calculate the area with the help of the new reference:

```
System.out.println(h2.area());
```

The result will be:

```
570.0
```

It is very important to note that it is the method `area` in class `BlockOfFlats` that is called, in spite of the fact that the reference has type "reference to `House`", because where redefined (overridden) methods are concerned, it is the *object's class* that determines the method to be chosen. The type of the reference is of no importance. Note that this is the opposite of the situation in relation to hidden instance variables.

All this goes by the name of *polymorphism*. When dealing with objects belonging to polymorphous classes, we can find operations going by the same name that, logically speaking, should do the same thing on the different objects but because of the nature of the object concerned, will do something different. Let us suppose, for example, that we have two different kinds of bank account, one where interest is calculated on a daily basis and another where a minimum amount must have been deposited for a certain length of time for the account to earn interest. Logically speaking, the operation "calculate interest" does the same thing for the two different types of bank account but the computation will be done in a different way. There is a mechanism in the object-oriented languages called *dynamic binding* which provides a standard procedure for dealing with the kind of objects we have discussed here. We do not have to determine the nature of the object ourselves; instead, a language mechanism sees to it that the correct operation is performed when the program is executed.

In Java, *dynamic binding* can best be explained by the following illustration. When a method m is called through a reference r, that is, when a call of the form r.m(*arguments*) is made, the Java interpreter will examine the kind of object r refers to. Let us suppose that the object belongs to the class c. If for class c there is a method called m that has parameters that match the given arguments in number and type, then this method is called. If such a method cannot be found in class c, the Java interpreter will check to see whether there is one in c's nearest superclass s1. If such a method can be found here, it is called. If it cannot be found in class s1, s1's nearest superclass s2 will be examined, and so on. The Java interpreter begins at the bottom in the inheritance hierarchy, searching its way up until it finds the method it is looking for. If we tried to write a program where an appropriate method could not be found either in class c or in one of its superclasses, we would get a compilation error.

In fact, earlier in the book we saw a number of examples where dynamic binding was used, and this was in programs using Swing components. These programs had in common the fact that they contained classes that had a method called paintComponent. This method is defined in class JComponent, a superclass for most Swing classes that describe GUI components. The subclasses of JComponent overrode the method paintComponent and defined their own version. (For example, we saw several examples where we wrote our own version of method paintComponent.) As we saw, the method paintComponent was called automatically every time a component had to be redrawn. The call was made with dynamic binding; as a result, different versions of method paintComponent were called for different kinds of graphics components.

Note that dynamic binding is quite a different mechanism to overloading, which we looked at in Section 2.11. Overloaded methods might have the same name but *different* parameters and the methods could be defined in the same class. We saw how the compiler chose the method appropriate to the parameters and the arguments given when the call was made. In the case of dynamic binding the methods will have *both* the same name and the same parameters but they must lie in different classes.

In Section 10.3 we saw that the reserved word **super** could be used inside a method in a subclass to access hidden instance variables in a superclass. The word **super** can also be used if we want to call overridden methods. For example, we can give an alternative version of the method `area` in class `BlockOfFlats`:

```
public double area() {
  return super.area() * 0.95;  // call area in class Building
}
```

Dynamic binding

A method `m` in a subclass that has the same name and parameters as an instance variable in the superclass *overrides* the method in the superclass.

If `r` is a reference variable and the call `r.m(arguments)` is made, the class of the object that `r` refers to determines the method to be called.
The type of the reference `r` is irrelevant. The search for the first appropriate method takes place from the bottom upwards in the class hierarchy.

We can write **super**.m in the subclass to access the method in the superclass.

Sometimes we may want to prevent a particular method from being overridden in subclasses. Then we can write the reserved word **final** in the definition of the method. If, for example, we had written in class `Building`

```
public class Building {
  ...
  public final double area() {// must not be overridden
    return length * width * noOfFloors;
  }
}
```

we would not have been allowed to redefine the method `area` in one of the subclasses of class `Building`, for example in class `BlockOfFlats`. We can use **final** as a safety measure to make sure that the actual method will not be changed in a subclass. In this connection, we should point out that methods defined with the word **private** cannot be overridden (they are, of course, not visible outside the class). Class methods, that is, methods defined with the word **static**, must not be overridden, either. Of course, it is not possible to override methods lying in classes that are defined with the word **final** (see page 329), as these classes cannot have subclasses.

10.5 Constructors and inheritance

Objects belonging to a subclass are initialized, as are other objects, by making use of constructors. When one of these is called, the data members inherited from the superclass must also be initialized. This will happen when a constructor for the superclass is called. The constructor will initialize the part of the object inherited from the super-class. The rest of the object will be initialized by the constructor defined especially for the subclass. In this section we shall see how this is done and consider the rules that apply. We continue to use class `Building`, with its subclasses, as an example.

In Section 2.10, we learned that if we failed to define a constructor for a class, the Java compiler would itself define a constructor without a parameter. This applies to all classes, both superclasses and subclasses. Up to now in this chapter, we have created new `Building` objects of different kinds by writing expressions having the form **new** `Building()`, **new** `House()` and **new** `BlockOfFlats()`. This worked well precisely because automatically generated constructors without parameters existed.

Meanwhile, we can define our own constructors, and this applies to subclasses as well. To demonstrate this, we begin by defining two constructors for the class `Building`:

```
public class Building {
    double length;
    double width;
    int numberOfFloors;
    int lastRenovation;

    Building() {}

    Building(double l, double w, int f) {
        length=l; width=w; noOfFloors=f;
    }

    as previously
}
```

The first constructor is one without parameters that does nothing. We only define it to be able to create new houses without indicating arguments. We should like to write

```
Building b = new Building();
```

The second constructor is one that makes it possible to indicate the length, width and number of floors for a building when it is created. For instance, we can now write:

```
Building b = new Building(10,20,3);
```

Of course, we saw in Section 2.10 that if we defined our own constructor as we have done here, the compiler would no longer define a parameterless constructor itself.

The following four steps take place when a constructor for a subclass is executed:

1. All the variables in the subclass are set to their default values (0, or equivalent).
2. A constructor for the superclass is called.
3. The instance variables in the subclass with explicit initialization expressions are initialized to these values.
4. The statements in the subclass's constructor are executed.

In order to demonstrate this, we shall define some constructors for the class House:

```
public class House extends Building {
  boolean additionallyInsulated;

  House(boolean insul) {
    additionallyInsulated=insul;
  }

  House() {
    additionallyInsulated=true;
  }

  House(double l, double w, int f, boolean insul) {
    super(l, w, f);
    additionallyInsulated=insul;
  }

  House(double l, double w, int f) {
    this(l, w, f, true);
  }
    as previously
}
```

The first constructor makes it possible to write something like

```
House h = new House(true);
```

In step 2 above, a constructor was called for the superclass. If nothing in particular has been indicated in the subclass's constructor, the superclass's *parameterless* constructor will always be called. In that case, if no parameterless constructor is available in the superclass, the program will be faulty. In this example, this means that the instance variables length, width and noOfFloors will all get the default value 0, as the parameterless constructor for class Building does nothing. The instance variable additionallyInsulated is then set to the given value.

The second constructor for the subclass House is a parameterless constructor. Because nothing in particular is said, this one will automatically call the parameterless constructor in superclass Building.

If, in step 2, we want a constructor other than the parameterless one to be called, we have to indicate this explicitly. In order to do this, we use the reserved word **super**. This is shown above in the third constructor for class House, where the constructor for the superclass with three parameters is called. Note that when we use the word **super** in this way to indicate the constructor to be used, the call of the superclass's constructor must be the *first statement* of the superclass's constructor. We can now create houses with expressions of the form

```
House h = new House(10,20,3,false);
```

We can also use the word **this** in subclasses to let a particular constructor call another for the same class, exactly as in Section 2.10. This is shown above, in the fourth constructor. Making use of this, we can give expressions of the form

```
House h = new House(10,20,3);
```

Then the instance variable additionallyInsulated will get the value **true**. What happens is that the fourth constructor is called first. It calls the third constructor, which in turn calls the superclass's constructor with three parameters.

These rules apply to all inheritance levels. If, for instance, we defined the following parameterless constructor for class BlockOfFlats:

```
BlockOfFlats() {}
```

it would call the parameterless constructor for class House.

10.6 The method finalize

Constructors are called automatically to initialize new objects. Similarly, there is a method called finalize that is called automatically just before an object is to be subjected to garbage collection (see page 56). This method is defined in the following way in class Object and is inherited by all classes:

```
protected void finalize() throws Throwable { }
```

As we can see, the method does nothing but it can be redefined in classes that have a special need to "clean up after them". This may apply to classes that use files which should be closed afterwards. This may look like this:

```
public class C extends A {

   ExtendedReader in = ExtendedReader.getFileReader(filename);

   public void finalize() throws Throwable  {
     in.close();        // clean up in this class
     super.finalize();  // clean up in the superclass
   }
   other methods
}
```

Note that we should always call the method finalize for the superclass. Constructors always call a constructor for the superclass automatically but there is no such mechanism for the method finalize.

In addition to files, there are other system resources that sometimes have to be set free explicitly, but in the large majority of cases, it is not necessary to redefine the method finalize. Finally, we should point out that method finalize may not be called every time an object is no longer required. If no garbage collection has to be carried out, `finalize` will not be called. If a program ends without garbage collection, the system resources used are usually set free by the operating system.

10.7 Object collections

Dynamic binding is a powerful mechanism that is central to object-oriented programming languages. It is often used in dealing with collections of several objects. The objects in a collection can be of different classes but these classes must have a common superclass. In Java this is not a problem, as all classes automatically have a common superclass, `Object`. Objects placed in a collection usually have a common property, for instance that they can be drawn on the screen or written out in a file. We can find an example of object collections in the standard GUI class `Container`. A `Container` object has an internal list of all the components included in the container, and all the objects in the list have in common the fact that they are of classes that are subclasses of the class `Component`. All the objects in the list can therefore be drawn on the screen by a call of the method `paint`.

To study collections of components, we shall begin with the following classes, which describe different kinds of vehicle. Class `Vehicle` is the superclass that all the classes will have in common. It has two subclasses, `MotorVehicle` and `Bike`. Class `MotorVehicle` has in turn the two subclasses `PrivateCar` and `Truck`. For each class, we have defined a simple constructor that initializes new objects of the class. Note that we have used the technique of calling the superclass's constructor in some of these constructors. We have also defined for class `Vehicle` a method called `print` that writes out information about the object concerned. This method has then been overridden in the subclasses. Note, too, that in the subclasses `PrivateCar` and `Truck` in the method `print`, we call the superclass's version of `print` to write out the part of the information that is found in the superclass. The different vehicle classes will look like this:

```java
public class Vehicle {
  public void print() {
    System.out.println("A vehicle");
  }
}

public class MotorVehicle extends Vehicle {
  String regNum;
  public MotorVehicle(String no) {
    regNum = no;
  }
  public void print() {
    System.out.println("A motor vehicle with reg no: "+ regNum);
  }
}
```

```
public class PrivateCar extends MotorVehicle {
   int numSeats;

   public PrivateCar(String no, int n) {
      super(no);
      numSeats = n;
   }

   public void print() {
      super.print();
      System.out.println("A private car with "+numSeats+" seats");
   }
}

public class Truck extends MotorVehicle {
   int maxL;

   public Truck(String no, int load) {
      super(no);
      maxL = load;
   }

   public void print() {
      super.print();
      System.out.println("A truck with "+maxL+" kg maximum load");
   }
}

public class Bike extends Vehicle {
   int numGears;

   public Bike(int g) {
      numGears = g;
   }

   public void print() {
      System.out.println("A bike with " + numGears + " gears");
   }
}
```

Let us now suppose that there is a company that hires out cars and bicycles. To keep track of all the company's vehicles, we use a computer program with the following array. We will assume that the company has a maximum of 100 different vehicles:

```
Vehicle[] veh = new Vehicle[100];
```

We can then let the different components in array veh describe different vehicles:

```
veh[0] = new PrivateCar("ABC123", 5);
veh[1] = new Truck("XYZ999", 10000);
veh[2] = new PrivateCar("PPP000", 6);
veh[3] = new Bike(10);
```

Note that in spite of the fact that the components in the array `veh` will be references to objects of class `Vehicle`, we are allowed to let the components refer to objects belonging to subclasses of this class. We say that we have a *heterogeneous object collection*, as the objects included in the collection are not of the same type.

Now let us suppose that we want to output information about all of the firm's vehicles. We can then construct a repetition statement that runs through all of the components in the array `veh` and gives information for all the components not equal to `null`.

```
for (int i=0; i<veh.length; i++)
   if (veh[i] != null) {
      veh[i].print();  // dynamic binding
      System.out.println();
   }
```

To output the information, we call the method `print` for every object. Note that these calls all take place with dynamic binding. This means that different versions of `print` will be called for different types of object. In our example, we get the printout:

```
A motor vehicle with reg no: ABC123
A private car with 5 seats

A motor vehicle with reg no: XYZ999
A truck with 10000 kg maximum load

A motor vehicle with reg no: PPP000
A private car with 6 seats

A bike with 10 gears
```

We have used a field to set up collections of objects, but we can also use class `Vector`. This can be used to handle any collection of objects, including heterogeneous collections of objects. As an example of this, we can now write a new version of the program lines that set up and print out collections of vehicles. Please note that we must do an explicit type conversion to class `Vehicle` when we read components in the vector. (Please refer to page 304.)

```
Vector u = new Vector();
u.add(new PrivateCar("ABC123", 5));
u.add(new Truck("XYZ999", 10000));
u.add(new PrivateCar("PPP000", 6));
u.add(new Bike(10));

for (ListIterator i=u.listIterator(); i.hasNext();) {
   Vehicle ve = (Vehicle) i.next();  // explicit type conversion
   ve.print();                       // dynamic binding
   System.out.println();
}
```

If any of the components had not been of class `Vehicle` or one of its subclasses, we would have had an execution error during type conversion. This worked out because

340

we had put only one vehicle into the vector. In a heterogeneous collection of objects, it can sometimes be necessary to check the type of a component before we do the type conversion. We then use the method `instanceof`. For example, you could write

```
for (ListIterator i=u.listIterator(); i.hasNext();) {
   Object o = i.next();
   if (o instanceof Vehicle)
      ((Vehicle) o).print();// safe explicit type conversion
   System.out.println();
}
```

10.8 Abstract classes

The method `print`, for the class `Vehicle` (see page 338), is really quite meaningless since, when we call it, the only result is that we get the printout, `"A vehicle"`. However, we still defined it because we wanted to be sure that a method `print` would be available for every object in one of the subclasses of `Vehicle`. Let us suppose, for example, that we declare a new subclass, `Tram`. We shall further suppose that we forgot to define a new method `print` for class `Tram`. Objects belonging to class `Tram` will then inherit the method `print` from class `Vehicle`. The method `print` must be available to all the subclasses of class `Vehicle` for us to be able to use dynamic binding. If we have a reference variable `ve`

```
Vehicle ve;
```

and we make the call

```
ve.print();
```

the method `print` must be available for all the objects that `ve` might refer to.

We do not have to find a "superfluous" method for a superclass in order to be sure that all the objects will have this method. What we can do instead is to declare an *abstract method*. An abstract method will not be implemented, so we cannot call it; it is merely a marker for a real method. We will now demonstrate this by turning the method `print` in class `Vehicle` into an abstract method. The definition of class `Vehicle` looks like this:

```
public abstract class Vehicle {
   public abstract void print();
}
```

The reserved word `abstract` indicates that `print` is an abstract method. There must be no body in the method definition because the method `print` will not be implemented. Instead, a semicolon is written after the head of the method definition.

In the first line, we have indicated that all of the class `Vehicle` is to be abstract. If a class contains one or more abstract methods, we have to indicate in this way that the class is to be abstract. (We are in fact allowed to declare classes as abstract even though there are no abstract methods in it.) The peculiar thing about an abstract class is that it is not allowed to create objects of such a class, for if it was, we could create objects with methods that were not implemented. We may only create objects of non-abstract classes where all the abstract methods have been overridden by "proper" methods. Thus, we may not create objects of class Vehicle, but one of the things we can do is to create objects of class Bike if this class has its own version of the method print.

```
public class Bike extends Vehicle {
    int numGears;

    public Bike(int g) {
        numGears = g;
    }

    public void print() { // overrides an abstract method
        System.out.println("A bike with " + numGears + " gears");
    }
}
```

If we define a new class that is a subclass of an abstract class, we are actually allowed not to define our own versions of the superclass's abstract methods. Then the new class must also be declared as abstract and we cannot create objects of the new class. For instance, if we removed the definition of the method print in class MotorVehicle, this class would also have to be declared as abstract. Then we would not be allowed to create objects of class MotorVehicle. However, we may create objects of the subclasses of class MotorVehicle as before, since these have defined their own versions of the method print.

We create an abstract class so that it can serve as a model for its subclasses. The abstract superclass defines the methods that must be present in all subclasses. Many of

---

Abstract methods and classes

A method can be declared as abstract

abstract *result_type* m(*parameters*);

Abstract methods have no implementation. A class with one or more abstract methods must be defined as an abstract class.

abstract class C {

  . . .

}

No objects of an abstract class can be created. Subclasses that do not have their own versions of all abstract methods must also be abstract.

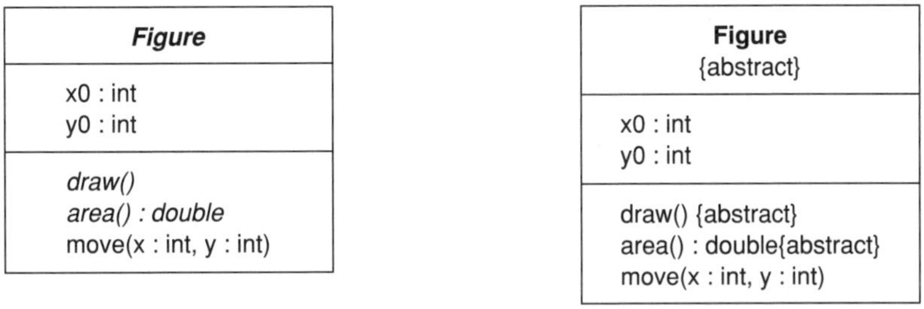

Figure
x0 : int y0 : int
draw() *area() : double* move(x : int, y : int)

Figure {abstract}
x0 : int y0 : int
draw() {abstract} area() : double{abstract} move(x : int, y : int)

Figure 10.4 An abstract class

the standard classes, such as the classes `Component` and `Container`, are abstract. We are not supposed to create objects of these classes, only of their subclasses.

Let us suppose, in another example, that we work with applications where geometric figures of different kinds are to be drawn on the screen. We can then obtain an abstract superclass, `Figure`. Starting with this class, we can define different subclasses for different kinds of figures, for example circles, rectangles or lines. The class `Figure` may contain the abstract methods `draw`, which draws a figure at the screen, and `area`, which calculates the area of a figure. But an abstract class may also contain normal methods which are not abstract. Suppose, for example, that the class `Figure` contains two instance variables `x0` and `y0` which define the starting point of a figure. If we let all subclasses of `Figure` have coordinates in relation to the point (`xo`, `y0`) then in class `Figure` we can define a non-abstract method `move` that moves a figure simply by changing the instance variables `x0` and `y0`.

Figure 10.4 demonstrates how abstract classes are described in UML. A diagram for an abstract class looks like an ordinary class diagram (see Figure 2.2 on page 45) but the class name and the abstract methods should be marked in a special way. There are two alternatives. You can either set the class name and the names of the abstract methods in italics, as in the diagram on the left in Figure 10.4, or you can use the marker {abstract} as in the diagram on the right in the figure.

10.9 Interface

The class `Bike`, which we studied in the earlier sections, is a subclass of class `Vehicle`. Now let us suppose that we want to draw bikes on the screen. One way to bring this about would be to define `Bike` as a subclass of the standard class `Canvas`. We would then be able to use all of the different standard methods to draw. However, this is not allowed in Java, since a class may have only one superclass. If we were able to have more than one, we would be making use of *multiple inheritance*, a mechanism found in C++, for instance, but one that is not allowed in Java. Multiple inheritance is a powerful mechanism but it can sometimes cause technical problems, and for this reason it is not found in Java. To compensate for this, Java has something called an *interface*.

As we have seen, some of the methods in an abstract class can be abstract, that is, they can lack implementation. We could say that an interface is a kind of abstract class where *all* of the methods are abstract. Because class Vehicle has only one method and this one is abstract, we can re-make class Vehicle into an interface:

```
public interface Vehicle {
   public void print();
}
```

This looks like a class definition but we write the word **interface** instead of **class**. Note that we do not need to write the word **abstract** for the method print. In an interface, all the methods are abstract, so we do not need to indicate anything in particular. (But we can write **abstract** if we like.)

It is true that a particular class may have only one superclass but it may inherit properties from several interfaces. This is what makes interfaces so useful. We can now define class Bike in the following way, for instance:

```
public class Bike extends Canvas implements Vehicle {
   int numGears;
   public Bike(int g) {
      numGears = g;
   }
   public void print() {
      System.out.println("A bike with " + numGears + " gears");
   }
   public void paint(Graphics g) {
      // draws the bike
   }
}
```

We have let Bike be a subclass of class Canvas but we have also allowed it to inherit properties from the interface Vehicle. When we inherit properties from an interface, we say that we *implement* the interface, and we use the reserved word **implements** to indicate this. To make this consistent with the other kinds of vehicle, we also have to redefine class MotorVehicle so that it implements the interface Vehicle, instead of being a subclass of class Vehicle.

```
public class MotorVehicle implements Vehicle {
   as previously
}
```

We are allowed to declare reference variables that refer to interfaces exactly as we declare reference variables that refer to classes. For instance, we can write:

```
Vehicle ve;  // reference to interface
```

However, we cannot create objects of class `Vehicle`, since an interface is like an abstract class. Consequently, the reference `ve` can never refer to an object of type `Vehicle`. But it can refer to objects of classes that implement the interface `Vehicle`. The two rules in Section 10.2 describing the relationship between references and subclasses also apply to interfaces, for which we can reformulate them:

If A *is a class and* Asub *is a subclass of* A *or if* A *is an interface and* Asub *is a class that implements* A, *then the following will apply: everywhere a value of type "reference to* A*" is required, an expression of the type "reference to* Asub*" can be given equally well. There will then be an automatic type conversion to the type "reference to* A*".*

For a reference variable r *that has the type "reference to* A*", the following will apply: if* A *is a class,* r *can refer to objects that are of class* A *or are of a subclass of* A. *If* A *is an interface,* r *can refer to objects that are of a class that implements* A.

So the following are allowed:

```
Bike   bi = new Bike(5);
Vehicle ve;
Canvas ca;
ve = bi;
ca = bi;
```

If a method in an interface is called, dynamic binding always takes place. In the call

```
ve.print();  // dynamic binding
```

the method `print` in class `Bike` is called, since the reference variable `ve` happens to refer to a `Bike` object.

Since an interface can only contain abstract methods and never "proper" ones, a class that implements an interface will never really inherit anything, but such a class is guaranteed to have defined its own versions of all the methods enumerated in the interface. So we use interfaces to indicate that a class has certain general properties. There is, for example, an interface called `Runnable` among the Java standard classes that contains a definition of only one method, a method called `run`. Classes that implement the interface `Runnable` will have the property that they can be executed in parallel with each other. To make this possible, they merely have to define their own version of the method `run`. (We shall return to this in Chapter 13.)

A class can implement more than one interface. Let us suppose, for example, that we have defined the two interfaces `Drawable` and `Storable`:

```
public interface Drawable {
  public void draw();
}

public interface Storable {
  public void store();
}
```

The following definition makes all objects of class Building drawable and storable:

```
class Building implements Drawable, Storable {
  public void draw() {
    ...
  }

  public void store() {
    ...
  }
    as previously
}
```

If a class implementing an interface does not contain its own definition of a method defined in the interface, the class must be declared as abstract. If we were to leave out the definition of the method store in class Building, this class would have to be declared as abstract and the method store would instead be defined in the subclasses of Building.

An interface can inherit other interfaces. It will then become a *sub-interface*:

```
public interface Vehicle extends Drawable, Storable {
  public void print();
}
```

Then all the classes implementing the interface Vehicle have to give their own definitions of the three methods draw, store and print. Note that an interface can inherit several other interfaces.

We can use references to interfaces instead of references to classes in collections of objects. For instance, we could create an array that contains drawable objects:

```
Drawable[] r = new Drawable[100];
r[0] = new PrivateCar("ABC123", 5);
r[1] = new Truck("XYZ999", 10000);
r[2] = new Bike(10);
r[3] = new Building();
```

This is a heterogeneous object collection, but because all the objects included in array r are of a class that implements the interface Drawable, there will be a method draw for all the objects. So we could write:

Interface

An interface is an abstract class that can contain only abstract methods. It may also contain constants that are `final` and `static`.

```
interface I {
    result_type m1(parameters);
    result_type m2(parameters);
    static final int k = constant_value;
}
```

No objects of an interface can be created.

A class can implement an interface. The abstract methods and constants are then inherited. A class can implement several interfaces.

```
class C implements I1, I2 {
    ...
}
```

Classes that do not have their own versions of all the abstract methods must be abstract. We can declare and work with references to interfaces in the same way as with references to classes.

```
for (int i=0; i<r.length; i++)
    if (r[i] != null)
        r[i].draw();
```

Of course, we can also use the standard class `Vector` to form a heterogeneous collection of drawable objects. We could then have written:

```
Vector v = new Vector();
v.add(new PrivateCar("ABC123", 5));
v.add(new Truck("XYZ999", 10000));
v.add(new Bike(10));
v.add(new Building());
```

We have to make an explicit type conversion to type `Drawable` for every object when we want to draw the objects in the collection. (This will be fine, since we know that all the objects that have been put into the vector are of a class that implements the interface `Drawable`.)

```
for (ListIterator i=v.listIterator(); i.hasNext();) {
    Drawable dr = (Drawable) = (Ritbar) i.next();
    dr.draw();
}
```

Apart from abstract methods, an interface may also contain definitions of constants and these may be defined as `final` and `static`. For instance, we can write:

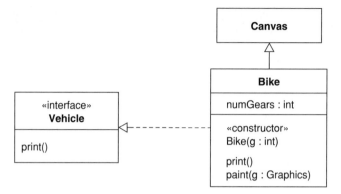

Figure 10.5 Interface diagram and interface implementation

```
public interface Storable {
    static final int blockSize = 1024;
    public void store();
}
```

Then all the classes implementing `Storable` can make use of the constant `blockSize`.

We shall round off the discussion of interfaces by demonstrating how interfaces are described in UML. On the left in Figure 10.5 there is diagram for the interface `Vehicle`. An interface diagram looks very much like an ordinary class diagram, but the stereotype «interface» should be written above the name of the interface. Since an interface cannot have instance variables the attribute compartment may be left out. Only the compartment with operations must be shown. An interface may only contain abstract operations. Therefore, it is not necessary to mark the operations as abstract by setting their names in italic or using the marker {abstract}.

On the right in Figure 10.5 a diagram for the class `Bike` is shown. (Compare this with the definition on page 344.) The dashed line with the hollow arrow means "implements" and the arrow to the class `Canvas` means, as before, that `Bike` is a subclass of `Canvas`. There is another, simpler, way to represent that a class implements an interface. We can draw a little circle. This is demonstrated in Figure 10.6.

If a class `C` uses an interface `I` which is implemented by one or more classes, we say that the class `C` is *dependent* on the interface `I`. If something is changed in `I` then the class `C` must also be changed. A *dependency relation* is shown in UML as a dashed line with an open arrow. Suppose, for instance, that we have a class `Owner`. An owner can own vehicles of different kinds and an owner must be able to call the method `print` to get a presentation of his or her vehicles. This means that the class `Owner` is dependent on the interface `Vehicle`. This is demonstrated in Figure 10.7.

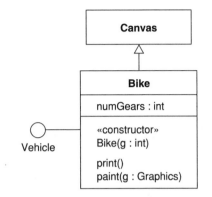

Figure 10.6 Interface implementation

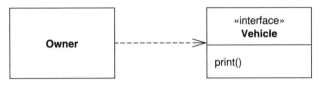

Figure 10.7 A dependency relation

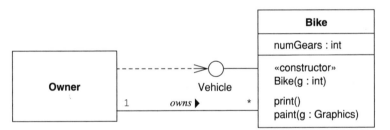

Figure 10.8 A dependency relation with association

If we want to show that the dependent class `c` is dependent on another class `c2` to implement a certain interface we can use the notation with the little circle. If, for instance, we want to describe that an `Owner` is dependent on class `Bike` to implement the interface `Vehicle` we can illustrate this as in Figure 10.8.

The dashed arrow shows the dependency. The solid line shows (as before) an association between objects of classes `Owner` and `Bike`.

10.10 An object-oriented example

It is now time to show a longer example constructed according to object-oriented principles. We shall write a program that allows the user to play the card game Twenty-one with the computer. The game is played in the following way: the user receives one card at a time and after each card, makes a decision whether or not to have another card. The user has to try to make the sum of a "hand" as near to 21 as possible, without exceeding this number. An ace is counted as either 1 or 14. If the number 21 is exceeded, the player loses and the computer wins. But if the player stops at a number under 21, the computer has to draw one card at a time, after each card deciding whether to continue or not. If the computer has more than 21 points or a score lower than the player's, the player wins; otherwise the computer wins. The computer therefore wins if both have the same number of points.

We begin by defining a class `Card` that describes cards. There is a constructor, so that we can initialize new cards, and methods so that we can look at a card's suit or value. In addition, there is a method `toString` that gives the card's value in the form of a text, for example `"Clubs Jack"`. The colours are represented by a whole number between 1 and 4. (1 = clubs, 2 = diamonds, 3 = hearts and 4 = spades.)

```
public class Card {
   private final static String[] stab =
                     {"Clubs", "Diamonds", "Hearts", "Spades"};
   private final static String[] vtab =
                     {"Ace", "2", "3", "4", "5", "6", "7",
                      "8","9", "10", "Jack", "Queen", "King"};
   private int s, v;
   public Card(int suit, int val) {
      if (suit < 1 || suit > 4 || val < 1 || val > 13) {
         System.out.println("Card: illegal arguments");
         System.exit(1);
      }
      s = suit;
      v = val;
   }
   public int suit() {     // 1=cl, 2=di, 3=he, 4=sp
      return s;
   }
   public int value() {    // Ace=1
      return v;
   }
   public String toString() {
      return stab[s-1] + " " + vtab[v-1];
   }
}
```

To describe a collection of cards, we then define a class `Cardstack`. An object of class `Cardstack` can describe either the cards in a player's hand or the whole deck of cards.

```java
public class Cardstack {
  private Card[] stack = new Card[52];
  private int no = 0;

  public int noOfCards() {
    return no;
  }

  public void throwCards() {
    no = 0;
  }

  public Card lookAt(int i) {
    return stack[no-i];
  }

  public void layTop(Card c) {
    stack[no++] = c;
  }

  public  Card dealTop() {
    return stack[--no];
  }

  public void newPack() {
    throwCards();
    for (int s=1; s<=4; s++)
      for (int v=1; v<=13; v++)
        layTop(new Card(s,v));
  }

  public void shuffle() {
    for (int i=1; i<1000; i++) {
      int n1 = (int) (Math.random() * no);
      int n2 = (int) (Math.random() * no);
      Card temp  = stack[n1];
      stack[n1] = stack[n2];
      stack[n2] = temp;
    }
  }
}
```

A stack of cards consists of, or "has", a maximum of 52 cards, and we put these into the array stack, which is a private instance variable. We also keep track of how many cards are currently in the stack by using the variable no. The method noOfCards gives us the number of cards currently in the stack. Because the variable no is initialized to 0, each new stack of cards will be empty from the beginning. We can call the method throwCards in order to remove all the cards from a stack.

The bottom card lies at place number 0 in the array stack, while the top card is in the position with the number no-1. In order to look at the cards without removing them

351

from the stack, we use the method `lookAt`. In the parameter `no` of the method `lookAt`, 1 means the top card, 2 the next one down, and so on. To take the right card, therefore, we must pick the card with the index `no-i` from the stack.

To add new cards to a stack of cards, we use the method `layTop`, and to take cards from the pack we call the method `dealTop`. In the method `dealTop`, it is extremely important that we write `--no` and not `no--` because the reduction in `no` must occur *before* we do the indexing. Similarly, it is important that in the method `layTop`, we write `no++` and not `++no`, since it is the *old* value of `no` we shall be indexing with.

If we want to change a stack of cards so that it contains a new deck of 52 cards, we can call the method `newPack`, in which we run through all the combinations of colours and values. The constructor for class `Card` is called once for each combination.

The method `shuffle` shuffles the cards in a stack, mixing them randomly. This is especially useful if the stack contains a new deck that has to be shuffled before the beginning of play. The method `shuffle` will run for 1000 rounds. At every round, it randomly chooses two whole numbers, `n1` and `n2`, in the interval 0 to `no-1`. It then changes the places of the cards for places `n1` and `n2` in the stack. The standard method `Math.random` is called to select random numbers. When it is called, this method will return a random real number x as result, where x is in the range $0 \leq x < 1$. We multiply this result by `no` and convert it to type **int**. We will then get a whole number in the interval 0 to `no-1`. (The decimals are removed in the conversion to type **int**.)

Note that both `Card` and `Cardstack` are completely independent of the game that will be played. They are quite general in character and could just as easily be used to write a program for a game of Patience.

Our next class is the class `Player`, which describes a participant in a game of Twenty-one. This class is, of course, intended only for this game:

```
public abstract class Player {
  protected Cardstack pack;
  protected Cardstack hand = new Cardstack();
  protected int p;  // actual points

  public Player(Cardstack st) {
    pack = st;
  }

  public abstract void play();

  public void newGame() {
    hand.throwCards();
    p = 0;
  }
}
```

```
public Card newCard() {
    Card c = pack.dealTop();
    hand.layTop(c);

    // calculate new points
    int numAces = 0;
    p = 0;
    for (int i=1; i<=hand.noOfCards(); i++) {
        int v = hand.lookAt(i).value();
        if (v == 1) { // an ace
            p += 14;
            numAces++;
        }
        else
            p += v;
    }

    for (int j=1; j<=numAces && p>21; j++)
        p -= 13;   // count an ace as 1
    return c;      // return the new card
}

public int points() {
    return p;
}
}
```

A player has three instance variables: hand is a stack of cards that describes the cards in the hand of the player, pack is a *reference* to the pack used in the game and p is used to save a player's actual points. The variable pack is an excellent example of the relation "knows". A player must know the pack of cards used in the game to be able to draw cards from it. The variable pack is therefore initialized in the constructor. As parameter the constructor will get a reference to the pack to be used. In other words, when a new player is created, this player will find out about the pack to be used. It is important for both players to use the same pack, so the relation "has" would not work here. If we had written in class Player

```
Cardstack pack = new Cardstack();   // ERROR!
```

each player would have his or her *own* pack to play with, and this would be entirely independent of the pack the other player had.

The method newGame is called every time a player is to begin a new game. Then all the cards used earlier are abandoned and the actual points are set at 0.

The method newCard is called every time the player has decided to take another card. The method draws the card at the top of the pack and puts it into the player's hand. The new points are then calculated. If the points come to more than 21, an attempt is made to calculate one or more of the aces as 1 instead of 14. The method `newCard` gives as result a reference to the new card drawn.

The method `points` is self-explanatory: it simply returns a player's actual points.

The class `Player` has been defined as an abstract class because it contains an abstract method, `play`. There are to be two kinds of players in our program, the person running the program and the computer, so we will define two subclasses of class `Player`, the classes `Human` and `Computer`. We define for each of the two subclasses its own variant of the method `play`. The subclass `Human` will look like this:

```java
import java.io.*;
public class Human extends Player {
   BufferedReader myIn = new BufferedReader
                        (new InputStreamReader(System.in));

   public Human(Cardstack k) {
      super(k);
   }

   public void play() {
      boolean newCardWanted = true;
      newGame();

      while (p < 21 && newCardWanted) {
         System.out.println("You got " + newCard() +
                            " and have " + p + " points");
         if (p < 21) {
            System.out.print("One more card? ");
            newCardWanted = answerIsYes();
         }
      }
   }

   // reads the answer and returns true if it is "yes"
   public boolean answerIsYes() {
      System.out.flush();
      String s = "";
      try {
         s = myIn.readLine();
      }
      catch (IOException e) {} // catch error signal
      return s.equals("") || s.equals("y") || s.equals("yes");
   }
}
```

In method `Player` we call the method `newCard` in the superclass to draw a new card. After each card, the card and the points total are printed out. (Please note that the method `toString` in the class `Card` is called automatically.) After this, the user is asked if he or she wants to draw another card. This is done with a method called `answerYes`. The line that the user then types is input to the `String` variable `s`. If the user just presses the Enter key, types a single "y" or types "yes", the answer is interpreted as *yes*. All other responses are interpreted as *no*. If the answer is *yes* the method returns `answerIsYes` value **true**, in other cases it returns the value **false**. (The call of `readLine` can generate an error signal, a so-called exception. A signal like this must be trapped or sent on. To avoid making the program too complicated, we choose to trap the signal by encapsulating the call in a **try** statement. We will discuss this game in greater detail in Chapter 11.)

The other subclass, the class `Computer`, is simpler. It looks like this:

```
public class Computer extends Player {
   private Player opponent;

   public Computer(Cardstack st, Player opp) {
      super(st);
      opponent = opp;
   }

   public void play() {
      newGame();
      while (p < 21 && p < opponent.points()) {
         System.out.println("The computer got " + newCard());
      }
      System.out.println("The computer has " + p + " points");
   }
}
```

A new card is taken in the method `play` as long as the computer's points come to less than those of its opponent. For the computer and the human player to know each other's points, the two opponents must know one another. We therefore use another "knows" relation. The private instance variable `opponent` can contain a reference to the opponent. This instance variable is initialized in the constructor with a parameter that is a reference to the opponent.

Now we only have to define the class `TwentyOne` that will begin the game. In this class there are three objects: the pack to be used, together with the two players (called `you` and `I`). Note that they are initialized so that both players will know the same pack of cards, and the computer player will know the opponent. The program begins as usual in the method `main`, where an object of class `TwentyOne` is created. The constructor is then called in which the game itself will start:

```java
public class TwentyOne {
   Cardstack pack = new Cardstack();
   Human you  = new Human(pack);
   Computer I = new Computer(pack, you);

   // Constructor
   TwentyOne() {
      System.out.println("Welcome to twenty-one");
      boolean newGameWanted = true;
      while (newGameWanted) {
         pack.newPack();
         pack.shuffle();
         you.play();
         if (you.points() > 21)
            System.out.println("You lost!");
         else if (you.points() == 21)
            System.out.println("You won!");
         else { // the computer must play
            I.play();
            if (I.points() <= 21 && I.points() >= you.points())
               System.out.println("You lost!");
            else
               System.out.println("You won!");
         }
         System.out.print("New game? ");
         newGameWanted = you.answerIsYes();
      }
   }

   public static void main(String[] arg) {
      TwentyOne t = new TwentyOne();
   }
}
```

Finally, here is an example of what the program can look like when it is run:

```
Welcome to twenty-one
You got Diamonds Ace and have 14 points
One more card? y
You got Clubs Jack and have 12 points
One more card? y
You got Spades 10 and have 22 points
You lost!
New game? y
You got Hearts 8 and have 8 points
One more card? y
You got Clubs 6 and have 14 points
One more card? y
You got Spades 4 and have 18 points
```

```
One more card? n
The computer got Hearts 7
The computer got Clubs 10
The computer got Diamonds 6
The computer has 23 points
You won!
New game? n
```

10.11 Exercises

1. Starting with class `Person` in Exercise 2 on page 79, construct a new derived class `Student`, with appropriate members. In addition, construct a new class `Course`, relating it to class `Student` in an acceptable way.

2. Starting with class `Person` in Exercise 2 on page 79 and from the class `MotorVehicle` on page 338, define a class `CarOwner` that describes a person who can be the owner of one or more vehicles. Make use of the standard class `Vector`.

3. In the previous exercise it was assumed that the owner of a vehicle was always a natural person "of flesh and bone". Write new class definitions which allow an owner to be a person in the legal sense, that is, a corporation of some sort. A corporation has, in turn, one or more owners. Beginning with an abstract superclass `Owner` and an interface `Thing`, show whether it is possible to define the situation that certain classes, for example persons, can be the owners of one or several things and that certain other classes, for example persons in the legal sense of corporations (entities), can be both owned and owners at the same time.

4. Different kinds of animal can be defined using inheritance. Define some animals by beginning with a class `Animal` and deriving the different animals from this class. Feel free to use such intermediate classes as `Mammal`, `Insect`, `Bird` and so on. Arrange for the class `Animal` to have an abstract method `cry` that describes the sound an animal makes. Implement this method in the different subclasses.

    Now declare an array of animals, writing statements to run through the array. Let all the animals in the array emit a cry.

5. Descriptions of geometric figures are often used as examples in the context of object-oriented programming. First, define a class `Point` that defines a point (x, y) in a two-dimensional coordinate system. Then declare an abstract class `Figure` that contains a starting point. Let class `Figure` have an abstract method `area`.

    In addition, define a number of subclasses of the class `Figure`, for example `Circle`, `Triangle` and `Rectangle`. Give them suitable instance variables. Let each subclass have its own version of the method `Area`.

Finally, declare an object of class `Vector` to describe a collection of figures and write the statements that are necessary to calculate and write out the area for all the figures in the collection.

6. Construct a class `Passenger` to define a passenger who travels by air. A trip can be composed of several flights (use class `Flight` on page 111). A passenger must therefore know these. There should be a constructor that initializes a passenger with the appropriate flight departures. Here you should check that times and flights correspond, so that the person will not take a flight that leaves before the previous flight has been completed. There should also be a method with which you can replace one flight by another. Check here, too, that times and flights correspond. If a flight is delayed, a passenger may need to change the flight that follows. Write a method that checks whether this is necessary.

7. Complete the class `Cardstack`, in Section 10.10, with an operation that combines two stacks of cards into one. (Make sure that the combined stack does not contain more than 52 cards.) Now use the classes `Card` and `Cardstack` to write a program that plays the card game *Starve The Fox*. This game is played by two players. First, all the cards are dealt so that each player gets a stack of 26 cards. One of the players plays his or her top card, after which the two players take it in turns to play a card. The player who first plays a higher card of the same suit as the card first played may then take all the cards on the table and put them under his or her stack. If the card that is first played happens to be an ace, it is counted as 1; aces are worth 14 points otherwise. The player who loses all his or her cards also loses the game.

Exceptions

Writing a computer program is no mean feat and even an experienced programmer can make mistakes. Three categories of common error can arise:

- *Compilation errors.* These are errors that arise because the rules of the language have not been followed. The compiler will discover them when an attempt is made to compile the program, and the result is normally a printout listing the various errors. Examples of ordinary compilation errors include a variable name wrongly spelt, a curly bracket omitted, a semicolon missing, or the wrong key pressed when the program has been entered.
- *Execution errors.* These are errors that arise when the program is run. The program may use the correct language and follow all of its rules but may still contain errors that prohibit its functioning normally during execution. Examples of such errors are attempting to index outside the boundaries of an array, attempting to use a reference variable that, at the time, does not refer to an object, or attempting to open a file that does not exist.
- *Logic errors.* These are errors due to faulty program design, the root of the problem being the algorithm used. This kind of error is the most difficult to find, since the program can be both compiled and run without error printout resulting. A logic error will reveal itself only when the program has been test run and an incorrect result is obtained. If tested data is unavailable, the programmer will find it difficult to be sure that his or her program is free from logic errors. A program may work for a particular set of input data but prove to be erroneous for another.

In this chapter we shall study errors of the second category, execution errors. Situations may arise during the execution of a program that can be regarded as exceptional. In fact, such situations are termed *exceptions*. There can be different kinds of exceptions.

When a method is being written, the algorithm should be as clear and easy to understand as possible. But if checks were inserted at each stage of the algorithm to handle every imaginable error and abnormal event, the algorithm would become very clumsy and hard to follow. In Java, there is a mechanism for handling exceptions.

A method in which the error arises generates an exception which, according to pre-determined rules, is passed on to other methods where the exception can be "caught" and dealt with.

Two separate stages can be distinguished when working with exceptions. In the first, an exception is generated, and in the second the exception is handled, "caught". We shall begin by describing what happens in the easier of these two stages, that is, how exceptions are generated.

11.1 Automatically generated exceptions

An exception is described by the use of an object that will belong to a subclass of the standard class `java.lang.Throwable`. There are two standardized subclasses of `Throwable`, the classes `java.lang.Error` and `java.lang.Exception`. These subclasses have in turn several different subclasses. The class `Error` and its subclasses are used by the Java interpreter to signal errors of different kinds, such as linking errors or lack of memory space, and will almost always lead to the program being interrupted.

Subclasses of `java.lang.Exception` are used to signal minor errors that can usually be caught by the program, possibly preventing program interruption. Such minor errors include so-called runtime errors, such as indexing outside array boundaries, or giving incorrect arguments for methods. Runtime errors are automatically signalled by the Java interpreter and are described with objects that are of a subclass of the class `java.lang.RuntimeException`, which in turn is a subclass of class `java.lang.Exception`. Runtime errors are usually produced by mistakes in the program itself. For example, an attempt to index outside an array's boundaries should not be found in a well-written program.

Another common type of error arises during input and output. We might try to open a non-existent file, or attempt to read from a file, in spite of the fact that *end of file* has been reached. This type of error is automatically signalled by the different classes in the package `java.io` and is described with subclasses of the class `java.io.IOException`, which is also a subclass of the class `java.lang.Exception`. Subclasses of the standard class `Exception` are shown in Figure 11.1. (There are more in other packages.)

When an exception occurs, normal execution is immediately interrupted, and control of the program is transferred to the part that catches the exception. Several activities, called threads, can be running in a Java program at the same time. (This will be described in Chapter 12.) If an exception is not caught, the task in which the exception occurred will be terminated abruptly. In a normal program not making use of a GUI, this usually leads to the program being interrupted. Printout is then produced informing the user of the kind of exception involved and the part of the program in which it

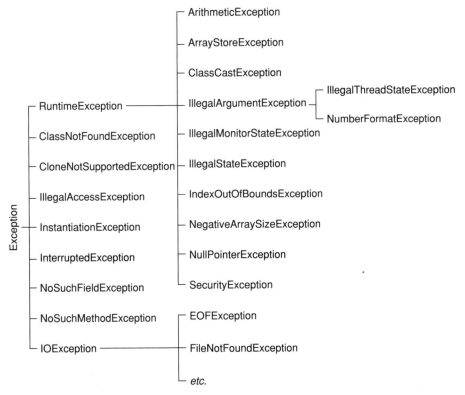

Figure 11.1 Exception classes

occurred. A stack trace is also produced. This is a printout giving the order of the calls of the various methods when the exception took place. Let us suppose that we have the following program lines in a method called `readAnswer`:

```
Std.out.println("Do you want to continue? ");
String s = Std.in.readLine();
if (s.equals("yes")) {
    ...
}
```

Let us further suppose that the user of the program writes Ctrl-Z (or Ctrl-D) to indicate that he or she does not want to continue. The method `readLine` will then return the value **null**. The variable s becomes equal to **null**, which means that we attempted to call the method `equals` with an empty reference. The Java interpreter will then generate an exception. Execution of the program is interrupted, producing the printout:

```
java.lang.NullPointerException
    at Extest.readAnswer(Extest.java:6)
    at Extest.main(Extest.java:17)
```

From this we can see that the error occurred in the method `readAnswer`, in line number 6 of the file `Extest.java`. We can also see that the method `readAnswer` was called from the method `main`, in line number 17 of the same file. This error is really the result of faulty programming and could have been avoided had the programmer had a little more foresight, forming the `if` statement in the following way:

```
if (s != null && s.equals("Yes"))
    ...
}
```

Let us suppose, in another example, that we define an array of whole numbers with 100 components and that we want to set the whole array to zero. We write the statements:

```
int[] a = new int[100];
for (int i=1; i<=100; i++)
   a[i] = 0;
```

When these lines are executed, the program will be interrupted, producing the error printout:

```
java.lang.ArrayIndexOutOfBoundsException: 100
   at Extest.initAll(Extest.java:12)
   at Extest.start(Extest.java:21)
   at Extest.main(Extest.java:27)
```

We have tried to index outside the array and we see from the error printout that an index value of 100 was involved. We also note that the error occurred in method `initAll`, in line 12. This method was called by the method `start` in line 21. The method `start` was in turn called by the method `main`, in line 27. Again, there is a programming error here. As we know, an array is indexed beginning at 0, which means that the last component should have the number 99 and not 100.

As a third example of automatically generated exceptions, we can look at the program `FileCopy2`, from page 146. The program reads in the name of the file to be copied. It then tries to connect a stream to the file with this name:

```
System.out.print("Input file? "); System.out.flush();
String name = myIn.readLine();
BufferedReader inFile = new BufferedReader
                            (new FileReader(name));
```

Let us suppose that we are running the program and indicate the file name `mydata.txt` as input data. If there is no file of that name, the program will be interrupted with the error printout:

```
java.io.FileNotFoundException: mydata.txt (cannot find file)
   at java.io.FileInputStream.open<Native Method>
   at java.io.FileInputStream.<init><FileInputStream.java:103>
```

```
    at java.io.FileInputStream.<init><FileInputStream.java:66>
    at java.io.FileReader.<init><FileReader.java:39>
    at FileCopy2.main(FileCopy2.java:11)
```

In the first line, we see that the faulty file name was `mydata.txt`. Then in the second line we learn that the error occurred in the method `open` in the class `FileInputStream`. Lines three and four show that this method was called from the constructor (`<init>` means constructor) in the class `FileInputStream`. The fifth line shows that this constructor was called from the constructor in class `FileReader`, and the last line says that this constructor was in turn called from line number 11 in our program.

This example clearly shows that an exception must arise if the user indicates an incorrect file name. On the other hand, the error could have been caught and interruption of the program avoided. We shall see how this is done later in the chapter.

The exception `ArithmeticException` is generated automatically when there is an error in calculations involving whole numbers, such as an attempt to divide by zero. On the other hand, errors arising in connection with calculations of the real numbers will not generate exceptions. In order to discover such errors, we have to make use of methods `isInfinite` and `isNaN`. (See page 52.)

11.2 Exceptions generated by the programmer

As is clear from this, several common types of error are signalled automatically by the Java interpreter. We can also generate exceptions ourselves by executing a **throw** statement. This has the general form

```
throw ex;
```

where *ex* is an object of an exception class.

All exception classes have definitions of the form:

```
public class class_name extends superclass_name {
    public class_name();
    public class_name(String s);
}
```

We see that there are two constructors, one without parameters and one that will have an argument of class `String`. We often create an exception object directly in the **throw** statement and then write an expression with one of the forms:

```
throw new E();
throw new E("a message");
```

Here, *E* will be the name of a subclass of the class `Throwable`. We normally only make use of subclasses of `Exception`. We can indicate either the name of one of the many standard classes, or of a subclass that we ourselves have defined. If we like, we can give a message as argument, and it can be read later when the exception has been caught. We can therefore use the message to insert extra information that could be useful, such as information about the reason for the exception.

If we wanted to generate an exception of the standard class ArithmeticException, we could write

```
throw new ArithmeticException("x too big");
```

On page 309, we showed an applet that drew a polygon on the screen and this applet got two parameters from the HTML file. The first parameter indicated the number of corners in the polygon and the second the polygon's radius. We can now complement the method init in this applet with statements that check the values of the parameters:

```
public void init()
{
   String s = getParameter("number");
   n = Integer.parseInt(s);
   if (n < 3)
     throw new IllegalArgumentException("number < 3");
   s = getParameter("radius");
   r = Integer.parseInt(s);
   if (r < 0)
     throw new IllegalArgumentException("the radius < 0");

   as before
}
```

If we now give incorrect arguments to the applet, execution will be interrupted and the message will be displayed in the web browser's message line. (If appletviewer is run, the message is written out in the text window appletviewer started from.)

We can also declare our own subclasses for Exception. We could give the definition:

```
public class CommunicationException extends Exception {
   public CommunicationException() {
     super();
   }
   public CommunicationException(String s) {
     super(s);
   }
}
```

We declared two constructors. This means that we can generate exceptions both with and without messages:

```
throw new CommunicationException("Timeout in reader");
throw new CommunicationException();
```

It is also possible to add instance variables in an exception class. For instance, in the class `CommunicationException`, we could have added an `int` that indicated the number of the actual communication channel. Then we could also have defined a third constructor enabling us to initialize the channel number. An example of an exception class with an extra instance variable is class `ArrayIndexOutOfBoundsException`. This has an `int` that indicates the incorrect index.

---

throw statement

```
throw new E();
throw new E("message");
```

where *E* is a subclass of `Exception`.
Normal execution is interrupted when a **throw** statement is executed.

11.3 Specification of exceptions

The technique of handling exceptions is based on catching exceptions occurring in the methods that have been called. Various means can be applied to deal with different kinds of exceptions. But how do we know what type of exception a method called can generate? One way of knowing this is to read the program code for the actual method but, of course, this is not possible in practice when applied to methods that are a part of large programs and which themselves call other methods. Another way is to read the documentation available about the actual method and hope that it contains information about the different kinds of exception that can be generated.

In Java this problem has been solved differently. A method declaration can contain a *specification* of the exceptions the method can generate. Suppose, for example, that we construct a method m and we know that only exceptions of type E1 and E2 can occur in this method. We can then define the method in the following way:

```
void m(parameters) throws E1, E2 {
   ...
}
```

At the end of the method head we write the reserved word **throws** followed by an enumeration of classes for the exceptions that can be generated. When we now want to make use of the method m, we will be aware of the kinds of exceptions we will have to catch. With "**throws** E1,E2,E3..." we write a "**throws** clause" but for the sake of simplicity we shall call it an *exception list*.

The exceptions that can be generated in a method are both the exceptions that the method itself generates by containing **throw** statements and those generated by other methods called by the actual method. Among these methods are methods in standard classes that can generate all the kinds of exceptions, as shown in Figure 11.1. It would therefore be inelegant, to say the least, if in every method we had to enumerate all the kinds of exceptions that this method was capable of generating. For this reason, exceptions have been divided into two categories: those that must be specified in exception lists and those that do not have to be specified. The former are called *checked* exceptions and the latter *unchecked* exceptions. Unchecked exceptions are those that belong to the class Error or one of its subclasses, or to class RuntimeException or one of its subclasses. Such exceptions then do not have to be enumerated in exception lists. This applies to exceptions normally generated by the system but not those generated by the programmer.

If the compiler discovers that a method might generate an exception of a kind not given in its exception list, we will get a compilation error. This means that if, in a method m1, we call another method m2 that can generate the checked exception E, then in m1 we must either ensure that the exception E is caught so that it cannot escape from m1, or include E in the exception list in m1. Let us suppose that we want to write a method readDouble that will read in a real number. As parameter we give the stream that we will read from. The method will look like this:

```
public static double readDouble(BufferedReader in)
                         throws IOException {
   String s = in.readLine();
   return Double.parseDouble(s);
}
```

Because the call of readLine can generate an exception of class IOException, this class will have to be enumerated in the exception list. The method parseDouble can generate an exception of class NumberFormatException, but exceptions of this class are unchecked exceptions and do not have to be given in the exception list.

If another method, for example the method main, now calls the method readDouble, then either this method must catch the exception IOException or give it in its own exception list. This might look as follows:

```
static BufferedReader myIn = new BufferedReader(new
                         InputStreamReader(System.in));

public static void main (String arg[])
                         throws IOException{
   ...
   double d = readDouble(myIn);
   ...
}
```

However, we must bear the following points in mind. First, if an exception of class E could be generated in a method, a superclass could be indicated for E in the method's exception list. For example, if we have a method that can generate an exception of class `FileNotFoundException`, this method's exception list might look like `throws IOException` since `FileNotFoundException` is a subclass of `IOException`.

Second, suppose that we have a method that overrides a method in a superclass, that is, a method that has the same name and parameters as the method in the superclass. Then for the method in the subclass, the checked exception classes indicated in its exception list must either also be found in the superclass's exception list, or be subclasses of classes in the superclass's exception list. The method in the subclass may also have fewer classes in its exception list.

Specification of exceptions

There must be an *exception list* in a method declaration where exceptions that might arise in the method without being caught are enumerated.

return type m(*parameters*) **throws** E1, E2, E3 {

Classes `Error` and `RuntimeException` and their subclasses need not be enumerated.

Alternatively, a superclass of the class concerned may be indicated in an exception list.

11.4 Catching exceptions

So far we have discussed how exceptions are generated but if they are not caught, the program will stop; in certain circumstances this is not acceptable. If we have a program that controls an industrial process of some sort, it is not acceptable for the program to stop abruptly when an exception occurs. The program must deal with what has happened, for example by writing a warning message to the operator, or closing down a critical process. It is also unacceptable for a program to stop because an operator happens to have entered incorrect input data into the program.

There are three levels of ambition in dealing with exceptions:

1. Take control of the exception and try to take suitable action to enable the program to continue.
2. Catch and identify the exception and pass it on to another part of the program to be dealt with.
3. Ignore the exception, in which case the program will stop.

The basic principle should be that the exception is dealt with in that part of the program where its effect can be handled most sensibly. The third level is of course the one that is easiest to apply. This is fine in the case of logic errors that have occurred while the program was being tested, before it was run properly. The right way is to deal with what has occurred outside the program, by correcting the program and so eliminating the error. We saw some examples of this type of error in Section 11.1.

We shall now write a new version of the method readDouble; see page 366. This is an example of ambition level 1, where we try to do something about an exception immediately. The method readDouble reads a real number from the stream indicated as parameter. Method readDouble calls the method parseDouble to convert the text the user has written into a number. If there is an error in something the user has written, the method parseDouble will generate an exception of type NumberFormatException. When we used the former version of the method readDouble, the program stopped when it occurred. However, in the new version we shall catch the error and give the user another chance to write correctly.

When we call a method that can generate exceptions, we must specifically indicate that we are prepared to catch these exceptions. This we do by making use of a **try** statement, which has the general form

```
try {
    statements
}
catch (E1 e1) {
    statements
}
catch (E2 e2) {
    statements
}
statements
```

where *E1* and *E2* represent names of exception classes and *e1* and *e2* are arbitrary parameter names. After the word **try**, a block is written which contains the statements to be performed and which might generate exceptions. (By "block" we mean a sequence of statements between curly brackets.) After this block, there should be one or more *handlers*. Each handler is introduced by the reserved word **catch** and has its own parameter, which will be of an exception class, that is, a subclass of Throwable.

The following things happen when the statements in the block after **try** are executed. If an exception does not occur, the statements are performed exactly as they usually are, and none of the handlers will be involved. If an exception of type *E* is generated by one of the statements after **try**, execution of this statement will be interrupted, and the program will instead jump to the first of the handlers that has a parameter of a type that matches *E*. When a handler has been found to catch the exception and the code in the handler has been executed, the exception will be cancelled. The execution process will then continue normally with the statement coming after the **try** statement, that is, with the statement that comes after the last of the handlers. Note that the program does not jump back to the statement that was interrupted inside the block. If we want to perform the statements in the `try` block again, we have to put the entire `try` statement into a repetition statement.

The rules state that when an exception of type E arises, control over it will be passed to the nearest handler whose type is the same as E, or is a superclass of E. By "nearest" we mean that the handler will be found in the `try` statement that was begun last, of all the `try` statements that are not yet terminated. This means that an exception is "forwarded" from the point where it arises, the interruption point, until there is a handler that can deal with it. Forwarding takes place in reverse order in respect of the path leading to the interruption. If a suitable handler cannot be found on the way back, the actual task (or thread) will be interrupted.

Incorporating use of the `try` statement, the method `readDouble` will now look as follows:

```
public static double readDouble(BufferedReader in)
                                    throws IOException {
    while(true)
      try {
         String s = in.readLine();
         return Double.parseDouble(s);
      }
      catch (NumberFormatException ne) {
         System.out.println("Incorrect number. Try again!");
      }
}
```

The reading of input lies in a `while` statement and can be repeated time and again. If the user had written a correct number, an exception would not be generated in the method `parse`. The `return` statement would then be executed normally and the method would return the number entered. If, on the other hand, the user enters incorrect input, an exception of type `NumberFormatException` is generated, and execution of the `return` statement is not terminated. Instead, there is a jump to the handler for exceptions of type `NumberFormatException`, resulting in error printout. Execution of the entire `try` statement is terminated but since the `try` statement lies inside the `while` statement, the `try` statement will be executed once more.

We have to retain `IOException` in the exception list, because the method `readLine` can generate exceptions of type `IOException`, and we have not caught such exceptions. As we know, this means that all other methods that call the method `readDouble` will either have to catch exceptions of type `IOException` themselves, or enumerate `IOException` in their exception list. This is not very elegant. In addition, errors of type `IOException` are often very serious, so it is unlikely that one of the methods calling `readDouble` will itself deal with this kind of error. We shall therefore extend the method `readDouble` with a handler to catch all errors of type `IOException`. If such an error should arise, the method `readDouble` will output a stack trace and terminate the program.

```
public static double readDouble(BufferedReader in) {
   while(true)
      try {
         String s = in.readLine();
         return Double.parseDouble(s);
      }
      catch (NumberFormatException ne) {
         System.out.println("Incorrect number. Try again!");
      }
      catch (IOException ie) {
         ie.printStackTrace();
         System.exit(1);
      }
}
```

The method `printStackTrace` is defined in class `Throwable` and so is inherited by all exception classes. Another useful method in class `Throwable` is the method `getMessage`. With this we can read the message inserted when an exception object has been created. For instance, in the handler, above, we could have written:

```
System.out.println(ie.getMessage());
```

The message would then have been written out. (We did not do this because the method `printStackTrace` also writes out the message.)

If there are several handlers in a **try** statement, it is important to place them in the right order. Because the rules say that an exception of type *E* will be dealt with by the first handler to have a parameter of type *E* or one of its superclasses, the most specific handlers should be put first. Let us suppose, for example, that we have a **try** statement that should be able to catch errors of types `IOException` and `EOFException`. Since `EOFException` is a subclass of `IOException`, we should put the handler for `EOFException` in front of the handler for `IOException`. Otherwise, we would finish in the handler for `IOException`, even in the case of exceptions of type `EOFException`.

Finally, we should mention that a **finally** part can be placed last in a **try** statement, after the handlers. This would have the form:

```
finally {
   statements
}
```

If a **finally** part is included, its statements will always be performed last of all. This will take place independently, whether the **try** statement has been executed normally,

---

try statement

```
try {
    statements
}
catch (E1 e1) {
    statements
}
catch (E2 e2) {
    statements
}
finally {
    statements
}
```

We can have any number of handlers (`catch` parts).
The `finally` part can be left out. (Takes place normally.)

If an exception occurs in the statements after `try`, there is a jump to the first handler (`catch` part) whose parameter matches the exception's type.
When the statements in the handler have been executed, the `try` statement is terminated and execution continues with the next statement.
There is never a jump back to the position where interruption occurred.
If there is no handler for an exception, the `try` statement is interrupted and the exception is sent on.
If there is a `finally` part, the statements in this are always executed last of all, regardless of whether an exception has arisen.

---

or an exception has occurred and we have finished in one of the `try` statement's handlers, or if an exception has occurred and has not been caught by one of the handlers.

11.5 Exercises

1. Write a method `openFile` that creates a new stream of class `BufferedReader` and connects the stream to a file. The file's name should be entered from the keyboard. If the file cannot be found, the user should get an error message and be requested to give another file name. As result, the method `openFile` should give a reference to the stream created.

2. On page 190 we studied the GUI program `Travel2` that read input data by making use of the class `JTextField`. Complement this program to display the text "Incorrect input data" in a dialog if the user enters incorrect numbers.

3. In Section 10.10, we used the classes `Card` and `CardStack`. The method `System.exit` is called in the constructor in class `Card` if the parameters are not correct. Change this so that an exception is generated instead; then insert suitable checks into methods `lookAt`, `layTop` and `dealTop`. (You may assume that there may be at most 52 cards in a stack of cards.) If there are errors in one of these methods, an exception will be generated. Declare your own exception class `CardError` and arrange for the generated exceptions to be of this class. Insert messages that explain the nature of the error.

Active objects

12

In Chapter 4, an object-oriented program was compared to a model of a real thing. An object-oriented program is built using a number of independent objects that communicate with each other by calling each other's methods. We can find active and passive things in reality, active things being ones that, on their own initiative, act or get other things to act. Passive things only do something when acted upon. If we look at traffic, for example, we could say that cars and traffic signals are active components of reality. Cars start, turn, brake and so on, while traffic signals change colour at intervals, which they themselves choose. In this context, streets or maps could be regarded as being passive, since a car drives into a street, while we can read a map. A bank account provides us with another example. A bank account is passive, while bank clerks and the bank's clients are active components in this context.

If we are able to represent real things in an object-oriented program, we should be able to differentiate between active and passive objects. This is, in fact, a perfectly natural development in the object-oriented way of looking at things. We create a program in which some objects are active and some are passive. If we create a program in which there is more than one active object, we create a *parallel program*, a program with several execution points. We sometimes also speak of *real-time programs*. A real-time program is usually one that collaborates with its environment and changes it. It could be a program that controls the different functions in an aeroplane, or one that supervises and controls a manufacturing process. What distinguishes a real-time program from others is that it has to comply with certain time constraints in order to change its environment before it is too late. (For instance, a program for an aeroplane that does not open out the plane's landing gear in time for the plane to touch down is not worth a great deal.)

Of the better-known programming languages, only Ada and Java can support the construction of parallel programs. (The other programming languages can do this but only by calling on functions in the operating system. Such programs then become affiliated with the actual operating system and cannot be moved.) Active objects in Java are described with the help of standard classes, while Ada has gone even further:

special constructions for parallel programming are built into the language itself. Ada was especially intended to be used for the programming of real-time programs operating within time constraints. Because Java is interpreted, it does not lend itself to such programs but it works extremely well in programs that are free of time constraints. There is nothing new in allowing several activities to exist in parallel in a computer. Operating systems that support multiple users, such as Unix, have always worked in this way. In one of these operating systems, each activity is called a *process*. In reality, the computer can execute only one process at a time, but by quickly switching between each process, the computer can give each user the illusion of having the computer to him/herself.

When you write parallel programs that contain several activities, you also switch between different activities. Each activity could be described by an operating system process, but switching between processes requires a considerable amount of processor power. For this reason, a simpler form of process is usually used in parallel programs, which does not require so much processor power. These processes are called *threads*. Each activity in the program is thus described by its own thread. In Section 12.2 we will study the basic standard class Thread, which is used to describe threads, but when we write programs that use Swing, we frequently do not need to use class Thread. You can get by with the simpler standard class javax.swing.Timer, so we will start by describing this class. (If you just want to learn how to write programs with dynamic Swing components, you can actually get by with just reading Section 12.1 in this chapter.)

12.1 Dynamic Swing components

It is possible to implement an active object which redraws an image at regular timed intervals. If you change the image slightly each time it is redrawn, you can make it look as if the illustration is moving. If you have a program that uses Swing components, this is relatively easy to do. In the package javax.swing there is actually a class called Timer which is very useful. An object of this class is executed as a separate thread in the background. A Timer object can generate regularly timed events of type ActionEvent. The frequency with which these events are generated and who listens to the events are specified as parameters to the constructor. The following declaration, for example, creates a Timer object that generates an event every 200 milliseconds. The variable 1 is a reference to a listener, an object that implements the interface ActionListener.

```
Timer t = new Timer(200, 1);
```

It is possible to add more listeners to the same Timer object by using the method addActionListener:

```
t.addActionListener(12);
```

To make a `Timer` start generating events, you must first call method `start`:

```
t.start();
```

After calling `start` the first event occurs after the number of milliseconds specified in the constructor. If you want a different time interval for the first event, you can change this by calling method `setInitialDelay`. At any time, you can stop a `Timer` by calling `stop` or restart it by calling `restart`. A sequence of events is normally generated, but you can instruct a `Timer` to generate a single event by calling method `setRepeats`.

javax.swing.Timer	
`new Timer(m, 1)`	creates a `Timer` which generates events every mth millisecond 1 is registered as the listener to the events
`t.addActionListener(1)`	registers 1 as listener to timer t
`t.start()`	starts the timer t, so that it generates events
`t.stop()`	stops the timer t, so that it stops generating events
`t.restart()`	restarts the timer t
`t.setDelay(m)`	changes the time interval to m milliseconds
`t.setInitialDelay(m)`	changes the time interval to the first event
`t.setRepeats(false)`	specifies that only one event should be generated

There is another standard class which is also called `Timer`. This is found in package `java.util`. This should not be confused with class `Timer` in the package `javax.swing`. If you have imported the package `java.util` into your program, you must explicitly specify which of the two `Timer` classes you mean. We do this by writing the package name in front of the class name. The declaration above must then be written as

```
javax.swing.Timer t = new javax.swing.Timer(200, 1);
```

As the first example, we will implement a program that generates the window in Figure 12.1. The window contains two digital clocks, one that displays local time and one that shows the time in New York. Both clocks are active components which are

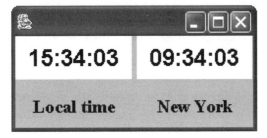

Figure 12.1

automatically incremented once a second. (This example is similar to the program DisplayClock on page 68, but we will provide a better and more general solution here.)

We start by declaring the class DigitalClock. This class should describe a component that can display texts. So we let the class be a subclass of class JLabel.

```java
import java.awt.*;
import javax.swing.*;
import java.awt.event.*;
import java.util.*;
import java.text.*;

public class DigitalClock extends JLabel
                          implements ActionListener {
  private DateFormat df = DateFormat.getTimeInstance();

  public DigitalClock() {      // Constructor
    setHorizontalAlignment(JLabel.CENTER);
    setOpaque(true);           // opaque background
    setBackground(Color.white);
    setFont(new Font("SansSerif", Font.BOLD, 24));
    javax.swing.Timer tim = new javax.swing.Timer(1000, this);
    tim.start();               // start the timer
  }

  public DigitalClock(String zon) { // Constructor
    this(); // call the parameterless constructor
    df.setTimeZone(TimeZone.getTimeZone(zon));
  }

  public void actionPerformed(ActionEvent e) {
    setText(df.format(new Date()));
  }
}
```

There are two constructors, one without parameters and one where you can specify the time zone you want as the parameter. Unless you specify a time zone, you automatically get the default time zone. The second constructor calls the parameterless constructor before it sets the time zone. In the constructor we create a Timer object and initialize it so that it generates an event every 100 milliseconds, i.e. once a second. We specify **this** as the listener, i.e. the current DigitalClock object.

Since the class DigitalClock should be a listener, it must implement interface ActionListener, which means that it should have a listener method actionPerformed. This will now be called by the Timer object once a second. During each call, it reads the computer's clock by creating a new Date object. By using editor df of class DateFormat the time that is read is converted to a text and setText is then called to change the text in this `JLabel` object. Note that we do not tick the clock forwards ourselves, as we did in class `Time` in the previous example. If we had done this, we would have risked having our digital clock run too slowly if the computer was occupied with other tasks, so that method `actionPerformed` was not called exactly once a second, and was somewhat delayed.

By using the class `DigitalClock` it is now easy for us to implement the program that generates the window in Figure 12.1.

```java
import java.awt.*;
import javax.swing.*;
import java.util.*;

public class ClockDemo extends JFrame {
    private DigitalClock c1 = new DigitalClock();
    private DigitalClock c2 = new DigitalClock("EST");

    public ClockDemo () {
        Container c = getContentPane();
        JLabel l1 = new JLabel("Local time", JLabel.CENTER);
        JLabel l2 = new JLabel("New York",  JLabel.CENTER);
        l1.setFont(new Font("Serif", Font.BOLD, 18));
        l2.setFont(new Font("Serif", Font.BOLD, 18));
        c.setLayout(new GridLayout(2,2,5,5));
        c.add(c1); c.add(c2); c.add(l1); c.add(l2);
        setSize(250,125);
        setVisible(true);
        setDefaultCloseOperation(EXIT_ON_CLOSE);
    }

    public static void main (String args[]) {
        ClockDemo kd = new ClockDemo();
    }
}
```

In the constructor in class `ClockDemo` we construct the window in Figure 12.1 with the help of four GUI components, `c1` and `c2` which are objects of class `DigitalClock` and `l1` and `l2` which are two simple (passive) `JLabel` objects. When the two objects `c1` and `c2` are created, the clocks will start automatically. In the constructor for object `c2` we have given the parameter `EST`, which refers to New York's time zone.

In Section 9.9 on page 299 we constructed an applet that draws a polygon. In the next example of using class `Timer` we will convert this applet into an autonomous program which displays a polygon that can move and rotate clockwise. When you run the program, it might look like Figure 12.2.

We will describe the actual polygon as an active object and will therefore define a class called `Poly`. We will use the same technique as we did in Chapter 7, where we

377

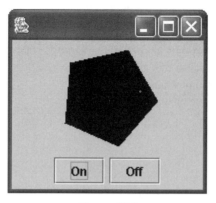

Figure 12.2

constructed our own GUI components. We let our new class `Poly` be a subclass of `JPanel` and write our own version of method `paintComponent`. We start by showing the class in its entirety, and then make some comments.

```java
import java.awt.*;
import javax.swing.*;
import java.awt.event.*;

public class Poly extends JPanel implements ActionListener {
   private int n, r;
   private double angle;
   private int[] x, y;
   private double dv = 5*2*Math.PI/360;  // 5 degrees
   private double turn = 0;
   private Timer tim = new Timer(100, this);

   public Poly(int number, int radius) { // constructor
      n = number; r = radius;
      x = new int[n];
      y = new int[n];
      angle = 2*Math.PI/n;
   }

   public void start() {
      tim.start();          // start the timer
   }

   public void stop() {
      tim.stop();           // stop the timer
   }

   public void actionPerformed(ActionEvent e) {
      // we get here each 100th ms
      turn = turn + dv;
      if (turn>2*Math.PI)
```

```
      turn -= 2*Math.PI;
    repaint();
  }

  public void paintComponent(Graphics g) {
    super.paintComponent(g);  // erase background
    int x0 = getSize().width/2;
    int y0 = getSize().height/2;
    // calculate new corners
    for (int i=0; i<n; i++) {
      double v = i*angle - turn;
      x[i] = x0 + (int)Math.round(r * Math.cos(v));
      y[i] = y0 - (int)Math.round(r * Math.sin(v));
    }
    // paint new picture
    g.fillPolygon(x, y, n);
  }
}
```

We use the same instance variables n, r, x0, y0, angle, x and y as in the applet in Section 9.9. The first five describe the number of corners, the radius, the centre of the circle and the angle between the corners of the polygon. The variables x and y are two arrays which contain the coordinates for the corners. In addition, we need a constant dv which specifies the amount the polygon should rotate in each unit of time and a variable turn which specifies how much the polygon has turned so far. We have assumed here that the polygon should be rotated 5 degrees in each unit of time, and that it has not been rotated from the beginning. All angles are measured in radians. The instance variable t is a Timer which is initialized so that it generates an event every 100 milliseconds. The object **this**, i.e. the current Poly object, is linked as a listener to the timer.

The constructor's parameters specify the numbers of corners and the radius. These are copied to instance variables. In the constructor, the arrays x and y are created. In addition, the angle between the corner points is calculated. On the other hand, the coordinates for the corner points are not calculated in the constructor. These are changed all the time, of course. Calculations are done in method paintComponent instead.

The methods start and stop can be called from outside to start and stop the timer t. If t is stopped, the polygon will be stationary, but it will rotate otherwise.

The variable turn specifies how much the polygon should be turned when it is drawn next time. In method actionPerformed, which is called by timer t every 100 ms, the variable turn is increased by dv radians. If this makes the polygon turn by more than a complete rotation (more than 2π radians), the variable turn is reduced by 2π, which corresponds to a full circle. After this, it calls repaint to redraw the polygon.

12. Active objects

Each time the polygon is redrawn, method `paintComponent` is called. (This is done by `repaint`.) The new coordinates for the corners of the polygon will then be calculated and placed in the arrays `x` and `y`. This calculation is done with the same formulae as on page 302. The only difference is that we must now consider that the polygon has been rotated. As previously, we divide a complete circle into n equal angles. From the angle thus obtained, we subtract the angle `turn`. (The reason that we subtract the angle `turn` and do not add it is that angles are measured anticlockwise when we call methods `sin` and `cos`. If we had added angle `turn` the polygon would then have turned anticlockwise.) The actual drawing is then done with standard method `fillPolygon`.

We can now implement the program that generates the window in Figure 12.2:

```
import java.awt.*;
import javax.swing.*;
import java.awt.event.*;
public class PolyDemo extends JFrame implements ActionListener {

    private JButton on = new JButton("On");
    private JButton off = new JButton("Off");
    private Poly y = new Poly(5, 50);

    public PolyDemo() {     // Constructor
        JPanel a = new JPanel();
        getContentPane().add(y, BorderLayout.CENTER);
        getContentPane().add(a, BorderLayout.SOUTH);
        a.add(on); a.add(off);
        on.addActionListener(this);
        off.addActionListener(this);
        setSize(200,180);
        setVisible(true);
        setDefaultCloseOperation(EXIT_ON_CLOSE);
    }

    public void actionPerformed(ActionEvent e) {
        if (e.getSource() == on)
            y.start();
        else
            y.stop();
    }

    public static void main (String args[]) {
        PolyDemo pd = new PolyDemo();
    }
}
```

The program places three Swing components in the window: two buttons with texts `On` and `Off` and an object of our class `Poly`. A listener is linked to the buttons, which starts or stops the timer in the `Poly` object. By clicking these buttons, the user can then get the polygon to rotate or stand still.

12.2 Threads

In the package `java.lang`, there is a standard class called `Thread`. In a parallel Java program, every activity is described as an instance of this class. A new activity can be created by defining a `Thread` object.

```
Thread a1 = new Thread();
```

In order to start execution of a thread, we call the method `start`:

```
a1.start();
```

In class `Thread` there is a method called `run`, and this method will be called automatically when `start` is called. The method `run` is intended to describe the activity itself. The thread will exist and be active right up to the point when method `run` has finished executing. Since method `run` in class `Thread` does not do anything, we have to define our own subclass of class `Thread` when we use this technique, letting this subclass have its own version of method `run`. But there is a big disadvantage to this technique. It so happens that we often want to let our classes inherit properties from some other class but because Java does not permit multiple inheritance, a class will not be able to inherit properties from another class if it is a subclass of `Thread`. For instance, it would not be possible to define a class that described active GUI components.

We will therefore go about it in a different way. When we create a new `Thread` object, we can connect another object to the thread. We could write

```
Thread a2 = new Thread(obj);
```

When we then start the thread by writing `a2.start()`, it is not the method `run` in the thread `a2` that will be called but instead, the method `run` in the object `obj`. For an object to be connected in this way to a thread, it must implement the interface `Runnable`. The only thing defined in the interface `Runnable` is the method `run`. Every class that implements the interface `Runnable` must therefore define its own version of method `run`. The method `run` usually contains a repetition statement that is repeated time and again, so that the activity can be sustained over a long period of time.

We shall now let each class `c`, which will describe active objects, have an instance variable of class `Thread`. We could say that every active object *has* its own thread. (Instead of saying that every active object *is* a thread, as we would have done if we had allowed the class to be a subclass of class `Thread`.) We call this instance variable `activity` and write the following declaration:

```
public Thread activity = new Thread(this);
```

By giving the parameter **this**, we indicate that the thread `activity` will execute the code in the actual object (**this**). For this to be permitted, our class `c` must implement the interface `Runnable` and have its own version of the method `run`.

The following example will best illustrate this: we will begin by defining a class `Writer` that describes active objects. A `Writer` will continually write out a particular text, pausing for a certain time between each printout. When we create a new writer, we indicate the text to be written out and the time interval as parameters of the constructor. In order to create a writer to write the text `Java` every tenth second, for instance, we make the declaration

```
Writer s = new Writer("Java", 10);
```

The writer is then started with the statement

```
s.activity.start();
```

Let us now see how class `Writer` is defined. It will implement the interface `Runnable` and so must have a method called `run`. It will also have a constructor.

```
public class Writer implements Runnable {
   public Thread activity = new Thread(this);
   private String text;
   private long interval;

   // constructor
   public Writer(String txt, long time) {
      text=txt;
      interval = time*1000;
   }

   public void run() {
      while(true) {
         try {
            Thread.sleep(interval); // wait
         }
         catch (InterruptedException e) { }
         System.out.print(text + " "); System.out.flush();
      }
   }
}
```

The constructor has two parameters: the text that will be written out and the time interval (indicated in seconds). When the constructor is called, the value of the parameters is kept in the instance variables `text` and `interval`. In the latter, the time interval is given in milliseconds, as a result of which the parameter will be multiplied by 1000.

The method `run` contains a continual **while** statement. The method `sleep` is called at every round, making the actual thread interrupt execution. The length of time it will pause before starting to execute again is indicated by the parameter, and this will be expressed in milliseconds. (There is another version of `sleep`, in which both milliseconds and nanoseconds can be indicated.) When the thread has been recalled to life, it will write out its text once and then pause again. The method `sleep` is a class method in the class `Thread`. We must therefore write the class name first. Because the method `sleep` can generate an exception of type `InterruptedException`, its call must lie in a **try** statement.

The method `interrupt` in class `Thread` can be called to interrupt an activity. For example, to interrupt the writer `s`, we make the statement

```
s.activity.interrupt();
```

The actual thread will not be interrupted immediately, as we might imagine. What happens is that we request the actual thread to terminate its activity *itself* in orderly fashion.[1] Exactly what happens when we call `interrupt` will depend on the circumstances of the actual thread. If it has called `sleep` and is paused, `sleep` will generate an exception of type `InterruptedException`. Otherwise, an interruption flag is set, indicating that the thread has been requested to stop. In both cases it is the thread itself that must check if it is to stop and so interrupt its execution. To illustrate how this works, we shall now write a new version of method `run` in class `Writer`:

```
public void run() {
   while(!Thread.interrupted()) {
      try {
         Thread.sleep(interval);
      }
      catch (InterruptedException e) {
         break; // interrupt the while statement
      }
      System.out.print(text + " "); System.out.flush();
   }
}
```

Before each round in the **while** statement, we check that the interruption flag has not been set; this is done by using the class method `interrupted` in class `Thread`. We must also catch the exception `InterruptedException`, which can be generated when `sleep` is called. If this exception arises, we interrupt the **while** statement.

These checks can appear inelegant when carried out in each active object, so to simplify matters, we can define our own subclass of class `Thread`. (This class can be found on the book's website.)

---

[1] In earlier versions of Java, there used to be a method `stop` that could be used to stop a thread forcibly but it has since been removed for reasons of program security.

```
public class XThread extends Thread {
    public static boolean delay(long millis) {
        if (interrupted())
            return false;
        try {
            sleep(millis);
        }
        catch (InterruptedException e) {
            return false;
        }
        return true;  // the thread has not been interrupted
    }
}
```

The new class XThread contains only a class method called delay, the idea here being that this method could be called instead of method sleep. Exactly as with method sleep, the method delay will have a number of milliseconds as argument. As result, delay will give a value that indicates whether or not the actual thread is to continue normally. The value **true** is then given if the actual thread has not been interrupted, and the value **false** if it has been interrupted. We can see that the method delay checks the interruption flag and in addition catches the exception arising in the call of sleep.

Through the use of class XThread we can now give a simpler (and final) version of the method run in class Writer. The only thing we need to do is to test whether, at each round, delay gives **true** as result. The whole class Writer will then look as follows:

```
public class Writer implements Runnable {
    public Thread activity = new Thread(this);
    private String text;
    private long interval;

    public Writer(String txt, long time) {
        text=txt;
        interval = time*1000;
    }

    public void run() {
        while(XThread.delay(interval)) {
            System.out.print(text + " "); System.out.flush();
        }
    }
}
```

To demonstrate how several active objects can execute in parallel, we shall write a program to write out the text Hocus every fifth second and the text Pocus every ninth second. The program will do this for one minute and will then be terminated. The printout will be:

```
Hocus Pocus Hocus Hocus Pocus Hocus Hocus Pocus Hocus Hocus
Pocus Hocus Pocus Hocus Hocus Pocus Hocus
```

The program will look like this:

```
public class HocusPocus {
  public static void main (String arg[]) {
    Writer w1 = new Writer("Hocus", 5),
           w2 = new Writer("Pocus", 9);
    w1.activity.start();
    w2.activity.start();
    XThread.delay(60000);  // wait one minute
    w1.activity.interrupt();
    w2.activity.interrupt();
  }
}
```

The program begins by creating and starting two writers, w1 and w2. The first will write out the text Hocus and the other, the text Pocus. The writers will execute in parallel and write out their texts for one minute. When one minute has elapsed, the program will request both writers to interrupt their activity.

When a Java program is started, a first thread is created automatically to call main. There will therefore be three threads in the program HocusPocus, since the two writers will each contain their own threads. Execution of a Java program will continue until all the threads have finished executing. In an ordinary, non-parallel program that contains only a single thread, the program will therefore terminate when main has finished executing, but in a program with several threads, we cannot be sure that the program will have finished executing when main has finished. For instance, if the writers had not interrupted their activity when interrupt was called, the program would not have finished, in spite of the fact that main had finished executing.

The method sleep in class Thread (and delay in class XThread) ensure that the actual thread has to wait for a certain time. Another method in class Thread that does this is the method join. We use join when we want to wait for another thread to finish. As an example, we will complement the program HocusPocus to make it end by writing the number of times Hocus and Pocus have been written out. The final printout will look like this:

```
11 Hocus and 6 Pocus have been written
```

In order to produce this result, we add a new instance variable to class Writer that will calculate the number of printouts:

```
public int number = 0;
```

(We write **public** for the sake of simplicity, so that the variable can be read from outside.) We also add the following statement at the end of the **while** statement in the method run:

```
number++;
```

Finally, we add the following statements last of all in method `main` in the class `HocusPocus`:

```
try {
   w1.activity.join(); // wait until w1 has finished
   w2.activity.join(); // wait until w2 has finished
}
catch (InterruptedException e) {}
System.out.println("\n" + w1.number + " Hocus and " +
                   w2.number + " Pocus have been written");
```

A call of `join` must be inserted into a **try** statement, since `join` can generate an exception if the actual thread is interrupted. This technique can be used to start a computation in a separate thread in the background. Something else can then be done while waiting for the result. Note that method `join` can be found in two other versions where a time expressed in milliseconds, or milliseconds and nanoseconds, can be given as argument. These methods can be used to produce *time out*. The actual thread will then only be paused for the given time, at most.

When a Java program with several threads is executed, the Java interpreter will alternate between the different threads. Where several threads are waiting to be run, the interpreter will choose the thread with the highest priority. We can ourselves read and change a thread's priority by making use of the methods `getPriority` and `setPriority`. The lowest priority value is `Thread.MIN_PRIORITY`, while the highest priority

java.lang.Thread	
new `Thread()`	creates a new thread
new `Thread(x)`	creates a new thread, connects the object `x` to the thread; `x` must belong to a class that implements `Runnable` (has a method `run`)
`t.start()`	starts the thread `t`; if the second constructor has been used the method `x.run` will be called, otherwise `t.run` is called
`t.interrupt()`	requests the thread `t` to finish executing
`interrupted()`	gives **true** if the thread executing is requested to finish
`sleep(m)`	lets the actual thread wait for `m` ms; gives `InterruptedException` if the thread has been requested to finish
`sleep(m,n)`	as above, but waits `m` ms plus `n` ns
`t.join()`	waits until the thread `t` has been terminated
`t.join(m)`	waits until `t` has been terminated, waits at most `m` ms
`t.join(m,n)`	waits until `t` has been terminated, waits at most `m` ms and `n` ns
`t.getPriority()`	gives the priority for the thread `t` (a whole number)
`t.setPriority(p)`	changes the priority for the thread `t` to `p` (a whole number)

value is `Thread.MAX_PRIORITY`. A thread will get the same priority as the thread that created it. Unless otherwise stated, all threads get the priority `Thread.NORM_PRIORITY`. When writing a program with several threads, we should let background activities have a low priority. We should also assign a high priority to any activities in response to signals from the user.

12.3 The class `java.util.Timer`

A new class was added in Java version 1.3, called `Timer` in the package `java.util`. (Do not confuse this class with class `Timer` in the package `javax.swing`.) The goal of the new class is to simplify handling of threads and to make programs more efficient. The idea is as follows. Instead of letting each activity execute its own thread, it uses a `Timer` object, which is an object that is executed by a single thread. The task of the `Timer` object is to schedule activities and periodically execute code from each object. The best way to explain how it works is to use an example. We will implement a new version of the `HocusPocus` program from Section 12.2. We start off with class `Writer`:

```java
import java.util.*;
public class Writer2 extends TimerTask {
    private String text;
    public int number = 0;

    public Writer2(String txt) {
        text=txt;
    }

    public void run() {
        System.out.print(text + " "); System.out.flush();
        number++;
    }
}
```

There are some important differences here compared with the version we showed on page 382. We first note that class `Writer2` is a subclass of a class called `TimerTask`. `TimerTask` is an abstract standard class which is used in combination with class `java.util.Timer`. If an object is to be able to call an active object, this object must belong to a subclass of class `TimerTask`. In the class `TimerTask` there is an abstract method called `run` which we must implement in our subclass. This method will be called by the `Timer` object at regular intervals. In method `run` we have to specify what should happen during each such call. The method `run` must not contain an eternal `while` statement as in our previous version. Please note that we do not define our own thread in the class. It is the `Timer` object that contains the thread and is responsible for ensuring that method `run` is called on the right occasions.

---

java.util.TimerTask

Must be used so that the object can be handled by timers of class `java.util.Timer`. We should create our own subclasses of this abstract class.

`tsk.cancel()`   stops the `TimerTask` object `tsk` from further execution

`tsk.run()`   specifies what should be done during each call. Must be implemented in its own subclass

---

The new version of class `HocusPocus` is as follows:

```
import java.util.*;
public class HocusPocus2 {
  public static void main (String arg[])
                                    throws InterruptedException {
    Timer t = new Timer();
    Writer2 w1 = new Writer2("Hocus"),
           w2 = new Writer2("Pocus");
    t.schedule(w1, 5000, 5000);
    t.schedule(w2, 9000, 9000);
    Thread.sleep(60000);  // wait one second
    w1.cancel();
    w2.cancel();

    System.out.println("\n" + w1.number + " Hocus and " +
                       w2.number + " Pocus has been written");
    t.cancel();  // stop the timer
  }
}
```

In the program, we create a `Timer` object `t` and two writers `w1` and `w2`. The `Timer` object `t` contains its own thread, which executes in the background. In the two calls of method `schedule`, `t` is instructed to call the method `run` in objects `w1` and `w2`. The second parameter specifies the number of milliseconds it should take until the first call and the last parameter specifies the number of milliseconds there should be between each call. These calls will then take place in `t`'s thread at the same time as the threads in `main` continue to be executed. The call of `sleep` means that `main` waits for one minute. (This call can generate exceptional events of type `InterruptedException`. This explains why we have written **throws** `InterruptedException` at the start of `main`.) After a minute, we specify that `w1` and `w2` should no longer be executed by the timer `t`. We do this by calling the method `cancel` for `w1` and `w2`. This method is in class `TimerTask` and thus has been inherited by our class `Writer2`.

At the end of `main` we call the method `cancel` for timer `t`. This call means that the actual timer `t` is terminated and its thread is broken off. If we had not done this call, it would have been remained as a background thread when `main` terminated and it would then have been impossible to terminate the program in the normal way.

If we compare this version of the program with the version we implemented in Section 12.2, we have achieved a couple of advantages. The first is that it becomes somewhat simpler. The class `Writer2` does not contain a thread of its own. This means that we avoid the problem of interrupting the thread in method `run`. Therefore we do not need our own help class `XThread`. The other advantage of using class `java.util.Timer` is that the programs become more efficient. Since all the active objects can be executed by a single thread, the system does not have to handle so many different threads. That might not be so apparent in this program, but in a program with a large number of active objects, it can be important.

java.util.Timer	
new `Timer()`	creates a new `Timer`

In the following calls, `tsk` will be an object which is a subclass of `TimerTask`. The parameter `d` should be of class `Date`.

`t.schedule(tsk, f, m)`	instructs `t` to call `tsk` with `m` ms between calls, the time to the first call is `f` ms
`t.schedule(tsk, d, m)`	instructs `t` to call `tsk` with `m` ms between calls, the first call is made at time `d`
`t.schedule(tsk, f)`	instructs `t` to call `tsk` *once* after `f` ms
`t.schedule(tsk, d)`	instructs `t` to call `tsk` *once*, at time `d`
`t.scheduleAtFixedRate(tsk,f,m)`	instructs `t` to call `tsk` with `m` ms between the *start* of each call, the time to the first call is `f` ms
`t.scheduleAtFixedRate(tsk,d,m)`	instructs `t` to call `tsk` with `m` ms between the *start* of each call, the first call is made at time `d`
`t.cancel()`	stops the timer `t` (and all its planned calls)

There is a further advantage to using class `java.util.Timer`. When you instruct a `Timer` object to call an active object, you can ask to have a specific time interval *between* each call. However, you can also specify that there should be a certain fixed time interval between the *start* of each call. This might appear to be a negligible difference, but if it takes a relatively long time to carry out a call for any reason (such as if garbage collection occurs), there will be a difference.

12.4 Synchronization of threads

When working with programs with several threads, we can be faced with problems entirely different from those encountered when dealing with ordinary programs. One such problem arises when two or more threads want to make use of a particular object at the same time. To illustrate this, we can return to class Account, from Chapter 3. (See page 88.) This class describes bank accounts. Objects belonging to class Account are passive objects that do not have an activity of their own but can be called by active objects. In class Account there was a method transaction that could be called when we wanted to credit an account or withdraw money from an account.

```
public class Account {
    private double balance;
    . . .
    public void transaction(double amount) {
        if (amount<0 && balance+amount<0)      // negative => withdrawal
            System.out.println("Withdrawal not possible!");
        else
            balance = balance+amount;
    }
}
```

Now let us suppose that we have declared an object of class Account:

```
Account a = new Account();
```

Let us further suppose that we have two active objects, cash, of class Cashpoint-Client, and giro, that are of class Transferor. The first object is executed each time a client withdraws money from a cash dispenser, and the second, when automatic transfers are made. There is a statement in both of these objects that looks like this:

```
a.transaction(b);
```

Let us suppose that a client withdraws $500 from a cash dispenser at the same time as an amount of $10,000 is automatically credited to his account. At the beginning, there was $13,958 in the account. The following course of events is then possible:

- The thread in the object cash called a.transaction and just had time to make the computation balance+amount, that is, 13,958 + (−500). The result was 13,458.
- The thread in the object cash is interrupted, and the thread in the object giro begins to execute. This calls a.transaction and performs the statement balance=balance +amount. Since the variable cash still has the value 13,958 before this statement is performed, the value of cash will be changed to 23,958.
- The thread in the object giro has finished executing for the moment. Execution of the thread in the object cash continues. This assigns its computed result of 13,458 to the variable balance.

The result of both these transactions will be that the balance was reduced by $500 in spite of $10,000 having been credited to the account!

To prevent this sort of thing happening, it is sometimes necessary to make sure that only one thread at a time has access to an object. (The balance would not have been incorrect if the thread in the object `cash` had been able to finish executing the entire method `transaction` before the thread in the object `giro` got access to the method.) This can be accomplished by indicating that certain methods are to be *synchronized*. This is done with the reserved word **synchronized**. We could write:

```
public class Account {
   private double balance;
   ...
   public synchronized void transaction(double amount) {
      if (amount<0 && balance+amount<0)    // negative => withdrawal
         System.out.println("Withdrawal not possible!");
      else
         balance = balance+amount;
   }
}
```

When a thread calls a synchronized method, a lock is put on the object to which the method belongs. If the thread in the object `cash` made the call

```
a.transaction(b);
```

a lock would be put on the object `a`. An object will remain locked until the call of the synchronized method has finished executing. If another thread attempts to call a synchronized method for a locked object, the thread will be obliged to wait until the object is no longer locked. Note that the second thread does not have to call the *same* synchronized method for the actual object, since there can be several synchronized methods in a class.

When we define a class to be used in a program with several threads, we should declare as synchronized all the methods that *change* something in the actual object. However, methods that merely read values should not be synchronized. A constructor does not need to be synchronized, since it can only be executed once for a particular object and this will happen before the other methods can be called.

Class methods (static methods) can also be declared as synchronized. This results in a lock that will apply to all the class methods for the actual class.

We should mention the existence in Java of *synchronized statements*. They have the form:

```
synchronized (obj)
   statement;
```

Of course, the statement can consist of a block – a sequence of statements between curly brackets. When one of these is performed, the object `obj` will be locked, and other threads wanting to perform synchronized statements on the object will have to wait. It is, however, better and safer to make use of synchronized methods than of synchronized statements. It is all too easy to forget to put a vital call into a synchronized statement.

In the program examples we have seen in this chapter so far, the different threads were executed independently of one another, but it is common for the different threads in a parallel program to need to communicate with each other. For example, a thread might have to perform a computation, the result of which might be needed in another thread. Then there must be a way for the first thread to tell the second when the computation has finished and there must be a way for the second thread to read the computed value. To ensure that threads sending data to each other will not have to wait unnecessarily, we often make use of an intermediary data buffer. The thread producing a result leaves it in the buffer, and the thread needing the result collects it from the buffer.

We will now give an example of this type of program. Let us suppose that we have a number of threads that compute results. We call these threads *producers*. These producers place their results in a buffer that functions like a queue. Each new result is placed last in the queue. Let us further suppose that there are threads wanting to read the computed values. These threads are called *consumers*. These consumers will collect the values from the buffer. Each time a value is collected, the value that is first in the queue is taken. This is shown in Figure 12.3, where we have drawn three producers and two consumers.

We begin by defining a class that describes a queue. We can easily construct a class of this kind as a subclass of the standard class `Vector`.

```
import java.util.*;
public class Queue extends Vector {

    public synchronized void putLast(Object obj) {
        add(obj);
```

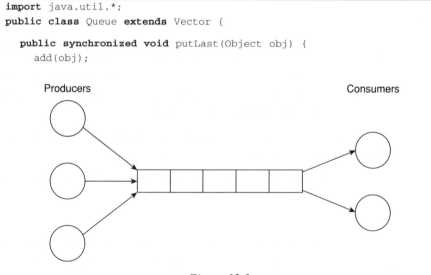

Figure 12.3

```
      notify();
   }

   public synchronized Object getFirst() {
      while (isEmpty())
         try {
            wait();
         }
         catch (InterruptedException e) {
            return null;
         }
      Object obj = get(0);
      remove(0);
      return obj;
   }
}
```

A queue is quite simply a `Vector`. To the subclass we have added two new methods, `putLast`, which puts an object last in the queue, and `getFirst`, which gets the object lying first in the queue. Both of these methods have been declared as synchronized, so that only one thread at a time can put in or take out objects in the queue.

The method `putLast` has as parameter the object that is to be put last in the queue. It is an easy matter to put the object there. We simply call the inherited method `add`, which puts an object last into a vector. The call of the method `notify` is interesting. This method is defined in the class `Object` and so is available for all classes. When `notify` is called, a signal is generated that says that something has happened to the actual object. In this case, we say that something has happened to the queue, which is that a new object has been inserted last in it.

The method `getFirst` gets and returns the first object from the queue but for it to go to collect something, the queue must have something in it. The method `isEmpty`, inherited from class `Vector`, will test whether a `Vector` is empty. If the queue is empty, we call the method `wait`. As with the method `notify`, this is defined in class `Object` and is available to all classes. When `wait` is called, execution of the actual thread is momentarily interrupted, while at the same time, the lock on the actual object is opened. In this way, threads other than the actual thread can execute synchronized methods. The interrupted thread is called to life again when another thread has called the method `notify` for the actual object. We then again test whether the condition we were waiting for has been fulfilled. In this case we were waiting for the queue not to be empty. Note that we shall always carry out this test in a **while** statement, so that we can wait again if the condition has not been fulfilled. (There may be other causes for the waiting thread to have been awakened.) Note, too, that the call of `wait` must always lie in a **try** statement, since it can generate an exception. The inherited methods `get` and `remove` are used last in the method `getFirst` to read and take away the first object (the one with the index number 0) from the queue.

Several threads can call `wait` for a particular object. They will then be passive and wait to be alerted again. When another thread then calls `notify` for the actual object, one of the waiting threads will be notified. There is also a method `notifyAll` that notifies all the threads waiting on the actual object concerned.

We shall now see how a queue can be utilized. The data that can be placed in a queue is of type `Object`, which means that we can put data of any class into a queue. We can also have different kinds of data. (Compare this with Section 10.7.) We begin by defining a class that produces data to be put into a queue. For the sake of simplicity, we will let this data be of class `String`. A producer is an active object that, time and again, puts a particular text into a queue. The producer will wait for a certain time between each bout of activity. The text and the time interval are given as parameters to the constructor, which also gets as parameter a reference to the queue to be used. The class `Producer` will then look like this:

```
public class Producer implements Runnable {
    public Thread activity = new Thread(this);
    private String text;
    private long interval;
    private Queue q;

    public Producer(String txt, long time, Queue k) {
        text=txt;
        interval = time*1000;
        q = k;
    }

    public void run() {
        while(XThread.delay(interval))
            q.putLast(text);
    }
}
```

The class `Consumer` is built up according to the same model, although it takes texts from the queue. This activity, too, is punctuated by time intervals. The texts that are collected are written out on the screen. The time interval and a reference to the queue to be used are given as parameters for the constructor:

```
public class Consumer implements Runnable {
    public Thread activity = new Thread(this);
    private long interval;
    private Queue q;

    public Consumer(long time, Queue k) {
        interval = time*1000;
        q = k;
    }
```

```
public void run() {
  while(XThread.delay(interval)) {
    System.out.print(q.getFirst() + " "); System.out.flush();
  }
}
}
```

Please note that objects of classes Producer and Consumer must each have their own threads so that synchronization will function correctly when they call methods in the class Queue. This means that we cannot use java.util.Timer here, since all the active objects would then be executed on the same thread.

We shall now bring everything together by writing a demonstration program that creates a queue, together with an arbitrary number of consumers and producers. When the program starts, it asks the user to indicate the number of producers and consumers required. The user also has to indicate the texts that the producers will generate and the time intervals to be used. When the program is run it might look like this:

```
Number of producers? 3
Producer no.1:
   Time interval? 5
   Text? Ole
Producer no.2:
   Time interval? 7
   Text? Dole
Producer no.3:
   Time interval? 9
   Text? Doff
Number of consumers? 2
Consumer no.1:
   Time interval? 4
Consumer no.2:
   Time interval? 8
Ole Dole Doff Ole Dole Ole Doff Ole Dole Ole Doff Dole Ole Ole
Dole Doff Ole Dole Ole Doff Dole
Number left in the queue: 4
```

The principal thread in method main starts the producers and consumers, then waits for a minute. After this time, the principal thread comes in again, reads and writes out the actual length of the queue, then interrupts the program forcibly by calling System.exit. (It could also have called the method interrupt for all the producers and consumers.) The method size, inherited by class Queue from class Vector, is called to find out the length of the queue. The thread in main raises its priority so that it will be certain of coming in before the other threads after one minute has elapsed. The program looks like this:

```java
import java.util.*;
import java.io.*;
public class OleDoleDoff {
  public static void main (String arg[])
            throws IOException, InterruptedException {
    Queue buf = new Queue();
    BufferedReader myIn = new BufferedReader
                        (new InputStreamReader(System.in));
    System.out.print("Number of producers? ");
    System.out.flush();
    String s = myIn.readLine();
    Producer[] p = new Producer[Integer.parseInt(s)];
    for (int i=0; i<p.length; i++) {
      System.out.println("Producer no.1 " + (i+1) +":");
      System.out.print(" Time interval ");System.out.flush();
      s = myIn.readLine();
      int time = Integer.parseInt(s);
      System.out.print(" Text? "); System.out.flush();
      s = myIn.readLine();
      p[i] = new Producer(s, time, buf);
    }

    System.out.print("Number of consumers? ");
    System.out.flush();
    s = myIn.readLine();
    Consumer[] c = new Consumer[Integer.parseInt(s)];
    for (int i=0; i<c.length; i++) {
      System.out.println("Consumer nr " + (i+1) +":");
      System.out.print("Time interval? ");System.out.flush();
      s = myIn.readLine();
      int time = Integer.parseInt(s);
      c[i] = new Consumer(time, buf);
    }

    // start activities
    Thread.currentThread().setPriority(Thread.MAX_PRIORITY);
    for (int i=0; i<p.length; i++)
      p[i].activity.start();
    for (int i=0; i<c.length; i++)
      c[i].activity.start();
    // wait
    Thread.sleep(60000);
    System.out.println("\nNumber left in the queue: " +
                    buf.size());
    System.exit(0);
  }
}
```

12.5 Threads and Swing

The appearance of Swing components on the screen can be influenced by several different types of event, such as key presses and mouse movements. Different parts of the program can also influence the appearance of components, such as by changing their contents. Events of this type can occur at the same time, but if we permitted all Swing components to be redrawn at the same time by different sections of the program, there would be chaos. You have to make sure that any changes to the appearance of Swing components are done one at a time. So when Swing was designed, a simple strategy was devised, which was that all changes to the Swing components should be done by one single thread in the program. This thread is called the *event-dispatching thread*. The event-dispatching thread is started automatically when Swing components are used in a program. This executes in the background and senses all external events, such as when the user presses a mouse button. The event-dispatching thread then works out what kind of external event it was, and calls suitable listeners. In other words, it is the event-dispatching thread that should execute the code found in listener methods, such as `actionPerformed`, which the programmer has defined. Since one normally puts the code that changes the appearance of Swing components in the listener methods, all changes will then be done in order, one at a time.

There is a general rule that the programmer must observe for this to work as intended, which is that *after a Swing component has been drawn on screen the first time, all operations that modify the component or depend on its state must be executed by the event-dispatching thread*. The easiest way to observe this rule is by *carrying out all operations in listener methods*, as we demonstrated at several places. You should also remember that you should *never call a listener method in a program yourself*. Calls are made automatically from the event-dispatching thread.

As we have seen, we can influence a component in another thread *before* it has been drawn the first time. This is what normally happens in a constructor, where we specify the basic properties of the component. This also applies in method `init` in an applet. In the programs we have seen so far, the code in the constructor has been executed by the same thread as the one that executes the method `main`. What you should remember is that *after you have called method `pack` or `setVisible`, you should not do further operations on the component in the constructor* (or in method `init` in an applet). For this reason, we have put the calls of `pack` and `setVisible` last in the constructors.

As long as you follow these simple rules, you do not have to worry about the event-dispatching thread. It should be pointed out that it is perfectly all right to use timers of class `javax.swing.Timer`, since they have been designed so that they make sure that the calls to the listener methods are executed by the event-dispatching thread.

The only times you have to look out is when you have programs with several threads and you want to access the Swing components for each thread. This is frequently a question of something that has happened in the program that is *not* an external event, but where the event should nevertheless influence the appearance of a Swing component. There are two auxiliary methods that you, as a programmer, can use to manage these situations: invokeLater and invokeAndWait. Both are class methods which are defined in class SwingUtilities.

We will give only a brief example here of using method invokeLater. Assume that in program OleDoleDoff on page 396 we want consumers to write out the messages they receive in a component of type JTextArea instead of in a command window. We can imagine that this component has been defined in method main and placed in a window with the following program lines:

```
JFrame f = new JFrame();
JTextArea a = new JTextArea(20, 50);
f.getContentPane().add(a);
f.pack();
f.setVisible(true);
```

Further down in the method main when we create an object of class Consumer, we provide a reference to text area a as a parameter to the constructor so that the Consumer object knows which text area it should write in.

```
c[i] = new Consumer(time, buf, a);
```

It is in class Consumer that the most important changes must be done:

```
import javax.swing.*;

public class Consumer implements Runnable {
   public Thread activity = new Thread(this);
   private long interval;
   private Queue q;
   private JTextArea a;

   public Consumer(long time, Queue k, JTextArea ar) {
      interval = time*1000;
      q = k;
      a = ar;
   }

   public void run() {
      Runner r = new Runner();
      while(XThread.delay(interval)) {
         SwingUtilities.invokeLater(r);
      }
   }
}
```

```
class Runner implements Runnable {  // internal class
  public void run() {
    a.append(q.getFirst() + " ");
  }
}
}
```

We first notice that the constructor has been given a further parameter, a reference to the text area we should write in. This reference is saved in the new instance variable a.

The method run, as before, contains a **while** statement which is executed repeatedly at a certain time interval between each iteration. It might be tempting, in method run, to insert the call at once:

```
a.append(q.getFirst() + " ");
```

to put the received message last in the text area. Had we done this, we would have broken the basic rule above, however. The code in method run in the class Consumer is not actually executed by the event-dispatching thread, it is executed by its own thread. What we have to do instead is to use method invokeLater to ensure that the call is done by the event-dispatching thread.

The method invokeLater should have a parameter which refers to a listener whose class implements the interface Runnable. This means, as we know, that the object must have a method called run. The method invokeLater will ensure that this method run is executed by the event thread. We have defined our own class called Runner, which implements the interface Runnable and which contains a method run. In this method, which will be executed by the event-dispatching thread, we have inserted the sensitive call of method append. Please note that the declaration of class Runner has been put inside the class Consumer. It is practical to do it this way. This is because the instance variables in a surrounding class are accessible from an inner class. In our case, we can directly use the instance variables a and q.

When you call method invokeLater a return takes place at once and execution continues directly in the current thread. You do not have to wait until the sensitive statements have been executed by the event-dispatching thread. If you have to wait, for example if you are going to read input data from a Swing component, instead of invokeLater you can use method invokeAndWait, which works in the same way but blocks the calling thread until the event-dispatching thread has carried out the relevant statements.

12.6 Threads in awt components

When you use awt components, in applets for example, you cannot use class Timer in the package javax.swing, but you can use class Thread instead. As an example, we

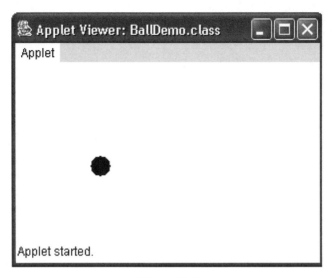

Figure 12.4

will construct an awt component which shows a ball that moves both horizontally and vertically. When the ball reaches the edge of the component, it bounces. We call the new class `Ball`. When we run an applet that displays a component of class `Ball` it can look like Figure 12.4.

The class `Ball` is as follows. The class describes active objects that are constructed on the same lines as class `Writer` in Section 12.2. (The reason that we do not use any of classes `javax.swing.Timer` and `java.util.Timer` is that they are not available in the most common web browsers.)

```java
import java.awt.*;

public class Ball extends Panel implements Runnable {
  private Thread activity;
  private int r, x0, y0;      // radius and centre of the ball
  private int xStep, yStep;   // movement

  public Ball(int radius, int xSpeed, int ySpeed) {
    r = radius; xStep = xSpeed; yStep = ySpeed;
    x0 = r; y0 = r;
  }

  public void start() {
    if (activity == null) {
      activity = new Thread(this);
      activity.start();
    }
  }
}
```

```
public void stop() {
   if (activity != null) {
      activity.interrupt();
      activity = null;
   }
}

public void run() {
   while (XThread.delay(100)) {
      if (x0-r+xStep < 0 || x0+r+xStep > getSize().width)
         xStep = -xStep;   // change direction
      x0 += xStep;
      if (y0-r+yStep < 0 || y0+r+yStep > getSize().height)
         yStep = -yStep;   // change direction
      y0 += yStep;
      repaint();
   }
}

public void paint(Graphics g) {
   g.fillOval(x0-r, y0-r, 2*r, 2*r);
}
}
```

When you call method start from outside, a new thread activity is created, which executes method run in the relevant Ball object. When you call method stop the thread is broken. In addition, the variable activity is set to **null**. This means that the memory space occupied by the terminated Thread object can be recycled by the system.

We allow the ball to move both horizontally and vertically on the screen. The instance variables x0 and y0 keep track of the current centre point of the ball and instance variables xStep and yStep specify the number of pixels that the polygon moves each time the ball is redrawn. In method run there is a **while** statement that is executed every 100 milliseconds. On each lap, the variables x0 and y0 are incremented by xStep and yStep. If xStep has a positive value, the ball moves right on the screen and if xStep has a negative value, the ball moves left. For yStep a positive value means downwards and a negative value means upwards. If the ball reaches an edge, we change the sign of xStep or yStep. The ball will then "bounce" and start to move in the opposite direction.

The applet that generates the window in Figure 12.4 is as follows:

```
import java.awt.*;
import java.applet.*;

public class BallDemo extends Applet {
   private Ball b;
```

```
public void init() {
    String s = getParameter("radius");
    int r = Integer.parseInt(s);
    s = getParameter("speed");
    int sp = Integer.parseInt(s);
    b = new Ball(r, sp, sp);
    setLayout(new GridLayout(1,1));
    add(b, BorderLayout.CENTER);
}

public void start() {
    b.start();
}

public void stop() {
    b.stop();
}
}
```

The radius and speed of the ball are given as parameters from the HTML code. The method init starts by reading these values. After this, a Ball object is created and placed in the centre of the applet. The parameters given are the radius and speeds. (For the sake of simplicity, we will make the ball move at the same speed along the x axis and y axis.)

The applet also contains the two methods start and stop. To explain their role, we will discuss how an applet is initiated and terminated. An applet is normally created by the web browser. As soon as the applet has been created, the web browser calls method init. The method init is thus called only once for a particular applet and the intention is that we should do everything in this method that we would have done in a constructor if it were not an applet.

When the web browser has called method init, it calls the method start. (Please note that this is a question of method start in the class Applet, not the method start in the class Thread.) This is done each time the web page with the relevant applet begins to be displayed. This can thus be done several times for a particular applet. If an applet contains a thread that you want to be active only when the applet is visible on the screen, this thread should be activated in method start.

When the web page with the applet is no longer displayed, the web browser automatically calls method stop in the applet. If the applet has a thread that displays a moving image, you should break this thread in method stop. If this is not done, the thread will continue to be executed.

A further method which you should know in class Applet is method destroy. This method is called by the web browser when an applet should cease to exist. You can then "tidy up", close files or break off background threads etc. which the applet has started.

It should be pointed out that methods `init`, `start`, `stop` and `destroy` are particular to applets. For ordinary objects we use a constructor, as you know, instead of `init`, and the method `finalize` (please refer to Section 10.6) more or less corresponds to method `destroy`.

Initialization and termination of applets	
`init`	is called when the applet is created, corresponds with the constructor for ordinary objects
`start`	is called when the web page containing the applet starts to be displayed
`stop`	is called when the web page containing the applet stops being displayed
`destroy`	is called when the applet should cease to exist, corresponds to `finalize` for ordinary objects

Please note that when you work with Swing components, you should *not* use the technique shown in this section but should use class `javax.swing.Timer` instead, which was described in Section 12.1, if at all possible. You then avoid the problem that all changes in Swing have to be done in the *event-dispatching thread*. (Please refer to Section 12.5.)

12.7 Reduction of flicker in awt components

If you test run the applet in Section 12.6, you will admittedly see a ball that moves on the screen, but it will not look good since the image will flicker a lot. This is a common problem when one uses awt components that draw moving images. There are various techniques that can be used to attempt to reduce the flicker. One technique is to avoid erasing, and another more general technique is to use so-called double buffering. Double buffering is automatically used when you use Swing components, without your having to do anything special.

12.7.1 Do not erase the component

When we call the method `repaint` for a graphics component, the method `paint` is not called directly. Instead, the call goes through yet another method called `update`. This method is defined in the class `Component` and looks roughly like this:

```
public void update(Graphics g) { // standard version
   g.setColor(getBackground());
   g.fillRect(0, 0, getSize().width, getSize().height);
   g.setColor(getForeground());
   paint(g);
}
```

The method `update` erases the entire component by filling it with background colour, and only then is the method `paint` called to draw the component once more. The flicker is caused by the whole component being erased and if this could be avoided, the flicker would be diminished.

In some cases, the component does not have to be erased. This is true where the method `paint` will draw over *everything* that needs to be redrawn. What we can do then is to redefine the method `update` in the class concerned. This is easy to do but the easiest way of going about it is to define a method that looks like this:

```
public void update(Graphics g) { // own version
   paint(g);
}
```

But we have to be careful. If `paint` does not redraw the entire component, it will draw on top of the component's old contents. For instance, if we redefined `update` in this way in our class `Ball`, from Section 12.6, a black track would gradually be displayed.

12.7.2 Double buffering

When we use double buffering, we do not draw directly on to the screen. Instead, we draw an invisible picture "on the side". Only when we have finished drawing the invisible picture will we copy it on to the visible screen, in one operation. As a result, the flicker will more or less disappear. To be able to use double buffering, we must declare and create an invisible picture. This will be an object of the standard class `Image`. In addition, a `Graphics` object, that is, a toolbox with graphics tools, must be connected to the invisible picture. (The class `Image` is defined in the package `java.awt`, as is class `Graphics`.) We therefore add the following two instance variables to our applet `PolyDemo`:

```
Image picture2;
Graphics g2;
```

We also add these initializations in method `init`:

```
picture2 = createImage(getSize().width, getSize().height);
g2 = picture2.getGraphics();
```

The method `createImage` will create a new, invisible picture. The dimensions the picture will have are given as parameters. We make this invisible picture exactly as large as the visible one on the screen. (The call of `getSize` is really a call of **this**.`getSize` and so will give the actual `Applet` object's size.)

In method `paint`, we draw our figure on to `picture2`, instead of drawing directly on to the screen; to achieve this, we use the `Graphics` object `g2`, instead of `g`. When the new coordinates of the corner points have been computed, this call is then made:

```
g2.fillPolygon(x, y, n);    // draw a new figure onto picture2
```

The invisible picture is then copied onto the screen and becomes visible through the call:

```
g.drawImage(picture2, 0, 0, this); // copy to the screen
```

The Graphics object g is connected to the visible screen, which is why we call the method drawImage for the object g. The first parameter for drawImage will be the picture to be drawn, and the next two will indicate where in the visible picture picture2 will begin to be drawn. We shall begin drawing in the upper left-hand corner and indicate the coordinates (0,0). The last parameter will be a reference to an object that can supervise the drawing of the picture. This object will belong to a subclass of Component. The easiest way is to allow the actual object to be the "supervisor", so we write this.

For this to work properly, we must also redefine the method update. In the standard version (see page 403), the visible picture is erased before the method paint is called. It was this erasing of the picture that caused the flicker. We do not have to erase the visible picture now, however, because a completely new picture is copied to the screen each time the above call is made. Instead, we have to erase the invisible picture picture2 each time, before we draw a new figure onto it. The new version of update will therefore look as follows. We have simply been erasing the invisible picture with the Graphics object g2, instead of the visible picture with g:

```
public void update(Graphics g) {  // our own version
  // efface picture2
  g2.setColor(getBackground());
  g2.fillRect(0, 0, getSize().width, getSize().height);
  g2.setColor(getForeground());
  paint(g);
}
```

These are all the changes needed to get applet BallDemo to produce a moving image that does not flicker so much. No changes are needed in BallDemo; it is only the class Ball that needs to be adjusted. This will be as follows:

```
import java.awt.*;
import java.applet.*;

public class Ball extends Panel implements Runnable {
  private Thread activity;
  private int r, x0, y0;       // radius and centre
  private int xStep, yStep;    // movement
  private Image im2;           // image for double buffering
  private Graphics g2;
```

```java
public Ball2(int radius, int xSpeed, int ySpeed) {
  r = radius; xStep = xSpeed; yStep = ySpeed;
  x0 = r; y0 = r;
}

public void start() {
  if (im2 == null) {
    im2 = createImage(getSize().width, getSize().height);
    g2 = im2.getGraphics();
  }
  if (activity == null) {
    activity = new Thread(this);
    activity.start();
  }
}

public void stop() {
  if (activity != null) {
    activity.interrupt();
    activity = null;
  }
}

public void run() {
  while (XThread.delay(100)) {
    if (x0-r+xStep < 0 || x0+r+xStep > getSize().width)
      xStep = -xStep;   // change direction
    x0 += xStep;
    if (y0-r+yStep < 0 || y0+r+yStep > getSize().height)
      yStep = -yStep;   // change direction
    y0 += yStep;
    repaint();
  }
}

public void update(Graphics g) {
  // efface im2
  g2.setColor(getBackground());
  g2.fillRect(0, 0, getSize().width, getSize().height);
  g2.setColor(getForeground());
  paint(g);
}

public void paint(Graphics g) {
  g2.fillOval(x0-r, y0-r, 2*r, 2*r);
  g.drawImage(im2, 0, 0, this); // copy to the screen
}

public void finalize() throws Throwable {
  g2.dispose();
  super.finalize();
}
}
```

Graphics objects demand a considerable amount of resources. It is therefore recommended to release these resources as soon as you no longer need them. One way to do this is to call method dispose. In our program, we ought to release object g2. When a Ball object ceases to exist, as we know, the system automatically calls method finalize. So in class Ball we have written our own version of this, where we have put in a call to dispose.

12.8 Exercises

1. Write a program to keep track of when a person has to take medicine. Whenever it is time to take medicine, a message such as "Take a Javacyl tablet now" should be produced. An active object for each medical element will be necessary. When the program is started, each medicine and information about how often it should be taken should be input.

2. Construct an applet with a digital clock that will show the duration of the user's visit to the relevant website.

3. Complement class Queue, in Section 12.4, with operations that make it possible for objects to be placed in order of priority into a queue. Objects with a higher priority will be put in front of objects with a lower priority. The priority of an object will be determined by the priority of the thread inserting the object.

4. Complement the applet Ball, on page 400, so that it emits a metallic sound every time the polygon touches a side.

5. Construct a Swing component that displays a set of traffic lights with red, amber and green lights. The traffic lights should change colour automatically at regular intervals. The time interval is given as parameter for the component's constructor.

6. Construct an active object displaying a red ball that is released from the top of the drawing area. The ball should rebound against the bottom of the drawing area. At every rebound, the ball will lose some of its height, finally coming to rest.

7. Construct an active object that displays an analogue clock with an ordinary clock face having hour, minute and second hands. The clock will move forward once per second. Use the formulae in the class Poly, on page 378, to calculate the angle the different hands are to have.

8. Construct a Swing version of the class Ball on page 400.

Events, listeners and actions

13

The computer world entered a new phase in the 1980s. An ever-increasing number of programs began to use graphical user interfaces (GUIs) and programs started to look much as they do today. Menus and buttons are an integral part of programs and we communicate with programs using a mouse. Prior to this, programs communicated with the user through a terminal similar to a typewriter. The program wrote out text at this terminal and the user entered text at the keyboard. Even if modern computer systems have a GUI, they still retain these typewriter-like terminals in a simulated form. For example, we can open a terminal window in a Unix system and an MS-DOS Prompt in Windows systems.

The transition from terminal-based communication to GUIs revolutionized and simplified the use of computers and made it possible for new categories of users to make use of them. A GUI program is event-driven and is constructed quite differently from a program that communicates through a terminal. Programmers had to learn new techniques. GUI programs are also more complex. To construct a GUI program within a reasonable time, we have to utilize libraries with ready-made functions, for example Xlib and Motif in Unix and Win API (Application Programming Interface) in Windows. It is important for programmers to master not only the programming language but also the many sets of ready-made functions.

This is why we have made use of GUIs from the very beginning of the book, describing their construction at the same time as discussing the more traditional basic programming techniques. In Chapter 6, where we discussed GUI components, we saw the first examples of event-driven programs, and we employed so-called listeners. In this chapter, we shall be looking at events and listeners in a little more detail. We shall also describe events that are generated by the user clicking with the mouse, or pressing a key at the keyboard.

13.1 Program structure

In a traditional program that communicates with the user via a terminal, we say that the reading of input data is *program-driven*. The program decides when it is time to read input data. It then outputs a request to the user. The program will wait until the user has written input data before it continues. The program `Travel` on page 138 was an example of this type of program. The program contains only one activity (a thread), and when this has finished executing, the program is terminated. In Java, this means that there is only one thread executing the method `main`. When `main` has reached its conclusion, the program has finished.

A GUI program has a completely different structure. We say that such a program is event-driven. Execution of an event-driven program takes place in two phases. The first is the initialization phase; we enter this phase as soon as the program starts. In Java, the initialization phase is executed by the thread that executes the method `main`. In the initialization phase, we declare and initialize the different GUI components that will be used by the program. We also define what are called *callback functions*, which will deal with the events that interest us. In Java, these callback functions are defined as methods in special *listeners*.

When the initialization phase is over, the program goes into its *waiting phase*. In most systems, this transition occurs at the end of the initialization phase, when we call a special wait function. In Java it is easier still, since it is completely automatic, without calls of any kind. In GUI programs, the Java interpreter starts a new thread in the background that takes care of the execution of the waiting phase. The initialization phase in Java ends when the thread that executed `main` comes to an end. We will remember from the previous chapter that a Java program executes until all the threads running have finished executing, so if there were no more threads, apart from the thread in `main`, the program would stop when `main` had finished.

The program remains in the waiting phase until *events* outside it occur. When we speak of outside events, we mean, for example, that the user clicks with the mouse, or presses a key. With the occurrence of an event of this kind, the callback function is called (in Java it is the listener) that was defined to deal with the event. It is therefore the user and not the program that will decide when it is time to enter data into the program. So we say that the program is event-driven.

An event-driven program, therefore, consists not of connected programs but of an initialization part and a number of callback functions (listener methods). The callback functions are never called in the ordinary way in a program. Instead, they are always called automatically when the corresponding event occurs.

13.2 Event classes

In Java, each event is described by means of special *event classes*. When an event occurs, an object is created of the class that describes the event. After this, a method is called in the listener that has been defined to listen to this type of event. The parameter given to the method in the listener is the newly created event object. All event classes have a common superclass called `EventObject`. Classes that describe events related to Java awt are found in a special package called `java.awt.event`. Several of these events are also used in Swing components. Classes particular to Swing include `ChangeEvent`, in package `javax.swing.event`.

For each event, there is a graphic component in which the event occurred. One way to find this component is to call the method `getSource`, which is defined in class `EventObject`, which all event classes inherit. You can also call method `getComponent` in all subclasses of class `ComponentEvent`, you can call the method `getContainer` for class `ContainerEvent` and you can call the method `getWindow` for class `WindowEvent`. In Table 13.1 there is a summary of the most common event classes which are used to describe various types of events.

A particular event class can be used to describe several similar events. The class `FocusEvent` is used for both events `focusGained` and `focusLost`, for example.

We should also mention here that we can call method `setActionCommand` for buttons and menu choices, to give each button or menu choice a unique name. (This does not need to be the same text as is written on the button or menu choice.) In the listener, you can then call method `getActionCommand` to find out the name of the button or menu choice that caused the event. This is useful if you do not have access to the variable name of the button or menu choice in the listener.

13.3 Listener classes and listener interface

To trap an event, you should create a *listener*. A listener is an object of a *listener class*. You are meant to define the listener class yourself. This class must contain special methods which the system automatically calls when an event occurs. There must be an interface for each and every event class which the listener class must implement. This listener interface will have the same name as the corresponding event class, but with `Listener` as a suffix instead of `Event`. For class `FocusEvent` there is an interface called `FocusListener`, for example, and for event class `KeyEvent` there is the interface `KeyListener`. The only exception to this rule is class `MouseEvent`. This has both an interface called `MouseListener` and one called `MouseMotionListener`. (The package `javax.swing.event` also contains an interface called `MouseInputListener`, which implements both interfaces `MouseListener` and `MouseMotionListener`.)

The methods the listener class must have are defined in the interface. The names of these methods are the same as the event names in the second column of Table 13.1. For instance, the methods `focusGained` and `focusLost` are defined in the interface `FocusListener`. A listener class for `FocusEvent` must, therefore, have the structure:

Table 13.1 Events

Event class	Events	Can be generated by
`ActionEvent`	`actionPerformed`	`AbstractButton` – button pressed `JTextField` – text changed `JComboBox` – alternative chosen
`ChangeEvent`	`stateChanged`	`JComponent` – state changed
`AdjustmentEvent`	`adjustmentValue-` `Changed`	`JScrollbar` – scroll bar changed
`ItemEvent`	`itemStateChanged`	`JToggleButton, Checkbox,` `Choice` – alternative chosen

`ComponentEvent`	`componentHidden`
	`componentMoved`
	`componentResized`
	`componentShown`
		`Component` – component hidden,
		moved, resized or shown

`ContainerEvent`	`componentAdded` `componentRemoved`	`Container` – a component added or removed
`FocusEvent`	`focusGained` `focusLost`	`Component` – the component gained or lost focus

`WindowEvent`	`windowActivated`
	`windowClosed`
	`windowClosing`
	`windowDeactivated`
	`windowDeiconified`
	`windowIconified`
	`windowOpened`
		`Window` – the window is opened,
		closed, is closing, is iconified,
		or restored

`KeyEvent`	`keyPressed`
	`keyReleased`
	`keyTyped`
		`Component` – a key has been
		pressed or released

`MouseEvent`	`mouseClicked`
	`mouseEntered`
	`mouseExited`
	`mousePressed`
	`mouseReleased`
		`Component` – mouse button
		pressed or released, the mouse
		moved into or out of the
		component

	`mouseDragged` `mouseMoved`	`Component` – mouse dragged or moved
`PropertyChangeEvent`	`propertyChange`	`JComponent` – properties changed

```
class MyListener implements FocusListener {
  public void focusGained(FocusEvent e) {
    ...
  }
```

```
public void focusLost(FocusEvent e) {
    ...
  }
}
```

As parameter, a listener method will always get an object of the current event class. The methods `focusGained` and `focusLost` have a parameter of type `FocusEvent`.

The class `MouseEvent` is, as mentioned above, an exception, as it has two different listener interfaces. The methods `mouseClicked`, `mouseEntered`, `mouseExited`, `mousePressed` and `mouseReleased` are defined in the interface `MouseListener`. The interface `MouseMotionListener` contains definitions of the methods `mouseDragged` and `mouseMoved`. If we want to define our own listener classes for `MouseEvent`, we might have to define two different listener classes, one for each interface.

A listener must be registered. We do this by calling the method `add?Listener` for the component the listener is to be connected to. The character `?` is then replaced by the name of the event. For example, if we wish to connect a listener of type `MyFocusListener` to the actual component, we can write:

```
FocusListener fl = new MyListener();
addFocusListener(fl);
```

In the examples we showed in Chapter 6, we made it easy for ourselves by allowing the class describing the surrounding component to be a listener class as well. For example, when we wanted to listen to events of the type `actionPerformed`, we made our program have the structure:

```
class C extends C0 implements ActionListener {

  public void actionPerformed(ActionEvent e) { // listener method
    ...
  }
  // constructors and other methods in C
  C() {
    addActionListener(this); // register the listener
    ...
  }
  ...
}
```

However, generally it is better to define a separate listener class. When we define a listener class, we normally define it *inside* the class where it is to be used, because we are allowed to define classes inside other classes in Java. We employ this procedure when we want to use a local class as an auxiliary class for another. When we have defined the listener class, we can create a listener from it. This might look as follows:

```
class C extends C0 {

    class MyListener implements FocusListener { // listener class
        public void focusGained(FocusEvent e) { // listener method
            ...
        }
        public void focusLost(FocusEvent e) { // listener method
            ...
        }
    }
    MyListener l = new MyListener(); // listener
    // constructors and other methods in C
    C() {
        addFocusListener(l); // register the listener
        ...
    }
    ...
}
```

One way of shortening this is by making use of something called an *anonymous class*.
We can then create an object with the required properties directly, without declaring a
class name. An alternative way of writing the above might be:

```
class C extends C0 {

    FocusListener l = new FocusListener() { // anonymous class
        public void focusGained(FocusEvent e) {
            ...
        }
        public void focusLost(FocusEvent e) {
            ...
        }
    };
    // constructors and other methods in C
    C() {
        addFocusListener(l); // register the listener
        ...
    }
    ...
}
```

Note that the definition of the anonymous class is included in the initialization by the
variable l and that initialization will be terminated by a semicolon.

13.4 Adapter classes

In Table 13.1 we saw that there were several event classes for which there was more
than one event. The class WindowEvent, for example, has seven different events. A

method is defined for each kind of event in the corresponding listener interface `WindowListener`. If we are to define our own listener class for `WindowEvent`, we will therefore have to define seven different listener methods in it. We might only wish to deal with a couple of kinds of event, in which case it would be inelegant to have to define listener methods for all the events that did not concern us. In order to avoid this, we have recourse to *adapter classes*, found in the package `java.awt.event`. There is an adapter class for every event class having more than one event. An adapter class is an abstract class that implements corresponding interfaces. An adapter class has the same name as the corresponding event class but with the suffix `Adapter`, instead of `Listener`. Consequently, there is an adapter class with the name `WindowAdapter` for class `WindowEvent`, and this class implements the interface `WindowListener`. All the listener methods in an adapter class are implemented with empty method bodies. In other words, nothing will happen if one of these listener methods is called, enabling us to construct our own listener classes as subclasses of the corresponding adapter class. In this way we can inherit all the methods and only have to redefine the methods that concern us. We can also use the technique of using anonymous classes when we inherit adapter classes.

13.5 Mouse

In this section, we shall be discussing the implications of clicking on a mouse button, or performing some other kind of operation with the mouse. The different kinds of events that can take place are listed in Table 13.1. If we wish to track events of the type `mouseDragged` or `mouseMoved`, we use a listener that implements the interface `MouseMotionListener`, or one that belongs to a subclass of the class `MouseMotionAdapter`. If we wish to track one or more of the other mouse events, we should use a listener that implements the interface `MouseListener`, or that belongs to a subclass of the class `MouseAdapter`. In both cases, the listener methods will get a parameter of class `MouseEvent`, and this parameter will contain information about what has taken place.

The following example will best illustrate this: we will construct a program that displays an empty window. Each time we click in the window, the program will write out which mouse button was used, whether it was a single click, double click or multiple click (three or more clicks). The printout will also tell us where in the window we clicked. Printout from the program will not be displayed in the window but will be displayed in a text window, at the side. The output might look as follows:

```
Single click with the left button at (73,58)
Single click with the right button at (95,103)
Single click with the left button at (69,108)
Double click with the left button at (69,108)
Single click with the left button at (138,97)
   CTRL pressed
Single click with the right button at (138,97)
   Shift pressed
```

The program also senses whether the Alt key, Shift key or Ctrl key was depressed when you clicked. The program listing follows.

```java
import javax.swing.*;
import java.awt.event.*;

public class MouseTest extends JFrame {
  MouseTest() {
    getContentPane().addMouseListener(l);
    setSize(200,200);
    setVisible(true);
    setDefaultCloseOperation(EXIT_ON_CLOSE);
  }

  MouseListener l = new MouseAdapter() {
    public void mouseClicked(MouseEvent e) {
      // how many clicks?
      String click;
      if (e.getClickCount() == 1)
        click = "Single click";
      else if (e.getClickCount() == 2)
        click = "Double click";
      else
        click = "Multiple click";

      // which mouse button?
      String button = "";
      if (SwingUtilities.isLeftMouseButton(e))
        button = "left button";
      else if (SwingUtilities.isMiddleMouseButton(e))
        button = "middle button";
      else if (SwingUtilities.isRightMouseButton(e))
        button = "right button";
      System.out.println(click + " with the " + button +
                    " at (" + e.getX() + "," + e.getY() +")");

      // was ALT, Shift, or CTRL pressed?
      if (e.isAltDown())
        System.out.println("    ALT pressed");
      if (e.isShiftDown())
        System.out.println("    Shift pressed");
      if (e.isControlDown())
        System.out.println("    CTRL pressed");
    }
  };

  public static void main (String arg[]) {
    MouseTest m = new MouseTest();
  }
}
```

The interesting thing here is the definition of listener 1. This is defined as a subclass of the class MouseAdapter, since we do not define methods for every different mouse event, only for the event mouseClicked.

We start by investigating whether it was a single click, double click or multiple click. We can get this information by calling the method getClickCount for the event in question. This method returns an integer which is the number of clicks.

After this, we find out which mouse button the user clicked. The class SwingUtilities contains methods isLeftMouseButton, isMiddleMouseButton and isRightMouseButton which can be used. Please note that these are class methods and that the event e should be given as a parameter.

The methods isAltDown, isShiftDown, isControlDown and isMetaDown are used to investigate whether the corresponding button was depressed when the event occurred.[1]

To find out where the user clicked in the window, we use methods getX and getY, which are defined in class MouseEvent. It would have been possible to call method getPoint, which returns an object of standard class Point. (See Section 2.12.)

java.awt.event.MouseEvent	
e.getX(), e.getY()	gives the x and y coordinates of the cursor location
e.getPoint()	gives a Point object which reports the cursor position
e.getClickCount()	specifies the number of times the user has clicked
e.getComponent()	gives the graphic component where the cursor is located
e.isControlDown()	reports whether the user held the Ctrl button down (in awt if the user has clicked the centre button!!)
e.isMetaDown()	reports whether the user held the Meta button down (in awt if the user has clicked the right button!!)
e.isAltDown()	reports whether the user held the Alt button down
e.isShiftDown()	reports whether the user held the Shift button down

The following methods report the button that was depressed:

```
SwingUtilities.isLeftMouseButton(e)
SwingUtilities.isMiddleMouseButton(e)
SwingUtilities.isRightMouseButton(e)
```

---

[1] If you program with awt components, however, the methods isControlDown and isMetaDown are not used to determine whether the keys were depressed, they are used to see which mouse button the user pressed instead. The method isControlDown returns the value **true** if the centre button (on a three-button mouse) was depressed and method isMetaDown specifies, in the same way, whether the right mouse button was depressed.

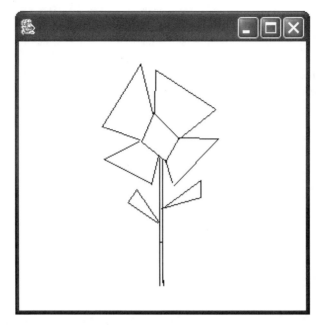

Figure 13.1 A simple drawing program

We will now give an example to demonstrate how other kinds of mouse events are dealt with. We shall write a simple drawing program that will allow the user to draw lines. The program will look like Figure 13.1 when it is run. When the user wants to draw a line, he or she puts the mouse where the line is to start and presses the mouse button, then keeps the mouse button pressed and moves (drags) the mouse to the point where the line is to stop. The user then releases the mouse button.

We shall use the standard class `Point`. We have to write our own class `Line`, because there is no standard class for lines. We define a line with two points, its end points. This class `Line` will look as follows. (Do not worry about why **implements** Serializable has been written here. This will be explained in Chapter 16.)

```
import java.awt.*;
import java.io.*;
public class Line implements Serializable {
   public Point p1, p2;

   public Line() {
      p1 = new Point();
      p2 = new Point();
   }

   public Line(Point a, Point b) {
      p1 = new Point(a);
```

```
      p2 = new Point(b);
   }

   public void draw(Graphics g) {
      g.drawLine(p1.x, p1.y, p2.x, p2.y);
   }
}
```

There are two constructors, one that is parameterless and one that has two points as parameters. We will also let the class `Line` have a method that draws a line on the screen; as parameter for this method we give a `Graphics` object that can be used for drawing.

We now use a vector to describe the lines we have drawn:

```
Vector lines = new Vector();
```

An instance variable `newL` of class `Line` is used to describe the line as it is being drawn. We let `newL` refer to a new line each time the user presses a mouse button. The line is initialized from the beginning, where the start and end points are the same, that is, giving the position of the mouse when the user first presses the mouse button.

```
newL = new Line(e.getPoint(), e.getPoint());
```

(Here, `e` is, as usual, the parameter of the listener.) When the user releases the mouse button, the mouse's position is read and the end point is changed in the line `newL`.

```
newL.p2 = e.getPoint();
```

The new line is then placed last in the vector:

```
lines.add(newL);
```

The method `paintComponent` is called automatically, in the usual way, each time the Swing component needs to be redrawn. In this method, we run through all the lines in the vector and draw them one at a time. We use an iterator to do this, as was described in Section 9.10 on page 302.

```
for (ListIterator i=lines.listIterator(); i.hasNext(); )
   ((Line) i.next()).draw(g);
```

The method `next` answers with a value of type `Object`. For this reason, an explicit type conversion must be done to type `Line`.

Each section can now be assembled into a complete class called `Painter`.

```
import javax.swing.*;
import java.awt.*;
import java.awt.event.*;
import java.util.*;
```

```
public class Painter extends JPanel {
  private Vector lines = new Vector();
  private Line newL;

  public Painter() {
    setBackground(Color.white);
    addMouseListener(l1);
  }

  public void paintComponent(Graphics g) {
    super.paintComponent(g);
    for (ListIterator i=lines.listIterator(); i.hasNext(); )
      ((Line) i.next()).draw(g);
  }

  MouseListener l1 = new MouseAdapter() {
    public void mousePressed(MouseEvent e) {
      newL = new Line(e.getPoint(), e.getPoint());
    }

    public void mouseReleased(MouseEvent e) {
      newL.p2 = e.getPoint();
      lines.add(newL);
      repaint();
    }
  };
}
```

We let the listener for the mouse listen to the two events that occur when the mouse is pressed and released. Note that `repaint` is called last in the method `mouseReleased`. All the lines in the window are then drawn, including the new line.

Now all we need is a class that contains the method `main` and generates the outer window. We let the window contain a component of class `Painter`.

```
import javax.swing.*;
import java.awt.*;
public class PaintProgram extends JFrame {
  public PaintProgram() {
    getContentPane().add(new Painter(), BorderLayout.CENTER);
    setSize(300,300);
    setVisible(true);
    setDefaultCloseOperation(EXIT_ON_CLOSE);
  }

  public static void main (String arg[]) {
    new PaintProgram();
  }
}
```

This drawing program serves its purpose but it has a major weakness: the line we are drawing cannot be seen until we have finished drawing it and release the mouse button. Let us therefore make a new, improved version of the class `Painter`.

We will use a technique called *XOR mode*. In a window, there is normally a background colour and a foreground colour; when a drawing command is given, everything is drawn with the colour in the foreground. In XOR mode, the drawing colour alternates between two different colours, the actual colour in the foreground and another one, the XOR colour, which we ourselves can specify. If we make several passes with the mouse in the same position on the screen, whatever is drawn will be displayed in these two, alternating colours. If we now choose the XOR colour so that it is the same as the background colour and we draw in the same place on the screen, we will be drawing with the foreground and background colours alternating: whatever we draw will therefore appear and disappear alternately. In XOR mode, therefore, we can erase a line we have just drawn by drawing it again.

To indicate that XOR mode is to be used, we call the method `setXORmode` for the `Graphics` object used. The XOR colour is given as parameter. If we want the current background colour to be used as the XOR colour, we write:

```
g.setXORMode(getBackground());
```

To return to the normal situation and drawing as usual, we make the call:

```
g.setPaintMode();
```

In the new version of the drawing program, we change over to XOR mode each time the user presses a mouse button and begins to draw a new line. We add a listener that listens to the mouse when it has been dragged, that is, moved with the button pressed. When this has been done, we read the mouse's actual position and update the line `newL` so that it will describe a line from `p1` (the point at which the mouse button was pressed) to the actual mouse position, point `p2`. We then draw the line `newL`. However, before we change `newL`, we redraw it. Because drawing takes place in XOR mode, the old line will be erased. When the program is run, it will look as though the line that is being drawn remains at its starting point `p1`, while the end point follows the movements of the mouse for as long as the mouse button is pressed. When the mouse button is released, we leave the XOR mode and begin to draw normally again. The new line is then drawn in its final version.

When all of this is combined, we will get the following class.

```
import javax.swing.*;
import java.awt.*;
import java.awt.event.*;
import java.util.*;
```

```
public class Painter extends JPanel {  // new version
  private Vector lines = new Vector();
  private Line newL;
  private Graphics g;

  public Painter() {
    setBackground(Color.white);
    addMouseListener(l1);
    addMouseMotionListener(l2);
  }

  public void paintComponent(Graphics g) {
    super.paintComponent(g);
    for (ListIterator i=lines.listIterator(); i.hasNext(); )
      ((Line) i.next()).draw(g);
  }

  MouseListener l1 = new MouseAdapter() {
    public void mousePressed(MouseEvent e) {
      g = ((Component) e.getSource()).getGraphics();
      newL = new Line(e.getPoint(), e.getPoint());
      g.setXORMode(getBackground()); // change over to XOR mode
    }

    public void mouseReleased(MouseEvent e) {
      newL.p2 = e.getPoint(); // set the end point
      lines.add(newL);
      g.setPaintMode();        // return to normal drawing
      newL.draw(g); //the line is finished, now draw it properly
    }
  };

  MouseMotionListener l2 = new MouseMotionAdapter() {
    public void mouseDragged(MouseEvent e) {
      newL.draw(g);                   // erase the line
      newL.p2 = e.getPoint();  // change the end point
      newL.draw(g);                   // redraw the line
    }
  };
}
```

Each time the mouse is depressed, i.e. each time we start to draw a new line, this sets the instance variable g so that it refers to the Graphics object which is currently being used. The reason that we cannot initialize g in the constructor is that the method getGraphics returns the value null before the component has been drawn the first time. In addition, it can happen that the component has been moved, which means that a new Graphics object must be used.

The method paintComponent is called if the window was concealed. All the lines must then be redrawn.

13.6 Keyboard

When the user presses a key on the keyboard, events described by the type `KeyEvent` are generated. These events are guided by the system to the GUI component that is in *focus* for the present. The component in focus is determined by the user, by clicking with the mouse or by using the Tab key (or Shift-Tab) in order to change between components. A component that is in focus is usually marked in some special way; it might be through a different colour or a change in its edges. For a component to be in focus, it must lie in the *active window*. The active window's frame is usually shown in a different colour. (In Windows, for example, the frame of an active window is often dark blue, while frames of non-active windows are grey.) The user will determine which window is to be active by clicking on it or by moving the mouse to it.

A window will recognize when it has become active by defining a listener that listens to `WindowActivated` events. In addition, there is a method `getFocusOwner` in class `Window` that returns a reference to the component in the actual window in focus. The method returns the value `null` if no component is in focus, which will happen if the window is not active. A particular component can expressly request to be in focus by calling the method `requestFocus`. For this request to succeed, the window in which the component lies must be the active window. A particular component can also define a listener that listens to the events `focusGained` and `focusLost`.

The component currently in focus can listen to all keyboard events, that is, events of class `KeyEvent`. To track such events, we have to create a listener that implements the interface `KeyListener`, or one that belongs to a subclass of class `KeyAdapter`. There are three different kinds of keyboard events: `keyPressed`, `keyReleased` and `keyTyped`.

---

java.awt.event.KeyEvent

Events of class `KeyEvent` are guided to the component that has focus.
This component must be found in the active window.
A component can call the method `requestFocus` to get focus.

`getKeyCode()`	gives the key number (virtual key code) upon `keyPressed` and `keyReleased` events
`VK_name`	constant with the key number for the key *name*
`getKeyText(n)`	translates the key number n to a text
`getKeyChar()`	gives a generated character (a `char`) upon `keyTyped` events
`getComponent()`	gives the GUI component in which the mouse finds itself
`isAltDown()`	indicates whether the user held down the Alt key
`isControlDown()`	indicates whether the user held down the Ctrl key
`isMetaDown()`	indicates whether the user held down the Meta key
`isShiftDown()`	indicates whether the user held down the Shift key

The first two are always generated when a key is pressed or released. The event `keyTyped` is generated if a key (or a combination of keys), which would have produced a visible character in an ordinary text window, is pressed. Note that `keyPressed` and `keyReleased` are always generated, even if the event `keyTyped` is also generated.

To demonstrate how this works, we shall construct a listener `l` that listens to all the kinds of key events. We connect this listener to a component with the statement:

```
addKeyListener(l);
```

In the listener, we will use the following methods defined in the class `KeyEvent`. The method `getKeyCode` gives a key number, a whole number that is unique for each key. This key number is called a "virtual key code". The method `getKeyCode` can be used when we track events such as `keyPressed` and `keyReleased` to find out which key was involved. There are also a number of whole number constants with different key numbers defined in class `KeyEvent`. All of these have a name beginning with `VK_`, for example, `VK_SPACE`, `VK_F3`, `VK_J` and `VK_9`, corresponding to a space, F3, the J key and the 9 key. We can use these constants when we wish to check which key was pressed or released. For instance, to check whether the user pressed the Enter key or the Tab key, we can write:

```
if (e.getKeyCode() == KeyEvent.VK_ENTER ||
    e.getKeyCode() == KeyEvent.VK_TAB)
```

(`e` is the parameter of the listener method here, that is, an object of class `KeyEvent`.) There is also a class method called `getKeyText` in the class `KeyEvent`. This gets a key number as parameter and translates this to a text with the name of the keys.

The method `getKeyCode` cannot be used for `keyTyped` events. The user may, of course, need to press two or more keys to generate a particular key character. (For instance, we use the Shift key and a letter key to generate a capital letter.) For `keyTyped` events, on the other hand, we can use the method `getKeyChar`. This will return a **char** indicating which key character was generated by pressure on the keys.

The methods `isAltDown`, `isControlDown`, `isMetaDown` and `isShiftDown`, inherited from class `InputEvent`, can be used to check whether one of the control keys was pressed.

We can now look at our listener `l`. It will display a message in the text window for every keyboard event and this will continue until the user presses the Esc key or Alt-Q. The program will then be terminated.

```
KeyListener l = new KeyAdapter() {
   public void keyPressed(KeyEvent e) {
      System.out.println("The " +
         KeyEvent.getKeyText(e.getKeyCode()) + " key was pressed");
      if (e.getKeyCode() == KeyEvent.VK_ESCAPE ||
```

```
        (e.getKeyCode() == KeyEvent.VK_Q && e.isAltDown()))
      System.exit(0);
  }

  public void keyReleased(KeyEvent e) {
    System.out.println("The " +
      KeyEvent.getKeyText(e.getKeyCode()) + " key was released");
  }

  public void keyTyped(KeyEvent e) {
    System.out.println("The " + e.getKeyChar() +
                       " character was generated");
    if (e.isAltDown())
      System.out.println("     ALT down");
    if (e.isControlDown())
      System.out.println("     CTRL down");
    if (e.isMetaDown())
      System.out.println("     Meta down");
    if (e.isShiftDown())
      System.out.println("     Shift down");
  }
};
```

Let us suppose that the user does the following: presses the PgUp key, presses the
7 key, holds the Shift key down and presses the 5 key, holds the Alt key down and
presses the G key, presses the F5 key and presses the Q key while holding down the
Alt key. Then the following text will be written out when the program is run.

```
The Page Up key was pressed
The Page Up key was released
The 7 key was pressed
The 7 character was generated
The 7 key was released
The Shift key was pressed
The 5 key was pressed
The % character was generated
   Shift down
The 5 key was released
The Shift key was released
The Alt key was pressed
The G key was pressed
The g character was generated
   Alt down
The G key was released
The Alt key was released
The F5 key was pressed
The F5 key was released
The Alt key was pressed
The Q key was pressed
```

From this we can see that we should listen to `keyPressed` and `keyReleased` events if we are interested in key presses and key releases and to `keyTyped` events when we are interested not in the key presses themselves but in the characters they generate.

As mentioned above, the Tab and Shift-Tab keys can be used to shift focus from one component to another. Programs frequently have more than one button, which the user can choose between. One then wants to be able to press the Enter key instead of clicking with the mouse. To achieve this, we can link listeners to the buttons that should be selectable in this way. We will start by creating a listener for keyboard events:

```
// Listener that makes it possible to click on a button
// using the Enter key
KeyListener enterListener = new KeyAdapter() {
   public void keyPressed(KeyEvent e) {
      if (e.getKeyCode() == KeyEvent.VK_ENTER &&
          e.getSource() instanceof AbstractButton)
         ((AbstractButton) e.getSource()).doClick();
   }
};
```

This listener can then be linked to an arbitrary number of buttons. For example, to link to a button `b`, you write

```
b.addKeyListener(enterListener);
```

The listener is called if you press any key when one of the linked buttons is in focus. In the listener, we check whether the Enter key has been pressed, and if the component is any kind of button. If this is the case, we call method `doClick` for the button, which has the same effect as if we had clicked the button with the mouse.

13.7 An advanced example – a game of tennis

In order to demonstrate how we can use listeners in a program employing multiple threads and displaying moving figures, we will construct a program that plays a game very much like tennis. The program will display a window that looks like Figure 13.2.

The game is played by two players, each of whom wields a racket, indicated by the black vertical lines on the short sides. Each player can move his or her racket up or down. The player on the right will use the keys ↑ and ↓, and the player on the left will use the A and Z keys as "up" and "down" keys.

A red ball bounces back and forth (and up and down) in the playing area, and each player has to hit the ball with the racket so that the ball does not touch the player's short side. If this does happen, the opponent gets a point. The point is displayed at the side of the playing area. When play begins, the ball travels relatively slowly from the left

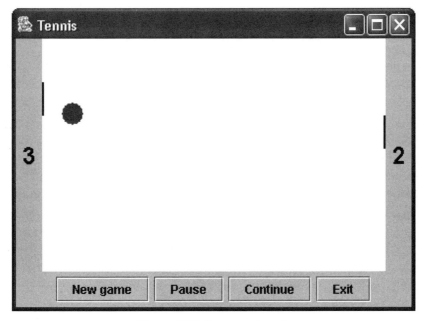

Figure 13.2 A game of tennis

but every time a player is able to hit the ball, its speed increases, making it more difficult to hit. The speed of the ball increases until one of the players misses it and it bounces against one of the short sides. The ball then returns to the speed it had at the beginning of the game. The game begins when we click on the "New game" button. A game is interrupted automatically when one of the players has reached 10 points. A game can be temporarily interrupted if the "Pause" button is clicked and continued when the "Continue" button is clicked. The actual game played can be interrupted and a new game begun instead, by clicking on the "New game" button.

There is an aspect of the program that is not obvious from the figure. The playing area's width and length can be changed at any time by dragging on the window. So the game can be made easier or more difficult, and play will be adjusted automatically to continue on the altered "court".

We will begin by describing the class Tennis, which will construct the window itself. The window contains four basic components: two JLabel objects that display the points, an object of class TennisCourt and a panel. The panel in turn contains four buttons. BorderLayout is used in the window. The JLabel objects are placed in the east and west positions, the panel is placed in the south, and the "court" in the centre.

We have defined the class TennisCourt ourselves. It is a subclass of the standard class JPanel and, in addition, describes an active object. It has four methods called from outside. The first one is the method init, which must be called before the first game is begun. It will have two arguments, references to the JLabel objects that will display the points. The other three methods are newGame, which sets the points to zero and starts a new game, stopGame, which temporarily stops the game, and startGame, which restarts a game. We shall return to class TennisCourt soon.

A listener is needed in class Tennis for the event actionPerformed, which occurs when the players click on a button. As usual, we arrange for the class itself to be the listener and define the method actionPerformed. The methods in class TennisCourt are called in this method. Note that requestFocus is called when the user has clicked on a button, so that the "court" will be in focus. This is important as otherwise we could not be certain that the court would recognize when the players pressed the keys.

```java
import java.awt.*;
import java.awt.event.*;
import javax.swing.*;

public class Tennis extends JFrame
                    implements ActionListener {
    private TennisCourt court = new TennisCourt();
    private JLabel points1 = new JLabel("0", JLabel.CENTER);
    private JLabel points2 = new JLabel("0", JLabel.CENTER);
    private JPanel pan = new JPanel();
    private JButton[] b = new JButton[4];
    private String[] s ={"New game","Pause","Continue","Exit"};

    public Tennis() {
        setTitle("Tennis");
        court.setPreferredSize(new Dimension(350,250));
        court.setBackground(Color.white);
        points1.setFont(new Font("SansSerif", Font.BOLD, 24));
        points2.setFont(new Font("SansSerif", Font.BOLD, 24));
        pan.setLayout(new FlowLayout());
        for (int i=0; i<b.length; i++) {
            b[i] = new JButton();
            b[i].setText(s[i]);
            b[i].addActionListener(this);
            pan.add(b[i]);
        }
        Container c = getContentPane();
        c.add(court, BorderLayout.CENTER);
        c.add(points1, BorderLayout.WEST);
        c.add(points2, BorderLayout.EAST);
        c.add(pan, BorderLayout.SOUTH);

        pack();
        court.init(points1, points2);
        setVisible(true);
    }
```

```
  public void actionPerformed(ActionEvent e) {
    court.requestFocus();
    if (e.getSource() == b[0])
      court.newGame();
    else if (e.getSource() == b[1])
      court.stopGame();
    else if (e.getSource() == b[2])
      court.startGame();
    else if (e.getSource() == b[3])
      System.exit(0);
  }

  public static void main(String[] arg) {
    Tennis s = new Tennis();
  }
}
```

The class `TennisCourt` becomes somewhat more complicated. We start by showing it in its entirety, and then make some comments.

```
class TennisCourt extends JPanel implements ActionListener {
  private Timer tim = new Timer(100, this);
  private JLabel points1, points2; // to display points
  private int p1, p2;              // actual points
  private int xMax, yMax;          // highest x and y coordinates
  private int r, x0, y0;           // the ball's radius and centre point
  private int xStep, yStep;        // the ball's "step" length
  private int v, v0 = 5;           // the ball's speed
  private int rLeft, rRight,       // the y coordinate for the
                                   // racket's upper edge
            rL, rStep;             // the racket's length and "step"

  public void init(JLabel l1, JLabel l2) {
    points1 = l1; points2 = l2;
    xMax = getSize().width-1;
    yMax = getSize().height-1;
    r   = yMax/20;    // compute the ball's radius
    rL = 3*r;         // compute the racket's length
    rStep = r;        // compute the racket's "step" length
    addKeyListener(kl);          // listen to the keyboard and
    addComponentListener(cl);    // changes in the court's size
    clear();
  }

  private void clear() {
    p1 = p2 = 0;    // set points to zero
    points1.setText(" 0 "); points2.setText(" 0 ");
    xStep = yStep = v = v0 = 5;  // speed at the beginning
    x0 = r + 1;                  // place the ball on the left side
```

```
    y0 = yMax/2;                     // in the middle of the short side
    rLeft= rRight = yMax/2-rL/2; //place the rackets in the middle
}

public void startGame() {
  tim.start();
}

public void stopGame() {
  tim.stop();
}

public void newGame() {
  stopGame();
  clear();
  startGame();
}

public void actionPerformed(ActionEvent e) {
  // we get here each 100th ms, called by the timer
  if (x0-r <= 0)  { // is the ball at the side on the left?
    if (y0 < rLeft || y0 > rLeft+rL) { // a miss?
      Toolkit.getDefaultToolkit().beep();    // beep
      points2.setText(" " + String.valueOf(++p2) + " ");
      if (p2 == 10) stopGame();
      v = v0;  // return to the speed at the beginning
    }
    else         // a hit
       v++;       // increase the speed
    xStep = v; // move to the right next time
  }
  else if (x0 + r>=xMax) {  // at the side on the right?
    if (y0 < rRight || y0 > rRight+rL) { // a miss?
      Toolkit.getDefaultToolkit().beep();    // beep
      points1.setText(" " + String.valueOf(++p1) + " ");
      if (p1 == 10) stopGame();
      v = v0;    // return to the speed at the beginning
    }
    else         // a hit
       v++;       // increase the speed
    xStep = -v; // move to the left next time
  }
  if (y0-r<=0 || y0+r>=yMax)  // at upper or lower edge?
     yStep = -yStep;            // change vertical direction
  x0 += xStep;  // move the ball horizontally
  y0 += yStep;  // move the ball vertically
  if (x0 < r)    // did the ball land too far to the left?
    x0 = r;
  else if (x0 > xMax-r)  // too far to the right?
    x0 = xMax-r+1;
```

```
    if (y0 < r)                 // did the ball land too far up?
      y0 = r;
    else if (y0 > yMax-r)  // did the ball land too far down?
      y0 = yMax-r+1;
    repaint();
  }

  public void paintComponent(Graphics g) {
    super.paintComponent(g);
    g.setColor(Color.red);
    g.fillOval(x0-r, y0-r, 2*r, 2*r);  // draw the ball
    g.setColor(Color.black);
    g.fillRect(0, rLeft, 2, rL);  // draw the racket on the left
    g.fillRect(xMax-1, rRight, 2, rL);  // draw the racket
                                        // on the right
  }

  KeyListener kl = new KeyAdapter() {
    public void keyPressed(KeyEvent e) {
      // a key has been pressed
      if (e.getKeyCode() == KeyEvent.VK_A)        // left up
        rLeft = Math.max(0, rLeft-rStep);
      else if (e.getKeyCode() == KeyEvent.VK_Z)   // left down
        rLeft = Math.min(yMax-rL, rLeft+rStep);
      if (e.getKeyCode() == KeyEvent.VK_UP)        // right up
        rRight = Math.max(0, rRight-rStep);
      else if (e.getKeyCode() == KeyEvent.VK_DOWN) // right down
        rRight = Math.min(yMax-rL, rRight+rStep);
    }
  };

  ComponentListener cl = new ComponentAdapter() {
    public void componentResized(ComponentEvent e) {
      // the size of the court has been changed
      xMax = e.getComponent().getSize().width-1;
      yMax = e.getComponent().getSize().height-1;
      e.getComponent().requestFocus();
      repaint();
    }
  };
}
```

Since we are dealing with a moving game, we let the court be an active object. The class `TennisCourt` will therefore follow the model from Section 12.1. This means that there is an instance variable `time` that refers to an object of class `javax.swing.Timer`. Class `TennisCourt` must also have a listener method called `actionPerformed` that is called by the timer. Each time this method is called the ball is moved. The instance variables `xStep` and `yStep` indicate the number of pixels the ball will move each time.

Similarly, the instance variable `rStep` indicates the number of pixels a racket can move up or down each time a player presses an "up" or a "down" key.

All the initializations that only have to be done once, each time the program is run, are made in the method `init`. For instance, the size of the ball and the rackets are computed from the size of the court. The reason for using a method `init` and not a constructor to carry out these initializations is that we must be able to read the size of the court. This cannot be done in a constructor, since the size is still unknown.

The method `clear` is called before each new game. The points for both of the players are set at zero, and the two rackets are put in the middle of the short sides.

The methods `startGame` and `stopGame` are simple. They only start or stop the timer. The method `newGame` is easy to construct. It only has to stop a game in session, set the points to zero and then start the game.

The method `actionPerformed` is the most complicated one here. It is called by the timer every hundredth millisecond. Then new coordinates are computed for the ball. A check is made to see whether the ball has reached one of the sides before it is moved. First, the sides on the left and the right are checked; if the ball is on one of these sides, there are two cases to consider. In the first case, the racket is not at the place where the ball hits the side. The opponent then gets a point, and the ball is given the speed it had at the beginning. To indicate clearly that one of the players has missed the ball, the program will emit a "beep". If, however, the racket is at the place where the ball hits the side, the speed of the ball is increased by one pixel per "step". If the ball hits the side, its direction must also be changed so that it is made to bounce.

When the method `actionPerformed` has checked whether the ball is to be found at one of the sides, it changes the ball's x and y coordinates. When these changes have been carried out, a small adjustment has to be made if parts of the ball should finish up outside the court. In this case, the ball is placed so that it is precisely at the side. Each call of the method `actionPerformed` is terminated with the method `repaint` being called so that the court can be redrawn with the ball in its new position.

Two listeners are needed in class `TennisCourt`. The listener `k1` listens to events generated by keys being pressed. We use the technique of anonymous listener classes and define the method `keyPressed`, which is called when a key is pressed. (We shall not worry about when keys are released.) A check is made in this method to see whether the key pressed is one of the four used as "up" and "down" keys. If it is, the corresponding racket is moved a step up or down. However, we have to be careful that we do not move a racket either above or below the court. This is most easily done using the methods `max` and `min` in the standard class `Math`.

We have defined the method `componentResized` in the other listener `c1`. This is called automatically if the user drags on the window, so that the size of the court is changed. If this happens, the variables `xMax` and `yMax` must be updated and the window redrawn.

This concludes our description of the tennis program. Of course, it was a little complicated but this was because we used several different techniques and combined them. We trust that it will serve as a model for other, similar programs.

13.8 Actions

When we have discussed how event-driven programs function, we have mainly focused on GUI components up to now. For example, we have said that "when the user clicks button B, the following will happen". One example is program TextEdit on page 211. During this discussion, we said "If you click the button Save the program will save the text displayed in the text area to the specified file". It is possible to turn the discussion round, however, and focus on the *actions* that the program must be able to carry out. For the program TextEditor we could say that "The program can save the text displayed in the text area to a file. In the program, we have chosen to link a button entitled Save to this action". This alternative way of reasoning is more flexible. The reason is that we can link several GUI components to the same action. In the program TextEditor, there could be a menu that contains the choice Save, in addition to the Save button. The person who used the program would then be able to carry out the action *Save* by either clicking the button Save or by selecting the menu choice Save. We could even link a particular keyboard shortcut to the action. In the program TextEditor we could link the keyboard shortcut Ctrl-S to the action *Save*. The person who used the program would then be able to save the text by pressing Ctrl-S on the keyboard.

An action in Java should be an object that belongs to a class that implements the interface Action. There is a ready-made class, AbstractAction, which you can utilize when you want to create your own actions. This class contains all the methods needed, except for method actionPerformed. This means that you must define the method actionPerformed yourself when you create subclasses of AbstractAction. To avoid having to define a complete subclass with constructors, it is easiest to make use of an anonymous subclass of AbstractAction and declare the Action object at once. For example, to declare an Action object called saveAction that describes the action *Save* in the program TextEditor we write:

```
Action saveAction = new AbstractAction() {
   public void actionPerformed(ActionEvent e) {
      try {
         FileWriter w = new FileWriter(namn.getText());
         area.write(w);
      }
      catch (IOException ie) {}
   }
};
```

In method `actionPerformed` there is the code that does the actual action. (We remember that in the program `TextEditor` the `name` is the text field in which the user has written the file name and `area` is the text area where the text is displayed.)

We can then link this action to any buttons we want to in the program. Assume that, as previously in program `TextEditor`, we had wanted a button called `save`:

```
JButton save = new JButton();
```

We now want to link an action to button `saveAction`. For this reason, we write

```
save.setAction(saveAction);
save.setText("Save");
```

When we link an action to a button, the action will automatically become a listener to the button. (In the program `TextEditor` we will thus remove the listener for button `save` and also remove the method `saveFile`.)

When you create an `Action` object you can supply a text and an icon which relates to the action as a parameter for the constructor. For example, we could have written

```
Action saveAction = new AbstractAction("Save") {
    etc.
```

or

```
Action saveAction = new AbstractAction("Save",
                                new ImageIcon("save.gif") {
    etc.
```

When you call method `setAction` for a button, the button is automatically given the text and the icon which have been defined for the event. If we had not defined any text or icon, the button would also lack text and an icon. In this case, we have to set them afterwards by using methods `setText` and `setIcon`, as we did above.

The method `setAction` is defined in class `AbstractButton`, so it can be used for all kinds of buttons and menu choices. (We have not considered menu choices yet, but they are a kind of button that inherits properties from class `AbstractButton`.) For example, if we had a menu choice called `saveItem`, we would have been able to link the action to this button as well, using the statements

```
saveItem.setAction(saveAction);
saveAction.setText("Save");
```

For actions, there is a method `setEnabled` which can be called to report whether an action should be activated or not. In the program `TextEditor` we could have wanted the action `saveAction` to be deactivated in the beginning, until there is something to save. We could then have added the following line to the program:

```
saveAction.setEnabled(false);
```

One neat property of actions is that when you call `SetEnabled`, all the buttons linked to the action in question are automatically activated. The buttons are automatically redrawn so that they show whether they are activated or not.

The Action interface

One that implements the interface `Action`. Describes an event.
Create an `Action` object by using the abstract class `AbstractAction` and define the method `actionPerformed` yourself:

```
Action a = new AbstractAction() {
   public void actionPerformed(ActionEvent e) {
      ...
   }
};
```

or

```
Action a = new AbstractAction(txt) { etc.
Action a = new AbstractAction(txt, icon) { etc.
```

`a.setEnabled(bool)`	specifies whether the action should be activated or not
`a.isEnabled()`	shows if the action is activated
`a.putValue(txt, obj)`	stores the object `obj` under the name `txt` in `a`
`a.getValue(txt)`	gives the object which is stored in `a` under the name `txt`
`b.setAction(a)`	links the action `a` to the button `b`

As shown in the fact box, the `Action` object has two methods `putValue` and `getValue`. These can be used to get an `Action` object to "remember" any property. A property has type `Object`, so you can store any type of property at all. If you want to store a property for an `Action` object, you just find a name for the property. You give this name in the form of a text which stores the property. You can use the name later on when you want to read the property.

We will also show how we can link a keyboard shortcut to an event. (This is a bit complicated, unfortunately.) Assume that in program `TextEditor` we want to be able to press Ctrl-S to save. To achieve this, we add the following lines to the program:

```
area.getInputMap().put(KeyStroke.getKeyStroke(KeyEvent.VK_S,
                        ActionEvent.CTRL_MASK), "save");
area.getActionMap().put("save", saveAction);
```

The first statement says that when the user presses the keys Ctrl-S an event should be created, called `"save"`. (You can invent any name you want for an action.) The second line says that this action should be performed by `Action` object `saveAction`. In the first statement there is a call to method `getKeyStroke`. We specify the relevant keyboard combination in this call. The details are shown in the fact box.

Connection of keyboard shortcuts to Action objects

To link the action `a` (of type `Action`) to a keyboard shortcut when the component `c` (of type `JComponent`) is in focus:

```
c.getInputMap().put(KeyStroke.getKeyStroke
                              (key, against), "name");
c.getActionMap().put("name", a);
```

This can also apply when `c` is not in focus if we write the first statement as

```
c.getInputMap(condition).put(KeyStroke.getKeyStroke
                              (key, against), "name");
```

key	should be `KeyEvent.VK_?`, where ? is the relevant key
against	should be `ActionEvent.ALT_MASK`, `ActionEvent.CTRL_MASK`, `ActionEvent.META_MASK`, `ActionEvent.SHIFT_MASK` or 0
name	a name you give to the keyboard shortcut
condition	should be `JComponent.WHEN_IN_FOCUSED_WINDOW`, or `JComponent.WHEN_ANCESTOR_OF_FOCUSED_COMPONENT`

Please note that the statements above are done for the component `area`. This means that the keyboard shortcut is linked to the action `saveAction` only when the component `area` is in focus. However, we can give a parameter to the method `getInputMap`. This parameter specifies when the link should apply. (Please refer to the fact box.)

As we know, we can usually use keyboard shortcuts to cut, copy and paste text in components that display editable text. In Swing, this can be done in all components that belong to one of the subclasses of `JTextComponent`, such as in a `JTextArea` component. For all these components, there is actually a number of pre-defined `Action` objects which are linked to the keyboard shortcut. This means that as a programmer, you do not have to create an action and link it to keyboard shortcut Ctrl-X, for instance. This action has already been defined. In most cases, such as in a text editor, you would want to let the user cut, copy and paste text, not just by using a keyboard shortcut but also by using a menu choice or by clicking a button. To permit this, we will have to link the pre-defined actions to the relevant menu choices or buttons in the program. We will show how this can be done here. Assume that in program `TextEditor` we have defined the following three buttons:

```
JButton cut = new JButton();
JButton copy = new JButton();
JButton paste = new JButton();
```

and we want to link the pre-defined actions for cutting, copying and pasting to these buttons. For each component, there is a table, a so-called `ActionMap`, which contains the names of the actions which are defined for the components. For each action name, the table contains a reference to the `Action` object which will carry out the action. On the following line, we define a variable `m` and let it refer to the action map for the component `area`.

```
ActionMap m = area.getActionMap();
```

We have previously used method `put` to insert a new action into the table. We are now going to use method `get` instead, to find references to the `Action` object which carries out the actions of cut, copy and paste. We must then know the names used for these actions in the table. These names are defined in class `DefaultEditorKit` (which is defined in package `javax.swing.text`). The name for the cut action is `cutAction`, for example. Using this, we can now read the references to the three actions and link them to our buttons.

```
cut   .setAction(m.get(DefaultEditorKit.cutAction));
copy  .setAction(m.get(DefaultEditorKit.copyAction));
paste.setAction(m.get(DefaultEditorKit.pasteAction));
```

The only thing that remains now is to put in the texts we want, or the icons on the buttons. For example, we could write

```
cut.setText("Cut");
copy.setText("Copy");
paste.setText("Paste");
```

We will finish off with an example that demonstrates how you can write flexible programs by using actions. We will implement a new version of the program `JButtonDemo` on page 176. This time the window will look as in Figure 13.3. The user is free to choose the language that the greeting is written in by clicking either a flag or

Figure 13.3 JButtonDemo

a button. The flag and the button for the language in question will then automatically be deactivated. The program has been designed so that it will be easy to add further languages. The program has the following appearance:

```java
import java.awt.*;
import java.awt.event.*;   // contains listener classes
import javax.swing.*;

public class JButtonDemo extends JFrame {
  private String[][] txt =
    {{"English", "flag_eng.gif", "Welcome!"},
     {"Deutsch", "flag_ger.gif", "Willkommen!"},
     {"Français", "flag_fra.gif", "Bienvenue!"},
     {"Svenska", "flag_swe.gif", "Välkommen!"}};

  private JButton[] b = new JButton[txt.length];
  private JButton[] f = new JButton[txt.length];
  private Action[] a = new Action[txt.length];
  private JLabel  lab = new JLabel();

  public JButtonDemo() { // constructor
    Container c = getContentPane();
    JPanel p1 = new JPanel();    // panel for buttons
    JPanel p2 = new JPanel();    // panel for flags
    c.add(p1, BorderLayout.NORTH);
    c.add(p2, BorderLayout.SOUTH);
    c.add(lab, BorderLayout.CENTER);
    c.setBackground(Color.white);
    lab.setHorizontalAlignment(JLabel.CENTER);
    lab.setFont(new Font("SansSerif", Font.ITALIC, 20));
    lab.setPreferredSize(new Dimension(100, 70));

    // one round for each language
    for (int i=0; i<b.length; i++) {
      // create an Action object for language no. i
      a[i] = new AbstractAction() {
        public void actionPerformed(ActionEvent e) {
          lab.setText((String) getValue("wel"));
          for (int j=0; j<a.length; j++)
            a[j].setEnabled(true);   // activate all actions
          setEnabled(false);   // deactivate this action
        }
      };

      // store text in the Action object
      a[i].putValue("wel", txt[i][2]);
      // create two buttons for language no. i
      b[i] = new JButton();
      f[i] = new JButton();
      p1.add(b[i]); p2.add(f[i]);
```

```
      // connect the Action object to the buttons
      b[i].setAction(a[i]);
      f[i].setAction(a[i]);

      // text and icon must be set AFTER the call of setAction
      b[i].setText(txt[i][0]);
      f[i].setIcon(new ImageIcon(txt[i][1]));
   }
   b[0].doClick();    // English from the beginning

   pack();
   setVisible(true);
   setDefaultCloseOperation(EXIT_ON_CLOSE);
   }

   public static void main (String[] arg) {
      JButtonDemo j = new JButtonDemo();
   }
}
```

The first thing declared in the class is an array `txt` which contains an element for each language. Each element consists of three texts in its turn, which specify the text on the button, the name of the image file containing the flag, and the greeting text. All that is needed to add more languages to the program is to add further lines to the array `txt`.

After this, two arrays containing buttons are declared. Each array has the same number of elements as the number of languages. Array `b` contains the buttons with the language names and array `f` contains the buttons with flags. In addition, an array `a` is declared containing actions (`Action` object). There are the same number of actions as there are languages, and each action should describe the measures needed to change to the relevant language.

The constructor contains a **for** statement which runs one lap for each language. An action is created for each language, which is put in the array `a`. Before we discuss how the actions are performed, we will study the code after the definition of the actions. For each action `a[i]` the method `putValue` is used to get the action to "remember" the text that should be displayed for the appropriate language. The texts are retrieved from the array `txt`. The action `a[0]`, for example, remembers the text `"Welcome!"` and the action `a[3]` text `"Välkommen!"`.

When this has been done, two buttons are created for the relevant language, button `b[i]`, which should display the language name, and a button `f[i]`, which should display a flag. The buttons with names are placed on a panel `p1` and the buttons with flags on another panel `p2`. The two buttons are then linked to the action for the current language and they are initialized so that they contain the correct text or image. The information is taken from the array `txt`.

Let us return to discussing how the actions are defined. We define our own version of method `actionPerformed`. In this method, we put the text first, which will be displayed in the greeting. Since we previously let the action "remember" the text, it can be retrieved with the aid of method `getValue`. After this, all the actions are activated. All buttons, both the ones containing text and the ones containing flags, are then drawn so that it shows they are activated. However, we then deactivate the action for the current language, which means that the buttons for this language will be displayed in deactivated format.

The last thing done in the constructor, after the actions and buttons have been created, is to call method `doClick` for button `b[0]`. The action `a[0]` will then be carried out. This leads to the greeting being displayed in English when the program is started.

13.9 Exercises

1. Assume that you have a class `F` which is a subclass of another class, `JFrame`. An object of class `F` can thus contain other components. Also assume that one of these components, a component called `first`, must always come into focus each time the window in question becomes active. Construct a listener for class `F` which ensures that component `first` is always in focus each time the window in question becomes active. Then construct a listener for component `first` which automatically makes the component's background colour blue each time the component is in focus.

2. Write a listener which can be linked to a button, a `JButton` object, which automatically makes the button's background colour red when the cursor is over the button.

3. The class `Component` has a method `setCursor` which can be used to change the appearance of the cursor. The argument for this method should be an object of class `Cursor`, which is also defined in package `java.awt`. In the class `Cursor` there is a class method `getPredefinedCursor` which returns a `Cursor` object. The argument of `getPredefinedCursor` should be an integer which specifies the appearance of the cursor. In the class `Cursor` there are a number of pre-defined integer constants that can be used. Some examples are `TEXT_CURSOR`, `HAND_CURSOR`, `WAIT_CURSOR` and `DEFAULT_CURSOR`.

    Construct a listener which automatically changes the appearance of the cursor so that it looks like a hand each time the mouse is moved to the component.

4. Complete the class `Painter` on page 422 so that you can cancel a line you have drawn. If you press the keys Ctrl-Z, the last line drawn should be deleted.

5. Several improvements to the tennis program in Section 13.7 could be imagined. When you have started a new game, for example, the ball is always in the centre

of the left-hand side and the ball always starts to move diagonally down to the right. Change this so that the ball ends up at random on the left or right side, and randomly goes upwards or downwards. The vertical position of the ball should also be random.

6. Another improvement to the tennis program, in addition to the one in Exercise 5, is as follows. Change it so that instead of having one button with text "New game", there are two buttons, one with the text "One player" and another with the text "Two players". When the user clicks the "Two players" button, the game should function as before, but when the user clicks the "One player" button, the left-hand player is replaced by the computer. The program should then automatically move the left-hand racket so that it always hits. Since the human player will then never get any points, there is no point in showing them. Instead, you should let the right-hand `JLabel` object show how many times the human player succeeded in hitting the ball before he or she lost at 10−0. The number of hits then becomes a measure of the skill of the player.

Menus, windows and dialogs

14

In Chapter 6 we discussed many different kinds of standard graphical components, but we did not deal with menus. We have deliberately waited until this chapter to look at menus. In this chapter, we will also study how to locate a tool bar in a window.

All the examples we have studied to date have used only one window on the screen, but sometimes you will have programs that need several windows. A text editor, for example, may need to have several text files open in separate windows at the same time for editing. This is easy to achieve in Java, and we will discuss how it's done in this chapter. We will also discuss how to create internal windows, that is, windows that are positioned inside a surrounding window. A special type of window is the dialog box. We have used dialogs in many places in this book, but in this chapter we will discuss different ways of creating dialogs in more detail.

14.1 Menus

In Swing there is a collection of classes with which you can construct menus. You can locate menus either on a menu bar at the top of the window, as is most common, or as a standalone popup menu that is displayed when you click a specific mouse button. Each menu can have an arbitrary number of menu items and one menu item can in turn be a new menu, called a sub-menu. It is also possible to define keyboard shortcuts so that certain combinations of key presses, for example Alt-C and Alt-X, select a specified menu item. Figure 14.1 shows the classes used to describe buttons and menus. We can see that the class JMenuItem, which is used to describe menu items, is a subclass of the class AbstractButton. This means that menu items are actually a kind of button in that they function in roughly the same way as components of the class JButton.

Figure 14.1 Menu classes

443

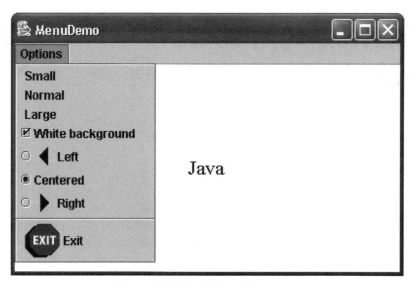

Figure 14.2 A window with a menu

14.1.1 Menu bars, menus and menu items

As an example, in this section we will construct the "Options" menu shown in Figure 14.2. With this menu, you can change the size and layout of text in a window. It will also be possible to choose a white or grey background.

You put a menu bar into a window. You do this by first declaring a `JMenuBar` object and then linking it to the window. You can put an arbitrary number of menus on the menu bar. We will start by defining the menu bar and the menus.

```
JMenuBar mb = new JMenuBar();
JMenu iMen  = new JMenu("Options");
```

We put the menu bar into the window and link the menus to the menu bar:

```
setJMenuBar(mb);
mb.add(iMen);
```

If you want, you can leave out the declaration of the variable `mb` and instead write:

```
setJMenuBar(new JMenuBar());
getJMenuBar().add(iMen);
```

A window can have only one menu bar, but you can put many menus onto the menu bar by invoking the method `add` many times. The menus are then positioned from left to right. If you want to put a help menu on the furthest right, instead of using the method `add` you can use the method `setHelpMenu`.

It's interesting to note that the class JMenuBar is a subclass of JComponent. This means that in actual fact you can locate menus anywhere you like in a window. For example, if you want to have the menu at the bottom of the window, you can use BorderLayout in the window and place the menu bar in the position SOUTH. You can also locate other components on a menu bar in addition to menu items.

JMenuBar

Inherit all characteristics from JComponent (see page 161).
Additionally has the following methods:

add(*c*)	puts the component c (e.g., a JMenu) on the menu
setHelpMenu(*m*)	locates the menu *m* furthest to the right on the menu bar
getMenuCount()	gives the number of menus on the menu bar
getMenu(*i*)	gives the menu number *i*
getHelpMenu()	gives the Help menu
setBorderPainted(*bool*)	specifies that a border is to be drawn around the bar

---

Once you have a menu, you can put a number of menu items on to it. Menu items are described by the class JMenuItem. Since this is a subclass of the class AbstractButton, the components of the class JMenuItem have all the characteristics shown in the fact box on page 179.

JMenuItem

Inherits all characteristics from the classes JComponent (page 161) and AbstractButton (page 179).

new JMenuItem()	creates a JMenuItem
new JMenuItem(txt)	creates a JMenuItem with the text txt
new JMenuItem(ic)	creates a JMenuItem with the icon ic
new JMenuItem(txt,ic)	creates a JMenuItem with the text txt and the icon ic
new JMenuItem(txt,KeyEvent.VK_X)	creates a JMenuItem with the tex txt and the keyboard shortcut Alt-X
new JMenuItem(a)	creates a JMenuItem with from the Action object a

---

Below we show how to create the first two items on the menu "Options" shown in Figure 14.2.

```
JMenuItem small  = new JMenuItem("Small");
JMenuItem normal = new JMenuItem("Normal");
```

Menu items can be added to the menu using the method `add`:

```
iMen.add(small); iMen.add(normal);
```

Alternatively, you can create and add menu items at the same time by writing:

```
JMenuItem small  = iMen.add("Small");
JMenuItem normal = iMen.add("Normal");
```

Just like ordinary buttons, menu items can have images as icons. The last menu item in Figure 14.2, for example, is created with the declaration:

```
JMenuItem exit = new JMenuItem("Exit",
                                    new ImageIcon("exit.gif"));
```

The two classes `JCheckboxMenuItem` and `JRadioButtonMenuItem` are subclasses of the class `JMenuItem`. They have the same characteristics as the classes `JCheckBox` and `JRadioButton`. See the fact box on page 181. The menu item that specifies the background colour in Figure 14.2 is of the type `JCheckboxMenuItem`. It is created with the declaration:

```
JCheckBoxMenuItem backgr = new JCheckBoxMenuItem
                            ("White background", true);
```

Menu items of this type have a small marker that indicates if the item is selected/ checked or not. Each time you select this item, it toggles between being checked or not checked. You can specify the default choice for this menu item in the constructor.

JCheckBoxMenuItem and JRadioButtonMenuItem

Inherits all characteristics from the classes `JMenuItem`, `JComponent` (page 161) and `AbstractButton` (page 179). The constructor is described in the fact box on page 181.

Menu items that indicate how the text is to be laid out in Figure 14.2 are created with the lines:

```
JRadioButtonMenuItem le = new JRadioButtonMenuItem("Left",
                            new ImageIcon("left.gif"),false);
JRadioButtonMenuItem ce = new JRadioButtonMenuItem
                            ("Centered", true);
JRadioButtonMenuItem ri = new JRadioButtonMenuItem("Right",
                            new ImageIcon("right.gif"),false);
```

Here, we let the first and last items have an icon, while the second just has a text. When you have radio buttons, you usually link them together in a group so that only one item at a time can be selected. You do this using the class `ButtonGroup` in the same way as we did when we had buttons of the type `JRadioButton`. (See page 181.)

```
ButtonGroup g = new ButtonGroup();
g.add(le); g.add(ce);   g.add(ri);
```

We want to have a horizontal line as a separator between the two last choices in the menu in Figure 14.2, which you can see in the figure. You can achieve this by invoking the method `addSeparator`.

JMenu

Inherits all characteristics from the classes `JComponent` (page 161) and `AbstractButton` (page 179).

new `JMenu(h)`	creates a new menu with the heading *h*
`add(c)`	puts the component *c* (e.g., a `JMenuItem`) on to the menu
`add(txt)`	creates a `JMenuItem` with the text *txt* and puts it on to the menu, returns the created `JMenuItem` object
`add(a)`	creates a `JMenuItem` that is linked to the `Action` object *a* and puts it on to the menu, returns the `JMenuItem` object
`addSeparator()`	puts a horizontal line in the menu
`insertSeparator(i)`	inserts a horizontal line in the menu, at position no. *i*
`getItemCount()`	gives the number of items on the line
`getItem(i)`	gives the number of the item *i*

Because a menu item is a kind of button, you can connect a listener to it of the type `ActionListener` in the regular way.

We will now show the complete program that generates the window in Figure 14.2.

```
import java.awt.*;
import java.awt.event.*;
import javax.swing.*;

public class MenuDemo extends JFrame
                      implements ActionListener {
  JLabel l = new JLabel("Java", JLabel.CENTER);
  Font smallFont  = new Font("Serif", Font.PLAIN, 10);
  Font normalFont = new Font("Serif", Font.PLAIN, 20);
  Font largeFont  = new Font("Serif", Font.PLAIN, 30);

  JMenuBar mb = new JMenuBar();
  JMenu iMen  = new JMenu("Options");
  JMenuItem small  = new JMenuItem("Small");
  JMenuItem normal = new JMenuItem("Normal");
  JMenuItem large  = new JMenuItem("Large");

  JCheckBoxMenuItem backgr = new JCheckBoxMenuItem
                             ("White background", true);
```

```
JRadioButtonMenuItem le = new JRadioButtonMenuItem("Left",
                            new ImageIcon("left.gif"),false);
JRadioButtonMenuItem ce = new JRadioButtonMenuItem
                                        ("Centered", true);
JRadioButtonMenuItem ri = new JRadioButtonMenuItem("Right",
                            new ImageIcon("right.gif"),false);
JMenuItem exit = new JMenuItem("Exit",
                            new ImageIcon("exit.gif"));

public MenuDemo() {      // Constructor
  getContentPane().add(l, BorderLayout.CENTER);
  l.setFont(normalFont);
  l.setBackground(Color.white);
  l.setOpaque(true);

  // add a menu and menu items
  setJMenuBar(mb);
  mb.add(iMen);
  iMen.add(small); iMen.add(normal); iMen.add(large);
  iMen.add(backgr);
  iMen.add(le); iMen.add(ce); iMen.add(ri);
  iMen.addSeparator();
  iMen.add(exit);

  // let the radio buttons form a group
  ButtonGroup g = new ButtonGroup();
  g.add(le); g.add(ce);  g.add(ri);

  // connect listeners to the menu items
  small.addActionListener(this);
  normal.addActionListener(this);
  large.addActionListener(this);
  backgr.addActionListener(this);
  le.addActionListener(this);
  ce.addActionListener(this);
  ri.addActionListener(this);
  exit.addActionListener(this);

  setTitle("MenuDemo");
  setSize(400,260);
  setDefaultCloseOperation(EXIT_ON_CLOSE);
  setVisible(true);
}

// listener method
public void actionPerformed(ActionEvent e) {
  if (e.getSource() == small)
    l.setFont(smallFont);

  else if (e.getSource() == normal)
    l.setFont(normalFont);
  else if (e.getSource() == large)
    l.setFont(largeFont);
```

```
      else if (e.getSource() == backgr)
        if (backgr.isSelected())
           l.setBackground(Color.white);
        else
           l.setBackground(Color.lightGray);
      else if (e.getSource() == le)
        l.setHorizontalAlignment(JLabel.LEFT);
      else if (e.getSource() == ce)
        l.setHorizontalAlignment(JLabel.CENTER);
      else if (e.getSource() == ri)
        l.setHorizontalAlignment(JLabel.RIGHT);
      else if (e.getSource() == exit)
        System.exit(0);
   }
   public static void main(String[] arg) {
     new MenuDemo();
   }
}
```

A `JLabel` object with the text "Java" is placed in the window. Since `BorderLayout` is used, the `JLabel` object is centred, and it will fill out the whole window. For simplicity's sake, we have let the object itself be the listener for the menu items. If you have a program with several menus, however, there will be many menu items for the listener to listen for. In such a case, it is better to define separate listeners for each menu. This means that the listeners don't need to process items from several different menus. This makes the program clearer.

14.1.2 Sub-menus

A menu item can, in turn, be a whole new menu – a sub-menu. When the user selects one of these menu items, a sub-menu is displayed. To demonstrate how to construct sub-menus, we will expand the menu in Figure 14.2 so that it will end up looking like the one in Figure 14.3. A new menu item "Color" has been added, and when this item is selected, a sub-menu is shown where the user can select which colour is to be used when printing the text in the window.

When you define menu items, the program can generally be simplified if you don't declare each item separately but use an array instead. We will demonstrate how to do this here. We will start by defining two arrays: one that contains the texts to be displayed for the items in the new sub-menu, and one that is used to define the corresponding `Color` object:

```
String[] colTxt = {"Black", "Red", "Blue", "Green"};
Color[] col = {Color.black, Color.red, Color.blue, Color.green};
```

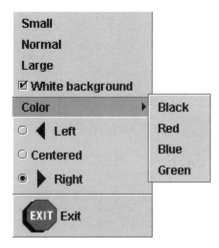

Figure 14.3 A menu with a sub-menu

We can now define the sub-menu and an array with references to the items the menu is to contain.

```
JMenu colMen= new JMenu("Color");
JMenuItem[] colItem = new JMenuItem[colTxt.length];
```

Note that we have not yet created the individual menu items. It's easiest to do this in the constructor in a `for` statement:

```
for (int i=0; i<colItem.length; i++) {
   colItem[i] = new JMenuItem(colTxt[i]);     // create menu item
   colMen.add(colItem[i]);                    // add to menu
   colItem[i].addActionListener(colListener); //connect listener
}
```

In the `for` statement, we also add the items in the menu and connect a listener to the menu items.

The new menu `colMen` is now complete. We could have added it as menu number two on the menu bar by writing the statement `mb.add(colMen)`, but instead we are going to place it as a sub-menu with the name "Color" on the original menu "Options". You do this with the following statement, which is inserted in the constructor:

```
iMen.insert(colMen, 4);
```

The item "Color" is placed as menu item number 4 (numbering starts at 0).

The only thing now remaining to do is to define the listener `colListener`, which will handle the events that occur when the user selects one of the items on the new menu. The listener will be as follows:

```
ActionListener colListener = new ActionListener() {
   public void actionPerformed(ActionEvent e) {
      for (int i=0; i<colItem.length; i++)
         if (e.getSource() == colItem[i])
      l.setForeground(col[i]);
   }
};
```

Because we are using an array, the listener can be made simple. It runs through all possible items on the colour menu and for each item listens to determine if it was this one the user clicked. If it was, the corresponding Color object is selected from the array col and specifies that the text is to be displayed in this colour.

14.1.3 Popup menus

Popup menus are menus that are not fixed to a menu bar. They can pop up anywhere at all in a window. A popup menu is opened when you click a specific mouse button (often the right button).

We will make a new change to the menus in the class MenuDemo. This time, we will let the "Options" menu regain its original appearance as shown in Figure 14.2. We will instead construct a popup menu that is displayed every time the user clicks on the right mouse button anywhere in the window. It will look like Figure 14.4. The menu pops up in the place in the window where the cursor happens to be.

A popup menu must be an object of the class JPopupMenu. We therefore define the colour menu here in the following way:

```
JPopupMenu colMen = new JPopupMenu("Color");
```

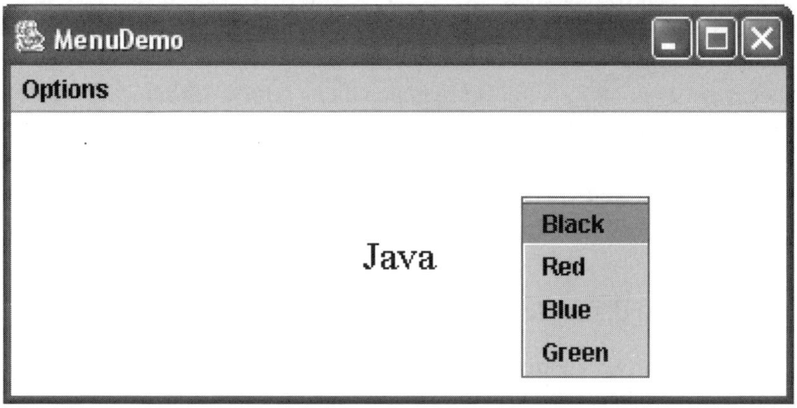

Figure 14.4 A window with a popup menu

451

The menu items are declared in exactly the same way as in the previous section, and we use the same `for` statement to create the items, to add them to the "Color" menu and to connect them to the listener `colListener`. This listener is also the same one we used in the previous section.

But because the "Color" menu is now going to be a popup menu, it will not be added to the menu bar or be an item on any menu accessed from the menu bar. Instead, we must ensure that the menu is displayed when the user clicks on the right mouse button. We do this by connecting a listener for mouse events to the component that the popup menu is to be displayed on. We call the listener `mListener`.

```
l.addMouseListener(mListener);
```

What remains now is to define `mListener`. Since there are many kinds of events described by the event class `MouseEvent` and we are only interested in the event `MousePressed`, we let `mListener` be a subclass of the class `MouseAdapter`. It will look like this:

```
MouseListener mListener = new MouseAdapter() {
    public void mousePressed(MouseEvent e) {
        if (SwingUtilities.isRightMouseButton(e))
            colMen.show(e.getComponent(), e.getX(), e.getY());
    }
};
```

The class `JPopupMenu` has a method called `show`. It has three parameters. The first parameter is to be a reference to the component on which the popup menu is to be displayed. The last two parameters specify the x and y coordinates of the point of the menu's upper left corner when it is displayed.

JPopupMenu	
new `PopupMenu()`	creates a popup menu
new `PopupMenu(`*h*`)`	creates a popup menu with the heading *h*
`show(`*co, x, y*`)`	displays the menu on top of the component *co* at the point (*x, y*)
The remaining methods are inherited from the class `JMenu`.	

14.1.4 Keyboard shortcuts in menus

In Swing there are two alternative ways of connecting keyboard shortcuts to menu items: you can use *mnemonics* or *accelerators*. We will start by describing mnemonics. When you use a shortcut of this type, the user can select the item by pressing the key

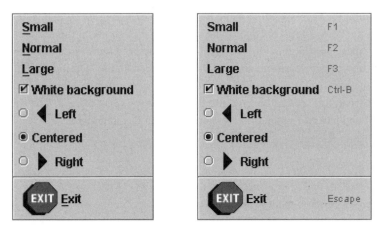

Figure 14.5 Menus with shortcuts

combination Alt-? where ? is to be a selected character found in the menu item's text. Generally, this is the initial letter. The selected character ? is shown underlined. In the left part of Figure 14.5 we have linked the shortcuts Alt-S, Alt-N and Alt-L to the first three items and the shortcut Alt-E to the last item, for example.

To connect a mnemonic shortcut to a menu item, you can use the method `setMnemonic` that the class `JMenuItem` has inherited from the superclass `JButtton`. To connect the shortcut Alt-E to the menu item "Exit", for example, we can add the invocation:

```
exit.setMnemonic(KeyEvent.VK_E);
```

Here, we use constants from the class `KeyEvent` (see page 423) to specify which character you want in the shortcut. It's also possible to connect a shortcut when you create the menu item by specifying an extra parameter in the constructor. To create the first three menu items in Figure 14.5 and connect shortcuts to them, we can declare the following, for example:

```
JMenuItem small  = new JMenuItem("Small",  KeyEvent.VK_S);
JMenuItem normal = new JMenuItem("Normal", KeyEvent.VK_N);
JMenuItem large  = new JMenuItem("Large",  KeyEvent.VK_L);
```

It is also possible to connect mnemonic shortcuts to entire menus. For example, the following statement connects the shortcut Alt-O to the "Options" menu in Figure 14.2:

```
iMen.setMnemonic(KeyEvent.VK_O);
```

This makes it possible for the user to select (that is, open) the "Options" menu by using the shortcut Alt-O.

Mnemonic shortcuts have two limitations. One is that you must always use the Alt key in combination with another key. The other limitation is that it's only possible to use the shortcut if the corresponding menu item is visible on the screen, that is, if the menu on which the item is found is open. The second type of shortcut, the accelerator, does not have these limitations. In the right-hand part of Figure 14.5 we have added shortcuts of type accelerator to some of the menu items in the "Options" menu. As you can see, the shortcut is displayed to the right of the menu item text. To connect this type of shortcut to a menu item, you use the method `setAccelerator`. The shortcuts in the right-hand part of Figure 14.5 were created with the statements:

```
small.setAccelerator(KeyStroke.getKeyStroke
                         (KeyEvent.VK_F1, 0));
normal.setAccelerator(KeyStroke.getKeyStroke
                         (KeyEvent.VK_F2, 0));
large.setAccelerator(KeyStroke.getKeyStroke
                         (KeyEvent.VK_F3, 0));
backgr.setAccelerator(KeyStroke.getKeyStroke
                         (KeyEvent.VK_B, ActionEvent.CTRL_MASK));
exit.setAccelerator(KeyStroke.getKeyStroke
                         (KeyEvent.VK_ESCAPE, 0));
```

You set the key combination you want by invoking the method `KeyStroke.getKey-Stroke`. The first parameter, which is a constant from the class `KeyEvent`, specifies the key. The second parameter specifies if a control key, such as CTRL, is to be held down. Possible values for the second parameter are `ActionEvent.ALT_MASK`, `Action-Event.CTRL_MASK`, `ActionEvent.META_MASK` and `ActionEvent.SHIFT_MASK`. You can also specify the value 0, which means that no control key is to be held down.

14.1.5 Menus and actions

As we discussed in Section 13.8, it is appropriate to use an action instead of a listener when you want it to be possible to start a certain action in the program in a number of alternative ways. For example, you want to be able to open a file either by selecting the item "Open" in a menu or by clicking a button in a tool bar. In this case, you would need to connect actions to the menu items. You can do this in two ways. Let's assume that, in the program `MenuDemo` on page 447, we have added an `Action` object called `exitAction`:

```
Action exitAction = new AbstractAction("Exit",
                                  new ImageIcon("exit.gif")) {
   public void actionPerformed(ActionEvent e) {
      System.exit(0);
   }
};
```

and that the menu item `exit` is defined instead in the following simple way:

```
JMenuItem exit = new JMenuItem();
```

We can then use the method setAction to connect the action to the menu item "Exit".

```
exit.setAction(exitAction);
```

You can also create menu items directly by using the method add for a menu. For example, we can write:

```
JMenuItem exit = iMen.add(exitAction);
```

Here, three things happen at once: A menu item is created, it is added to the menu iMen and the action exitAction is connected to the created menu item. The method add gives the created menu item as its return value.

We will also demonstrate how you can create menus in a very compact way using arrays and actions. The technique demonstrated here is useful when you have menu items that do the same thing but where some detail, such as the colour or font, is different. As an example, we show how you can create the sub-menu in Figure 14.3 in the program MenuDemo on page 447 in another way. We declare the following:

```
String[] colTxt = {"Black", "Red", "Blue", "Green"};
Color[] col = {Color.black, Color.red, Color.blue, Color.green};
Action[] a = new Action[col.length];
JMenu colMen = new JMenu("Color");
```

We then insert the lines below into the constructor:

```
iMen.insert(colMen, 4);  // add the sub-menu to the menu iMen
for (int i=0; i<colTxt.length; i++) {
   a[i] = new AbstractAction(colTxt[i]) {
      public void actionPerformed(ActionEvent e) {
         l.setForeground((Color) getValue("color"));
      }
   };
   colMen.add(a[i]);
   a[i].putValue("color", col[i]);
}
```

We use the same technique as in the program JButtonDemo on page 438. In the for statement, which does one loop per colour, a new action is created for each loop and added to the menu. This way, a new menu item is automatically created. At the end of each loop, we let the new action "remember" a colour. We do this by storing a Color object from the array col in the action. We give the saved value the name "color". We use this name inside the method actionPerformed, where we want the action to get information on which colour it should change to.

In the next section, where we discuss tool bars, we will show how you can also connect the actions we have created in this section to a set of buttons.

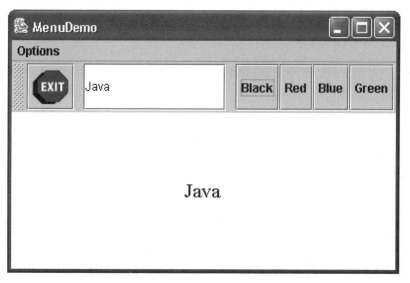

Figure 14.6 A window with a tool bar

14.2 Tool bars – the class `JToolBar`

In many programs such as word processors and browsers, you can have a tool bar under the menu bar. A tool bar generally contains buttons with which you can access tools for common tasks/actions in the program, for example to save your file or print it. In Swing you can use the class `JToolBar` to create similar tool bars. You can put whatever components you like in a tool bar, but generally we use buttons, and often buttons with an icon. Figure 14.6 shows what a tool bar might look like. There, we have extended the program `MenuDemo` on page 447 so that it also generates a tool bar. We have also designed the program so that the "Options" menu looks like Figure 14.3 on page 450. The first thing you need is a `JToolBar` object, which can be declared with the line:

```
JToolBar tb = new JToolBar();
```

A `JToolBar` object is a common Swing component and thus can be positioned like other components, but the sensible thing is to position the tool bar using `BorderLayout` in the container in which the tool bar is to be placed. You can then position the tool bar at one of the extremities (the points of the compass). The most natural place to put a tool bar is in the `NORTH` position. The other three points of the compass should be left empty. In the program `MenuDemo` we insert the following statement into the constructor:

```
getContentPane().add(tb, BorderLayout.NORTH);
```

Let's discuss the positioning of the components on the tool bar. The class `JToolBar` is a container that uses a `BoxLayout`. Therefore, you can position components in the regular way by using the method add. It's also possible to add an Action object to a JToolBar, which we will shortly demonstrate. This automatically creates a button that is connected to the specified Action object.

There are to be five buttons and a text field on our tool bar in Figure 14.6. The text field is a component of the type JTextField. It can be declared using the line:

```
JTextField txtF = new JTextField("Java");
```

When the user enters a text in the text field, the text in the JLabel object l in the middle of the window changes to this text. It is done by a simple listener that we connect to the text field txtF.

```
txtF.addActionListener(new ActionListener() {
    public void actionPerformed(ActionEvent e) {
        l.setText(txtF.getText());
    }
});
```

When you click the "Exit" button in the tool bar, the same action should occur as when you select the item "Exit" on the menu; and when you click any of the colour buttons in the tool bar, the same action should occur as when you select one of the equivalent items in the sub-menu shown in Figure 14.3. To accomplish this easily, we let the program contain the Action objects discussed in Section 14.1.5. In other words, the program contains the Action object exitAction and the array a, which contains references to the four Action objects that change the text to the different colours we have defined. The "Exit" button is created and positioned using the following statement, which also connects the button to the action exitAction:

```
JButton be = tb.add(exitAction);
```

(You could also have created the button first and then invoked the method setAction.) Then we add the text field txtF. Since we want a small space on both the left and right of the text field, we also add a separator.

```
tb.addSeparator();
tb.add(txtF);
tb.addSeparator();
```

Finally, we position the buttons for the different colours on the tool bar and connect them at the same time to the same Action objects that the corresponding items in the "Color" sub-menu are connected to, that is, to the Action objects in the array a.

```
for (int i=0; i<a.length; i++) {
    JButton bu = tb.add(a[i]);
    bu.setMaximumSize(new Dimension(bu.getPreferredSize().width,
                                    be.getPreferredSize().height));
}
```

We have invoked setMaximumSize to increase the height of the four buttons so that they will be the same height as the "Exit" button be.

457

JToolBar

Is a container with a `BoxLayout`.
Below, *ori* is equivalent to `JToolBar.HORIZONTAL` or `JToolBar.VERTICAL`.

new `JToolBar()`	creates a horizontal tool bar
new `JToolBar(`*ori*`)`	creates a tool bar with the orientation *ori*
new `JToolBar(`*h*`)`	creates a horizontal tool bar with the heading *h*
new `JToolBar(`*h*, *ori*`)`	creates a tool bar with the heading *h* and the orientation *ori*
`add(`*c*`)`	places the component `c` in the tool bar
`add(`*a*`)`	creates a `JButton` that is connected to the `Action` object *a* and places it in the tool bar, returns the `JButton` object
`addSeparator()`	puts a space on the tool bar
`setOrientation(`*ori*`)`	sets the orientation to be *ori*
`setFloatable(`*bool*`)`	specifies if the tool bar is to be floatable/movable or not
`getComponentAtIndex(`*i*`)`	gets the component number *i* on the tool bar

Tool bars are a bit different from other objects. They can be moved around. Even if you have located a tool bar in a certain position, for example in the NORTH position, the user can move it to another position using the mouse. (You do this by grasping hold of the "rough" area to the far left of the tool bar.) If the user has dragged the tool bar to the EAST position, it might look like Figure 14.7.

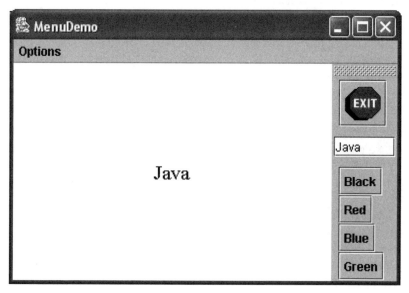

Figure 14.7 A window with a tool bar that has been moved

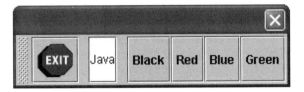

Figure 14.8 A tool bar outside its window

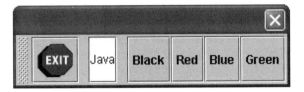

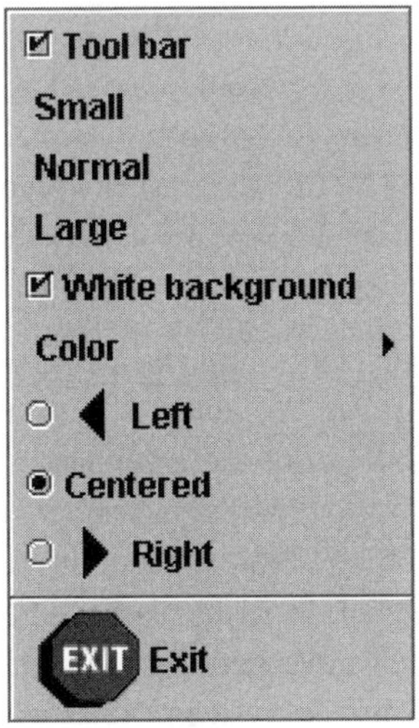

Figure 14.9

It's even possible to drag a tool bar so that it ends up outside the window to which it belongs. The tool bar then becomes a little window of its own. This is shown in Figure 14.8.

If you want the user to be able to move a tool bar, you can invoke the method `setFloatable`. The following statement makes the tool bar `tb` unmovable.

```
tb.setFloatable(false);
```

In programs that use tool bars, it is generally possible for the user to control whether or not the tool bar is displayed by selecting a menu item to this effect. For example, let's assume that we want to extend the menu in the program `MenuDemo` so that it contains the item "Tool bar" as shown in Figure 14.9. The following lines can be added to the program:

```
JCheckBoxMenuItem visibleToolBar = new JCheckBoxMenuItem
                          ("Tool bar", true);
iMen.insert(visibleToolBar, 0);
visibleToolBar.addActionListener(new ActionListener() {
  public void actionPerformed(ActionEvent e) {
    if (visibleToolBar.isSelected())
```

459

```
         tb.setVisible(true);
     else
         tb.setVisible(false);
   }
});
```

14.3 Common characteristics of top-level components

Graphical components that can be displayed independently as separate windows on the screen or as a separate component in a web browser are called *top-level containers*. Figure 14.10 shows the classes that describe such components. All the classes in the figure are subclasses of the class `Container`. Components at the top level can thus contain other graphical components.

The class `Window` describes standalone windows. All graphical components that can be displayed in a window of their own are subclasses of the class `Window`. A component of the class `Window` or its Swing version `JWindow` has no frame. You therefore seldom use the classes `Window` and `JWindow` directly, but rather define instead objects of one or other of the classes `JFrame` or `JDialog` (or `Frame` or `Dialog` if you are using awt). These classes inherit some useful methods from the class `Window`. One example is the method `pack`, which we have used in several programs. A list of some of the methods that are common to top-level components is given in the fact box. These methods (with the exception of the method `addWindowListener`) also exist for the class `JInternalFrame`, which we will discuss in Section 14.5.

The classes `Applet` and `JApplet` are not subclasses of `Window`. Since applets are not standalone windows but are displayed in web pages, these classes lack the methods used for handling windows.

The awt classes `Window`, `Frame`, `Dialog` and `Applet` are ordinary containers. In other words, using the method `add`, you can place components directly in a component of

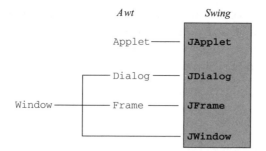

Figure 14.10 Top-level containers

JWindow, JFrame, JInternalFrame and JDialog	
`dispose()`	deletes the window and frees all the resources it uses
`setVisible(b)`	shows or hides the window, `b` is of type `boolean`
`isShowing()`	indicates if the window is visible or not
`getFocusOwner()`	gets the component in the window that is in focus (or `null`)
`pack()`	positions the window's sub-components and sets their sizes
`toBack()`	places the window to the back
`toFront()`	places the window to the front
`setLocation(x,y)`	specifies where the upper left corner is to be placed
`setLocation(p)`	specifies where the upper left corner is to be placed, p is of the class `Point`
`getLocationOnScreen()`	returns the window's location as a `Point` object
`getContentPane()`	gives the content pane (also for `JApplet`)
`setContentPane(c)`	changes the content pane (also for `JApplet`)
`getGlassPane()`	gives a glass pane (also for `JApplet`)
`setGlassPane(c)`	changes the glass pane (also for `JApplet`)
`getJMenuBar()`	gives the menu bar (also for `JApplet`)
`setJMenuBar(c)`	changes the menu bar (also for `JApplet`)
`addWindowListener(l)`	specifies that the listener `l` will track events of the class `WindowEvent` (not for `JInternalFrame`)

one of these classes. However, the top-level classes in Swing have a more complex construction. As we mentioned in Section 6.1, a component of any of these classes contains a single child component, namely a `JRootPane`. This contains in turn two other components: a `glassPane`, which you can position on top of the window, and a `JLayeredPane`, which arranges the window's other components in layers on the screen. One of these layers is the window's `contentPane` and you can also have a `JMenuBar` on this layer. As luck would have it, the average programmer doesn't need to know about or use the classes `JRootPane` or `JLayeredPane`. Normally, you just use a window's `contentPane` and menu bar, and possibly a glass pane. All the top-level classes have simple methods with which you can access and change/edit `content-Panes`, menu bars and glass panes.

What is important to remember when you have top-level components in Swing is that you should never place child components directly in the window. You should always place them in the window's `contentPane`, and we have seen dozens of examples of this.

We will now discuss how you can use the `glassPane`. You can place a glass pane over any window at all. We can take the program `TextEdit` on page 211 as an example. We will add a number of program lines that will result in the program looking like

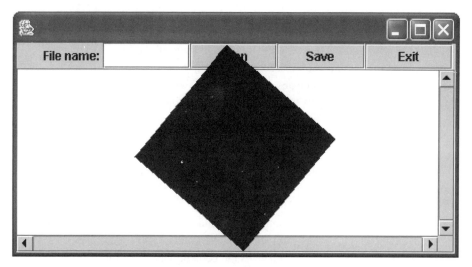

Figure 14.11 Transparent glass pane

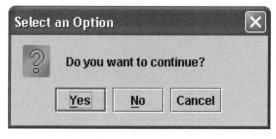

Figure 14.12

Figure 14.11 when you start it. On top of the window is a glass pane with a rotating square. The glass pane is transparent, so that you can see the window under it. However, it is not possible to use the program in the regular way. The glass pane captures all mouse clicks made in the window and as soon as you click anywhere in the window, the dialog shown in Figure 14.12 opens. If the user clicks on the Yes button in this dialog box, the glass pane disappears and the program TextEdit functions again as normal.

We don't change any lines in the program on page 211. We just make some additions that we put into a private method called createGlass. We add an invocation of the new method first in the constructor in the class TextEdit:

```
public TextEdit() {     // constructor
   createGlass();
   as before
}
```

The method `createGlass` is as follows:

```
private void createGlass() {
    final JPanel glass = (JPanel) getGlassPane();
    glass.setLayout(new BorderLayout());
    Poly po = new Poly(4, 100);  // see page 378
    po.setOpaque(false);
    po.start();       // let the polygon rotate
    glass.add(po);
    glass.setVisible(true);

    // listener for mouse clicks
    glass.addMouseListener(new MouseAdapter() {
        public void mouseClicked(MouseEvent e) {
            if (JOptionPane.showConfirmDialog(null,
                "Do you want to continue? ") == 0)
                glass.setVisible(false);
            else
                System.exit(0);
        }
    });
    // listener for mouse motions
    glass.addMouseMotionListener(new MouseMotionAdapter() {});
}
```

First, the method `getGlassPane` is invoked, which gives a reference to the window's glass pane. The reference is put into a variable called `glass`. The return type from the method `getGlassPane` is `Component`, but in actual fact, you get a reference to a `JPanel` as the result, which is why we can do a type conversion. We then use our class `Poly` from page 378 to create an active object that has a square. We start the active object so that the square starts to rotate and then place the active object in the middle of the glass pane. The glass pane is then made visible, which means that the square is displayed.

We connect two listeners to the glass pane. The first captures all clicks of the mouse and the other all movements of the mouse. Since the glass pane covers the window completely, no mouse events will occur in the underlying content pane. The glass pane therefore blocks the program's normal functions. We use the technique of anonymous classes described in Section 13.3. We put a listener method into the first listener class, which is invoked when the user has clicked a mouse button. When this happens, the dialog in Figure 14.12 is generated. If the user clicks on the Yes button in the dialog, the window's glass pane is made invisible. The underlying content pane then comes to the front and the program starts functioning normally again.

Naturally, it would have been just as good putting any picture on the glass pane. If, for example, we had a file called `picture.jpg` containing an image, we could have placed it instead of the square in the glass pane using the following statements:

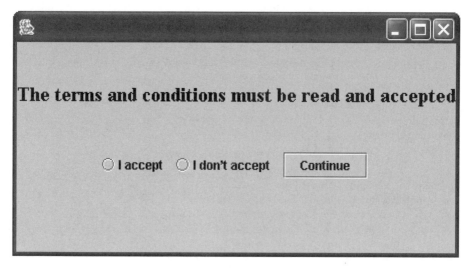

Figure 14.13 Opaque glass pane

```
JLabel l = new JLabel(new ImageIcon("picture.jpg"));
glass.add(l);
```

We will now show one more example of where a glass pane is used. This time, we will use an opaque glass pane, which functions like a cover over the window. Here again we will use the program TextEdit as an example. When you start the program, it looks like Figure 14.13. The user must click one of the radio buttons and then click the Continue button. If the user selects the left-hand radio button, the opaque glass pane disappears and the program TextEdit functions normally again. If the user selects the right-hand radio button, the program exits.

Here too, we put all the code that has to do with the glass pane into our own private method in the class TextEdit. We call this new method createCover. The only change we need to make in the existing code is to insert an invocation into the constructor:

```
public TextEdit() {       // constructor
    createCover();
    as before
}
```

The method createCover looks like this:

```
private void createCover() {
    final JPanel glass = (JPanel) getGlassPane();
    glass.setOpaque(true);
    glass.setLayout(new GridLayout(2,1));
    JLabel l = new JLabel(
            "The terms and conditions must be read and accepted",
            JLabel.CENTER);
```

```
l.setFont(new Font("Serif", Font.BOLD, 20));
glass.add(l);

// create a panel with two radio buttons and one button
JPanel buttons = new JPanel();
final JRadioButton yes = new JRadioButton(
                            "I accept");
final JRadioButton no = new JRadioButton(
                            "I don't accept");
ButtonGroup g = new ButtonGroup();
g.add(yes); g.add(no);
JButton cont = new JButton("Continue");
buttons.setLayout(new FlowLayout());
buttons.add(yes); buttons.add(no); buttons.add(cont);
glass.add(buttons);
glass.setVisible(true);

// listener method for the button 'Continue'
cont.addActionListener(new ActionListener() {
  public void actionPerformed(ActionEvent e) {
    if (yes.isSelected())
      glass.setVisible(false);
    else if (no.isSelected())
      System.exit(0);
  }
});

// listeners for mouse clicks and mouse movements
glass.addMouseListener(new MouseAdapter() {});
glass.addMouseMotionListener(new MouseMotionAdapter() {});
}
```

14.4 The class JFrame

The class JFrame describes a window that has a frame and can have menus. The first window in a standalone graphical program is usually of this class. We have seen many examples of this. In this section, we will discuss how you can generate new windows by creating new JFrame objects. We will also discuss the problems that arise when you want to close windows in a program that uses several windows.

When a window is opened, closed or minimized to an icon, events are generated. These events are described in the event class WindowEvent. Table 13.1 on page 412 shows different types of events that can occur. The event windowActivated occurs, for example, when a window becomes active because the user has moved the mouse to it and selected it. The event windowClosed occurs when the window is closed by the program through the invocation of the method dispose. windowClosing occurs when the user has clicked the window's Close button or equivalent.

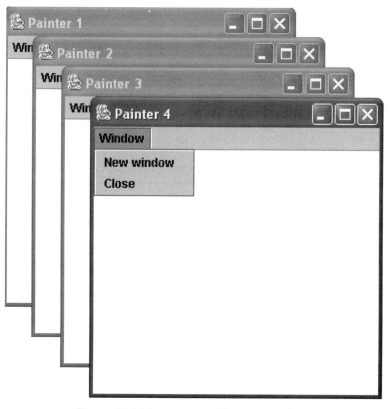

Figure 14.14 A program with many windows

As an example of this, we will make a new version of the drawing program from Section 13.5. Figure 14.14 shows what the screen will look like when you run the new version of the program. When you start the program, the window that lies uppermost to the left (Painter 1) is displayed automatically. We have put a menu bar with two items in each window. Each time you select "New window", a new window is opened on the screen. The figure shows what the screen will look like when you have opened four windows. The drawing windows function fully independently of each other, and you can draw lines in them just as was shown in Section 13.5.

We will keep the class `Painter` on page 422 as it is without making any changes whatsoever in it. What we will do here is to write a new version of the class `PaintProgram` on page 420. We call this new version `PaintWindow`. It looks like this:

```
import javax.swing.*;
import java.awt.*;
import java.awt.event.*;

public class PaintWindow extends JFrame
                              implements ActionListener {
```

```
private static int totalNo = 0;  // total number of windows
private static int nextNo  = 0;  // number of next window
private int no;                  // this window's number

private JMenuBar mb = new JMenuBar();
private JMenu men   = new JMenu("Window");
private JMenuItem newItem = new JMenuItem("New window");
private JMenuItem closeItem = new JMenuItem("Close");

public PaintWindow() {
  totalNo++;        // increase the total number of windows
  no = nextNo++;    // assign a number to this window
  setTitle("Painter " + (no+1));
  setLocation(30*no, 30*no);

  setJMenuBar(mb);
  mb.add(men);
  men.add(newItem); men.add(closeItem);
  getContentPane().add(new Painter(), BorderLayout.CENTER);

  // connect listener to the menu items and the window
  newItem.addActionListener(this);
  closeItem.addActionListener(this);
  addWindowListener(wl);

  setSize(300,300);
  setVisible(true);
  setDefaultCloseOperation(WindowConstants.DISPOSE_ON_CLOSE);
}

public void actionPerformed(ActionEvent e) {
  if (e.getSource() == newItem)
    new PaintWindow();
  else if (e.getSource() == closeItem)
    dispose();
}

private WindowListener wl = new WindowAdapter() {
  public void windowClosed(WindowEvent e) {
    // will be called when dispose is called
    if (--totalNo == 0) // is the final window closing?
      System.exit(0);
  }
};

public static void main (String arg[]) {
  new PaintWindow();
}
}
```

Each object of the class PaintWindow gets a unique number no. The number starts from zero, that is, the first window gets the number zero. In addition, there are two counters.

The first, `totalNo`, keeps track of the total number of windows open; and the second, `nextNo`, contains the number that the next window you open will be assigned. Both of these counters are, of course, class variables.

The execution starts normally in the method `main`. There, the first `PaintWindow` object is created. Each time a new `PaintWindow` object is created, the constructor is invoked. There, you give the new object a unique number and increment the class variables `totalNo` and `nextNo`.

When a new window has been created, the method `setTitle` is invoked to specify what text will be put in the window's frame. (Since the numbering is from zero, we must add 1.)

When a new window is displayed on the screen, it is placed in the upper left corner unless you specify otherwise. Since we don't want the windows to be displayed right on top of each other, we specify explicitly where a new window is to be placed. You can do this by invoking the method `setLocation`, which determines where the window's upper left corner is to be placed. We want each new window to be displaced 30 image points down and to the right.

In the constructor in the class `PaintWindow` we create, as in the class `PaintProgram` on page 420, a component of the class `Painter` and place it in the middle of the window. What's new here is that we also create a menu with two items. As usual, we let the class itself be the listener to the two menu items.

The interesting part is what occurs in the listener. When the user clicks on the menu item "New window" the program creates a new object of the class `PaintWindow`. When you create a new `JFrame` it is initially invisible, but since the constructor in the class `PaintWindow` calls `setVisible` the new window will be visible.

Let's also discuss what happens when you click the `Close` button or on the Close symbol in the frame of the window. In most programs, we have previously added the call:

```
setDefaultCloseOperation(EXIT_ON_CLOSE);
```

in the constructor, which has meant that the program exits when you click the Close symbol. However, we cannot do that here. If the program exited, *all* the windows would be closed when you clicked the Close symbol in one window. Instead, we have written:

```
setDefaultCloseOperation(WindowConstants.DISPOSE_ON_CLOSE);
```

which means that the method `dispose` is invoked for the window to be closed. For the same reason, we cannot write the following in the listener to the menu item "Close":

```
System.exit(0);
```

Then too, all windows would close when you went to close only one of them. Instead, we have the listener for the `Close` button in the invocation:

```
dispose();
```

When `dispose` is invoked, an event is generated of type `windowClosed`. In the class `PaintWindow` we have added a listener that listens for this event. The listener is designed in such a way that it counts down the counter `totalNo` and exits the program when it can't find any visible windows left. Thus, the program will behave as we want it to: if you close one window, the others remain open, but if there is only one window left to close, and you close it, the program exits.

JFrame

See also the fact box on page 461.

new JFrame()	creates a new, initially invisible, window
new JFrame(*text*)	creates a new, initially invisible, window with the title *text*
setTitle(*text*)	sets the title in the window frame to *text*
setDefaultCloseOperation(op)	specifies what will happen when the window is closed. op is `WindowConstants.DO_NOTHING_ON_CLOSE`, `WindowConstants.HIDE_ON_CLOSE`, `WindowConstants.DISPOSE_ON_CLOSE` or `EXIT_ON_CLOSE`
setResizable(*bool*)	defines if it will be possible to resize the window
setIconImage(*im*)	specifies that the image *im* is to be used as the window's icon
getIconImage()	gives a reference to the window's icon image
setState(s)	s will have the value `Frame.ICONIFIED` or `Frame.NORMAL`
getState()	gives the value `Frame.ICONIFIED` or `Frame.NORMAL`
getFrames()	gives an array with the `Frame` objects created by the program
setDefaultLookAndFeelDecorated(bool)	class method, see page 267

14.5 Internal windows

Some programs such as word-processing programs have a window that in turn may contain internal windows. If, for example, you want to edit several documents at the same time, each document can be opened in its own internal window. An internal window cannot be moved outside of its surrounding window, the program's start window. It is relatively easy to construct programs with internal windows when you use Swing. To demonstrate this, we will make a new version of the program from the previous section, which displayed drawing windows. When you run the new version, it will look like Figure 14.15. (Compare this with Figure 14.14 on page 466.)

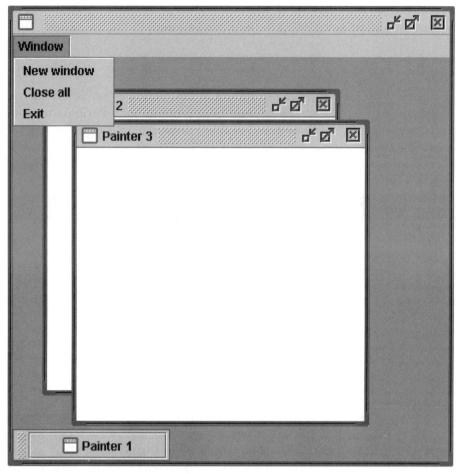

Figure 14.15 A program with internal windows

The program has a surrounding start window with a menu. This menu includes the item "New window". When the user selects this item, a new internal window is created. In each internal window, you can draw pictures using the mouse, as in the windows in Figure 14.14. These internal windows are located with a certain displacement in relation to each other. The user can move the internal windows by dragging them with the mouse. By clicking the symbols in the window's frame, the user can close the window, minimize it to an icon or maximize it so that it covers the entire area of the start window's pane. (The figure shows what the window will look like after the user has minimized drawing window number 1 to an icon.)

Internal windows are constructed in Swing using the class JInternalFrame. This class has roughly the same characteristics as the class JFrame (see the fact box).

JInternalFrame

See also the fact box on page 461.

`new JInternalFrame()`	creates an internal window
`new JInternalFrame(`*txt*`)`	creates an internal window with the title *txt*
`new JInternalFrame(`*txt, res, clo, max, ico*`)`	creates an internal window with the title *txt*. Other arguments of type **boolean** specify if the size can be changed, the window can be closed, and maximized or minimized
`setTitle(`*text*`)`	sets the title in the window frame to *text*
`setDefaultCloseOperation(op)`	specifies the close operation `op` is `WindowConstants.DO_NOTHING_ON_CLOSE`, `WindowConstants.HIDE_ON_CLOSE` or `WindowConstants.DISPOSE_ON_CLOSE`
`setResizable(`*bool*`)`	defines whether it is possible to resize the window or not
`setClosable(`*bool*`)`	defines if it is possible to close the window or not
`setMaximizable(`*bool*`)`	defines if the window can be maximized or not
`setIconifiable(`*bool*`)`	defines whether or not the window can be minimized
`setMaximum(`*bool*`)`	maximizes or resets the window
`setIcon(`*bool*`)`	converts the window into an icon or resets it
`isClosed()`	indicates if the window is closed or not
`isMaximum()`	indicates if the window is maximized or not
`isIcon()`	indicates if the window is an icon or not
`isSelected()`	indicates if the window is selected or not
`moveToBack()`	moves the window to the back
`moveToFront()`	moves the window to the front
`setFrameIcon(ic)`	indicates that the icon `ic` is to be displayed in the frame
`getDesktopPane()`	gives the `DesktopPane` in which this window is located
`addInternalFrameListener(l)`	specifies that the `InternalFrameListener` `l` is to handle events of the class `InternalFrameEvent`

We start by constructing a class `IntPaintWindow` which describes the internal windows in Figure 14.15. We let the class be a subclass of `JInternalFrame`.

```java
import javax.swing.*;
import java.awt.*;

public class IntPaintWindow extends JInternalFrame {
    public IntPaintWindow(String title) {
        super(title, true, true, true, true);
        getContentPane().add(new Painter(), BorderLayout.CENTER);
        setSize(300, 300);
        setVisible(true);
    }
}
```

As can be seen, this class is very simple. It contains only one constructor. (The many parameters of the superclass's constructor indicate that the window is resizable, that it can be closed, that it can be maximized so that it fills the entire surrounding window pane and that it can be minimized to an icon.) Compare the class `IntPaintWindow` with the class `PaintWindow` on page 466. As in that class, we let the window contain a single component, namely, a component of the class `Painter`. Our new class `IntPaint-Window` is much simpler than the class `PaintWindow`, since we have removed the menu and the class variables that keep track of the number of windows, etc. The new class doesn't have any `main` method either, of course.

A component of the class `JInternalFrame` is a normal Swing component that must be placed in a `Container`. In practice, you should always place it in a container of the type `JDesktopPane`. This type of component is a special `Container` that is meant to contain internal windows. We can make the following declaration, for example:

```
JDesktopPane desktop = new JDesktopPane();
```

You position the components in the container in the regular way using the method `add`. For example, we can write:

```
JInternalFrame f = new JInternalFrame();
desktop.add(f);
```

When you position an internal window in a `JDesktopPane` component, you must specify how large the internal window is to be and also where it is to be located.

JDesktopPane	
Special container used for internal windows. Subclass of `JComponent`. See also the fact box on page 161.	
`new JDesktopPane()`	creates a `JDesktopPane`
`getSelectedFrame()`	gives the internal window that is selected
`setSelectedFrame(f)`	selects the internal window `f`
`getAllFrames()`	gives an array with all the internal windows
`setDragMode(m)`	`m` is to be a `JDesktopPane.LIVE_DRAG_MODE` or `JDesktopPane.OUTLINE_DRAG_MODE`

The next step in our program is to construct a class that generates the surrounding window in Figure 14.15. We call this class `Folder`. Since it is to generate a normal external window, we let it be a subclass of `JFrame`. We let the window have a menu with three items: "New window", "Close all" and "Exit". When you select the second item, all internal windows are closed, but the program does not exit. The menus are placed in the window and listeners are connected to them in the regular way. The class `Folder` looks like this:

```java
import javax.swing.*;
import java.awt.*;
import java.awt.event.*;
import java.util.*;

public class Folder extends JFrame implements ActionListener{
  private JMenuBar mb = new JMenuBar();
  private JMenu men    = new JMenu("Window");
  private JMenuItem newItem = new JMenuItem("New window");
  private JMenuItem closeItem = new JMenuItem("Close all");
  private JMenuItem exit = new JMenuItem("Exit");

  private JDesktopPane bord = new JDesktopPane();
  private int n; // number of internal windows

  public Folder() {
    setContentPane(bord);
    setJMenuBar(mb);
    mb.add(men);
    men.add(newItem); men.add(closeItem); men.add(exit);

    // connect listener to the menu alternatives
    newItem.addActionListener(this);
    closeItem.addActionListener(this);
    exit.addActionListener(this);
    setSize(450, 450);
    setVisible(true);
    setDefaultCloseOperation(EXIT_ON_CLOSE);
  }

  public void actionPerformed(ActionEvent e) {
    if (e.getSource() == newItem) {
      IntPaintWindow f = new IntPaintWindow("Painter "+ (n+1));
      bord.add(f);
      int x = Math.min(30*n, bord.getWidth() -f.getWidth());
      int y = Math.min(30*n, bord.getHeight()-f.getHeight());
      f.setLocation(x, y);

      f.moveToFront();    // put the new window on top
      n++;
    }
    else if (e.getSource() == closeItem) {
      JInternalFrame[] a = bord.getAllFrames();
      for (int i=0; i<a.length; i++)
        a[i].dispose();    // close all windows
      n = 0;
    }
    else if (e.getSource() == exit)
      System.exit(0);
  }
```

```
public static void main (String arg[]) {
    // Metal Look & Feel in the outermost frame
    JFrame.setDefaultLookAndFeelDecorated(true);
    new Folder();
}
}
```

Pay particular attention to the fact that we create an object `bord` of the class `JDesktopPane` in the class, and that we then let this component comprise the window's content pane:

```
setContentPane(bord);
```

Each time the user selects the item "New window" a new component of the type `IntPaintWindow` is created and placed in the `JDesktopPane` component `bord`.

```
JInternalFrame f = new IntPaintWindow("Painter " + (n+1));
bord.add(f);
```

(The variable `n` is used to keep track of the internal window's number.) In the program, we let the internal windows determine their own size. However, we set their location in the listener by invoking the method `setLocation`. We calculate the x and y coordinates of the internal windows' upper left corners. This is done so that the windows are displaced somewhat in relation to each other, but we have also added a barrier so that no window ever ends up so far to the right or so far down that it cannot be seen.

If you don't set the Look & Feel (see Section 8.5) to be used, the internal window will have the "Metal" look by default. To give our program a consistent appearance, we have therefore chosen to give the outer frame the Metal look as well. You do this by invoking the method `setDefaultLookAndFeelDecorated` in the method `main`.

You could also have done the reverse. You could let the outside frame keep its look and feel and instead let the internal windows have the same look and feel as the outside one. You can do this by inserting the following lines first in the constructor in the class `Folder`:

```
String look = UIManager.getSystemLookAndFeelClassName();
try {
    UIManager.setLookAndFeel(look);
    SwingUtilities.updateComponentTreeUI(this);
}
catch (Exception ex) {}
```

If the program was run under Windows, for example, this would mean that all windows would get the "Windows" look and feel.

14.6 Dialogs

In programs with a GUI, you often use dialogs to display messages or ask the user for a response. Previously in this book, we have shown several examples of this. Some dialogs can be visible at the same time as the user does other things in the program. They don't hinder the program's other functions. These kinds of dialogs are called *non-modal dialogs*. However, generally you use *modal dialogs*. A modal dialog bars all other input to the program as long as it remains open. For example, the user cannot click in any other window in the program. All the dialogs we have constructed previously in this book have been modal. A model dialog may contain an important message to the user or a question to which the user must give a response immediately for the program to be able to continue. (See Figure 1.9 on page 25, for example.) Modal dialogs may also contain text fields that the user needs to enter some data in. (See Figure 1.6 on page 13, for example.)

There are three different ways of creating dialogs when using Swing:

1. Invoke one of the class methods `showXxxDialog` in the class `JOptionPane`.
2. Create a component of the class `JOptionPane` and place it in a dialog box.
3. Create a component of the class `JDialog` and place components in it.

We will describe these three options in detail below. Option 1 is the simplest and luckily can be used in most instances. It's this option that we have used up to now in this book. The most important limitation of Option 1 is that it can only be used to create modal dialogs. If you want a non-modal dialog box, you must use one of the other two options. In most cases, Option 2 can be used instead.

Using the class `JOptionPane` you can create dialogs that have a standardized appearance. The purpose of the class `JOptionPane` is to make it as easy as possible for the programmer to create dialogs. Option 3 is only needed if you want to have a dialog with a special appearance that cannot be achieved using the class `JOptionPane`. In other words, you must use Option 3 if you have chosen not to use Swing, for example, in an applet. In this case, you must create an object of the awt class `Dialog` instead of `JDialog`.

14.6.1 Class methods in the class `JOptionPane`

In the class `JOptionPane` there is a group of class methods called `showMessageDialog`, `showConfirmDialog`, `showInputDialog` and `showOptionDialog`. These can be used to create dialogs in programs that use ordinary (external) windows. The methods exist in several, superimposed versions with different parameters. There is also an equivalent group of class methods called `showInternalMessageDialog`, `showInternalConfirm-Dialog`, `showInternalInputDialog` and `showInternalOptionDialog`. You use these if you want dialogs in a program with internal windows. We will describe here the first group of methods. The methods `showInternalMessageDialog` etc. function in exactly the same way as the methods of the same names in the first group.

When you invoke any of the class methods `showXxxDialog` a dialog of the class `JDialog` is automatically created. As the only component in this dialog box, there is a container of the type `JOptionPane`. The invoked class method automatically positions the components to be found in the dialog in this container. A dialog created in this way can contain the following components (see Figure 1.6 on page 13, for example):

- A *title* in the frame of the dialog box
- An *icon*
- A *message*
- A *text field* for input
- A bar with *buttons* for various options.

The components included in any dialog and precisely how they will be arranged depend on the class methods invoked and the parameters given. The fact box shows a list of the various parameters that may occur and a list of all the various superimposed versions of the class methods.

The icon that is displayed is dependent on the type of message. Figure 14.16 shows the standard icons used for questions, information, warnings and errors, respectively. If the message is of the type `PLAIN_MESSAGE` no icon is displayed. In addition, you can select another icon yourself by declaring the parameter `icon`.

Figure 14.16 Standard icons for dialogs

We will now give examples of how to invoke the various class methods. In all of the examples, we assume that the variable `f` is a reference to an object of the class `JFrame` (or a subclass of it). For example, the following declaration can be made:

```
JFrame f = new JFrame();
```

showMessageDialog

This method is used to generate dialogs with messages. The dialog will contain an icon, a message text and a button with the text "OK". The method exists in three versions. You can select the text to be displayed, the title to be displayed in the frame and the type of message it is going to be. You can also specify a special icon if you wish.

The class methods JOptionPane.showXxxDialog

The following parameters may occur in these methods:

par   *Parent.* Specifies which window the dialog will be displayed on. `null` means that the dialog is displayed in the middle of the screen

mess   *Message.* What is shown in the window, often a text, but can be any object at all

mType   *Type of message.* Determines which icon is to be displayed in the dialog box. (Can be changed by the parameter `icon`.) Permitted values are: QUESTION_MESSAGE, INFORMATION_MESSAGE, WARNING_MESSAGE, ERROR_MESSAGE and PLAIN_MESSAGE

bType   *Type of buttons.* Determines which buttons are found at the bottom of the dialog box. (Can be changed by the parameter `opt`.) Possible values: DEFAULT_OPTION, YES_NO_OPTION, YES_NO_CANCEL_OPTION and OK_CANCEL_OPTION

opt   *Options.* Determines which buttons are to be found. Normally an array with texts but can be an array with any objects, e.g., icons

ic   *Icon.* Determines which icon is to be displayed. May be `null`

title   *Title.* Gives the text that will be displayed in the frame of the dialog box

val   An array. Specifies the values that can be selected in the input field

init   *Initial value.* Specifies the default value to be displayed in the text field

Class method	**Return type**
`showMessageDialog(par, mess)`	**void**
`showMessageDialog(par, mess, title, mType)`	**void**
`showMessageDialog(par, mess, title, mType, ic)`	**void**
`showInputDialog(mess)`	String
`showInputDialog(mess, init)`	String
`showInputDialog(par, mess)`	String
`showInputDialog(par, mess, init)`	String
`showInputDialog(par, mess, title, mType)`	String
`showInputDialog(par, mess, title, mType, ic, val, init)`	Object
`showConfirmDialog(par, mess)`	**int**
`showConfirmDialog(par, mess, title, bType)`	**int**
`showConfirmDialog(par, mess, title, bType, mType)`	**int**
`showConfirmDialog(par, mess, title, bType, mType, ic)`	**int**
`showOptionDialog(par,mess,title,bType,mType,ic,opt,init)`	**int**

An example of the application of this method is given in Figure 1.7 on page 17. We will show a couple more examples. The two dialogs in Figure 14.17 were generated by the invocation

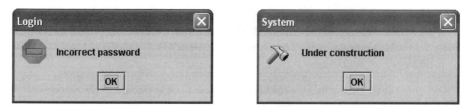

Figure 14.17 Message dialogs

```
JOptionPane.showMessageDialog(f, "Incorrect password", "Login",
                            JOptionPane.ERROR_MESSAGE);

JOptionPane.showMessageDialog(f, "Under construction","System",
        JOptionPane.PLAIN_MESSAGE, new ImageIcon("hammer.gif"));
```

showInputDialog

An example of a dialog that has been created with this method is shown in Figure 1.6 on page 13. In this type of dialog, generated by the method showInputDialog, there is an input field in which the user can enter data. In all versions of the method, except in the last in the box, the input field is a text field, that is, a component of the type JTextField. When the method is invoked, it gives the text the user wrote in the text field as the result. If the user cancels the input by clicking the "Cancel" button, for example, or in the Close symbol in the frame of the dialog box, the value null is returned. The last version of the method showInputDialog given in the box is of particular interest. When you invoke this method, you give an array with the values the user can choose from as one of the parameters. This is generally an array containing texts. For example, we can have the following program lines:

```
String[] colors = {"white", "black", "blue", "red", "yellow"};
String input = (String) JOptionPane.showInputDialog
   (f, "Choose color", "Order", JOptionPane.PLAIN_MESSAGE,
    new ImageIcon("palett.gif"), colors, colors[0]);
```

The dialog's appearance is demonstrated in Figure 14.18.

The input box now becomes a list in which the user can choose one item. In the left part of the figure, you can see what the dialog looks like when it opens. The item "white" is shown initially, since this has been stated as the last parameter in the invocation of showInputDialog. In the right-hand part of the figure, you can see what the dialog looks like when the user has selected one of the items on the list. When the user has made his or her choice and clicked the OK button, the selected option will be given as the return value from the method showInputDialog. In this version of the method, the return value is of the type Object so we must do a type conversion

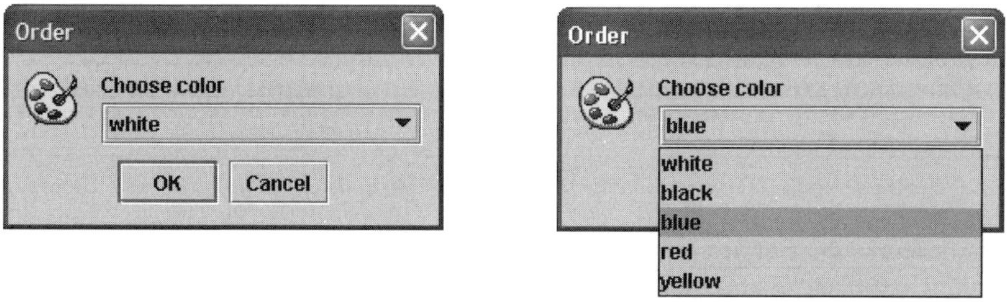

Figure 14.18 Dialog with list for selection of input

to the type `String` to be able to allocate the result to the variable `input`. If, for example, the user selects the item "blue", then the variable `input` will contain the text `"blue"`.

showConfirmDialog

In dialogs created with this method, the user can answer a question by clicking a button. You can specify the buttons to be found by specifying the parameter `bType` in the box. You can choose to just have an OK button (the option `DEFAULT_OPTION`); to have two buttons with the texts "Yes" and "No", respectively; to have three buttons with the texts "Yes", "No" and "Cancel", respectively; or to have two buttons with the texts "OK" and "Cancel", respectively. If you don't specify the parameter `bType` you get the option with three buttons automatically. We will show a couple of examples. The following program lines generate the dialogs in Figure 14.19.

```
int i = JOptionPane.showConfirmDialog(f, "Replace old files?");
int j = JOptionPane.showConfirmDialog(f, "Download now?",
                "Installation", JOptionPane.OK_CANCEL_OPTION);
```

The return value is the number of the button the user selects. The numbering is normally from zero, with the left-hand button having the number zero. If the user closes the dialog by clicking the Close symbol in the frame, the value –1 is returned. If you don't want keep track of the numbers of the buttons, you can instead compare

Figure 14.19 Dialogs for asking questions

the result obtained with the constants `YES_OPTION`, `NO_OPTION`, `CANCEL_OPTION` `OK_OPTION` and `CLOSED_OPTION`.

showOptionDialog

This is the most general of the class methods. With its help, you can affect all the parameters in the fact box on page 477. In particular, you can specify your own set of buttons. (If you do this, the parameter `bType` will be meaningless.) The method `showOptionDialog` returns an integer, as does `showConfirmDialog`, which is the number of the button the user selected. In our first example, we want to create the dialog in Figure 14.20.

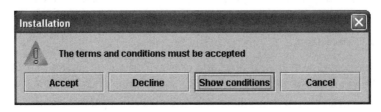

Figure 14.20 Dialog created with showOptionDialog

This can be done with the program lines below. We declare an array a that contains the texts to be shown on the buttons. In the last parameter for the method `showOptionDialog` we indicate which of the buttons is to be selected as the default selection.

```
String[] a = {"Accept", "Decline",
              "Show conditions", "Cancel"};
int answer = JOptionPane.showOptionDialog
              (f, "The terms and conditions must be accepted",
              "Installation", JOptionPane.DEFAULT_OPTION,
              JOptionPane.WARNING_MESSAGE, null, a, a[2]);
```

In the next example, we will show how you can create a dialog with icons on the buttons. We will generate the dialog shown in Figure 14.21.

![Mouse options dialog with four directional arrow buttons]

Figure 14.21 Dialog with icons on the buttons

This can be done with the following program lines. This time, we define an array in which the elements are icons.

```
Object[] arrows = {new ImageIcon("arrowup.gif"),
                   new ImageIcon("arrowdown.gif"),
                   new ImageIcon("arrowleft.gif"),
                   new ImageIcon("arrowright.gif")};
int r = JOptionPane.showOptionDialog
        (f, "Indicate direction for scrolling", "Mouse options",
        JOptionPane.DEFAULT_OPTION, JOptionPane.PLAIN_MESSAGE,
        new ImageIcon("mouse.gif"), arrows, arrows[1]);
```

14.6.2 Objects of the class `JOptionPane`

If you want to create a non-modal dialog box, it's easiest to create an object of the class `JOptionPane` and then put it into a `JDialog`. Even if you want to have a modal dialog box, it can sometimes be an advantage to use this technique instead of using the class methods `showXxxDialog` from the previous section. This applies when you want to be able to show a certain dialog several times during the execution of the program. Each time you invoke one of the class methods, a *new* dialog is created, in which all the components are to be placed. Naturally, this takes some time. If instead you use the technique that we will demonstrate in this section, a specific dialog is created only once. Execution of the program will therefore be faster.

Objects of the class `JOptionPane` can be given the same characteristics as the objects generated using the class methods `showXxxDialog`. In other words, you can specify the message and the icons to be displayed and the buttons to be found in the dialog box. (You can also have an input field where the user enters data, but since it is complicated to access the information the user enters before the dialog is closed, we will not discuss this here.) You can specify the characteristics for a dialog using the parameters for the constructor or by invoking one or more of the methods `setXxx`. A list of the various possibilities is given in the fact box.

We will start with a simple example. The following program lines generate the non-modal dialog shown in Figure 14.22.

```
JOptionPane jo = new JOptionPane
                      ("This is a demonstration program",
                      JOptionPane.INFORMATION_MESSAGE);
JDialog d1 = jo.createDialog(f, "Demo");
d1.setModal(false);
d1.setVisible(true);
```

In the first lines, a `JOptionPane` object `jo` is created. The method `createDialog` creates a new dialog of the type `JDialog` and places `jo` automatically as the only component in the new dialog box. We assume as before that the variable `f` indicates the window

---

JOptionPane

Here, the same parameters are used as in the fact box on page 477.

Constructors:

```
new JOptionPane()
new JOptionPane(mess)
new JOptionPane(mess, mType)
new JOptionPane(mess, mType, bType)
new JOptionPane(mess, mType, bType, ic)
new JOptionPane(mess, mType, bType, ic, opt)
new JOptionPane(mess, mType, bType, ic, opt, init)
```

Methods that specify characteristics:

```
setMessage(mess)
setMessageType(mType)
setOptions(opt)
setOptionType(bType)
setIcon(ic)
setInitialValue(init)
```

Other methods:

`createDialog(par, title)` creates and returns a `JDialog` with this `JOptionPane` as the only component

`createInternalFrame(par, title)` creates and returns a `JInternalFrame` with this `JOptionPane` as the only component

`getOptions()` gives `null` if you haven't defined any options of your own

`getValue()` returns the option (of the type `Object`) the user has selected. Gives `null` if the user closes the dialog without selecting any of the options, gives `JOptionPane.UNINITIALIZED_VALUE` if no choice has been made yet, gives the number of the button (an `Integer`) if no options of your own exist, gives the text on the button (a `String`) if your own options exist

---

Figure 14.22 A non-modal dialog box

Figure 14.23 Dialogs with answer options

(of the type JFrame) that we want the dialog to be displayed over. In the last two lines, we specify that the dialog is to be non-modal and that it is to be visible.

A non-modal dialog like the one we have just constructed does not prevent the program from executing other functions. In our example, the program therefore will not stop at the invocation of setVisible. The execution will go directly on to the next line in the program. A non-modal dialog remains visible until the user selects one of the buttons or closes the dialog by clicking the Close symbol in the frame.

Even when you create dialogs in this way, you can track which button the user has selected in the program. As an example, we will look at how to construct the two dialogs shown in Figure 14.23.

The left-hand dialog in the figure can be created with the following program lines:

```
JOptionPane op=new JOptionPane("Register now?");
op.setMessageType(JOptionPane.QUESTION_MESSAGE);
op.setOptionType(JOptionPane.YES_NO_OPTION);
JDialog d = op.createDialog(f, "Registration");
d.setVisible(true);
```

If you want the dialog to be non-modal, you add the invocation d.setModal(false) before the invocation of setVisible.

Since we have specified that buttons are to be of the type YES_NO_OPTION we get two buttons with the texts "Yes" and "No", respectively. If instead we want to have three buttons as in the right-hand dialog in the figure, instead of invoking the method setOptionType we should write:

```
String[] alternative = {"Yes", "No", "Later"};
op.setOptions(alternative);
```

To know which button the user has selected, you can invoke the method getValue for the JOptionPane object in the program. If the user closes the dialog by clicking the Close symbol in the frame, this method returns the value null. Otherwise, a value of the type Object is returned. If this is a non-modal dialog box, it may still be open when you invoke getValue and the user has not yet selected any button. In this case getValue returns the special value JOptionPane.UNINITIALIZED_VALUE. In other cases, the user has closed the dialog by clicking one of the buttons. If you have a dialog that has only the standard buttons, that is, buttons determined by specifying the parameter `bType` when you created the dialog box, `getValue` will return the number of the selected button. This number is given as an object of the wrapper class `Integer`. Finally, if you specified yourself which buttons you wanted by specifying the parameter `opt` when you created the dialog box, `getValue` will return a `String` that contains the text on the selected button. To demonstrate the various values that the method `getValue` can return, we write the following program lines:

```
if (op.getValue() == null)
   System.out.println("Dialog closed");
else if (op.getValue() == JOptionPane.UNINITIALIZED_VALUE)
   System.out.println("No alternative chosen");
else if (op.getOptions() == null) { // standard buttons
   int no = ((Integer) op.getValue()).intValue();
   System.out.println("Alternative no " + no + " chosen");
}
else {    // self made buttons
   String txt = (String) op.getValue();
   System.out.println("The button \"" + txt + "\" chosen");
}
```

14.6.3 Direct usage of the class `JDialog`

The basic class for creating dialogs is the class `JDialog`. It is used automatically when you use the help methods in the class `JOptionPane`, but you can also use it directly. The class `JDialog` has largely the same characteristics as the class `JFrame` (see fact box) and can be used in roughly the same way. The actual difference is that a `JDialog` can

---

JDialog

See also the fact box on page 461.

In the constructor `par` designates the parent window and `title` the title text in the frame. The parameter `par` can be either a `Frame` or a `Dialog`.

new `JDialog()`	creates a non-modal dialog box without parent
new `JDialog(par)`	creates a non-modal dialog box
new `JDialog(par, modal)`	creates a dialog box (`modal` is **boolean**)
new `JDialog(par, title)`	creates a non-modal dialog box
new `JDialog(par, title, modal)`	creates a dialog box (`modal` is **boolean**)
`setModal(`*bool*`)`	defines whether the dialog box is to be modal or not
`isModal()`	indicates if the dialog box is modal or not
`setUndecorated(`*bool*`)`	specifies that the dialog will not have a frame

---

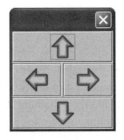

Figure 14.24 Dialog with a special appearance

be made modal so that this it temporarily suspends execution and blocks input to other components in the program.

In most cases, it is more convenient to use the help class JOptionPane than to work with the class JDialog directly, but there are a couple of instances when you cannot use the class JOptionPane. The first example is when you want to have a dialog with an appearance that is special and which cannot be generated by the class JOption-Pane. Assume, for example, that we want a dialog as shown in Figure 14.24. We can achieve this by creating a JDialog component on which we place four JButton components, each of which may contain its own icon. The following program lines are needed:

```
JDialog arrows = new JDialog(f);
final JButton up = new JButton(new ImageIcon("arrowup.gif"));
final JButton down = new JButton(new ImageIcon("arrowdown.gif"));
final JButton le = new JButton(new ImageIcon("arrowleft.gif"));
final JButton ri = new JButton(new ImageIcon("arrowright.gif"));
Container c = arrows.getContentPane();
c.add(up,BorderLayout.NORTH);   c.add(down, BorderLayout.SOUTH);
c.add(le,  BorderLayout.WEST);  c.add(ri,   BorderLayout.EAST);
arrows.pack();
arrows.setResizable(false);
arrows.setModal(false);
arrows.setVisible(true);
```

The reason why the buttons must be declared as **final** is that this is required to be able to access them in a listener. (See below.) We have chosen here to make the dialog non-modal so that it can be open while the program continues to execute.

As previously, we assume that f is a reference to the window that is to be the parent of the dialog box. When you create dialog boxes directly, they will not automatically be positioned on top of the parent window, as occurs when you use the help class JOptionPane. You must set the location of the dialog box yourself by invoking the method setLocation. For example, to locate our dialog box arrows immediately to the right of the parent window with the upper edge at the same height, we write:

```
arrows.setLocation(f.getLocation().x + f.getWidth()
                   f.getLocation().y);
```

What happens then when the user clicks on any of the arrows? If this occurs, an event of the type `ActionEvent` will be generated, as one would expect. If we want to do something when this occurs, we must first of course define a listener and connect it to the buttons. For example, we can add the following program lines. (In a real program, you would do something more intelligent than just give printouts.)

```
ActionListener l = new ActionListener () {
   public void actionPerformed(ActionEvent e) {
      if (e.getSource() == up)
        System.out.println("down");
      else if (e.getSource() == down)
        System.out.println("down");
      else if (e.getSource() == ri)
        System.out.println("right");
      else if (e.getSource() == le)
        System.out.println("left");
   }
};

up.addActionListener(l);
down.addActionListener(l);
le.addActionListener(l);
ri.addActionListener(l);
```

The other case where you need to create dialogs directly without using the help class `JOptionPane` is when you have chosen not to use Swing. You might have constructed an applet that should be able to run in most web browsers. Here, we will construct our own class `YesNoDialog` which you can use to generate simple modal dialogs like the one in Figure 14.25.

The purpose of this is to be able to create dialogs by writing in the following way:

```
YesNoDialog d = new YesNoDialog(f, "Download now?");
if (d.answer == 0)
   System.out.println("Download started ...");
```

Figure 14.25 Dialog constructed with awt components

The parameter f will be a reference to the window you want the dialog to be placed on. The dialog is opened automatically in the constructor. Since it is modal, you will not come to the if statement until the user has clicked one of the buttons or closed the dialog. The class YesNoDialog contains an instance variable called answer which you can examine when the dialog has been closed. This contains the number of the button the user clicked. If the user closed the dialog by clicking the Close symbol in the frame, the variable answer will have the value −1.

Let us finally look at the class YesNoDialog.

```java
import java.awt.*;
import java.awt.event.*;

public class YesNoDialog extends Dialog
                         implements ActionListener {
  private Button yes = new Button("Yes");
  private Button no  = new Button("No");
  public int answer  = -1;

  public YesNoDialog(Frame f, String question) {
    super(f, true);   // make the dialog modal
    Panel p = new Panel();
    p.setLayout(new FlowLayout());
    add(new Label(question), BorderLayout.CENTER);
    add(p, BorderLayout.SOUTH);
    p.add(yes); p.add(no);
    yes. addActionListener(this);
    no.addActionListener(this);
    pack();
    // place the dialog in the middle of f
    setLocation(f.getLocation().x+f.getWidth()/2-getWidth()/2,
                f.getLocation().y+f.getHeight()/2-getHeight()/2);
    setVisible(true);
  }

  // listener method
  public void actionPerformed(ActionEvent e) {
    if (e.getSource() == yes)
      answer = 0;
    else if (e.getSource() == no)
      answer = 1;
    setVisible(false);    // close the dialog
  }
}
```

We have let the class be a subclass of Dialog, which is an awt class. It has largely the same characteristics as its subclass JDialog. Before the dialog is displayed, the starting point is set so that the dialog is centred on top of the parent window f. You come to the listener when the user has clicked one of the two buttons. This is where the variable answer is set. In addition, the window is closed so that execution can proceed again.

Of course, you can construct more general classes according to this same model. For example, you can create a class that makes it possible for the programmer who uses it to select the number of buttons and the texts on these buttons in the dialog him/herself. The constructor will then have an additional parameter that contains an array with texts. However, we will leave this up to the reader.[1]

14.7 The class JFileChooser

A special but very useful class is JFileChooser, which is used to create dialogs where the user can specify a file name. It's very easy to use the class JFileChooser in a program. To create a dialog to be used when you want to open a file, you make the following declaration, for example:

```
JFileChooser fc = new JFileChooser();
```

When you then want to display the dialog box, you invoke the method showOpen-Dialog. The invocation might be as follows:

```
int result = fc.showOpenDialog(f);
```

The parameter f will be a reference to the window you want the dialog to be opened on. (This parameter can be null. In that case, the dialog will be displayed in the centre of the screen.) The appearance of the dialog will depend on the Look & Feel that has been used. If you haven't explicitly specified the Look & Feel (see Section 8.5) the dialog will have the default "Metal" look and feel. It would look like Figure 14.26.

If you don't specify anything in particular, you will come to the folder "My Documents" if you are running Windows. If you are running Unix, you will come to the user's home directory. If you want the dialog to start in another folder/directory, you can state a parameter with the start folder's name in the constructor. For example, we can define the dialog fc in the following way:

```
JFileChooser fc = new JFileChooser("C:\\Program\\JProg\\data");
```

The dialog will then start in the folder C:\Program\JProg\data. (Note that you need to double the character \ since this is regarded as a special character in Java.)

Generally, you will want the dialog to show the same folder as the program itself is executing in. To find out which folder this is, you can invoke the standard function

---

[1] The package extra, which is available on this book's website, contains several ready-made dialog classes that you can use when you are programming using awt.

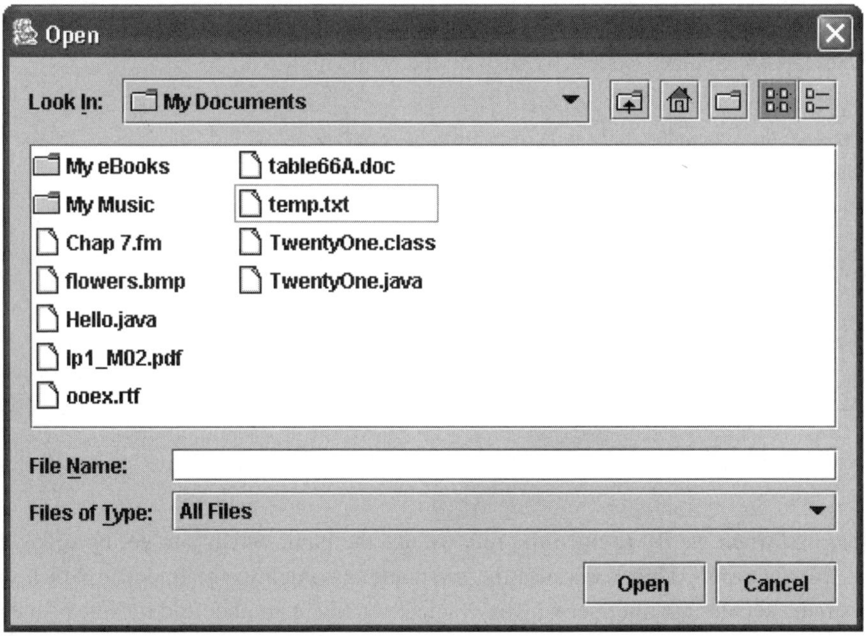

Figure 14.26 Dialog generated by JFileChooser

`System.getProperty` using the parameter `"user.dir"`. Using this, we can define `fc` in the following way:

```
String currentFolder = System.getProperty("user.dir");
JFileChooser fc = new JFileChooser(currentFolder);
```

The invocation of `showOpenDialog` gives an integer as the result. If this integer has the value `JFileChooser.APPROVE_OPTION` the user has selected the file that he or she wants to open. If the result value is instead `JFileChooser.CANCEL_OPTION` the user has clicked the "Cancel" button or closed the dialog with the Close symbol in the frame. If errors occur, the result value `JFileChooser.ERROR_OPTION` may be given.

If the result value was `JFileChooser.APPROVE_OPTION` you can invoke the method `getFile` to find out which file the user has selected. The method `getFile` returns a value of the class `File`. This is a class you can use to describe files. We will discuss this in Section 16.6. The only thing we need to know about it now is that it contains the two methods `getName` and `getAbsolutePath`. You can use these to find out the name of the file. The first gives the file name only, for example `example.txt`, and the other gives the absolute path to the file, for example `C:\Temp\example.txt`.

As an example, we show some statements that can be used to open a text file. As in Section 5.5.2, let's assume that we have declared a stream of the class `BufferedReader`:

```
BufferedReader inFile;
```

When the file is to be opened, we then do the following:

```
int result = fc.showOpenDialog(null);
if (result == JFileChooser.APPROVE_OPTION) {
   String name = fc.getSelectedFile().getName();
   String path = fc.getSelectedFile().getAbsolutePath();
   try {
      inFile = new BufferedReader(new FileReader(path));
   }
   catch (FileNotFoundException e) {
      JOptionPane.showMessageDialog(f, "Cannot open " + name);
   }
}
else
   // the user closed the dialog, do something sensible
   ...
```

Note that when we try to open the file, we use the path, which you get by invoking getAbsolutePath. This is because the file name is related to the folder in which the program executes and the user may have selected a file in another folder. Note also that it is not certain that the selected file actually exists. The user may have written in the file name instead of clicking a file in the list. The constructor of the class FileReader throws an exception FileNotFoundException if the entered file cannot be found (doesn't exist). This kind of event must be dealt with. In this example, we have used a normal dialog box to tell the user that the file could not be found.

If instead you want to *save* a file, you should display the file dialog by invoking the method showSaveDialog instead of the method showOpenDialog. For example, we write:

```
int result = fc.showSaveDialog(null);
```

This will give you a dialog for saving files. In Figure 14.26, for example, it would say "Save" in the frame and on the left button instead of "Open". In addition, you can specify any text (see the fact box). You can use the same JFileChooser object to both open and save files and simply show it with different versions of the method showXxxDialog. This can be an advantage since a JFileChooser object remembers which folder was last displayed. The next time you display the file dialog, it will open in the same folder.

The class JFileChooser has additional methods that you ought to be aware of. A couple of these are setSelectedFile and setCurrentDirectory. They both have an object of the type File as their only argument. The method setSelectedFile indicates which file is to be the default selection when the dialog opens and setCurrentDirectory specifies which folder (directory) the dialog initially will display. (The parameter

490

`null` means that the user's home directory, or "My Documents" in Windows, is displayed.)

You can control which files are displayed in the file dialog. For example, if you are writing a text-editing program, you might only want to see files with the extension `.txt`; and if you are writing an image-processing program, you might only want to display files with the extensions `.gif` and `.jpg`. You can achieve this by using a so-called filter. There is a built-in filter that is normally active. It filters out hidden files. You can control whether hidden files should be displayed or concealed by invoking the method `setFileHidingEnabled`.

In the dialog box, there is a list of filters the user can choose from. You can add or remove filters from this list. If you don't do anything special in a file dialog there is a

JFileChooser	
new `JFileChooser()`	gives a file dialog that starts in the user's home directory
new `JFileChooser(`*start*`)`	gives a file dialog that starts in *start* (a `String` or `File`)
`showOpenDialog(`*parent*`)`	displays the dialog with an "Open" button, gives the value `APPROVE_OPTION` if the user selected a file
`showSaveDialog(`*parent*`)`	displays the dialog with a "Save" button, gives the value `APPROVE_OPTION` if the user selected a file
`showDialog(`*parent, txt*`)`	displays the dialog with the text *txt* on the button, gives the value `APPROVE_OPTION` if the user selected a file
`setDialogTitle(`*txt*`)`	specifies the text of the title in the dialog's frame
`getSelectedFile()`	gives a description (of class `File`) of the selected file
`setSelectedFile(f)`	specifies that `f` (a `File`) is to be selected by default
`f.getName()`	gives the name of the file `f` (of the class `File`)
`f.getAbsolutePath()`	gives the path of the file `f` (of the class `File`)
`setCurrentDirectory(f)`	specifies which directory will be displayed, `f` is a `File`
`getCurrentDirectory()`	gives a description (a `File`) of the current directory
`rescanCurrentDirectory()`	updates the view of the files in the current directory
`setFileSelectionMode(m)`	specifies which types of files can be selected, `m` is `FILES_ONLY`, `DIRECTORIES_ONLY` or `FILES_AND_DIRECTORIES`
`setFileHidingEnabled(`*bool*`)`	specifies if hidden files are to be shown
`addChoosableFileFilter(t)`	specifies that the filter `t` can be selected
`setAcceptAllFileFilterUsed(`*bool*`)`	specifies that the filter "All files" can be selected
`removeChoosableFileFilter(t)`	specifies that the filter `t` cannot be selected
`setFileFilter(t)`	specifies that the filter `t` is to be selected by default

491

single filter, called "All files". You can use the method setAcceptAllFileFilterUsed to specify whether you want this filter to be included in the list or not. You can also define your own filters, which we will show how to do here.

A filter is an object that belongs to a subclass of the abstract class FileFilter, which is found in the package javax.swing.filechooser. As yet, there are no ready-made subclasses of this class – so you have to define them yourself. The class FileFilter contains two abstract methods that you must define in a subclass of their own. These are the methods accept and getDescription. The method accept gets a file description (an object of the class File) as a parameter. The method accept should return a value of the type **boolean** which specifies whether the selected file is to be visible in the file dialog or not. The method getDescription should return a String. This is to contain the text to be displayed in the list of filters that the user can choose from.

This is most easily seen with an example of how it works. Let's assume that we have constructed a text editor that can edit text files. The text editor has some additional special features that make it suitable for use for editing program files containing C, C++ or Java programs. For this reason, we want the dialog for opening files to have three filters: one for showing all files, one that only shows files with the extension .txt and one that shows only files with the extensions .c .h .cpp or .java . We can achieve this by writing the following in that part of the program in which the file dialog is defined:

```
JFileChooser fc = new JFileChooser();
NameFilter t1 = new NameFilter(".txt");
NameFilter t2 = new NameFilter(".c .h .cpp .java");
fc.addChoosableFileFilter(t1);
fc.addChoosableFileFilter(t2);
fc.setFileFilter(t1);
```

We declare two filters, t1 and t2, of the class NameFilter. We then add these two filters to the list of selectable filters. On the last line, we say that the filter t1 is to be the default filter. The class NameFilter is a class we have constructed ourselves. It is used to create filters that filter file names with certain extensions. You set which file extensions are to be used as a parameter for the constructor when you create your filters. Figure 14.27 shows how a dialog created with the statements above would look.

We will now study the class NameFilter. (Since this is generally useful, it is also defined in the package extra found on this book's website.) The class contains a constructor and the methods accept and getDescription. It is a subclass to the class FileFilter in the package javax.swing.filechooser. Now as it happens, the package java.io contains another class that is also called FileFilter. To specify which of these two classes we mean, we must therefore write out the full name of the class FileFilter.

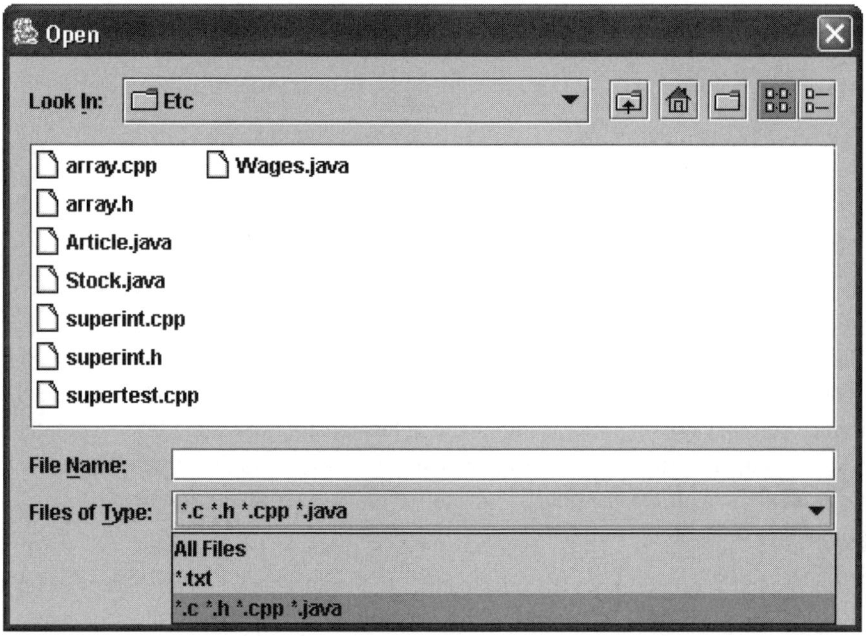

Figure 14.27 Dialog with selectable file filters

```
import javax.swing.filechooser.*;
import java.io.*;
import java.util.*;

public class NameFilter
                    extends javax.swing.filechooser.FileFilter {
  private String[] suf;              // contains suffix
  private String description = "";

  public NameFilter(String suffix) {
    StringTokenizer tok = new StringTokenizer(suffix);
    suf = new String[tok.countTokens()];
    for (int i=0; i<suf.length; i++) {
      suf[i] = tok.nextToken();   // next suffix
      description += "*" + suf[i] + " ";
    }
  }

  public boolean accept(File f) { // will f be accepted?
    if (f.isDirectory()) {
      return true;
    }
    for (int i=0; i<suf.length; i++) {
      if (f.getName().endsWith(suf[i]))
```

```
            return true;
        }
        return false;
    }

    public String getDescription() {  // description of files
        return description;               // to be accepted
    }
}
```

The constructor has a parameter of the type `String`. This contains the various file extensions with spaces between them. A `StringTokenizer` (see Section 5.3.3 on page 127) is used in the constructor to pick out individual file extensions. These are put into an internal array called `suf`. Each element in this field will contain a file extension. The instance variable `description` is initialized in the constructor so that it will contain the text to be shown in the list of filters in the dialog box. For example, if you have invoked the constructor with the parameter `".c .h .cpp .java"`, the variable `description` will contain the text `"*.c *.h *.cpp *.java"`.

The method `accept` examines the selected file. If it is a folder (directory), or if its name ends with any of the extensions in the array `suf`, the file (or folder or directory) will be displayed in the dialog box. The method `accept` therefore returns the value **true** in these cases. For other files, the value **false** is returned.

The method `getDescription`, finally, is very simple. It simply returns the text constructed in the constructor.

14.8 Example – a text editor

As the conclusion of this chapter, a new, improved version of the text editor that was discussed in Section 6.12 follows below. In this new version, we will use most of the building blocks dealt with in this chapter: modal dialogs, file dialogs, tool bars and menus. The purpose of this example is to show how the building blocks function together in a bigger, more realistic example. Figure 14.28 shows what the screen will look like when you run the new version of the text editor.

The buttons in Section 6.12 have been replaced by two menus: "File" and "Edit". The "File" menu has the items "New", "Open", "Save", "Save as" and "Exit". The "Edit" menu has the items "Cut", "Copy" and "Paste". In addition to the menus, there is a tool bar with buttons for the items "New", "Open", "Save", "Cut", "Copy" and "Paste". It is also possible to use the common keyboard shortcuts Ctrl-X, Ctrl-C and Ctrl-V to cut, copy and paste.

When you select "Open" or "Save as", a file dialog is displayed where you can enter the file name in the regular way. (Figure 14.26 shows a file dialog of this kind.) If you

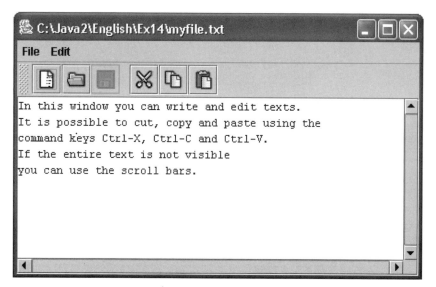

Figure 14.28 A text editor

try to open a file that cannot be found, a modal dialog will be displayed with a message. Each time you specify that you want to edit a new text or read a new file, the program will check if the text in question has been changed. If it has, the user gets a message asking if he or she wants to save the text. This question is shown in a dialog box. The choices "Save" and "Save as" are inactive if you have selected "New" and not yet entered anything in the window. "Save" is additionally inactive when you have just opened a file but not yet made any changes. If you have selected "New" and entered new text and then select "Save", the program will instead execute the command "Save as" automatically so that you have the option of specifying what the file is to be called.

The program permits you to edit files saved in different folders/directories. The absolute path to the file you are editing is shown at all times in the window frame.

The program will now be shown in its entirety. Since the user should be able to give the command either from the menu or via the button on the tool bar, the program uses actions. A separate action is defined for each of the commands ("New", "Open", "Save" etc.). These actions are then linked to both the menus and the tool bar. To access the `Action` objects corresponding to the shortcuts for cut, copy and paste, we use the technique described on page 435. File management is done in the same way as in the previous version (see Section 6.12). The text area inside the window is also handled in the same way as in the previous version of the program. The program does not contain any new constructions not dealt with previously. We therefore leave it up to the reader to go through the program text and look at how the program is constructed.

```java
import java.awt.*;
import java.awt.event.*;
import java.io.*;
import javax.swing.*;
import javax.swing.text.*;

class TextEdit extends JFrame {

    private JTextArea area = new JTextArea(10,60);
    private JFileChooser dialog =
                new JFileChooser(System.getProperty("user.dir"));

    private String currentFile = "unnamed";
    private boolean changed = false;

    // Constructor
    public TextEdit() {
        // Put the text area in a JScrollPane
        area.setFont(new Font("Monospaced", Font.PLAIN, 12));
        JScrollPane scroll = new JScrollPane(area,
                            JScrollPane.VERTICAL_SCROLLBAR_ALWAYS,
                            JScrollPane.HORIZONTAL_SCROLLBAR_ALWAYS);
        getContentPane().add(scroll,  BorderLayout.CENTER);

        // The menu bar
        JMenuBar mb = new JMenuBar();
        setJMenuBar(mb);
        JMenu fileMenu = new JMenu("File");
        JMenu editMenu = new JMenu("Edit");
        mb.add(fileMenu); mb.add(editMenu);

        // The File menu
        fileMenu.add(newFile); fileMenu.add(open);
        fileMenu.add(save); fileMenu.add(saveAs);
        fileMenu.addSeparator(); fileMenu.add(exit);
        for (int i = 0; i<4; i++)
            fileMenu.getItem(i).setIcon(null);   // no icons

        // The Edit menu
        editMenu.add(cut); editMenu.add(copy); editMenu.add(paste);
        editMenu.getItem(0).setText("Cut");
        editMenu.getItem(1).setText("Copy");
        editMenu.getItem(2).setText("Paste");

        // The tool bar
        JToolBar tools = new JToolBar();
        getContentPane().add(tools, BorderLayout.NORTH);
        tools.add(newFile); tools.add(open);
        tools.add(save); tools.addSeparator();
        JButton cuB=tools.add(cut), coB=tools.add(copy),
                paB=tools.add(paste);
        cuB.setText(null); cuB.setIcon(new ImageIcon("cut.gif"));
```

```java
      coB.setText(null); coB.setIcon(new ImageIcon("copy.gif"));
      paB.setText(null); paB.setIcon(new ImageIcon("paste.gif"));

      save.setEnabled(false);
      saveAs.setEnabled(false);

      setDefaultCloseOperation(EXIT_ON_CLOSE);
      pack();
      area.addKeyListener(kl); // to note changes in the text
      setTitle(currentFile);
      setVisible(true);
   }

   // Listener for text changes
   private KeyListener kl = new KeyAdapter() {
      // the user has pressed a key in the text window
      public void keyPressed(KeyEvent e) {
         changed = true;
         save.setEnabled(true);
         saveAs.setEnabled(true);
      }
   };

   // Define the actions
   Action newFile = new AbstractAction("New",
                                      new ImageIcon("new.gif")) {
      public void actionPerformed(ActionEvent e) {
         saveOld();
         area.setText("");   // empty the text area
         currentFile = "unnamed";
         setTitle(currentFile);
         changed = false;
         save.setEnabled(false);
         saveAs.setEnabled(false);
      }
   };

   Action open = new AbstractAction("Open ...",
                                      new ImageIcon("open.gif")){
      public void actionPerformed(ActionEvent e) {
         saveOld();
         if (dialog.showOpenDialog(null)==
                              JFileChooser.APPROVE_OPTION) {
            readFile(dialog.getSelectedFile().getAbsolutePath());
         }
         saveAs.setEnabled(true);
      }
   };

   Action save = new AbstractAction("Save",
                                      new ImageIcon("save.gif")){
```

```
    public void actionPerformed(ActionEvent e) {
      if (!currentFile.equals("unnamed"))
        saveFile(currentFile);
      else
        saveFileAs();
    }
};

Action saveAs = new AbstractAction("Save as ...") {
  public void actionPerformed(ActionEvent e) {
    saveFileAs();
  }
};

Action exit = new AbstractAction("Exit") {
  public void actionPerformed(ActionEvent e) {
    saveOld();
    System.exit(0);
  }
};

ActionMap m = area.getActionMap();
Action cut   = m.get(DefaultEditorKit.cutAction);
Action copy = m.get(DefaultEditorKit.copyAction);
Action paste = m.get(DefaultEditorKit.pasteAction);

// Internal methods

private void saveFileAs() {
  if (dialog.showSaveDialog(null)==
                                JFileChooser.APPROVE_OPTION)
    saveFile(dialog.getSelectedFile().getAbsolutePath());
}

private void saveOld() {
  if (changed) {
    if (JOptionPane.showConfirmDialog
        (this, "Save " + currentFile + "?", "",
        JOptionPane.YES_NO_OPTION) == JOptionPane.YES_OPTION)
    saveFile(currentFile);
  }
}

private void readFile(String fileName) {
  try {
    FileReader r = new FileReader(fileName);
    area.read(r, null);
    r.close();
    currentFile = fileName;
    setTitle(currentFile);
    changed = false;
  }
```

```
      catch (IOException e) {
        Toolkit.getDefaultToolkit().beep();   // beep
        JOptionPane.showMessageDialog
              (this, "Cannot find the file " + fileName);
      }
    }

    private void saveFile(String fileName) {
      try {
        FileWriter w = new FileWriter(fileName);
        area.write(w);
        w.close();
        currentFile = fileName;
        setTitle(currentFile);
        changed = false;
        save.setEnabled(false);
      }
      catch (IOException e) {}
    }

    public static void main (String[] arg) {
      new TextEdit();
    }
  }
```

14.9 Exercises

1. Redo the class `Travel2` on page 190 so that you can do several calculations in different windows at the same time. Add a button that you can click when you want to start a new calculation in parallel with the current one.

2. Make changes in the class `TextEdit` in Section 14.8 so that a new editing window opens automatically when the user selects "New". The text in the existing window must not be deleted as a consequence. Ensure that the new window does not end up being positioned on top of the old one, but with a slight displacement.

3. Do the same as in the previous exercise, but use an *internal* window for each file to be edited. Place the menus in the surrounding external window.

4. Add shortcuts for the menu items "New", "Open", "Save" and "Exit" in the class `TextEdit` in Section 14.8. In addition, add *tool tips* to the buttons in the tool bar.

5. Redo the program `JToggleDemo` on page 182 so that the radio buttons are shown in a separate, non-modal dialog to the side of the main window.

6. Rewrite the program `TwentyOne` in Section 10.10 so that it uses dialogs to communicate with the user.

7. Solve Exercise 8 on page 152 but let the program have a GUI and use the class `JFileChooser` to fetch the file name into the program.

8. Add to the program `PaintProgram` on page 420 so that it contains a help menu with one item. When the user selects this item, a box explaining how to draw a picture is displayed.

9. Extend the program `PaintProgram` on page 420 so that it contains a menu containing the items "Open", "Save" and "Exit". When you select "Open" or "Save", the program should display a file dialog in which the user can enter a file name. You can save the picture drawn by printing the start and end points of the lines to a text file.

10. Add the items "Find" and "Find/Replace" to the "Edit" menu in the class `TextEdit` in Section 14.8. The first item is used to look for a certain text and the other to find and replace one text with another.

Images and sounds

15

Previously in this book, we have seen many examples of how you can display images in Swing by positioning icons with images on top of graphical components, for example components of the type `JLabel` and `JButton`. In this chapter, we will discuss the class `Image`, which is the underlying class used when you handle images. The class `Image` is useful if you want to have more control over how images are downloaded and displayed. We will also look at how to construct your own icons, for example icons with scalable images. At the end of this chapter, we will learn how to play audio files in your programs and applets.

15.1 Downloading and display of images

When you are going to download a file with an image from the Internet, you must state where the file is. To do this, you use an object of the class `URL` (Uniform Resource Locator). Each `URL` object represents a unique address on the Internet. The `URL` class is defined in the package `java.net`. We will discuss the class `URL` in more detail in Chapter 17. Here, we will only show how to create a `URL` object based on an Internet address. The simplest way is to give the address as a text. For example, you can write:

```
URL u = new URL("http://www.xyz.se/pub/example/picture1.gif");
```

As an example, we will study a program called `ImageDemo` which loads an image from another computer and displays it. The image to be displayed is specified as a parameter for `main` (see Section 9.8). For example, if we start the program with the command:

```
java ImageDemo http://www.cs.chalmers.se/~skanshol/Java_eng/dog.gif
```

the image in Figure 15.1 is displayed.

We let the window, as its only component, have a `JLabel` with an icon on top of it. With the help of the class `ImageIcon`, we create the icon. In our earlier examples, we used the name of the image file as the argument for the constructor, but this time, we are going to use the fact that the class `ImageIcon` also has a constructor that has a `URL` object as a parameter.

Figure 15.1 A program that downloads and displays an image

```
import javax.swing.*;
import java.awt.*;
import java.net.*;     // contains the class URL

public class ImageDemo extends JFrame {

    public ImageDemo(String name) {
        URL u = null;
        try {
            u = new URL(name);
        }
        catch (MalformedURLException e) {
            System.out.println("Incorrect URL: " + name);
            System.exit(0);
        }
        // create a JLabel containing the downloaded picture
        JLabel l = new JLabel(new ImageIcon(u));
        getContentPane().add(l);
        setDefaultCloseOperation(EXIT_ON_CLOSE);
        setSize(400,210);
        // display the URL address in the frame
        setTitle(u.getHost()+u.getFile());
        getContentPane().setBackground(Color.white);
        setVisible(true);
    }

    public static void main(String[] arg) {
        new ImageDemo(arg[0]);  // URL address from the command line
    }
}
```

The constructor for the class URL generates an exception of the type MalformedURL-
Exception if you have specified an incorrect protocol in the URL address. For this
reason, you need to encapsulate the construction of the URL object in a **try** statement. In the program, we have also used the methods getHost and getFile, which
are defined in the class URL, to be able to show the Internet address in the window
frame.

An icon of the class ImageIcon contains an internal object of the class Image that
describes an image. The class Image can handle the image formats GIF, JPEG and
PNG. Animated images can also be displayed. We will now discuss how to use the
class Image to have more control over the downloading and displaying of images.

In the class java.awt.Toolkit there is a method called getImage that you can use to
download (get) an image. This method is available in two versions. The first of these
has a parameter of the type URL. If u is a URL object, you can start downloading an
image by writing:

```
Image im = Toolkit.getDefaultToolkit().getImage(u);
```

The second version of getImage can be used when you want to display an image that
is stored in a file on your own computer. You enter the file name as a parameter:

```
Image im = Toolkit.GetDefaultToolkit().
              getImage("C:\\myFiles\\pictures\\myPicture.gif");
```

To demonstrate this, we make a small change in the program ImageDemo. We don't let
the class ImageIcon manage the downloading of the image any longer – we do this
separately. Only after this do we create a JLabel with an ImageIcon object. To achieve
this, we replace the line:

```
JLabel l = new JLabel(new ImageIcon(u));
```

with the two lines:

```
Image im = Toolkit.getDefaultToolkit().getImage(u);
JLabel l = new JLabel(new ImageIcon(im));
```

A *standalone program* such as ImageDemo can download files from any computer,
but for security reasons, an *applet* may not read or write files that are located on a
computer other than the one where the applet itself is located (that is, the computer
that the applet has been downloaded from). This also applies to image files. It's
very easy to find out the web address for the applet itself in the applet. You invoke a
method called getCodeBase. This returns a URL object containing the address of the
applet's class file. There is also a similar method called getDocumentBase. This
returns a URL object containing the address of the HTML file that the applet is started
from.

To read an image file into the applet you don't use the method `getImage` in the class `Toolkit`. Instead, you use a version of the method `getImage` that is defined in the class `Applet`. The version of the method `getImage` that is suitable to use has two parameters. The first is a `URL` object and the second is an address relative to the first parameter. The relative address is stated as a text. To get the value of the first parameter for the method `getImage` you can simply invoke `getCodeBase` (or perhaps `getDocumentBase`). If the image file is called `pic1.gif`, for example, and is found in the same directory as the applet, you can load the image into the applet with the line:

```
Image im = getImage(getCodeBase(), "pic1.gif");
```

If image files are placed in a separate directory, you can of course state a relative path for the invocation `getImage`.

```
Image im = getImage(getCodeBase(), "pictures/pic1.gif");
```

In both cases, the applet is movable, on the condition that the file `pic1.gif` is moved with it. If no file with the specified name exists, `getImage` will return the value **null**.

We will study a very simple applet that does the same thing as the program `ImageDemo`, that is, it is given the name of an image file as a parameter and displays the image. When you execute the applet in a web browser, it would look like Figure 15.2.

The HTML file that the applet is started from looks like this:

Figure 15.2 An applet that displays an image

```
<html>
  <head><title>ImageAppl</title></head>
  <body>
  <applet code=ImageAppl.class width=208 height=198 align=right>
    <param name=pictureName value=dog.gif>
  </applet>
  <H1>Welcome to the
  <br>
  Java Gallery</H1>
  </body>
</html>
```

When the applet is initialized, it reads the image's file name. Thereafter, it fetches
the file to an Image object with the name img. To make it more usable, we should construct the applet without using Swing components, in which case we will not have
access to the classes JLabel and ImageIcon. Instead we define our own simple class
ImagePanel. This class is a subclass of the awt class Panel and encapsulates an image
so that it can be used as a graphical component. The class ImagePanel looks like this:

```
import java.awt.*;
public class ImagePanel extends Panel {

  private Image im;

  public ImagePanel(Image img) {  // constructor
    im = img;
    setSize(im.getWidth(this), im.getHeight(this));
  }

  public void paint(Graphics g) {
    g.drawImage(im, 0, 0, this);
  }
}
```

Using this class, we can now construct the applet.

```
import java.applet.*;
import java.awt.*;
public class ImageAppl extends Applet {
  Image img;

  public void init() {
    String name = getParameter("pictureName");
    img = getImage(getCodeBase(), name);
    setLayout(new BorderLayout());
    add(new ImagePanel(img));
    setBackground(Color.white);
  }
}
```

The image is drawn with the help of the method drawImage. The first parameter in drawImage is the image. The next two parameters indicate where to start drawing the image. Here, we want to start drawing the image in the upper left corner and so we specify the coordinates (0.0). The last parameter must be a reference to an object that can track the drawing of the image. This object is to be a subclass of Component. The simplest way to do this is to let the object be the supervisor and so we write **this**.

The method drawImage is available in several different versions. One of these additionally has two parameters that specify the height and width of the image when it is drawn. Using these, you can also scale the image. The original size of the image can be read using the method getWidth and getHeight. To make the image half the size when it is drawn, you can write, for example:

```
g.drawImage(im, 0, 0, im.getWidth(this)/2,
                       im.getHeight(this)/2,this);
```

Note that the methods getWidth and getHeight and the method drawImage must have a reference to a Component object as a parameter. **this** can generally be used.

The class Image
The following methods are used in standalone programs:
`Toolkit.getDefaultToolkit().getImage(`*url*`)`   initializes the download of an image with the URL address *url*
The following methods are used in applets:
`getDocumentBase()`   gives a URL with the address to the HTML file's directory `getCodeBase()`   gives a URL with the address to the class file's directory `getImage(`*url, filename*`)`   initializes the download of an image with the name   *filename* stated relative to the URL address *url*
The following methods are used to manage Image objects. *comp* is a graphical component such as **this**.

`im.getWidth(`*comp*`)`   returns the width for the image im
`im.getHeight(`*comp*`)`   returns the height for the image im
`g.drawImage(im, `*x,y,comp*`)`   draws the image im starting at the position (*x,y*)
`g.drawImage(im, `*x,y,b,h,comp*`)`   draws the image im starting at the position (*x,y*),
                         rescaled to the size *b×h*
`g.drawImage(im, `*x,y,c,comp*`)`   as above, but with the background color *c*
`g.drawImage(im, `*x,y,b,h,c,comp*`)`   as above, but with the background color *c*
`g.drawImage`   is also found in versions where you can draw, scale and rotate
                part of an image (see the documentation of the class Graphics)

As we all know, it can take a long time to download an image from the Internet. The method getImage (this applies both to the version defined in the class Toolkit and the one defined in the class Applet) doesn't wait for the entire image to be downloaded – it starts a parallel thread that downloads the data in the background. This means that when you return from the call of getImage the full image doesn't need to be available yet. The method drawImage also works for incomplete images. If the entire image hasn't been downloaded yet, only part of it is drawn.

If you want to, you can track the downloading of an image. You use the class MediaTracker in the package java.awt to do this. You first create an object of the class MediaTracker. You need to give a reference to the object as a parameter for the constructor. In other words, you write this:

```
MediaTracker mt = new MediaTracker(this);
```

Then you use a method called addImage to register the images you want to track. In addition to the image, the method needs an ID number. This is an integer that you decide yourself. If you want the image to have the number 0, for example, you write:

```
mt.addImage(img, 0);
```

In addition, there is a set of methods that you can use to check the status of the image download. The method checkID checks if the download of a certain image is complete. (See the fact box.) The method waitForID is of particular interest, because you can use it to wait until the download of an image is complete. We will add to our applet ImageAppl a number of statements that will result in waiting to start drawing the image until the entire image has been downloaded. We rewrite the applet as follows:

```
import java.applet.*;
import java.awt.*;

public class ImageAppl extends Applet {
    Image img;

    public void init() {
        String name = getParameter("pictureName");
        img = getImage(getCodeBase(), name);
        showStatus("Loads " + name);
        MediaTracker mt = new MediaTracker(this);
        mt.addImage(img, 0);
        try {mt.waitForID(0);}
        catch(InterruptedException e){}
        showStatus("Loading finished");
        setLayout(new BorderLayout());
        add(new ImagePanel(img));
        setBackground(Color.white);
    }
}
```

As before, we initialize the download of the image by invoking the method `getImage`. Then we use the method `showStatus` to tell the user what is happening. The method `showStatus` is defined in the class `Applet`. When you invoke this method, the message you give as parameter is displayed in the web browser's message bar, normally at the bottom of the window frame.

We then create a `MediaTracker` object and register that the image is to be tracked. We give the image the ID number 0. The method `waitForID` is then invoked to wait until the download is complete. Give the ID number of the image you want to wait for as a parameter. Since the method `waitForID` can generate an exception of the type `InterruptedException`, the invocation must be put inside a **try** statement.

MediaTracker
new `MediaTracker(this)`   creates a `MediaTracker` object
`addImage(im,n)`   registers that the image `im` with ID number `n` is to be tracked
`removeImage(im)`   registers that the image `im` should no longer be tracked
`checkAll()`   gives **true** if all tracked images have been loaded
`checkID(n)`   gives **true** if the image with the ID number `n` has been loaded
`isErrorID(n)`   gives **true** if the loading of the image number `n` failed
`isErrorAny()`   gives **true** if the loading of any image failed
`waitForID(n)`   waits until the loading of image number `n` is complete
`waitForID(n,ms)`   as above, but wait at the most `ms` milliseconds
`waitForAll()`   waits until all images have been loaded
`waitForAll(ms)`   as above, but waits at most `ms` milliseconds

15.2 Icons

The possibility of displaying icons and buttons on `JLabel` objects is one of the most appreciated additions in Swing compared with awt. To create an icon with an image, we use the standard class `IconImage`, as we already know. An icon need not be of this class, however. It is possible to construct your own icon classes. In this section, we will demonstrate how. We will display icons that we have drawn with the help of the regular drawing tools (`drawLine`, `drawRect` etc.) and also icons that contain images whose size can be varied.

15.2.1 The interface `Icon`

Icons that can be placed on components of the type `JLabel` and `JButton` must be of a class that implements the standard interface `Icon`. There are only three methods in this interface, which all classes that implement the interface must have. These are the methods `getIconWidth` and `getIconHeight` which give the icon's width and height, and the method `paintIcon`. The last draws the icon. As a parameter, it gets a reference to the graphical component on which the icon is to be drawn and two coordinates that specify where the drawing is to begin. In addition, it gets a reference to a graphical "toolkit" of the type `Graphics` which gives access to the various drawing tools.

The interface Icon
Must be implemented by all classes that describe icons.

`getIconWidth()`	gives the icon's width
`getIconHeight()`	gives the icon's height
`paintIcon(co, graph, x, y)`	draws the icon on the component co starting at the position x, y. graph is of the type Graphics

The standard class `ImageIcon`, which is used to create icons with images, implements the interface `Image`.

ImageIcon
In addition to the methods in the `Icon` interface, it includes the following:

new `ImageIcon()`	creates an uninitialized `ImageIcon` object
new `ImageIcon(filename)`	creates an icon with the image in the file *filename*
new `ImageIcon(url)`	creates an icon, image to be downloaded from *url*
new `ImageIcon(image)`	creates an `ImageIcon` with the image *image*
`getImage()`	gives the image to be displayed
`setImage(image)`	sets the image to be displayed
`loadImage(image)`	sets the image to be displayed, waits until download is done

15.2.2 A simple icon class

As an example, we will construct our own icon class with the name `OvalIcon`. This can be used to create icons that have a circle/ring or oval shape. The icons can be drawn as outlines only or filled. Figure 15.3 shows two buttons on which we have put icons of our class `OvalIcon`. One of the icons is filled and the other not.

Here is our class `OvalIcon`. The class has four instance variables that hold the icon's characteristics: its width, height and colour, and whether it is filled or not. Since the class is to implement the interface `Icon` it must have the three methods `getIconWidth`, `getIconHeight` and `paintIcon`. In addition to these, we have added a constructor. Using the parameters of this constructor, you can specify the icon's characteristics.

Figure 15.3 Buttons with their own icons

```java
import javax.swing.*;
import java.awt.*;

public class OvalIcon implements Icon {

  private int w, h;        // width and height
  private Color color;
  private boolean filled;

  public OvalIcon(int width, int height, Color col, boolean fi){
    w = width; h = height; color = col; filled = fi;
  }

  public int getIconWidth() {
    return w;
  }

  public int getIconHeight() {
    return h;
  }

  public void paintIcon(Component c, Graphics g, int x, int y) {
    g.setColor(color);
    if (filled)
      g.fillOval(x, y, w, h);
    else
      g.drawOval(x, y, w, h);
  }
}
```

As can be seen, it's quite simple. The methods `getIconWidth` and `getIconHeight` need only return the two instance variables `w` and `h` and the method `paintIcon` can use the drawing tools `fillOval` and `drawOval`.

The statements that generate the buttons in Figure 15.3 might be as follows:

```java
OvalIcon iOn = new OvalIcon(25, 25, Color.black, false);
OvalIcon iOff = new OvalIcon(25, 25, Color.red, true);
JButton on = new JButton("On", iOn);
JButton off = new JButton("Off", iOff);
on.setHorizontalTextPosition(JButton.CENTER);
```

```
off.setHorizontalTextPosition(JButton.CENTER);
on.setVerticalTextPosition(JButton.BOTTOM);
off.setVerticalTextPosition(JButton.BOTTOM);
getContentPane().setLayout(new FlowLayout());
getContentPane().add(on); getContentPane().add(off);
```

15.2.3 Icons with variable size

Icons of the type `OvalIcon` always have a fixed size that you decide when you create them. We will now demonstrate how you can construct an icon whose size varies and adapts itself to the component on which it is drawn. For example, we will construct a class `CrossRingIcon` that can be used when you want to display the board for a board game. Figure 15.4 shows how this would look. We have constructed a board for playing noughts and crosses (tic-tac-toe).

On each button, there is an icon of the class `CrossRingIcon`. (The empty buttons also have icons, but these don't draw anything.) If the size of the window changes, the sizes of the icons will also change so that they always adapt themselves to the sizes of the buttons. We will start by showing the statements that generate the buttons in the figure. First, we declare two 2-dimensional arrays – one with buttons and one with icons:

```
JButton[][] b = new JButton[3][3];
CrossRingIcon[][] i = new CrossRingIcon[3][3];
```

Then the buttons and icons are created and positioned:

```
getContentPane().setLayout(new GridLayout(3,3));
for (int r=0; r<b.length; r++)
   for (int k=0; k<b[r].length; k++) {
      i[r][k] = new CrossRingIcon();
```

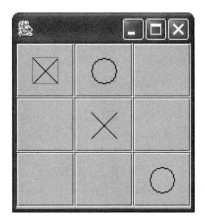

Figure 15.4 Buttons with icons of variable size

```
      b[r][k] = new JButton(i[r][k]);
      i[r][k].setParent(b[r][k]);
      getContentPane().add(b[r][k]);
   }
```

For an icon to be able to adapt its size to the component on which it is to be drawn (the parent component), it must know what this component is. For this reason, there is a method `setParent` in the class `CrossRingIcon` that you need to invoke to tell the icon which component is its parent.

To specify if an icon is to be drawn as a ring/circle or cross, or remain empty, we invoke the method `setSymbol`. This parameter should have one of the constants EMPTY, CROSS or RING, which are defined in the class `CrossRingIcon`. To see the diagram shown in the figure we have made the following invocation:

```
   i[0][0].setSymbol(CrossRingIcon.CROSS);
   i[0][1].setSymbol(CrossRingIcon.RING);
   i[1][1].setSymbol(CrossRingIcon.CROSS);
   i[2][2].setSymbol(CrossRingIcon.RING);
```

It's now time to see what the class `CrossRingIcon` looks like. This class, too, implements the interface `Icon`.

```
import javax.swing.*;
import java.awt.*;

public class CrossRingIcon implements Icon {

   private JComponent p;      // parent component
   private int symbol = EMPTY;

   public static final int EMPTY=0, CROSS=1, RING=2;

   // Constructors
   public CrossRingIcon() { }

   public CrossRingIcon(int s) {
      setSymbol(s);
   }

   // Methods
   public void setParent(JComponent parent) {
      p = parent;
   }

   public void setSymbol(int s) {
      if (s >= EMPTY && s <= RING)
         symbol=s;
   }

   public int getSymbol() {
      return symbol;
   }
```

```
    // Internal method
    private int size() {
      // calculate the smaller of the parent's width and height
      return Math.min
        (p.getWidth() -p.getInsets().left-p.getInsets().right,
          p.getHeight()-p.getInsets().top -p.getInsets().bottom);
    }

    public int getIconWidth() {
      return size();
    }

    public int getIconHeight() {
      return size();
    }

    public void paintIcon(Component c, Graphics g, int x, int y) {
      g.setColor(Color.black);
      if (symbol == CROSS) {
        g.drawLine(x, y, x+getIconWidth(), y+getIconHeight());
        g.drawLine(x, y+getIconHeight(), x+getIconWidth(), y);
      }
      else if (symbol == RING)
        g.drawOval(x, y, getIconWidth(), getIconHeight());
    }
}
```

An icon of this type has two instance variables: one that will contain a reference to the parent component, and one that identifies which symbol is to be drawn. There are two constructors: one that is parameterless, and one where you state which symbol is to be drawn. If you select the parameterless constructor, the symbol will be EMPTY, which means that nothing at all will be drawn. There are methods for setting the parent component and for changing and reading the current symbol.

Since the rings and crosses are to be symmetrical, we always let the height and width be the same for each icon. The methods getIconWidth and getIconHeight required by the interface Icon therefore return the same value. This value is calculated in the auxiliary method size. In this method, the size of the parent component is checked and the smallest value of its height and width are selected. In the calculation, the amount of space used for the parent component's border is deducted.

Finally, the method paintIcon checks which symbol is to be drawn. To know how big the symbol should be, the methods getIconWidth and getIconHeight are invoked. Note that the drawing of the ring or cross starts at the point x, y.

15.2.4 Images with variable size

A limitation of the standard class ImageIcon is that it isn't possible to change the size of the image when displayed. For example, if the component on which the icon is drawn is smaller than the image, only part of the image will be displayed. So we will construct a subclass DynamicImageIcon of the class ImageIcon which makes it possible to rescale the image so that it adapts itself to the size of the parent component. As for the class OvalIcon, we let the class have an instance variable that contains a reference to the parent component. We also define a method called setParent that you can invoke to specify which component is the parent component. If the user doesn't invoke this method, the icon will not know what size the image should be. In that case, the image will take its original size. (In other words, in that case the class DynamicImageIcon will function in exactly the same way as its superclass ImageIcon.)

In the class DynamicImageIcon the three methods getIconWidth, getIconHeight and paintIcon are redefined. In addition, a new method called getIconSize is defined, which calculates the icon's size (width and height). The class looks as follows. (It is also found in the package extra on this book's website.)

```java
import javax.swing.*;
import java.awt.*;
import java.net.*;

public class DynamicImageIcon extends ImageIcon {

  private JComponent p;      // parent component

  // Constructors
  public DynamicImageIcon(String filename) {
    super(filename);
  }

  public DynamicImageIcon(URL location) {
    super(location);
  }

  public DynamicImageIcon(Image image) {
    super(image);
  }

  // Methods
  public void setParent(JComponent parent) {
    p = parent;
  }

  public Dimension getIconSize() {
    // calculate the initial size of the picture
    int iw = getImage().getWidth(component),
        ih = getImage().getHeight(component);
    if (p == null)
      return new Dimension(iw, ih); // no parent given
    else {
      // calculate the size of the parent component
      int pw, ph;
```

```
      pw=p.getWidth() -p.getInsets().left-p.getInsets().right;
      ph=p.getHeight()-p.getInsets().top -p.getInsets().bottom;
      if (pw/(double)ph < iw/(double)ih)
         return new Dimension(pw, pw*ih/iw); // the width decides
      else
         return new Dimension(ph*iw/ih, ph); // the height decides
   }
}

public int getIconWidth() {
   return getIconSize().width;
}

public int getIconHeight() {
   return getIconSize().height;
}

public void paintIcon(Component c, Graphics g, int x, int y) {
   g.drawImage(getImage(), x, y, getIconWidth(),
            getIconHeight(), component);
}
}
```

The most complicated method, not surprisingly, is getIconSize. It starts by calculating the original size of the image. (To be able to do this, getWidth and getHeight are invoked. As we have seen previously, both of these methods must have a component as the parameter. Here, we cannot use **this**, since our class DynamicImageIcon is not a subclass of Component. In the superclass IconImage, however, there is an instance variable called component that can be used.) If no parent component is specified, that is, if p is equal to **null**, you let the size of the icon be the same as the image size. If there is a parent component, you calculate its size. Then you compare the ratios of width and height for the parent and the image to decide if the image's size should be determined by the parent's width or height.

Figure 15.5 shows how it would look if you use the class DynamicImageIcon. The window contains three JLabel components. A DynamicImageIcon has been positioned on each such component. The following shows the lines of the program to construct the window:

Figure 15.5 Use of the class DynamicIconImage

```
DynamicImageIcon d1 = new DynamicImageIcon("dog.gif");
DynamicImageIcon d2 = new DynamicImageIcon("exit.gif");
DynamicImageIcon d3 = new DynamicImageIcon("hammer.gif");
JLabel l1 = new JLabel(d1, JLabel.CENTER);
JLabel l2 = new JLabel(d2, JLabel.CENTER);
JLabel l3 = new JLabel(d3, JLabel.CENTER);
d1.setParent(l1); d2.setParent(l2); d3.setParent(l3);
Container c = getContentPane();
c.setLayout(new GridLayout(1,3));
c.add(l1); c.add(l2); c.add(l3);
```

15.3 Moving images

The classes Image and ImageIcon can handle animated images stored as files in GIF format, for example. However, you can also achieve moving images with the technology used in movies. You can display a series of different images in the same position on the screen. If the images thus displayed differ only slightly, and you change to the next image at an appropriate time interval, the effect is of a movie. (This is the same idea we used in Chapter 12 when we looked at how to use active objects to achieve moving images.) In this section, we will demonstrate how. The images can, of course, be displayed directly in an applet or in the start window of a standalone application, but to make it a bit more general, we will start by constructing a class FilmViewer. Instances of this class will become active objects that can display moving images. So that this class also can be used in an applet that doesn't use Swing, we will avoid using Swing components. We therefore let the FilmViewer be a subclass of the class Canvas.

We use the same technique as in Section 12.2 to construct active objects. We let the class Movie have an instance variable that is a Thread object. This thread is connected to the current object. The class Movie therefore has to implement the interface Runnable and have a method run, in which the actual execution of the thread will take place. In the class Movie we shall also define the methods start and stop.

There are two constructors in the class Movie, and both will have an array of images as a parameter. The images in this array are the frames of the film to be shown. When the activity is started, the film will be shown repeatedly. One constructor will have another parameter that is an integer, used to indicate the time interval required between each display of the film frames. Time is indicated in milliseconds. (If we make use of the first constructor, where we cannot indicate a time interval, this interval will automatically be set to 500 ms.) The class Movie will look like this:

```
import java.awt.*;
public class Movie extends Canvas implements Runnable {
    private Thread activity;
    private Image[] filmFrames;
```

```
  private int interval;
  private int no;  // no. of the next frame to be displayed

  // constructors
  public Movie(Image[] filmFrames) {
    this(filmFrames, 500);
  }

  public Movie(Image[] filmFrames, int interval) {
    this.filmFrames = filmFrames;
    this.interval = interval;
    // wait until all the frames have been loaded
    MediaTracker mt = new MediaTracker(this);
    for (int i=0; i<filmFrames.length; i++)
      mt.addImage(filmFrames[i], i);
    try {mt.waitForAll();}
    catch (InterruptedException e){}
    // make the film screen as large as the frames
    setSize(filmFrames[0].getWidth(this),
            filmFrames[0].getHeight(this));
  }

  public void run() {
    while (XThread.delay(interval)) {
      repaint();
      no = (no+1) % filmFrames.length;
    }
  }

  public void update(Graphics g) {  // own version that
    paint(g);                       // does not erase
  }

  public void paint(Graphics g) {
    g.drawImage(filmFrames[no], 0, 0, this);
  }

  public void start() {
    if (activity == null) {
      activity = new Thread(this);
      activity.start();
    }
  }

  public void stop() {
    if (activity != null) {
      activity.interrupt();
      activity = null;
    }
  }
}
```

The method `run` contains an eternal top that will make one turn per time interval. At each turn, `repaint` is invoked so that the component can be redrawn. The integer variable `no` is used to keep track of the frame waiting to be displayed. The variable is increased by 1 at each turn. By making use of the `%` operator, we ensure that `no` will automatically be equal to 0 when `no+1` is equal to the number of frames.

We will recall from Section 12.7 that the method `repaint` in turn calls the method `update`. The standard version of `update` will erase the entire component but this is not necessary, as we will draw a new image to fill the entire component in any case. To avoid flicker, we redefine the method `update` so that it will not erase.

Note that we could have done the drawing ourselves in the method `run` and would not have had to define the methods `update` and `paint`, but we chose to do things as we did, to be consistent and to follow the same pattern as we had before. Then again, this version works better in the places where `repaint` is automatically invoked, that is, when the window has been completely or partially hidden.

We will now show how the class `Movie` can be used. We write an applet `Animation`, which will show a moving film – an animation. The HTML file that the applet will start from might look like this:

```html
<html>
  <head>
    <title>Animation</title>
  </head>
  <body>
    <applet code=Animation.class width=300 height=150>
      <param name=number value=10>
      <param name=fileName value=film>
    </applet>
  </body>
</html>
```

As parameters, the applet will have both a number of frames and a text indicating the names of the image files. If the second parameter, as in this example, has the value `film`, the frames will be in files with the names `film1.gif`, `film2.gif` and so on.

Now comes the applet `Animation`. We cannot show a picture of how it will look, as moving images are a little difficult to show in a book. (If the reader would like to test run it, he or she can make use of the two image files `T1.gif` and `T2.gif`, which can be found in the demonstration example `Animator`, in J2SDK.)

```java
import java.awt.*;
import java.applet.*;
public class Animation extends Applet {
  private Movie m;
```

518

```
public void init() {
   int n = Integer.parseInt(getParameter("number"));
   String fileName = getParameter("fileName");
   Image[] frames = new Image[n];
   for (int i=0; i<n; i++)
      frames[i] =getImage(getCodeBase(), fileName+(i+1)+".gif");
   m = new Movie(frames);
   add(m);
}

public void start() {
   m.start();
}

public void stop() {
   m.stop();
}
}
```

15.4 Sounds in applets

Handling sound in Java is quite easy. Java is able to deal with sound files in AU, AIFF, WAW, TYPE 0 MIDI and TYPE 1 MIDI format. Everything to do with sound is defined in the package `java.applet`. A sound sequence is represented by the class `AudioClip`. We load a sound file in an applet in the same way as we load an image file, except that we use the method `getAudioClip` instead of `getImage`. For instance, to read in the sound file `beep.au`, we write:

```
AudioClip a = getAudioClip(getCodeBase(), "beep.au");
```

Sound files, too, must be in the same computer as the applet. Therefore we can use the form of `getAudioClip` where the first parameter is a URL address and the second is a text that describes the corresponding file name.

The class `AudioClip` is very simple. It has only three methods: `play` is used to start the sound file playing once, `stop` interrupts playing and `loop` starts playing the sound file again and again. For example, to start the file `beep.au` playing, we can write:

```
a.play();
```

java.applet.AudioClip	
Describes a sound file.	
`play()`	starts playing the sound file
`stop()`	stops playing the sound file
`loop()`	plays the sound file repeatedly

But if we want the sound file to play only once, we can do this rather more simply in the class `Applet`. We use the method `play` and write, for example:

```
play(getCodeBase(), "beep.au");
```

Sound methods in the class Applet	
newAudioClip (*url*)	a class method that gives the sound file with the URL address *url*
getAudioClip (*url*, *filename*)	gives the sound file with the name *filename*, given in relation to the URL address *url*
play (*url*, *filename*)	plays the sound file with the name *filename*, given in relation to the URL address *url*

We will now show an applet that gets the name of a sound file as a parameter. The applet retrieves the file and starts it playing over and over again. The filename is displayed in the window as follows:

```
import java.awt.*;
import java.applet.*;

public class SoundDemo extends Applet {
    AudioClip a;
    String fileName;

    public void init() {
        fileName = getParameter("fileName");
        a = getAudioClip(getCodeBase(), fileName);
        a.loop();
        add(new Label("Playing " + fileName));
    }

    public void start() {
        a.loop();
    }

    public void stop() {
        a.stop();
    }
}
```

We start playing the sound file in the method `start` and stop it in the method `stop`. This means that the sound file will automatically begin to play when the web page is displayed. As soon as another page is shown, the sound will stop. If we had not stopped the sound the sound file would have continued to play, even when we changed web page.

15.5 Sounds in standalone applications

It is also easy to play sound files in standalone applications. We make use of the method `newAudioClip`. For practical reasons, the method has been defined in class `Applet`, although it has nothing whatever to do with applets. As parameter, `newAudio-Clip` will have a URL object that gives the web address of the sound file to be played. So we have to begin by defining a URL object. For instance, we can write:

```
URL u = new URL("http://www.xyz.se/pub/Java_dir/noise.au");
```

We can then load the sound file.

```
AudioClip a = Applet.newAudioClip(u);
```

Here we have a standalone application that corresponds to the applet `SoundDemo` from the previous section. The sound file's name will be given as parameter for `main`:

```java
import java.awt.*;
import java.applet.*;
import java.net.*;

public class SoundPlayer extends Frame {
    URL u;
    AudioClip a;

    SoundPlayer(String fileName) {
        try {
            u = new URL(fileName);
        }
        catch (MalformedURLException e) {
            System.out.println("Illegal URL: " + fileName);
        }
        a = Applet.newAudioClip(u);
        a.loop();

        setSize(400,200);
        add(new Label("Playing " + fileName));
        setVisible(true);
    }

    public static void main (String arg[]) {
        new SoundPlayer(arg[0]);
    }
}
```

As before, the constructor for the class URL can generate an exception of the type `MalformedURLException`. Therefore, a **try** statement must be used.

521

15.6 Exercises

1. Extend the applet `ImageAppl` on page 505 so that it will not draw the image until the entire image has been downloaded. While the image is being downloaded, a small rectangle with an appropriate appearance is to be drawn in the place where the image will be drawn once it is downloaded.

2. Write a program that downloads images and displays them. In addition to the image, the window should contain a `JTextField` in which the user can enter the URL address for the image to be displayed. Each time the user enters a new URL, the previous image is to be erased and the new one loaded and displayed instead.

3. Expand the program in Exercise 2 so that a slider (of the class `JSlider`) is also displayed in the window, graduated from 0.5 to 2. Using this slider, the user will be able to zoom the image to make it bigger or smaller. Each time a new image starts being displayed, the slider should be automatically reset to 1, which means that the image is displayed in its original size. Use the class `DynamicImageIcon`.

4. Expand the program in Exercise 2 so that there is an additional `JTextField` component. In this component, the user can enter the URL address of a sound file that will be played repeatedly in the background.

5. Add a method to the class `Movie` on page 516 that makes it possible to view a film/movie just once.

6. Add to the class `Movie` on page 516 so that it can show movies/films with sound. Construct new constructors that have an `AudioClip` object as a parameter. Then use this expanded version of `FilmViewer` to make a new version of the applet `Animation` on page 518. In the new version, you must also specify the name of the sound file as a parameter in the HTML file.

7. Add a suitable background sound to the applet `BallDemo` on page 401. (Search on your computer for a suitable sound file that can be used.)

Streams and files

16

In Chapter 3 we discussed how we could read and write texts in a text window. We also saw how we could read and write files containing text. To do this we used streams. It is now time to generalize the description of streams so that we can put into context what we have learnt so far. In this chapter we shall also discuss binary files, that is, files that do not contain text. We will be looking at sequential files, which can be described by using streams, and direct-access files, which are handled by a special class.

A stream is a kind of communication path for data from a *source* to a *destination*. When data flows into a program, we speak of an *input stream*, and of an *output stream* when data flows out of the program. As we saw in Chapter 3, the source or destination of a stream can be anything, a file, for example, or a distant computer. Streams are used in a program so that data can be handled uniformly, regardless of what the source or destination might be.

In the package java.io there are several classes that describe streams with different characteristics. There are many different classes of streams; they fall into two distinct categories: *byte streams* and *char streams*. In byte streams, data is transferred in the form of bytes, that is, in groups of 8 bits. Groups of this kind are described most easily by the built-in type **byte**. In char streams, data is transferred in Unicode format (see Section 9.1) of 16 bits, and this kind of data is described by the built-in type **char**. Char streams are intended to handle data containing text, while byte streams are meant to take care of the other kind of data, binary data. When Java was first created, it only used byte streams but char streams were introduced in Version 1.1 because it was found that byte streams could not handle Unicode characters properly. It is easy to differentiate between the classes that describe byte streams and those that describe char streams. All the classes that describe byte streams contain the word Stream in their names, while all those describing char streams have the word Reader or Writer in their names.

When char streams were introduced, a couple of the classes in earlier versions of Java became obsolete (or *deprecated* as it is called in the literature). These were the classes

523

`StringBufferInputStream` and `LineNumberInputStream`. We will not be discussing these classes. The class `PrintStream` could have been included with these two but it has been retained for historical reasons. (This is discussed further in Section 16.3.10.)

All the examples in this chapter deal with files called for standalone programs because, for security reasons, applets cannot read and write files on a local computer. In addition, they cannot discover information about files or directories.

16.1 An overview

Streams can be connected in much the same way we connect hoses, and the flow of data from one stream can be input directly into another. In Figure 5.4 on page 133, for example, we saw how three streams were connected to transmit input data from the keyboard to the program. Streams can be connected in many different ways. It is actually quite complex and confusing. So we shall try to introduce some order by presenting two "connection charts" that will demonstrate how different streams are connected. Properties unique to the different streams, methods for instance, will be discussed later in the chapter.

Byte input streams

To describe complicated classes, a diagram showing their inheritance structure is useful. In this way, we can see that all classes involved in the reading of byte streams are subclasses of the class `InputStream`. Perhaps more interesting is to see how streams can be connected. We shall therefore study a connection chart instead; see Figure 16.1. The chart is divided into two parts. Byte streams are described in the upper half, and char streams in the lower half. We shall begin by looking at byte streams.

Data flows from left to right in the chart. The source of this flow is on the extreme left, while the program that reads data from the stream is furthest to the right. There are four classes describing streams that can be connected to a source: `InputStream`, `File-InputStream`, `ByteArrayInputStream` and `PipedInputStream`. The class `InputStream` describes a general input stream, and the type of source is not specified. It is an abstract class, which means that it is not possible to create instances of it. One way of gaining access to a stream of this class is to call a special method giving a stream as result. For example, the class `URL`, which we studied in Section 15.1, has a method with the name `openStream` that can be used to create a stream whose source is a file on another computer.

The class `FileInputStream` is used when the source of the flow is a file. The name of the file can be indicated directly when the stream is created.

```
FileInputStream fin = new FileInputStream(file_name);
```

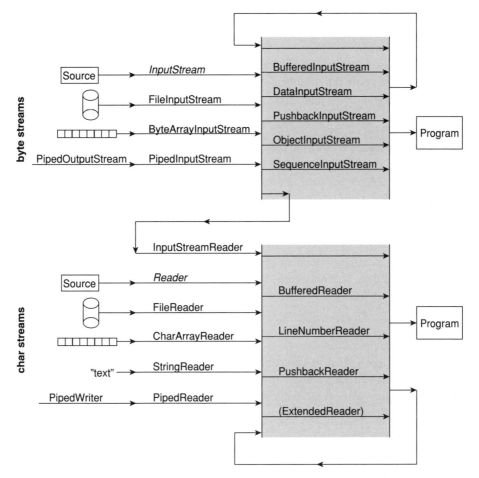

Figure 16.1 A connection chart for input streams

The class `ByteArrayInputStream` can be used when we want to retrieve data from an array of bytes. By using a stream, we can "read" from the array just as if the data came from a file. We write this in the following way:

```
byte[] a = new byte[1000];
... // here input data is placed in a
ByteArrayInputStream bin = new ByteArrayInputStream(a);
```

We use the class `PipedInputStream` when we want two objects to communicate with each other. We arrange for one object to enter an output stream of class `PipedOutput-Stream` and the other to read from an input stream of class `PipedInputStream`.

In Figure 16.1, the upper shaded area gives the streams that can be connected to a byte input stream. The arrow at the top (the one without text) illustrates that it is not necessary to make any connection at all, since the program will read directly from the original input stream here. Because the four classes to the left in the figure have only primitive methods for reading, we may often want to connect to another stream. In the shaded area, we can see that there are five different classes to choose from. For instance, we can connect to a stream of class `BufferedInputStream` to make reading a little more efficient. If we want to connect a buffer to the stream `fin`, we can write:

```
BufferedInputStream bufin = new BufferedInputStream(fin);
```

When we now come to read from the stream `bufin`, this stream will, in turn, read from the stream `fin`. Often, we do not need to access the first stream directly. We do not then need to give it a name but instead can write:

```
BufferedInputStream bufin = new BufferedInputStream
                              (new FileInputStream(file_name));
```

The arrow going in the opposite direction at the top of Figure 16.1 tells us that we can connect to an arbitrary number of streams in this way. If we wanted to be able to read numerical data in binary form quickly, we could connect to a stream of class `DataInputStream` like this:

```
DataInputStream din = new DataInputStream(bufin);
```

The classes `BufferedInputStream`, `DataInputStream`, `PushbackInputStream` and `ObjectInputStream` have in common a constructor in which we indicate the input stream to which the new stream is to be connected. The class `SequenceInputStream`, however, is somewhat special. It enables us to connect two or more input streams to a single stream. We shall show in Section 16.2.14 how this is done.

Char input streams

Input streams used for the reading of Unicode characters are given in the lower half of Figure 16.1. All of these classes are subclasses of class `Reader`. Class `Reader` describes a general input stream, where data flowing into the stream is of type **char**. The source type is not specified. Class `Reader`, like class `InputStream`, is abstract, so we cannot create our own objects of this class. Instead, we shall use one of the other classes indicated at the bottom on the left in Figure 16.1.

The most important of the non-abstract classes is class `InputStreamReader`. With it, we can create a char input stream that, in turn, will read from a stream of class `InputStream`. We could write:

```
InputStream s = initialized in some way;
InputStreamReader r = new InputStreamReader(s);
```

When we read from stream `r`, stream `r` will, in turn, read from stream `s`. The data flowing in stream `s` is in the form of bytes of 8 bits, because `s` is a byte stream, but the data read from stream `r` will be in the form of Unicode with 16 bits. To deal with this in class `InputStreamReader`, a *translation* is made from 8-bit bytes to 16-bit Unicode. We shall discuss in Section 16.2.3 how this is done. Class `InputStreamReader` is, effectively, a bridge between byte streams and char streams; see Figure 16.1.

The class `FileReader`, a subclass of `InputStreamReader`, enables us to read directly from a file. `FileReader` also makes translations from 8-bit bytes to 16-bit Unicode.

Perhaps the simplest of these classes are `CharArrayReader` and `StringReader`. These are used to connect a stream to an array of **char** or a `String` object. The stream will then enable us to "read" from the array or `String` object. These classes function in the same way as the stream `ByteArrayInputStream`. No conversions will be necessary, as data in a **char** array and a `String` object will already exist in Unicode format.

Like the class `PipedInputStream`, class `PipedReader` is used in a program when we want two active objects to communicate with each other through a stream.

The lower shaded area in Figure 16.1 gives the connections that can be made in a char stream. We can read directly from an original char stream, as indicated by the arrow at the top of this section, or we can connect to streams of one of the classes indicated. The arrow pointing in the opposite direction illustrates that we can connect an arbitrary number of streams. Connections are made in the same way as for byte streams, that is, we indicate the stream we want to connect to in the constructor.

We have included our own auxiliary class `ExtendedReader`, shown in Figure 16.1 in brackets, which we introduced in Section 5.4.2. We included this class to show that it follows the same pattern as the other classes. Note, however, that it is not a standard class. As we saw in Chapter 5, class `ExtendedReader` contains a set of methods that helps the programmer when entering data in the form of text. This class is a subclass of class `BufferedReader`, so we do not have to connect an extra buffer when we use it. If `r`, as above, is a stream of class `Reader`, we can write directly:

```
ExtendedReader er = new ExtendedReader(r);
```

Byte output streams

In the chart in Figure 16.2 we show how output streams are connected. Output streams, containing data in the form of 8-bit bytes, are shown in the upper part of the figure. The program writing to a stream is shown furthest to the left, and on the extreme right we find the different destinations this stream can have. We shall begin by discussing the classes for those streams connected to a destination, that is, the classes indicated furthest to the right.

The class `OutputStream` is an abstract class that is a superclass of all the classes handling byte output streams and describes a general output stream. The destination of

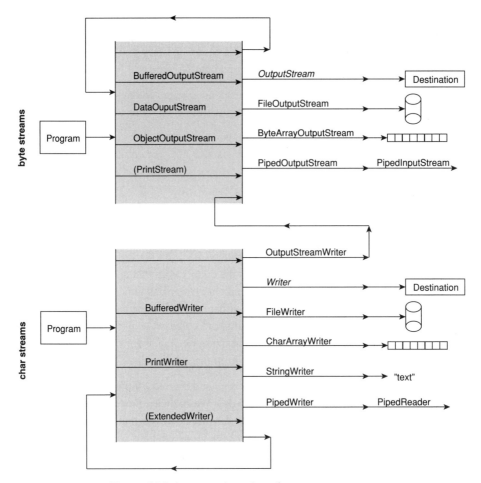

Figure 16.2 A connection chart for output streams

this stream is not specified. We cannot create our own instances of this class. However, we can call special methods that give a stream of this kind as result. (For example, the method getOutputStream in class Socket, to be discussed in Chapter 17, gives an OutputStream that we can write in when we want to send data to another computer.)

If we want to write data to a file, we can use the class FileOutputStream. We can indicate the file's name directly when we create the stream:

```
FileOutputStream fout = new FileOutputStream(file_name);
```

We can also let the destination be an array of bytes and "write" to the array by using the stream, exactly as we might write in a file.

We use class `PipedOutputStream` when we want to be able to send data through a stream from one active object to another. The active object that sends the data will use a stream of class `PipedOutputStream`, and the active object that receives the data will make use of class `PipedInputStream`.

The shaded area at the top of Figure 16.2 shows the connections that can be made to a byte output stream. The difference, when compared with input streams, is that a connection is made *in front of* the stream connected to a destination. For example, if we wanted to use a buffer when outputting data, we could connect a stream of class `BufferedOutputStream`.

```
BufferedOutputStream bout = new BufferedOutputStream(fout);
```

The arrow in the opposite direction indicates, as before, that several streams can be connected in this way. If we wanted to write out numerical data in binary form in a file using buffering, we could write the following stream:

```
DataOutputStream dout = new DataOutputStream(bout);
```

Char output streams

How we connect char output streams is shown in the lower part of Figure 16.2. The classes furthest to the right are those that describe streams that can be connected directly to a destination. The abstract class `Writer` is a superclass to all the classes that describe char output streams. The most important of the non-abstract classes is `OutputStreamWriter`. This is a link between char streams and byte streams. When we write in a stream of class `OutputStreamWriter`, the 16-bit Unicode characters we write are translated into a sequence of 8-bit bytes so that they can be output in the byte stream to which the `OutputStreamWriter` stream is connected. (This translation process is described in Section 16.3.2). If `fout`, as above, is a stream of class `FileOutputStream`, we could create the stream:

```
OutputStreamWriter ow = new OutputStreamWriter(fout);
```

Then the data we wrote would be translated into bytes and stored in the file to which stream `fout` is connected. If we want to write to a file in this way, however, we could simplify things somewhat by using a stream of class `FileWriter` instead.

We use the classes `CharArrayWriter` and `StringWriter` when we want to utilize a stream to "write" to a char array or a `String` object. As we saw earlier, the class `PipedWriter` is employed when two active objects are to make use of char streams to communicate with each other.

The connections that can be made in a char output stream are shown in the lower shaded area of Figure 16.2. Several streams can be connected in sequence in this way, and connections are made in the same way as for byte streams.

The class `PrintWriter` contains methods, `println` for example, which are useful when writing out data of the simple, built-in types, with printout in text form.

In Figure 16.2, class `ExtendedWriter` has also been included, in spite of the fact that we ourselves constructed it and it is not a standard class. It was included to show that it fits into the chart and follows the same pattern as the other classes of char output streams. As we saw in Section 5.4.2, the class `ExtendedWriter` is a subclass of class `PrintWriter`. It will therefore contain methods for the printout of different forms of data in text form. The difference, when compared with class `PrintWriter`, is that the data we output can be edited. As we saw in Chapter 5, we were able to control the number of positions and decimals we wanted to have in the printout.

Two arrows are, in fact, missing from Figure 16.2. Both the class `PrintWriter` and its subclass `ExtendedWriter` can also be connected to an `OutputStream` but we did not want to complicate the chart further.

16.2 Streams for inputting

We shall now discuss, in a little more detail, the different stream classes. Many of the methods and constructors can generate exceptions of class `IOException` (or of one of its subclasses). We will therefore assume that such exceptions have been dealt with by using a **try** statement or through writing **throws** `IOException`.

Let us begin with streams for inputting. There are similar streams for byte streams and char streams, so we can describe the two different categories of streams in parallel. Input streams of the classes `DataInputStream` and `ObjectInputStream` must be discussed together with their corresponding output streams. We will not deal with them in this section, therefore, but later on in this chapter.

16.2.1 `InputStream`

The class `InputStream` is a superclass for all the classes handling the inputting of byte streams. The class is abstract, so we cannot create our own instances of it. It defines the fundamental methods for reading that all of its subclasses must have. The most important of these methods is `read`, which exists in three versions. The simplest form of `read` reads a single byte. This method will wait until there is a byte to read from the stream, or until the stream has finished. The value read is then given as result by the call. If the stream has finished, a value of –1 will be returned. Let us suppose that we have a byte input stream `s`. We can then read the stream with the following statements:

```
byte b;
int i;
while((i = s.read()) != -1) { // read until end of stream
```

```
    b = (byte) i; // type conversion from int to byte
    // do something with b
    ...
}
```

We should note an important point here: the method `read` returns not a value of type `byte` but one of type **int**. If we want to have the value read in the form of a `byte`, we must make an explicit type conversion, as shown in the example.

The two other versions of `read` have an array of bytes as parameter and can read more than one byte at a time. One of these versions has three parameters: an array of bytes that we can read to, a start index in the array and the maximum number of bytes to be read. A call of this method can look like this:

```
numberRead = s.read(a, startPos, maxNumber);
```

We suppose that `a` is an array of type **byte**[] and that `numberRead`, `startPos` and `maxNumber` are variables of type **int**. This call of `read` essentially reads `maxNumber` bytes from the stream `s` and places the values read into the array `a`, beginning in the position `startPos`. The call will give the number of bytes read as result. If the stream completes, the value –1 is given as result. This version of `read` reads as many bytes as are immediately accessible in the stream and will then return. However, it will never read more bytes than the maximum number indicated. So it will not wait until there are at least `maxNumber` bytes available. If no data is available when the call is made, `read` will wait until at least one byte is available. So we cannot be sure that this version of `read` will always read the number of bytes given as parameter.

The third version of `read` has only one parameter, the byte array that we will read to. The start position will then be equal to zero and the maximum number of bytes equal to the length of the array. The call `s.read(a)` is therefore the same thing as `s.read(a,0,a.length)`. By using the third version of `read`, we can obtain a more efficient reading from the stream `s` than in the example, above, when we read only one byte at a time.

```
byte[] a = new byte[1024];
int n;
while ((n = s.read(a)) != -1) { // read until end of stream
    // do something with bytes number 0 to n-1 in the array a
    ...
}
```

It is the job of the subclasses to make their own versions of the method `read` to ensure it works as efficiently as possible.

If we would like to test the number of bytes that can be read from a stream in advance without having to wait, we can call the method `available`. It must also be redefined in the subclasses, as the variant in class `InputStream` will always give a value of 0 as result.

If we want to skip a certain number of bytes in an input stream, we can call the method `skip`. As parameter it will have the number of bytes we want to skip and as result it will give the number of bytes it actually skipped. If the stream completes, a value of −1 will be returned. The result value has type `long`. So we can write:

```
long numberSkipped = s.skip(n);
```

We may sometimes have to go back to data in a stream. We might have to read for a while to see what kind of input data is coming and then go back to deal with it as we would like to. We might then want to use the methods `mark` and `reset`. The method `mark` is used to mark the place to which we will want to return. As parameter this method will have the maximum number of bytes we can read before we go back. To return to the place in the stream last marked, we use the method `reset`. Note that we cannot go back in this way with all streams. To test whether a particular stream supports the methods `mark` and `reset`, we can call the method `markSupported`. This may look like this:

```
if (s.markSupported()) {
   s.mark(512); // remember this place in the stream
   // read at most another 512 bytes
   ...
   s.reset(); // return to the marked place
}
```

The last method in class `InputStream` is the method `close`, which is called to close the stream and return all the resources associated with it:

```
s.close();
```

The class InputStream		The class Reader	
`int`	`read()`	`int`	`read()`
`int`	`read(`**`byte`**`[] b)`	`int`	`read(`**`char`**`[] b)`
`int`	`read(`**`byte`**`[] b,` `int off, int len)`	`int`	`read(`**`char`**`[] b,` `int off, int len)`
`long`	`skip(`**`int`**` n)`	`long`	`skip(`**`int`**` n)`
`int`	`available()`	`boolean`	`ready()`
`boolean`	`markSupported()`	`boolean`	`markSupported()`
`void`	`mark(`**`int`**` limit)`	`void`	`mark(`**`int`**` limit)`
`void`	`reset()`	`void`	`reset()`
`void`	`close()`	`void`	`close()`

16.2.2 `Reader`

The class `Reader` is an abstract class that is superclass to all of the classes involved in the inputting of char streams. Class `Reader` directly corresponds to class `InputStream`, and the two classes have, with a minor exception, exactly the same methods. The exception here is that the method `available` does not exist for class `Reader`. Instead, there is a method with the name `ready` that we can call to check whether there is a character directly available in a stream, without our having to wait. The method `ready` gives a **boolean** as result. If we have a **char** stream r, we can write, for example:

```
if (r.ready()) {
    ...
```

The only other difference, when compared with class `InputStream`, is that the two versions of the method `read` that can read several characters at a time will have an array of **char** as parameter, instead of an array of **bytes**. The first, simplest version of `read` will return, as before, an **int** but we have to make a type conversion of this **int** to a **char**, instead of to a **byte**. This might look as follows:

```
char c;
int i;
while((i = r.read()) != -1) { // read until the stream finishes
    c = (char) i;  // type conversion from int to char
    // do something with c
    ...
}
```

16.2.3 `InputStreamReader`

The class `InputStreamReader` is, as we saw on page 526, a link between byte streams and char streams. It is used when we want to read a byte stream and translate the bytes we read into characters in the Unicode format. As we know, Java uses 16-bit Unicode internally in the program but we cannot be sure that this format is used externally to store text. If, for example, we want to read in data stored in a text file, this information is usually held in ASCII or LATIN_1 format, with 8 bits for each character that can be written. And we cannot be sure either that each character will be represented by a equal number of bytes. An example of a code where the different characters can be represented by a different number of bytes is the UTF 8 code, where a character is represented as one byte, or several bytes in succession.

When we create a stream of class `InputStreamReader`, we can indicate how the bytes that will be input data for the stream are to be coded. There are two constructors. We can write either:

```
new InputStreamReader(input_stream)
```

or

```
new InputStreamReader(input_stream, "code_name")
```

533

The inputting stream indicated as parameter will be of class `InputStream`. If we choose the first version, the translation will take place from the code that is the default for the conventions in use. (This is controlled by the default `Locale` that applies.) In English installations, this code is the same as LATIN_1. If we want to translate from another code, we should use the other form of the constructor. The code name is a text. For example, UTF 8 code is called `"UTF8"`, LATIN_1 is called `"8859_1"`, and the code in MS-DOS that corresponds most closely to LATIN_1 is called `"Cp850"`. (We can see which codes are available if we read the documentation for the command `native2ascii` included in J2SDK.) If we want to know the coding that is the default for the installation we are using, we can call the standard method `getProperty`.

```
String code = System.getProperty("file.encoding");
```

16.2.4 `FileInputStream`

We use this class when we want to create a byte stream that reads from a file. There are three different constructors:

```
new FileInputStream(file_name)   // file_name has type String
new FileInputStream(file)        // file has type File
new FileInputStream(fd)          // fd has type FileDescriptor
```

The first constructor will simply have as parameter the file name in the form of a `String`. In the second constructor, we indicate the file to be read by giving as parameter an object of the standard class `File`. This is a class with which we can get information on files and directories. Each `File` object will describe a file or a directory. We shall discuss this class in Section 16.6. The third constructor has as parameter an object of class `FileDescriptor`. This is a standard class that is a kind of reference to a file at a low level. We do not need to use this class.

16.2.5 `FileReader`

This class is a subclass of class `InputStreamReader`. It therefore translates a stream of bytes to a stream of **char**. We use this class when we want to read a text file, that is, a file that contains text, which will be coded in the standard format applicable to the actual installation. If the text is coded in some other way, we instead have to use class `InputStreamReader` and connect it to an object of class `FileInputStream`. Class `FileReader`, just like `FileInputStream`, has three different constructors, where a file name, a `File` object or a `FileDescriptor` object can be indicated as parameter. The first form

```
new FileReader(file_name)   // file_name has type String
```

is equivalent to

```
new InputStreamReader(new FileInputStream(file_name))
```

16.2.6 `ByteArrayInputStream` and `CharArrayReader`

On page 525 we saw that we could use a stream of class `ByteArrayInputStream` when we wanted to read input data from an array of bytes. If we have declared an array

```
byte[] a = new byte[1000];
```

then we can create a stream that reads from this array:

```
ByteArrayInputStream s = new ByteArrayInputStream(a);
```

There is also an alternative form of constructor where we can indicate that only a certain part of an array will constitute the input data to the stream:

```
new ByteArrayInputStream(array, startpos, number)
```

When we read from a stream of this kind, it looks just as though we were reading from a file or some other external source.

We use the class `CharArrayReader` when we want to create a char stream that reads data from a char array. No conversions are necessary, since the array will already contain data in Unicode format. We proceed as we would for class `ByteArrayInputStream`, the only difference being that the array will be of type **char**[] instead of **byte**[].

16.2.7 `StringReader`

This class functions in the same way as class `CharArrayReader`. The only difference is that input data will come from a `String` object instead of from a **char** array. There is only one constructor, and it will have an object of class `String` as parameter:

```
new StringReader(text) // text has type String
```

16.2.8 `PipedInputStream` and `PipedReader`

These classes are used together with the classes `PipedOutputStream` and `PipedWriter` when two active objects communicate through streams. We will be giving examples of how they are used in Section 16.3.7.

16.2.9 `FilterInputStream` and `FilterReader`

The classes `FilterInputStream` and `FilterReader` describe input streams that can be connected after another input stream. As their names suggest, they will be used to describe streams which in some way "filter" the data entered. (Class `FilterInputStream` is superclass for classes `BufferedInputStream`, `DataInputStream` and `PushbackInputStream` and class `FilterReader` is superclass for class `PushbackReader`.) The filter classes `FilterInputStream` and `FilterReader` have a single constructor that as parameter has another input stream named `in`. What happens when one of the methods in the filter classes is called is that the corresponding method in the stream `in` is called. If a `FilterInputStream` or a `FilterReader` were connected to a stream, therefore, data would flow straight through without being changed.

We should, of course, define our own subclasses of the filter classes. (The class `FilterReader` is, in fact, an abstract class and cannot be used directly.) In these subclasses we can redefine whichever methods we want to. Of course, it would be interesting to redefine the different versions of the method `read` so that `read` first read from the input stream `in` and then in some way changed or "filtered" the data that had been read. The method `read` can be found in all three versions (see Section 16.2.1) in class `FilterInputStream`, and these should be redefined in a subclass. We need to redefine only two versions of method `read` in subclasses of `FilterReader` but the version with only a **char** array as parameter does not have to be redefined.

We shall now give an example of how we can create our own filter class. The following class, a subclass of the filter class `FilterReader`, describes a filter that translates all the capitals in a char stream to lower-case letters:

```java
import java.io.*;

public class ToLowerCaseReader extends FilterReader {

  // constructor
  public ToLowerCaseReader(Reader r) {
    super(r);
  }

  // redefine the methods read
  public int read() throws IOException {
    int i = in.read();
    if (i == -1)
      return -1;
    else
      return (int) Character.toLowerCase((char) i);
  }

  public int read(char[] cbuf, int off, int len)
                                    throws IOException {
    int n = in.read(cbuf, off, len);
    for (int i=off; i<off+n; i++)
      cbuf[i] = Character.toLowerCase(cbuf[i]);
    return n;
  }
}
```

There are a couple of things here to note. The first is that we have to call the superclass's constructor in the constructor so that the input stream `in` can be correctly initialized. The other is that the input stream `in` is inherited by our subclass and is directly accessible in all methods.

We have used the method `toLowerCase` in the wrapper class `Character` (see page 51) to do the job of translating. This method will leave unchanged all characters that are not capital letters.

Here is an example of how our new filter class can be used when we want to read text from the keyboard and output the text entered, with all the capitals changed to lower-case letters:

```
import java.io.*;
import extra.*;

class FilterDemo {

   public static void main(String[] arg) throws IOException {
      BufferedReader r = new BufferedReader
                         (new ToLowerCaseReader
                         (new InputStreamReader
                         (System.in, "Cp437")));
      String s;
      while ((s=r.readLine()) != null)
         Std.out.println(s);
   }
}
```

Data flows in from the keyboard through the standard stream `System.in`, which is a stream of type `InputStream`. In order to translate the 8-bit bytes in this stream to 16-bit `char`, an `InputStreamReader` is used. We have supposed here that the program will be run in an MS-DOS window. The LATIN_1 coding is not used in MS-DOS, so we have indicated in the constructor of the intermediate `InputStreamReader` stream that "Cp437" coding is to be used.

When in the program we call the method `readLine` (defined in the class `Buffered-Reader`), this method will in turn call the method `read` in class `ToLowerCaseReader`. All the capitals will then be translated into lower-case letters.

16.2.10 `BufferedInputStream` and `BufferedReader`

It can be very inefficient, when reading from an external source such as a file, to read only one `byte` or one `char` at a time. Data transfer will go much more quickly if we can read whole blocks at a time; we can do this with the classes `BufferedInputStream` and `BufferedReader`. They will disengage internal reading from external reading by using a buffer where data that has been read is stored temporarily. When we call the method `read` in a buffered stream, the stream can read in advance and fill the buffer. It is useful to use a buffered stream that is directly connected to the first input stream. There will be two constructors. The first has as its only parameter the input stream from which buffered stream will read. The second also has, apart from this stream, a whole number that indicates the number of bytes or char for which the buffer will have space. (When we use the first of these constructors, we use a default value.) If `rin` is an input stream of class `Reader`, we can write, for instance:

```
BufferedReader br = new BufferedReader(rin, 1024);
```

The classes `BufferedInputStream` and `BufferedReader` contain all the methods that were defined in classes `InputStream` and `Reader`. Class `BufferedReader` also contains a new method that is very useful, the method `readLine`, which can read a whole line at a time. This method is so useful that a stream of class `BufferedReader` is often used simply to gain access to it. The method `readLine` was demonstrated in Section 5.4.1.

16.2.11 `ExtendedReader`

In spite of the fact that there are so many standard classes for handling streams, oddly enough, there is no standard class that makes it possible for the programmer to read data of different types from a char stream with ease. The class `BufferedReader` has, as we stated above, the method `readLine` but that is the only one. If we want to read numerical data from a char stream, putting it into normal numerical variables, for example, in variables of type **int** and **double**, then there are no ready-made aids at hand. We must, as we saw in Section 5.4.1, first enter data in text form, then make type conversions using a wrapper class or an object of class `NumberFormat`. (Another alternative is to use an object of class `StringTokenizer` and connect this object to the input stream. This is general but a bit complicated.)

For this reason, we have chosen in this book to construct and use our own class `ExtendedReader`. This is a subclass of the class `BufferedReader` and has all of its properties. It has the same constructors, for instance. The stream `Std.in`, which we used when reading from the keyboard, is a stream of class `ExtendedReader`. It is declared in the following way in class `Std`:

```
public static final ExtendedReader in = new ExtendedReader
                    (new InputStreamReader(System.in,code), 1);
```

The variable `code` is a `String` that contains the code's name. If we are running a PC with an English version of Windows, `code` will contain the text `"Cp437"`. (To find out which platform and language will apply, the calls `System.getProperty("os.name")` and `System.getProperty("user.language")` are made in the class `Std`.) The "one" in the constructor means that the buffer will contain only one character. We chose such a small buffer because `Std.in` is essentially intended for interactive inputting. So it will work better if the buffer contains only the one character.

As we stated in Section 5.4.2, there is a set of methods in class `ExtendedReader` that makes it easier for the programmer to read different types of data from an input stream. There are also methods that can facilitate inputting in other ways; see the fact box on page 136. Class `ExtendedReader` is accessible through the website of this book.

16.2.12 `LineNumberReader`

This class is a subclass of class `BufferedReader`. It will therefore have all the properties of `BufferedReader`. An extra property is that it can keep track of line numbers. There are two new methods. The method `getLineNumber` lacks parameters and gives as result the actual line number. The method `setLineNumber` has a whole number as parameter and assigns a number to the actual line. If `lno` is a stream of class `LineNumberReader`, the following call will give the actual line the number 100. Consecutive lines will then get the numbers 101, and so on:

```
lno.setLineNumber(100);
```

16.2.13 `PushbackInputStream` and `PushbackReader`

Sometimes we may need to read a little bit ahead to see the type of data coming in a stream. Depending on the kind of data, we might then want to handle it in different ways; for instance, we might want to read this data in a different part of our program. We can then make use of the classes `PushbackInputStream` and `PushbackReader`, which will allow us to push back data that has already been read into the input stream so that this data can be read again. There are two constructors. The first has only an input stream as parameter. We could write:

```
PushbackReader pr = new PushbackReader(rin);
```

If we use this constructor, we will be able to push back only a single character or byte into the stream. The other constructor includes another parameter. By using this one, we can indicate the maximum number of characters or bytes we want to push back:

```
PushbackReader pr = new PushbackReader(rin, 100);
```

Apart from all the methods inherited from the classes `InputStream` and `Reader`, classes `PushbackInputStream` and `PushbackReader` also have a method with the name `unread`. There are three variants of this method. The first has only one parameter, and this will indicate the **byte** or **char** to be pushed back into the stream. In the following example, for instance, we read one character. If this should turn out to be a letter, the character will be the beginning of a name. We then push this character back into the stream and call another method to read in and deal with the whole name:

```
char c = (char) pr.read();
if (Character.isLetter(c)) {
  pr.unread(c);
  dealWithName(pr);
}
```

The two other variants of unread allow us to push back more than one byte or character. They have an array of bytes and a char, respectively, as parameter. In one variant, all the data in the array is pushed back into the stream and in the other, a sub-interval can be indicated in the array; then only the data in this sub-interval will be pushed back. For example, we can write:

```
char[] a = new char[50];
pr.unread(a);            // all 50 characters are pushed back
pr.unread(a, 10, 5);    // characters 10-14 are pushed back
```

16.2.14 `SequenceInputStream`

We use this class when we want to connect several streams to form one stream. To connect two input streams s1 and s2 into one, we can write, for example:

```
SequenceInputStream s = new SequenceInputStream(s1, s2);
```

When we then read from the stream s, all the data in stream s1 will be read first, followed by all the data in stream s2. If we want to connect more than two streams, we can give as argument for the constructor an iterator that refers to a data collection consisting of several input streams. For example, we can use the class Vector to create a collection of three input streams s1, s2 and s3.

```
Vector v = new Vector();
v.addElement(s1);
v.addElement(s2);
v.addElement(s3);
```

We can then create a SequenceInputStream that connects the three streams.

```
SequenceInputStream t = new SequenceInputStream(v.elements());
```

When we then read from the stream t, stream s1 will be read first, then stream s2 and finally stream s3.

16.3 Streams for outputting

In this section we shall look rather more closely at the streams that are used with outputting. We shall discuss byte streams and char streams in parallel, as they have similar classes. But we shall not discuss the classes DataOutputStream and Object-OutputStream until Section 16.4.

16.3.1 `OutputStream` and `Writer`

These two classes are abstract. `OutputStream` is superclass for all classes that describe byte output streams, while `Writer` is superclass for all the classes that describe char output streams. The methods `write`, `flush` and `close`, available for all output streams, are defined in the classes `OutputStream` and `Writer`.

The method `write` can be found in several different versions. The simplest of these writes out a single byte or char to a stream. Let us suppose that `out` is a reference to an output stream and `d` a simple variable of type **byte** or **char** (depending on whether a byte or char stream is involved). Then we can make the call:

```
out.write(d);
```

The next two versions of `write` will write out several bytes or char to a stream at a time. These versions will have an array as parameter. We can either write out the whole of the array to the stream, or only a part of it. If we suppose that `a` is an array of **byte** or **char**, we could make the statements:

```
out.write(a);  // writes out the entire array
out.write(a, startpos, number);  // writes out a sub-array
```

We have supposed that `startpos` and `number` are of type **int**.

There are two other versions of the method `write` for class `Writer` (but not for `OutputStream`), with which we can write out a `String` or part of a `String`. If `w` is a stream of class `Writer` and `txt` a `String` object, we could for instance make the statements:

```
w.write(txt);  // writes out a text
w.write(txt, startpos, number);  // writes out part of a text
```

When we write to an output stream, we cannot be entirely certain that the data we write will immediately reach the stream's destination. If, for instance, we wrote to a file, we could not be certain that the data would immediately land in the file. This is because the stream may use a buffer in which the data might be temporarily stored. If we want to be certain that data will really be written out, we can call the method `flush`. This will empty any buffers and output data to the stream's destination. We simply make the statement:

```
out.flush();
```

We saw earlier that it was important to use `flush` when we were dealing with interactive programs that wrote out questions in a text window.

The last method in the classes `OutputStream` and `Writer` is `close`, which closes a stream and releases all its resources. This method normally calls the method `flush` to empty all the buffers before the stream is closed.

The class OutputStream	The class Writer
void flush()	**void** flush()
void close()	**void** close()
void write(**int** b)	**void** write(**int** b)
void write(**byte**[] b)	**void** write(**char**[] b)
void write(**byte**[] b,	**void** write(**char**[] b,
int off, int len)	int off, int len)
	void write(String str)
	void write(String str,
	int off, int len)

16.3.2 `OutputStreamWriter`

As we saw on page 529, the class `OutputStreamWriter` is used to translate a char output stream to a byte output stream. The 16-bit Unicode characters in the char stream will be translated into a sequence of 8-bit bytes. These can then be sent on to their destination, which might be a file for storing them.

When we create a stream of class `OutputStreamWriter`, we can indicate how the bytes, which will be output data from the stream, are to be coded. There are two constructors. We can write either:

```
new OutputStreamWriter(output_stream)
```

or

```
new OutputStreamWriter(output_stream, "code_name")
```

The outputting stream indicated as parameter will be of class `OutputStream`. If we use the first constructor, translation will take place to the default code for the conventions being used. In English installations this code is the same as LATIN_1. (Available codes are given in the documentation of the command `native2ascii` in J2SDK.)

16.3.3 `FileOutputStream`

We use this class when we want to store a byte stream in a file. There are four different constructors:

```
new FileOutputStream(file_name) // file_name has type String
new FileOutputStream(file_name, append) // file_name has type String
new FileOutputStream(file) // file has type File
new FileOutputStream(fd) // fd has type FileDescriptor
```

The first and second constructors will have as parameter a file name in the form of a `String`. In the second constructor, the parameter *append* is a **boolean** that indicates whether we are to overwrite an existing file or add new data at the end of the file. The value `true` means that new data has been added to the end of the file. In the third constructor, we indicate the file to be written by giving as parameter an object of the standard class `File`; see Section 16.6. The third constructor has as parameter an object of class `FileDescriptor`. This class gives a reference to a file at a low level.

16.3.4 `FileWriter`

This class is a subclass of the class `OutputStreamWriter`. It will therefore translate a stream of `char` to a stream of bytes. We use this class when we want to store text in a file. The text in the file will be coded in the standard format applying to the actual installation. If we want the text to be coded in some other way, we must use the class `OutputStreamWriter` and connect it to an object of class `FileOutputStream`. The class `FileWriter`, like class `FileOutputStream`, has four different constructors in which we can indicate as parameter a file name, a file name and a `boolean`, a `File` object, or a `FileDescriptor` object. We could write

```
new FileWriter(file_name)  // file_name has type String
```

which would be equivalent to

```
new OutputStreamWriter(new FileOutputStream(file_name))
```

16.3.5 `ByteArrayOutputStream` and `CharArrayWriter`

We use these two classes when we want to "write out" data in an array. This array will exist as a buffer inside the stream object itself. When we use a stream of class `ByteArrayOutputStream`, the buffer is of type `byte[]`, while the buffer will, of course, be of type `char[]` when an object of class `CharArrayWriter` is used. The buffer will automatically increase in size as new data is written out.

It is quite easy to create a stream of one of these classes. We simply write:

```
ByteArrayOutputStream bas = new ByteArrayOutputStream();
CharArrayWriter       caw = new CharArrayWriter();
```

The constructors can also be found in an alternative form, where a size can be indicated for the internal buffer at the outset:

```
ByteArrayOutputStream bas = new ByteArrayOutputStream(size);
CharArrayWriter       caw = new CharArrayWriter(size);
```

Streams of these classes contain the methods that all output streams have. For instance, we could write data using the method `write`:

```
bas.write(b);
```

To find out the number of data elements actually in the internal buffer, we can call the method `size`, which will give a whole number as result. We could make the call:

```
bas.size()
```

Of course, we will want to have access to the buffer when we have written data to a stream. Then we can use the method `toByteArray`, or `toCharArray`. For example, we could write:

```
byte[] ba = bas.toByteArray();
char[] ca = caw.toCharArray();
```

The method `toString`, which translates data in the internal buffer to a `String` object, is also available for both classes:

```
String s1 = bas.toString();
String s2 = caw.toString();
```

This translation is self-evident in the case of a stream of class `CharArrayWriter`, since the buffer will already contain components of type **char**. If we have a stream of class `ByteArrayOutputStream`, translation must take place from a sequence of bytes to a text. This is the same problem that arose when we had to read from a byte stream and translate the stream to a char stream. There are therefore two different versions of the method `toString` in class `ByteArrayOutputStream`. The first, which was used above, lacks parameters, making the translation in accordance with the default code for the actual installation. The second version of `toString` has a code name as parameter, exactly like the constructor of class `InputStreamReader`. We can then indicate how the bytes in the buffer should be decoded. We could write:

```
String s3 = bas.toString("UTF-8");
```

The last of the new methods in classes `ByteArrayOutputStream` and `CharArrayWriter` is the method `reset`. New printout will begin in the internal buffer in the stream – the old content will, of course, be destroyed – if we make the following call:

```
bas.reset();
```

16.3.6 `StringWriter`

This class may remind us of the class `CharArrayWriter` but the internal buffer is not of type **char**[]. It is an object of the standard class `StringBuffer`. We have not discussed `StringBuffer` but it suffices to say that like class `String`, it can contain text. The difference is that the text in a `StringBuffer` object can be changed.

The class `StringWriter` has two constructors, one with no parameters, where a default value is used for the initial size of the buffer, and one where the buffer size is given:

```
StringWriter sw = new StringWriter();
StringWriter sw2 = new StringWriter(size);
```

We can, of course, write to a stream of type StringWriter with the method write.

```
sw.write("Java");
```

To access the text written in the buffer, we can call the method toString.

```
String s = sw.toString();
```

There is also a method with the name getBuffer that can be used to access the internal buffer. The result will be an object of type StringBuffer.

The class StringWriter is useful when we want to use the aids offered by streams for editing text without having to write out the text to a file. Let us suppose, for example, that we want to show a JLabel object containing a current balance. This will look as in Figure 16.3.

Figure 16.3 An example of the use of StringWriter

When we create a JLabel object, we will indicate, as parameter for the constructor, a String object containing the desired text. We can create this String object by writing in a stream of class StringWriter. To edit the text, we first connect a stream of class ExtendedWriter. This might look as follows:

```
double balance;
...  // compute balance
// edit the text
StringWriter    sw = new StringWriter();
ExtendedWriter out = new ExtendedWriter(sw);
out.print("Balance:");
out.setFillChar('*'); out.print(balance,15,2); out.flush();
// display the text
getContentPane().add(new JLabel(sw.toString(), JLabel.CENTER));
```

16.3.7 PipedOutputStream and PipedWriter

We can let two active objects send data to each other through streams. Here we will show a schematic example to demonstrate how this is done. Let us suppose that we have two active objects, obj1 and obj2. When obj1 is executing, it sometimes requires a computation to be done. It will therefore send input data for computation to obj2, which carries out the computation and returns the answer to obj1. We let obj1 and obj2 be objects of the classes C1 and C2, respectively:

```
class C1 implements Runnable {
   private Thread activity = new Thread(this);
   InputStream in;
   OutputStream out;

   public C1(InputStream in, OutputStream out) {
      this.in = in;
      this.out = out;
      activity.start();
   }

   public void run() {
      while (true) {
         byte b;
         ... // put input data in b
         // send input data to obj2
         out.write(b);
         ... // do something else
         // read the answer from obj2
         byte answer = (byte)in.read();
         ...
      }
   }
}

class C2 implements Runnable {
   private Thread activity = new Thread(this);
   InputStream in;
   OutputStream out;

   public C2(InputStream in, OutputStream out) {
      this.in = in;
      this.out = out;
      activity.start();
   }

   public void run() {
      int inputData;
      while ((inputData = in.read()) != -1) {
         byte result;
         ... // compute the result
         out.write(result);
      }
   }
}
```

546

We see that internally, both of these classes have their own input and output stream. These are initialized in the constructors. We will be using two communication streams, stream A, going from `obj1` to `obj2`, and stream B, going in the opposite direction. To achieve this, we will have to create four stream objects, two going in each direction:

```
PipedOutputStream  outA = new PipedOutputStream();
PipedInputStream   inA  = new PipedInputStream(outA);
PipedOutputStream  outB = new PipedOutputStream();
PipedInputStream   inB  = new PipedInputStream(outB);
```

Stream `outA` is the stream in which `obj1` will write. This will be connected to `inA`, which is the stream `obj2` will read from. We connect two streams of this kind by giving one stream as parameter of the other's constructor. (We could just as well have put the declarations in the reverse order and given `inA` as parameter for the constructor of `outA`.) The streams `outB` and `inB` are similarly connected. There is another way to connect streams. Both streams can be created without arguments for the constructor, and the method `connect` is then called for one of the streams; the other stream is then given as parameter.

When two streams have been connected correctly, we merely have to declare the two active objects `obj1` and `obj2` and let them start:

```
C1 obj1 = new C1(inB, outA);
C2 obj2 = new C2(inA, outB);
```

We used classes `PipedInputStream` and `PipedOutputStream` in this example but `PipedReader` and `PipedWriter` work in exactly the same way.

16.3.8 `FilterOutputStream` and `FilterWriter`

The classes `FilterOutputStream` and `FilterWriter` describe output streams that can be connected in front of another output stream. They can be used to create streams that "filter" data before they are output. (The class `FilterOutputStream` is a superclass of the classes `BufferedOutputStream`, `DataOutputStream` and `PushbackOutputStream`.) The filter classes have a single constructor that has another output stream as parameter. This output stream is called `out`. When one of the methods in the filter classes is called, the corresponding method in stream `out` will also be called.

We have to define our own subclasses of the filter classes so that data can be changed in a filter stream. The different versions of the method `write` should be redefined in the subclasses, so that they will first "filter" data, then write out the filtered data in the output stream `out`. The three versions of method `write`, which was defined in the superclass `OutputStream` (see Section 16.3.1), can be found in the class `FilterOutputStream` and these should be redefined in a subclass. In subclasses of `FilterWriter` we only have to redefine the following three versions of method `write`:

```
write(c)                      // writes out a char
write(a, startpos, number)  // writes out part of a char array
write(s, startpos, number)  // writes out part of a string
```

16.3.9 `BufferedOutputStream` and `BufferedWriter`

Writing one **byte** or one **char** at a time to an external destination such as a file often wastes time. It is much quicker to output entire blocks of data. The classes `BufferedOutputStream` and `BufferedWriter` collect data in an internal buffer and write it out in blocks. It can often be useful to use a buffer stream that is connected directly in front of the last output stream. To connect a buffer before printout to a char stream that writes in a file, we might for instance make the declaration:

```
BufferedWriter bw = new BufferedWriter(new FileWriter(file_name));
```

There are two different constructors in the classes `BufferedOutputStream` and `BufferedWriter`. Both have as parameter the output stream to which buffer stream will write. We can also indicate, in the second constructor, the number of bytes or char the buffer will hold. (A default value is used in the first constructor.) If `fout` is an output stream of class `FileOutputStream`, we might write:

```
BufferedOutputStream bos = new BufferedOutputStream(fout, 1024);
```

The classes `BufferedOutputStream` and `BufferedWriter` contain all the methods that were defined in classes `OutputStream` and `Writer`. Apart from these, there is a method `newLine`, in class `BufferedWriter`, which writes out an end-of-line marker. As we will remember from Section 9.1, an end-of-line marker can look different on different platforms. The character '\n' is used in a Unix system, while in MS-DOS, the two characters '\r' and '\n' are employed. If we use the method `newLine`, instead of writing out these characters ourselves, the combination of characters that apply on the actual platform will be written out. We can then move the program we have constructed between different platforms.

16.3.10 `PrintStream` and `PrintWriter`

The class `PrintStream` was defined in Version 1.0 of Java. It was intended to be used for writing out texts in an ordinary 8-bit character format, to a text window, for example, or to a text file, but `PrintStream` could only write out text correctly when LATIN_1 coding was used. When char streams were introduced in Java 1.1, therefore, it was a good time to remove class `PrintStream`. It was replaced by class `Print-Writer`, which can handle character codes properly. Class `PrintStream` was spared the fate of being made obsolete by the pre-defined streams `System.out` and `System.err`, both of which are of class `PrintStream`. So the class was allowed to remain.

The classes PrintStream and PrintWriter are unusual in that they have the methods print and println. These have a single parameter and write out the value of the parameter in text form. The methods print and println are defined in several versions. The parameter can be of any of the simple built-in types, of class String, or a char array. There is also a version that has a parameter of class Object. When we call print or println, the parameter will be translated from its internal, binary form to text. If class PrintOutput is used, we get a sequence of 8-bit characters, while the use of PrintWriter will result in a sequence of 16-bit **char**. We have seen several examples in the book where methods print and println were used when we wrote to the streams System.out and Std.out. Note, however, that versions of print and println with more than one parameter are not defined in either PrintStream or PrintWriter; they are defined in our own class ExtendedWriter; see next section.

Class PrintStream has no accessible constructor but class PrintWriter has no fewer than four of them. The first two have an output stream as their only parameter, and this can be either of class Writer or of class OutputStream. If bw is a stream of class BufferedWriter and bos a stream of class BufferedOutputStream we could write:

```
PrintWriter pw1 = new PrintWriter(bw);
PrintWriter pw2 = new PrintWriter(bos);
```

The two other constructors have one more parameter. This is a **boolean** that will indicate whether flush should be called automatically or not when the method println is used. We could write, for example:

```
PrintWriter pw3 = new PrintWriter(new BufferedWriter
                        (new FileWriter(file_name)),true);
```

16.3.11 ExtendedWriter

Naturally, the classes PrintOutput and PrintWriter are valuable when outputting data in text form. However, they are incomplete, as there is no simple way of formatting printout. For instance, we must use a formatter of type NumberFormat when we write out a real number and want to control the number of decimals. This was why we defined our own class ExtendedWriter.

Class ExtendedWriter is a subclass of class PrintWriter and has the same four constructors as this class. All the versions of print and println in class PrintWriter can also be found in class ExtendedWriter. Some have been directly inherited, while others have been redefined. In addition to these methods, there are also a number of new methods with which output can be formatted. A set of instance methods in class ExtendedWriter was given in the fact box on page 137, and in Section 5.4.2 we showed examples of how some of them were used.

Class ExtendedWriter also contains a set of useful class methods that can be used to format text without the text having to be written in a stream. These methods will instead return a String that contains the formatted text. A set of these methods was given in the fact box on page 141. We shall now give an example of another way of producing the text in Figure 16.3; see page 545. We wrote to a stream of class StringWriter before, but this can be simplified by using the class method formatNum, in the class ExtendedWriter.

```
double balance;
...  // compute the balance
// edit the text
String s= ExtendedWriter.formatNum(balance,15,2,'*');

// display the text
getContentPane().add(new JLabel(s));
```

The streams Std.out and Std.err are of class ExtendedWriter. Std.out is initialized in the following way in class Std:

```
public static final ExtendedWriter out = new ExtendedWriter
                (new OutputStreamWriter(System.out, code), true);
```

A char stream is connected to the pre-defined stream System.out. The code that will be used in the translation is indicated by the String variable code. (Compare this with the stream Std.in in Section 16.2.11.) The parameter **true** indicates that flush will be called automatically with every call of println.

16.4 Streams with binary data

Our discussions up to now have mainly concerned the reading and writing of streams containing text. The original source or the final destination of a stream has been a text file or a text window. Text files and text windows are usually intended for communication with people. On the other hand, when a program produces output data to be read by another program, it is not necessary to store data in text form. It is generally more efficient to store the data in the same binary format as it has been in the program. For instance, if we wish to store an **int** variable in a file, we can use 32 bits, or 4 bytes, instead of decoding the variable and representing it by a sequence of character codes. Files containing data stored in this binary format are usually called *binary files*.

There are two ways in Java of handling streams with binary data. If we only have to deal with simple data such as can be described by Java's simple, built-in types, we can use the classes DataInputStream and DataOutputStream. If we are handling more complicated data, data described by classes, we shall have to use the classes ObjectInputStream and ObjectOutputStream. We can also store simple data in binary form in direct-access files, in which case we do not use streams but instead make use of the class RandomAccessFile. We shall discuss this in Section 16.5.

Apart from the classes we have named here, there are four interfaces: DataInput, DataOutput, ObjectInput and ObjectOutput. All the methods in class DataInput-Stream are defined in the interface DataInput. The class DataInputStream therefore implements the interface DataInput. Similarly, the class DataOutputStream implements the interface DataOutput, the class ObjectInputStream the interface ObjectInput, and the class ObjectOutputStream the interface ObjectOutput. The interfaces have been defined in parallel with the classes because it will then be possible to define other classes that implement the interfaces. The class RandomAccessFile is an example of this. It does not describe a stream but it still implements both the interface DataInput and the interface DataOutput.

16.4.1 DataInputStream and DataOutputStream

These two classes are subclasses of FilterInputStream and FilterOutputStream, respectively. They can be connected to a stream when we want to read or write simple data in binary form. The different methods in these classes are shown in the fact box. Those methods with a direct equivalent in both classes are shown in the upper part of the table. If we output data with one of the printout methods and then input with the corresponding input method, we will get exactly the same data as we printed out. We see that there is an input method, together with its corresponding output method, for each one of the eight simple, built-in types. In addition, there are the methods writeUTF and readUTF that print out and read in texts coded in UTF 8 code. Note that the methods readChar and writeChar read and write 16-bit **char** values.

There are three methods in the interface DataOutput that lack an equivalent in the interface DataInput. The method writeChars writes out all the characters in a text of 16 bits per character, while the method writeBytes writes out a text of 8 bits per character. The three methods with the name write write out a single byte, or several bytes, from an array. We discussed how these functioned in Section 16.3.1. The method size indicates the total number of bytes that have been written to the stream.

Some methods in the interface DataInput also lack equivalents in the interface DataOutput. There are integer types in the programming languages C and C++ that are "unsigned". A variable of this type can only contain numbers that are greater than, or equal to, zero. There are no "unsigned" integer types in Java, but the methods readUnsignedByte and readUnsignedShort can be used to input data of this kind. The result type will then be an **int**.

The two methods readFully function in the same way as the methods read, inherited from the class InputStream; see Section 16.2.1. The difference is that the methods readFully always wait until *all* data has been input to the array given as parameter. As

The interface DataInput	The interface DataOutput
boolean readBoolean()	**void** writeBoolean(**boolean** v)
char readChar()	**void** writeChar(**int** v)
byte readByte()	**void** writeByte(**int** v)
short readShort()	**void** writeShort(**int** v)
int readInt()	**void** writeInt(**int** v)
long readLong()	**void** writeLong(**long** v)
float readFloat()	**void** writeFloat(**float** v)
double readDouble()	**void** writeDouble(**double** v)
String readUTF()	**void** writeUTF(String s)
int readUnsignedByte()	**void** writeChars(String s)
int readUnsignedShort()	**void** writeBytes(String s)
void readFully(**byte**[] b)	**void** write(**int** b)
void readFully(**byte**[] b,	**void** write(**byte**[] b)
int off, **int** len)	**void** write(**byte**[] b,
void skipBytes(**int** n)	**int** off, **int** len)
String readLine()	**int** size()

we saw earlier, the methods read did not always do this. They only waited until at least one byte could be read. The method skipBytes skips over a number of bytes in the input stream. It differs from the method skip in class InputStream in that it waits until *all* the bytes needing to be skipped have been skipped.

The method readLine is a remnant from Java 1.0. It has been eliminated from the class DataInputStream as char streams should be used to read text. As we saw earlier, there is an equivalent method in the class BufferedReader.

By way of an example, we will show how an array of **double** can be stored in a binary file. We will suppose that the file's name has been given as parameter for main:

```
DataOutputStream out = new DataOutputStream
                        (new FileOutputStream(arg[0]));
double a[] = new double[100];
... // compute data and store in the array
// write out the array to the file
out.writeInt(a.length);
for (int i=0; i<a.length; i++)
   out.writeDouble(a[i]);
out.close();
```

Note that we first write out the array's length as an **int**, then all the components in the array. We can now write another program that reads in the file and re-creates the array:

```
DataInputStream in = new DataInputStream
                     (new FileInputStream(arg[0]));
int n = in.readInt(); // read the array's length
double z[] = new double[n];
// read in the array's components
for (int i=0; i<z.length; i++)
   z[i] = in.readDouble();
```

Note that data is stored in the file in binary format. If we tried to read the file as text, in a text editor, for instance, we would get nothing but gobbledegook on the screen.

16.4.2 `ObjectInputStream` and `ObjectOutputStream`

To write out and read in binary data of the simple, built-in types is relatively straightforward. Each value written will always have a definite length. For example, an `int` is always four bytes long. We need only a moment's thought to realize that it must be a much more complicated matter to write out data objects described by classes, when much of the data is considerably more complex. We also have to store information about the object so that it can be re-created. In addition, a particular object can have instance variables referring to other objects, and these other objects will have to be written out. Then these objects can, in turn, contain references to other objects that must be written out, and so on. An object that contains references to other objects forms a kind of tree structure in a system's primary memory and when this tree is written out to a stream, it has to be "flattened out". In Java, we say that we *serialize* the object. In spite of all of this, it is surprisingly straightforward to read whole objects in Java. This is because the classes `ObjectInputStream` and `ObjectOutputStream` are extremely sophisticated and will do the whole job. We really only have to use two methods: `readObject` and `writeObject`. Classes `ObjectInputStream` and `Object-OutputStream` also implement the interfaces `DataInput` and `DataOutput`, respectively, so that all the methods in the fact box opposite will also be available.

We can create streams of the classes `ObjectInputStream` and `ObjectOutputStream` in the usual way. As parameter for the constructor, we indicate another stream to which the new stream will be connected. So, if `sin` and `sout` are of classes `InputStream` and `OutputStream` respectively, we can write:

```
ObjectInputStream  in  = new ObjectInputStream(sin);
ObjectOutputStream out = new ObjectOutputStream(sout);
```

There is one requirement that must be satisfied if we are to be able to write out an object `obj` in a stream: the class `C` to which `obj` belongs must implement the interface `Serializable`, or the interface `Externalizable`. This does not apply only to class `C`. If `obj` contains a reference to another object, the class of this object must also implement one of these interfaces. The interface `Externalizable` is used when we want full control over the input and output processes. We shall not go further into this here but will content ourselves with a discussion of the interface Serializable. This is a particularly simple interface. It contains no methods and is merely a sort of marker indicating that we are allowing objects of the class to be serialized. We could declare a class C:

```
public class C implements Serializable {
    the usual definitions of variables and methods
}
```

If we indicate that a class is to be serializable, this will also apply to all of the class's subclasses. Many of the standard classes in Java will implement the interface Serial-izable. This is true for class Component, so it follows that all GUI components can be serialized. The class Vector is another example of a standard class that implements the interface Serializable.

Let us now suppose that we have an object obj of the class C. We can then write obj to the stream out with the following simple statement:

```
out.writeObject(obj);
```

To read in and re-create an object is almost as simple. We write:

```
obj = (C) in.readObject();  // explicit type conversion
```

The method readObject returns a reference of type Object. To assign this to the variable obj, we have to make an explicit type conversion to the class concerned. Both methods can generate an exception of class IOException. The method readObject can, in addition, give an exception of class ClassNotFoundException.

In certain types of application programs, text editors or GUI programs, for instance, the user can save his or her work, loading it later to continue with it. A number of games also offer this possibility. When constructing such programs, the classes ObjectInput-Stream and ObjectOutputStream might be very useful. If there is an object in the program that describes the actual condition, we can save this condition simply by writing out the object to a file. The object can be read from the file later. For example, in Section 13.5, we wrote a program in which we could draw lines. To keep track of the lines in a figure, we used a vector; see class Painter on page 420.

```
Vector lines = new Vector();
```

Into this we put objects of class Line; see page 420. Each time the user drew a new line, we added a new Line object to the vector. We can save the whole figure the user drew by writing out the object lines in a file.

When we are to save and load an object in this type of application program, we can use the two class methods storeObject and loadObject, shown below. Both will get a file name as parameter. The method `storeObject` will in addition get as parameter a reference to the object to be saved. Both of these methods will catch any exceptions that might arise:

```
public static void storeObject(Object obj, String name) {
   try {
      ObjectOutputStream out = new ObjectOutputStream
                                 (new FileOutputStream(name));
      out.writeObject(obj);
      out.close();
   }
   catch (IOException ie) {
      ie.printStackTrace(); System.exit(1); }
}
```

```
public static Object loadObject(String name) {
   Object obj = null;
   try {
      ObjectInputStream in = new ObjectInputStream
                                 (new FileInputStream(name));
      obj = in.readObject();
      in.close();
   }
   catch (IOException ie) {
       ie.printStackTrace(); System.exit(1); }
   catch (ClassNotFoundException ce) {
       ce.printStackTrace(); System.exit(2); }
   return obj;
}
```

The method `loadObject` returns a reference to class `Object`. So we must use an explicit type conversion when we call it. For example, to read in a saved vector v from the file saved, we can make the statement:

```
v = (Vector) loadObject("saved");
```

For example, let's go back to the program `PaintProgram` on page 420. Now assume that we want it to be possible to save the pictures we have drawn in a file and to be able to load and do more work on pictures we have saved previously. So what we do is add a new menu in the drawing program containing the options "New", "Open" and "Save". With this addition, the class `PaintProgram` will look like this:

```
import javax.swing.*;
import java.awt.*;
import java.awt.event.*;
import java.util.*;       .
import java.io.*;
```

```java
public class PaintProgram extends JFrame
                          implements ActionListener {
  private JMenuBar mb = new JMenuBar();
  private JMenu file = new JMenu("File");
  private JMenuItem[] fileItems = { new JMenuItem("New"),
                                    new JMenuItem("Open"),
                                    new JMenuItem("Save") };
  private JFileChooser fc = new JFileChooser();
  Painter p = new Painter();

  PaintProgram() {
    setJMenuBar(mb);
    mb.add(file);
    for (int i=0; i<fileItems.length; i++) {
      file.add(fileItems[i]);
      fileItems[i].addActionListener(this);
    }
    getContentPane().add(p, BorderLayout.CENTER);
    setSize(300,300);
    setVisible(true);
    setDefaultCloseOperation(EXIT_ON_CLOSE);
  }

  public void actionPerformed(ActionEvent e) {    // listener
    if (e.getSource() == fileItems[0])   // New
      p.clear();
    else if (e.getSource() == fileItems[1]) { // Open
      if (fc.showOpenDialog(null) ==JFileChooser.APPROVE_OPTION)
        p.set((Vector)
          loadObject(fc.getSelectedFile().getAbsolutePath()));
    }

    else if (e.getSource() == fileItems[2]) {   // Save
      if (fc.showSaveDialog(null) ==JFileChooser.APPROVE_OPTION)
        storeObject(p.get(),
                    fc.getSelectedFile().getAbsolutePath());
    }
  }

  public static void storeObject(Object obj, String name) {
    as on page 555
  }

  public static Object loadObject(String namne) {
    as on page 555
  }
  public static void main (String arg[]) {
    new PaintProgram();
  }
}
```

When the user selects one of these menu options, you come to the listener. You get the name of the file you want to save or open by using a file dialog of the class `FileChooser`. In the listener, three new methods `clear`, `set` and `get` are called in the class `Painter` (see page 422). These look like this:

```
// Additions to class Painter
public void clear() {
   lines.clear();
   repaint();
}
public void set(Vector l) {
   lines = l;
   repaint();
}
public Vector get() {
   return lines;
}
```

16.5 Direct-access files

When we read data from a file or write data to a file by using streams, we have to read or write in a sequence from beginning to end. However, we may sometimes want to be able to move back and forth in a file, more or less as we do when indexing in an array. We can do this by using the class `RandomAccessFile`. This class does not describe a stream but implements both of the interfaces `DataInput` and `DataOutput`. It will therefore have all the methods that were defined in the fact box on page 552. In addition, there are three versions of `read` defined in class `InputStream`; see the fact box on page 532. This means that data can be read and written by using class `Random-AccessFile` in exactly the same way as is done with the classes `DataInputStream` and `DataOutputStream`. Note that class `RandomAccessFile` handles binary data seen as a sequence of bytes. There is no "char version" of `RandomAccessFile`.

When we create an object of class `RandomAccessFile`, we will give two parameters. The first, which can be either a `String` with a file name or an object of class `File`, will indicate the file concerned. The second is a text that must be equal to `"r"` or `"rw"`. It will indicate whether we only want to read from the file, or want to be able to both read and write. To create a `RandomAccessFile` object that makes it possible for us to both read and write the file `"diverse.dat"`, we can write, for instance:

```
RandomAccessFile f = new RandomAccessFile("diverse.dat", "rw");
```

What is interesting about direct-access files is that the class `RandomAccessFile` will automatically keep track of an actual position in the file. The actual position is the place in the file where the next byte will be read from or written to. This actual position is automatically moved forward when we read or write in the file. The actual position is represented by a whole number of type `long` that will give the number of bytes from the beginning of the file. Numbering will take place from 0. There are four interesting methods: `getFilePointer`, `seek`, `length` and `setLength`. The methods `getFilePointer` and `length` are the simplest. They lack parameters and give as result the actual position and the file's total length expressed in number of bytes, respectively. The method `seek` moves the actual position to the place indicated by the parameter. If we wanted to move back the actual position by 10 bytes, we could write:

```
f.seek(f.getFilePointer() - 10);
```

The last method, `setLength`, is used to change a file's total length. The required length is given as parameter. To shorten the file `f` by 100 bytes, for example, we can write:

```
f.setLength(f.length() - 100);
```

If we indicate as parameter a length that is greater than the old length, the file will be lengthened, and the new part will consist of bytes with an undefined content.

---

java.io.RandomAccessFile

new `RandomAccessFile(`*name, mode*`)`	*name* is a `String` or a `File` object
	mode is `"r"` (read) or `"rw"` (read/write)
`getFilePointer()`	gives actual position
`seek(pos)`	moves actual position
`length()`	gives the file's length
`setLength(n)`	changes the file's length

In addition, the methods in the interfaces `DataInput` and `DataOutput` are included.

Direct-access files are often used to store databases of different kinds. Booking programs, programs that keep track of booked and available places, for example in hotels and at concerts, often make use of direct-access files. Stock-keeping programs, which will keep track of the number of articles in stock, are another example. What distinguishes this type of program from others is that direct-access files are used to store *entries*. A file will contain a number of entries of the same kind. An entry is a group of data that belongs together. It may describe a particular room in a hotel, for instance, or a certain article in a stock-keeping program. Entries are stored in binary form in a file, so there will be *no* conversion to characters. Data in the file will have exactly the same appearance as in the system's primary memory. When we read and write entries from and to files, we normally transfer a whole entry at a time.

In Java, we shall, of course, describe entries using classes. A class that will describe an entry must be very simple, however. It must contain only simple data. In addition, all the entries in a direct-access file must have the same length if we are to locate them easily. This will pose problems, for example, if a class contains String objects, for then we have to be sure that these will always contain the same number of characters. If necessary, spaces have to be filled out with blank characters, or text has to be cut out. As an example, we shall show the class Account, which describes bank accounts. We will let this class have four instance variables: account number, balance, the account-holder's name and address. Simple data types can describe the account number and balance (long and double, respectively) but the name and address will be objects of class String. We therefore have to ensure that these will have the same lengths for all accounts. We will make the name consist of 20 characters and the address of 30 characters. To keep track of these lengths, we define the constant class variables nameL and addrL. We shall also define a constant class variable that gives the length of the whole entry. Since the account number and the balance consist of 8 bytes each (see the fact box on page 49), the total length will be equal to 8+8+nameL+addrL. The class variables will not be included in this, as we will not be storing them in the entries.

```java
import java.io.*;
import extra.*;
public class Account {
   public long     number;
   public double balance;
   public String name = "";
   public String addr = "";

   public final static int nameL = 20;
   public final static int addrL = 30;
   public final static int length = 8 + 8 + nameL + addrL;

   public void write(DataOutput out) throws IOException {
      // writes entries with a fixed length
      out.writeLong(number);
      out.writeDouble(balance);
      out.writeBytes(ExtendedWriter.toFixedLength(name,nameL));
      out.writeBytes(ExtendedWriter.toFixedLength(addr,addrL));
   }

   public void read(DataInput in) throws IOException {
      // reads entries with a fixed length
      number = in.readLong();
      balance  = in.readDouble();
      byte[] nameBuf = new byte[nameL];
      in.readFully(nameBuf);
      name = new String(nameBuf);
      byte[] addrBuf = new byte[addrL];
      in.readFully(addrBuf);
      addr =   new String(addrBuf);
   }
}
```

In this class we have defined two methods that are used when we want to read and write `Account` entries. They will get as parameter a reference to the interfaces `DataOutput` and `DataInput` and can therefore be called with an object of class `RandomAccessFile` as parameter, as this class implements both these interfaces. We can also give parameters of the classes `DataOutputStream` and `DataInputStream`, respectively, if we wish to write or read `Account` entries sequentially. The method `write` writes out the four components. The texts are adjusted before the account-holder's name and address are written out, to ensure they will be precisely 20 and 30 characters long, respectively. This can easily be done using the class method `toFixedLength`, in the class `ExtendedWriter`. The method `read` will do the opposite. It first reads the two simple components and then reads in exactly 20 bytes and 30 bytes, respectively, placing them in two arrays having these lengths. These arrays are then re-made into `String` objects and put into the object.

We shall now look at a class `AccountDatabase` that keeps track of bank accounts. Information about the different accounts lies stored in a direct-access file. When we create an object of class `AccountDatabase`, we give the file's name as parameter of the constructor. The class `AccountDatabase` contains the methods `open`, `close`, `finalize` and `transaction`. (In Exercise 5 on page 569 we also define a method that opens a new account.) The method `open` creates an object of class `RandomAccessFile`. This object is then used in class `AccountDatabase` to read and write in a file. The method `close` calls `close` for the object `file`. The method `finalize` is called automatic-ally when an `AccountDatabase` object ceases to exist. The most interesting method here is `transaction`. Before dealing with this method, we shall first show the class `AccountDatabase`:

```
import java.io.*;
public class AccountDatabase {
   private RandomAccessFile file;
   private String fileName;
   private Account record = new Account();

   // constructor
   public AccountDatabase(String fileName) throws IOException {
     this.fileName = fileName;
     open();
   }

   public void open() throws IOException {
     if (file == null)
        file = new RandomAccessFile(fileName, "rw");
   }

   public void close() throws IOException {
     if (file != null) {
        file.close();
```

```
      file = null;
    }
  }

  public void finalize() throws Throwable  {
    close();
    super.finalize();
  }

  public synchronized boolean transaction(long accounNo,
          double amount, Account result) throws IOException {
    // binary search
    boolean found = false;
    long recordNo = 0, first = 0,
         last = file.length()/Account.length-1;
    while (!found && first <= last) {
      recordNo = (first+last)/2; // the middle of the interval
      file.seek(recordNo*Account.length);  // move to the middle
      record.read(file);          // read the entry in the middle
      if (accounNo < record.number)
        last = recordNo-1;        // search in the half on the left
      else if (accounNo > record.number)
        first = recordNo+1;       // search in the half on the right
      else
        found = true;             // the entry is found
    }
    if (!found) {
      result.number = -1;
      return false;
    }
    // the account exists,
    // give account information in the parameter result
    result.number  = record.number;
    result.balance = record.balance;
    result.name = record.name;
    result.addr = record.addr;
    if (amount>0 || record.balance+amount>=0) {
      // deposit or permitted withdrawal
      record.balance += amount;
      // update the file
      file.seek(recordNo*Account.length);
      record.write(file);
      result.balance  = record.balance;
      return true;
    }
    else
      return false;
  }
}
```

The method `transaction` is called when we want to carry out a transaction on a particular account. It has three parameters: an account number, an amount and an object of class `Account`. The first two are input parameters for the method. The account number, of course, indicates the account on which the transaction is made, and the amount will indicate the sum to be deposited or withdrawn. The amount will be positive for deposits and negative for withdrawals. The third parameter is an output parameter with the name `result`, which will be a reference to an object of class `Account`. When the transaction has been carried out, the method `transaction` will fill in the result in the output parameter `result`. The method `transaction` also returns a value of type **boolean** that will indicate whether the transaction has been successful or not. A transaction may be unsuccessful for two reasons: first, an account with the given account number may not exist, in which case the method will put the value −1 in the place for the account number in the output parameter `result`; second, if the transaction involves a withdrawal of more money than is in the account. Then the withdrawal will be refused.

Note that the method `transaction` is defined as **synchronized**. This means that only one thread at a time can execute this method. There is therefore no risk of information for an account in the database being incorrect when we have a program of several threads, with some of these attempting to update the account at the same time.

Let us now see how the method `transaction` functions internally. The instance variable `file` is used to handle the direct-access file with the account entries. Let us suppose that the file entries have been sorted in numerical order. The entries in the file are numbered from 0 upwards. Since all the entries are of equal length, we can calculate the initial position in the file for a particular entry by multiplying the entry's number by its size. A binary search is used to find a particular entry in the file; compare this with our discussion in Section 9.5. Since the file's length is calculated in bytes, the number of entries in the file can be calculated by dividing the file's length by the size of the entry. The length of the file is obtained by calling the method `length`, while the entry's size is given by the class variable `length` in class `Account`. The variable `recordNo` contains the number of the next entry to be read from the file. It will be set from the beginning to the number of the file's most central entry. The method `seek` is used to move to the correct place in the file. When we call this method, we have to multiply by the size of the entry, since the position in the file is indicated in bytes.

The instance variable `record` is declared in class `AccountDatabase`. This variable is of class `Account` and is used when we are going to read and write entries in the file. We read or write a whole entry at a time with the methods `read` and `write`, which we defined in class `Account`.

If we do not find the entry with a binary search, we put the value −1 into the account number in the output parameter `result` and then return the value **false** to indicate that the search has been unsuccessful. If the entry was found, we copy the information in the file to the output parameter `result`. We then try to carry out the transaction, and if a withdrawal is involved, we check to see whether there is enough money in the account. If there is not, we will return the value `false`.

We will now show a small demonstration program that uses the class `AccountData-base`. Let us suppose that the program is run by a bank clerk. Whenever there is a new client, the program will ask for an account number and an amount. A positive amount will mean a deposit and a negative amount a withdrawal. The program will then look for the entry in the database containing the account number indicated. If there is an entry with this number, the program will carry out the given transaction and update the actual account entry in the database. Here is an example of how this might look:

```
Account no? 123456
Amount? -50
Elisabeth Bergman
1 Coffee Lane, Longdale
New balance: 434.00

Account no? 178520
Amount? 100
Incorrect account no

Account no? 234567
Amount? -500
Charles Wilson
19 Bean Road, Notown
Balance: 224.50
Withdrawal cannot be done!
```

The program is as follows. We will suppose that the account file is called `accounts`:

```java
import java.io.*;
import extra.*;

public class BankDemo {
   public static void main(String[] arg) throws IOException {
      AccountDatabase  b = new AccountDatabase("accounts");
      Account acc = new Account();    // output parameter
      while(true) {
         Std.out.print("Account no? ");
         if (!Std.in.more())
            break;
         long no = Std.in.readLong();
         Std.out.print("Amount? ");
         if (!Std.in.more())
            break;
         double amount = Std.in.readDouble();
```

```
      boolean transOK = b.transaction(no, amount, acc);
      // the result can be found in the acc
      if (acc.number > 0) {   // account number OK
        Std.out.println(acc.name);
        Std.out.println(acc.addr);
        if (transOK) {
          Std.out.print("New balance: ");
          Std.out.println(acc.balance, 1, 2);
        }
        else {
          Std.out.print("Balance: ");
          Std.out.println(acc.balance, 1, 2);
          Std.out.println("Withdrawal cannot be done!");
        }
      }
      else
        Std.out.println("Incorrect account no");
      Std.out.println();
    }
  }
}
```

This concludes our description of direct-access files. We might perhaps ask ourselves if it would not have been possible to use the classes ObjectOutputStream and ObjectInputStream, writing and reading whole entries to a file, instead of constructing our own methods read and write in class Account. There are two problems here: the first is that when we use ObjectOutputStream more information than the values of the instance variables is stored, taking up a lot of extra space in the file, which is not a good thing if the file has to hold a great number of entries; the other problem is that all the entries have to be of the same length if we are to be able to search properly in a direct-access file. However, there is one way of solving this second problem, enabling us to combine the flexibility of classes ObjectOutputStream and ObjectInputStream with the quick search a direct-access file allows. Two direct-access files can be used: one where the different objects are stored sequentially and one where we store only the object's search key (for example, the account number) for every object, together with its position and length in the first file. We shall leave this task as an exercise.

16.6 The class File

The class File is used when we want to access information about individual files or directories (folders). It also contains methods to remove files, change the names of files and create new files and directories. Note that the class File is not used to read or write to a file. For this we have to make use of the stream classes discussed earlier in this chapter. Of course, we can also use the class RandomAccessFile. The class File contains a number of methods. A list of these is given in the fact box. The names of these methods will usually explain what they do. We will only give examples of how some of the methods are used; for a complete description of all their details we refer the reader to the online documentation.

java.io.File	
`File(String path)`	`boolean mkdir()`
`File(String path,String name)`	`boolean mkdirs()`
`File(File dir, String name)`	`boolean createNewFile()`
	`boolean delete()`
`String    getName()`	`boolean renameTo(File dest)`
`String    getPath()`	`boolean equals(Object obj)`
`String    getAbsolutePath()`	`int compareTo(File file)`
`String    getCanonicalPath()`	`int compareTo(Object o)`
`String    getParent()`	`String toString()`
`File      getAbsoluteFile()`	`URL    toURL()`
`File      getCanonicalFile()`	`String[] list()`
`File      getParentFile()`	`String[] list`
`void      deleteOnExit()`	`          (FilenameFilter filter)`
`boolean   exists()`	`File[] listFiles()`
`boolean   canWrite()`	`File[] listFiles`
`boolean   canRead()`	`          (FilenameFilter filter)`
`boolean   setReadOnly()`	`int hashCode()`
`boolean   isFile()`	`static File createTempFile`
`boolean   isDirectory()`	`(String prefix, String suffix)`
`boolean   isAbsolute()`	`static File createTempFile`
`boolean   isHidden()`	`(String prefix, String suffix,`
`long      lastModified()`	` File dir)`
`boolean   setLastModified()`	`static File[] listRoots()`
`long      length()`	`static separator`

As we can see, there are three constructors. We indicate the file's name as a text in the first one. The name can be either relative or absolute. A relative file name is indicated in relation to the *current directory* in which the program is executing, while an absolute file name contains the complete *path* of the file. In the second constructor, the name of the directory is indicated as first parameter and the file's relative name as second parameter. In the third constructor, we use another `File` object to indicate the directory in question. For example, we can write:

```
File f1 = new File("Diverse");
File f2 = new File("C:\\Diverse\\my_file.txt");
File f3 = new File(f1, "Demo.java");
```

Note that there does not have to be a real file with the given name for us to be able to create a `File` object. We might, for instance, want to create a `File` object to use later for the creation of a new directory of that name, or to rename a file. The full file name can be either relative or absolute and will depend not on the constructor we have used but the parameters we have given for it. We can use the method isAbsolute to check whether a File object contains an absolute or a relative file name. The method getName will give the simple file name without the name of the directory, while the method getPath gives the file's name, including the name of the directory. The method getAbsolutePath will give the file's name in its absolute form. If we want to compose our own file names, we can make use of the class variable separator, which contains the character (or possibly, characters) that will appear between the file names in an absolute name. For example, if we are running Windows, separator will contain the character \. In Unix, the character would be /.

We now give an example of a program that will write out the name of the current directory. A list of the names of all the files in this directory is then given and the length of each file is indicated. Every file that is a directory is indicated by the character /, which appears first in the name. To find the name of the current directory, the class method System.getProperty is called, with "user.dir" as parameter. The method list is called to get a list of all the files in the directory.

```java
import java.io.*;
public class FileDemo {
  public static void main(String[] arg) {
    String name = System.getProperty("user.dir");
    File f = new File(name);    // describes current directory
    System.out.println(f.getAbsolutePath());

    String[] l = f.list();
    System.out.println("Number of files: " + l.length);
    for (int i=0; i<l.length; i++) {
      File g = new File(l[i]); // describes a file in the
                               // directory
      if (g.isDirectory())
        System.out.print("/");
      else
        System.out.print(" ");
      System.out.print(l[i]);
      System.out.println("   " + g.length());
    }
  }
}
```

We can also show an example of how we can create new directories. The following program lines will create two new directories. The directory new_directory will land in the current directory and the directory example will end up in the directory C:\temp:

```
File d1 = new File("new_directory");
d1.mkdir();
File d2 = new File("C:\\temp\\example");
d2.mkdir();
```

It is also a simple matter to change the names of file or directories or to remove them. The following lines will change the name of the directory new_directory to newDirectory and remove a file called old.txt:

```
File d3 = new File("newDirectory");
d1.renameTo(d3);
File f4 = new File("old.txt");
f4.delete();
```

The method list in an earlier example gave a list of *all* the files in the current directory, but this method exists in an alternative version that we can use if we only want to have a list of certain files in a directory. For instance, we might want a list of all the files containing Java programs, in which case this list would only contain files with the suffix ".java". This alternative version of the method list has as parameter a reference to an object that implements the interface FilenameFilter. There is only one method defined in this interface, that is, the method accept, with the definition:

```
public boolean accept(File dir, String name);
```

Every class that implements the interface FilenameFilter must therefore have its own version of this method. When the method list is to create a list of files, it calls the method accept for each file. If accept returns the value **true**, the actual file will be included in the list, otherwise it will not be included. The method accept has two parameters. The first is a File object that describes the directory in which the file lies, and the second is the name of the file.

There are no ready-made standard classes that implement the interface FilenameFilter. We have to define such interfaces ourselves. We will now show a class of our own that can be useful for filtering out files with certain suffixes. We call the class SuffixFilter. It has a single constructor that has as parameter the suffix we want to filter out. To get a list with all the file names that contain Java programs, for instance, we can make the statements:

```
SuffixFilter filter = new SuffixFilter("java");
String[] = f.list(filter);
```

We shall now show what the class SuffixFilter looks like. It contains only one constructor and its own version of the method accept. For every file, a check is made to see whether its name ends with the desired suffix. If so, we check to see whether we can read the file. To do this, we create a new File object that describes the file.

```
import java.io.*;

public class SuffixFilter implements FilenameFilter {
   public String suffix;

   public SuffixFilter(String suffix) {
      this.suffix = suffix;
   }

   public boolean accept(File dir, String name) {
      return name.endsWith("." + suffix) &&   // ends with suffix?
             (new File(dir, name)).canRead(); // can be read?
   }
}
```

16.7 Exercises

1. We have saved a secret message in a text file with the name `secret.txt`. The message has been encoded so that no unauthorized person may easily read it. Each letter in the message has been coded to another letter by using the following table:

   ```
   code letters:   guwyrmqpsaeicbnozlfhdkjxtv
   original text:  abcdefghijklmnopqrstuvwxyz
   ```

   If, for example, the file contains the text "inybrt jgshsbq jrybrfygt rsqph oc", the decoded message will be "rodney waiting wednesday eight pm". Write a program to read the file with the secret message and write it out in plain language. The program should begin by reading in the code (the first line in the above table) from the keyboard.

2. A command that is often used in the Unix operating system is one called `cat`. The task here is to write your own version `Cat` of this program. Feel free to use the class `SequenceInputStream`. We should be able to use the program `Cat` to combine files but could also use it to write out the contents of one or more files at the terminal. The command to run the program should have the form:

   ```
   java Cat f1 f2 f3 ...
   ```

   An arbitrary number of file names are therefore given as parameters for `main`. If no parameters are given, the program should read from standard input. The program should write out the files one at a time to standard output. If we want to concatenate files, standard output can be redirected. For example, the following command will mean that `fc` will contain a copy of `fa` concatenated with `fb`.

   ```
   java Cat fa fb > fc
   ```

   Note that a redirection is not an argument that is sent to `main`, so the program will only get `fa` and `fb` as arguments on this line.

3. In Section 10.7 we worked with a class `Vehicle` that had several subclasses. We showed how we could describe a collection of different kinds of vehicle by using class `Vector`. The exercise now is to write the program lines necessary for such a vector to be saved in a file. In addition, write program lines to enable us later to read in information about all vehicles and store them in a vector. Use the classes `ObjectOutputStream` and `ObjectInputStream`.

4. Information about a number of persons has been collected in a file as part of some statistical research. Each person is described by an object of a class `Person` (which you must define yourself), and information is stored using the class `ObjectOutputStream`. A person's name, height, weight, shoe size, age and civil status are included in this class `Person`. To deal with the data in the file properly, you will also have to know a person's sex but this information has not been stored.

Write a program that will read the file and create two new files, one containing only women and one only men. For every person in the file, the program will ask the operator whether the person is a woman or a man. A person will be described in the new files by a new class that also contains a person's sex.

5. Extend the class `AccountDatabase` in Section 16.5 with a method that opens a new account. The account-holder's name and address will be given as parameters for the method, which should give as result the number of the new account. The method should choose account numbers arbitrarily. Having checked that an account number is available, the method should then create a new entry, putting it into the correct position in the direct-access file to ensure that this file remains sorted.

6. When we handle files, they are usually sorted. (The direct-access file with the bank account in Section 16.5 was an example of this.) Some particular component among the entries, for instance a civic registration number, or a car registration number, is normally chosen to institute the sort procedure. This component is called the *sort key*. A problem can occur if there are two sorted files with entries of the same type and a new, sorted file has to be made containing the entries of both files. The new file should also be sorted. We say that the two original files have been *merged*. Write a program that merges two files containing entries of the same length that define cars. The sort key is the car registration number. You may yourself decide what the other entries are to be.

7. Let us suppose that the time of day is defined by a text string in the format "hh.mm.ss". Write a class method that updates a time of day by adding a certain number of seconds (which can be greater than 60). The method should have two parameters: a `String` object that contains a time of day and a whole number that will indicate the number of seconds to be added. As result, the method should give a `String` object that describes the updated time. *Tip*: Use the technique of connecting streams to texts.

8. It is difficult to use the technique of serialization together with direct access, since the objects stored in a file will have different lengths. A trick we can use to find the stored objects quickly is to use two direct-access files. In one of the files, the *data file*, all of the objects are stored in serialized format. The file is not sorted. In the other file, the *index file*, we store entries of equal length. There is an entry for every object stored in the data file. Every entry in the index file contains three pieces of information: the object's search key, the object's initial position in the data file and the number of bytes that the object will occupy in the data file. The index file is sorted. We shall, of course, use the classes `ObjectInputStream` and `ObjectOutputStream` when we are to read and write in the data file, but we cannot connect streams directly to a direct-access file. What we can do is to use byte arrays. When we read from the data file, we read the number of bytes that the active object occupies. We then use a `ByteArrayInputStream` and an `ObjectInput-Stream` to read the array. We reverse this process when outputting to the data file.

Let us now suppose that information about the different kinds of motor vehicles has been stored in this way. (The class definitions in Section 10.7 can be used.) Your task is to write a method that will find a motor vehicle with a particular registration number and to write out information about this vehicle on the screen. The registration number is given as parameter for the method.

Communication

17

The many examples in this book have shown us that it is relatively easy to write GUI programs in Java. We have even been able to produce programs with moving pictures and sound. It may come as something of a surprise, therefore, to learn that the best is yet to come – the resources we have in Java for communications. It is very easy to write Java programs that can communicate with other computers in various ways. This opens new vistas for "ordinary" programmers who are not experts in data communication. In this chapter, we shall be looking at the different ways of communicating. We will see how we can examine and retrieve a file from another computer, how we can send quick messages in the form of datagrams, how we can use multicast to send messages to several computers at the same time and how we can establish a connection and write client–server programs. For security reasons, certain restrictions apply to applets. For this reason, most of the examples have been worked out as independent applications. Communication in applets will be discussed in a separate section.

17.1 The class URL

In Section 15.1 we used the class URL. A URL object points to a file on the Internet. The URL class is defined in the package java.net. There are several different constructors in the class URL (see the fact box). In the simplest of these, you simply state the address as a text. For example, you can write:

```
URL u = new URL("http://www.xyz.se/pub/Java_dir/image1.gif");
```

A URL address can contain several different parts. First should always be the name of a *protocol*. This is followed by a name that may include the host name. It may also contain a port number. The protocol indicates how you will communicate with the remote computer. The most common protocol for web browsers is http. Another common protocol is file, which you can use when you want to refer to a file on your own computer. If you are running Windows, you might write, for example:

```
URL u = new URL("file:C:\\own\\images\\myimage.gif");
```

java.net.URL	
new URL(*addr*)	creates a URL object with the address *addr*
new URL(*prot, host, file*)	creates a URL object with the address *prot+host+file*
new URL(*prot, host, portno, file*)	creates a URL object with the address *prot+host+portno+file*
new URL(u,*file*)	creates a URL object on the basis of the URL object u and the corresponding address *file*
getContent()	gives whatever the URL object refers to; return type: Object
openConnection()	gives a URLConnection object
openStream()	gives whatever the URL object refers to; return type: InputStream
getHost()	gives the host name
getFile()	gives the corresponding file name
getProtocol()	gives the protocol that is used
getPort()	gives the port number
toExternalForm()	gives the complete address as a text

When you have created a URL object in your program, you can load whatever it is that the URL object refers to. In the URL class, there are three different methods you can use for this: getContent, openConnection and openStream. The simplest of these is getContent. The method getContent results in an object that contains whatever it is that the URL object refers to. The result type is Object, since a URL object can refer to any kind of data at all on the Internet. If a URL object refers to a file with an image, the method getContent, for example, will return an object of the class java.awt.image.ImageProducer. If you want a bit more control over what happens, you can open a URL connection. The URL class includes a method called openConnection which is used for this purpose. This results in a reference to an object of the class URLConnection. For example, you can write:

```
URLConnection uc = u.openConnection();
```

When we have created the connection, we can indicate how we want it to be used. If we only want to read the file on the distant computer, we can write:

```
uc.setDoInput(true);
```

There is also a corresponding method with the name setDoOutput that indicates whether we want to write in the file or not.

Then we can establish the connection with the command:

```
uc.connect();
```

When this has been done, we can access the distant file and read its properties. If we want to know how long the file is, for example, we can write:

```
int length = uc.getContentLength();
```

To read the file, we call the method getInputStream, which connects a stream to the file:

```
InputStream in = uc.getInputStream();
```

Similarly, we can use the method getOutputStream if we want to write to the file. (Actually, the methods setDoInput and connect are superfluous in this example, as the default value is **true** for setDoInput, and the method getInputStream will itself call connect if this has not already been done.)

We can then read the stream in the usual way to copy the file to our own computer. If we want to do this to a new file on our computer, we will first have to create an output stream to which we can copy. This can be done by the declaration:

```
FileOutputStream out = new FileOutputStream(arg[1]);
```

(We suppose that the name of the new file has been given as the second parameter for main.) We can now copy the distant file to our own computer with the program lines:

```
int i, n = 0;
while ((i=in.read()) >= 0) {
        out.write((byte) i);
        n++;
}
System.out.println(n + " bytes copied");
```

java.net.URLConnection	
url.openConnection()	gives a URLConnection object for the URL object url
setDoInput (*bool*)	indicates whether or not we wish to read the file
setDoOutput (*bool*)	indicates whether or not we wish to write to the file
connect()	makes the connection
getInputStream()	gives an input stream that is connected to the file
getOutputStream()	gives an output stream that is connected to the file
getContent()	same as the method getContent in the class URL
getContentLength()	gives the file's length
getContentType()	gives a text that describes the file's type
getDate()	gives the file's date of creation
getLastModified()	gives the date when the file was last modified
A point in time t is returned as the number of milliseconds since 1 January 1970 and can easily be converted to a Date object: **new** Date(*t*). (See page 146.)	

Note that this could be done rather more easily if we merely wanted to read the file, without reading its properties. Then we would not have to create a `URLConnection` object but could instead directly get an input stream connected to the file on the distant computer by calling the method `getFile` in the class `URL`. We simply write:

```
InputStream in = u.openStream();
```

Since the file in the above example will be copied exactly as it is, we have been able to read it with a byte stream and copy one byte at a time. We will now give another example where a text file will be copied. Let us suppose that, on some central computer, we have a text file containing information about current temperatures in different locations. The reading of every temperature can be found in its own line in the file, where each line contains the name of the location, the temperature read and the time a temperature was reported. The program we will now be looking at will download the file from the central computer and present the current temperatures in a window on the screen. When the program is run, it could look as in Figure 17.1.

The file is written out in a `JTextArea` component. At the bottom, in a `JLabel` object, we can see the time when the downloaded file was last updated in the central computer. There is also a button on which the user can click to download a new, more current copy from the central computer. We make use of `BorderLayout` and place the text area in the "Center" position. The `Label` object and the "Update" button are put into a panel, which in turn is placed in the "South" position in the window. When we start the program, we give the `URL` address as parameter for `main`. This might look as follows:

```
java TemperatureDisplay http://www.weather.xx/pub/temperatures
```

Here is the program:

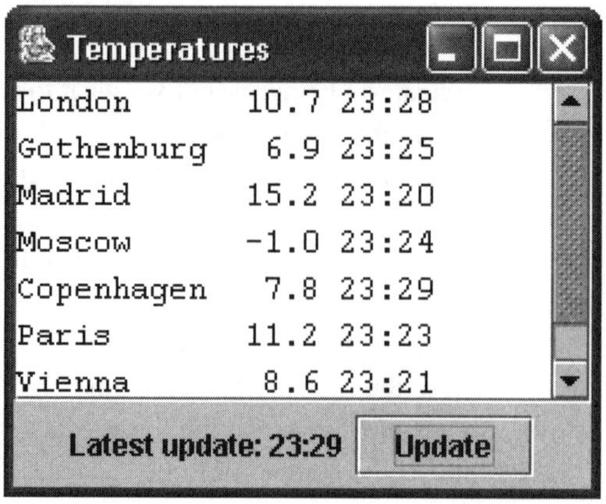

Figure 17.1 Downloading of a text file

```
import javax.swing.*;
import java.awt.*;
import java.awt.event.*;
import java.net.*;
import java.io.*;
import java.util.*;
import java.text.*;
public class TemperatureDisplay extends JFrame
                                implements ActionListener {
  JTextArea ta = new JTextArea("",0,0);
  JScrollPane sp = new JScrollPane(ta);
  JPanel  p  = new JPanel();
  JLabel  la = new JLabel();
  JButton up = new JButton("Update");
  URL u;

  public TemperatureDisplay(String address) {
    try {
      u = new URL(address);
      update();  // download the file
    }
    catch (MalformedURLException e) {
      e.printStackTrace();
    }
    setTitle("Temperatures");
    ta.setEditable(false);
    ta.setFont(new Font("Monospaced", Font.PLAIN, 14));
    ta.setBackground(Color.white);
    la.setBackground(Color.lightGray);
    getContentPane().add(sp, BorderLayout.CENTER);
    getContentPane().add(p, BorderLayout.SOUTH);
    p.add(la); p.add(up);
    up.addActionListener(this);
    setSize(250,200);
    setVisible(true);
    setDefaultCloseOperation(EXIT_ON_CLOSE);
  }

  private void update() { // downloads and displays the file
    try {
      // open a connection, connect a text stream to the file
      URLConnection c = u.openConnection();
      BufferedReader in = new BufferedReader
                (new InputStreamReader(c.getInputStream()));
      // read the file and display it in the text area
      ta.read(in, null);
      in.close();

      // read in, format and display the updated date
      Date d = new Date(c.getLastModified());
```

575

```
        DateFormat  f = DateFormat.getTimeInstance
                       (DateFormat.SHORT);
        la.setText("Latest update: "+ f.format(d));
      }
    catch (IOException e) {
        e.printStackTrace();
      }
   }

  public void actionPerformed(ActionEvent e) {
     // when the user has clicked on the button
     if (e.getSource() == up)
        update();
   }

  public static void main(String[] arg) {
     new TemperatureDisplay(arg[0]); // address as parameter
   }
 }
```

As usual, the configuration of the window is done in the constructor, and initialization of the URL object referring to the file of temperatures is also done there. Note that the constructor for class URL can generate an exception of type MalformedURLException, and this must be dealt with or sent on.

The real work is done in the method update. This is called both from the constructor, when the file is to be downloaded for the first time, and from the listener when the user has clicked on the button. We have to connect a char stream to the input stream, as the file to be downloaded is a text file. We use a stream of class BufferedReader. As we will remember, a stream of class BufferedReader cannot be directly connected to a stream of class InputStream without the use of an intermediary stream of class InputStreamReader.

The method getLastModified gives a time in the form of a whole number value of type long, and this value is used as parameter of the constructor for the class Date. We will then get a Date object that describes the time. We will make use of a DateFormat object to display this value in the desired form.

17.2 Ports and sockets

As we know, a URL address describes the address of a file on the Internet. A computer not only can have files on the Internet but can also offer different kinds of services. One of these is the opportunity to send and receive data by using the HTTP protocol; another, to give the exact time and date for the computer. To keep track of the different kinds of services, we use something called a *port*. Each service is assigned a particular port, identified by a whole number. For instance, port number 80 is used for HTTP

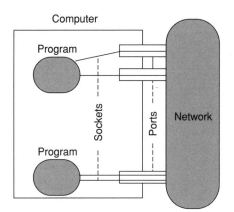

Figure 17.2 Ports and sockets

communication, port number 21 for FTP communication, and port number 13 gives the exact time and date. If we want to have a particular service from a certain computer, we have to indicate both the computer's name on the Internet and the port number we wish to use. Port numbers are whole numbers in the interval 0 to 65,535. Numbers up to 1024 are reserved for different forms of standard service, while those over 1024 can be freely used when programs providing a service are written. We can think of a port as a connection point on a computer, a sort of "virtual input". (Compare this with the input points on the back of a computer, TV or stereo amplifier.)

When we want to get on the Internet to communicate with other computers through a program, we have to connect a "virtual line" through the "virtual input" out to the Internet. This "virtual line" is called a *socket*. So a socket is a kind of channel for data. Only one socket is usually drawn through a particular port but it is possible to have several sockets running through a port. A program can also make use of several ports and sockets. Figure 17.2 gives a diagrammatic view of ports and sockets.

We shall utilize ports and sockets in the following sections in order to communicate through programs. There are two main principles according to which communication can proceed. We can either send *datagrams*, independent packets of data that contain the address of their destination, or we can set up a *connection* between two computers and send data through this connection. In the first case, that is, when we use datagrams, we have the option of using *multicast*, a means of sending data packets at the same time to several connected members of a particular group.

17.3 Datagrams

A datagram is a packet of data sent over the Internet. It will contain the address of both the sender and the receiver, where this address is indicated as the computer's address with the port number added. Sending a datagram can be compared to sending an ordinary letter through the post. There is no guarantee that it will actually reach the receiver, and if several datagrams are sent, we cannot be certain that they will arrive in the same order as they are sent.

Datagrams in Java are described by the class `java.net.DatagramPacket`. One of the things a datagram will contain is the receiver's Internet address. Internet addresses are described by the class `java.net.InetAddress`. This class has no constructors. Instead we create an `InetAddress` object by calling one of the class methods `getLocalHost` and `getByName`. The first lacks parameters and gives the Internet address of our own computer. The method `getByName` has a text as parameter. This text will contain the Internet address either as a symbolic name, for example, `www.xyz.pqr.com`, or as an IP address, such as `206.26.48.100`. For example, we can write:

```
InetAddress toAddr = InetAddress.getByName("www.xyz.pqr.com");
```

java.net.InetAddress	
`getLocalHost()`	class method, gives the `InetAddress` of one's own computer
`getByName(name)`	class method, gives the `InetAddress` of the computer *name*; *name* can be indicated as a symbolic name or an IP address
`getHostName()`	gives the computer name for this `InetAddress`
`getHostAddress()`	gives the IP address for this `InetAddress`
`isMulticastAddress()`	indicates whether this `InetAddress` can be used to send multicast messages (messages to several receivers)
`equals(iAddr)`	checks whether this `InetAddress` is the same as `iAddr`

If we have given an incorrect address as parameter, we will get an exception of type `UnknownHostException`.

A datagram will of course contain the data that is being sent, and this will be in the form of an array of bytes. The data to be sent must therefore be converted into this form. For instance, if we want to send a text of type `String`, the text can be converted to an array of bytes with the method `getBytes`:

```
String message = "Hello";
byte[] data = message.getBytes();
```

We can now put together a datagram by creating a new object of the class `DatagramPacket`:

```
DatagramPacket packet = new DatagramPacket(data, data.length,
                                           toAddr, toPort);
```

As we can see, the length of the byte array must also be given as parameter. The last parameter is a whole number that indicates the port number of the receiving computer.

When we have created a datagram, we can send it. To do this, we have to create a socket on the sender computer, that is, a "line" to an appropriate port to send it through. The class `DatagramSocket` describes such a socket, which is very easy to create. We simply write:

```
DatagramSocket socket = new DatagramSocket();
```

Alternatively, we can indicate a port number as parameter for the constructor. If we do not do this, the constructor will automatically choose a vacant port. The constructor for the class can generate an exception of type `SocketException` if something goes wrong.

Everything is now ready to send the message. This is done with the method `send`.

```
socket.send(packet);
```

If for some reason the transmission is not successful, an exception of type `IOException` is generated.

java.net.DatagramSocket	
`new DatagramSocket(port)`	creates a socket through the port `port`
`new DatagramSocket()`	creates a socket through a vacant port
`send(pack)`	sends the datagram `pack`
`receive(pack)`	receives the datagram `pack`
`setSoTimeout(m)`	indicates that `receive` will wait at most `m` ms; gives `InterruptedIOException` at time out
`close()`	breaks the connection
`getLocalPort()`	gives the number for the port the socket is tied to

We can combine all of this into a small program that sends a number of messages to an arbitrary receiver. The receiver's Internet address and port number are given as parameter for `main` when we start the program. For example, we can write:

```
java MessageSender www.xyz.pqr.com 15318
```

java.net.DatagramPacket	
`new DatagramPacket(data, len, iAddr, port)`	
	creates a datagram with the content `data` (a bytes array) of length `len`; will be sent to the port `port` at `iAddr`
`new DatagramPacket(data, len)`	
	creates a datagram for reception, `data` is a byte array of length `len`
`getData()`	gives data that has been sent (or will be sent)
`getLength()`	gives the length of data that has been (or will be) sent
`getAddress()`	gives the sender's `InetAddress` (on reception)
`getPort()`	gives the sender's port number (on reception)

We then enter the messages we want to send, one message to each line. The program will look as follows:

```java
import java.net.*;
import java.io.*;
public class MessageSender {
  public static void main(String[] arg) throws
            UnknownHostException, SocketException, IOException {
    BufferedReader in = new BufferedReader
                        (new InputStreamReader(System.in));
    InetAddress toAddr = InetAddress.getByName(arg[0]);
    int toPort = Integer.parseInt(arg[1]);
    // create a socket to send through
    DatagramSocket socket = new DatagramSocket();
    while (true) {
      // read in the message from the keyboard
      System.out.print("? ");System.out.flush();
      String message = in.readLine();
      if (message == null)
        break;
      // convert the message from a String to a byte array
      byte[] data = message.getBytes();
      // prepare a data packet and send it
      DatagramPacket packet = new DatagramPacket(data,
                              data.length, toAddr, toPort);
      socket.send(packet);
    }
  }
}
```

Now it is time to take a look at what is happening at the receiving end. The receiver must also create a socket, that is, a "line" to the program from the socket the messages will come through. This is done by the creation of a Socket object. This time we must use the form of the constructor where we explicitly indicate the port to be used. For example, we write:

```java
DatagramSocket socket = new DatagramSocket(15318);
```

The next step is to create an object of class DatagramPacket. The incoming datagram will be placed in this object. We do not indicate an Internet address or port number when we create it, as it will be used for reception of the datagram. However, we must indicate as parameter an array of bytes in which the incoming message will be placed. The size of the array must also be given.

```java
DatagramPacket packet = new DatagramPacket(data, data.length);
```

For example, the array data is declared in the following way:

```java
byte[] data = new byte[256];
```

When we want to receive a datagram, we simply call the method `receive`. The listener in the actual port and program will wait until the datagram comes through the port.

```
socket.receive(packet);
```

This method can generate an exception of type `IOException` if reception is unsuccessful.

When the datagram has been received, it can be examined with the methods `getData`, `getLength`, `getAddress` and `getPort`. The first two will give the byte array received and its length. The other two will give the sender's `InetAddress` and port number. Data received will be in the form of an array of bytes, so this array must be converted to the type we want the message to have. For example, if the received message should be a text, we can use the constructor for class `String` that initializes a `String` with part of a byte array. The first parameter will be the array, the second the start index in the array and the third the number of bytes we want to include. For example, we can write:

```
String message = new String(packet.getData(), 0,
                                    packet.getLength());
```

We will combine this into a program that can execute in the receiving computer. When we start the program, we give as parameter the number of the port we want to listen to:

```
java MessageReceiver 15318
```

Here is the entire program:

```
import java.net.*;
import java.io.*;
public class MessageReceiver {
  public static void main(String[] arg)
                          throws SocketException, IOException {
    int myPort = Integer.parseInt(arg[0]);
    // create the socket that will listen at the port
    DatagramSocket socket = new DatagramSocket(myPort);
    byte[] data = new byte[256];
    while (true) {
      // create a datagram to receive the next message in
      DatagramPacket packet =
                      new DatagramPacket(data, data.length);
      // wait for the next message
      socket.receive(packet);
      System.out.println("Message from " +
                          packet.getAddress().getHostName());
      // convert the message from bytes to String
      String message = new String(packet.getData(), 0,
                                  packet.getLength());
      System.out.println(message);
    }
  }
}
```

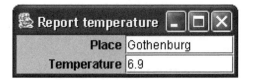

Figure 17.3 Reporting temperatures

Let us look at another example of communication through datagrams. This time, communication in both directions will be shown, and we will be making use of time out. In Section 17.1, we wrote a program that retrieved information about temperatures from a file in a central computer. We will now look at how we can read temperatures at different stations and report these temperatures to a central computer, which will receive the information and store it in a file. We begin by discussing the stations where the temperatures are read. The program `TemperatureReader` is run at each station. When it is run, a window is displayed like the one in Figure 17.3. The user fills in the name of the location together with the current temperature, and every time he or she presses the Enter key, this information will be sent to the central computer.

When the program is started at a station, the name and port number of the central computer are given as arguments. This can have the appearance:

```
java TemperatureReader www.weather.se 9963
```

We will now show the whole program, followed by the commentary:

```
import javax.swing.*;
import java.awt.*;
import java.awt.event.*;
import java.net.*;
import java.io.*;
import extra.*;

public class TemperatureReader extends JFrame
                                implements ActionListener {
    final int placeLen = 10;
    final int temLen = 6;
    JTextField place = new JTextField(10),
               tem = new JTextField();
    InetAddress    iadr;
    DatagramSocket socket;
    int port;

    public TemperatureReader(String toAddress, int portNo)
                throws UnknownHostException, SocketException {
        // create a socket for sending and receiving
        iadr = InetAddress.getByName(toAddress);
        port = portNo;
```

```java
      socket = new DatagramSocket();
      socket.setSoTimeout(10000);
      // prepare the window's layout
      setTitle("Report temperature");
      Container c = getContentPane();
      c.setLayout(new GridLayout(2, 2));
      c.add(new JLabel("Place ", JLabel.RIGHT)); c.add(place);
      c.add(new JLabel("Temperature ", JLabel.RIGHT)); c.add(tem);
      place.addActionListener(this);
      tem.addActionListener(this);
      pack();
      setVisible(true);
      setDefaultCloseOperation(EXIT_ON_CLOSE);
   }
   private void report(String where, double temp) {
      // read the location and temperature from the window
      String mess = ExtendedWriter.toFixedLength(where,placeLen)+
                    ExtendedWriter.formatNum(temp, temLen, 1);
      byte[] data = mess.getBytes(); // convert the text into bytes
      for (int i=1; i<=3; i++) {   // make three attempts to send
        // create a datagram with the message
        DatagramPacket packet = new DatagramPacket(data,
                                      data.length, iadr, port);
        try {
          socket.send(packet);
          socket.receive(packet);  // wait until an answer has come
          // convert the received bytes into a String
          String answer = new String(packet.getData(), 0,
                                packet.getLength());
          if (answer.equals("OK"))
            return;    // the attempt to send was successful
        }
        catch(IOException ie) {} // time out or error
      }
      // all attempts to send were unsuccessful
      System.out.println("Communication error");
   }
   public void actionPerformed(ActionEvent e) {
      // the user has pressed the Enter key
      if (e.getSource()==place || e.getSource()==tem)
        report(place.getText(), Parse.toDouble(tem.getText()));
   }
   public static void main(String[] arg)
               throws UnknownHostException, SocketException {
      // retrieve the Internet address and port number from arg
      new TemperatureReader(arg[0], Integer.parseInt(arg[1]));
   }
}
```

A socket is created in the constructor for the sending and reception of datagrams. The method `setSoTimeout` is called to set the time out at reception to 10 seconds. When we then call the method `receive` to receive datagrams at the socket, an exception of type `TimeoutError` will be generated if no datagram has arrived within 10 seconds.

When the user has written data in the window and pressed the Enter key, the method `actionPerformed` is called. This in turn calls the method `report`. Every time this method is called, input information will be retrieved from the window and sent to the central computer in the form of a datagram. This datagram will contain text and have a fixed length. The location will be indicated in 10 characters and the temperature in six characters. The temperature will be given with one decimal. The class methods `toFixedLength` and `formatNum` in class `ExtendedWriter` (see page 141) are used to format data into this form. Conversion from type `String` to an array of bytes is then done, as before, with the method `getBytes` in class `String`.

When the message has been formatted and converted, it is sent as a datagram to the central computer. Because datagrams are a little unreliable, the method `report` will wait until the central computer sends a datagram with the text `"OK"` as a receipt for the message. Note that we can use the same socket and datagram packet for both sending and receiving. If a receipt does not come within 10 seconds, the message is sent once more. The method `report` will make a maximum of three attempts at sending. If all of these are unsuccessful, an error message is given. The class `TimeoutError`, which is generated at time out, is a subclass of the class `IOError`. All the errors can therefore be caught in the same handler.

Let us now turn to the central computer, where the program `TemperatureCentral` is executed. This program will be listening for incoming messages from the different stations. When a message comes, the program will update the file that contains the temperatures. The line applying to the station in question will be updated. We give two arguments when we start the program. The first is the name of the file and the second is the number of the port at which the program will listen. We can write:

```
java TemperatureCentral /pub/temperatures 9963
```

The program consists of two main parts, a constructor and the method `store`. The program listens in the constructor at the receiving port, receives the messages and sends the receipt. Every time a message is received, a check is made to see that it has the correct length. If it has, the method `store` is called to store the message in the file.

The program will look as follows:

```
import java.net.*;
import java.io.*;
import java.text.*;
import java.util.*;
```

```java
public class TemperatureCentral {
  final int placeLen = 10;
  final int temLen = 6;
  String fileName;
  DateFormat f = DateFormat.getTimeInstance(DateFormat.SHORT);

  public TemperatureCentral(String fileName, int portNo)
                                    throws SocketException {
    this.fileName = fileName;
    // create a socket for receiving and sending
    DatagramSocket socket = new DatagramSocket(portNo);

    // create a bytes array for receiving and sending
    byte[] data = new byte[placeLen+temLen];
    byte[] OKData = "OK".getBytes();
    while (true)
    try {
      // create a datagram to receive messages
      DatagramPacket packet =
                      new DatagramPacket(data, data.length);
      socket.receive(packet);  // wait for a message
      // create a datagram to send receipts
      DatagramPacket OKPacket =
            new DatagramPacket(OKData,OKData.length,
                      packet.getAddress(), packet.getPort());
      socket.send(OKPacket);    // send a receipt
      // check that the message has the correct length
      if (packet.getLength() == placeLen+temLen)
        store(packet.getData());  // store in the file
    }
    catch (IOException e) {}
  }

  private void store(byte[] data) throws IOException {
    // translate the name of the location from bytes to String
    String place = new String(data, 0, placeLen);

    // open the file of temperature
    RandomAccessFile file = new RandomAccessFile(fileName,"rw");
    // search the file for the current location
    String line;
    long pos = 0;  // actual position in the file
    while ((line = file.readLine()) != null) {
      if (line.substring(0,placeLen).equals(place)) {
        // line found
        file.seek(pos);  // go back to the line's start position
        break;
      }
      pos =file.getFilePointer();  //remember the line's position
    }
    // write over the old line
```

```
      file.write(data); // data contains both location and temp.
      // write date
      file.writeBytes(" " + f.format(new Date()) + "\n");
      file.close();
   }

   public static void main(String[] arg)
                      throws SocketException {
      // retrieve the file name and port number from the arguments
      new TemperatureCentral(arg[0], Integer.parseInt(arg[1]));
   }
}
```

The method `store` handles the file as a direct-access file and therefore uses a stream of class `RandomAccessFile` to update the file. Because a `RandomAccessFile` is a binary file, data in the file is stored as a sequence of bytes, and when the datagram is received it will be in this form.

Lines are of a fixed length in the file. All lines will therefore be of equal length. The file will look as in Figure 17.1. To update the file, we have to find the line that contains data about the current location, overwriting this line with the new information. The file will be read line by line until the correct line has been found. Before a line is read, the method `getFilePointer` is called to see where in the file the line began. When the correct line has been found, we only have to call the method `seek` to go back to the beginning of the line. If a line does not already exist in the file for the current location, a new line will be added at the end of it.

When the old line is overwritten (or a new line written at the end), we can write out the message from the datagram directly, as this message will have the correct form (an array of bytes). The current date is written out last in the line. To format the time properly, we will use an editor of class `DateFormat` (see page 149).

17.4 Multicast

It might be the case that, in certain applications, we will want to send messages to several receivers at a time. Instead of sending a message to a specific receiver, then, we will send it to a group of receivers. A message of this kind is called a *multicast message*, and the group of receivers is known as a *multicast group*. The sender of a multicast message is normally included in a multicast group but this is not necessarily so. When we want to send or receive multicast messages in Java, we create a socket of class `MulticastSocket`, which is a subclass of the class `DatagramSocket`. As parameter, we indicate the port to be used.

```
MulticastSocket so = new MulticastSocket(16718);
```

A multicast message is sent in the form of a datagram. As we know, one of the things a datagram contains is the receiver's Internet address. When we send a multicast message, we do not indicate an Internet address for some particular receiver. Instead, we use an imaginary *multicast address* that all the receivers in the group know and listen to. This type of multicast address will be an IP address in the interval 224.0.0.1 to 239.255.255.255. Every receiver wanting to belong to a particular multicast group must report this by calling the method joinGroup in class MulticastSocket. If the imaginary multicast address is 234.235.236.237, we can write, for example:

```
iaddr = InetAddress.getByName("234.235.236.237");
so.joinGroup(iaddr);
```

The method joinGroup will have a parameter of type InetAddress so, as in the last section, we will have to use the class method getByName to convert the text with the IP address to an InetAddress object. In order to leave a multicast group, we will call the method leaveGroup.

Methods can then be sent and received, as for ordinary datagrams, with the methods send and receive.

java.net.MulticastSocket	
new MulticastSocket(port)	creates a multicast socket through the port port
send(pack)	sends the datagram pack
receive(pack)	receives the datagram pack
joinGroup(iaddr)	joins the multicast group with the multicast address iaddr (of class InetAddress)
leaveGroup(iaddr)	leaves the multicast group with the multicast address iaddr (of class InetAddress)
close()	breaks the connection

In order to demonstrate the use of multicast, we will construct a so-called chat program. This is a program where we can get connected to the Net and chat with several people at the same time. When our chat program is run, a window is displayed that could look like the one in Figure 17.4.

The program is extremely simple to run. In the middle of the window there is a text area in which all the messages, even those we write ourselves, are displayed. At the bottom, there is a text field where we can write our own messages. To terminate the program, we click on "Disconnect". This program is called Chat. When we start it, we can indicate as parameter what we want to call ourselves. If we write nothing, we will be assigned the name "Anonymous". To start the program that will generate Figure 17.4 we write:

```
java Chat Hanna
```

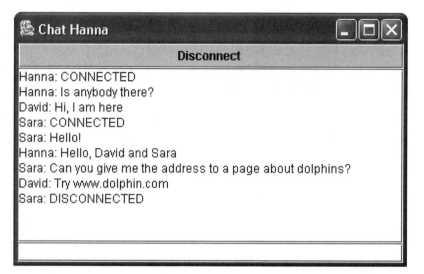

Figure 17.4 A chat program

The program makes use of two parallel threads. The normal thread (the one that is active when the program starts) deals with the messages the user writes in the text field and sends them out to all of the other members of the multicast group. An active object, which reads in multicast messages from the Net and displays them in the text area, is used in parallel with this thread. The two threads execute in parallel and will not affect one another. A user's name is automatically inserted first when a message is sent out. Automatic messages are also generated when we connect and disconnect. We will also receive our own messages, as a multicast message is sent to all the members in a multicast group.

Let us begin by looking at the class that describes the active object that deals with the reception of multicast messages. The constructor has two parameters, the socket that we will read from and the text area that the messages will be displayed in. Because the receiver will be an active object, it will in the usual way have a thread, started in the constructor. The work itself is done in the method run, which uses a repetition statement that reads a message at every loop. Every message read in is displayed in the text area. The method run will execute until IOException occurs, which will happen when the socket it is reading from is closed. Here is the class Receiver:

```
import javax.swing.*;
import java.awt.*;
import java.awt.event.*;
import java.net.*;
import java.io.*;
```

```
class Receiver implements Runnable {
  Thread activity = new Thread(this);
  MulticastSocket so;
  JTextArea  txt;

  // constructor
  Receiver(MulticastSocket sock, JTextArea txtAr) {
    so = sock;
    txt = txtAr;
    activity.start();
  }

  public void run() {
    byte[] data = new byte[1024]; // space for received data
    while (true)
      try {
        // create a datagram for reception
        DatagramPacket packet =
                        new DatagramPacket(data, data.length);
        // wait for next message
        so.receive(packet);
        // convert the message to a String
        String mess = new String(data, 0, packet.getLength());
        txt.append(mess + "\n"); // display the message
      }
      catch (IOException e) {break;} // occurs when so is closed
  }
}
```

The rest of the program is composed of the class `Chat`, which prepares the window's layout and deals with the sending of messages. Execution will begin, as usual, in the method `main` and this will in turn call the constructor. Given as parameters are the name the user has chosen, a multicast address in the form of an IP address and the port number to be used. For the sake of simplicity, we have used the fixed IP address `234.235.236.237` and the port number `9876`. The class `Chat` looks like this:

```
public class Chat extends JFrame implements ActionListener {
  String name;       // the name the user has chosen
  InetAddress iadr; // the multicast address
  int port;
  MulticastSocket so;
  JTextArea  txt    = new JTextArea();    // display the messages
  JScrollPane sp    = new JScrollPane(txt);
  JTextField writeField =new JTextField();//for our own messages
  JButton stop = new JButton("Disconnect");

  // constructor
  public Chat(String userName, String groupAddr, int portNo)
                                        throws IOException {
```

```
      // deal with the parameters
      name = userName;
      iadr = InetAddress.getByName(groupAddr);
      port = portNo;

      // create socket and start communication
      so = new MulticastSocket(port);
      so.joinGroup(iadr);
      new Receiver(so, txt);    // create and start reception
      sendMessage("CONNECTED");

      // prepare layout for the window
      setTitle("Chat " + name);
      txt.setEditable(false);
      getContentPane().add(stop, BorderLayout.NORTH);
      getContentPane().add(sp, BorderLayout.CENTER);
      getContentPane().add(writeField, BorderLayout.SOUTH);
      stop.addActionListener(this);
      writeField.addActionListener(this);
      setSize(400,250);
      setVisible(true);
      setDefaultCloseOperation(EXIT_ON_CLOSE);
   }

   private void sendMessage(String s) {
      // convert the message to an array of bytes
      byte[] data = (name + ": " + s).getBytes();
      // create and send a datagram packet
      DatagramPacket packet =
            new DatagramPacket(data,  data.length, iadr, port);
      try {so.send(packet);} catch (IOException ie) {}
   }

   public void actionPerformed(ActionEvent e) {
      if (e.getSource() == writeField) {
        // the user has written his/her own message
        sendMessage(writeField.getText());
        writeField.setText("");
      }
      else if (e.getSource() == stop) {
        // the user has pressed the "Disconnect" button
        sendMessage("DISCONNECTED");
        try {so.leaveGroup(iadr);} catch (IOException ie) {}
        so.close();       // close the socket
        dispose();        // remove the window
        System.exit(0); // terminate the program
      }
   }

   public static void main(String[] arg) throws IOException {
      String name = "Anonymous";
```

590

```
    if (arg.length > 0)
      name = arg[0];
    new Chat(name, "234.235.236.237", 9876);
  }
}
```

All our own messages are sent in the method `sendMessage`, which gets the message as parameter. Note that the method `sendMessage` will put the user's name first in the datagram sent.

17.5 Establishing client–server connections

Communicating by means of datagrams has the advantage of being quite simple. The disadvantage is the lack of security. As we pointed out earlier, we cannot be certain that when we send a datagram, it will really reach the receiver; neither can we be certain that the datagrams we send will arrive in the same order as they were sent. In many applications, this is not terribly important. In our example concerning temperature readings, it would not have been a catastrophe if one reading was lost. In the chat program, too, one message missing would not have meant a great deal. In certain applications, however, it is important to know that we can count on the means of communication. If this is the case, we cannot make use of datagrams. Instead, we have to establish a virtual connection between the two parties that are to communicate. This works much as when we use an ordinary telephone. First the connection is made and then, when contact has been established, communication takes place on the line. The information sent on an established line does not, like a datagram, need to be divided into packets containing sender and receiver addresses. Instead, information is transferred as a continual flow of data. This idea is illustrated in Figure 17.5. What we do is to extend the "virtual line", that is, the socket, of the calling party so that it goes through the port of the receiving computer straight to the program the caller is to communicate with.

In this section we shall demonstrate the establishment of connections in relation to the client–server technique. When this technique is used, there is a computer, or *server*, which provides a service. Other computers, or *clients*, can be associated with the server to gain access to this service. A server can often handle several clients at the same time. An example of an ordinary client–server system is that of databases, where current information is available at a centrally situated computer. An example is a database that contains information concerning the booking of seats on an aeroplane. Clients can be connected to the database to find out about available seats and to make bookings. In this kind of system, it is very important for the server to deal with several different clients so that a seat is not booked more than once. It is also important for communication between a server and its clients to be reliable.

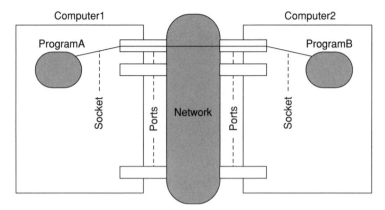

Figure 17.5 Established connections

A client that wants to connect to a server will create a new socket, where the server's address and port number are indicated. We can write:

```
Socket  s = new Socket("www.xyz.serv.se", 13781);
```

Note that we use the class `Socket` (not `DatagramSocket`). The constructor generates an exception of class `IOException` or `UnknownHostException` (a subclass of `IOException`) if a connection is unsuccessful.

When the connection is ready, we call the methods `getInputStream` and `getOutput-Stream` in class `Socket` to get access to two streams in the connection, one for each direction of communication. These streams are of the fundamental classes `InputStream` and `OutputStream`. We can, of course, connect other streams to them, in the way discussed in Chapter 16. If we want to be able to read and write simple data in binary form, we can connect, for example, streams of the classes `DataInputStream` and `DataOutputStream`, respectively.

```
DataInputStream   in =new DataInputStream(s.getInputStream());
DataOutputStream out=new DataOutputStream(s.getOutputStream());
```

java.net.Socket
Created by a client.

new `Socket(addr, port)`	connects to the port `port` in the server `addr` (a `String`)
`getInputStream()`	gives a stream to read data from the other computer
`getOutputStream()`	gives a stream to send data to the other computer
`getInetAddress()`	gives the other computer's `InetAddress`
`close()`	breaks the connection

This is all that needs to be done in the client to establish the connection. Let us now turn to the server. The server must be listening to discover whether there is a client wanting to make a connection. This is done by means of a special `ServerSocket` that can be created in the following way:

```
ServerSocket listenerSock = new ServerSocket(13781);
```

As parameter for the constructor we give the number of the port we will be listening to. The method `accept` is then called in order to wait for a client, and we do not return from this method until a client has been connected. The method `accept` will then give as return value the socket the client uses to communicate in. This can have the following appearance:

```
Socket clientSock = listenerSock.accept();
```

The server, just like the client, can now use the methods `getInputStream` and `getOutput-Stream` to create two streams of the classes `DataInputStream` and `DataOutputStream` if simple data in binary form has to be read and written.

```
DataInputStream  in = new DataInputStream
                              (clientSock.getInputStream());
DataOutputStream out = new DataOutputStream
                              (clientSock.getOutputStream());
```

java.net.ServerSocket	
Created by a server.	
`new ServerSocket(port)`	gives a socket that will listen in the port `port`
`accept()`	waits until a client has been connected; returns the `Socket` created by the client
`close()`	breaks the connection

There is a small difficulty here, however. Because several clients will normally join the connection to a server, it is not a good idea to let the server get stuck with one client. We shall therefore create a new active object (with its own parallel thread) for each client connected. Meanwhile, the original thread can continue to listen at the port to see whether there is another client wanting to be connected. The server will then have the structure:

```
while (true) {
   // wait until the next client gets connected
   Socket clientSock = listenerSock.accept();
   // create a new active object,
   // give the client's socket as parameter
   new ActiveObject(clientSock);
}
```

The class `ActiveObject` is a class we define ourselves. We can establish the two communication streams in class `ActiveObject` by means of the client's socket, which is given as parameter for the constructor.

We shall now study the client–server technique in a rather simplified, yet complete, example. We shall set up a system for deposits and withdrawals on a bank account. Clients of the bank will be able to make deposits and withdrawals at different branches far apart from each other by communicating with a central computer through a network. The local computer at each branch is tended by a clerk, who uses a program to book the deposits and withdrawals that clients wish to make. Naturally, the clerk will also be able to check that there is enough money in an account to enable a withdrawal to be made. In the central computer, which represents the server in our example, there is a database that keeps track of clients' accounts. When the distant computers connect to the system and want to carry out various transactions, the server will use its database to enter the transactions. It will then send the result back to the distant computers.

Our example will be a little simpler than one that would be required of a real system. For example, we do not require the bank clerk to communicate with the central computer by means of a special password. We also let the program executed by the branches use a simple text window to communicate with the bank clerk. (Although it would not be difficult to put on a GUI, we do not do so in this example, because the principles of communication are clearer in a program that uses a simple text window.)

We shall deal with the server first. In Section 16.5, which dealt with direct-access files, we constructed a class `AccountDatabase`, which described a simple database that kept track of bank accounts. In this example, we will use class `AccountDatabase` in the server, and nothing needs to be changed. This class will function exactly as before. We remember from Section 16.5 that we made use of a direct-access file in which information about the accounts was stored. When we created an object of class `AccountDatabase`, we were asked to give the name of the file as parameter for the constructor. Then, to perform transactions in the database, we were asked to use the method `transaction`. This method was to have three parameters: an account number, an amount and an object of class `Account`. The first two were input parameters, and the third was an output parameter that was a reference to an object of class `Account` (defined on page 559). When the transaction had been carried out, the method `transaction` filled in the result in the `Account` object. The method `transaction` also returned a value of type **boolean**, which indicated whether the transaction was successful or not.

The server in our example is made up of two classes. The first is the class `BankServer`, which listens for new clients. It is constructed according to the model that we sketched above. The only method in class `BankServer` is `main`. When we start the server, we give as parameter for `main` the number of the port the server will listen to. The class `BankServer` is as follows:

```
import java.io.*;
import java.net.*;

public class BankServer {
  public static AccountDatabase dbase;

  public static void main(String[] arg) throws IOException {
    int listenerPort = Integer.parseInt(arg[0]);
    // create a socket to listen for new clients
    ServerSocket listenerSock = new ServerSocket(listenerPort);
    System.out.println("Server running. Port no "+listenerPort);

    // open the database for the account
    dbase = new AccountDatabase("accounts");

    while (true) {
      // wait until the next client gets connected
      Socket clientSock = listenerSock.accept();
      System.out.println(clientSock.getInetAddress().
                      getHostName() + " connected");
      // create a new active object
      new ClientHandler(clientSock);
    }
  }
}
```

The class `BankServer` creates the `AccountDatabase` object that handles the file with the accounts. To ensure that all the `ClientHandler`s can gain access to this `Account-Database` object, a reference to it is put as a class variable (static variable) in class `BankServer`. A new active object of class `ClientHandler` is created every time a new client gets connected to the server. This object will then take care of the new client.

The class `ClientHandler` is relatively simple. The constructor will get as parameter a reference to the client's socket, and it will use this socket to create the two streams required to communicate with the client.

```
class ClientHandler implements Runnable {
  public Thread activity = new Thread(this);
  Socket so;
  DataInputStream  streamIn;
  DataOutputStream streamOut;

  // constructor
  public ClientHandler(Socket s) throws IOException {
    so = s;
    // open streams to the client
    streamIn  = new DataInputStream (so.getInputStream());
    streamOut = new DataOutputStream(so.getOutputStream());
    activity.start();
  }
```

```
public void run() {
   Account acc = new Account();
   while (true)
     // new transaction
     try {
       // retrieve account number and amount from the client
       long no       = streamIn.readLong();
       double amount = streamIn.readDouble();
       // perform the transaction
       boolean transOK = BankServer.dbase.
                         transaction(no, amount, acc);

       // send the answer to the client
       streamOut.writeBoolean(transOK);   // result value
       acc.write(streamOut);              // output parameter
     }
     catch(IOException e) {break;} //when the client disconnects
   System.out.println(so.getInetAddress().getHostName() +
                 "disconnected");
   try {so.close();}
   catch (IOException e) {}
 }
}
```

The transactions are performed in the method run. In this, there is a repetition statement that executes one loop per transaction. The repetition is interrupted if we get an IOException. This will happen if, for instance, the client breaks the connection. Input data sent by the client is retrieved first in every transaction. This will apply to the account number and the amount of the transaction. Note that we use streams of the classes DataInputStream and DataOutputStream, so data will be transferred in binary form. The methods readLong and readDouble are called to read the input data the client has sent. When the transaction has been carried out in the database, the result is sent back to the client. The result value, of type **boolean**, is sent first, followed by the Account object that contains the output data. The method write, which is defined in class Account, is used to output the contents of the Account object to the stream.

This is all we need to have in the server. Let us now look at the client programs executing at the various bank branches. We define a class BankClient. This looks almost exactly like the class BankDemo on page 563. The class BankDemo called the account database directly to perform the different transactions but in class BankClient, these calls will take place through the server. The server's address and port number are given as parameter for main when we start the program. For example, we write:

```
java BankClient www.bank.serv.se 17916
```

When the program BankClient is run, it will look exactly the same as when we run the BankDemo program. The class BankClient will look like this:

```
import java.io.*;
import java.net.*;
import extra.*;
public class BankClient {

  public static void main(String[] arg) throws IOException{
    String toComputer = arg[0];
    int toPort = Integer.parseInt(arg[1]);

    // try to connect to the server
    Socket so = new Socket(toComputer, toPort);
    Std.out.println("Connecting to " + toComputer +
                    " port no " + toPort);
    // create streams to the server
    DataInputStream  streamIn = new DataInputStream
                                   (so.getInputStream());

    DataOutputStream streamOut = new DataOutputStream
                                   (so.getOutputStream());

    while(true) {
      // read input data for transaction
      Std.out.print("Account no? ");
      if (!Std.in.more())
        break;
      long accountNo = Std.in.readLong();
      Std.out.print("Amount? ");
      if (!Std.in.more())
        break;
      double amount = Std.in.readDouble();

      // ask the server to perform the transaction
      streamOut.writeLong(accountNo);
      streamOut.writeDouble(amount);

      // read answer from the server
      boolean transOK = streamIn.readBoolean();
      Account acc = new Account();
      acc.read(streamIn);

      // analyse the result
      if (acc.number > 0) {  // account number OK
        Std.out.println(acc.name);
        Std.out.println(acc.addr);
        if (transOK) {
          Std.out.print("New balance: ");
          Std.out.println(acc.balance, 1, 2);
        }
        else {
          Std.out.print("Balance: ");
          Std.out.println(acc.balance, 1, 2);
```

```
            Std.out.println("Withdrawal cannot be done!");
        }
    }
    else
        Std.out.println("Incorrect account no");
    Std.out.println();
    }

    so.close();
    }
}
```

Input data for the transaction is sent in binary form in the output stream to the server. The answer will then return in the input stream. The result value from the method transaction (a value of type **boolean**) will come first, followed by the Account object that has been filled up. The method read in class Account is used to read the account number in binary form from the stream.

17.6 E-mail

You can send and receive e-mails in a Java program. The classes required for this go under the collective name of JavaMail API. These classes are not included in J2SDK, however – they have to be downloaded separately. You can download them from the web address java.sun.com/products/javamail/. There, you will also find instructions on how to install the classes on your computer.

We will content ourselves here with describing how to send e-mail, which is the most useful function. To do this, you must carry out a number of steps and use several of the extension classes. This a bit complicated. To make it as simple as possible, in our package extra, which is found on the book's website, we have added a class Mail that contains a couple of easy-to-use methods. We will use them here.

The first thing you need to do in a program before you can send any e-mails is to state which mail server is to be used. You get this piece of information from your Internet Service Provider. For example, let's assume that you have found out that you should use a server with the name mail.theServer.com. So you add the following call first in your program:

```
 Mail.setServer("mail.theServer.com");
```

This only needs to be done once. For this to work, of course, you need to have imported the package extra into the program. Thereafter, you can call the method send in the package Mail to send an e-mail. This method is available in three variants. In the simplest variant, you state the sender's and receiver's e-mail addresses, the subject of the e-mail and the message text. All parameters are of the type String. There is also a variant that allows you to attach a file. You enter the file name as a parameter.

```
try {
  Mail.send("David_Swing@anisp.se","MJava@servY.com",
          "Reminder", "Don't forget the meeting\nBye\nDavid",
          "agenda.doc");
}
catch (Exception ex) {
// transmission failed
}
```

The method send generates an exception (of the type MessagingException) if something doesn't work. For this reason, you need to encapsulate the call in a try statement.

The method send is also found in a more complete version in which you can state several receivers, several receivers of copies of the message and where you can send an arbitrary number of files as attachments. (See fact box.)

extra.Mail

Mail.setServer(s)   s is the name (a String) of the mail server to be used.

The following methods can be used to send an e-mail.

```
Mail.send(from, to, subject, text)
Mail.send(from, to, subject, text, filename)
Mail.send(from, toArr, copyArr, subject, text, filenameArr)
```

The parameters from, to, subject, text and filename are of the type String.
The parameters toArr, copyArr and filenameArr are of the type String[].

On page 319 we wrote a program called Order. This was used to order Christmas magazines, etc. When you run the program, you get a printout of all the orders placed in the command window. We will now adapt this program so that instead it sends an e-mail for each order placed. For the order shown in Figure 9.10 the program will send a message, for example:

```
From: agentX@aServer.com
To: bookstore@servY.se
Subject: Order number 1

Susan Wilson, 22 First Lane, Rumford
   The Nutcracker $11
   Santa's Sled Race $7
   The Christmas Coloring Book $8
Total cost: $26
```

The following changes are needed in the program Order: In the method main we add the following line right at the beginning:

```
Mail.setServer("mail.theServer.com");
```

Then we change the part of the listener where you end up when the user has clicked on the button `"Order"`:

```
else if (e.getSource() == best) {    // button Order
   String name = JOptionPane.showInputDialog
                                  ("Name and address?");
   if (name != null) {
     // send order by e-mail
     String text = name + "\n"; // text will contain the message
     for (int i=0; i < mod2.size(); i++)
       text += "     " + mod2.get(i) + "\n";
     text += costLabel.getText();
     try {
       Mail.send("agentX@aServer.com",
                 "bookstore@servY.se",
                 "Order number " + ++no, text);
     }
     catch (Exception ex) {
       JOptionPane.showMessageDialog(null,
                                     "Transmission failed");
     }
     // prepare for next customer
     l1.clearSelection();    // no selections in list 1
     mod2.clear();           // clear list 2
   }
}
```

17.7 Applets and communication

We will remember that an applet is not allowed, for security reasons, to use a local file system. There are also a number of restrictions that apply to communication through applets. Briefly, we can say that an applet may only establish a connection to the computer from which it has been downloaded. The client–server relationship may be used in an applet if the applet is the client and the server is in the computer from which the applet has been downloaded. When we want to create a connection in an applet to a server, we can write, for instance:

```
Socket so = new Socket(getCodeBase().getHost(), 9876);
```

This enables us to construct web pages with applets which, when they are downloaded to another computer, can be connected back to the host to get different kinds of services. (See Exercises 3 and 4 on page 604.)

We will now show another form of communication that can be used in applets. For every applet, there is an environment provided by the web browser or `appletviewer` the applet started from. This environment is described by the class `AppletContext`, in the packet `java.applet`. If in an applet we want to access the `AppletContext` object that describes the actual environment, we can call the method `getAppletContext`.

The class `AppletContext` contains several interesting methods. We have already discussed some of them, for example `showStatus`, as they are also available to the class `Applet`. An interesting method in the class `AppletContext` is `showDocument`, used to request the web browser to download and display a particular web page. This method exists in two variants. The first has one parameter, a `URL` object that describes the web address for the web page we wish to display. For example, we can write:

```
URL webURL = new URL("http://www.awl-he.com");
getAppletContext().showDocument(webURL);
```

Then the page displayed in the web browser will be replaced by the page indicated by the `URL` address. The second variant of `showDocument` has two parameters: the first parameter is, as before, a `URL` object; the second is a text that indicates how the page chosen is to be displayed. This text can be one of the following: `"_self"`, which indicates that the page containing the applet will be replaced, `"_top"`, which indicates that the web browser's top window will be replaced, `"_blank"`, which indicates that the given page will be displayed in a new top window (without a name) and `"_parent"`, which indicates that the window that is parent to the applet's window will be replaced. We can also give a text with a name as second parameter. The page will then be displayed in a window of this name. If there is no window with the given name, a new window will be created at the top. For instance, we can write:

```
getAppletContext().showDocument(webURL, "_blank");
```

We will now make use of this to construct an applet that displays an arbitrary picture. When the user clicks on the picture, a certain given web page will be displayed in a new window. The picture and the web page to be displayed will be indicated as parameters of the applet in the HTML file the applet started from. This file might look like this:

```
<html>
  <head> <title>PictureDemo</title> </head>
  <body>
    <applet code=PictureDemo.class width=400 height=150>
      <param name=pictureName value=image1.gif>
      <param name=wwwPage value=http://www.studentlitteratur.se>
    </applet>
  </body>
</html>
```

This applet will be an extended version of the one that was discussed in Section 15.1 We must add a listener that listens for mouse clicks. When a mouse click occurs, we will check to see whether the mouse is inside the picture. If it is, the method showDocument is called to display the web page indicated.

We use the standard class Rectangle (in the packet java.awt) to simplify the task of finding out whether the mouse is in the picture. We construct a rectangle that is exactly as big as the picture and placed in the same position. It is easy to create a rectangle. We indicate only the coordinates of the rectangle's upper left-hand corner and the rectangle's length and width. We use the class Rectangle because this class has a method with the name contains that checks to see whether a certain point, of the standard class Point, lies in the rectangle or not.

We also take this opportunity to reveal a little trick that we have only touched on in an exercise. When the user moves the mouse so that the mouse's cursor lands inside the picture, we will let the cursor change its appearance so that it looks like a pointing hand. If the cursor is moved outside the picture, it will resume its standard appearance. To produce this effect, we use the method setCursor, defined in the class Component and thus accessible in all GUI components. As argument, setCursor will have an object of class Cursor, which is also defined in the packet java.awt. There is a class method getPredefinedCursor in class Cursor that returns a Cursor object. As argument, getPredefinedCursor will have a whole number that indicates the appearance we want for the mouse cursor. In class Cursor there are a number of pre-defined whole number constants that can be used. Some examples are TEXT_CURSOR, HAND_CURSOR, WAIT_CURSOR and DEFAULT_CURSOR.

With these additions, the applet will have the following appearance:

```java
import java.applet.*;
import java.awt.*;
import java.awt.event.*;
import java.net.*;

public class PictureDemo extends Applet {
    Image im;
    int x0 = 10, y0 = 50;
    Rectangle r;
    URL webURL;

    public void init() {
        // retrieve the name of the file with the picture
        String name  = getParameter("pictureName");
        // begin to load the picture
        im = getImage(getCodeBase(), name);
        showStatus("Loading " + name);

        // wait until the picture has been loaded
        MediaTracker mt = new MediaTracker(this);
        mt.addImage(im, 0);
        try {mt.waitForID(0);}
```

```
    catch(InterruptedException e){}
    showStatus("Loading finished");

    // create a rectangle that describes the picture's surface
    r = new Rectangle(x0, y0, im.getWidth(this),
                              im.getHeight(this));

    // retrieve the address of the desired web page
    String wwwPage = getParameter("wwwPage");
    try {
      webURL = new URL(wwwPage);
    }
    catch(MalformedURLException e) {
      showStatus("Illegal parameter: " + wwwPage);
    }
    // listen to mouse clicks and movements
    addMouseListener(l1);
    addMouseMotionListener(l2);
  }
  // listeners called when the mouse is clicked
  MouseListener l1 = new MouseAdapter() {
    public void mouseClicked(MouseEvent e) {
      if (!e.isControlDown() && !e.isMetaDown())
        // the left-hand button
        if (r.contains(e.getPoint()))
          // the user has clicked on the picture
          // request the web browser to display a new window
          // with the indicated page
          getAppletContext().showDocument(webURL, "New page");
    }
  };

  // listeners called when mouse is moved
  MouseMotionListener l2 = new MouseMotionAdapter() {
    public void mouseMoved(MouseEvent e) {
      // check whether mouse is in the picture or not
      // and choose appropriate cursor
      if (r.contains(e.getPoint()))
        setCursor(Cursor.getPredefinedCursor
                  (Cursor.HAND_CURSOR));
      else
        setCursor(Cursor.getPredefinedCursor
                  (Cursor.DEFAULT_CURSOR));
    }
  };

  public void paint(Graphics g) {
    g.drawImage(im, x0, y0, this);
  }
}
```

17.8 Exercises

1. Reconstruct our system involving temperature readings in Sections 17.1 and 17.3 to exclude the idea of a central computer that keeps track of all the temperatures. The stations should instead send out multicast messages containing the current temperatures to all interested parties. Every computer that is interested will then keep track of all the temperatures itself.

2. Construct a client–server system for customer support. Customers will be able to run a program that connects them to a server and will be able to put questions to and receive answers from someone at customer service running the server program. Both the customer program and the server will use a GUI where we can enter our own text and see what our correspondent writes to us. The server program should open a new window for every new customer joining the connection. The window should close when a customer breaks the connection.

3. On a certain web page, we want to give the user the possibility of leaving a message for the web page's owner. To this end, we put an applet on the page that can send a message back to the computer from which the web page was downloaded. The applet should contain a button with the text "Leave message". If we click on this button, a new window should pop up with a text area in which we can write a message. The message should be sent automatically when we have finished writing it. Now construct the applet!

4. Construct the server program required to receive such messages as are generated by the applet in Exercise 3. Messages received should be written out.

A bit of everything

18

In this penultimate chapter we shall deal with some language constructs that we did not need in the earlier chapters of the book but which we should know to get a more complete picture of Java.

18.1 Comments and documentation

All our programs call for some kind of comment. Comments fall into two categories. The first is for those who will be reading the program code itself and possibly making changes to it. These comments are intended to make the program easier to read and understand. They can also be of a technical nature, their aim being to clarify complex constructions in the code. The other category is for those who will want to use ready-made classes or methods but are not interested in knowing what the code looks like inside these classes or methods. This type of comment might describe the parameters a method has.

In Java, there are three types of comment. We have constantly used one type, the kind that is introduced by the pair of parallel lines, //. Everything on the *same* line after this can be understood to be a comment:

```
...  // This is a comment
```

Another kind of comment is introduced by the characters /* and is terminated by the characters */. A comment of this kind can extend to several lines:

```
/* This is a comment
   that continues for several lines */
```

The final pair of characters should not be forgotten. If they are, the rest of the program will be understood to be a comment. This kind of comment is useful for long explanations. We can also use them when we are testing a program and want to exclude part of the program temporarily. We can then make this part a comment.

We provide the first two types of comment for whoever would like to study the program code itself. The third type is provided as an aid for the use of ready-made classes and is therefore called a *documentation comment*. This is introduced by the character combination /** and is terminated by the combination */. Like the second type of comment, a documentation comment can comprise several lines:

```
/** This is a documentation comment.
  * We often begin each line with the character *
  * so that the comment will be clear
  * but this is not necessary.
  */
```

Comments of the form /*...*/ and documentation comments appear exactly the same to the Java compiler. They contain only text, and the compiler will skip this. The interesting thing about documentation comments is that they can be used with the program javadoc, included in J2SDK. The javadoc program can be started by the command

```
javadoc parameter1 parameter2 parameter3 ...
```

In this way we can indicate an arbitrary number of parameters. Each parameter can be either the name of a Java package or the name of a file that contains a Java program. If it is a file, the file name must end with .java. (We can also indicate different options in front of the parameters; see the J2SDK documentation for details.) The javadoc program reads the program code for the packages or files given as parameters and produces a set of HTML files containing documentation on all the classes, interfaces, methods, constructors and variables that are marked as public or protected. An HTML file is produced for every file with program code. javadoc also produces an HTML file that displays inheritance structure and one that contains an index with all the methods and variables. The files that are generated will land in the same directory we are in when we give the command. (However, this can be changed if we use the options.) We can read the generated HTML files with a web browser, Internet Explorer, for instance. The javadoc program is extremely useful. For instance, the HTML files in J2SDK that contain documentation on all the standard classes were produced by javadoc.

What does this have to do with comments? When javadoc produces HTML documentation files, the documentation comments in the program listings are put into the files. The idea is to put a documentation comment in front of every class, interface, constructor, variable or method that is to be documented. These documentation comments can be arbitrarily long but first there should always be a sentence, terminated by a period, describing what is being documented. The first sentence will be included in the general summary of the class in question. The text in a documentation comment can contain simple HTML commands such as <i>, which indicates that the text will be in italics, or <code>, which signals that the font for program listings will be used. HTML commands that affect the structure of the document may not be used, however.

606

Special *tags* can also be inserted in a documentation comment. These tags always begin with the character @ and must be written at the beginning of the line (or directly after an introductory asterisk, *). Some examples of tags are:

```
@author the name of the author
@version text
@see class
@see class# attribute
@param parameter nameparameter description
@return description of return value
@exception class name description
```

When javadoc discovers a tag, it generates documentation in a standardized format. For an exception tag, for example, it will generate a "Throws" section, where the exceptions that can be generated will appear.

To give a more complete example of what this might look like, we show here a new version of our own class Line, from Section 13.5:

```java
package extra;
import java.awt.*;
import java.io.*;
/**
 * The <code>Line</code> class represents a line between two
 * points in a two-dimensional coordinate space.
 * For example:
 * <pre>
 *    Line l = new Line(new Point(1,0), new Point(2,1));
 * </pre>
 * @version 1.0
 * @author  Jan Skansholm
 * @see     java.awt.Point
 */
public class Line implements Serializable {
  /**
   * The first end point.
   */
  public Point p1;
  /**
   * The second end point.
   */
  public Point p2;
  /**
   * Constructs a line with start and end points at (0,0).
   */
  public Line() {
    p1 = new Point();
```

```
    p2 = new Point();
  }

  /**
   * Constructs a line with the specified start and end points.
   * @param a the first end point.
   * @param b the second end point.
   */
  public Line(Point a, Point b) {
    p1 = new Point(a);
    p2 = new Point(b);
  }

  /**
   * Draws a line between the end points.
   * @param g The graphics context to use for painting.
   */
  public void draw(Graphics g) {
    g.drawLine(p1.x, p1.y, p2.x, p2.y);
  }
}
```

18.2 More operators

We have already discussed most of the operators in Java earlier in the book. In this section, we shall examine the operators we have not met so far.

18.2.1 Bit operators and the binary storing of whole numbers

Most of the language constructs in Java have been inherited from the programming language C++, which in turn is a development of C. From the beginning, C was constructed to be used for writing programs that worked closely with a computer's operating system and hardware. In this context, we often need to be able to handle individual bits in a memory cell. In C, C++ and Java, there are a number of operators with which we can handle whole number variables as though they contained groups of bits rather than whole numbers. In this section, we shall give a brief account of these operators. The reader will need to know more about how whole numbers are stored in binary form to understand everything in this section. So we shall begin with a short review.

A computer's memory consists of a number of memory cells. Each of these consists of a certain number of bits, and each bit can contain a binary digit (a zero or a one). It is therefore natural for numbers to be stored in binary form in the memory. Let us look then at the *binary number system*. The decimal number system is the dominating system in our culture (probably because we have 10 fingers). If, for example, we write the number 158.32, we automatically assume that it is expressed in the decimal number system, with a base of 10. This means that we interpret the number 158.32 as

$$1 \times 10^2 + 5 \times 10^1 + 8 \times 10^0 + 3 \times 10^{-1} + 2 \times 10^{-2}$$

More generally, we can say that a decimal number

$$a_n a_{n-1} \ldots a_1 a_0 . d_1 d_2 \ldots d_m$$

(where the as indicate whole number figures and the ds, decimals) really means

$$a_n \times 10^n + a_{n-1} \times 10^{n-1} + \ldots + a_1 \times 10^1 + a_0 \times 10^0 + d_1 \times 10^{-1} + d_2 \times 10^{-2} + \ldots + d_m \times 10^{-m}$$

If we now use the base 2 instead of 10, we can similarly interpret the binary number

$$b_n b_{n-1} \ldots b_1 b_0 . c_1 c_2 \ldots c_m$$

as

$$b_n \times 2^n + b_{n-1} \times 2^{n-1} + \ldots + b_1 \times 2^1 + b_0 \times 2^0 + c_1 \times 2^{-1} + c_2 \times 2^{-2} + \ldots + c_m \times 2^{-m}$$

The bs here indicate binary whole number digits and the cs give the fraction. The binary number 10111.101, for example, can be interpreted as

$$1 \times 2^4 + 0 \times 2^3 + 1 \times 2^2 + 1 \times 2^1 + 1 \times 2^0 + 1 \times 2^{-1} + 0 \times 2^{-2} + 1 \times 2^{-3}$$

or, if we wish

$$16 + 0 + 4 + 2 + 1 + 0.5 + 0 + 0.125 = 23.625$$

A certain number of bits are used when a whole number is stored in a computer. The number of bits used will depend on the type. In Java, for example, 32 bits are used for type `int` and 16 bits for type `short`. If we want to store the number 23 with 16 bits, we will get the binary configuration:

```
0000000000010111
```

If we let each bit represent a binary digit, we will get an *unsigned* form. The largest number that can be stored in an unsigned form with N bits will then be $2^N - 1$. If we have 16 bits, the largest number we can store will then be $2^{16} - 1 = 65\,535$. The unsigned form cannot be used to store negative numbers.

Unsigned forms are not used in Java. Instead, we use another form called *two's complement*. With this form, we can store both positive and negative whole numbers.

In the two's complement form, the bit furthest to the left will give the number's sign. A zero indicates that it is a positive number and a one that it is negative. The largest positive number that can be stored in the two's complement form with 16 bits will then be

```
0111111111111111
```

This turns out to be $2^{15} - 1 = 32\,767$. In the two's complement form, the number -1 is stored with 16 bits as

```
1111111111111111
```

We get the number -2 by subtracting a binary 1 from this to give

```
1111111111111110
```

The number -3 will then be

```
1111111111111101
```

By continuing to subtract, we find that the smallest whole number (that is, the largest negative number) that can be stored in the two's complement form with 16 bits will be

```
1000000000000000
```

This turns out to be the number $-2^{15} = -32\,768$. We can generally say that if a whole number is stored in the two's complement form with N bits, the smallest number that can be stored will be -2^{N-1} and the largest will be $2^{N-1} - 1$.

The values of the standard types `byte`, `short`, `int` and `long` are represented in the two's complement form but programmers do not normally have to know anything about the storing process. The compiler takes care of that.

Let us now turn to the operations of bit operators. Note that these are defined only for whole number types. The ~ operator is the simplest. It has only one operand. As result it gives a bit configuration where all the zeros in the operand have been exchanged for ones, and vice versa. Let us look at an example. (In the following statements we will suppose that all the variables have type `int`.)

```
a = 7;     // a = 0000 0000 0000 0000 0000 0000 0000 0111
b = 20;    // b = 0000 0000 0000 0000 0000 0000 0001 0100
c = ~a;    // c = 1111 1111 1111 1111 1111 1111 1111 1000
```

The operators &, | and ^ carry out the operations *and*, *or* and *exclusive or*, bit by bit. 'Exclusive or' means that a particular bit in the result will be a one if exactly one of the operands contains a one in the corresponding position. If none or both of the operands contain a one, the result bit will be equal to 0.

```
d = a & b;   // d = 0000 0000 0000 0000 0000 0000 0000 0100
e = a | b;   // e = 0000 0000 0000 0000 0000 0000 0001 0111
f = a ^ b;   // f = 0000 0000 0000 0000 0000 0000 0001 0011
```

Bit operators
Are defined only for whole number types. Carry out the operations bit by bit.

~	changes 0 <-> 1	<<	shift left
&	*and*, bit by bit	>>	arithmetic shift right
|	*or*, bit by bit	>>>	logical shift right
^	*exclusive or*		

The operators << and >> carry out *shift left* and *shift right*, respectively, that is, they move the bits to the right or the left. The left-hand operand contains the bit configuration to be moved, and the right-hand operand will indicate the number of places the bits are to be moved. Zeros are always moved in from the right when a left shift is carried out. If a number is shifted one place to the left, this means the number will be multiplied by 2. Similarly, a shift to the right will mean that the number is divided by 2. If we use the operator >> to perform a shift right and the value to be moved is positive, zeros are shifted in from the left. If, on the other hand, the value is negative, ones will be moved in from the left. So when we use the operator >>, the number shifted will keep its sign. We say, therefore, that the >> operator performs an *arithmetic shift*. There is another operator, >>>, which performs a *logical shift*. It will always move zeros in from the left, regardless of whether the number to be shifted is positive or negative. Here are some examples:

```
g = b << 5;    // g = 0000 0000 0000 0000 0000 0010 1000 0000
h = c >> 2;    // h = 1111 1111 1111 1111 1111 1111 1111 1110
i = c >>> 2;   // i = 0011 1111 1111 1111 1111 1111 1111 1110
```

We often use the & operator to perform *masking*, that is, selecting certain bits. For example, the following statement will select eight bits in the bit configuration contained by the variable i:

```
j = i & 0xf00f; // j = 0000 0000 0000 0000 1111 0000 0000 1110
```

The | operator can be used to insert ones into certain bits. The following statement will ensure that there are ones in the eight bits furthest to the right:

```
k = j | 0x00ff; // k = 0000 0000 0000 0000 1111 0000 1111 1111
```

Note that none of the operators we have shown here will affect their operands. If we want operators that can do this, we can use the corresponding assignment operators, which also exist. We can write, for example:

```
a &= 0x000f;
```

which is the same thing as writing

```
a = a & 0x000f;
```

In fact, the & and | operators can also be used with operands of type `boolean`, in which case they will not perform operations bit by bit. They are logical operators, exactly like && and ||. On page 53, we stated that the && and || operators were always computed from left to right and that the right-hand operand was not always computed. The & and | operators do not necessarily work in this way. They *always* compute both operands. This can be useful when the right-hand operand has a side-effect of some kind.

18.2.2 The conditional operator

There is an operator which we can do without but which we should recognize and understand. This is the *conditional operator*. We use it to form *conditional expressions*. Let us suppose that we want to know which of the variables x and y is the larger, then to assign the larger value to the variable z. This is easily done with an `if` statement:

```
if (x>y)
    z = x;
else
    z = y;
```

but we can also use a conditional expression:

```
z = (x>y) ? x : y;
```

The conditional operator has three operands. The first is a test expression. If the test expression is true, the second operand, the one after the question mark ?, is computed, and the result of the whole conditional expression will be equal to this operand. However, if the test expression is false, the third operand is computed, the one after the colon :, and the result of the conditional expression will be equal to this operand. A conditional expression will therefore leave a value as result. The type the result has will be determined by the last two operands. These should have the same type.

The conditional operator

expression1 ? expression2 : expression3

If *expression1* is `true`, the result will be equal to *expression2*, otherwise the result will be equal to *expression3*.
expression2 and *expression3* should have the same type.

As an example, we shall show some program lines that write out a text string s, with the aim that all the tab characters are translated into three blank characters. Other characters will be written out unchanged. (We suppose that the variable c has type `char`.)

```
for (int i=0; i<s.length(); i++)
   System.out.print(s.charAt(i) == '\t'
                    ? "    " : s.substring(i,i+1));
```

The result of the conditional expression is of class `String`. Note that we could not have written `s.charAt(i)` as the final operand, since the last two operands would have got different types, and a `String` cannot be assigned to a `char`.

18.3 More statements

There are a number of statements in Java that we have not used. We shall describe them in this section.

18.3.1 The `switch` statement

A `switch` statement can be used instead of an `if` statement when we are offered several options. As an example, we shall show part of a program that simulates a simple calculator. The program reads in expressions of the form *x op y*. Let us suppose that we have read in *x* and *y* and that the values are in two variables *x* and *y* of type `double`. Let us further suppose that the operator *op* has been read in to a variable of type `char`. The expression's value can then be computed with the following `switch` statement.

```
switch(op) {
  case '+':
    System.out.println(x+y);
    break;
  case '-':
    System.out.println(x-y);
    break;
  case '*':
    System.out.println(x*y);
    break;
  case '/':
    if (y != 0)
      System.out.println(x/y);
    else
      System.out.println("Division by zero");
    break;
  default:
    System.out.println("Incorrect operator");
}
```

A `switch` statement is introduced by the word `switch`. A *test expression* in brackets, which must be of an integer type, or of the type `char`, then follows this word. Every alternative statement is introduced by the word `case`. The expressions that come after case, the case expressions, must be constants, and two or more case expressions cannot have the same value. There may also be a default alternative. The test expression is computed first when a switch statement is executed. The value of the test expression is compared with the values of the different case expressions. If the test expression has the same value as a case expression, there will be a jump to the statement after this case expression. If none of the case expressions has the same value as the test expression, there is a jump to the statement after the word default. If the default alternative is missing and none of the case expressions is appropriate, nothing will be done in the switch statement. Note that there must be a break statement at the end of every alternative. The break statement will terminate the alternative, and there will be a jump to the end of the switch statement. If there is no break statement in a particular alternative, execution will continue with the statements in the next alternative!

We can make the example more complete by adding the lines that read the values of the variables x, op and y. We read one line at a time and use the method parse in the class NumberFormat to decode the number. It's this method that is used inside the class Parse on page 122. We have not gone through the method parse but briefly, it can be said that it is to have two parameters. The first should be the text to be decoded and the second an object of the class ParsePosition. The second parameter is used to indicate where in the text the decoding is to start. After the call, you can also use it to see where the decoding finished. The class ParsePosition has two methods getIndex and setIndex that are used for this purpose. See the example below:

```
BufferedReader in = new BufferedReader
                        (new InputStreamReader(System.in));
NumberFormat   nf  = NumberFormat.getInstance(Locale.US);
ParsePosition pos = new ParsePosition(0);  // start position 0
String line;
while ((line=in.readLine()) != null) {
  pos.setIndex(0);                      // indicate where x begins
  double x = nf.parse(rad, pos).doubleValue();
  char op  = rad.charAt(pos.getIndex());
  pos.setIndex(pos.getIndex()+1); // indicate where x begins
  double y = nf.parse(rad, pos).doubleValue();;
  switch(op) {
    as previously
  }
}
```

We are allowed to have several case expressions for a particular alternative in a switch statement. Let us suppose, for example, that we want to calculate the number of characters of different kinds in a text. Then the following statement can be used.

```
switch(c) {
  case '0': case '1': case '2': case '3': case '4':
  case '5': case '6': case '7': case '8': case '9':
    numberOfFigures++;
    break;
  case ' ': case '\t': case '\n':
    numberOfWhite++;
    break;
  default:
    numberOfOthers++;
}
```

Unfortunately, this is not very elegant, as the word `case` has to be repeated.

---

switch statement

```
switch(test_expression) {
  case constant_value1:
    statements
    break;
  case constant_value2:
    statements
    break;
  ...
  default:
    statements
}
```

The expressions after `case` must have different values. The `default` alternative can be left out. Several `case` expressions can be found in front of a particular alternative. There is a jump to the alternative for which *test_expression* is the same as *constant_value*. If no alternative fits, there is a jump to the `default` alternative.

18.3.2 The `do` statement

In this book, we have used `while` statements and `for` statements to produce repetition but there is a third repetition statement, the `do` statement. It has the form:

```
do
    statement
while (expression);
```

This statement is similar to the `while` statement, the difference being that the test expression is computed and tested *after* instead of before every loop. This means that the statement inside the `do` statement must always be performed at least once. We can use curly brackets if there is more than one statement to be performed at every loop. Then we usually write the `do` statement in the following way:

```
do {
    statements
} while (expression);
```

It is useful to write the right-hand curly bracket first, on the last line. Then we will not be fooled into thinking that the word `while` is the beginning of a statement.

An example now follows of the type of program where it can be useful to use a `do` statement. Repeated computations are made in the program (in the method `res`) for different kinds of input data. The user is asked, after each computation, whether further computations are to be carried out:

```
BufferedReader in = new BufferedReader
                    (new InputStreamReader(System.in));
String answer;
do {
    System.out.print("Give input data: "); System.out.flush();
    double x = Double.parseDouble(in.readLine());
    System.out.println("Result=" + res(x));
    System.out.print("Continue? (y, n) "); System.out.flush();
    answer = in.readLine();
} while (answer.charAt(0) == 'y');
```

18.3.3 Statements with labels

Every statement (or declaration) in Java can be provided with a *label*. A label is a kind of name written in front of the statement. Here is an example:

```
start: int n = in.readInt();
loop1: for (int i=0; i<n; i++)
```

Labels can be useful in connection with `break` and `continue` statements.

18.3.4 The `break` statement

We have made use of `break` statements on several occasions. A break statement can be used to jump out of a repetition statement or a `switch` statement. If we only write `break`, we will jump from the *nearest* surrounding statement. This jump always takes place to the first statement after the statement we jump from. Here is an example:

```
loop1: for (i=0; i<n; i++) {
    statement1
    loop2: for (j=0; j<n; j++) {
        if (a[i][j] == 0)
            break;  // there is a jump to statement3
        statement2
    }
```

```
    statement3
  }
statement4
```

The nearest surrounding statement is the innermost `for` statement.

We can also indicate a label after the word `break`. We then make a jump from the statement that has this label. We will change our example. We now make a jump out of the `for` statement (the one with the label `loop1`).

```
loop1: for (i=0; i<n; i++) {
  statement1
  loop2: for (j=0; j<n; j++) {
    if (a[i][j] == 0)
      break loop1; // there is a jump to statement4
    statement2
  }
  statement3
}
statement4
```

18.3.5 The `continue` statement

This (rather strange) statement is also inherited from the programming language C. We can manage without it but it is important to recognize it and understand what it does if we happen to come across it in some program code. A `continue` statement can be found inside a repetition statement. We can either simply write `continue`, or indicate the label of a surrounding repetition statement:

```
continue;
continue label;
```

If we do not include a label, the `continue` statement will apply to the nearest surrounding repetition statement; otherwise it will apply to the repetition statement that has been indicated. A `continue` statement, like a `break` statement, will interrupt execution at the actual position and make a jump. However, there is no jump out of the repetition statement. Instead, the *actual loop* in the repetition statement is interrupted, whereupon execution continues immediately with the next loop. We shall first show an example where a label has not been indicated, when the actual loop in the inner `for` statement will be interrupted:

```
loop1: for (i=0; i<n; i++) {
  statement1
  loop2: for (j=0; j<n; j++) {
    if (a[i][j] == 0)
      continue; // continue immediately after statement2
```

```
        statement2
    }
    statement3
}
statement4
```

If we indicate the label `loop1` after `continue`, the actual loop in the outer `for` statement will be interrupted instead. This looks as follows:

```
loop1: for (i=0; i<n; i++) {
    statement1
    loop2: for (j=0; j<n; j++) {
        if (a[i][j] == 0)
            continue loop1; // continue immediately after statement3
        statement2
    }
    statement3
}
statement4
```

18.4 Recursion

We have seen how a method can call other methods. A method is even allowed to call itself; when this happens, it is called a *recursive method*. It is convenient to use recursive methods when we have to find solutions to certain kinds of problems. It is most appropriate to use recursion when we are faced with problems that are specified recursively from the very beginning; this is often the case with certain mathematical problems. The most common example of a recursive method (this one is found in most books on programming) is the one that will compute n factorial, *n!*, of a whole number *n*. The factorial of a number *n* can be defined in the following way:

$$n! = \begin{cases} 1 & \text{if } n = 0 \\ 1 \times 2 \times 3 \times \ldots \times n & \text{if } n > 0 \end{cases}$$

Naturally, we can easily calculate this product by means of a repetition statement. The following method will get a number `n` as parameter and will compute the factorial of the number.

```
static int nfac1(int n) {
    int prod = 1;
    for (int i=1; i<=n; i++)
        prod = prod * i;
    return prod;
}
```

Let us now see how we can make use of recursion instead. Another way of defining the factorial of a number is

$$n! = \begin{cases} 1 & \text{if } n = 0 \\ n(n-1)! & \text{if } n > 0 \end{cases}$$

There is an obvious case (*n*=0) and one where we use induction to express the solution by means of values already defined. This way of writing the definition will lead naturally to the following method. Here it is the last but one line that interests us: it calls `nfac` itself.

```
static int nfac(int n) {
   if (n <= 0)
      return 1;
   else
      return n * nfac(n-1);
}
```

Those of us unfamiliar with recursion usually find it a little strange but we should remember a basic rule: recursive method calls work in *exactly the same way* as other method calls. (See the fact box on page 65.) There are no special rules for recursion, so when a method is called (by itself or by another method) the arguments will be computed first. Memory space is then generated for the parameters of the method called, and the arguments are copied into this. New memory space is generated for the parameters and for the *local* variables with *every* new call. If a particular method is called several times, *every* edition of the method will have its *own edition* of parameters and local variables. The statements in the method called are then performed. When these statements have finished, we return to the point from which the method was called. If a method calls itself, we hence return to a point within the method itself. Let us take a concrete example and look at exactly what happens. Let us suppose that the method `nfac` is defined in the class `C` and that we write the statement

```
m = C.nfac(3);
```

The method `nfac` is called. It will generate space for the parameter `n`, and this will have the value 3. Since `n` is greater than 0, the statement after **else** will be performed. There is now a new call of the method `nfac`. The value of the argument `n-1` is 2. A new space is generated for the parameter `n`, and this space will get the value 2. From this moment, there will, therefore, be two different parameters, both with the name `n`. The first one, with the value 3, belongs to the first edition of `nfac`, and the second, with the value 2, belongs to the second edition of `nfac`.

In the second edition, `n` is also greater than zero, and the statement after **else** is performed. `nfac` is called here for a third time, and yet another parameter `n` is generated, this time with the value 1. The statement after `else` will also be performed in the third edition of `nfac`, as 1 is greater than 0. The method `nfac` is called for the fourth time, and a parameter with the name n is created once again. This one will have the value 0. Four parameters with the name n will therefore be in existence at the same time.

The condition after `if` will be true in the fourth edition of `nfac`. So the statement

```
return 1;
```

will be executed. Exactly as we would expect, the method is terminated, the result value is 1, and there is a jump to the point from which the call took place. Since the fourth call of `nfac` took place from the statement

```
return n * nfac(n-1);
```

the jump will be to that statement. As the result value is 1, the expression n*1 will be computed. But what value does n have? In the fourth edition of `nfac`, n had the value 0 but the fourth edition is now finished. We have returned to the third edition and n had the value 1 there, so the expression 1*1 will be computed. Now we can finish executing the `return` statement and this means that the third edition of `nfac` will also be terminated. The result will be 1 and there is another jump to the point where the call took place. We therefore return again to the statement

```
return n * nfac(n-1);
```

As we return to the second edition of `nfac`, n will have the value 2 this time, so the expression 2*1 will be computed. Edition number two is terminated with the return value 2, and once again there is a jump to the point of the call, that is, to the statement

```
return n * nfac(n-1);
```

We have now returned to edition number one of `nfac`. In this edition, n had the value 3. As the result value of the expression `nfac(n-1)` was 2, the expression 3*2 will be computed. So edition number one of `nfac` will give a result value of 6. Edition number one is now terminated and there is another jump back. The first call of `nfac` took place from the statement

```
m = C.nfac(3);
```

so the jump will be to this statement. The variable m will be assigned the value 6.

Recursive solutions always follow the same idea. Faced with a problem, we first identify one (or more) simple, special case where the solution is self-evident ($n=0$, in `nfac`). We now try to formulate the problem so that it becomes simpler in some way (($n-1$)! is simpler than n!). We can then imagine that the method we are writing already exists and that it can solve the simpler problem.

Recursive method
A method that directly or indirectly calls itself. When executed, there are as many editions of the method as the number of calls that have been made but not terminated. Every edition of the method has parameters and local variables with their own unique values.

As an example, we shall construct a recursive method that reads from an input stream and writes it out *backwards* to an output stream. We use the following recursive idea:

1. Try to read the input stream's first byte and save it.
   If it could be read, do the following:

   1.1 Read in the rest of the input stream and write it out backwards.

   1.2 Write out the input stream's first byte.

The obvious, special case is that the input stream is empty. So, we do nothing at all. In step 1.1, we suppose that there is already a method that can read in a stream and write it out backwards. We make use of this method to solve the simpler problem that arises when the input stream is one byte shorter than it was at the beginning. By means of this algorithm, we can construct the following Java program, which reads a file and copies it backwards to another file. The names of the files are given as parameters of `main`. The copying of the files is done by the recursive method `backwards`.

```java
import java.io.*;
class CopyBack {
   static InputStream   in;
   static OutputStream out;

   static void backwards() throws IOException {
      int c;
      if ((c = in.read()) != -1) {
         backwards();
         out.write(c);
      }
   }

   public static void main(String[] arg) throws IOException {
      in  = new FileInputStream (arg[0]);
      out = new FileOutputStream(arg[1]);
      backwards();
   }
}
```

Reading takes place by means of the method `read`, which reads one byte at a time. When the file is finished, `read` returns the value −1. The method `backwards` will exist in as many editions (plus one) as the number of bytes in the stream. The first edition will read the first byte in the stream. This edition will not be terminated until all of the other editions have been terminated. The last thing that happens, therefore, is that the first byte is written out. Note that every edition of the method `backwards` has its own, unique edition of the local variable `c`. So, at most, there is the same number of `c`s as there are bytes in the file.

Note that the method `backwards` makes use of the *class* variables `in` and `out`. These only exist in one edition, which is shared by all the other editions of the method `backwards`. We also could have given the streams `in` and `out` as parameters of the method `backwards` but this would have been unnecessary, as we would then have had as many copies of these parameters as the number of editions of the method `backwards`.

The recursive method has been a class method (static method) in the examples we have seen here. Naturally, we could also have used recursion in an ordinary instance method. Note, however, that the objects' *instance* variables exist in only one edition per object. It is only the recursive method's parameters and *local* variables that exist in as many editions as the number of calls.

Recursion will normally arise because a method calls itself. This is called *direct recursion*. We can also have *indirect recursion*. For example, a method `m1` can call another method `m2`, which in turn calls `m1`. We then say that `m1` and `m2` are *mutually recursive*. Recursion can even arise over several stages (for example, `m1` can call `m2`, which calls `m3`, which then calls `m1`).

In some cases, it can be useful to have recursive methods with arrays as parameters. To demonstrate this, we write a method `sum`, the task of which is to compute the sum of all the components in an array of whole numbers. This method has two parameters. The first is the array that will be summed and the second is an `int` that indicates where in the array summing is to begin. If we want to add up the entire array, we will give this second parameter the value 0. For example, the following statements will result in the value 69 being written out:

```
int a[] = {1, 3, 5, 2, 4, 7, 10, 20, 15, 2};
System.out.println(sum(a, 0)); // 69 is written out
```

The method `sum` will look like this:

```
static int sum(int[] a, int startPos) {
   if (startPos>=a.length)
      return 0;
   else
      return a[startPos] + sum(a, startPos+1);
}
```

The recursive idea is a simple one. In the most obvious case the start position is greater than, or equal to, the length of the array. The chosen part of the array will therefore lack components and the sum will be equal to zero. If the start position is less than the length of the array, we can calculate the sum of the elements by adding the value in the start position to the sum of all the remaining components in the array. The method sum will call itself recursively in order to compute the sum of the remaining components.

18.5 Exercises

1. Insert documentation comments into one of your own classes, then use the javadoc program to document your class.

2. Let us suppose that the variable c of type **byte** contains two small whole numbers in the interval 0 to 15. One of the whole numbers is stored in the four left-hand bits in c, and the other in the four right-hand bits. Write a program to output the sum of the two small numbers.

3. Let us suppose that we use an array a of the element type **byte** to store an array of logical values. Every logical value is to be represented by only one bit. There will therefore be room for eight logical values in every **byte**. Write part of a program to show how we can index in the array. In other words, given a variable k, we have to produce the logical value number k.

4. Write a program that reads a date in the format yyyy-mm-dd. The program should write out the day number of the date during the year, that is, a number between 1 and 365, or 366 if it is a leap year. (Leap years are years that are divisible by 4 but years exactly divisible by 100 are not leap years, except those divisible by 400, which are.) Use a **switch** statement with the different months as an alternative.

5. A trade union is offered an agreement over a number of years in accordance with the following model:
    In the first year (year 1), every employee will get a monthly wage of $2,000.
    In the following years (year 2, 3, 4, etc.) employees will get an increase of 4% on the previous year's wages and, in addition, a general increment of $60.

    Write a recursive method that will compute a monthly wage in a particular year. The function will have the number of a year as its only parameter.

6. Write a recursive method sgd that will compute the greatest common divisor of two positive whole numbers m and n on the basis of the following definition:

$$sgd(m, n) = \begin{cases} m & \text{if } m = n \\ sgd(m-n, n) & \text{if } m > n \\ sgd(m, n-m) & \text{otherwise} \end{cases}$$

7. Write a recursive variant of the method `binarySearch` on page 297.

Standard classes for data structures

When you program, you often need to use different types of data structures in order to keep track of the data objects you are working with. The class `Vector`, which we discussed in Section 9.10, is an example of a class that you can use to build data structures. In version 1.1 and earlier versions of Java there was only the class `Vector` (and its subclass `Stack`) available for creating data structures, but in J2SDK a whole new group of classes was introduced. In this chapter, we give an overview of these classes. They are all found in the package `java.util`. Since data structures have different properties, in Java they have been divided into two groups: *collections* and *maps*.

19.1 Collections – the `Collection` interface

A collection contains several objects. The objects in a collection are called the collection's *elements*. There are two categories of collections: lists and sets. A *list* is an ordered sequence of elements. Each element is found in a certain position in the list and you can indicate this position using an *index* (an integer). The same element is allowed to occur in several positions in a list. A *set* is a collection in which one and the same element may occur only once at most. Elements in a set do not need to be sorted in any particular order. You don't use indexes to get to individual elements.

In Figure 19.1, we show the interfaces and classes that are used to describe collections. The interfaces are shown in the shaded area of the figure. The interface `Collection` describes properties that are common to all classes in a collection. This interface has two sub-interfaces: `List` and `Set`. The latter also has the sub-interface `SortedSet`, which describes sets where the elements are internally sorted. On the right in the figure are shown the standard classes that implement these interfaces. For example, we can see that the class `Vector` implements the interface `List`. We might think that it is unnecessary to have several standard classes that implement the same interface. They have the same methods, which can be used in the same way. The reason is that there are often alternative technical solutions that can be used inside the classes. These classes

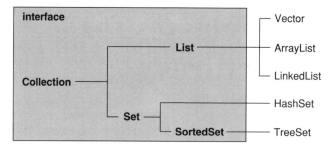

Figure 19.1 Interfaces and classes for collections

will then have different properties. It is true that they implement all of the methods but they may do this with varying degrees of success. For example, the classes `Vector` and `ArrayList` are good at changing individual elements inside a list but they are ineffective when it comes to inserting new elements, for example, in the list's first position. The opposite is the case with the class `LinkedList`. The point is that we should make use of the class that is best suited for the operations we have to carry out most often.

The standard classes that implement the interface `Collection`, that is, the classes `Vector`, `ArrayList`, `LinkedList`, `HashSet` and `TreeSet`, have another property that can be interesting to know. They all implement the interface `Serializable`. So we can output whole lists and sets to streams. We can easily store a list or a set in a file, therefore; see Section 16.4.2 on page 553.

Constructors

All collections have (at least) two constructors, one without parameters and one that has another collection as parameter. We can create a copy of a collection by means of the second constructor. The copy does not have to be organized in the same way as the original. For example, we can write:

```
HashSet h = new HashSet();
... // place elements in the set h
LinkedList l = new LinkedList(h); // make a copy of h
```

Methods

In the fact box we list the methods defined in the interface `Collection` and which, therefore, all the collection classes must have. Most of the methods do not need explanation. All the parameters that indicate objects are of the class `Object` to enable us to put any kind of object into a collection. For example, to insert a text last in the list `l`, we can write:

```
l.add(new String("a text"));
```

The interface java.util.Collection	
`add(o)`	inserts the object o into the collection (In a list, o is inserted last. In a set, o is only inserted if it does not already exist)
`addAll(s)`	inserts all objects in the collection s into the actual collection
`clear()`	removes all the elements from the collection
`contains(o)`	checks whether the object o is in the collection
`containsAll(s)`	checks whether all the objects in the collection s are in the actual collection
`equals(s)`	checks whether this collection is equal to the collection s. Two collections are equal if they are of the same category (list or set) and have the same elements (in the same order, for lists)
`isEmpty()`	checks whether this collection lacks elements
`iterator()`	returns an iterator of class `Iterator` that can be used to run through this collection
`remove(o)`	removes the object o from the collection if it is there
`removeAll(s)`	removes all the objects in the collection s from the collection
`retainAll(s)`	removes all the objects except those in the collection s
`size()`	gives the number of elements in the collection
`toArray()`	returns an array with all the elements in this collection
`toArray(a)`	a is an array. Returns an array with all the elements in this collection that have the same type as the elements in a

The method `iterator` returns an iterator of the class `Iterator`. This is a simpler version of the class `ListIterator`, which we described on page 305 in connection with vectors. The class `Iterator` only allows you to run through a collection from the beginning. It has the three methods `hasNext`, which checks to see if there is a next element, `next`, which gives the next element and `remove`, which removes the element that the last call of `next` gave as its result. Let's assume, for example, that we have put objects of the class `String` in list l. We can then run through the list and remove all elements that contain the text `"old"`.

```
for (Iterator i=l.iterator(); i.hasNext(); ) {
    String s = (String) i.next();
    if (s.indexOf("old") != -1)
        i.remove();
}
```

Methods in the class `Collections`

Apart from the interface `Collection`, there is also a *class* `Collections` (with an s at the end), which contains some class methods that can be of interest. For example, we can find here the methods min and max, which can be used to get the least or the greatest element in a collection. In order to find the greatest element in the list l, for example, we can write:

```
Object obj = Collections.max(l);
```

The objects in the collection must be *naturally comparable* if this is to work. More precisely, they must implement the interface Comparable. The only method in the interface Comparable is the method compareTo. This has another object obj as parameter and compares the current object with this one. The result value is a whole number. If the objects are equal, a value of 0 is returned; if the active object is smaller than the parameter obj, a negative value is returned, and if the active object is greater than the parameter obj, a positive value is returned. Many standard classes are naturally comparable. This applies, for example, to the classes Date, File and URL, as well as the wrapper classes Integer, Double, etc. The class String is also naturally comparable but the comparisons will not give the correct alphabetical order. If we want to compare texts, it is better to use a collator (see below).

The methods min and max can be found in alternative versions that can be used for objects that are not naturally comparable. We then have to give an extra parameter. To find the smallest element in the set h, we can write, for example:

```
Object obj = Collections.max(h, comp);
```

Here comp will be an object of a class that implements the interface Comparator. This interface has only the method compare, which will have two objects as parameters. The result value is (exactly as for the method compareTo, above) a whole number indicating which of the objects was the greater. The class Collator, which we used in Section 9.2, implements the interface Comparator. So we can use an object of this class as an extra parameter for the methods min and max when we want to search for the smallest and the largest element in a collection of texts.

The class Collections also contains two constants, EMPTY_SET and EMPTY_LIST, which we can use when we want to check whether a list or a set is empty.

When we construct programs with parallel threads, note that the collection classes ArrayList, LinkedList, HashSet and TreeSet are not synchronized (their methods have not been marked with the word **synchronized**). This means that errors can arise if several threads use a collection at the same time. To remedy this, we can use one of the class methods, synchronizedList, synchronizedSet and synchronizedSortedSet, in the class Collections. For example, to get a synchronized list that can be used in a program with parallel trees, we can write:

```
List list = Collections.synchronizedList(new LinkedList());
```

19.2 Lists

Properties peculiar to lists are defined in the interface `List`. The new methods that have been added are shown in the next fact box. For example, we can find methods here to access individual elements by the use of indexing:

```
l.add(5,new String("Java"));    // insert the text "Java" in
                                // position 5
String s = (String) l.get(5);   // retrieve the text in position 5
```

The interface java.util.List	
`add(k,o)`	interposes the object `o` in position number `k` in the list
`addAll(k,s)`	interposes all the objects in collection `s` in position number `k` in the list
`get(k)`	returns the object in position number `k`
`indexOf(o)`	gives the index for the object `o`, or −1 if `o` cannot be found in the list
`lastIndexOf(o)`	as `indexOf(o)`, but searches from the back
`listIterator()`	returns a `ListIterator` that begins in position number 0
`listIterator(k)`	returns a `ListIterator` that begins in position number `k`
`remove(k)`	removes the object in position number `k`
`set(k,o)`	replaces the element in position no. `k` i with the object `o`
`subList(i,j)`	gives the part of the list that includes the elements `i` to `j-1`

In addition, all the methods in the interface `java.util.Collection` are included.

The method `subList` is useful when we want to change a part of a list. An example:

```
l.subList(3,8).clear(); // remove the elements 3-7
```

The method `listIterator` gives an object of type `ListIterator` as discussed in Section 9.10. See the fact box on page 305.

Methods in the class `Collections`

The class `Collections` also contains some useful class methods for lists. The method `fill` will replace all the elements in a list with a certain value:

```
Collections.fill(l, "Java"); // puts "Java" in all elements in l
```

The method `nCopies` forms a list that consists of `n` similar objects:

```
List zeros = Collections.nCopies(100,new Integer(0));
```

The method `copy` copies all the elements in a list to another list. We can write:

```
Collections.copy(lTo, lFrom);
```

The list we copy to must be at least as long as the one we copy from. If it is longer, the extra elements will remain unchanged.

There are methods that will move elements in a list. The method `reverse` puts elements in reverse order, the method `shuffle` puts elements in an arbitrary order, while the method `sort` will sort elements. For example, we can write:

```
Collections.sort(l);
```

The method `binarySearch` searches for a particular element in a list:

```
int pos = Collections.binarySearch(l, searchedObj);
```

As we have shown here, the methods `sort` and `binarySearch`, in their simplest versions, require the elements in the list to implement the interface `Comparable`. In other words, they should have a `compareTo` method. If this is not the case, we can use alternative versions of `sort` and `binarySearch` where we give an object that implements the interface `Comparator` as an extra parameter. If we want to sort alphabetically a list containing texts, we can use a collator of the type `Collator`; see Section 9.2. If the list `l` contains texts, we can sort it with the following statements:

```
Collator co = Collator.getInstance();
co.setStrength(Collator.PRIMARY);
Collections.sort(l,co);
```

Implementing lists

As we saw in Figure 19.1, there are in Java three standard classes that implement the interface `List`. These are the classes `Vector`, `ArrayList` and `LinkedList`. The first two make use internally of an array to describe the list. The class `Vector` is included for historical reasons. We described this in Section 9.10, and all the methods are shown in the fact box on page 306. The class `ArrayList` has roughly the same properties as the class `Vector`, the biggest difference being that it is not synchronized. Class `ArrayList` has the methods in the fact box on page 306.

Implementing a list with an array is effective when we want to carry out operations that make use of indexing to read and change individual elements. This is not the case, however, when we want to interpose new elements in a list or remove elements, as we have to move the elements, which can take some time if the array is a large one. If we often have to carry out this type of operation, it is more convenient to use the class `LinkedList`. This makes use of a completely different technique, that of a doubly linked list, to make the implementation.

A *linked list* consists of a number of *nodes*. Each node contains both a reference to the next node and a reference to an element to be found in the list. There are, therefore, as

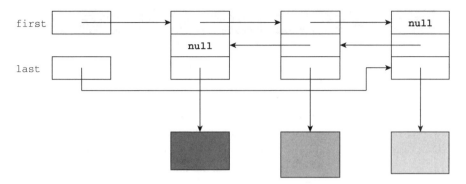

Figure 19.2 A doubly linked list

many nodes in the list as there are elements. If every node in addition contains a reference to the previous node, then we have a *doubly linked list*. This can look as in Figure 19.2. The shaded boxes indicate the elements of the list themselves. There are also two references, called `first` and `last` in the figure, which refer to the first and last nodes. We make use of these references as starting points whenever we want to perform an operation on the list. The value `null` has been used to indicate when the list has ended. There is also another technique, where we let the list be circular, that is, the last node refers forwards to the first and the first node refers backwards to the last one.

It lies outside the scope of this book to go into the details of how we implement a linked list. As luck would have it, we do not have to know this to make use of the standard class `LinkedList`. However, we should know that we can interpose new elements anywhere in a linked list without having to move the old elements. We simply create a new node that refers to the new element and link in this node at the required point in the list by changing references; neither do we have to move elements when we want to remove an element. As we have direct references to the beginning and end of the list, we can access the first and last elements very quickly. It is also particularly easy to insert or remove elements at the beginning and end of the list. On the other hand, it may take some time to access elements inside the list, as we will always have to run through it from the beginning or the end. So we can see that lists implemented as linked lists have quite different properties from lists implemented with arrays. This explains why there are standard classes that use both techniques.

As the class `LinkedList` is especially suitable in applications where we have to deal with the beginning and the end of a list, there is a set of extra methods for these operations in class `LinkedList`. These are called `addFirst`, `addLast`, etc. In addition, class `LinkedList`, like the classes `Vector` and `ArrayList`, has the method `clone`; see the fact box.

Extra methods in java.util.LinkedList	
`addFirst(o)`	inserts the object o first in the list
`addLast(o)`	inserts the object o last in the list
`getFirst()`	returns the first object in the list
`getLast()`	returns the last object in the list
`removeFirst()`	removes the first object from the list
`removeLast()`	removes the last object from the list
`clone()`	returns a copy of the list (the references to the objects in the list are copied, not the objects themselves)

19.3 Sets

The properties applying to sets are defined in the interface `Set`. No new methods are defined in this interface in addition to those that apply for all collections and that are shown in the fact box on page 627. What is particular to this interface is that the constructors and the method `add` must be designed in such a manner that no element can be added to the set more than once. If we try to add an element that is already there, nothing will happen.

Note also that there is a method `singleton` in the class `Collections` with which we can create a set that contains a single element:

```
Set s = Collections.singleton(new String("Sole"));
```

Sorted sets

Sorted sets have some unique properties. These are described in the interface `SortedSet`. We must be able to compare the elements of a set with one another in order to be able to sort it. We can do this if the elements are naturally comparable, that is, they implement the interface `Comparable` and have a method `compareTo`. If, when we create a sorted set, the elements are not naturally comparable, we will have to indicate that a special collator is to be used. This collator will be an object that implements the interface `Comparator`, that is, it will have a `compare` method. (We discussed the interfaces `Comparable` and `Comparator` on page 628.)

A class, for example the standard class `TreeSet`, which implements the interface `SortedSet`, should have (at least) the following four constructors:

```
TreeSet()
TreeSet(Comparator comp)
TreeSet(Collection coll)
TreeSet(SortedSet ss)
```

The first creates an empty set. All the elements to be placed in the set must be naturally comparable. The second constructor also creates an empty set but does not require elements to be naturally comparable. Instead, we give a collator to be used as parameter. The third constructor creates a sorted set of the elements included in the collection that is given as parameter. These elements must be naturally comparable. The last constructor gets a sorted set as parameter and creates a copy of this set.

There are methods in the interface `SortedSet` that are typical for sorted sets. These are shown in the fact box. What distinguishes a sorted set from an ordinary one is, of course, that the elements of a sorted set are internally sorted. So we shall get the elements in sorted order when we use an iterator.

The interface java.util.SortedSet	
`first()`	returns the set's smallest element
`last()`	returns the set's largest element
`headSet(toE)`	returns a sorted subset with all the elements that are smaller than the element `toE`
`tailSet(fromE)`	returns a sorted subset with all the elements that are larger than, or equal to, the element `fromE`
`subSet(fromE,toE)`	returns a sorted subset with all the elements that are larger than, or equal to, the element `fromE` and smaller than the element `toE`
`comparator()`	returns the collator that is used, or **null**, if the elements are naturally comparable

In addition, all the methods in the interface `java.util.Collection` are included.

As an example of this, we shall show a program that reads a file containing a text and which writes out all the words included in the text. The name of the file is given as parameter for `main`. The printout of the words will be sorted in alphabetical order and words that occur several times in the text will be found in only one place in the printout. All the words are written out in capitals. The program has the following appearance. (To simplify the program, we use the classes in the package `extra`.)

```java
import java.util.*;
import java.text.*;
import java.io.*;
import extra.*;
public class TextAnalysis {
    public static void main(String[] arg)  {
        String word;
        Collator co = Collator.getInstance();  // compare texts
```

```
        co.setStrength(Collator.PRIMARY);
        TreeSet wordSet = new TreeSet(co);
        // open the file
        ExtendedReader r = ExtendedReader.getFileReader(arg[0]);
        // read one word at a time and add to the set
        while((word = nextWord(r)) != null)
            wordSet.add(word.toUpperCase());
        // write out all the words
        for (Iterator i=wordSet.iterator(); i.hasNext(); )
            Std.out.println(i.next());
    }

    // The method nextWord reads a word, gives null at end of file
    public static String nextWord(ExtendedReader r) {
        String s ="";
        int c;
        // skip all the characters that are not letters
        while ((c=r.lookAhead()) != -1 &&
                 !Character.isLetter((char) c))
            c = r.readChar(); // skip this character

        // form a word from the letters that follow
        while ((c=r.lookAhead()) != -1 &&
                 Character.isLetter((char) c))
            s = s + (char)r.readChar();  // insert this letter into s
        if (s.length() == 0)
            return null;    // at end of file
        else
            return s;
    }
}
```

A sorted set, wordSet, is created in the method main. In order to get the correct
alphabetical order, we give a collator of class Collator as parameter for the
constructor; see Section 9.2. One word at a time is then read from the file and added to
the set. When all the words have been read, an iterator is used to run through the set.
Words are read in from the file in the method nextWord. In this method we first skip
all the characters that are not letters. (We use the method lookAhead so that the
algorithm will be as simple as possible. This method looks ahead to the next character,
without taking it out of the stream.) Then we read in one letter at a time until we get a
character that is not a letter. The letters that are read are put together to form a word,
which is then returned from the method.

Implementing sets

In Java there are two standard classes for sets, TreeSet and HashSet. TreeSet forms
sorted sets and HashSet, unsorted sets. The class TreeSet is implemented with the

class `TreeMap`, and the class `HashSet` with the class `HashMap`. These classes will be discussed in the next section, which deals with maps. We shall not go into details now but confine ourselves to giving some general properties of the classes `TreeSet` and `HashSet`.

The class `TreeSet` sorts elements into a *binary search tree*. It allows us to search, add or remove elements relatively quickly. (The time it takes is proportional to the logarithm of the number of elements in the set.) Running through the set with an iterator is done in the fastest way possible. (The time this takes is proportional to the number of elements in the set.)

The class `HashSet` uses a *hash table* internally. If configured correctly, this can be an extremely fast way to search, add or remove elements. (The time it takes is constant and not proportional to the number of elements in the set.) On the other hand, a hash table can be inefficient if we want to run through all the elements in a set. There is also another disadvantage. For it to work correctly, we have to reserve a little more memory space for the hash table than there are elements in the set.

In conclusion, we can say that if we want to run through a set, it would be best to use the class `TreeSet`, certainly if we will perform the operation frequently. If we want to sort elements, we must use `TreeSet`, since `HashSet` does not sort elements. If we do not need to run through the set, we can find it more appropriate to use the class `HashSet`. It will then be much faster to search, add or remove elements.

19.4 Maps

A *map* is a table where we use a *search key* to access information. An example of this is a motor-vehicle registration office. The search key in this case is a car's registration number. If we know the registration number, we can retrieve information about a car, the make and model, for instance. We say that the search key in a map is *mapped* on to a *value* (the information). So a search key and its accompanying value form a pair, called a *mapping*. The term *key–value pair* is often used. A search key can only be mapped on to *one* value. (One car cannot have several registration numbers.) A particular search key can therefore be found only once in a map. On the other hand, a particular value can occur several times. For example, if we have a map where the search keys are the names of people and the values are ages, it would be possible for several people to have the same age.

In Figure 19.3 are shown the standard interfaces and standard classes in Java for describing maps. The interfaces are shown in the shaded part of the figure. The interface `Map` describes properties that all maps have in common. The sub-interface `SortedMap` describes maps where the search keys are sorted internally. To the right in the figure are shown the three standard classes, `Hashtable`, `HashMap` and `TreeMap`,

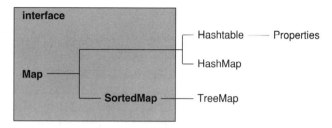

Figure 19.3 Interfaces and classes for mappings

which implement these interfaces. The class `Hashtable` also has a subclass `Properties`, which, among other things, is used to represent system properties.

One point worth noting is that all the three standard classes `Hashtable`, `HashMap` and `TreeMap` also implement the interface `Serializable`, so we can write out a whole map to a file without difficulty; see Section 16.4.2.

Constructors

All maps have (at least) two constructors, one without parameters and one that has another map as parameter. We can use the second of these if we want to create a copy of a map. For example, we can write:

```
TreeMap tab1 = new TreeMap();
... // insert mappings in tab1
HashMap tab2 = new HashMap(tab1);
```

Methods

The fact box lists the methods in the interface `Map`. These methods can be found in all the classes that implement the interface, that is, in the classes `Hashtable`, `HashMap` and `TreeMap`, and which, therefore, must be implemented by all the map classes. The most important methods are `put` and `get`, which are used to insert mappings in the map and to look up the value of a particular search key. Both keys and values are of type `Object`, so that we can have any kind of object as key and value. For example, to insert a mapping that says that the person David is 17 years old, we can write:

```
tab1.add("David", new Integer(17));
```

If in a car registration `reg` we want to get information about the car with registration number ABC123, we can write:

```
MotorVehicle mv = (MotorVehicle) reg.get("ABC123");
```

The interface java.util.Map	
put(key,value)	inserts a mapping in the map. Any previous values of key are replaced. The old value is returned
putAll(tab)	inserts all the mappings to be found in another map, tab, into this map
remove(key)	removes the mapping for key from the map
clear()	removes all the mappings from the map
get(key)	returns the value for key, or **null** if key cannot be found
containsKey(n)	checks whether the key n can be found in the map
containsValue(v)	checks whether one or more keys are mapped on to the value v
isEmpty()	checks whether this map lacks mappings
size()	gives the number of mappings in the map
equals(tab)	checks whether the map has the same mappings as tab
keySet()	returns a set (Set) with all the keys in this map
values()	returns a collection (Collection) with all the values in the map
entrySet()	returns a set (Set) with all the mappings in the map Every mapping has the type Map.Entry
Map.Entry	class that represents a mapping. Includes the methods getKey, getValue and setValue

The classes HashMap and TreeMap are, unlike class Hashtable, unsynchronized. (Their methods have not been marked with the word **synchronized**.) This is a point to ponder if we are writing programs with several threads. To get a synchronized map, we can use the class method synchronizedMap in the class Collections:

```
Map m = Collections.synchronizedMap(new TreeMap());
```

19.5 The class TreeMap

With the class TreeMap, we can create *sorted* maps. The class TreeMap implements the interface SortedMap. What distinguishes a sorted map from an ordinary one is that we get *sorted* sets as result if we call one of the methods keySet and entrySet. Search keys are stored in sorted order in sorted maps. For search keys to be sorted, they must be naturally comparable. In other words, they must implement the interface Comparable. If they do, they will have a method compareTo. If the elements are not naturally comparable and we want to create a sorted map, we have to indicate that we will use a special collator. This will be an object that implements the interface Comparator, that is, it will have a method compare; see page 628.

The class `TreeMap`, which implements the interface `SortedMap`, has four constructors:

```
TreeMap()
TreeMap(Comparator comp)
TreeMap(Map m)
TreeMap(SortedMap sm)
```

The first creates an empty map and requires all the search keys that will be put into the map to be naturally comparable. We can use the second constructor when search keys are not naturally comparable. We then give as parameter a collator that we will use. The third constructor creates a sorted map of the mappings included in the table given as parameter. Search keys must be naturally comparable. The last constructor gets a sorted map as parameter and creates a copy of this table. The same sort order is used.

The methods characteristic of sorted maps have been defined in the interface `SortedMap`; see the fact box. The class `TreeMap` also has all the methods in the interface `Map`. There is also a method `clone` to enable us to create copies of a table.

The interface java.util.SortedMap	
`firstKey()`	returns the smallest search key
`lastKey()`	returns the largest search key
`headMap(toK)`	returns a map with all the mappings where the search key is smaller than `toK`
`tailMap(fromK)`	returns a map with all the mappings where the search key is larger than, or equal to, `fromK`
`subMap(fromK,toK)`	returns a map with all the mappings where the search key is larger than, or equal to, `fromK` and smaller than `toK`
`comparator()`	returns the collator that is used, or `null` if the search keys are naturally comparable

In addition, there are all the methods in the interface `java.util.Map`.

We shall now write a new variant of our text analysis program on page 633 to show how the class `TreeMap` can be used. That program read a text from a file and wrote out all the words included in the text in alphabetical order. In the new variant of that program, we shall write out not only the words included in the text but also the number of times the word occurs. As before, the words will be written out in alphabetical order. We merely have to reconstruct the method `main`. The rest of the class `TextAnalysis` will remain as before. We will now use a sorted map, where the words are search keys. For each search key, we let the value be an object of class `Integer`. This object will contain the number of times the word in question occurs in the text. The program will look as follows:

```
public static void main(String[] arg)  {
  String word;
  Collator co = Collator.getInstance();  // compare texts
  co.setStrength(Collator.PRIMARY);
  // create the map
  TreeMap wordTable = new TreeMap(co);
  // open the file
  ExtendedReader r = ExtendedReader.getFileReader(arg[0]);
  // read one word at a time
  while((word = nextWord(r)) != null) {
    word = word.toUpperCase(); // translate to capitals
    // look up the word in the table
    Integer number = (Integer) wordTable.get(word);
    if (number == null)
      number = new Integer(0); // the word did not exist before
    // insert the word into the table
    wordTable.put(word, new Integer(number.intValue()+1));
  }

  // create a sorted set with all the pairs of words and numbers
  Set mappings = wordTable.entrySet();
  // write out all the pairs
  for (Iterator i=mappings.iterator(); i.hasNext(); ) {
    Map.Entry e = (Map.Entry) i.next();
    Std.out.println(e.getKey() + "   " + e.getValue());
  }
}
```

We look up a word in the table every time it has been read from the file. If the word could be found in the table, we will get as result an object of the class Integer. If the word did not exist before, we will get as result the value null. We then insert the word that has been read into the table and increase the number by 1 for this word. When the whole text has been read, we use the method entrySet to form a set of all the mappings, that is, pairs of words and corresponding numbers. The mappings are of the class Map.Entry; see the fact box on page 637. We then use an iterator to run through these pairs and output the information.

The class TreeMap is implemented by means of a *binary search tree*. A *tree* is a programming construct that is built with a number of *nodes*. Unlike ordinary trees, the *root* comes at the top. Each node contains references to its nodes underneath, which are called its *children*. In a *binary* tree, each node has at most two children. Apart from the references to its children, each node contains information of some kind. In a tree used to create maps, there will be one node per mapping. So each node will contain a reference to a search key and a reference to the corresponding value. We do not have the space to go into more detail here but we can show the principles involved in a figure. If we had a map that was used to count the number of words in a text, it might

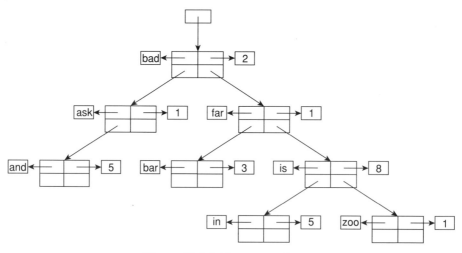

Figure 19.4 A binary search tree

look something like Figure 19.4. For example, from the figure we can see that the word "and" has occurred five times and the word "is" eight times.

But how has this construct been sorted? If we look carefully, we shall see that the search keys have been ingeniously placed. For every node, the search key is larger than all the search keys in the node's left-hand children and all the children of these nodes, grandchildren, etc. For instance, the word "bad" is larger than both the word "ask" and the word "and". Similarly, the search key in every node is smaller than the search key in the node's right-hand children and all the children of these nodes, etc. The word "far", for example, is smaller than the word "is", "in" or "zoo".

We can make use of the fact that the search keys have been deployed in this way when we have to search for a particular key. The reference at the top of the figure is always used as a starting point, and from there on we search downwards in the tree. For every node we search through, we compare the search key in this node with the one we are looking for. If the node contains a search key that is larger than the one we are looking for, we continue the search in the node's left-hand children, and if the node contains a search key that is smaller than the one we are looking for, we continue the search in the node's right-hand children. We continue in this way until either we come across the search key we are looking for or we reach the end of the tree. If a tree is balanced, that is, if each level is filled out before a new one is started, a search can be quite fast, as the maximum number of comparisons that must be made to find a particular word is proportional to the number of *levels* in the tree, not the number of words.

If we wish to form a sorted list of words or mappings, we begin with an empty list and use the following recursive algorithm:

If the tree lacks nodes, do nothing.

Otherwise, do the following:

> Call this algorithm for the sub-tree that has the root's left-hand child as root.
>
> Place the root's search word (and value) last in the list.
>
> Call this algorithm for the sub-tree that has the root's right-hand child as root.

By way of a summary, we can state the following for maps that have been created with the class `TreeMap`: searches, insertions and removals of mappings can be done relatively quickly. (The time required is in proportion to the logarithm of the number of search keys.) We can easily form *sorted* lists of search words and mappings.

19.6 The classes `Hashtable` and `HashMap`

For fast searches where we are not interested in having sorted lists of search keys and mappings, we should use one of the classes `Hashtable` and `HashMap`. Both classes function in the same way. They both implement the interface `Map`, shown in the fact box on page 637. The only real difference between these classes is that `HashMap` is not synchronized, while `Hashtable` is. The class `Hashtable` has remained for historical reasons, having been in earlier versions of Java. Apart from the methods in the interface `Map`, it contains some methods that are shown in the fact box below. The method `clone` can also be found in the class `HashMap`.

Extra methods in java.util.Hashtable	
`contains(v)`	same as the method `containsValue`
`keys()`	gives an iterator of the class `Enumeration`, which runs through all the search keys in the table
`elements()`	gives an iterator of the class `Enumeration`, which runs through all the values in the table
`clone()`	returns a copy of the table (references to the objects in the table are copied and not the objects themselves)

The classes `Hashtable` and `HashMap` make use of something called a *hash table*, as we would expect, given their names. A hash table is constructed for fast searches. As we know, an array is the programming construct that produces the fastest searches. If we know the index of a particular element, we can immediately look it up in an array. Ideally, we would always use arrays for our searches but the search keys always have to be whole numbers so that they can be used as indexes in the array. In addition, a search key has to lie within a limited interval, otherwise the array would have to be unacceptably large. Despite these limitations, we still make use of arrays in hash tables. One of these is shown in Figure 19.5, with the array at the top. All the `ks` indicate search keys, and all the `vs` their corresponding values.

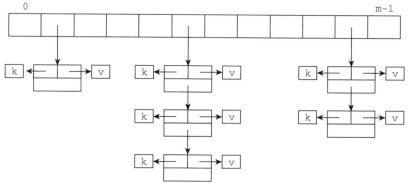

Figure 19.5 A hash table

To index with a search key in an array, we first have to translate the search key into a whole number. The translation of search keys into whole numbers is done by a *hash function*. For example, if the search key is a text, the hash function will compute a whole number on the basis of this text. (The whole number for a text can, for instance, be calculated as the sum of the LATIN_1 codes for the characters included in the text.) We then use the resulting whole number h to index in the array. We use the value h%m as the index to ensure indexing will not take place outside the array. Here m is the size of the array, and the operator % gives the remainder when h is divided by m. Of course, different hash functions are required for different types of search key. A method called hashCode, which corresponds to the hash function, is defined in the class Object. If objects of a certain class are to be used as search keys, the class must have defined its own version of the hashCode method. Several standard classes, for example the class String, have their own version of this method. For objects of a certain class to be used as search keys, the class must also have defined its own version of the method equals to ensure search keys can be compared with each other.

The problem with hash functions is that several values can be translated into the same whole number. (If, for example, we add the LATIN_1 codes for the texts "fat" and "gas", we will get the same total.) We then get a *collision*. Several different search keys can therefore get the same index in an array. To solve this problem, we do not let each element in an array contain a single value but a list of search keys and corresponding values, that is, a list of mappings. In Figure 19.5, for example, we can see that collisions have arisen for two elements in the array.

Naturally, we would prefer it if there were no collisions at all. We would then find the search key immediately, without having to search through a list. We could avoid collisions if we had a perfect hash function that translated all the different search keys into different indices. In most cases, it is not possible to construct such a hash function but it is important that the hash function should be so designed that it will spread the different search keys as evenly as possible in an array. The risk of a collision will also decrease, of course, if the array is a large one, so we usually let the array be larger than the number of search keys. For hash tables we use the word *capacity* to indicate the number of elements in the array. We also indicate a *load factor*, which is the ratio of the number of mappings (that is, the number of search keys) to the capacity. We should have a low load factor in order to diminish the risk of collisions but this requires more memory space. In practice, the risk of a collision is high if the load factor exceeds 0.75.

The classes `Hashtable` and `HashMap` have four constructors, the two that all maps have (see page 636) and two extra ones, where we can choose the capacity and load factor; see the fact box. If we choose the capacity ourselves, we should let it be a prime number. If we insert so many mappings in a hash table that the load factor is exceeded, the hash table's capacity will be increased automatically (doubled). All of the old mappings in the table will then be moved around, which will naturally take a little time. If we know in advance roughly how many mappings the hash table is to hold, it would be best to use one of the constructors in which we can indicate the capacity ourselves.

Constructors in java.util.Hashtable and java.util.HashMap	
`HashMap()` `Hashtable()`	creates an empty hash table with a default value for the capacity. The load factor will be 0.75
`HashMap(map)` `Hashtable(map)`	creates a hash table that contains all the mappings in the map `map`. The load factor will be 0.75
`HashMap(cp)` `Hashtable(cp)`	creates an empty hash table with capacity `cp` and load factor 0.75
`HashMap(cp,f)` `Hashtable(cp,f)`	creates an empty hash table with capacity `cp` and load factor `f`

As an example, we shall show one of our own classes, by means of which we can translate a text that contains the name of a colour to an object of the standard class `Color`. Our class will be called `Colors`. It will have a class method `get` that has a `String` as parameter and returns a `Color` object. For example, we will be able to write:

```
Color col = Colors.get("orange");
```

The method `get` will be designed such that it will not make any difference whether we indicate the name of a colour with a capital or small letter. The class `Colors` will have the appearance shown below. It makes use internally of a hash table that is initialized in a static initializer. There are 13 colours to be inserted into the table. The hash table's capacity has therefore been given as 19. This is a prime number and gives a load factor under 0.75. We look up colours in the hash table in the method `get` but before we do this, we translate the name of the colour to small letters. If the given name of a colour is missing from the table, the colour black will be returned.

```java
import java.awt.*;
import java.util.*;
public class Colors {

    private static Hashtable tab = new Hashtable(19);

    // initialize the hash table
    static {
        tab.put("black",    Color.black);
        tab.put("blue",     Color.blue);
        tab.put("cyan",     Color.black);
        etc., for other pre-defined colours
    }

    public static Color get(String name) {
        Object c = tab.get(name.toLowerCase());
        if (c != null)
            return (Color) c;
        else
            return Color.black;
    }
}
```

19.7 The class `Properties`

The last class we shall be discussing in this survey is the standard class `Properties`. This class is a subclass of the class `Hashtable`. We use it to create maps where both the search keys and the values are of type `String`. We therefore use the class `Properties` to map *key words* on to texts. We call a map of class `Properties` a *property table*.

A unique property of class `Properties` is that we can connect, to a certain `Properties` object p1, another `Properties` object p2, which contains default values. So if we are searching for a particular key word in p1 and this key word cannot be found, the search will automatically continue in p2. If the search word is found in p2, we will get the value that is stored there. This takes place recursively. If the searched word cannot be found in p2 either, and if p2 in turn has a third `Properties` object with default values, the search will proceed to p3, and so on.

Another unique property of the class `Properties` is that we can store a map in a text file, a *property file*. We can also read in a property file and put the mappings indicated there into a property table. A property file will contain lines of the form:

```
keyword=the text that applies for this keyword
```

java.util.Properties	
Properties()	creates an empty table without default values for search words
Properties(pdef)	creates an empty table and indicates that the Properties object pdef contains default values for the search words
put(searchWord,txt)	inserts a map in the table. Earlier values for searchWord are replaced. The old value is returned
setProperty(searchWord,txt)	the same as put(searchWord,txt)
getProperty(searchWord)	gives the text for searchWord
getProperty(searchWord,txt)	the same as getProperty(searchWord,txt), but gives the result txt if searchWord is missing
store(out,rubric)	saves the table as a property file in the output stream out; rubric is inserted as comment in the first line
load(in)	reads a property file from the input stream in and inserts the mappings into the table
propertyNames()	gives an iterator of class Enumeration that runs through all the search words in the table
list(out)	outputs the table in out (an OutputStream or a Writer)

A keyword will appear first on every line; then, after the equals sign (or a colon), will come the text that is to be the value for this keyword. The text to the right of the equals sign can contain blank characters. If we want special characters to be included in the text, we can make use of the escape sequences shown in the fact box on page 272. If a text is too long to be contained in a line, we can conclude the line with the character \ and continue on a new line. Lines introduced with the character # or ! are considered to be comments and are skipped when we read in the mappings. Property files often allow us to make programs exactly as we want them to be, without having to change the program code. Colours, fonts and sizes are examples of the things that we can change by using property files. We shall give an example of this shortly.

The Java interpreter makes use of a property table, that is, an object of the class Properties, to describe system properties. Some of the keywords that can be found in this table are java.version, os.name, user.language and user.timezone. In the standard class java.lang.System there is a method getProperties that we can use to get access to a system's property table. For example, we can make the following statement to get a printout of the actual system properties:

```
System.getProperties().list(System.out);
```

A system's property table is initialized automatically at the start of a program. If we use D arguments when we start our program (see page 148), the mappings we write there will also end up in the system's property table. The methods in the class System that have to do with the system's property table are shown in the following revision table. Note that we can both read and change individual properties. We can even replace the system's property table with one of our own.

Some of the methods in java.lang.System	
getProperties()	returns the system's property table
setProperties(p)	replaces the system's property table with p
getProperty(word)	gives the text for word in the system's property table
getProperty(word,txt)	the same as setProperty(word,txt) but gives the result txt if word is missing
setProperty(word,txt)	inserts a mapping in the system's property table. Earlier values are replaced. The old value is returned

We shall conclude by showing a new version of the program Greeting on page 31, which showed a message in a window on the screen. In the new version we use a property file called Greeting.properties to control the font, together with the foreground and background colours to be used. We shall also arrange for the message itself to be included in the property file. This can look as follows:

```
# Properties for the program Greeting
background=yellow
fontName=SansSerif
fontStyle=ITALIC
fontSize=24
message=Goodbye and Thank You!
```

The program uses a property table that is initialized from the property file. It then looks up the different properties that are required in the table. Default values have been indicated for each property. The class Colors, which we showed on page 644, is used to translate the names of the colours indicated in the property file to objects of the standard class Color. The new version of the class Greeting looks like this:

```
import java.awt.*;
import javax.swing.*;
import java.util.*;
import java.io.*;
public class Greeting {
   public static void main (String[] arg) {
      Welcome2 w2 = new Welcome2();   // create a Welcome2 object
   }
}

class Welcome2 extends JFrame {
   public Welcome2() {
```

```java
    // create and initialize the property table
    Properties p = new Properties();
    try {
      p.load(new FileInputStream("Greeting.properties"));
    }
    catch (IOException e) {}

    // create a Label object with the message
    String mess  = p.getProperty("message",  "Welcome");
    JLabel l = new JLabel(mess, JLabel.CENTER);
    getContentPane().add(l);
    l.setOpaque(true);

    // retrieve the font
    String fName  = p.getProperty("fontName",  "Serif");
    String fStyle = p.getProperty("fontStyle", "PLAIN");
    // translate the style to an int constant
    int ifStyle;
    if (fStyle.equals("BOLD") )
      ifStyle = Font.BOLD;
    else if (fStyle.equals("ITALIC"))
      ifStyle = Font.ITALIC;
    else
      ifStyle = Font.PLAIN;
    int fSize = Integer.parseInt
                (p.getProperty("fontSize", "24"));
    l.setFont(new Font(fName, ifStyle, fSize));

    // set the foreground colour
    String fColor = p.getProperty("foreground",  "black");
    l.setForeground(Colors.get(fColor));

    // set the background colour
    String bColor = p.getProperty("background",  "white");
    l.setBackground(Colors.get(bColor));

    setSize(400,150);
    setVisible(true);
    setDefaultCloseOperation(EXIT_ON_CLOSE);
  }
}
```

If the property file has the content shown opposite, the program will look as in Figure
19.6 when it is run.

Figure 19.6 Using a property file

19.8 Exercises

1. Change the program `TextAnalysis` on page 633 so that it will only write out words that are reserved words in Java. (See Appendix A.) Use a set that contains the reserved words and check to see whether the words read in are present in this set.

2. Solve Exercise 6 on page 323 in a different way, using a map to map article designations on to objects of the class `Article`. Use the classes `ObjectInputStream` and `ObjectOutputStream` to read in and write out the map.

3. Instead of having several property tables in a program, it can be more useful to combine the mappings we read in from a particular property file of system properties so that we have only one property table to search. Write statements that will form a new property table of this kind and replace the system's property table with the new one.

Appendix A
Reserved words and operators

The reserved words in Java are shown in Table A.1. The words written in brackets are reserved but not used in the language at the moment, although they may be used in future versions of Java.

Table A.1 Reserved words

abstract	default	(goto)	(operator)	synchronized
boolean	do	if	(outer)	this
break	double	implements	package	throw
byte	else	import	private	throws
(byvalue)	extends	(inner)	protected	transient
case	false	instanceof	public	true
(cast)	final	int	(rest)	try
catch	finally	interface	return	(var)
char	float	long	short	void
class	for	native	static	volatile
(const)	(future)	new	super	while
continue	(generic)	null	switch	

A compilation of the operators in Java is given in Table A.2. Operators with only one operand, *unary* operators, have been placed in the first two boxes, while operators with two operands have been placed in the other boxes. (The exception is the conditional operator, which has three operands.) The operators have been listed in order of priority, with the operator in the first box having highest priority. Operators in the same box have the same priority. (In the table, the symbol a is used to indicate an arbitrary expression.)

Table A.2 Operators

postfix, increase and decrease	`a++  a--`
prefix, increase and decrease	`++a  --a`
unary + and −	`+a  -a`
the bit operator NOT	`~a`
logical NOT	`!a`
multiplication, division, remainder	`*  /  %`
addition, subtraction	`+  -`
shift	`<<  >>  >>>`
less than and greater than	`<  >  <=  >=`
test of an object's class	`instanceof`
equality, inequality	`==  !=`
the bit operator AND	`&`
the bit operator XOR	`^`
the bit operator OR	`|`
logical AND	`&&`
logical OR	`||`
the conditional operator	`?:`
assignment operators	`=  +=  -=  *=  /=  %=`
	`&=  ^=  |=`
	`<<=  >>=  >>>=`

Appendix B
LATIN_1 codes

Table B.1 LATIN_1 codes

\u0000	*nul*	\u0020	*space*	\u0040	@	\u0060	`
\u0001	*soh*	\u0021	!	\u0041	A	\u0061	a
\u0002	*stx*	\u0022	"	\u0042	B	\u0062	b
\u0003	*etx*	\u0023	#	\u0043	C	\u0063	c
\u0004	*eot*	\u0024	$	\u0044	D	\u0064	d
\u0005	*enq*	\u0025	%	\u0045	E	\u0065	e
\u0006	*ack*	\u0026	&	\u0046	F	\u0066	f
\u0007	*bel*	\u0027	'	\u0047	G	\u0067	g
\u0008	*bs*	\u0028	(	\u0048	H	\u0068	h
\u0009	*ht*	\u0029	)	\u0049	I	\u0069	i
\u000A	*lf*	\u002A	*	\u004A	J	\u006A	j
\u000B	*vt*	\u002B	+	\u004B	K	\u006B	k
\u000C	*ff*	\u002C	,	\u004C	L	\u006C	l
\u000D	*cr*	\u002D	-	\u004D	M	\u006D	m
\u000E	*so*	\u002E	.	\u004E	N	\u006E	n
\u000F	*si*	\u002F	/	\u004F	O	\u006F	o
\u0010	*dle*	\u0030	0	\u0050	P	\u0070	p
\u0011	*dc1*	\u0031	1	\u0051	Q	\u0071	q
\u0012	*dc2*	\u0032	2	\u0052	R	\u0072	r
\u0013	*dc3*	\u0033	3	\u0053	S	\u0073	s
\u0014	*dc4*	\u0034	4	\u0054	T	\u0074	t
\u0015	*nak*	\u0035	5	\u0055	U	\u0075	u
\u0016	*syn*	\u0036	6	\u0056	V	\u0076	v
\u0017	*etb*	\u0037	7	\u0057	W	\u0077	w
\u0018	*can*	\u0038	8	\u0058	X	\u0078	x
\u0019	*em*	\u0039	9	\u0059	Y	\u0079	y
\u001A	*sub*	\u003A	:	\u005A	Z	\u007A	z
\u001B	*esc*	\u003B	;	\u005B	[	\u007B	{
\u001C	*fs*	\u003C	<	\u005C	\	\u007C		
\u001D	*gs*	\u003D	=	\u005D	]	\u007D	}
\u001E	*rs*	\u003E	>	\u005E	^	\u007E	~
\u001F	*us*	\u003F	?	\u005F	_	\u007F	*del*

Table B.1 (Continued)

\u0080		\u00A0	*nbsp*	\u00C0	À	\u00E0	à
\u0081		\u00A1	¡	\u00C1	Á	\u00E1	á
\u0082		\u00A2	¢	\u00C2	Â	\u00E2	â
\u0083		\u00A3	£	\u00C3	Ã	\u00E3	ã
\u0084	*ind*	\u00A4	¤	\u00C4	Ä	\u00E4	ä
\u0085	*nel*	\u00A5	¥	\u00C5	Å	\u00E5	å
\u0086	*ssa*	\u00A6	¦	\u00C6	Æ	\u00E6	æ
\u0087	*esa*	\u00A7	§	\u00C7	Ç	\u00E7	ç
\u0088	*hts*	\u00A8	¨	\u00C8	È	\u00E8	è
\u0089	*htj*	\u00A9	©	\u00C9	É	\u00E9	é
\u008A	*vts*	\u00AA	ª	\u00CA	Ê	\u00EA	ê
\u008B	*pld*	\u00AB	«	\u00CB	Ë	\u00EB	ë
\u008C	*plu*	\u00AC	¬	\u00CC	Ì	\u00EC	ì
\u008D	*ri*	\u00AD	-	\u00CD	Í	\u00ED	í
\u008E	*ss2*	\u00AE	®	\u00CE	Î	\u00EE	î
\u008F	*ss3*	\u00AF	¯	\u00CF	Ï	\u00EF	ï
\u0090	*dcs*	\u00B0	°	\u00D0	Ð	\u00F0	ð
\u0091	*pul*	\u00B1	±	\u00D1	Ñ	\u00F1	ñ
\u0092	*pu2*	\u00B2	²	\u00D2	Ò	\u00F2	ò
\u0093	*sts*	\u00B3	³	\u00D3	Ó	\u00F3	ó
\u0094	*cch*	\u00B4	´	\u00D4	Ô	\u00F4	ô
\u0095	*mw*	\u00B5	µ	\u00D5	Õ	\u00F5	õ
\u0096	*spa*	\u00B6	¶	\u00D6	Ö	\u00F6	ö
\u0097	*epa*	\u00B7	·	\u00D7	×	\u00F7	÷
\u0098		\u00B8	¸	\u00D8	Ø	\u00F8	ø
\u0099		\u00B9	¹	\u00D9	Ù	\u00F9	ù
\u009A		\u00BA	º	\u00DA	Ú	\u00FA	ú
\u009B	*csi*	\u00BB	»	\u00DB	Û	\u00FB	û
\u009C	*st*	\u00BC	¼	\u00DC	Ü	\u00FC	ü
\u009D	*osc*	\u00BD	½	\u00DD	Ý	\u00FD	ý
\u009E	*pm*	\u00BE	¾	\u00DE	Þ	\u00FE	þ
\u009F	*apc*	\u00BF	¿	\u00DF	ß	\u00FF	ÿ

The characters included in LATIN_1 are shown in Table B1. These characters correspond to the first 256 characters in Unicode, so the Unicode sequences of the characters have also been shown. Some characters, such as *esc* and *del*, relate to system control and are not represented by graphic symbols. In the table, the symbolic names of these characters have been written in italics.

Index

Page numbers written in bold refer to facts tables.